CW00695829

Collins School Bible

NEW TESTAMENT

Good News New Testament

Second Edition

Study Notes by Michael Keene

Collins Educational

An Imprint of HarperCollinsPublishers

Published by Collins Educational
An Imprint of HarperCollins*Publishers* Ltd
77–85 Fulham Palace Road
London W6 8JB

www.**Collins**Education.com
On-line support for schools and colleges

Good News New Testament – Second Edition © 1994
Text, illustrations and helps are copyright
New Testament © American Bible Society 1966, 1971,
1976, 1992
Study notes and maps © HarperCollins*Publishers* Ltd 1998

First published 1998

Reprinted 2000

ISBN 0 00 322134 2

British Library Cataloguing in Publication Data
A catalogue record for this book is available
from the British Library

You might also like to visit
www.**fire**and**water**.co.uk
The book lover's website

Commissioning Editor: Domenica de Rosa
Edited by Thomas Allain-Chapman
Cover design by Clinton Banbury
Cover photograph: John Fryer/Circa Photo Library
Page design and typesetting by Derek Lee
Maps by John Booth
Picture research by Katie Anderson
Production by Sue Cashin
Printed and bound by Printing Express Ltd., Hong Kong

Acknowledgements

The publishers would like to thank the following for
permission to reproduce photographs:

p. 2 David Frith; p. 4 Kurt M. Westerman/Anzenber/
Colorific!; p. 5 Alex Keene & Jo MacLennan (The Walking
Camera); p. 9 Kim Westerkov/Tony Stone Worldwide;
p. 11 Alex Keene & Jo MacLennan (The Walking Camera);
p. 16 John Paul Kay/Still Pictures; p. 18, 21, 23, 26 Alex
Keene & Jo MacLennan (The Walking Camera); p. 33 James
Nachtwey/Magnum Photos; p. 34, 36 Alex Keene & Jo
MacLennan (The Walking Camera); p. 38 Bridgeman Art
Library; p. 40 Alex Keene & Jo MacLennan (The Walking
Camera); p. 43 Bridgeman Art Library; p. 46 Carlos Reyes-
Manzo/Andes Press Agency; p. 52 Alex Keene & Jo
MacLennan (The Walking Camera); p. 57 HarperCollins
Publishers Ltd; p. 59, 62, 63 Alex Keene & Jo MacLennan
(The Walking Camera); p. 66 Tony Latham/Tony Stone
Worldwide; p. 67 Alex Keene & Jo MacLennan (The
Walking Camera); p. 70 Index/Bridgeman Art Library;
p. 71 Alex Keene & Jo MacLennan (The Walking Camera);
p. 72 Mark Edwards/Still Pictures; p. 77, 82, 83 Alex Keene
& Jo MacLennan (The Walking Camera); p. 88 Telegraph
Colour Library; p. 93, 99, 101, 103 Alex Keene & Jo
MacLennan (The Walking Camera); p. 106 Bridgeman Art
Library; p. 112 Alex Keene & Jo MacLennan (The Walking
Camera); p. 115 Carlos Reyes-Manzo/Andes Press Agency;
p. 118, 122, 127, 128 Alex Keene & Jo MacLennan (The
Walking Camera); p. 131 Bridgeman Art Library; p. 135,
138, 141 Alex Keene & Jo MacLennan (The Walking
Camera); p. 143 Bridgeman Art Library; p.149, 156 Alex
Keene & Jo MacLennan (The Walking Camera); p.169
Barnaby's Picture Library; p. 172, 173, 174, 179, 184 Alex
Keene & Jo MacLennan (The Walking Camera); p. 188
Carlos Reyes-Manzo/Andes Press Agency; p. 190 Alex
Keene & Jo MacLennan (The Walking Camera); p.192
Abbas/Magnum Photos; p. 196, 201, 203, 211, 215, 216,
217, 224, 227, 229, 233, 235, 240, 241, 245, 255 Alex
Keene & Jo MacLennan (The Walking Camera); p. 262, 267
Carlos Reyes-Manzo/Andes Press Agency; p. 272, 280 Alex
Keene & Jo MacLennan (The Walking Camera)

Quotation Rights for the Good News Bible

Authors and publishers may use up to one thousand
(1,000) verses from the Good News Bible text in church,
religious and other publications, without the need to seek
and receive written permission. However, the extent of
quotation must not comprise a complete book, nor should
it amount to more than 50% of the work. The following
copyright notice must appear on the title or copyright
page: "Scriptures quoted from the *Good News Bible*
published by The Bible Societies/HarperCollins Publishers
Ltd., UK American Bible Society, 1966, 1971, 1976, 1992",
and two copies of any publication quoting from GNB
should be sent to the address below.

When quotations from GNB are used in non-saleable
media, such as church bulletins, orders of service, posters,
transparencies or similar media, a complete copyright
notice is not required, but the initials GNB must appear at
the end of each quotation.

Requests for quotations in excess of one thousand (1,000)
verses in any publication must be directed to and written
approval received from Bible Society, Stonehill Green,
Westlea, Swindon SN5 7DG.

The *United Bible Societies* is a world-wide fellowship of
National Bible Societies working in more than 180
countries. Their aim is to reach all people with the Bible or
some part of it in a language they can understand and at a
price they can afford. More than 500 million Scriptures are
distributed every year. You are invited to share in this work
by your prayers and gifts. The Bible Society in your country
will be very happy to provide details of its activity.

Contents

Part I

Contents

Contents

THE BOOKS OF THE NEW TESTAMENT
Alphabetically Arranged

List of Maps

Preface

to the Good News New Testament – Second Edition

The New Testament is the book about Jesus Christ. Its name means that it is the record of God's new covenant with his people. This covenant, or agreement, is the good news of God's promise to save those who believe in Jesus Christ as Lord and Saviour.

The twenty-seven books which make up the New Testament were written by perhaps as many as twelve different authors over a period of some fifty years.

The four Gospels tell the story of the life, teaching, deeds, death, and resurrection of Jesus. They are followed by the Acts of the Apostles, which traces the spread of the gospel for some thirty years from Jerusalem to Rome, the capital of the Empire. The letters of Paul were all written to meet specific needs faced by early Christians. The eight books that follow, known as the General Letters, are varied: some of them are addressed to believers everywhere, while others are written to individual churches or persons.

The last book in the New Testament is different from all the others. Its teaching concerning the victory of the Kingdom of God and the lordship of Christ is conveyed by means of visions, images, and symbols, many of which are very difficult for the modern reader to understand. But its central message, which may also be taken as the theme of the whole New Testament, is clearly proclaimed: "The power to rule over the world belongs now to our Lord and his Messiah, and he will rule for ever and ever!" (Revelation 11.15).

This translation of the New Testament has been prepared by the United Bible Societies for people everywhere for whom English is either their mother tongue or a language they learn. It does not conform to traditional vocabulary or style, but seeks to express the meaning of the Greek text in words and forms accepted as standard by people everywhere who use English as a means of communication.

The translator, Dr Robert G Bratcher, was assisted in his task by a panel of specialists, and the translation was reviewed and approved by the Translations Committee and the Board of the American Bible Society.

In view of the differences in vocabulary and form which exist between the American and the British use of the English language, this British edition has been published, incorporating such changes as are in keeping with British usage. Final approval of this text was given by the General Committee of the British and Foreign Bible Society.

In December 1986, as it had become plain that there was a need for revisions to the *Good News Bible,* the ABS Board of Managers approved the undertaking of revision work. This was restricted to two main areas of concern that had been raised and discussed since the first appearance of the *Good News* translation: (1) passages in which the English style was unnecessarily masculine-oriented, and (2) passages in which either the style of the translation or the terms used had given rise to problems for some readers.

The first stage of the revision process was to invite all English-language Bible Societies and English-speaking UBS translations consultants to submit proposals for revisions. These were collected, along with those invited from numerous scholarly consultants in the USA and representatives of various American churches. The proposals were then assembled for review by the same group of experts, who brought to the project special skills including translation, linguistics, English usage, literary style, biblical studies, and theology. In four stages, agreement was sought on which proposals were necessary and valid, and at each of these stages the number of proposals under consideration was reduced until widespread agreement was reached. On the recommendation of the programme committee of the ABS Board of Trustees, and its Translations subcommittee, the ABS Board acted to approve the revisions for the *Good News Bible* Second Edition in September 1990. These revisions have been adapted for use in British usage editions of the *Good News Bible.*

In the decade and a half since publication of the full *Good News Bible,* the built-in masculine linguistic biases of both the ancient languages and the English language caused some Bible readers to feel excluded from being addressed by the scriptural Word. This concern led to the revision of most major English translations during the 1980s. Increasingly, *Good News Bible* readers wrote to ask the Bible Societies to take the concern into consideration in preparing any revision. In practical terms it means that, where references in particular passages are to both men and women, the revision aims at language that is not exclusively male-oriented. At the same time, however, great care was taken not to distort the historical situation of the male-dominated culture of Bible times.

The text from which this translation was made is the Third Edition (1975) of the Greek New Testament prepared by an international committee of New Testament scholars, sponsored by the United Bible Societies. There are many places in the New Testament where the various Greek manuscripts and ancient versions have different texts; some of the more important of these *variant readings* appear in the footnotes. In many places the Greek text may be understood and translated in two or more different ways; and some of these *alternative renderings* are also given in footnotes.

How to Use this Book

The New Testament is made up of 27 separate books. We usually refer to a book by the key words in its title. For instance, *The Gospel according to Mark* is known as *Mark*, and *The Acts of the Apostles* we call *Acts*. You will find a full list of the books in the New Testament on page iv.

Each book is divided into chapters, and each of these chapters are divided into short sections called verses. These divisions are the same in all translations and editions of the Bible in all languages. This enables us to find the same passage in different versions with ease and accuracy. Here is a typical chapter and verse reference:

1 Corinthians 13.1–13

There are two letters to the Corinthians in the New Testament. This number indicates which one is referred to here. Several other books are referred to by number as well as by name
(e.g. 1 Thessalonians, 3 John).

These numbers refer to verses, in this case, verses one to thirteen (inclusive) of chapter thirteen. The beginning of each verse is indicated either by a coloured number in the margin or a small number within the text itself.

The book's title. You will be able to find out which page each book starts on by looking at the contents pages. Sometimes, references will only give an abbreviated title,
e.g. 1 Cor 13.1–13.
A key to these abbreviations is given on page iv.

This is the chapter number. If you look at the top of each page in the New Testament, the numbers of the chapters featured on each page are given to help you find particular passages. Four books (Philemon, 2 John, 3 John and Jude) are so short that they are not divided into chapters, only verses.

References which cover more than one chapter give the chapter and verse at which the passage begins and ends, separated by a long dash (e.g. Luke 1.26—2.20).

The system of book, chapter and verse reference is common to all Bibles. This book has some additional features designed to make it easier for you to find your way around the New Testament and enhance your study of it.

The first section contains notes, tables, timelines, diagrams and a map which give information on the background, events and people of the New Testament.

The text of the New Testament itself is set out with clear headings and chapter and verse numbers. As you can see from the page opposite, the miracles, parables and teachings of Jesus are sign-posted. Underneath the heading at the start of each section, references to any similar passages in other books are given. Some pages also feature footnotes on the sources or translations of particular words or passages.

At the beginning of each book of the New Testament you will find an *Introduction* which gives an overview of the content of that book. Below this, the *Outline of Contents* lists the main topics or events covered in the book along with references for these sections.

Studying ... Boxes

A little further into each book you will find a *Studying* ... box, which provides concise notes to help you in your study. Each box sets out to answer five crucial questions about the origins and purpose of the book:

Who wrote it?
When?
Where from?
For whom?
Why?

In addition to answering these questions, *Studying* ... boxes list key points about each book, such as distinctive features of style and important themes.

The information given in the *Studying* ... boxes takes account of the opinions of respected, recent biblical scholars. Of course, some facts are less certain than others, and in some cases there are facts we simply do not know. These notes will, however, help you gain an idea of the circumstances in which these important writings came into being.

Social Issues

Information and questions for discussion on important social issues can be found on pages 304–12, together with references to relevant passages in the New Testament.

Glossary

Finally, there is a glossary to help you with unfamiliar words, names and places.

How to Use this Book

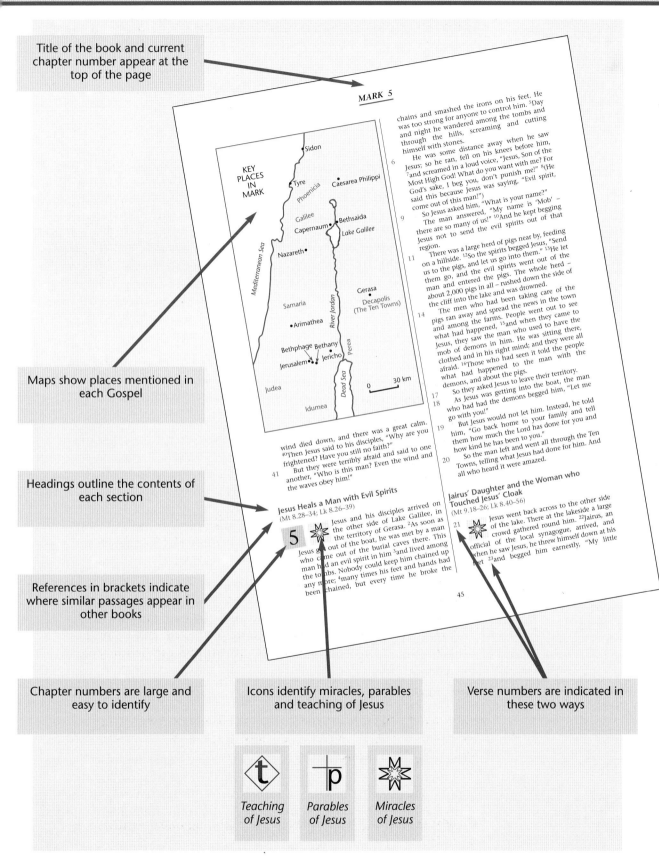

Title of the book and current chapter number appear at the top of the page

Maps show places mentioned in each Gospel

Headings outline the contents of each section

References in brackets indicate where similar passages appear in other books

Chapter numbers are large and easy to identify

Icons identify miracles, parables and teaching of Jesus

Verse numbers are indicated in these two ways

MARK 5

KEY PLACES IN MARK

- Sidon
- Tyre
- Caesarea Philippi
- Phoenicia
- Galilee
- Bethsaida
- Capernaum
- Lake Galilee
- Nazareth
- Mediterranean Sea
- Samaria
- River Jordan
- Gerasa
- Decapolis (The Ten Towns)
- Arimathea
- Perea
- Bethphage Bethany
- Jerusalem Jericho
- Judea
- Dead Sea
- Idumea

0   30 km

chains and smashed the irons on his feet. He was too strong for anyone to control him. ⁵Day and night he wandered among the tombs and through the hills, screaming and cutting himself with stones.

6 He was some distance away when he saw Jesus; so he ran, fell on his knees before him, ⁷and screamed in a loud voice, "Jesus, Son of the Most High God! What do you want with me? For God's sake, I beg you, don't punish me!" ⁸(He said this because Jesus was saying, "Evil spirit, come out of this man!")

9 So Jesus asked him, "What is your name?" The man answered, "My name is 'Mob' – there are so many of us!" ¹⁰And he kept begging Jesus not to send the evil spirits out of that region.

11 There was a large herd of pigs near by, feeding on a hillside. ¹²So the spirits begged Jesus, "Send us to the pigs, and let us go into them." ¹³He let them go, and the evil spirits went out of the man and entered the pigs. The whole herd – about 2,000 pigs in all – rushed down the side of the cliff into the lake and was drowned.

14 The men who had been taking care of the pigs ran away and spread the news in the town and among the farms. People went out to see what had happened, ¹⁵and when they came to Jesus, they saw the man who used to have the mob of demons in him. He was sitting there, clothed and in his right mind; and they were all afraid. ¹⁶Those who had seen it told the people what had happened to the man with the demons, and about the pigs.

17 So they asked Jesus to leave their territory.

18 As Jesus was getting into the boat, the man who had had the demons begged him, "Let me go with you!"

19 But Jesus would not let him. Instead, he told him, "Go back home to your family and tell them how much the Lord has done for you and how kind he has been to you."

20 So the man left and went all through the Ten Towns, telling what Jesus had done for him. And all who heard it were amazed.

wind died down, and there was a great calm. ⁴⁰Then Jesus said to his disciples, "Why are you frightened? Have you still no faith?"

41 But they were terribly afraid and said to one another, "Who is this man? Even the wind and the waves obey him!"

Jesus Heals a Man with Evil Spirits
(Mt 8.28–34; Lk 8.26–39)

5 Jesus and his disciples arrived on the other side of Lake Galilee, in the territory of Gerasa. ²As soon as Jesus got out of the boat, he was met by a man who came out of the burial caves there. This man had an evil spirit in him ³and lived among the tombs. Nobody could keep him chained up any more; ⁴many times his feet and hands had been chained, but every time he broke the

Jairus' Daughter and the Woman who Touched Jesus' Cloak
(Mt 9.18–26; Lk 8.40–56)

21 Jesus went back across to the other side of the lake. There at the lakeside a large crowd gathered round him. ²²Jairus, an official of the local synagogue, arrived, and when he saw Jesus, he threw himself down at his feet ²³and begged him earnestly, "My little

45

t Teaching of Jesus

p Parables of Jesus

Miracles of Jesus

Introducing the New Testament

The first gatherings of Christians probably followed the practice of the Jewish synagogue and had regular readings from the Jewish Scriptures (which Christians later called the Old Testament) in their services. At the same time, since they were worshipping Jesus, it was natural for an eye-witness or two to pass on some information that they remembered about him. Since the disciples – now called apostles – had spent more time than anyone else with Jesus, their recollections were the most highly valued. As the Church grew, however, and the eye-witnesses began to die, so it became increasingly necessary for this information to be written down. In this way the four Gospels – Matthew, Mark, Luke and John – came into existence.

Mark, using the recollections of Peter, was the first Gospel and was probably written between 65 and 70 CE. Obviously the Gospels were widely circulated and valued among the different Christian communities and given a central place in all worship.

The Gospels, though, were not the first books in the New Testament to be written. The Apostles, and other Church leaders, had already written letters, also called "epistles", which had been sent to individuals and churches throughout the Roman Empire. These gave general guidance on the Christian life and beliefs. The usefulness of these letters for the Church generally was soon recognized with them being read and re-read. The Acts of the Apostles was also warmly received since this continued the story begun by Luke in his Gospel.

The New Testament, then, is a collection of books which were written by many different authors for different reasons and which were gradually collected together into the New Testament as we know it. By the fourth century CE, the books of the New Testament had been joined to the Jewish Scriptures – which Christians now called the Old Testament – to form the Bible. These books can be grouped together as follows:

The Gospels

The word "Gospel" means "Good News". The Gospels are placed at the beginning of the New Testament because they are its most important books. They are the only important records that we have about the life and teaching – the Good News – of Jesus, but they are not biographies. Only two of them, for instance, tell us anything about the birth of Jesus

– Matthew and Luke. Just one Gospel, Luke, records any incident in the boyhood of Jesus.

The whole of Mark's Gospel, and the vast majority of Matthew and Luke, are taken up with a short period of time at the end of the life of Jesus. More remarkably, over 30 per cent of Mark and more than 20 per cent of Matthew and Luke are devoted to the last week in the life of Jesus. John, you may have noticed, is the odd one out of the four Gospels. See the section "Studying the Synoptic Gospels" on page xxii for more details.

The Acts of the Apostles

This book, written by Luke, describes how Christianity spread from Palestine to the lands around the Mediterranean Sea between the Day of Pentecost and the imprisonment of Paul in Rome around 61 CE.

The Letters

Most of the letters, or epistles as they are sometimes called, in the New Testament were written by Paul to explain some aspect of Christian belief or behaviour. All of Paul's letters were written earlier than the first Gospel. The first of the letters, 1 Thessalonians, was probably written in 49 CE.

The New Testament also contains letters written by other church leaders such as Peter, James, John and Jude.

The Revelation to John

This book, the last to be written, is the odd one out in the New Testament. It is an "apocalyptic" work, written to encourage Christians who were undergoing severe persecution. Using strange images and symbols, Revelation encourages Christians to believe that God is in control of the events right up to the end of the world.

Timeline: The Life of Jesus

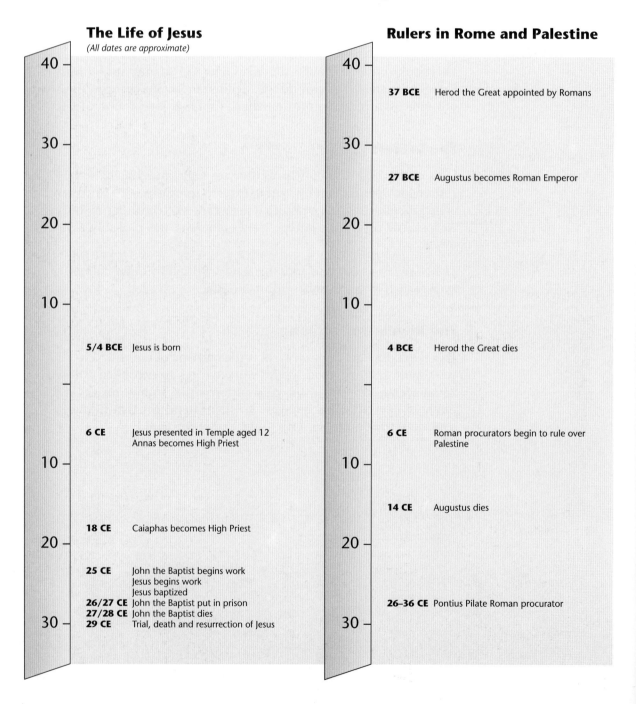

The Life of Jesus
(All dates are approximate)

5/4 BCE	Jesus is born
6 CE	Jesus presented in Temple aged 12 Annas becomes High Priest
18 CE	Caiaphas becomes High Priest
25 CE	John the Baptist begins work Jesus begins work Jesus baptized
26/27 CE	John the Baptist put in prison
27/28 CE	John the Baptist dies
29 CE	Trial, death and resurrection of Jesus

Rulers in Rome and Palestine

37 BCE	Herod the Great appointed by Romans
27 BCE	Augustus becomes Roman Emperor
4 BCE	Herod the Great dies
6 CE	Roman procurators begin to rule over Palestine
14 CE	Augustus dies
26–36 CE	Pontius Pilate Roman procurator

Timeline: The Early Church

Events in the Early Church
(All dates are approximate)

29 CE	Holy Spirit given to disciples at Pentecost
29–30CE	Stephen martyred
34 CE	Paul converted on road to Damascus
43 CE	James martyred; Peter imprisoned
45–47 CE	Paul's first missionary journey
49–50 CE	Council at Jerusalem
49 CE	Paul writes first letter – 1 Thessalonians
50–52 CE	Paul's second missionary journey
53–57 CE	Paul's third missionary journey
57 CE	Paul's Letter to the Romans written
64 CE	Paul dies in Rome; Christians persecuted by Nero
65–70 CE	Mark's Gospel written
80–85 CE	Luke's Gospel written
85–90 CE	Matthew's Gospel written
88 CE	Domitian persecutes Christians in Rome
90–95 CE	John's Gospel written

Events and Rulers in Palestine

37 CE	Herod Agrippa I ruler of Batanaea
39 CE	Herod Antipas (ruler of Galilee) exiled to Gaul
41 CE	Herod Agrippa I king of Judea and Samaria
44 CE	Herod Agrippa I dies
66 CE	First Jewish Revolt begins
70 CE	Jerusalem destroyed by Romans

Roman Emperors

14–37 CE	Tiberius
37–41 CE	Gaius (Caligula)
41–54 CE	Claudius
54–68 CE	Nero
69–78 CE	Vespasian
79–81 CE	Titus
81–96 CE	Domitian

Timeline markers (all three columns): 30, 40, 50, 60, 70, 80, 90

New Testament Places

THE WORLD OF THE NEW TESTAMENT

Political and Religious Groups at the Time of Jesus

The Romans

In the New Testament
Matthew 22.15–22
Luke 2.1–7

The Romans had occupied the land of Palestine ever since Pompey led his army into Jerusalem in 63 BCE. They appointed a governor to rule over each province in their Empire, and he was responsible to the Emperor for maintaining law and order. Augustus, who was Roman Emperor until 14 CE, ordered a census throughout the Empire in the year in which Jesus was born. This required every male to return to the city or town where he owned property. This meant that Jesus was born in Bethlehem, the city of Joseph's ancestor, King David. In 26 CE, Emperor Tiberius appointed Pontius Pilate as governor (procurator) of Palestine, and it was he who condemned Jesus to death.

The Romans allowed the Jews complete freedom in religious matters – freedom to keep the Sabbath (the Jewish day of rest), for instance – but they kept a very strict control over the country in other matters. Any civil unrest, like the riot in which Barabbas had been involved (Mark 15.6–15) was ruthlessly crushed.

Herod's Party (The Herodians)

In the Gospels
Matthew 22.15–17
Mark 3.6

While we know relatively little about them, it is clear that the Herodians were a political party which supported Herod Antipas, ruler of Galilee and Perea. These territories had been given to him by the Roman Emperor in 4 CE, and he needed Roman approval in order to keep his hold on power. He managed to hold on until 39 CE, when he was forced into exile in Gaul.

Afraid that Jesus would cause unrest and upset the Romans, Herod's party took a hostile attitude to Jesus. The Gospels record how they tried to trap Jesus with questions and plotted to kill him.

The Zealots (Patriots)

In the Gospels
Luke 6.15

Motivated by "zeal" for the Jewish Law, the Zealots (later called "dagger-carriers") were fiercely opposed to Roman control of Palestine. Simon, a disciple of Jesus, was a Zealot, although as a group they did not believe that Jesus was the Messiah. They believed instead that God would send a Messiah who would become a political and military leader to deliver the Jews from the Romans. They played a major part in the uprising (some 30 years after Jesus' death) of 66 CE, which resulted in the destruction of Jerusalem in 70 CE.

The Pharisees

In the Gospels
Matthew 23.1–36
Mark 7.3–4
Luke 18.9–14

The Pharisees were a Jewish sect which was formed in the second century BCE. Their name meant "the separated ones", and what separated them from other Jews was their strict adherence to Jewish Law (the Torah). Not only were they careful to observe every minute detail of the Law, they encouraged others to do the same.

The Pharisees believed in angels, demons, the immortality of the soul and life after death. They frequently disagreed with Jesus, for instance over fasting (Mark 2.18), Sabbath observance (Mark 2.24) and divorce (Mark 10.2). They rejected Jesus as the Jewish Messiah, attacking him for associating with the outcasts in society, like tax collectors and prostitutes (Matthew 9.9–12). Despite this, a few individuals among the Pharisees, such as Nicodemus (John 3) and Simon (Luke 7.36–50), appear to have been open to Jesus and his teaching.

The Sadducees

In the Gospels
Matthew 3.7–10;
16.1–12
Luke 20. 27–40

Begun in second century BCE, the Sadducees were a wealthy, upper-class Jewish party. They defended the Law (the Torah) strongly, but it seems they did not recognize the writings of the Prophets as authoritative. They rejected the idea that the soul was immortal and did not believe in an afterlife, and their opinions are evident in the question they put to Jesus in Luke 20.

Like other upper-class groups such as Herod's party, they encouraged co-operation with the Roman authorities. Since they provided the Chief Priest, the most important Jewish leader under Roman rule, they stood to lose power if the Romans were overthrown.

Teachers of the Law (Scribes)

In the Gospels
Matthew 16.21
Mark 11.15–19
Luke 19.45–48

The Scribes were experts in understanding the Law of Moses (the Torah), and this gave them considerable influence in Jewish society. Many scribes were also Pharisees, and only a few were priests. They denied the right of Jesus to reinterpret the Law, and their bitter opposition to his teaching led them to work with the Pharisees to bring about Jesus' death.

The Samaritans

In the Gospels
Luke 9.51–56
Luke 10.25–37
John 4.1–42

The Samaritans are unique amongst the groups mentioned in the Bible in that they still exist today. At some time, long before the time of Jesus, the Samaritans separated themselves from other Jews to follow a way of life which they still largely continue. They only accepted the Torah as Holy Scripture, kept the Sabbath Day with great strictness, imposed the laws relating to food and hygiene without allowing any exceptions, and maintained that their holy mountain, Gerizim, was the place where God should be worshipped. A small group of Samaritans still live in Nablus and Jaffa and worship on Mount Gerizim.

Key Events in the Gospels

Birth of Jesus	Matthew 1.18–25; Luke 1.26—2.20
Ministry of John the Baptist	Matthew 3.1–12; Mark 1.1–8; Luke 3.1–20
Baptism of Jesus	Matthew 3.13–17; Mark 1.9–11; Luke 3.21,22
Temptations of Jesus	Matthew 4.1–11; Mark 1.12–13; Luke 4.1–13
Jesus chooses twelve disciples	Matthew 10.2–4; Mark 3.13–19; Luke 6.12–16
The Sermon on the Mount	Matthew 5—7
Jesus feeds 5,000 people	Matthew 14.13–21; Mark 6.30–44; Luke 9.10–17; John 6.1–15
Jesus feeds 4,000 people	Matthew 15.29–39; Mark 8.1–13
Peter's confession at Caesarea Philippi	Matthew 16.13–20; Mark 8.27–30; Luke 9.18–27
The transfiguration	Matthew 17.1–13; Mark 9.2–13; Luke 9.26–36
Parable of the Good Samaritan	Luke 10.30–37
Jesus enters Jerusalem	Matthew 21.1–11; Mark 11.1–11; Luke 19.29–40; John 12.12–16
The Last Supper	Matthew 26.17–30; Mark 14.12–26; Luke 22.7–38
The Garden of Gethsemane	Matthew 26.36–46; Mark 14.32–42; Luke 22.39–46
Arrest of Jesus	Matthew 26.47–56; Mark 14.43–52; Luke 22.47–53; John 18.1–11
Denial of Peter	Matthew 26.69–75; Mark 14.66–72; Luke 22.54–62; John 18.15–18,25–27
Jesus before Pilate	Matthew 27.11–26; Mark 15.1–15; Luke 23.1–25; John 18.28—19.16
The crucifixion	Matthew 27.32–44; Mark 15.21–32; Luke 23.26–43; John 19.17–27
The death of Jesus	Matthew 27.45–53; Mark 15.33–41; Luke 23.44–49; John 19.28–37
The burial of Jesus	Matthew 27.57–66; Mark 15.42–47; Luke 23.50–56; John 19.38–42
The resurrection	Matthew 28.1–10; Mark 16.1–8; Luke 24.1–12; John 20.1–31

Studying the Synoptic Gospels

For further information on the four Gospels, see:
Studying Matthew on page 2
Studying Mark on page 41
Studying Luke on page 65
Studying John on page 105

There are four Gospels in the New Testament, and three of them – Matthew, Mark and Luke – have a great deal in common. So much, in fact, that they are called the "Synoptic Gospels". This means that they can be "seen together" as presenting a common approach to the life and death of Jesus. The fourth Gospel, John, is often described as a "spiritual" Gospel since it has very different material to the other three and little in common with them.

Most scholars today believe that Mark was the first Gospel to be written. Then Matthew and Luke used the information in Mark to write their own accounts. Since much of Mark's information seemed to come from Peter in the first place, his Gospel was considered to be very reliable.

The Synoptic Problem

Of the 661 verses in Mark, all but 31 have parallels in Matthew or Luke. Over 600 of these parallels are in Matthew and at least 350 are found in Luke.

Matthew and Luke have some 200 verses, largely sayings of Jesus, in common with each other which are not found in Mark. It is thought that they had access to a document which has long since disappeared (if it ever existed) for this information. Scholars today call this document "Q", from the German word meaning "source". Even if "Q" never existed as a separate document it is useful to use it to cover material shared by Matthew and Luke but not found in Mark.

There is a considerable amount of material found in Matthew's Gospel which is not in the other two. It seems that some 250 verses are unique to Matthew alone. This material, Matthew's special source, is known to scholars as "M". No one knows whether it actually existed or not.

There is also material in Luke's Gospel which is not found in either Mark or Matthew. This material includes almost 50 per cent of all the information included in Luke. It includes a number of famous parables (the lost sheep, coin and son of Luke 15) as well as Luke's distinctive description of the birth of Jesus (chapters 1 and 2). This material is known as "L" – Luke's special source.

Similarities and Differences

The following diagram displays the similarities and differences between the three Synoptic Gospels. As well as listing the material unique to each of the Gospel accounts, the diagram also shows the proportion of material in each Gospel found in one or both of the other Synoptics.

Only found in Matthew – M

Dream of Joseph (1.20–24)
Wise Men visit Jesus (2.1–12)
Escape of Jesus with his family to Egypt
(2.13–15)
Slaughter by Herod of the young children
(2.16–18)
Suicide of Judas (27.3–10)
Dream of Pilate's wife (27.19)
Dead returning to life (27.52)
Bribery of the guards (28.11–15)
Emphasis on baptism in the last words of
Jesus (28.19–20)

Q

identical material

MATTHEW

Only found in Mark

Parable of the growing seed (4.26–29)
Healing of a deaf mute (7.31–37)
Healing of a blind man in Bethsaida
(8.22–26)

identical material

MARK

Only found in Luke – L

Events connected with the birth of John the
Baptist and Jesus (1.5–80)
Birth of Jesus and events from his early life
(2.1–52)
Jesus is rejected by his home town. (4.16–30)
Miraculous catch of fish (5.1–11)
Bringing a widow's only son back to life
(7.11–17)
A sinful woman anoints Jesus (7.36–50)
Women travelling with Jesus (8.1–3)
Events, teaching and miracles leading up to
Jesus' death (10.1—18.14)
Jesus and Zaccheus, the tax-collector
(19.1–27)
Jesus on trial before Herod (23.6–12)
Last words of Jesus before his ascension into
heaven (24.44–49)

Q

identical material

LUKE

Looking at the similarities and differences in material between the three accounts, it seems Mark was written first and became an important source for Matthew and Luke. As well as Mark's account, both Matthew and Luke used information from another unknown source ("Q"). Matthew also included material from an additional source ("M") and Luke from a further source ("L").

The way in which the three Synoptic Gospels may have come about can be illustrated in this diagram.

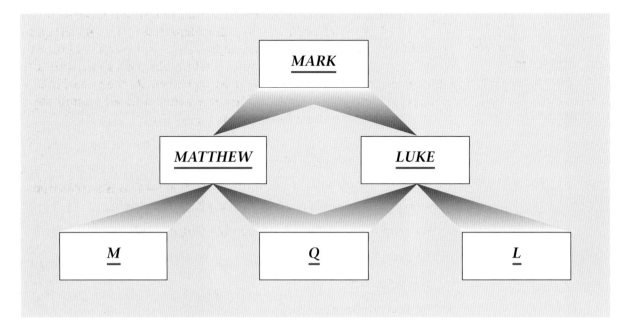

Explaining the link between the Gospels of Matthew, Mark and Luke is called the "Synoptic Problem". The way that we have explained how the Gospels may have come about is called "source criticism".

The Teaching of Jesus

Passages in the Gospels which record major teachings of Jesus are marked with this icon to make them easier to find.

As well as narrating the important events in the life of Jesus, the Gospels set out to include the most important things he said. The Gospels record Jesus' teaching about the nature of God and about his own status as God's Messiah, prayer, moral issues, and much more. Often, Jesus taught the people by telling them parables, stories which contained hidden meanings (see page xxvi). At the end of this book, Jesus' views on a number of issues which continue to dominate human life today are discussed (see pages 304–12).

The Sermon on the Mount

The Sermon on the Mount is found in Matthew 5—7. It is a collection of the key teachings of Jesus about many topics, including:

- The people who will receive God's blessing (5.1–12)
- The Law (5.17–20)
- Anger (5.21–26)
- Lust and adultery (5.27–30)
- Divorce (5.31–32)
- Retaliation and loving one's enemies (5.38–48)
- Giving to those in need (6.1–4)
- Prayer (6.5–14)
- Money (6.19–24)
- Worrying (6.25–34)
- Criticising others (7.1–6)

Some of the material Matthew groups together in the Sermon on the Mount appears in similar form in Luke 6.20–49. This shorter collection of teachings is sometimes referred to as the Sermon on the Plain.

The Parables of Jesus

Where the parables of Jesus occur in the Gospels they are marked with this icon to make them easier to find.

The first recorded words of Jesus found in Mark's Gospel are "The right time has come and the Kingdom of God is near" (Mark 1.15). The theme of the Kingdom of God, or the Kingdom of heaven as it was often called, dominated the teaching of Jesus. It referred to God's rule or reign as king – the spiritual sphere over which God rules. Nearly all the teaching of Jesus about this Kingdom was given in the form of parables.

The Jewish rabbis of the time often taught the people through parables. This was a form of teaching by means of using a comparison. Parables were stories which contained a meaning or message over and above the obvious meaning of the story. Often this took the form of an extended simile – a "like" saying – as when Jesus often said "The Kingdom of heaven is like …"

The Synoptic Gospels record around 40 different parables, as the table opposite shows:

The Parables of Jesus

Parable	Matthew	Mark	Luke
A lamp under a bowl	5.14–15	4.21–22	8.16;11.33
The two house builders	7.24–27	6.47–49	
Cloth and wineskins	9.16–17	2.21–22	5.36–38
The sower and the soils	13.3–9,18–23	4.3–9,13–20	8.5–8,11–15
The weeds	13.24–30,36–43		
The mustard seed	13.31–32	4.30–32	13.18,19
The yeast	13.33		13.20–21
The hidden treasure	13.44		
The pearl	13.45–46		
The net	13.47–50		
The lost sheep	18.12–14		15.4–7
The unforgiving servant	18.21–34		
The workers in the vineyard	20.1–16		
The two sons	21.28–32		
The tenants in the vineyard	21.33–44	12.1–11	20.9–18
The feast	22.2–14		14.16–24
The faithful and the unfaithful servant	24.45–51		12.42–48
The ten young women	25.1–13		
The three servants	25.14–30		19.12–27
The sheep and the goats	25.31–46		
The growing seed		4.26–29	
The watchful servants	13.35–37	12.35–40	
The money and the moneylender			7.41–43
The Good Samaritan			10.30–37
The friend in need			11.5–8
The rich fool			12.16–21
The unfruitful fig tree			13.6–9
The tower and the king			14.28–33
The lost coin			15.8–10
The lost son			15.11–32
The shrewd manager			16.1–8
The rich man and Lazarus			16.19–31
The widow and the judge			18.2–8
The Pharisee and the tax collector			18.10–14

The Miracles of Jesus

Passages in the Gospels which record the miracles of Jesus are marked with this icon to make them easier to find.

The writers of the books of the Bible believed that God could, and did, intervene in the course of nature and in the lives of individuals. The word "miracle" came from the Greek word meaning "wonder", and a miracle was an event which caused people to stop and wonder. A miracle was an act of supernatural power, and people were aware that Jesus could only perform his miracles by the power of God. In John's Gospel the miracles were called "signs" since they demonstrated God's power to the people. The miracles recorded in the Gospels fall into three categories:

(a) Those which demonstrate the power of Jesus over the forces of nature. Three miracles demonstrate this most clearly – Jesus calming the storm on the sea of Galilee, Jesus feeding the hungry people and Jesus walking on the water.

(b) Those which show the power of Jesus over the evil spirits which caused distress, illness and suffering to people. Sometimes he demanded faith from those being cured but, on other occasions, he performed a miracle without the person even being present. Throughout his ministry Jesus is presented in the Synoptic Gospels as being in a continual battle with the forces of evil and darkness.

(c) Those in which Jesus brought the dead back to life. This happens on three occasions – the raising of Jairus' daughter, the raising of the widow of Nain's son and the bringing of Lazarus back to life.

The Miracles of Jesus

(a) Jesus and the Forces of Nature

	Matthew	Mark	Luke	John
Calming the storm	8.23–27	4.35–41	8.22–25	
Walking on the water	14.22–33	6.45–52		6.16–21
Feeding 5,000 people	14.13–21	6.30–44	9.10–17	6.1–15
Feeding 4,000 people	15.32–38	8.1–9		
Coin in the fish's mouth	17.24–27			
Fig-tree wither	21.18–22	11.12–14,20–24		
Catch of fish			5.1–11	
Water into wine				2.1–11
Catch of fish				21.1–11

(b) Healing Miracles

	Matthew	Mark	Luke	John
Man with leprosy	8.1–4	1.40–45	5.12–16	
Roman soldier's servant	8.5–13		7.1–10	
Peter's mother-in-law	8.14–17	1.29–34	4.38–41	
Two men from Gadara	8.28–34	5.1–20	8.26–39	
Paralysed man	9.1–7	2.1–12	5.17–26	
Woman with bleeding	9.20–22	5.25–29	8.43–48	
Two blind men	9.27–31			
Mute possessed man	9.32–34			
Man with paralysed hand	12.9–14	3.1–6	6.6–11	
Blind and mute man	12.23		11.14–15	
Canaanite woman's daughter	15.21–28	7.24–30		
Boy with a demon	17.14–21	9.14–29	9.37–43	
Two blind men	20.29–34	10.46–52	18.35–43	
Deaf mute		7.31–37		
Man possessed		1.21–28	4.31–37	
Blind man at Bethsaida		8.22–26		
Crippled woman			13.10–17	
Man with swollen limbs			14.1–6	
Ten men with leprosy			17.11–19	
The high priest's servant			22.49–51	
Official's son				4.43–54
Sick man				5.1–18
Man born blind				9.1–12

(c) Returning the dead to Life

	Matthew	Mark	Luke	John
Jairus' daughter	9.18–19,23–26	5.21–24,35–43	8.40–42,49–56	
Widow of Nain's son			7.11–17	
Lazarus				11.1–44

Although the events of the Gospels span several years (over thirty in the case of Matthew and Luke), they are all dominated by the events of seven days. The story of the week leading up to the death and resurrection of Jesus occupies some 30 per cent of Mark's Gospel, and the events of Holy Week (as Christians refer to it) are re-enacted each year in the services leading up to the festival of Easter.

You will find a map of Jerusalem, where all the events of the last week took place, on page 54.

Sunday

Jesus enters Jerusalem

In the Gospels
Matthew 21.1–11
Mark 11.1–11
Luke 19.28–40
John 12.12–19

Crowds waving branches and shouting "God bless him who comes in the Lord's name!" greet Jesus as he arrives in the city. He rides on a donkey, fulfilling the words of the Old Testament prophet, Zechariah.

Monday

Jesus clears the Temple

In the Gospels
Matthew 21.12–13
Mark 11.15–17
Luke 19.45–46

Angry that the Temple courts were filled not with people worshipping God but with money-changers and merchants, Jesus drives out the traders and knocks over their stalls. He quotes the prophets Isaiah and Jeremiah, saying that God's Temple should be a house of prayer, but it has instead become a hideout for thieves.

Tuesday

Judas agrees to betray Jesus

In the Gospels
Matthew 26.14–16
Mark 14.10–11
Luke 22.3–6

Judas, one of Jesus' twelve disciples, approaches the chief priests and offers to help them arrest Jesus at a suitable time and place. They eagerly accept his offer and promise him money.

Thursday

The Last Supper

Jesus shares the traditional Passover meal with his disciples, during which he instructs them to eat bread, saying "This is my body" and to drink wine, saying "This is my blood". During the meal, Jesus also predicts that Judas will betray him, and that Peter will deny him three times.

Jesus in Gethsemane

When the meal is over, Jesus goes to the Garden of Gethsemane (an olive orchard on the Mount of Olives) to pray. Jesus asks the disciples to pray with him, but they fall asleep while he prays that he might escape the suffering which he knows is to follow.

Jesus is betrayed and arrested

Judas leads the temple guard to Gethsemane, where he identifies Jesus by kissing him. Jesus does not resist arrest, but asks that his disciples be allowed to go free.

Friday

Jesus' trial and Peter's denial

In the early hours of Friday, Jesus is brought before the teachers of the Law and the elders to be tried. While he waits outside, Peter is accused three times of being a disciple of Jesus, and each time he denies it. Jesus is later brought before Pontius Pilate, the Roman governor, who condemns Jesus to be flogged and later to be crucified.

Jesus is crucified

Jesus is led out to Golgotha ("The Place of the Skull"), where he is crucified along with two thieves. Between noon and three o'clock, while Jesus hangs on the cross, the sky is dark. At three o'clock, Jesus gives a loud cry and dies. That evening, before the Sabbath begins, his body is taken down and buried by a rich man, Joseph of Arimathea. The tomb is sealed and Roman guards are stationed outside it.

Sunday

The resurrection

Early on Sunday morning, some women followers of Jesus go to the tomb, hoping to anoint his body. They find the stone rolled away and the tomb empty. Men in shining clothes tell them that Jesus has been raised from the dead. Jesus himself later appears to many of his followers.

Who were the Disciples?

The Gospels record that Jesus chose twelve disciples, or apostles, to accompany him on his travels, to share his work and continue it after his death and resurrection (Mark 3.13–18; Luke 6.12–16). While many other followers of Jesus play important roles in the Gospels (especially the women followers of Jesus mentioned in Luke 8.1–3), it is the disciples whom Jesus commands to carry the Good News to the whole world (Matthew 28.18–20).

Simon Peter

In the New Testament
Matthew 4.18–20
Mark 8.27–33
Luke 22.31–34
John 21.15–19
Acts 2.14–41
Acts 10.1—11.18

Known as Simon, Son of John, until Jesus renamed him Peter ("the rock"), Simon Peter was earning his living as a fisherman on Lake Galilee when he met Jesus. A member of the "inner circle" of disciples with James and John, he shared many important occasions with Jesus, like the Transfiguration. Peter became the first disciple to recognize Jesus as the Messiah at Caesarea Philippi, yet he denied knowing Jesus three times during his trial. When the Holy Spirit was given to the disciples on the Day of Pentecost, it was Peter who stood up and addressed the crowds, calling them to believe in Jesus and be baptized. Peter became the leader of church in Jerusalem, and would later disagree with Paul over admitting Gentile (non-Jewish) believers into the Church.

James

In the New Testament
Mark 10.35–40
Luke 9.51–56
Acts 12.1–2

Son of Zebedee, and brother of John (together called "the sons of thunder"), James was another fisherman who became a member of the "inner circle" of disciples along with Peter and John. Along with John, he asked Jesus for a place of honour in his Kingdom. Elsewhere in the Gospels he is eager to call down fire from heaven on those who had refused to listen to the message of Jesus. James' execution by Herod Agrippa I is recorded in Acts, and tradition has it that he wrote the Letter of James.

John

In the New Testament
Mark 1.19–20; 10.35–40
Luke 9.51–56
John 19.26–27;
21.20–24

Son of Zebedee, and brother of James (together called "the sons of thunder"), John is usually mentioned in the Gospels along with his brother. He later became a leader of the church in Jerusalem, and tradition credits him with writing the fourth Gospel, along with 1, 2 and 3 John and Revelation.

Andrew

In the New Testament
Matthew 4.18–20
John 1.35–42
John 12.20–22

Simon Peter's brother, Andrew was also a fisherman. According to John's Gospel, it was Andrew who first told his brother about Jesus, saying, "We have found the Messiah."

Philip

In the New Testament
John 1.43–46; 6.1–7;
12.20–22; 14.8–14

Philip too was a fisherman. He is mentioned individually on more than one occasion in John's Gospel. He tells Nathanael about Jesus, and later questions how 5,000 people are to be fed with a few loaves and fish.

Bartholomew (Nathanael)

In the New Testament
John 1.45–51; 21.1–13

John records that Nathanael rejected Jesus at the beginning because he came from Nazareth, but he later followed him.

Matthew (Levi)

In the New Testament
Matthew 9.9–13
Mark 2.13–17
Luke 5. 27–32

A former tax collector, Matthew abandoned a corrupt career to follow Jesus, inviting Jesus to share a meal with friends at his home. Tradition has it that he wrote the Gospel which bears his name.

Thomas

In the New Testament
John 14.5–7; 20.24–29;
21.1–13

The best-known incident concerning Thomas in the Gospels comes after the resurrection of Jesus. Thomas refused to believe that Jesus had risen from the dead and appeared to the other disciples until he could see and feel him for himself.

James

This James was the son of Alphaeus.

Thaddaeus

Also called Judas, son of James – not to be confused with Judas Iscariot, who betrayed Jesus.

Simon the Patriot (Zealot)

Member of the Zealot party (see page xix).

Judas Iscariot

In the New Testament
Matthew 26.20–25;
27.3–8
Luke 22.47–48
John 12.1–8

Judas clashed with Jesus when he criticised the woman who poured expensive ointment over Jesus, saying that it should have been sold and the money given to the poor. He betrayed Jesus into the hands of the chief priests and later killed himself.

The Gospel according to MATTHEW

INTRODUCTION

The Gospel according to Matthew tells the good news that Jesus is the promised Saviour, the one through whom God fulfilled the promises he made to his people in the Old Testament. This good news is not only for the Jewish people, among whom Jesus was born and lived, but for the whole world.

Matthew is carefully arranged. It begins with the birth of Jesus, describes his baptism and temptation, and then takes up his ministry of preaching, teaching, and healing in Galilee. After this the Gospel records Jesus' journey from Galilee to Jerusalem and the events of Jesus' last week, culminating in his crucifixion and resurrection.

This Gospel presents Jesus as the great Teacher, who has the authority to interpret the Law of God, and who teaches about God's kingdom. Much of his teaching is gathered by subject matter into five collections: (1) The Sermon on the Mount, which concerns the character, duties, privileges, and destiny of the citizens of the Kingdom of heaven (chapters 5–7); (2) Instructions to the twelve disciples for their mission (chapter 10); (3) Parables about the Kingdom of heaven (chapter 13); (4) Teaching on the meaning of discipleship (chapter 18); and (5) Teaching about the end of the present age and the coming of the Kingdom of heaven (chapters 24–25).

Outline of Contents

The Ancestors of Jesus Christ
(Lk 3.23–38)

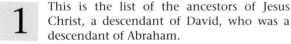

1 This is the list of the ancestors of Jesus Christ, a descendant of David, who was a descendant of Abraham.

2–6a From Abraham to King David, the following ancestors are listed: Abraham, Isaac, Jacob, Judah and his brothers; then Perez and Zerah (their mother was Tamar), Hezron, Ram, Amminadab, Nahshon, Salmon, Boaz (his mother was Rahab), Obed (his mother was Ruth), Jesse, and King David.

6b–11 From David to the time when the people of Israel were taken into exile in Babylon, the following ancestors are listed: David, Solomon (his mother was the woman who had been Uriah's wife), Rehoboam, Abijah, Asa, Jehoshaphat, Jehoram, Uzziah, Jotham, Ahaz, Hezekiah, Manasseh, Amon, Josiah, and Jehoiachin and his brothers.

12–16 From the time after the exile in Babylon to the birth of Jesus, the following ancestors are listed: Jehoiachin, Shealtiel, Zerubbabel, Abiud, Eliakim, Azor, Zadok, Achim, Eliud, Eleazar, Matthan, Jacob, and Joseph, who married Mary, the mother of Jesus, who was called the Messiah.

17 So then, there were fourteen generations from Abraham to David, and fourteen from David to the exile in Babylon, and fourteen from then to the birth of the Messiah.

The Birth of Jesus Christ
(Lk 2.1–7)

18 This was how the birth of Jesus Christ took place. His mother Mary was engaged to Joseph,

Studying
MATTHEW

Who wrote it? Traditionally Matthew, a tax collector and disciple – more likely an unknown author, who may have known Matthew.

When? Probably 85–90 CE. Destruction of Jerusalem in 70 CE seems a distant past event. Author used *Mark* together with other sources – especially a sayings source ("Q") and his own material ("M"). One of the Synoptic Gospels, along with *Mark* and *Luke*.

Where from? Most likely Antioch of Syria, where Matthew may have founded a church.

For whom? Mainly Jewish readers – many Jewish customs and references are not explained.

Why? There was tension between Jews and Christians in the area. Author supports Christian claim that Jesus was the Messiah, frequently quoting from Jewish Scriptures.

KEY POINTS

- Only *Matthew* and *Luke* record the birth of Jesus. Quotes from Isaiah 7 to indicate that Jesus was born to a virgin.
- Matthew alone brings scattered fragments of the teaching of Jesus together into the Sermon on the Mount (Matthew 5–7).
- Matthew has two favourite descriptions of Jesus – the Son of God and the Son of Man.

but before they were married, she found out that she was going to have a baby by the Holy Spirit. [19]Joseph was a man who always did what was right, but he did not want to disgrace Mary publicly; so he made plans to break the engagement privately. [20]While he was thinking about this, an angel of the Lord appeared to him in a dream and said, "Joseph, descendant of David, do not be afraid to take Mary to be your wife. For it is by the Holy Spirit that she has conceived. [21]She will have a son, and you will name him Jesus – because he will save his people from their sins."

[22] Now all this happened in order to make what the Lord had said through the prophet come true, [23]"A virgin will become pregnant and have a son, and he will be called Immanuel" (which means, "God is with us").

[24] So when Joseph woke up, he married Mary, as the angel of the Lord had told him to do. [25]But he had no sexual relations with her before she gave birth to her son. And Joseph named him Jesus.

Visitors from the East

2 Jesus was born in the town of Bethlehem in Judea, during the time when Herod was king. Soon afterwards, some men who studied the stars came from the east to Jerusalem [2]and asked, "Where is the baby born to be the king of the Jews? We saw his star when it came up in the east, and we have come to worship him."

[3] When King Herod heard about this, he was very upset, and so was everyone else in Jerusalem. [4]He called together all the chief priests and the teachers of the Law and asked them, "Where will the Messiah be born?"

[5] "In the town of Bethlehem in Judea," they answered. "For this is what the prophet wrote:

[6] 'Bethlehem in the land of Judah,
   you are by no means the least of the
      leading cities of Judah;
   for from you will come a leader
      who will guide my people Israel.'"

[7] So Herod called the visitors from the east to a secret meeting and found out from them the exact time the star had appeared. [8]Then he sent them to Bethlehem with these instructions: "Go and make a careful search for the child, and when you find him, let me know, so that I too may go and worship him."

[9–10] And so they left, and on their way they saw

A mosaic showing the wise men who visited Jesus carrying gifts

the same star they had seen in the east. When they saw it, how happy they were, what joy was theirs! It went ahead of them until it stopped over the place where the child was. [11]They went into the house, and when they saw the child with his mother Mary, they knelt down and worshipped him. They brought out their gifts of gold, frankincense, and myrrh, and presented them to him.

12   Then they returned to their country by another road, since God had warned them in a dream not to go back to Herod.

The Escape to Egypt

13   After they had left, an angel of the Lord appeared in a dream to Joseph and said, "Herod will be looking for the child in order to kill him. So get up, take the child and his mother and escape to Egypt, and stay there until I tell you to leave."

14   Joseph got up, took the child and his mother, and left during the night for Egypt, [15]where he stayed until Herod died. This was done to make what the Lord had said through the prophet come true, "I called my Son out of Egypt."

The Killing of the Children

16   When Herod realized that the visitors from the east had tricked him, he was furious. He gave orders to kill all the boys in Bethlehem and its neighbourhood who were two years old and younger – this was done in accordance with what he had learned from the visitors about the time when the star had appeared.

17   In this way what the prophet Jeremiah had said came true:

18   "A sound is heard in Ramah,
         the sound of bitter weeping.
      Rachel is crying for her children;
         she refuses to be comforted,
         for they are dead."

The Return from Egypt

19   After Herod died, an angel of the Lord appeared in a dream to Joseph in Egypt [20]and said, "Get up, take the child and his mother, and go back to the land of Israel, because those who tried to kill the child are dead." [21]So Joseph got up, took the child and his mother, and went back to Israel.

22   But when Joseph heard that Archelaus had succeeded his father Herod as king of Judea, he was afraid to go there. He was given more

instructions in a dream, so he went to the province of Galilee [23]and made his home in a town named Nazareth. And so what the prophets had said came true: "He will be called a Nazarene."

The Preaching of John the Baptist
(Mk 1.1–8; Lk 3.1–18; Jn 1.19–28)

3 At that time John the Baptist came to the desert of Judea and started preaching. [2]"Turn away from your sins," he said, "because the Kingdom of heaven is near!" [3]John was the man the prophet Isaiah was talking about when he said:

> "Someone is shouting in the desert,
>   'Prepare a road for the Lord;
>   make a straight path for him to travel!'"

4   John's clothes were made of camel's hair; he wore a leather belt round his waist, and his food was locusts and wild honey. [5]People came to him from Jerusalem, from the whole province of Judea, and from all the country near the River Jordan. [6]They confessed their sins, and he baptized them in the Jordan.

7   When John saw many Pharisees and Sadducees coming to him to be baptized, he said to them, "You snakes – who told you that you could escape from the punishment God is about to send? [8]Do those things that will show that you have turned from your sins. [9]And don't think you can escape punishment by saying that Abraham is your ancestor. I tell you that God can take these stones and make descendants for Abraham! [10]The axe is ready to cut down the trees at the roots; every tree that does not bear good fruit will be cut down and thrown in the fire. [11]I baptize you with water to show that you have repented, but the one who will come after me will baptize you with the Holy Spirit and fire. He is much greater than I am; and I am not good enough even to carry his sandals. [12]He has his winnowing shovel with him to thresh out all the grain. He will gather his wheat into his barn, but he will burn the chaff in a fire that never goes out."

The Baptism of Jesus
(Mk 1.9–11; Lk 3.21–22)

13   At that time Jesus arrived from Galilee and came to John at the Jordan to be baptized by him. [14]But John tried to make him change his mind. "I ought to be baptized by you," John said, "and yet you have come to me!"

15   But Jesus answered him, "Let it be so for now.

For in this way we shall do all that God requires." So John agreed.

16 As soon as Jesus was baptized, he came up out of the water. Then heaven was opened to him, and he saw the Spirit of God coming down like a dove and alighting on him. [17]Then a voice said from heaven, "This is my own dear Son, with whom I am pleased."

The Temptation of Jesus
(Mk 1.12–13; Lk 4.1–13)

4 Then the Spirit led Jesus into the desert to be tempted by the Devil. [2]After spending 40 days and nights without food, Jesus was hungry. [3]Then the Devil came to him and said, "If you are God's Son, order these stones to turn into bread."

4 But Jesus answered, "The scripture says, 'Human beings cannot live on bread alone, but need every word that God speaks.'"

5 Then the Devil took Jesus to Jerusalem, the Holy City, set him on the highest point of the Temple, [6]and said to him, "If you are God's Son, throw yourself down, for the scripture says:

'God will give orders to his angels about you;
    they will hold you up with their hands,
    so that not even your feet will be hurt on
        the stones.'"

7 Jesus answered, "But the scripture also says, 'Do not put the Lord your God to the test.'"

8 Then the Devil took Jesus to a very high mountain and showed him all the kingdoms of the world in all their greatness. [9]"All this I will give you," the Devil said, "if you kneel down and worship me."

10 Then Jesus answered, "Go away, Satan! The scripture says, 'Worship the Lord your God and serve only him!'"

11 Then the Devil left Jesus; and angels came and helped him.

Jesus Begins his Work in Galilee
(Mk 1.14–15; Lk 4.14–15)

12 When Jesus heard that John had been put in prison, he went away to Galilee. [13]He did not stay in Nazareth, but went to live in Capernaum, a town by Lake Galilee, in the territory of Zebulun and Naphtali. [14]This was done to make what the prophet Isaiah had said come true:

15 "Land of Zebulun and land of Naphtali,
    on the road to the sea, on the other side of
        the Jordan,
    Galilee, land of the Gentiles!

16 The people who live in darkness
        will see a great light.
    On those who live in the dark land of death
        the light will shine."

17 From that time Jesus began to preach his message: "Turn away from your sins, because the Kingdom of heaven is near!"

Jesus Calls Four Fishermen
(Mk 1.16–20; Lk 5.1–11)

18 As Jesus walked along the shore of Lake Galilee, he saw two brothers who were fishermen, Simon (called Peter) and his brother Andrew, catching fish in the lake with a net. [19]Jesus said to them, "Come with me, and I will teach you to catch people." [20]At once they left their nets and went with him.

21 He went on and saw two other brothers, James and John, the sons of Zebedee. They were in their boat with their father Zebedee, getting their nets ready. Jesus called them, [22]and at once they left the boat and their father, and went with him.

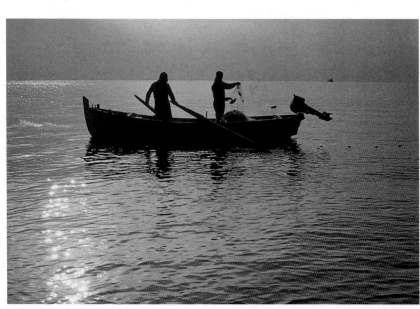

Fishermen working on Lake Galilee

Jesus Teaches, Preaches, and Heals
(Lk 6.17–19)

23 Jesus went all over Galilee, teaching in the synagogues, preaching the Good News about the Kingdom, and healing people who had all kinds of disease and sickness. [24]The news about him spread through the whole country of Syria, so that people brought to him all those who were sick, suffering from all kinds of diseases and disorders: people with demons, and epileptics, and paralytics – and Jesus healed them all. [25]Large crowds followed him from Galilee and the Ten Towns, from Jerusalem, Judea, and the land on the other side of the Jordan.

THE SERMON ON THE MOUNT
5.1—7.29

 5 Jesus saw the crowds and went up a hill, where he sat down. His disciples gathered round him, [2]and he began to teach them:

True Happiness
(Lk 6.20–23)

3 "Happy are those who know they are
     spiritually poor;
     the Kingdom of heaven belongs to them!
4 Happy are those who mourn;
     God will comfort them!
5 Happy are those who are humble;
     they will receive what God has promised!
6 Happy are those whose greatest desire is to
     do what God requires;
     God will satisfy them fully!
7 Happy are those who are merciful to others;
     God will be merciful to them!
8 Happy are the pure in heart;
     they will see God!
9 Happy are those who work for peace;
     God will call them his children!
10 Happy are those who are persecuted because
     they do what God requires;
     the Kingdom of heaven belongs to them!

11 "Happy are you when people insult you and persecute you and tell all kinds of evil lies against you because you are my followers. [12]Be happy and glad, for a great reward is kept for you in heaven. This is how the prophets who lived before you were persecuted.

Salt and Light
(Mk 9.50; Lk 14.34–35)

13 "You are like salt for the whole human race. But if salt loses its saltiness, there is no way to make it salty again. It has become worthless, so it is thrown out and people trample on it.
14 "You are like light for the whole world. A city built on a hill cannot be hidden. [15]No one lights a lamp and puts it under a bowl; instead he puts it on the lampstand, where it gives light for everyone in the house. [16]In the same way your light must shine before people, so that they will see the good things you do and praise your Father in heaven.

A Torah (Law) scroll with a yad to help the reader follow the text (5.17–20)

Teaching about the Law

17 "Do not think that I have come to do away with the Law of Moses and the teachings of the prophets. I have not come to do away with them, but to make their teachings come true. [18]Remember that as long as heaven and earth last, not the least point nor the smallest detail of the Law will be done away with – not until the end of all things.[a] [19]So then, whoever disobeys even the least important of the commandments and teaches others to do the same, will be least in the Kingdom of heaven. On the other hand, whoever obeys the Law and teaches others to do the same, will be great in the Kingdom of heaven. [20]I tell you, then, that you will be able to enter the Kingdom of heaven only if you are more faithful than the teachers of the Law and the Pharisees in doing what God requires.

[a] **5.18** the end of all things; *or* all its teachings come true.

Teaching about Anger
(Lk 12.57–59)

21 "You have heard that people were told in the past, 'Do not commit murder; anyone who does will be brought to trial.' ²²But now I tell you: whoever is angry[a] with his brother will be brought to trial, whoever calls his brother 'You good-for-nothing!' will be brought before the Council, and whoever calls his brother a worthless fool will be in danger of going to the fire of hell. ²³So if you are about to offer your gift to God at the altar and there you remember that your brother has something against you, ²⁴leave your gift there in front of the altar, go at once and make peace with your brother, and then come back and offer your gift to God.

25 "If someone brings a lawsuit against you and takes you to court, settle the dispute with him while there is time, before you get to court. Once you are there, he will hand you over to the judge, who will hand you over to the police, and you will be put in jail. ²⁶There you will stay, I tell you, until you pay the last penny of your fine.

Teaching about Adultery

27 "You have heard that it was said, 'Do not commit adultery.' ²⁸But now I tell you: anyone who looks at a woman and wants to possess her is guilty of committing adultery with her in his heart. ²⁹So if your right eye causes you to sin, take it out and throw it away! It is much better for you to lose a part of your body than to have your whole body thrown into hell. ³⁰If your right hand causes you to sin, cut it off and throw it away! It is much better for you to lose one of your limbs than for your whole body to go to hell.

Teaching about Divorce
(Mt 19.9; Mk 10.11–12; Lk 16.18)

31 "It was also said, 'Anyone who divorces his wife must give her a written notice of divorce.' ³²But now I tell you: if a man divorces his wife, for any cause other than her unfaithfulness, then he is guilty of making her commit adultery if she marries again; and the man who marries her commits adultery also.

Teaching about Vows

33 "You have also heard that people were told in the past, 'Do not break your promise, but do

---

[a] **5.22** whoever is angry; *some manuscripts have* whoever without cause is angry

what you have vowed to the Lord to do.' ³⁴But now I tell you: do not use any vow when you make a promise. Do not swear by heaven, for it is God's throne; ³⁵nor by earth, for it is the resting place for his feet; nor by Jerusalem, for it is the city of the great King. ³⁶Do not even swear by your head, because you cannot make a single hair white or black. ³⁷Just say 'Yes' or 'No' – anything else you say comes from the Evil One.

Teaching about Revenge
(Lk 6.29–30)

38 "You have heard that it was said, 'An eye for an eye, and a tooth for a tooth.' ³⁹But now I tell you: do not take revenge on someone who wrongs you. If anyone slaps you on the right cheek, let him slap your left cheek too. ⁴⁰And if someone takes you to court to sue you for your shirt, let him have your coat as well. ⁴¹And if one of the occupation troops forces you to carry his pack one kilometre, carry it two kilometres. ⁴²When someone asks you for something, give it to him; when someone wants to borrow something, lend it to him.

Love for Enemies
(Lk 6.27–28, 32–36)

43 "You have heard that it was said, 'Love your friends, hate your enemies.' ⁴⁴But now I tell you: love your enemies and pray for those who persecute you, ⁴⁵so that you may become the children of your Father in heaven. For he makes his sun to shine on bad and good people alike, and gives rain to those who do good and to those who do evil. ⁴⁶Why should God reward you if you love only the people who love you? Even the tax collectors do that! ⁴⁷And if you speak only to your friends, have you done anything out of the ordinary? Even the pagans do that! ⁴⁸You must be perfect – just as your Father in heaven is perfect!

Teaching about Charity

6 "Make certain you do not perform your religious duties in public so that people will see what you do. If you do these things publicly, you will not have any reward from your Father in heaven.

2 "So when you give something to a needy person, do not make a big show of it, as the hypocrites do in the houses of worship and on the streets. They do it so that people will praise

them. I assure you, they have already been paid in full. ³But when you help a needy person, do it in such a way that even your closest friend will not know about it. ⁴Then it will be a private matter. And your Father, who sees what you do in private, will reward you.

Teaching about Prayer
(Lk 11.2–4)

5   "When you pray, do not be like the hypocrites! They love to stand up and pray in the houses of worship and on the street corners, so that everyone will see them. I assure you, they have already been paid in full. ⁶But when you pray, go to your room, close the door, and pray to your Father, who is unseen. And your Father, who sees what you do in private, will reward you.

7   "When you pray, do not use a lot of meaningless words, as the pagans do, who think that their gods will hear them because their prayers are long. ⁸Do not be like them. Your Father already knows what you need before you ask him. ⁹This, then, is how you should pray:

'Our Father in heaven:
    May your holy name be honoured;
10   may your Kingdom come;
    may your will be done on earth as it is in heaven.
11   Give us today the food we need.ᵃ
12   Forgive us the wrongs we have done,
    as we forgive the wrongs that others have done to us.
13   Do not bring us to hard testing,
    but keep us safe from the Evil One.'ᵇ

14   "If you forgive others the wrongs they have done to you, your Father in heaven will also forgive you. ¹⁵But if you do not forgive others, then your Father will not forgive the wrongs you have done.

Teaching about Fasting

16   "And when you fast, do not put on a sad face as the hypocrites do. They neglect their appearance so that everyone will see that they are fasting. I assure you, they have already been paid in full. ¹⁷When you go without food, wash your face and comb your hair, ¹⁸so that others

cannot know that you are fasting – only your Father, who is unseen, will know. And your Father, who sees what you do in private, will reward you.

Riches in Heaven
(Lk 12.33–34)

19   "Do not store up riches for yourselves here on earth, where moths and rust destroy, and robbers break in and steal. ²⁰Instead, store up riches for yourselves in heaven, where moths and rust cannot destroy, and robbers cannot break in and steal. ²¹For your heart will always be where your riches are.

The Light of the Body
(Lk 11.34–36)

22   "The eyes are like a lamp for the body. If your eyes are sound, your whole body will be full of light; ²³but if your eyes are no good, your body will be in darkness. So if the light in you is darkness, how terribly dark it will be!

God and Possessions
(Lk 16.13; 12.22–31)

24   "No one can be a slave of two masters; he will hate one and love the other; he will be loyal to one and despise the other. You cannot serve both God and money.

25   "This is why I tell you not to be worried about the food and drink you need in order to stay alive, or about clothes for your body. After all, isn't life worth more than food? And isn't the body worth more than clothes? ²⁶Look at the birds: they do not sow seeds, gather a harvest and put it in barns; yet your Father in heaven takes care of them! Aren't you worth much more than birds? ²⁷Can any of you live a bit longerᶜ by worrying about it?

28   "And why worry about clothes? Look how the wild flowers grow: they do not work or make clothes for themselves. ²⁹But I tell you that not even King Solomon with all his wealth had clothes as beautiful as one of these flowers. ³⁰It is God who clothes the wild grass – grass that is here today and gone tomorrow, burnt up in the oven. Won't he be all the more sure to clothe you? How little faith you have!

31   "So do not start worrying: 'Where will my food come from? or my drink? or my clothes?' ³²(These are the things the pagans are always

ᵃ **6.11** we need; *or* for today; *or* for tomorrow.
ᵇ **6.13** *Some manuscripts add* For yours is the kingdom, and the power, and the glory for ever. Amen.

ᶜ **6.27** live a bit longer; *or* grow a bit taller.

concerned about.) Your Father in heaven knows that you need all these things. ³³Instead, be concerned above everything else with the Kingdom of God and with what he requires of you, and he will provide you with all these other things. ³⁴So do not worry about tomorrow; it will have enough worries of its own. There is no need to add to the troubles each day brings.

Judging Others
(Lk 6.37–38, 41–42)

7 ⟨t⟩ "Do not judge others, so that God will not judge you, ²for God will judge you in the same way as you judge others, and he will apply to you the same rules you apply to others. ³Why, then, do you look at the speck in your brother's eye, and pay no attention to the log in your own eye? ⁴How dare you say to your brother, 'Please, let me take that speck out of your eye,' when you have a log in your own eye? ⁵You hypocrite! First take the log out of your own eye, and then you will be able to see clearly to take the speck out of your brother's eye.

6   "Do not give what is holy to dogs – they will only turn and attack you. Do not throw your pearls in front of pigs – they will only trample them underfoot.

Ask, Seek, Knock
(Lk 11.9–13)

7   "Ask, and you will receive; seek, and you will find; knock, and the door will be opened to you. ⁸For everyone who asks will receive, and anyone who seeks will find, and the door will be opened to those who knock. ⁹Would any of you who are fathers give your son a stone when he asks for bread? ¹⁰Or would you give him a snake when he asks for a fish? ¹¹Bad as you are, you know how to give good things to your children. How much more, then, will your Father in heaven give good things to those who ask him!

12   "Do for others what you want them to do for you: this is the meaning of the Law of Moses and of the teachings of the prophets.

The Narrow Gate
(Lk 13.24)

13   "Go in through the narrow gate, because the gate to hell is wide and the road that leads to it is easy, and there are many who travel it. ¹⁴But the gate to life is narrow and the way that leads to it is hard, and there are few people who find it.

A Tree and its Fruit
(Lk 6.43–44)

15   "Be on your guard against false prophets; they come to you looking like sheep on the outside, but on the inside they are really like wild wolves. ¹⁶You will know them by what they do. Thorn bushes do not bear grapes, and briars do not bear figs. ¹⁷A healthy tree bears good fruit, but a poor tree bears bad fruit. ¹⁸A healthy tree cannot bear bad fruit, and a poor tree cannot bear good fruit. ¹⁹And any tree that does not bear good fruit is cut down and thrown in the fire. ²⁰So then, you will know the false prophets by what they do.

I Never Knew You
(Lk 13.25–27)

21   "Not everyone who calls me 'Lord, Lord' will enter the Kingdom of heaven, but only those who do what my Father in heaven wants them to do. ²²When Judgement Day comes, many will say to me, 'Lord, Lord! In your name we spoke God's message, by your name we drove out many demons and performed many miracles!' ²³Then I will say to them, 'I never knew you. Get away from me, you wicked people!'

The Two House Builders
(Lk 6.47–49)

24   ⟨p⟩ "So then, anyone who hears these words of mine and obeys them is like a wise man who built his house on rock. ²⁵The rain poured down, the rivers overflowed, and the wind blew hard against that house. But it did not fall, because it was built on rock.

26   "But anyone who hears these words of mine and does not obey them is like a foolish man who built his house on sand. ²⁷The rain poured down, the rivers overflowed, the wind blew hard against that house, and it fell. And what a terrible fall that was!"

The Authority of Jesus

28   When Jesus finished saying these things, the crowd was amazed at the way he taught. ²⁹He wasn't like the teachers of the Law; instead, he taught with authority.

Jesus Heals a Man
(Mk 1.40–45; Lk 5.12–16)

8 ⟨M⟩ When Jesus came down from the hill, large crowds followed him. ²Then a man suffering from a dreaded skin disease came to him, knelt down before him, and said, "Sir, if you want to, you can make me clean."[a]

3 Jesus stretched out his hand and touched him. "I do want to," he answered. "Be clean!" At once the man was healed of his disease. [4]Then Jesus said to him, "Listen! Don't tell anyone, but go straight to the priest and let him examine you; then in order to prove to everyone that you are cured, offer the sacrifice that Moses ordered."

Jesus Heals a Roman Officer's Servant
(Lk 7.1–10)

5 When Jesus entered Capernaum, a Roman officer met him and begged for help: [6]"Sir, my servant is sick in bed at home, unable to move and suffering terribly."

7 "I will go and make him well," Jesus said.

8 "Oh no, sir," answered the officer. "I do not deserve to have you come into my house. Just give the order, and my servant will get well. [9]I, too, am a man under the authority of superior officers, and I have soldiers under me. I order this one, 'Go!' and he goes; and I order that one, 'Come!' and he comes; and I order my slave, 'Do this!' and he does it."

10 When Jesus heard this, he was surprised and said to the people following him, "I tell you, I have never found anyone in Israel with faith like this. [11]I assure you that many will come from the east and the west and sit down with Abraham, Isaac, and Jacob at the feast in the Kingdom of heaven. [12]But those who should be in the Kingdom will be thrown out into the darkness, where they will cry and grind their teeth." [13]Then Jesus said to the officer, "Go home, and what you believe will be done for you."

And the officer's servant was healed that very moment.

Jesus Heals Many People
(Mk 1.29–34; Lk 4.38–41)

14 Jesus went to Peter's home, and there he saw Peter's mother-in-law sick in bed with a fever. [15]He touched her hand; the fever left her, and she got up and began to wait on him.

16 When evening came, people brought to Jesus many who had demons in them. Jesus drove out the evil spirits with a word and healed all who were sick. [17]He did this to make what the prophet Isaiah had said come true, "He himself took our sickness and carried away our diseases."

The Would-be Followers of Jesus
(Lk 9.57–62)

18 When Jesus noticed the crowd round him, he ordered his disciples to go to the other side of the lake. [19]A teacher of the Law came to him. "Teacher," he said, "I am ready to go with you wherever you go."

20 Jesus answered him, "Foxes have holes, and birds have nests, but the Son of Man has nowhere to lie down and rest."

21 Another man, who was a disciple, said, "Sir, first let me go back and bury my father."

22 "Follow me," Jesus answered, "and let the dead bury their own dead."

Jesus Calms a Storm
(Mk 4.35–41; Lk 8.22–25)

23 Jesus got into a boat, and his disciples went with him. [24]Suddenly a fierce storm hit the lake, and the boat was in danger of sinking. But Jesus was asleep. [25]The disciples went to him and woke him up. "Save us, Lord!" they said. "We are about to die!"

26 "Why are you so frightened?" Jesus answered. "How little faith you have!" Then he got up and ordered the winds and the waves to stop, and there was a great calm.

---

[a] **8.2** MAKE ME CLEAN: *This disease was considered to make a person ritually unclean.*

27 Everyone was amazed. "What kind of man is this?" they said. "Even the winds and the waves obey him!"

Jesus Heals Two Men with Demons
(Mk 5.1–20; Lk 8.26–39)

28 When Jesus came to the territory of Gadara on the other side of the lake, he was met by two men who came out of the burial caves there. These men had demons in them and were so fierce that no one dared travel on that road. ²⁹At once they screamed, "What do you want with us, you Son of God? Have you come to punish us before the right time?"

30 Not far away there was a large herd of pigs feeding. ³¹So the demons begged Jesus, "If you are going to drive us out, send us into that herd of pigs."

32 "Go," Jesus told them; so they left and went off into the pigs. The whole herd rushed down the side of the cliff into the lake and was drowned.

33 The men who had been taking care of the pigs ran away and went into the town, where they told the whole story and what had happened to the men with the demons. ³⁴So everyone from the town went out to meet Jesus; and when they saw him, they begged him to leave their territory.

Jesus Heals a Paralysed Man
(Mk 2.1–12; Lk 5.17–26)

9 Jesus got into the boat and went back across the lake to his own town,ᵃ ²where some people brought to him a paralysed man, lying on a bed. When Jesus saw how much faith they had, he said to the paralysed man, "Courage, my son! Your sins are forgiven."

3 Then some teachers of the Law said to themselves, "This man is speaking blasphemy!"

4 Jesus perceived what they were thinking, so he said, "Why are you thinking such evil things? ⁵Is it easier to say, 'Your sins are forgiven,' or to say, 'Get up and walk'? ⁶I will prove to you, then, that the Son of Man has authority on earth to forgive sins." So he said to the paralysed man, "Get up, pick up your bed, and go home!"

7 The man got up and went home. ⁸When the people saw it, they were afraid, and praised God for giving such authority to people.

ᵃ **9.1** HIS OWN TOWN: *Capernaum (see 4.13).*

Jesus Calls Matthew
(Mk 2.13–17; Lk 5.27–32)

9 Jesus left that place, and as he walked along, he saw a tax collector, named Matthew, sitting in his office. He said to him, "Follow me."

Matthew got up and followed him.

10 While Jesus was having a meal in Matthew's house,ᵇ many tax collectors and other outcasts came and joined Jesus and his disciples at the table. ¹¹Some Pharisees saw this and asked his disciples, "Why does your teacher eat with such people?"

12 Jesus heard them and answered, "People who are well do not need a doctor, but only those who are sick. ¹³Go and find out what is meant by the scripture that says: 'It is kindness that I want, not animal sacrifices.' I have not come to call respectable people, but outcasts."

The Question about Fasting
(Mk 2.18–22; Lk 5.33–39)

14 Then the followers of John the Baptist came to Jesus, asking, "Why is it that we and the Pharisees fast often, but your disciples don't fast at all?"

15 Jesus answered, "Do you expect the guests at a wedding party to be sad as long as the bridegroom is with them? Of course not! But the day will come when the bridegroom will be taken away from them, and then they will fast.

16 "No one patches up an old coat with a piece of new cloth, for the new patch will shrink and make an even bigger hole in the coat. ¹⁷Nor does anyone pour new wine into used wineskins, for the skins will burst, the wine will pour out, and the skins will be ruined. Instead, new wine is poured into fresh wineskins, and both will keep in good condition."

The Official's Daughter and the Woman who Touched Jesus' Cloak
(Mk 5.21–43; Lk 8.40–56)

18 While Jesus was saying this, a Jewish official came to him, knelt down before him, and said, "My daughter has just died; but come and place your hands on her, and she will live."

19 So Jesus got up and followed him, and his disciples went along with him.

20 A woman who had suffered from severe

ᵇ **9.10** in Matthew's house; *or* in his (*that is,* Jesus') house.

bleeding for twelve years came up behind Jesus and touched the edge of his cloak. [21]She said to herself, "If I only touch his cloak, I will get well."

22 Jesus turned round and saw her, and said, "Courage, my daughter! Your faith has made you well." At that very moment the woman became well.

23 Then Jesus went into the official's house. When he saw the musicians for the funeral and the people all stirred up, [24]he said, "Get out, everybody! The little girl is not dead – she is only sleeping!" Then they all laughed at him. [25]But as soon as the people had been put out, Jesus went into the girl's room and took hold of her hand, and she got up. [26]The news about this spread all over that part of the country.

The inside of a synagogue showing the bimah (reading-seat) and the Star of David (9.35)

Jesus Heals Two Blind Men

27 Jesus left that place, and as he walked along, two blind men started following him. "Take pity on us, Son of David!" they shouted.

28 When Jesus had gone indoors, the two blind men came to him, and he asked them, "Do you believe that I can heal you?"

"Yes, sir!" they answered.

29 Then Jesus touched their eyes and said, "Let it happen, then, just as you believe!" – [30]and their sight was restored. Jesus spoke sternly to them, "Don't tell this to anyone!"

31 But they left and spread the news about Jesus all over that part of the country.

Jesus Heals a Man who could not Speak

32 As the men were leaving, some people brought to Jesus a man who could not talk because he had a demon. [33]But as soon as the demon was driven out, the man started talking, and everyone was amazed. "We have never seen anything like this in Israel!" they exclaimed.

34 But the Pharisees said, "It is the chief of the demons who gives Jesus the power to drive out demons."

Jesus has Pity for the People

35 Jesus went round visiting all the towns and villages. He taught in the synagogues, preached the Good News about the Kingdom, and healed people with every kind of disease and sickness. [36]As he saw the crowds, his heart was filled with pity for them, because they were worried and helpless, like sheep without a shepherd. [37]So he said to his disciples, "The harvest is large, but there are few workers to gather it in. [38]Pray to the owner of the harvest that he will send out workers to gather in his harvest."

The Twelve Apostles
(Mk 3.13–19; Lk 6.12–16)

10 Jesus called his twelve disciples together and gave them authority to drive out evil spirits and to heal every disease and every sickness. [2]These are the names of the twelve apostles: first, Simon (called Peter) and his brother Andrew; James and his brother John, the sons of Zebedee; [3]Philip and Bartholomew; Thomas and Matthew, the tax collector; James son of Alphaeus, and Thaddaeus; [4]Simon the Patriot, and Judas Iscariot, who betrayed Jesus.

The Mission of the Twelve
(Mk 6.7–13; Lk 9.1–6)

5 These twelve men were sent out by Jesus with the following instructions: "Do not go to any Gentile territory or any Samaritan towns. [6]Instead, you are to go to the lost sheep of the people of Israel. [7]Go and preach, 'The Kingdom of heaven is near!' [8]Heal the sick, bring the dead back to life, heal those who suffer from dreaded skin diseases, and drive out demons. You have received without paying, so give without being paid. [9]Do not carry any gold, silver, or copper money in your pockets; [10]do not carry a beggar's bag for the journey or

an extra shirt or shoes or a stick. Workers should be given what they need.

11 "When you come to a town or village, go in and look for someone who is willing to welcome you, and stay with him until you leave that place. [12]When you go into a house, say, 'Peace be with you.' [13]If the people in that house welcome you, let your greeting of peace remain; but if they do not welcome you, then take back your greeting. [14]And if some home or town will not welcome you or listen to you, then leave that place and shake the dust off your feet. [15]I assure you that on the Judgement Day God will show more mercy to the people of Sodom and Gomorrah than to the people of that town!

Coming Persecutions
(Mk 13.9–13; Lk 21.12–17)

16 "Listen! I am sending you out just like sheep to a pack of wolves. You must be as cautious as snakes and as gentle as doves. [17]Watch out, for there will be those who will arrest you and take you to court, and they will whip you in the synagogues. [18]For my sake you will be brought to trial before rulers and kings, to tell the Good News to them and to the Gentiles. [19]When they bring you to trial, do not worry about what you are going to say or how you will say it; when the time comes, you will be given what you will say. [20]For the words you will speak will not be yours; they will come from the Spirit of your Father speaking through you.

21 "Men will hand over their own brothers to be put to death, and fathers will do the same to their children; children will turn against their parents and have them put to death. [22]Everyone will hate you because of me. But whoever holds out to the end will be saved. [23]When they persecute you in one town, run away to another one. I assure you that you will not finish your work in all the towns of Israel before the Son of Man comes.

24 "No pupil is greater than his teacher; no slave is greater than his master. [25]So a pupil should be satisfied to become like his teacher, and a slave like his master. If the head of the family is called Beelzebul, the members of the family will be called even worse names!

Whom to Fear
(Lk 12.2–7)

26 "So do not be afraid of people. Whatever is now covered up will be uncovered, and every secret will be made known. [27]What I am telling you in the dark you must repeat in broad daylight, and what you have heard in private you must announce from the housetops. [28]Do not be afraid of those who kill the body but cannot kill the soul; rather be afraid of God, who can destroy both body and soul in hell. [29]For only a penny you can buy two sparrows, yet not one sparrow falls to the ground without your Father's consent. [30]As for you, even the hairs of your head have all been counted. [31]So do not be afraid; you are worth much more than many sparrows!

Confessing and Rejecting Christ
(Lk 12.8–9)

32 "For those who declare publicly that they belong to me, I will do the same before my Father in heaven. [33]But if anyone rejects me publicly, I will reject him before my Father in heaven.

Not Peace, but a Sword
(Lk 12.51–53; 14.26–27)

34 "Do not think that I have come to bring peace to the world. No, I did not come to bring peace, but a sword. [35]I came to set sons against their fathers, daughters against their mothers, daughters-in-law against their mothers-in-law; [36]your worst enemies will be the members of your own family.

37 "Those who love their father or mother more than me are not fit to be my disciples; those who love their son or daughter more than me are not fit to be my disciples. [38]Those who do not take up their cross and follow in my steps are not fit to be my disciples. [39]Those who try to gain their own life will lose it; but those who lose their life for my sake will gain it.

Rewards
(Mk 9.41)

40 "Whoever welcomes you welcomes me; and whoever welcomes me welcomes the one who sent me. [41]Whoever welcomes God's messenger because he is God's messenger, will share in his reward. And whoever welcomes a good man because he is good, will share in his reward. [42]You can be sure that whoever gives even a drink of cold water to one of the least of these my followers because he is my follower, will certainly receive a reward."

KEY PLACES IN MATTHEW

Sidon
Phoenicia
Tyre
Caesarea Philippi
Chorazin Capernaum
Galilee Bethsaida
Lake Galilee
Nazareth Gadara
River Jordan
Samaria
Arimathea
Bethphage
Perea
Jerusalem Jericho
Judea Bethany
Bethlehem
Idumea
Dead Sea
Mediterranean Sea
Nile Delta
Egypt
0 60 km

The Messengers from John the Baptist
(Lk 7.18–35)

11 When Jesus finished giving these instructions to his twelve disciples, he left that place and went off to teach and preach in the towns near there.

2 When John the Baptist heard in prison about the things that Christ was doing, he sent some of his disciples to him. [3]"Tell us," they asked Jesus, "are you the one John said was going to come, or should we expect someone else?"

4 Jesus answered, "Go back and tell John what you are hearing and seeing: [5]the blind can see, the lame can walk, those who suffer from dreaded skin diseases are made clean,[a] the deaf hear, the dead are brought back to life, and the Good News is preached to the poor. [6]How happy are those who have no doubts about me!"

7 While John's disciples were leaving, Jesus spoke about him to the crowds: "When you went out to John in the desert, what did you expect to see? A blade of grass bending in the wind? [8]What did you go out to see? A man dressed up in fancy clothes? People who dress like that live in palaces! [9]Tell me, what did you go out to see? A prophet? Yes indeed, but you saw much more than a prophet. [10]For John is the one of whom the scripture says: 'God said, I will send my messenger ahead of you to open the way for you.' [11]I assure you that John the Baptist is greater than anyone who has ever lived. But the one who is least in the Kingdom of heaven is greater than John. [12]From the time John preached his message until this very day the Kingdom of heaven has suffered violent attacks,[b] and violent men try to seize it. [13]Until the time of John all the prophets and the Law of Moses spoke about the Kingdom; [14]and if you are willing to believe their message, John is Elijah, whose coming was predicted. [15]Listen, then, if you have ears!

16 "Now, to what can I compare the people of this day? They are like children sitting in the

---

[a] **11.5** MADE CLEAN: *See 8.2.*

[b] **11.12** has suffered violent attacks; *or* has been coming violently.

market place. One group shouts to the other, [17]'We played wedding music for you, but you wouldn't dance! We sang funeral songs, but you wouldn't cry!' [18]When John came, he fasted and drank no wine, and everyone said, 'He has a demon in him!' [19]When the Son of Man came, he ate and drank, and everyone said, 'Look at this man! He is a glutton and a drinker, a friend of tax collectors and other outcasts!' God's wisdom, however, is shown to be true by its results."

The Unbelieving Towns
(Lk 10.13–15)

20   The people in the towns where Jesus had performed most of his miracles did not turn from their sins, so he reproached those towns. [21]"How terrible it will be for you, Chorazin! How terrible for you too, Bethsaida! If the miracles which were performed in you had been performed in Tyre and Sidon, the people there would long ago have put on sackcloth and sprinkled ashes on themselves, to show that they had turned from their sins! [22]I assure you that on the Judgement Day God will show more mercy to the people of Tyre and Sidon than to you! [23]And as for you, Capernaum! Did you want to lift yourself up to heaven? You will be thrown down to hell! If the miracles which were performed in you had been performed in Sodom, it would still be in existence today! [24]You can be sure that on the Judgement Day God will show more mercy to Sodom than to you!"

Come to Me and Rest
(Lk 10.21–22)

25   At that time Jesus said, "Father, Lord of heaven and earth! I thank you because you have shown to the unlearned what you have hidden from the wise and learned. [26]Yes, Father, this was how you wanted it to happen.

27   "My Father has given me all things. No one knows the Son except the Father, and no one knows the Father except the Son and those to whom the Son chooses to reveal him.

28   "Come to me, all of you who are tired from carrying heavy loads, and I will give you rest. [29]Take my yoke and put it on you, and learn from me, because I am gentle and humble in spirit; and you will find rest. [30]For the yoke I will give you is easy, and the load I will put on you is light."

The Question about the Sabbath
(Mk 2.23–28; Lk 6.1–5)

12   Not long afterwards Jesus was walking through some cornfields on the Sabbath. His disciples were hungry, so they began to pick ears of corn and eat the grain. [2]When the Pharisees saw this, they said to Jesus, "Look, it is against our Law for your disciples to do this on the Sabbath!"

3   Jesus answered, "Have you never read what David did that time when he and his men were hungry? [4]He went into the house of God, and he and his men ate the bread offered to God, even though it was against the Law for them to eat it – only the priests were allowed to eat that bread. [5]Or have you not read in the Law of Moses that every Sabbath the priests in the Temple actually break the Sabbath law, yet they are not guilty? [6]I tell you that there is something here greater than the Temple. [7]The scripture says, 'It is kindness that I want, not animal sacrifices.' If you really knew what this means, you would not condemn people who are not guilty; [8]for the Son of Man is Lord of the Sabbath."

The Man with a Paralysed Hand
(Mk 3.1–6; Lk 6.6–11)

9   Jesus left that place and went to a synagogue, [10]where there was a man who had a paralysed hand. Some people were there who wanted to accuse Jesus of doing wrong, so they asked him, "Is it against our Law to heal on the Sabbath?"

11   Jesus answered, "What if one of you has a sheep and it falls into a deep hole on the Sabbath? Will you not take hold of it and lift it out? [12]And a human being is worth much more than a sheep! So then, our Law does allow us to help someone on the Sabbath." [13]Then he said to the man with the paralysed hand, "Stretch out your hand."

He stretched it out, and it became well again, just like the other one. [14]Then the Pharisees left and made plans to kill Jesus.

God's Chosen Servant

15   When Jesus heard about the plot against him, he went away from that place; and large crowds followed him. He healed all those who were ill [16]and gave them orders not to tell others about him. [17]He did this so as to make what God had said through the prophet Isaiah come true:

18   "Here is my servant, whom I have chosen,
          the one I love, and with whom I am
            pleased.
        I will send my Spirit upon him,
          and he will announce my judgement to
            the nations.
19   He will not argue or shout,
          or make loud speeches in the streets.
20   He will not break off a bent reed,
          or put out a flickering lamp.
        He will persist until he causes justice to
            triumph,
21   and in him all peoples will put their hope."

Jesus and Beelzebul

(Mk 3.20–30; Lk 11.14–23)

22   Then some people brought to Jesus a
        man who was blind and could not talk
        because he had a demon. Jesus healed
the man, so that he was able to talk and see.
²³The crowds were all amazed at what Jesus had
done. "Could he be the Son of David?" they
asked.
24   When the Pharisees heard this, they replied,
"He drives out demons only because their ruler
Beelzebul gives him power to do so."
25   Jesus knew what they were thinking, so he
said to them, "Any country that divides itself
into groups which fight each other will not last
very long. And any town or family that divides
itself into groups which fight each other will fall
apart. ²⁶So if one group is fighting another in
Satan's kingdom, this means that it is already
divided into groups and will soon fall apart!
²⁷You say that I drive out demons because
Beelzebul gives me the power to do so. Well,
then, who gives your followers the power to
drive them out? What your own followers do
proves that you are wrong! ²⁸No, it is not
Beelzebul, but God's Spirit, who gives me the
power to drive out demons, which proves that
the Kingdom of God has already come upon you.
29   "No one can break into a strong man's house
and take away his belongings unless he first ties
up the strong man; then he can plunder his
house.
30   "Anyone who is not for me is really against
me; anyone who does not help me gather is
really scattering. ³¹And so I tell you that people
can be forgiven any sin and any evil thing they
say;ᵃ but whoever says evil things against the
Holy Spirit will not be forgiven. ³²Anyone who

ᵃ **12.31** evil thing they say; *or* evil thing they say
against God.

says something against the Son of Man can be
forgiven; but whoever says something against the
Holy Spirit will not be forgiven – now or ever.

A Tree and its Fruit

(Lk 6.43–45)

33   "To have good fruit you must have a healthy
        tree; if you have a poor tree, you will have bad
        fruit. A tree is known by the kind of fruit it bears.
        ³⁴You snakes – how can you say good things
        when you are evil? For the mouth speaks what
        the heart is full of. ³⁵A good person brings good
        things out of a treasure of good things; a bad
        person brings bad things out of a treasure of bad
        things.
36   "You can be sure that on Judgement Day
        everyone will have to give account of every
        useless word he has ever spoken. ³⁷Your words
        will be used to judge you – to declare you either
        innocent or guilty."

The Demand for a Miracle

(Mk 8.11–12; Lk 11.29–32)

38   Then some teachers of the Law and some
        Pharisees spoke up. "Teacher," they said, "we
        want to see you perform a miracle."
39   "How evil and godless are the people of this
        day!" Jesus exclaimed. "You ask me for a
        miracle? No! The only miracle you will be given
        is the miracle of the prophet Jonah. ⁴⁰In the
        same way that Jonah spent three days and
        nights in the big fish, so will the Son of Man
        spend three days and nights in the depths of the
        earth. ⁴¹On Judgement Day the people of
        Nineveh will stand up and accuse you, because
        they turned from their sins when they heard
        Jonah preach; and I tell you that there is some-
        thing here greater than Jonah! ⁴²On Judgement
        Day the Queen of Sheba will stand up and
        accuse you, because she travelled all the way
        from her country to listen to King Solomon's
        wise teaching; and I assure you that there is
        something here greater than Solomon!

The Return of the Evil Spirit

(Lk 11.24–26)

43   "When an evil spirit goes out of a person, it
        travels over dry country looking for a place to
        rest. If it can't find one, ⁴⁴it says to itself, 'I will
        go back to my house.' So it goes back and finds
        the house empty, clean, and all tidy. ⁴⁵Then it
        goes out and brings along seven other spirits
        even worse than itself, and they come and live

there. So when it is all over, that person is in a worse state than he was at the beginning. This is what will happen to the evil people of this day."

Jesus' Mother and Brothers
(Mk 3.31–35; Lk 8.19–21)

46 Jesus was still talking to the people when his mother and brothers arrived. They stood outside, asking to speak with him. [47]So one of the people there said to him, "Look, your mother and brothers are standing outside, and they want to speak with you."[a]

48 Jesus answered, "Who is my mother? Who are my brothers?" [49]Then he pointed to his disciples and said, "Look! Here are my mother and my brothers! [50]Whoever does what my Father in heaven wants him to do is my brother, my sister, and my mother."

The Parable of the Sower
(Mk 4.1–9; Lk 8.4–8)

13 ✝ℙ That same day Jesus left the house and went to the lakeside, where he sat down to teach. [2]The crowd that gathered round him was so large that he got into a boat and sat in it, while the crowd stood on the shore. [3]He used parables to tell them many things.

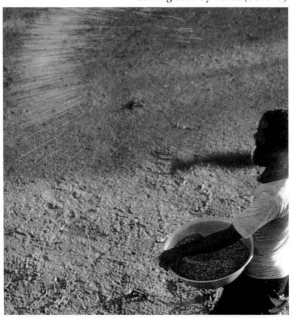

Sowing seed by hand (13.1–9)

"Once there was a man who went out to sow corn. [4]As he scattered the seed in the field, some of it fell along the path, and the birds came and ate it up. [5]Some of it fell on rocky ground, where there was little soil. The seeds soon sprouted, because the soil wasn't deep. [6]But when the sun came up, it burnt the young plants; and because the roots had not grown deep enough, the plants soon dried up. [7]Some of the seed fell among thorn bushes, which grew up and choked the plants. [8]But some seeds fell in good soil, and the plants produced corn; some produced a hundred grains, others sixty, and others thirty."

9 And Jesus concluded, "Listen, then, if you have ears!"

The Purpose of the Parables
(Mk 4.10–12; Lk 8.9–10)

10 Then the disciples came to Jesus and asked him, "Why do you use parables when you talk to the people?"

11 Jesus answered, "The knowledge about the secrets of the Kingdom of heaven has been given to you, but not to them. [12]For the person who has something will be given more, so that he will have more than enough; but the person who has nothing will have taken away from him even the little he has. [13]The reason I use parables in talking to them is that they look, but do not see, and they listen, but do not hear or understand. [14]So the prophecy of Isaiah applies to them:

'This people will listen and listen, but not
        understand;
    they will look and look, but not see,

15 because their minds are dull,
    and they have stopped up their ears
    and have closed their eyes.
Otherwise, their eyes would see,
    their ears would hear,
    their minds would understand,
and they would turn to me, says God,
    and I would heal them.'

16 "As for you, how fortunate you are! Your eyes see and your ears hear. [17]I assure you that many prophets and many of God's people wanted very much to see what you see, but they could not, and to hear what you hear, but they did not.

Jesus Explains the Parable of the Sower
(Mk 4.13–20; Lk 8.11–15)

18 "Listen, then, and learn what the parable of the sower means. [19]Those who hear the message

about the Kingdom but do not understand it are like the seeds that fell along the path. The Evil One comes and snatches away what was sown in them. 20The seeds that fell on rocky ground stand for those who receive the message gladly as soon as they hear it. 21But it does not sink deep into them, and they don't last long. So when trouble or persecution comes because of the message, they give up at once. 22The seeds that fell among thorn bushes stand for those who hear the message; but the worries about this life and the love for riches choke the message, and they don't bear fruit. 23And the seeds sown in the good soil stand for those who hear the message and understand it: they bear fruit, some as much as a hundred, others sixty, and others thirty."

The Parable of the Weeds

24 Jesus told them another parable: "The Kingdom of heaven is like this. A man sowed good seed in his field. 25One night, when everyone was asleep, an enemy came and sowed weeds among the wheat and went away. 26When the plants grew and the ears of corn began to form, then the weeds showed up. 27The man's servants came to him and said, 'Sir, it was good seed you sowed in your field; where did the weeds come from?' 28'It was some enemy who did this,' he answered. 'Do you want us to go and pull up the weeds?' they asked him. 29'No,' he answered, 'because as you gather the weeds you might pull up some of the wheat along with them. 30Let the wheat and the weeds both grow together until harvest. Then I will tell the harvest workers to pull up the weeds first, tie them in bundles and burn them, and then to gather in the wheat and put it in my barn.'"

The Parable of the Mustard Seed

(Mk 4.30–32; Lk 13.18–19)

31 Jesus told them another parable: "The Kingdom of heaven is like this. A man takes a mustard seed and sows it in his field. 32It is the smallest of all seeds, but when it grows up, it is the biggest of all plants. It becomes a tree, so that birds come and make their nests in its branches."

The Parable of the Yeast

(Lk 13.20–21)

33 Jesus told them still another parable: "The Kingdom of heaven is like this. A woman takes some yeast and mixes it with forty litres of flour until the whole batch of dough rises."

Jesus' Use of Parables

(Mk 4.33–34)

34 Jesus used parables to tell all these things to the crowds; he would not say a thing to them without using a parable. 35He did this to make what the prophet had said come true:

> "I will use parables when I speak to them;
> I will tell them things unknown since the creation of the world."

Jesus Explains the Parable of the Weeds

36 When Jesus had left the crowd and gone indoors, his disciples came to him and said, "Tell us what the parable about the weeds in the field means."

37 Jesus answered, "The man who sowed the good seed is the Son of Man; 38the field is the world; the good seed is the people who belong to the Kingdom; the weeds are the people who belong to the Evil One; 39and the enemy who sowed the weeds is the Devil. The harvest is the end of the age, and the harvest workers are angels. 40Just as the weeds are gathered up and burnt in the fire, so the same thing will happen at the end of the age: 41the Son of Man will send out his angels to gather up out of his Kingdom all those who cause people to sin and all others who do evil things, 42and they will throw them into the fiery furnace, where they will cry and grind their teeth. 43Then God's people will shine like the sun in their Father's Kingdom. Listen, then, if you have ears!

The Parable of the Hidden Treasure

44 "The Kingdom of heaven is like this. A man happens to find a treasure hidden in a field. He covers it up again, and is so happy that he goes and sells everything he has, and then goes back and buys that field.

The Parable of the Pearl

45 "Also, the Kingdom of heaven is like this. A man is looking for fine pearls, 46and when he finds one that is unusually fine, he goes and sells everything he has, and buys that pearl.

The Parable of the Net

47 "Also, the Kingdom of heaven is like this. Some fishermen throw their net out in the lake and catch all kinds of fish. ⁴⁸When the net is full, they pull it to shore and sit down to divide the fish: the good ones go into their buckets, the worthless ones are thrown away. ⁴⁹It will be like this at the end of the age: the angels will go out and gather up the evil people from among the good ⁵⁰and will throw them into the fiery furnace, where they will cry and grind their teeth.

New Truths and Old

51 "Do you understand these things?" Jesus asked them.

"Yes," they answered.

52 So he replied, "This means, then, that every teacher of the Law who becomes a disciple in the Kingdom of heaven is like the owner of a house who takes new and old things out of his storeroom."

Jesus is Rejected at Nazareth
(Mk 6.1–6; Lk 4.16–30)

53 When Jesus finished telling these parables, he left that place ⁵⁴and went back to his home town. He taught in the synagogue, and those who heard him were amazed. "Where did he get such wisdom?" they asked. "And what about his miracles? ⁵⁵Isn't he the carpenter's son? Isn't Mary his mother, and aren't James, Joseph, Simon, and Judas his brothers? ⁵⁶Aren't all his sisters living here? Where did he get all this?" ⁵⁷And so they rejected him.

Jesus said to them, "A prophet is respected everywhere except in his home town and by his own family." ⁵⁸Because they did not have faith, he did not perform many miracles there.

The Death of John the Baptist
(Mk 6.14–29; Lk 9.7–9)

14 At that time Herod, the ruler of Galilee, heard about Jesus. ²"He is really John the Baptist, who has come back to life," he told his officials. "That is why he has this power to perform miracles."

3 For Herod had earlier ordered John's arrest, and he had him chained and put in prison. He had done this because of Herodias, his brother Philip's wife. ⁴For some time John the Baptist had told Herod, "It isn't right for you to be married to Herodias!" ⁵Herod wanted to kill him, but he was afraid of the Jewish people, because they considered John to be a prophet.

6 On Herod's birthday the daughter of Herodias danced in front of the whole group. Herod was so pleased ⁷that he promised her, "I swear that I will give you anything you ask for!"

8 At her mother's suggestion she asked him, "Give me here and now the head of John the Baptist on a dish!"

9 The king was sad, but because of the promise he had made in front of all his guests he gave orders that her wish be granted. ¹⁰So he had John beheaded in prison. ¹¹The head was brought in on a dish and given to the girl, who took it to her mother. ¹²John's disciples came, carried away his body, and buried it; then they went and told Jesus.

This church banner recalls Jesus' feeding of 5,000 people (14.13–21)

MATTHEW 15

Jesus Feeds a Great Crowd
(Mk 6.30–44; Lk 9.10–17; Jn 6.1–14)

13 When Jesus heard the news about John, he left there in a boat and went to a lonely place by himself. The people heard about it, so they left their towns and followed him by land. ¹⁴Jesus got out of the boat, and when he saw the large crowd, his heart was filled with pity for them, and he healed those who were ill.

15 That evening his disciples came to him and said, "It is already very late, and this is a lonely place. Send the people away and let them go to the villages to buy food for themselves."

16 "They don't have to leave," answered Jesus. "You yourselves give them something to eat!"

17 "All we have here are five loaves and two fish," they replied.

18 "Then bring them here to me," Jesus said. ¹⁹He ordered the people to sit down on the grass; then he took the five loaves and the two fish, looked up to heaven, and gave thanks to God. He broke the loaves and gave them to the disciples, and the disciples gave them to the people. ²⁰Everyone ate and had enough. Then the disciples took up twelve baskets full of what was left over. ²¹The number of men who ate was about 5,000, not counting the women and children.

Jesus Walks on the Water
(Mk 6.45–52; Jn 6.15–21)

22 Then Jesus made the disciples get into the boat and go on ahead to the other side of the lake, while he sent the people away. ²³After sending the people away, he went up a hill by himself to pray. When evening came, Jesus was there alone; ²⁴and by this time the boat was far out in the lake, tossed about by the waves, because the wind was blowing against it.

25 Between three and six o'clock in the morning Jesus came to the disciples, walking on the water. ²⁶When they saw him walking on the water, they were terrified. "It's a ghost!" they said, and screamed with fear.

27 Jesus spoke to them at once. "Courage!" he said. "It is I. Don't be afraid!"

28 Then Peter spoke up. "Lord, if it is really you, order me to come out on the water to you."

29 "Come!" answered Jesus. So Peter got out of the boat and started walking on the water to Jesus. ³⁰But when he noticed the strong wind, he was afraid and started to sink down in the water. "Save me, Lord!" he cried.

31 At once Jesus reached out and grabbed hold of him and said, "How little faith you have! Why did you doubt?"

32 They both got into the boat, and the wind died down. ³³Then the disciples in the boat worshipped Jesus. "Truly you are the Son of God!" they exclaimed.

Jesus Heals the Sick in Gennesaret
(Mk 6.53–56)

34 They crossed the lake and came to land at Gennesaret, ³⁵where the people recognized Jesus. So they sent for the sick people in all the surrounding country and brought them to Jesus. ³⁶They begged him to let those who were ill at least touch the edge of his cloak; and all who touched it were made well.

The Teaching of the Ancestors
(Mk 7.1–13)

15 Then some Pharisees and teachers of the Law came from Jerusalem to Jesus and asked him, ²"Why is it that your disciples disobey the teaching handed down by our ancestors? They don't wash their hands in the proper way before they eat!"

3 Jesus answered, "And why do you disobey God's command and follow your own teaching? ⁴For God said, 'Respect your father and your mother,' and 'Whoever curses his father or his mother is to be put to death.' ⁵But you teach that if a person has something he could use to help his father or mother, but says, 'This belongs to God,' ⁶he does not need to honour his father.ᵃ In this way you disregard God's command, in order to follow your own teaching. ⁷You hypocrites! How right Isaiah was when he prophesied about you!

8 'These people, says God, honour me with their words,
   but their heart is really far away from me.
9 It is no use for them to worship me,
   because they teach human rules as though they were my laws!'"

The Things that Make a Person Unclean
(Mk 7.14–23)

10 Then Jesus called the crowd to him and said to them, "Listen and understand! ¹¹It is not what

ᵃ **15.6** his father; *some manuscripts have* his father or mother.

19

goes into a person's mouth that makes him ritually unclean; rather, what comes out of it makes him unclean."

12 Then the disciples came to him and said, "Do you know that the Pharisees had their feelings hurt by what you said?"

13 "Every plant which my Father in heaven did not plant will be pulled up," answered Jesus. [14]"Don't worry about them! They are blind leaders of the blind; and when one blind man leads another, both fall into a ditch."

15 Peter spoke up, "Explain this saying to us."

16 Jesus said to them, "You are still no more intelligent than the others. [17]Don't you understand? Anything that goes into a person's mouth goes into his stomach and then on out of his body. [18]But the things that come out of the mouth come from the heart, and these are the things that make a person ritually unclean. [19]For from his heart come the evil ideas which lead him to kill, commit adultery, and do other immoral things; to rob, lie, and slander others. [20]These are the things that make a person unclean. But to eat without washing your hands as they say you should – this doesn't make a person unclean."

A Woman's Faith
(Mk 7.24–30)

21 Jesus left that place and went off to the territory near the cities of Tyre and Sidon. [22]A Canaanite woman who lived in that region came to him. "Son of David!" she cried out. "Have mercy on me, sir! My daughter has a demon and is in a terrible condition."

23 But Jesus did not say a word to her. His disciples came to him and begged him, "Send her away! She is following us and making all this noise!"

24 Then Jesus replied, "I have been sent only to the lost sheep of the people of Israel."

25 At this the woman came and fell at his feet. "Help me, sir!" she said.

26 Jesus answered, "It isn't right to take the children's food and throw it to the dogs."

27 "That's true, sir," she answered; "but even the dogs eat the leftovers that fall from their masters' table."

28 So Jesus answered her, "You are a woman of great faith! What you want will be done for you." And at that very moment her daughter was healed.

Jesus Heals Many People

29 Jesus left there and went along by Lake Galilee. He climbed a hill and sat down. [30]Large crowds came to him, bringing with them the lame, the blind, the crippled, the dumb, and many other sick people, whom they placed at Jesus' feet; and he healed them. [31]The people were amazed as they saw the dumb speaking, the crippled made whole, the lame walking, and the blind seeing; and they praised the God of Israel.

Jesus Feeds Another Great Crowd
(Mk 8.1–10)

32 Jesus called his disciples to him and said, "I feel sorry for these people, because they have been with me for three days and now have nothing to eat. I don't want to send them away without feeding them, for they might faint on their way home."

33 The disciples asked him, "Where will we find enough food in this desert to feed this crowd?"

34 "How much bread have you?" Jesus asked.
"Seven loaves," they answered, "and a few small fish."

35 So Jesus ordered the crowd to sit down on the ground. [36]Then he took the seven loaves and the fish, gave thanks to God, broke them, and gave them to the disciples; and the disciples gave them to the people. [37]They all ate and had enough. Then the disciples took up seven baskets full of pieces left over. [38]The number of men who ate was 4,000, not counting the women and children.

39 Then Jesus sent the people away, got into a boat, and went to the territory of Magadan.

The Demand for a Miracle
(Mk 8.11–13; Lk 12.54–56)

16 Some Pharisees and Sadducees who came to Jesus wanted to trap him, so they asked him to perform a miracle for them, to show that God approved of him. [2]But Jesus answered, "When the sun is setting, you say, 'We are going to have fine weather, because the sky is red.' [3]And early in the morning you say, 'It is going to rain, because the sky is red and dark.' You can predict the weather by looking at the sky, but you cannot interpret the signs concerning these times![a] [4]How evil and

---

[a] **16.3** Some manuscripts do not have the words of Jesus in verses 2–3.

godless are the people of this day! You ask me for a miracle? No! The only miracle you will be given is the miracle of Jonah."

So he left them and went away.

The Yeast of the Pharisees and Sadducees
(Mk 8.14–21)

5 When the disciples crossed over to the other side of the lake, they forgot to take any bread. ⁶Jesus said to them, "Take care; be on your guard against the yeast of the Pharisees and Sadducees."

7 They started discussing among themselves, "He says this because we didn't bring any bread."

8 Jesus knew what they were saying, so he asked them, "Why are you discussing among yourselves about not having any bread? How little faith you have! ⁹Don't you understand yet? Don't you remember when I broke the five loaves for the five thousand men? How many baskets did you fill? ¹⁰And what about the seven loaves for the four thousand men? How many baskets did you fill? ¹¹How is it that you don't understand that I was not talking to you about bread? Guard yourselves from the yeast of the Pharisees and Sadducees!"

12 Then the disciples understood that he was not warning them to guard themselves from the yeast used in bread but from the teaching of the Pharisees and Sadducees.

Peter's Declaration about Jesus
(Mk 8.27–30; Lk 9.18–21)

13 Jesus went to the territory near the town of Caesarea Philippi, where he asked his disciples, "Who do people say the Son of Man is?"

14 "Some say John the Baptist," they answered. "Others say Elijah, while others say Jeremiah or some other prophet."

15 "What about you?" he asked them. "Who do you say I am?"

16 Simon Peter answered, "You are the Messiah, the Son of the living God."

17 "Good for you, Simon son of John!" answered Jesus. "For this truth did not come to you from any human being, but it was given to you directly by my Father in heaven. ¹⁸And so I tell you, Peter: you are a rock, and on this rock foundation I will build my church, and not even death will ever be able to overcome it. ¹⁹I will give you the keys of the Kingdom of heaven; what you prohibit on earth will be prohibited in heaven, and what you permit on earth will be permitted in heaven."

20 Then Jesus ordered his disciples not to tell anyone that he was the Messiah.

Jesus Speaks about his Suffering and Death
(Mk 8.31—9.1; Lk 9.22–27)

21 From that time on Jesus began to say plainly to his disciples, "I must go to Jerusalem and suffer much from the elders, the chief priests, and the teachers of the Law. I will be put to death, but three days later I will be raised to life."

22 Peter took him aside and began to rebuke him. "God forbid it, Lord!" he said. "That must never happen to you!"

23 Jesus turned around and said to Peter, "Get away from me, Satan! You are an obstacle in my way, because these thoughts of yours don't come from God, but from human nature."

Peter holding the keys to the Kingdom of heaven (16.19)

24 Then Jesus said to his disciples, "If anyone wants to come with me, he must forget self, carry his cross, and follow me. ²⁵For whoever wants to save his own life will lose it; but whoever loses his life for my sake will find it. ²⁶Will people gain anything if they win the whole world but lose their life? Of course not! There is nothing they can give to regain their life. ²⁷For the Son of Man is about to come in the glory of his Father with his angels, and then he will reward each one according to his deeds. ²⁸I assure you that there are some here who will not die until they have seen the Son of Man come as King."

The Transfiguration
(Mk 9.2–13; Lk 9.28–36)

17 Six days later Jesus took with him Peter and the brothers James and John and led them up a high mountain where they were alone. ²As they looked on, a change came over Jesus: his face was shining like the sun, and his clothes were dazzling white. ³Then the three disciples saw Moses and Elijah talking with Jesus. ⁴So Peter spoke up and said to Jesus, "Lord, how good it is that we are here! If you wish, I will make three tents here, one for you, one for Moses, and one for Elijah."

5 While he was talking, a shining cloud came over them, and a voice from the cloud said, "This is my own dear Son, with whom I am pleased – listen to him!"

6 When the disciples heard the voice, they were so terrified that they threw themselves face downwards on the ground. ⁷Jesus came to them and touched them. "Get up," he said. "Don't be afraid!" ⁸So they looked up and saw no one there but Jesus.

9 As they came down the mountain, Jesus ordered them, "Don't tell anyone about this vision you have seen until the Son of Man has been raised from death."

10 Then the disciples asked Jesus, "Why do the teachers of the Law say that Elijah has to come first?"

11 "Elijah is indeed coming first," answered Jesus, "and he will get everything ready. ¹²But I tell you that Elijah has already come and people did not recognize him, but treated him just as they pleased. In the same way they will also ill-treat the Son of Man."

13 Then the disciples understood that he was talking to them about John the Baptist.

Jesus Heals a Boy with a Demon
(Mk 9.14–29; Lk 9.37–43a)

14 When they returned to the crowd, a man came to Jesus, knelt before him, ¹⁵and said, "Sir, have mercy on my son! He is an epileptic and has such terrible fits that he often falls in the fire or into water. ¹⁶I brought him to your disciples, but they could not heal him."

17 Jesus answered, "How unbelieving and wrong you people are! How long must I stay with you? How long do I have to put up with you? Bring the boy here to me!" ¹⁸Jesus gave a command to the demon, and it went out of the boy, and at that very moment he was healed.

19 Then the disciples came to Jesus in private and asked him, "Why couldn't we drive the demon out?"

20 "It was because you haven't enough faith," answered Jesus. "I assure you that if you have faith as big as a mustard seed, you can say to this hill, 'Go from here to there!' and it will go. You could do anything!"^a

Jesus Speaks Again about his Death
(Mk 9.30–32; Lk 9.43b–45)

22 When the disciples all came together in Galilee, Jesus said to them, "The Son of Man is about to be handed over to people ²³who will kill him; but three days later he will be raised to life."

The disciples became very sad.

Payment of the Temple Tax

24 When Jesus and his disciples came to Capernaum, the collectors of the temple tax came to Peter and asked, "Does your teacher pay the temple tax?"

25 "Of course," Peter answered.

When Peter went into the house, Jesus spoke up first, "Simon, what is your opinion? Who pays duties or taxes to the kings of this world? The citizens of the country or the foreigners?"

26 "The foreigners," answered Peter.

"Well, then," replied Jesus, "that means that the citizens don't have to pay. ²⁷But we don't want to offend these people. So go to the lake and drop in a line. Pull up the first fish you hook, and in its mouth you will find a coin worth enough for my temple tax and yours. Take it and pay them our taxes."

---

^a **17.20** *Some manuscripts add verse 21:* But only prayer and fasting can drive this kind out; nothing else can *(see Mk 9.29).*

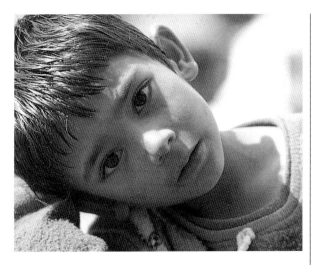

Who is the Greatest?
(Mk 9.33–37; Lk 9.46–48)

18 ◇t◇ At that time the disciples came to Jesus, asking, "Who is the greatest in the Kingdom of heaven?"

2 So Jesus called a child, made him stand in front of them, ³and said, "I assure you that unless you change and become like children, you will never enter the Kingdom of heaven. The greatest in the Kingdom of heaven is the one who humbles himself and becomes like this child. ⁵And whoever welcomes in my name one such child as this, welcomes me.

Temptations to Sin
(Mk 9.42–48; Lk 17.1–2)

6 "If anyone should cause one of these little ones to lose his faith in me, it would be better for that person to have a large millstone tied round his neck and be drowned in the deep sea. ⁷How terrible for the world that there are things that make people lose their faith! Such things will always happen – but how terrible for the one who causes them!

8 "If your hand or your foot makes you lose your faith, cut it off and throw it away! It is better for you to enter life without a hand or a foot than to keep both hands and both feet and be thrown into the eternal fire. ⁹And if your eye makes you lose your faith, take it out and throw it away! It is better for you to enter life with only one eye than to keep both eyes and be thrown into the fire of hell.

ª **18.10** *Some manuscripts add verse 11: For the Son of Man came to save the lost (see Lk 19.10).*

The Parable of the Lost Sheep
(Lk 15.3–7)

10 ┼p "See that you don't despise any of these little ones. Their angels in heaven, I tell you, are always in the presence of my Father in heaven.ª

12 "What do you think a man does who has a hundred sheep and one of them gets lost? He will leave the other ninety-nine grazing on the hillside and go and look for the lost sheep. ¹³When he finds it, I tell you, he feels far happier over this one sheep than over the ninety-nine that did not get lost. ¹⁴In just the same way yourᵇ Father in heaven does not want any of these little ones to be lost.

A Brother or Sister who Sins

15 ◇t◇ "If your brother sins against you,ᶜ go to him and show him his fault. But do it privately, just between yourselves. If he listens to you, you have won your brother back. ¹⁶But if he will not listen to you, take one or two other persons with you, so that 'every accusation may be upheld by the testimony of two or more witnesses,' as the scripture says. ¹⁷And if he will not listen to them, then tell the whole thing to the church. Finally, if he will not listen to the church, treat him as though he were a pagan or a tax collector.

Prohibiting and Permitting

18 "And so I tell all of you: what you prohibit on earth will be prohibited in heaven, and what you permit on earth will be permitted in heaven.

19 "And I tell you more: whenever two of you on earth agree about anything you pray for, it will be done for you by my Father in heaven. ²⁰For where two or three come together in my name, I am there with them."

The Parable of the Unforgiving Servant

21 ┼p Then Peter came to Jesus and asked, "Lord, if my brother keeps on sinning against me, how many times do I have to forgive him? Seven times?"

22 "No, not seven times," answered Jesus, "but seventy times seven,ᵈ ²³because the Kingdom of heaven is like this. Once there was a king who decided to check on his servants' accounts. ²⁴He

---

ᵇ **18.14** your; *some manuscripts have* my.
ᶜ **18.15** *Some manuscripts do not have* against you.
ᵈ **18.22** seventy times seven; *or* seventy-seven times.

had just begun to do so when one of them was brought in who owed him millions of pounds. [25]The servant did not have enough to pay his debt, so the king ordered him to be sold as a slave, with his wife and his children and all that he had, in order to pay the debt. [26]The servant fell on his knees before the king. 'Be patient with me,' he begged, 'and I will pay you everything!' [27]The king felt sorry for him, so he forgave him the debt and let him go.

28   "Then the man went out and met one of his fellow-servants who owed him a few pounds. He grabbed him and started choking him. 'Pay back what you owe me!' he said. [29]His fellow-servant fell down and begged him, 'Be patient with me, and I will pay you back!' [30]But he refused; instead, he had him thrown into jail until he should pay the debt. [31]When the other servants saw what had happened, they were very upset and went to the king and told him everything. [32]So he called the servant in. 'You worthless slave!' he said. 'I forgave you the whole amount you owed me, just because you asked me to. [33]You should have had mercy on your fellow-servant, just as I had mercy on you.' [34]The king was very angry, and he sent the servant to jail to be punished until he should pay back the whole amount."

35   And Jesus concluded, "That is how my Father in heaven will treat every one of you unless you forgive your brother from your heart."

Jesus Teaches about Divorce
(Mk 10.1–12)

 When Jesus finished saying these things, he left Galilee and went to the territory of Judea on the other side of the River Jordan. [2]Large crowds followed him, and he healed them there.

3   Some Pharisees came to him and tried to trap him by asking, "Does our Law allow a man to divorce his wife for whatever reason he wishes?"

4   Jesus answered, "Haven't you read the scripture that says that in the beginning the Creator made people male and female? [5]And God said, 'For this reason a man will leave his father and mother and unite with his wife, and the two will become one.' [6]So they are no longer two, but one. No human being must separate, then, what God has joined together."

7   The Pharisees asked him, "Why, then, did Moses give the law for a man to hand his wife a divorce notice and send her away?"

8   Jesus answered, "Moses gave you permission to divorce your wives because you are so hard to teach. But it was not like that at the time of creation. [9]I tell you, then, that any man who divorces his wife for any cause other than her unfaithfulness, commits adultery if he marries some other woman."

10   His disciples said to him, "If this is how it is between a man and his wife, it is better not to marry."

11   Jesus answered, "This teaching does not apply to everyone, but only to those to whom God has given it. [12]For there are different reasons why men cannot marry: some, because they were born that way; others, because men made them that way; and others do not marry for the sake of the Kingdom of heaven. Let him who can accept this teaching do so."

Jesus Blesses Little Children
(Mk 10.13–16; Lk 18.15–17)

13   Some people brought children to Jesus for him to place his hands on them and to pray for them, but the disciples scolded the people. [14]Jesus said, "Let the children come to me and do not stop them, because the Kingdom of heaven belongs to such as these."

15   He placed his hands on them and then went away.

The Rich Young Man
(Mk 10.17–31; Lk 18.18–30)

16   Once a man came to Jesus. "Teacher," he asked, "what good thing must I do to receive eternal life?"

17   "Why do you ask me concerning what is good?" answered Jesus. "There is only One who is good. Keep the commandments if you want to enter life."

18   "What commandments?" he asked.

Jesus answered, "Do not commit murder; do not commit adultery; do not steal; do not accuse anyone falsely; [19]respect your father and your mother; and love your neighbour as you love yourself."

20   "I have obeyed all these commandments," the young man replied. "What else do I need to do?"

21   Jesus said to him, "If you want to be perfect, go and sell all you have and give the money to the poor, and you will have riches in heaven; then come and follow me."

22   When the young man heard this, he went away sad, because he was very rich.

23   Jesus then said to his disciples, "I assure you: it will be very hard for rich people to enter the Kingdom of heaven. [24]I repeat: it is much harder for a rich person to enter the Kingdom of God

than for a camel to go through the eye of a needle."

25 When the disciples heard this, they were completely amazed. "Who, then, can be saved?" they asked.

26 Jesus looked straight at them and answered, "This is impossible for human beings, but for God everything is possible."

27 Then Peter spoke up. "Look," he said, "we have left everything and followed you. What will we have?"

28 Jesus said to them, "You can be sure that when the Son of Man sits on his glorious throne in the New Age, then you twelve followers of mine will also sit on thrones, to rule the twelve tribes of Israel. 29And everyone who has left houses or brothers or sisters or father or mother or children or fields for my sake, will receive a hundred times more and will be given eternal life. 30But many who now are first will be last, and many who now are last will be first.

The Workers in the Vineyard

20 ⳨p
"The Kingdom of heaven is like this. Once there was a man who went out early in the morning to hire some men to work in his vineyard. 2He agreed to pay them the regular wage, a silver coin a day, and sent them to work in his vineyard. 3He went out again to the market place at nine o'clock and saw some men standing there doing nothing, 4so he told them, 'You also go and work in the vineyard, and I will pay you a fair wage.' 5So they went. Then at twelve o'clock and again at three o'clock he did the same thing. 6It was nearly five o'clock when he went to the market place and saw some other men still standing there. 'Why are you wasting the whole day here doing nothing?' he asked them. 7'No one hired us,' they answered. 'Well, then, you also go and work in the vineyard,' he told them.

8 "When evening came, the owner told his foreman, 'Call the workers and pay them their wages, starting with those who were hired last and ending with those who were hired first.' 9The men who had begun to work at five o'clock were paid a silver coin each. 10So when the men who were the first to be hired came to be paid, they thought they would get more; but they too were given a silver coin each. 11They took their money and started grumbling against the employer. 12'These men who were hired last worked only one hour,' they said, 'while we put up with a whole day's work in the hot sun – yet you paid them the same as you paid us!'

13 " 'Listen, friend,' the owner answered one of them, 'I have not cheated you. After all, you agreed to do a day's work for one silver coin. 14Now take your pay and go home. I want to give this man who was hired last as much as I have given you. 15Don't I have the right to do as I wish with my own money? Or are you jealous because I am generous?' "

16 And Jesus concluded, "So those who are last will be first, and those who are first will be last."

Jesus Speaks a Third Time about his Death
(Mk 10.32–34; Lk 18.31–34)

17 As Jesus was going up to Jerusalem, he took the twelve disciples aside and spoke to them privately, as they walked along. 18"Listen," he told them, "we are going up to Jerusalem, where the Son of Man will be handed over to the chief priests and the teachers of the Law. They will condemn him to death 19and then hand him over to the Gentiles, who will mock him, whip him, and crucify him; but three days later he will be raised to life."

A Mother's Request
(Mk 10.35–45)

20 Then the wife of Zebedee came to Jesus with her two sons, bowed before him, and asked him a favour.

21 "What do you want?" Jesus asked her.

She answered, "Promise me that these two sons of mine will sit at your right and your left when you are King."

22 "You don't know what you are asking for," Jesus answered the sons. "Can you drink the cup of suffering that I am about to drink?"

"We can," they answered.

23 "You will indeed drink from my cup," Jesus told them, "but I do not have the right to choose who will sit at my right and my left. These places belong to those for whom my Father has prepared them."

24 When the other ten disciples heard about this, they became angry with the two brothers. 25So Jesus called them all together and said, "You know that the rulers of the heathen have power over them, and the leaders have complete authority. 26This, however, is not the way it shall be among you. If one of you wants to be great, he must be the servant of the rest; 27and if one of you wants to be first, he must be your slave – 28like the Son of Man, who did not come to be served, but to serve and to give his life to redeem many people."

A procession on Palm Sunday recalls Jesus' entry into Jerusalem

Jesus Heals Two Blind Men
(Mk 10.46–52; Lk 18.35–43)

29 As Jesus and his disciples were leaving Jericho, a large crowd was following. ³⁰Two blind men who were sitting by the road heard that Jesus was passing by, so they began to shout, "Son of David! Take pity on us, sir!"

31 The crowd scolded them and told them to be quiet. But they shouted even more loudly, "Son of David! Take pity on us, sir!"

32 Jesus stopped and called them. "What do you want me to do for you?" he asked them.

33 "Sir," they answered, "we want you to give us our sight!"

34 Jesus had pity on them and touched their eyes; at once they were able to see, and they followed him.

The Triumphant Entry into Jerusalem
(Mk 11.1–11; Lk 19.28–40; Jn 12.12–19)

21 As Jesus and his disciples approached Jerusalem, they came to Bethphage at the Mount of Olives. There Jesus sent two of the disciples on ahead ²with these instructions: "Go to the village there ahead of you, and at once you will find a donkey tied up with her colt beside her. Untie them and bring them to me. ³And if anyone says anything, tell him, 'The Master[a] needs them'; and then he will let them go at once."

4 This happened in order to make what the prophet had said come true:

5 "Tell the city of Zion,
   Look, your king is coming to you!
He is humble and rides on a donkey
   and on a colt, the foal of a donkey."

6 So the disciples went and did what Jesus had told them to do: ⁷they brought the donkey and the colt, threw their cloaks over them, and Jesus got on. ⁸A large crowd of people spread their cloaks on the road while others cut branches from the trees and spread them on the road. ⁹The crowds walking in front of Jesus and those walking behind began to shout, "Praise to David's Son! God bless him who comes in the name of the Lord! Praise God!"

10 When Jesus entered Jerusalem, the whole city

[a] **21.3** The Master; *or* Their owner.

was thrown into an uproar. "Who is he?" the people asked.

11 "This is the prophet Jesus, from Nazareth in Galilee," the crowds answered.

Jesus Goes to the Temple
(Mk 11.15–19; Lk 19.45–48; Jn 2.13–22)

12 Jesus went into the Temple and drove out all those who were buying and selling there. He overturned the tables of the moneychangers and the stools of those who sold pigeons, 13and said to them, "It is written in the Scriptures that God said, 'My Temple will be called a house of prayer.' But you are making it a hideout for thieves!"

14 The blind and the crippled came to him in the Temple, and he healed them. 15The chief priests and the teachers of the Law became angry when they saw the wonderful things he was doing and the children shouting in the Temple, "Praise to David's Son!" 16So they asked Jesus, "Do you hear what they are saying?"

"Indeed I do," answered Jesus. "Haven't you ever read this scripture? 'You have trained children and babies to offer perfect praise.'"

17 Jesus left them and went out of the city to Bethany, where he spent the night.

Jesus Curses the Fig Tree
(Mk 11.12–14, 20–24)

18 On his way back to the city early next morning, Jesus was hungry. 19He saw a fig tree by the side of the road and went to it, but found nothing on it except leaves. So he said to the tree, "You will never again bear fruit!" At once the fig tree dried up.

20 The disciples saw this and were astounded. "How did the fig tree dry up so quickly?" they asked.

21 Jesus answered, "I assure you that if you believe and do not doubt, you will be able to do what I have done to this fig tree. And not only this, but you will even be able to say to this hill, 'Get up and throw yourself in the sea,' and it will. 22If you believe, you will receive whatever you ask for in prayer."

The Question about Jesus' Authority
(Mk 11.27–33; Lk 20.1–8)

23 Jesus came back to the Temple; and as he taught, the chief priests and the elders came to him and asked, "What right have you to do these things? Who gave you this right?"

24 Jesus answered them, "I will ask you just one question, and if you give me an answer, I will tell you what right I have to do these things. 25Where did John's right to baptize come from: was it from God or from human beings?"

They started to argue among themselves, "What shall we say? If we answer, 'From God,' he will say to us, 'Why, then, did you not believe John?' 26But if we say, 'From human beings,' we are afraid of what the people might do, because they are all convinced that John was a prophet." 27So they answered Jesus, "We don't know."

And he said to them, "Neither will I tell you, then, by what right I do these things.

The Parable of the Two Sons

28 "Now, what do you think? There was once a man who had two sons. He went to the elder one and said, 'Son, go and work in the vineyard today.' 29'I don't want to,' he answered, but later he changed his mind and went. 30Then the father went to the other son and said the same thing. 'Yes, sir,' he answered, but he did not go. 31Which one of the two did what his father wanted?"

"The elder one," they answered.

So Jesus said to them, "I tell you: the tax collectors and the prostitutes are going into the Kingdom of God ahead of you. 32For John the Baptist came to you showing you the right path to take, and you would not believe him; but the tax collectors and the prostitutes believed him. Even when you saw this, you did not later change your minds and believe him.

The Parable of the Tenants in the Vineyard
(Mk 12.1–12; Lk 20.9–19)

33 "Listen to another parable," Jesus said. "There was once a landowner who planted a vineyard, put a fence around it, dug a hole for the winepress, and built a watchtower. Then he let out the vineyard to tenants and went on a journey. 34When the time came to gather the grapes, he sent his slaves to the tenants to receive his share of the harvest. 35The tenants seized his slaves, beat one, killed another, and stoned another. 36Again the man sent other slaves, more than the first time, and the tenants treated them the same way. 37Last of all he sent his son to them. 'Surely they will respect my son,' he said. 38But when the tenants saw the son, they said to themselves, 'This is the owner's son. Come on, let's kill him, and we will get his property!'

[39]So they seized him, threw him out of the vineyard, and killed him.

40 "Now, when the owner of the vineyard comes, what will he do to those tenants?" Jesus asked.

41 "He will certainly kill those evil men," they answered, "and let the vineyard out to other tenants, who will give him his share of the harvest at the right time."

42 Jesus said to them, "Haven't you ever read what the Scriptures say?

'The stone which the builders rejected as
worthless
turned out to be the most important of all.
This was done by the Lord;
what a wonderful sight it is!'

43 "And so I tell you," added Jesus, "the Kingdom of God will be taken away from you and given to a people who will produce the proper fruits."[a]

45 The chief priests and the Pharisees heard Jesus' parables and knew that he was talking about them, [46]so they tried to arrest him. But they were afraid of the crowds, who considered Jesus to be a prophet.

The Parable of the Wedding Feast
(Lk 14.15–24)

22 Jesus again used parables in talking to the people. [2]"The Kingdom of heaven is like this. Once there was a king who prepared a wedding feast for his son. [3]He sent his servants to tell the invited guests to come to the feast, but they did not want to come. [4]So he sent other servants with this message for the guests: 'My feast is ready now; my bullocks and prize calves have been butchered, and everything is ready. Come to the wedding feast!' [5]But the invited guests paid no attention and went about their business: one went to his farm, another to his shop, [6]while others grabbed the servants, beat them, and killed them. [7]The king was very angry; so he sent his soldiers, who killed those murderers and burnt down their city. [8]Then he called his servants and said to them, 'My wedding feast is ready, but the people I invited did not deserve it. [9]Now go to the main streets and invite to the feast as many people as you find.' [10]So the servants went out into the streets and gathered all the people they could find, good and bad alike; and the wedding hall was filled with people.

---

[a] **21.43** *Some manuscripts add verse 44:* Whoever falls on this stone will be cut to pieces; and if the stone falls on someone, it will crush him to dust *(see Lk 20.18).*

11 "The king went in to look at the guests and saw a man who was not wearing wedding clothes. [12]'Friend, how did you get in here without wedding clothes?' the king asked him. But the man said nothing. [13]Then the king told the servants, 'Tie him up hand and foot, and throw him outside in the dark. There he will cry and grind his teeth.'"

14 And Jesus concluded, "Many are invited, but few are chosen."

The Question about Paying Taxes
(Mk 12.13–17; Lk 20.20–26)

15 The Pharisees went off and made a plan to trap Jesus with questions. [16]Then they sent to him some of their disciples and some members of Herod's party. "Teacher," they said, "we know that you tell the truth. You teach the truth about God's will for people, without worrying about what others think, because you pay no attention to anyone's status. [17]Tell us, then, what do you think? Is it against our Law to pay taxes to the Roman Emperor, or not?"

18 Jesus, however, was aware of their evil plan, and so he said, "You hypocrites! Why are you trying to trap me? [19]Show me the coin for paying the tax!"

They brought him the coin, [20]and he asked them, "Whose face and name are these?"

21 "The Emperor's," they answered.

So Jesus said to them, "Well, then, pay the Emperor what belongs to the Emperor, and pay God what belongs to God."

22 When they heard this, they were amazed; and they left him and went away.

The Question about Rising from Death
(Mk 12.18–27; Lk 20.27–40)

23 That same day some Sadducees came to Jesus and claimed that people will not rise from death. [24]"Teacher," they said, "Moses said that if a man who has no children dies, his brother must marry the widow so that they can have children who will be considered the dead man's children. [25]Now, there were seven brothers who used to live here. The eldest got married and died without having children, so he left his widow to his brother. [26]The same thing happened to the second brother, to the third, and finally to all seven. [27]Last of all, the woman died. [28]Now, on the day when the dead rise to life, whose wife will she be? All of them had married her."

29 Jesus answered them, "How wrong you are! It is because you don't know the Scriptures or

God's power. [30]For when the dead rise to life, they will be like the angels in heaven and will not marry. [31]Now, as for the dead rising to life: haven't you ever read what God has told you? He said, [32]'I am the God of Abraham, the God of Isaac, and the God of Jacob.' He is the God of the living, not of the dead."

33   When the crowds heard this, they were amazed at his teaching.

The Great Commandment
(Mk 12.28–34; Lk 10.25–28)

34   When the Pharisees heard that Jesus had silenced the Sadducees, they came together, [35]and one of them, a teacher of the Law, tried to trap him with a question. [36]"Teacher," he asked, "which is the greatest commandment in the Law?"

37   Jesus answered, " 'Love the Lord your God with all your heart, with all your soul, and with all your mind.' [38]This is the greatest and the most important commandment. [39]The second most important commandment is like it: 'Love your neighbour as you love yourself.' [40]The whole Law of Moses and the teachings of the prophets depend on these two commandments."

The Question about the Messiah
(Mk 12.35–37; Lk 20.41–44)

41   When some Pharisees gathered together, Jesus asked them, [42]"What do you think about the Messiah? Whose descendant is he?"

"He is David's descendant," they answered.

43   "Why, then," Jesus asked, "did the Spirit inspire David to call him 'Lord'? David said,

44   'The Lord said to my Lord:
Sit here on my right
until I put your enemies under your feet.'

45   If, then, David called him 'Lord', how can the Messiah be David's descendant?"

46   No one was able to give Jesus any answer, and from that day on no one dared to ask him any more questions.

Jesus Warns against the Teachers of the Law and the Pharisees
(Mk 12.38–39; Lk 11.43, 46; 20.45–46)

 Then Jesus spoke to the crowds and to his disciples. [2]"The teachers of the Law and the Pharisees are the authorized interpreters of Moses' Law. [3]So you must obey and follow everything they tell you to do; do not, however, imitate their actions, because they don't practise what they preach. [4]They tie on to people's backs loads that are heavy and hard to carry, yet they aren't willing even to lift a finger to help them carry those loads. [5]They do everything so that people will see them. Look at the straps with scripture verses on them which they wear on their foreheads and arms, and notice how large they are! Notice also how long are the tassels on their cloaks![a] [6]They love the best places at feasts and the reserved seats in the synagogues; [7]they love to be greeted with respect in the market places and to be called 'Teacher'. [8]You must not be called 'Teacher', because you are all members of one family and have only one Teacher. [9]And you must not call anyone here on earth 'Father', because you have only the one Father in heaven. [10]Nor should you be called 'Leader', because your one and only leader is the Messiah. [11]The greatest one among you must be your servant. [12]Whoever makes himself great will be humbled, and whoever humbles himself will be made great.

Jesus Condemns their Hypocrisy
(Mk 12.40; Lk 11.39–42, 44, 52; 20.47)

13   "How terrible for you, teachers of the Law and Pharisees! You hypocrites! You lock the door to the Kingdom of heaven in people's faces, and you yourselves don't go in, nor do you allow in those who are trying to enter![b]

15   "How terrible for you, teachers of the Law and Pharisees! You hypocrites! You sail the seas and cross whole countries to win one convert; and when you succeed, you make him twice as deserving of going to hell as you yourselves are!

16   "How terrible for you, blind guides! You teach, 'If someone swears by the Temple, he isn't bound by his vow; but if he swears by the gold in the Temple, he is bound.' [17]Blind fools! Which is more important, the gold or the Temple which makes the gold holy? [18]You also teach, 'If someone swears by the altar, he isn't bound by his vow; but if he swears by the gift on the altar, he is bound.' [19]How blind you are! Which is the more important, the gift or the

---

[a] **23.5** TASSELS ON THEIR CLOAKS: *These tassels were worn as a sign of devotion to God (see Num 15.37–41).*

[b] **23.13** *Some manuscripts add verse 14:* How terrible for you, teachers of the Law and Pharisees! You hypocrites! You take advantage of widows and rob them of their homes, and then make a show of saying long prayers! Because of this your punishment will be all the worse! *(see Mk 12.40).*

altar which makes the gift holy? ²⁰So then, when a person swears by the altar, he is swearing by it and by all the gifts on it; ²¹and when he swears by the Temple, he is swearing by it and by God, who lives there; ²²and when someone swears by heaven, he is swearing by God's throne and by him who sits on it.

23 "How terrible for you, teachers of the Law and Pharisees! You hypocrites! You give to God a tenth even of the seasoning herbs, such as mint, dill, and cumin, but you neglect to obey the really important teachings of the Law, such as justice and mercy and honesty. These you should practise, without neglecting the others. ²⁴Blind guides! You strain a fly out of your drink, but swallow a camel!

25 "How terrible for you, teachers of the Law and Pharisees! You hypocrites! You clean the outside of your cup and plate, while the inside is full of what you have obtained by violence and selfishness. ²⁶Blind Pharisee! Clean what is inside the cup first, and then the outside will be clean too!

27 "How terrible for you, teachers of the Law and Pharisees! You hypocrites! You are like whitewashed tombs, which look fine on the outside but are full of bones and decaying corpses on the inside. ²⁸In the same way, on the outside you appear good to everybody, but inside you are full of hypocrisy and sins.

Jesus Predicts their Punishment
(Lk 11.47–51)

29 "How terrible for you, teachers of the Law and Pharisees! You hypocrites! You make fine tombs for the prophets and decorate the monuments of those who lived good lives; ³⁰and you claim that if you had lived during the time of your ancestors, you would not have done what they did and killed the prophets. ³¹So you actually admit that you are the descendants of those who murdered the prophets! ³²Go on, then, and finish what your ancestors started! ³³You snakes and children of snakes! How do you expect to escape from being condemned to hell? ³⁴And so I tell you that I will send you prophets and wise men and teachers; you will kill some of them, crucify others, and whip others in the synagogues and chase them from town to town. ³⁵As a result, the punishment for the murder of all innocent people will fall on you, from the murder of innocent Abel to the murder of Zachariah son of Berachiah, whom you murdered between the Temple and the altar. ³⁶I tell you indeed: the punishment for all these murders will fall on the people of this day!

Jesus' Love for Jerusalem
(Lk 13.34–35)

37 "Jerusalem, Jerusalem! You kill the prophets and stone the messengers God has sent you! How many times have I wanted to put my arms round all your people, just as a hen gathers her chicks under her wings, but you would not let me! ³⁸And so your Temple will be abandoned and empty. ³⁹From now on, I tell you, you will never see me again until you say, 'God bless him who comes in the name of the Lord.'"

Jesus Speaks of the Destruction of the Temple
(Mk 13.1–2; Lk 21.5–6)

24 Jesus left and was going away from the Temple when his disciples came to him to call his attention to its buildings. ²"Yes," he said, "you may well look at all these. I tell you this: not a single stone here will be left in its place; every one of them will be thrown down."

Troubles and Persecutions
(Mk 13.3–13; Lk 21.7–19)

3 As Jesus sat on the Mount of Olives, the disciples came to him in private. "Tell us when all this will be," they asked, "and what will happen to show that it is the time for your coming and the end of the age."

4 Jesus answered, "Be on your guard, and do not let anyone deceive you. ⁵Many men, claiming to speak for me, will come and say, 'I am the Messiah!' and they will deceive many people. ⁶You are going to hear the noise of battles close by and the news of battles far away; but do not be troubled. Such things must happen, but they do not mean that the end has come. ⁷Countries will fight each other, kingdoms will attack one another. There will be famines and earthquakes everywhere. ⁸All these things are like the first pains of childbirth.

9 "Then you will be arrested and handed over to be punished and be put to death. All nations will hate you because of me. ¹⁰Many will give up their faith at that time; they will betray one another and hate one another. ¹¹Then many false prophets will appear and deceive many people. ¹²Such will be the spread of evil that many people's love will grow cold. ¹³But whoever holds out to the end will be saved. ¹⁴And this Good News about the Kingdom will be preached through all the world for a witness to all nations; and then the end will come.

The Awful Horror
(Mk 13.14–23; Lk 21.20–24)

15   "You will see 'The Awful Horror' of which the prophet Daniel spoke. It will be standing in the holy place." (Note to the reader: be sure to understand what this means!) [16]"Then those who are in Judea must run away to the hills. [17]Someone who is on the roof of his house must not take the time to go down and get his belongings from the house. [18]Someone who is in the field must not go back to get his cloak. [19]How terrible it will be in those days for women who are pregnant and for mothers with little babies! [20]Pray to God that you will not have to run away during the winter or on a Sabbath! [21]For the trouble at that time will be far more terrible than any there has ever been, from the beginning of the world to this very day. Nor will there ever be anything like it again. [22]But God has already reduced the number of days; had he not done so, nobody would survive. For the sake of his chosen people, however, God will reduce the days.

23   "Then, if anyone says to you, 'Look, here is the Messiah!' or 'There he is!' – do not believe it. [24]For false Messiahs and false prophets will appear; they will perform great miracles and wonders in order to deceive even God's chosen people, if possible. [25]Listen! I have told you this before the time comes.

26   "Or, if people should tell you, 'Look, he is out in the desert!' – don't go there; or if they say, 'Look, he is hiding here!' – don't believe it. [27]For the Son of Man will come like the lightning which flashes across the whole sky from the east to the west.

28   "Wherever there is a dead body, the vultures will gather.

The Coming of the Son of Man
(Mk 13.24–27; Lk 21.25–28)

29   "Soon after the trouble of those days, the sun will grow dark, the moon will no longer shine, the stars will fall from heaven, and the powers in space will be driven from their courses. [30]Then the sign of the Son of Man will appear in the sky; and all the peoples of earth will weep as they see the Son of Man coming on the clouds of heaven with power and great glory. [31]The great trumpet will sound, and he will send out his angels to the four corners of the earth, and they will gather his chosen people from one end of the world to the other.

The Lesson of the Fig Tree
(Mk 13.28–31; Lk 21.29–33)

32   "Let the fig tree teach you a lesson. When its branches become green and tender and it starts putting out leaves, you know that summer is near. [33]In the same way, when you see all these things, you will know that the time is near, ready to begin.[a] [34]Remember that all these things will happen before the people now living have all died. [35]Heaven and earth will pass away, but my words will never pass away.

No One Knows the Day and Hour
(Mk 13.32–37; Lk 17.26–30, 34–36)

36   "No one knows, however, when that day and hour will come – neither the angels in heaven nor the Son;[b] the Father alone knows. [37]The coming of the Son of Man will be like what happened in the time of Noah. [38]In the days before the flood people ate and drank, men and women married, up to the very day Noah went into the boat; [39]yet they did not realize what was happening until the flood came and swept them all away. That is how it will be when the Son of Man comes. [40]At that time two men will be working in a field: one will be taken away, the other will be left behind. [41]Two women will be at a mill grinding meal: one will be taken away, the other will be left behind.

42   "Be on your guard, then, because you do not know what day your Lord will come. [43]If the owner of a house knew the time when the thief would come, you can be sure that he would stay awake and not let the thief break into his house. [44]So then, you also must always be ready, because the Son of Man will come at an hour when you are not expecting him.

The Faithful or the Unfaithful Servant
(Lk 12.41–48)

45   "Who, then, is a faithful and wise servant? It is the one that his master has placed in charge of the other servants to give them their food at the proper time. [46]How happy that servant is if his master finds him doing this when he comes home! [47]Indeed, I tell you, the master will put that servant in charge of all his property. [48]But if he is a bad servant, he will tell himself that his master will not come back for a long time, [49]and

[a] **24.33** the time is near, ready to begin; *or* he is near, ready to come.
[b] **24.36** *Some manuscripts do not have* nor the Son.

he will begin to beat his fellow-servants and to eat and drink with drunkards. [50]Then that servant's master will come back one day when the servant does not expect him and at a time he does not know. [51]The master will cut him in pieces[a] and make him share the fate of the hypocrites. There he will cry and grind his teeth.

The Parable of the Ten Young Women

25 ☩**p** "At that time the Kingdom of heaven will be like this. Once there were ten young women who took their oil lamps and went out to meet the bridegroom. [2]Five of them were foolish, and the other five were wise. [3]The foolish ones took their lamps but did not take any extra oil with them, [4]while the wise ones took containers full of oil for their lamps. [5]The bridegroom was late in coming, so the women began to nod and fall asleep.

6 "It was already midnight when the cry rang out, 'Here is the bridegroom! Come and meet him!' [7]The ten women woke up and trimmed their lamps. [8]Then the foolish ones said to the wise ones, 'Let us have some of your oil, because our lamps are going out.' [9]'No, indeed,' the wise ones answered, 'there is not enough for you and for us. Go to the shop and buy some for yourselves.' [10]So the foolish women went off to buy some oil; and while they were gone, the bridegroom arrived. The five who were ready went in with him to the wedding feast, and the door was closed.

11 "Later the other women arrived. 'Sir, sir! Let us in!' they cried out. [12]'Certainly not! I don't know you,' the bridegroom answered."

13 And Jesus concluded, "Be on your guard, then, because you do not know the day or the hour.

The Parable of the Three Servants
(Lk 19.11–27)

14 ☩**p** "At that time the Kingdom of heaven will be like this. Once there was a man who was about to go on a journey; he called his servants and put them in charge of his property. [15]He gave to each one according to his ability: to one he gave five thousand gold coins, to another he gave two thousand, and to another he gave one thousand. Then he left on his journey. [16]The servant who had received five thousand coins went at once and invested his money and earned another five thousand. [17]In the same way the servant who had received two

thousand coins earned another two thousand. [18]But the servant who had received one thousand coins went off, dug a hole in the ground, and hid his master's money.

19 "After a long time the master of those servants came back and settled accounts with them. [20]The servant who had received five thousand coins came in and handed over the other five thousand. 'You gave me five thousand coins, sir,' he said. 'Look! Here are another five thousand that I have earned.' [21]'Well done, you good and faithful servant!' said his master. 'You have been faithful in managing small amounts, so I will put you in charge of large amounts. Come on in and share my happiness!'

22 "Then the servant who had been given two thousand coins came in and said, 'You gave me two thousand coins, sir. Look! Here are another two thousand that I have earned.' [23]'Well done, you good and faithful servant!' said his master. 'You have been faithful in managing small amounts, so I will put you in charge of large amounts. Come on in and share my happiness!'

24 "Then the servant who had received one thousand coins came in and said, 'Sir, I know you are a hard man; you reap harvests where you did not sow, and you gather crops where you did not scatter seed. [25]I was afraid, so I went off and hid your money in the ground. Look! Here is what belongs to you.'

26 "'You bad and lazy servant!' his master said. 'You knew, did you, that I reap harvests where I did not sow, and gather crops where I did not scatter seed? [27]Well, then, you should have deposited my money in the bank, and I would have received it all back with interest when I returned. [28]Now, take the money away from him and give it to the one who has ten thousand coins. [29]For to every person who has something, even more will be given, and he will have more than enough; but the person who has nothing, even the little that he has will be taken away from him. [30]As for this useless servant – throw him outside in the darkness; there he will cry and grind his teeth.'

The Final Judgement

31 ☩**p** "When the Son of Man comes as King and all the angels with him, he will sit on his royal throne, [32]and the people of all the nations will be gathered before him. Then he will divide them into two groups, just as a shepherd separates the sheep from the goats. [33]He will put the righteous people on his right and the others on his left. [34]Then the King will

---

[a] **24.51** cut him in pieces; *or* throw him out.

say to the people on his right, 'Come, you that are blessed by my Father! Come and possess the kingdom which has been prepared for you ever since the creation of the world. ³⁵I was hungry and you fed me, thirsty and you gave me a drink; I was a stranger and you received me in your homes, ³⁶naked and you clothed me; I was sick and you took care of me, in prison and you visited me.'

37   "The righteous will then answer him, 'When, Lord, did we ever see you hungry and feed you, or thirsty and give you a drink? ³⁸When did we ever see you a stranger and welcome you in our homes, or naked and clothe you? ³⁹When did we ever see you sick or in prison, and visit you?' ⁴⁰The King will reply, 'I tell you, whenever you did this for one of the least important of these members of my family, you did it for me!'

41   "Then he will say to those on his left, 'Away from me, you that are under God's curse! Away to the eternal fire which has been prepared for the Devil and his angels! ⁴²I was hungry but you would not feed me, thirsty but you would not give me a drink; ⁴³I was a stranger but you would not welcome me in your homes, naked but you would not clothe me; I was sick and in prison but you would not take care of me.'

44   "Then they will answer him, 'When, Lord, did we ever see you hungry or thirsty or a stranger or naked or sick or in prison, and would not help you?' ⁴⁵The King will reply, 'I tell you, whenever you refused to help one of these least important ones, you refused to help me.'

An aid worker providing help for someone in great need

⁴⁶These, then, will be sent off to eternal punishment, but the righteous will go to eternal life."

The Plot against Jesus
(Mk 14.1–2; Lk 22.1–2; Jn 11.45–53)

26 When Jesus had finished teaching all these things, he said to his disciples, ²"In two days, as you know, it will be the Passover Festival, and the Son of Man will be handed over to be crucified."

3   Then the chief priests and the elders met together in the palace of Caiaphas, the High Priest, ⁴and made plans to arrest Jesus secretly and put him to death. ⁵"We must not do it during the festival," they said, "or the people will riot."

Jesus is Anointed at Bethany
(Mk 14.3–9; Jn 12.1–8)

6   Jesus was in Bethany at the house of Simon, a man who had suffered from a dreaded skin disease. ⁷While Jesus was eating, a woman came to him with an alabaster jar filled with an expensive perfume, which she poured on his head. ⁸The disciples saw this and became angry. "Why all this waste?" they asked. ⁹"This perfume could have been sold for a large amount and the money given to the poor!"

10   Jesus knew what they were saying, so he said to them, "Why are you bothering this woman? It is a fine and beautiful thing that she has done for me. ¹¹You will always have poor people with you, but you will not always have me. ¹²What she did was to pour this perfume on my body to get me ready for burial. ¹³Now, I assure you that wherever this gospel is preached all over the world, what she has done will be told in memory of her."

Judas Agrees to Betray Jesus
(Mk 14.10–11; Lk 22.3–6)

14   Then one of the twelve disciples – the one named Judas Iscariot – went to the chief priests ¹⁵and asked, "What will you give me if I betray Jesus to you?" They counted out 30 silver coins and gave them to him. ¹⁶From then on Judas was looking for a good chance to hand Jesus over to them.

Jesus Eats the Passover Meal with his Disciples
(Mk 14.12–21; Lk 22.7–13, 21–23; Jn 13.21–30)

17   On the first day of the Festival of Unleavened Bread the disciples came to Jesus and asked him,

A wood-carving showing Jesus with his disciples at the Last Supper (26.17–25)

"Where do you want us to get the Passover meal ready for you?"

18 "Go to a certain man in the city," he said to them, "and tell him: 'The Teacher says, My hour has come; my disciples and I will celebrate the Passover at your house.'"

19 The disciples did as Jesus had told them and prepared the Passover meal.

20 When it was evening, Jesus and the twelve disciples sat down to eat. 21During the meal Jesus said, "I tell you, one of you will betray me."

22 The disciples were very upset and began to ask him, one after the other, "Surely, Lord, you don't mean me?"

23 Jesus answered, "One who dips his bread in the dish with me will betray me. 24The Son of Man will die as the Scriptures say he will, but how terrible for that man who betrays the Son of Man! It would have been better for that man if he had never been born!"

25 Judas, the traitor, spoke up. "Surely, Teacher, you don't mean me?" he asked.

Jesus answered, "So you say."

The Lord's Supper
(Mk 14.22–26; Lk 22.14–20; 1 Cor. 11.23–25)

26 While they were eating, Jesus took a piece of bread, gave a prayer of thanks, broke it, and gave it to his disciples. "Take and eat it," he said; "this is my body."

27 Then he took a cup, gave thanks to God, and gave it to them. "Drink it, all of you," he said; 28"this is my blood, which seals God's covenant, my blood poured out for many for the forgiveness of sins. 29I tell you, I will never again drink this wine until the day I drink the new wine with you in my Father's Kingdom."

30 Then they sang a hymn and went out to the Mount of Olives.

Jesus Predicts Peter's Denial
(Mk 14.27–31; Lk 22.31–34; Jn 13.36–38)

31 Then Jesus said to them, "This very night all of you will run away and leave me, for the scripture says, 'God will kill the shepherd, and the sheep of the flock will be scattered.' 32But after I am raised to life, I will go to Galilee ahead of you."

33 Peter spoke up and said to Jesus, "I will never leave you, even though all the rest do!"

34 Jesus said to Peter, "I tell you that before the cock crows tonight, you will say three times that you do not know me."

35 Peter answered, "I will never say that, even if I have to die with you!"

And all the other disciples said the same thing.

Jesus Prays in Gethsemane
(Mk 14.32–42; Lk 22.39–46)

36 Then Jesus went with his disciples to a place called Gethsemane, and he said to them, "Sit here while I go over there and pray." 37He took with him Peter and the two sons of Zebedee. Grief and anguish came over him, 38and he said to them, "The sorrow in my heart is so great that it almost crushes me. Stay here and keep watch with me."

39 He went a little farther on, threw himself face downwards on the ground, and prayed, "My Father, if it is possible, take this cup of suffering from me! Yet not what I want, but what you want."

40 Then he returned to the three disciples and found them asleep; and he said to Peter, "How is it that you three were not able to keep watch with me even for one hour? 41Keep watch and pray that you will not fall into temptation. The spirit is willing, but the flesh is weak."

42 Once more Jesus went away and prayed, "My Father, if this cup of suffering cannot be taken away unless I drink it, your will be done." 43He returned once more and found the disciples asleep; they could not keep their eyes open.

44 Again Jesus left them, went away, and prayed the third time, saying the same words. 45Then he returned to the disciples and said, "Are you still sleeping and resting? Look! The hour has come for the Son of Man to be handed over to the power of sinners. 46Get up, let us go. Look, here is the man who is betraying me!"

The Arrest of Jesus

(Mk 14.43–50; Lk 22.47–53; Jn 18.3–12)

47   Jesus was still speaking when Judas, one of the twelve disciples, arrived. With him was a large crowd armed with swords and clubs and sent by the chief priests and the elders. ⁴⁸The traitor had given the crowd a signal: "The man I kiss is the one you want. Arrest him!"

49   Judas went straight to Jesus and said, "Peace be with you, Teacher," and kissed him.

50   Jesus answered, "Be quick about it, friend!"ᵃ

Then they came up, arrested Jesus, and held him tight. ⁵¹One of those who were with Jesus drew his sword and struck at the High Priest's slave, cutting off his ear. ⁵²"Put your sword back in its place," Jesus said to him. "All who take the sword will die by the sword. ⁵³Don't you know that I could call on my Father for help, and at once he would send me more than twelve armies of angels? ⁵⁴But in that case, how could the Scriptures come true which say that this is what must happen?"

55   Then Jesus spoke to the crowd, "Did you have to come with swords and clubs to capture me, as though I were an outlaw? Every day I sat down and taught in the Temple, and you did not arrest me. ⁵⁶But all this has happened in order to make what the prophets wrote in the Scriptures come true."

Then all the disciples left him and ran away.

Jesus Before the Council

(Mk 14.53–65; Lk 22.54–55, 63–71; Jn 18.13–14, 19–24)

57   Those who had arrested Jesus took him to the house of Caiaphas, the High Priest, where the teachers of the Law and the elders had gathered together. ⁵⁸Peter followed from a distance, as far as the courtyard of the High Priest's house. He went into the courtyard and sat down with the guards to see how it would all come out. ⁵⁹The chief priests and the whole Council tried to find some false evidence against Jesus to put him to death; ⁶⁰but they could not find any, even though many people came forward and told lies about him. Finally two men stepped up ⁶¹and said, "This man said, 'I am able to tear down God's Temple and three days later build it up again.'"

62   The High Priest stood up and said to Jesus, "Have you no answer to give to this accusation against you?" ⁶³But Jesus kept quiet. Again the High Priest spoke to him, "In the name of the living God I now put you on oath: tell us if you are the Messiah, the Son of God."

64   Jesus answered him, "So you say. But I tell all of you: from this time on you will see the Son of Man sitting on the right of the Almighty and coming on the clouds of heaven!"

65   At this the High Priest tore his clothes and said, "Blasphemy! We don't need any more witnesses! You have just heard his blasphemy! ⁶⁶What do you think?"

They answered, "He is guilty and must die."

67   Then they spat in his face and beat him; and those who slapped him ⁶⁸said, "Prophesy for us, Messiah! Guess who hit you!"

Peter Denies Jesus

(Mk 14.66–72; Lk 22.56–62; Jn 18.15–18, 25–27)

69   Peter was sitting outside in the courtyard when one of the High Priest's servant women came to him and said, "You, too, were with Jesus of Galilee."

70   But he denied it in front of them all. "I don't know what you are talking about," he answered, ⁷¹and went on out to the entrance of the courtyard. Another servant woman saw him and said to the men there, "He was with Jesus of Nazareth."

72   Again Peter denied it and answered, "I swear that I don't know that man!"

73   After a little while the men standing there came to Peter. "Of course you are one of them," they said. "After all, the way you speak gives you away!"

74   Then Peter said, "I swear that I am telling the truth! May God punish me if I am not! I do not know that man!"

Just then a cock crowed, ⁷⁵and Peter remembered what Jesus had told him: "Before the cock crows, you will say three times that you do not know me." He went out and wept bitterly.

Jesus is Taken to Pilate

(Mk 15.1; Lk 23.1–2; Jn 18.28–32)

27 Early in the morning all the chief priests and the elders made their plans against Jesus to put him to death. ²They put him in chains, led him off, and handed him over to Pilate, the Roman governor.

ᵃ **26.50** Be quick about it, friend!; *or* Why are you here, friend?

The Death of Judas
(Acts 1.18–19)

3   When Judas, the traitor, learnt that Jesus had been condemned, he repented and took back the 30 silver coins to the chief priests and the elders. [4]"I have sinned by betraying an innocent man to death!" he said.

"What do we care about that?" they answered. "That is your business!"

5   Judas threw the coins down in the Temple and left; then he went off and hanged himself.

6   The chief priests picked up the coins and said, "This is blood money, and it is against our Law to put it in the temple treasury." [7]After reaching an agreement about it, they used the money to buy Potter's Field, as a cemetery for foreigners. [8]That is why that field is called "Field of Blood" to this very day.

9   Then what the prophet Jeremiah had said came true: "They took the thirty silver coins, the amount the people of Israel had agreed to pay for him, [10]and used the money to buy the potter's field, as the Lord had commanded me."

Pilate Questions Jesus
(Mk 15.2–5; Lk 23.3–5; Jn 18.33–38)

11   Jesus stood before the Roman governor, who questioned him. "Are you the king of the Jews?" he asked.

A Station of the Cross showing Jesus before Pontius Pilate

"So you say," answered Jesus. [12]But he said nothing in response to the accusations of the chief priests and elders.

13   So Pilate said to him, "Don't you hear all these things they accuse you of?"

14   But Jesus refused to answer a single word, with the result that the Governor was greatly surprised.

Jesus is Sentenced to Death
(Mk 15.6–15; Lk 23.13–25; Jn 18.39—19.16)

15   At every Passover Festival the Roman governor was in the habit of setting free any one prisoner the crowd asked for. [16]At that time there was a well-known prisoner named Jesus Barabbas. [17]So when the crowd gathered, Pilate asked them, "Which one do you want me to set free for you? Jesus Barabbas or Jesus called the Messiah?" [18]He knew very well that the Jewish authorities had handed Jesus over to him because they were jealous.

19   While Pilate was sitting in the judgement hall, his wife sent him a message: "Have nothing to do with that innocent man, because in a dream last night I suffered much on account of him."

20   The chief priests and the elders persuaded the crowd to ask Pilate to set Barabbas free and have Jesus put to death. [21]But Pilate asked the crowd, "Which one of these two do you want me to set free for you?"

"Barabbas!" they answered.

22   "What, then, shall I do with Jesus called the Messiah?" Pilate asked them.

"Crucify him!" they all answered.

23   But Pilate asked, "What crime has he committed?"

Then they started shouting at the top of their voices: "Crucify him!"

24   When Pilate saw that it was no use to go on, but that a riot might break out, he took some water, washed his hands in front of the crowd, and said, "I am not responsible for the death of this man! This is your doing!"

25   The whole crowd answered, "Let the responsibility for his death fall on us and our children!"

26   Then Pilate set Barabbas free for them; and after he had Jesus whipped, he handed him over to be crucified.

The Soldiers Mock Jesus
(Mk 15.16–20; Jn 19.2–3)

27   Then Pilate's soldiers took Jesus into the governor's palace, and the whole company gathered round him. [28]They stripped off his clothes and put a scarlet robe on him. [29]Then they made a

crown out of thorny branches and placed it on his head, and put a stick in his right hand; then they knelt before him and mocked him. "Long live the King of the Jews!" they said. ³⁰They spat on him, and took the stick and hit him over the head. ³¹When they had finished mocking him, they took the robe off and put his own clothes back on him. Then they led him out to crucify him.

Jesus is Crucified
(Mk 15.21–32; Lk 23.26–43; Jn 19.17–27)

32   As they were going out, they met a man from Cyrene named Simon, and the soldiers forced him to carry Jesus' cross. ³³They came to a place called Golgotha, which means, "The Place of the Skull". ³⁴There they offered Jesus wine mixed with a bitter substance; but after tasting it, he would not drink it.

35   They crucified him and then divided his clothes among them by throwing dice. ³⁶After that they sat there and watched him. ³⁷Above his head they put the written notice of the accusation against him: "This is Jesus, the King of the Jews." ³⁸Then they crucified two bandits with Jesus, one on his right and the other on his left.

39   People passing by shook their heads and hurled insults at Jesus: ⁴⁰"You were going to tear down the Temple and build it up again in three days! Save yourself if you are God's Son! Come on down from the cross!"

41   In the same way the chief priests and the teachers of the Law and the elders jeered at him: ⁴²"He saved others, but he cannot save himself! Isn't he the king of Israel? If he comes down off the cross now, we will believe in him! ⁴³He trusts in God and claims to be God's Son. Well, then, let us see if God wants to save him now!"

44   Even the bandits who had been crucified with him insulted him in the same way.

The Death of Jesus
(Mk 15.33–41; Lk 23.44–49; Jn 19.28–30)

45   At noon the whole country was covered with darkness, which lasted for three hours. ⁴⁶At about three o'clock Jesus cried out with a loud shout, *"Eli, Eli, lema sabachthani?"* which means, "My God, my God, why did you abandon me?"

47   Some of the people standing there heard him and said, "He is calling for Elijah!" ⁴⁸One of them ran up at once, took a sponge, soaked it in cheap wine, put it on the end of a stick, and tried to make him drink it.

49   But the others said, "Wait, let us see if Elijah is coming to save him!"

50   Jesus again gave a loud cry and breathed his last.

51   Then the curtain hanging in the Temple was torn in two from top to bottom. The earth shook, the rocks split apart, ⁵²the graves broke open, and many of God's people who had died were raised to life. ⁵³They left the graves, and after Jesus rose from death, they went into the Holy City, where many people saw them.

54   When the army officer and the soldiers with him who were watching Jesus saw the earthquake and everything else that happened, they were terrified and said, "He really was the Son of God!"

55   There were many women there, looking on from a distance, who had followed Jesus from Galilee and helped him. ⁵⁶Among them were Mary Magdalene, Mary the mother of James and Joseph, and the wife of Zebedee.

The Burial of Jesus
(Mk 15.42–47; Lk 23.50–56; Jn 19.38–42)

57   When it was evening, a rich man from Arimathea arrived; his name was Joseph, and he also was a disciple of Jesus. ⁵⁸He went into the presence of Pilate and asked for the body of Jesus. Pilate gave orders for the body to be given to Joseph. ⁵⁹So Joseph took it, wrapped it in a new linen sheet, ⁶⁰and placed it in his own tomb, which he had just recently dug out of solid rock. Then he rolled a large stone across the entrance to the tomb and went away. ⁶¹Mary Magdalene and the other Mary were sitting there, facing the tomb.

The Guard at the Tomb

62   The next day, which was a Sabbath, the chief priests and the Pharisees met with Pilate ⁶³and said, "Sir, we remember that while that liar was still alive he said, 'I will be raised to life three days later.' ⁶⁴Give orders, then, for his tomb to be carefully guarded until the third day, so that his disciples will not be able to go and steal the body, and then tell the people that he was raised from death. This last lie would be even worse than the first one."

65   "Take a guard," Pilate told them; "go and make the tomb as secure as you can."

66   So they left and made the tomb secure by putting a seal on the stone and leaving the guard on watch.

The Resurrection
(Mk 16.1–10; Lk 24.1–12; Jn 20.1–10)

28 After the Sabbath, as Sunday morning was dawning, Mary Magdalene and the other Mary went to look at the tomb. ²Suddenly there was a violent earthquake; an angel of the Lord came down from heaven, rolled the stone away, and sat on it. ³His appearance was like lightning, and his clothes were white as snow. ⁴The guards were so afraid that they trembled and became like dead men.

5 The angel spoke to the women. "You must not be afraid," he said. "I know you are looking for Jesus, who was crucified. ⁶He is not here; he has been raised, just as he said. Come here and see the place where he was lying. ⁷Go quickly now, and tell his disciples, 'He has been raised from death, and now he is going to Galilee ahead of you; there you will see him!' Remember what I have told you."

8 So they left the tomb in a hurry, afraid and yet filled with joy, and ran to tell his disciples.

9 Suddenly Jesus met them and said, "Peace be with you." They came up to him, took hold of his feet, and worshipped him. ¹⁰"Do not be afraid," Jesus said to them. "Go and tell my brothers to go to Galilee, and there they will see me."

The Report of the Guard

11 While the women went on their way, some of the soldiers guarding the tomb went back to the city and told the chief priests everything that had happened. ¹²The chief priests met with the elders and made their plan; they gave a large sum of money to the soldiers ¹³and said, "You are to say that his disciples came during the night and stole his body while you were asleep. ¹⁴And if the Governor should hear of this, we will convince him that you are innocent, and you will have nothing to worry about."

An image of the Resurrection in a 15th-century Book of Hours

15 The guards took the money and did what they were told to do. And so that is the report spread round by the Jews to this very day.

Jesus Appears to his Disciples
(Mk 16.14–18; Lk 24.36–49; Jn 20.19–23; Acts 1.6–8)

16 The eleven disciples went to the hill in Galilee where Jesus had told them to go. ¹⁷When they saw him, they worshipped him, even though some of them doubted. ¹⁸Jesus drew near and said to them, "I have been given all authority in heaven and on earth. ¹⁹Go, then, to all peoples everywhere and make them my disciples: baptize them in the name of the Father, the Son, and the Holy Spirit, ²⁰and teach them to obey everything I have commanded you. And I will be with you always, to the end of the age."

The Gospel according to MARK

INTRODUCTION

The Gospel according to Mark begins with the statement that it is "the Good News about Jesus Christ, the Son of God". Jesus is pictured as a man of action and authority. His authority is seen in his teaching, in his power over demons, and in forgiving people's sins. Jesus speaks of himself as the Son of Man, who came to give his life to set people free from sin.

Mark presents the story of Jesus in a straightforward, vigorous way, with emphasis on what Jesus did, rather than on his words and teachings. After a brief prologue about John the Baptist and the baptism and temptation of Jesus, the writer immediately takes up Jesus' ministry of healing and teaching. As time goes on, the followers of Jesus come to understand him better, but Jesus' opponents become more hostile. The closing chapters report the events of Jesus' last week of earthly life, especially his crucifixion and resurrection.

The two endings to the Gospel, which are enclosed in brackets, are generally regarded as written by someone other than the author of *Mark*.

Outline of Contents

The Preaching of John the Baptist
(Mt 3.1–12; Lk 3.1–18; Jn 1.19–28)

1 This is the Good News about Jesus Christ, the Son of God.[a] 2It began as the prophet Isaiah had written:

"God said, 'I will send my messenger ahead
    of you
  to clear the way for you.'
3 Someone is shouting in the desert,
    'Get the road ready for the Lord;
    make a straight path for him to travel!'"

4 So John appeared in the desert, baptizing and preaching.[b] "Turn away from your sins and be baptized," he told the people, "and God will forgive your sins." 5Many people from the province of Judea and the city of Jerusalem went out to hear John. They confessed their sins, and he baptized them in the River Jordan.

6 John wore clothes made of camel's hair, with a leather belt round his waist, and his food was locusts and wild honey. 7He announced to the people, "The man who will come after me is much greater than I am. I am not good enough even to bend down and untie his sandals. 8I baptize you with water, but he will baptize you with the Holy Spirit."

The Baptism and Temptation of Jesus
(Mt 3.13—4.11; Lk 3.21-22; 4 1–13)

9 Not long afterwards Jesus came from Nazareth in the province of Galilee, and was baptized by John in the Jordan. 10As soon as Jesus came up out of the water, he saw heaven opening and the Spirit coming down on him like a dove. 11And a voice came from heaven,

---

[a] **1.1** *Some manuscripts do not have* the Son of God.
[b] **1.4** John appeared in the desert, baptizing and preaching; *some manuscripts have* John the Baptist appeared in the desert, preaching.

"You are my own dear Son. I am pleased with you."

12 At once the Spirit made him go into the desert, [13]where he stayed 40 days, being tempted by Satan. Wild animals were there also, but angels came and helped him.

Jesus Calls Four Fishermen
(Mt 4.12–22; Lk 4.14–15; 5.1–11)

A synagogue showing the scrolls of the Torah in the Ark (1.21–28)

14 After John had been put in prison, Jesus went to Galilee and preached the Good News from God. [15]"The right time has come," he said, "and the Kingdom of God is near! Turn away from your sins and believe the Good News!"

16 As Jesus walked along the shore of Lake Galilee, he saw two fishermen, Simon and his brother Andrew, catching fish with a net. [17]Jesus said to them, "Come with me, and I will teach you to catch people." [18]At once they left their nets and went with him.

19 He went a little farther on and saw two other brothers, James and John, the sons of Zebedee. They were in their boat getting their nets ready. [20]As soon as Jesus saw them, he called them; they left their father Zebedee in the boat with the hired men and went with Jesus.

A Man with an Evil Spirit
(Lk 4.31–37)

21 Jesus and his disciples came to the town of Capernaum, and on the next Sabbath Jesus went to the synagogue and began to teach. [22]The people who heard him were amazed at the way he taught, for he wasn't like the teachers of the Law; instead, he taught with authority.

23 Just then a man with an evil spirit in him came into the synagogue and screamed, [24]"What do you want with us, Jesus of Nazareth? Are you here to destroy us? I know who you are – you are God's holy messenger!"

25 Jesus ordered the spirit, "Be quiet, and come out of the man!"

26 The evil spirit shook the man hard, gave a loud scream, and came out of him. [27]The people were all so amazed that they started saying to one another, "What is this? Is it some kind of new teaching? This man has authority to give orders to the evil spirits, and they obey him!"

28 And so the news about Jesus spread quickly everywhere in the province of Galilee.

Jesus Heals Many People
(Mt 8.14–17; Lk 4.38–41)

29 Jesus and his disciples, including James and John, left the synagogue and went straight to the home of Simon and Andrew. [30]Simon's mother-in-law was sick in bed with a fever, and as soon as Jesus arrived, he was told about her. [31]He went to her, took her by the hand, and helped her up. The fever left her, and she began to wait on them.

32 After the sun had set and evening had come, people brought to Jesus all the sick and those who had demons. [33]All the people of the town gathered in front of the house. [34]Jesus healed many who were sick with all kinds of diseases and drove out many demons. He would not let the demons say anything, because they knew who he was.

Jesus Preaches in Galilee
(Lk 4.42–44)

35 Very early the next morning, long before daylight, Jesus got up and left the house. He went out of the town to a lonely place, where he prayed. [36]But Simon and his companions went out searching for him, [37]and when they found him, they said, "Everyone is looking for you."

38 But Jesus answered, "We must go on to the other villages round here. I have to preach in them also, because that is why I came."

39 So he travelled all over Galilee, preaching in the synagogues and driving out demons.

Capernaum (handwritten annotation)

Jesus Heals a Man
(Mt 8.1–4; Lk 5.12–16)

40 ✳ A man suffering from a dreaded skin disease came to Jesus, knelt down, and begged him for help. "If you want to," he said, "you can make me clean."[a]

41 Jesus was filled with pity,[b] and stretched out his hand and touched him. "I do want to," he answered. "Be clean!" [42]At once the disease left the man, and he was clean. [43]Then Jesus spoke sternly to him and sent him away at once, [44]after saying to him, "Listen, don't tell anyone about this. But go straight to the priest and let him examine you; then in order to prove to everyone that you are cured, offer the sacrifice that Moses ordered."

45 But the man went away and began to spread the news everywhere. Indeed, he talked so much that Jesus could not go into a town publicly. Instead, he stayed out in lonely places, and people came to him from everywhere.

Jesus Heals a Paralysed Man
(Mt 9.1–8; Lk 5.17–26)

2 ✳ A few days later Jesus went back to Capernaum, and the news spread that he was at home. [2]So many people came together that there was no room left, not even out in front of the door. Jesus was preaching the message to them [3]when four men arrived, carrying a paralysed man to Jesus. [4]Because of the crowd, however, they could not get the man to him. So they made a hole in the roof right above the place where Jesus was. When they had made an opening, they let the man down, lying on his mat. [5]Seeing how much faith they had, Jesus said to the paralysed man, "My son, your sins are forgiven."

6 Some teachers of the Law who were sitting there thought to themselves, [7]"How does he dare to talk like this? This is blasphemy! God is the only one who can forgive sins!"

8 At once Jesus knew what they were thinking, so he said to them, "Why do you think such things? [9]Is it easier to say to this paralysed man, 'Your sins are forgiven', or to say, 'Get up, pick up your mat, and walk'? [10]I will prove to you, then, that the Son of Man has authority on earth to forgive sins." So he said to the paralysed man, [11]"I tell you, get up, pick up your mat, and go home!"

---

[a] **1.40** MAKE ME CLEAN: *This disease was considered to make a person ritually unclean.*

[b] **1.41** pity; *some manuscripts have* anger.

Studying
MARK

Who wrote it? Early Christians agreed it was written by John Mark. Papias, a bishop in 130 CE, said Mark was Peter's "interpreter" who "wrote down accurately … all that he remembered of what Christ had said or done". Mark accompanied Paul on his early travels (Acts 12.25).
When? 65–75 CE. First Gospel written, one of the Synoptic Gospels along with *Matthew* and *Luke*.
Where from? Almost certainly Rome.
For whom? One Gentile (non-Jewish) community, probably church in Rome.
Why? The church in Rome was persecuted from 65–67 CE following a fire in 64 CE, for which the Christians were wrongly blamed. Writer wanted to encourage them by showing how Jesus faced up to death. Also wanted to record invaluable information about Jesus before key eye-witnesses died.

KEY POINTS
- The shortest Gospel, *Mark* presents a simple and straightforward account of Jesus' life.
- Mark presents a very human picture of Jesus – he falls asleep, gets angry with disciples.
- The suffering and death of Jesus take up about 30% of this Gospel – more than in any other.
- Emphasizes Jesus' role as teacher – he is called "rabbi" (teacher) on 39 occasions.
- Stresses that Jesus was God's Messiah but wanted this kept secret.

12 While they all watched, the man got up, picked up his mat, and hurried away. They were all completely amazed and praised God, saying, "We have never seen anything like this!"

Jesus Calls Levi
(Mt 9.9–13; Lk 5.27–32)

13 Jesus went back again to the shore of Lake Galilee. A crowd came to him, and he started teaching them. [14]As he walked along, he saw a tax collector, Levi son of Alphaeus, sitting in his office. Jesus said to him, "Follow me." Levi got up and followed him.

15 Later on Jesus was having a meal in Levi's house.[c] A large number of tax collectors and other outcasts were following Jesus, and many of them joined him and his disciples at the table. [16]Some teachers of the Law, who were Pharisees, saw that Jesus was eating with these outcasts and tax collectors, so they asked his disciples, "Why does he eat with such people?"

17 Jesus heard them and answered, "People who

---

[c] **2.15** in Levi's house; *or* in his *(that is,* Jesus') house.

---

are well do not need a doctor, but only those who are sick. I have not come to call respectable people, but outcasts."

The Question about Fasting
(Mt 9.14–17; Lk 5.33–39)

18   On one occasion the followers of John the Baptist and the Pharisees were fasting. Some people came to Jesus and asked him, "Why is it that the disciples of John the Baptist and the disciples of the Pharisees fast, but yours do not?"

19   Jesus answered, "Do you expect the guests at a wedding party to go without food? Of course not! As long as the bridegroom is with them, they will not do that. ²⁰But the day will come when the bridegroom will be taken away from them, and then they will fast.

21   "No one uses a piece of new cloth to patch up an old coat, because the new patch will shrink and tear off some of the old cloth, making an even bigger hole. ²²Nor does anyone pour new wine into used wineskins, because the wine will burst the skins, and both the wine and the skins will be ruined. Instead, new wine must be poured into fresh wineskins."

The Question about the Sabbath
(Mt 12.1–8; Lk 6.1–5)

23   Jesus was walking through some cornfields on the Sabbath. As his disciples walked along with him, they began to pick the ears of corn. ²⁴So the Pharisees said to Jesus, "Look, it is against our Law for your disciples to do that on the Sabbath!"

25   Jesus answered, "Have you never read what David did that time when he needed something to eat? He and his men were hungry, ²⁶so he went into the house of God and ate the bread offered to God. This happened when Abiathar was the High Priest. According to our Law only the priests may eat this bread – but David ate it and even gave it to his men."

27   And Jesus concluded, "The Sabbath was made for the good of human beings; they were not made for the Sabbath. ²⁸So the Son of Man is Lord even of the Sabbath."

The Man with a Paralysed Hand
(Mt 12.9–14; Lk 6.6–11)

 Then Jesus went back to the synagogue, where there was a man who had a paralysed hand. ²Some people were there who wanted to accuse Jesus of doing wrong; so they watched him closely to see whether he would heal the man on the Sabbath. ³Jesus said to the man, "Come up here to the front." ⁴Then he asked the people, "What does our Law allow us to do on the Sabbath? To help or to harm? To save someone's life or to destroy it?"

But they did not say a thing. ⁵Jesus was angry as he looked round at them, but at the same time he felt sorry for them, because they were so stubborn and wrong. Then he said to the man, "Stretch out your hand." He stretched it out, and it became well again. ⁶So the Pharisees left the synagogue and met at once with some members of Herod's party, and they made plans to kill Jesus.

A Crowd by the Lake

7   Jesus and his disciples went away to Lake Galilee, and a large crowd followed him. They had come from Galilee, from Judea, ⁸from Jerusalem, from the territory of Idumea, from the territory on the east side of the Jordan, and from the region round the cities of Tyre and Sidon. All these people came to Jesus because they had heard of the things he was doing. ⁹The crowd was so large that Jesus told his disciples to get a boat ready for him, so that the people would not crush him. ¹⁰He had healed many people, and all those who were ill kept pushing their way to him in order to touch him. ¹¹And whenever the people who had evil spirits in them saw him, they would fall down before him and scream, "You are the Son of God!"

12   Jesus sternly ordered the evil spirits not to tell anyone who he was.

Jesus Chooses the Twelve Apostles
(Mt 10.1–4; Lk 6.12–16)

13   Then Jesus went up a hill and called to himself the men he wanted. They came to him, ¹⁴and he chose twelve, whom he named apostles. "I have chosen you to be with me," he told them. "I will also send you out to preach, ¹⁵and you will have authority to drive out demons."

16   These are the twelve he chose: Simon (Jesus gave him the name Peter); ¹⁷James and his brother John, the sons of Zebedee (Jesus gave them the name Boanerges, which means "Men of Thunder"); ¹⁸Andrew, Philip, Bartholomew, Matthew, Thomas, James son of Alphaeus, Thaddaeus, Simon the Patriot, ¹⁹and Judas Iscariot, who betrayed Jesus.

27   "No one can break into a strong man's house and take away his belongings unless he first ties up the strong man; then he can plunder his house.

28   "I assure you that people can be forgiven all their sins and all the evil things they may say.[a] [29]But whoever says evil things against the Holy Spirit will never be forgiven, because he has committed an eternal sin." [30](Jesus said this because some people were saying, "He has an evil spirit in him.")

Jesus' Mother and Brothers
(Mt 12.46–50; Lk 8.19–21)

31   Then Jesus' mother and brothers arrived. They stood outside the house and sent in a message, asking for him. [32]A crowd was sitting round Jesus, and they said to him, "Look, your mother and your brothers and sisters are outside, and they want you."

33   Jesus answered, "Who is my mother? Who are my brothers?" [34]He looked at the people sitting round him and said, "Look! Here are my mother and my brothers! [35]Whoever does what God wants him to do is my brother, my sister, my mother."

The Parable of the Sower
(Mt 13.1–9; Lk 8.4–8)

4 ▯p   Again Jesus began to teach beside Lake Galilee. The crowd that gathered round him was so large that he got into a boat and sat in it. The boat was out in the water, and the crowd stood on the shore at the water's edge. [2]He used parables to teach them many things, saying to them:

3   "Listen! Once there was a man who went out to sow corn. [4]As he scattered the seed in the field, some of it fell along the path, and the birds came and ate it up. [5]Some of it fell on rocky ground, where there was little soil. The seeds soon sprouted, because the soil wasn't deep. [6]Then, when the sun came up, it burnt the young plants; and because the roots had not grown deep enough, the plants soon dried up. [7]Some of the seed fell among thorn bushes, which grew up and choked the plants, and they didn't produce any corn. [8]But some seeds fell in good soil, and the plants sprouted, grew, and produced corn: some had thirty grains, others sixty, and others a hundred."

A 15th-century image of St Andrew, one of the apostles

Jesus and Beelzebul
(Mt 12.22–32; Lk 11.14–23; 12.10)

20   ◇t   Then Jesus went home. Again such a large crowd gathered that Jesus and his disciples had no time to eat. [21]When his family heard about it, they set out to take charge of him, because people were saying, "He's gone mad!"

22   Some teachers of the Law who had come from Jerusalem were saying, "He has Beelzebul in him! It is the chief of the demons who gives him the power to drive them out."

23   So Jesus called them to him and spoke to them in parables: "How can Satan drive out Satan? [24]If a country divides itself into groups which fight each other, that country will fall apart. [25]If a family divides itself into groups which fight each other, that family will fall apart. [26]So if Satan's kingdom divides into groups, it cannot last, but will fall apart and come to an end.

---

[a] **3.28** evil things they may say; *or* evil things they may say against God.

43

9   And Jesus concluded, "Listen, then, if you have ears!"

The Purpose of the Parables
(Mt 13.10–17; Lk 8.9–10)

10   When Jesus was alone, some of those who had heard him came to him with the twelve disciples and asked him to explain the parables. ¹¹"You have been given the secret of the Kingdom of God," Jesus answered. "But the others, who are on the outside, hear all things by means of parables, ¹²so that,

'They may look and look,
    yet not see;
they may listen and listen,
    yet not understand.
For if they did, they would turn to God,
    and he would forgive them.'"

Jesus Explains the Parable of the Sower
(Mt 13.18–23; Lk 8.11–15)

13   Then Jesus asked them, "Don't you understand this parable? How, then, will you ever understand any parable? ¹⁴The sower sows God's message. ¹⁵Some people are like the seeds that fall along the path; as soon as they hear the message, Satan comes and takes it away. ¹⁶Other people are like the seeds that fall on rocky ground. As soon as they hear the message, they receive it gladly. ¹⁷But it does not sink deep into them, and they don't last long. So when trouble or persecution comes because of the message, they give up at once. ¹⁸Other people are like the seeds sown among the thorn bushes. These are the ones who hear the message, ¹⁹but the worries about this life, the love for riches, and all other kinds of desires crowd in and choke the message, and they don't bear fruit. ²⁰But other people are like the seeds sown in good soil. They hear the message, accept it, and bear fruit: some thirty, some sixty, and some a hundred."

A Lamp under a Bowl
(Lk 8.16–18)

21   Jesus continued, "Does anyone ever bring in a lamp and put it under a bowl or under the bed? Doesn't he put it on the lampstand? ²²Whatever is hidden away will be brought out into the open, and whatever is covered up will be uncovered. ²³Listen, then, if you have ears!"

24   He also said to them, "Pay attention to what you hear! The same rules you use to judge others will be used by God to judge you – but with even greater severity. ²⁵Those who have something will be given more, and those who have nothing will have taken away from them even the little they have."

The Parable of the Growing Seed

26   Jesus went on to say, "The Kingdom of God is like this. A man scatters seed in his field. ²⁷He sleeps at night, is up and about during the day, and all the while the seeds are sprouting and growing. Yet he does not know how it happens. ²⁸The soil itself makes the plants grow and bear fruit; first the tender stalk appears, then the ear, and finally the ear full of corn. ²⁹When the corn is ripe, the man starts cutting it with his sickle, because harvest time has come.

The Parable of the Mustard Seed
(Mt 13.31–32, 34; Lk 13.18–19)

30   "What shall we say the Kingdom of God is like?" asked Jesus. "What parable shall we use to explain it? ³¹It is like this. A man takes a mustard seed, the smallest seed in the world, and plants it in the ground. ³²After a while it grows up and becomes the biggest of all plants. It puts out such large branches that the birds come and make their nests in its shade."

33   Jesus preached his message to the people, using many other parables like these; he told them as much as they could understand. ³⁴He would not speak to them without using parables, but when he was alone with his disciples, he would explain everything to them.

Jesus Calms a Storm
(Mt 8.23–27; Lk 8.22–25)

35   On the evening of that same day Jesus said to his disciples, "Let us go across to the other side of the lake." ³⁶So they left the crowd; the disciples got into the boat in which Jesus was already sitting, and they took him with them. Other boats were there too. ³⁷Suddenly a strong wind blew up, and the waves began to spill over into the boat, so that it was about to fill with water. ³⁸Jesus was in the back of the boat, sleeping with his head on a pillow. The disciples woke him up and said, "Teacher, don't you care that we are about to die?"

39   Jesus stood up and commanded the wind, "Be quiet!" and he said to the waves, "Be still!" The

KEY
PLACES
IN
MARK

Sidon

Tyre

Phoenicia

Caesarea Philippi

Galilee

Capernaum • • Bethsaida

Lake Galilee

Nazareth •

Mediterranean Sea

Samaria

River Jordan

Gerasa
•
Decapolis
(The Ten Towns)

• Arimathea

Bethphage Bethany
•
Jerusalem • • ↓ Jericho

Perea

Dead Sea

Judea

0   30 km

Idumea

---

chains and smashed the irons on his feet. He was too strong for anyone to control him. ⁵Day and night he wandered among the tombs and through the hills, screaming and cutting himself with stones.

6   He was some distance away when he saw Jesus; so he ran, fell on his knees before him, ⁷and screamed in a loud voice, "Jesus, Son of the Most High God! What do you want with me? For God's sake, I beg you, don't punish me!" ⁸(He said this because Jesus was saying, "Evil spirit, come out of this man!")

9   So Jesus asked him, "What is your name?"

The man answered, "My name is 'Mob' – there are so many of us!" ¹⁰And he kept begging Jesus not to send the evil spirits out of that region.

11 There was a large herd of pigs near by, feeding on a hillside. ¹²So the spirits begged Jesus, "Send us to the pigs, and let us go into them." ¹³He let them go, and the evil spirits went out of the man and entered the pigs. The whole herd – about 2,000 pigs in all – rushed down the side of the cliff into the lake and was drowned.

14 The men who had been taking care of the pigs ran away and spread the news in the town and among the farms. People went out to see what had happened, ¹⁵and when they came to Jesus, they saw the man who used to have the mob of demons in him. He was sitting there, clothed and in his right mind; and they were all afraid. ¹⁶Those who had seen it told the people what had happened to the man with the demons, and about the pigs.

17 So they asked Jesus to leave their territory.

18 As Jesus was getting into the boat, the man who had had the demons begged him, "Let me go with you!"

19 But Jesus would not let him. Instead, he told him, "Go back home to your family and tell them how much the Lord has done for you and how kind he has been to you."

20 So the man left and went all through the Ten Towns, telling what Jesus had done for him. And all who heard it were amazed.

Jairus' Daughter and the Woman who Touched Jesus' Cloak
(Mt 9.18–26; Lk 8.40–56)

21 Jesus went back across to the other side of the lake. There at the lakeside a large crowd gathered round him. ²²Jairus, an official of the local synagogue, arrived, and when he saw Jesus, he threw himself down at his feet ²³and begged him earnestly, "My little

---

wind died down, and there was a great calm. ⁴⁰Then Jesus said to his disciples, "Why are you frightened? Have you still no faith?"

41 But they were terribly afraid and said to one another, "Who is this man? Even the wind and the waves obey him!"

Jesus Heals a Man with Evil Spirits
(Mt 8.28–34; Lk 8.26–39)

5   Jesus and his disciples arrived on the other side of Lake Galilee, in the territory of Gerasa. ²As soon as Jesus got out of the boat, he was met by a man who came out of the burial caves there. This man had an evil spirit in him ³and lived among the tombs. Nobody could keep him chained up any more; ⁴many times his feet and hands had been chained, but every time he broke the

daughter is very ill. Please come and place your hands on her, so that she will get well and live!"

24 Then Jesus started off with him. So many people were going along with Jesus that they were crowding him from every side.

25 There was a woman who had suffered terribly from severe bleeding for twelve years, 26even though she had been treated by many doctors. She had spent all her money, but instead of getting better she got worse all the time. 27She had heard about Jesus, so she came in the crowd behind him, 28saying to herself, "If I just touch his clothes, I will get well."

29 She touched his cloak, and her bleeding stopped at once; and she had the feeling inside herself that she was healed of her trouble. 30At once Jesus knew that power had gone out of him, so he turned round in the crowd and asked, "Who touched my clothes?"

31 His disciples answered, "You see how the people are crowding you; why do you ask who touched you?"

32 But Jesus kept looking round to see who had done it. 33The woman realized what had happened to her, so she came, trembling with fear, knelt at his feet, and told him the whole truth. 34Jesus said to her, "My daughter, your faith has made you well. Go in peace, and be healed of your trouble."

35 While Jesus was saying this, some messengers came from Jairus' house and told him, "Your daughter has died. Why bother the Teacher any longer?"

36 Jesus paid no attention to[a] what they said, but told him, "Don't be afraid, only believe." 37Then he did not let anyone else go on with him except Peter and James and his brother John. 38They arrived at Jairus' house, where Jesus saw the confusion and heard all the loud crying and wailing. 39He went in and said to them, "Why all this confusion? Why are you crying? The child is not dead – she is only sleeping!"

40 They laughed at him, so he put them all out, took the child's father and mother and his three disciples, and went into the room where the child was lying. 41He took her by the hand and said to her, "*Talitha, koum,*" which means, "Little girl, I tell you to get up!"

42 She got up at once and started walking around. (She was twelve years old.) When this happened, they were completely amazed. 43But Jesus gave them strict orders not to tell anyone, and he said, "Give her something to eat."

---

[a] **5.36** paid no attention to; *or* overheard.

Jesus is Rejected at Nazareth
(Mt 13.53–58; Lk 4.16–30)

6 Jesus left that place and went back to his home town, followed by his disciples. 2On the Sabbath he began to teach in the synagogue. Many people were there; and when they heard him, they were all amazed. "Where did he get all this?" they asked. "What wisdom is this that has been given him? How does he perform miracles? 3Isn't he the carpenter, the son of Mary, and the brother of James, Joseph, Judas, and Simon? Aren't his sisters living here?" And so they rejected him.

4 Jesus said to them, "Prophets are respected everywhere except in their own home town and by their relatives and their family."

5 He was not able to perform any miracles there, except that he placed his hands on a few sick people and healed them. 6He was greatly surprised, because the people did not have faith.

Jesus Sends out the Twelve Disciples
(Mt 10.5–15; Lk 9.1–6)

Then Jesus went to the villages round there, teaching the people. 7He called the twelve disciples together and sent them out two by two. He gave them authority over the evil spirits 8and ordered them, "Don't take anything with you on

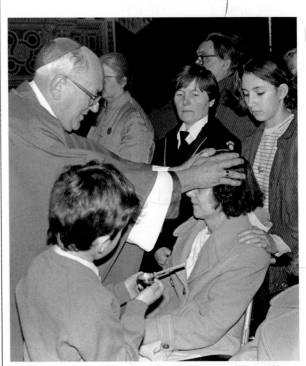

A priest anoints the sick with oil and lays hands on them (6.13)

your journey except a stick – no bread, no beggar's bag, no money in your pockets. 9Wear sandals, but don't carry an extra shirt." 10He also said, "Wherever you are welcomed, stay in the same house until you leave that place. 11If you come to a town where people do not welcome you or will not listen to you, leave it and shake the dust off your feet. That will be a warning to them!"

12   So they went out and preached that people should turn away from their sins. 13They drove out many demons, and rubbed olive oil on many sick people and healed them.

The Death of John the Baptist
(Mt 14.1–12; Lk 9.7–9)

14   Now King Herod[a] heard about all this, because Jesus' reputation had spread everywhere. Some people were saying, "John the Baptist has come back to life! That is why he has this power to perform miracles."

15   Others, however, said, "He is Elijah."

    Others said, "He is a prophet, like one of the prophets of long ago."

16   When Herod heard it, he said, "He is John the Baptist! I had his head cut off, but he has come back to life!" 17Herod himself had ordered John's arrest, and he had him chained and put in prison. Herod did this because of Herodias, whom he had married, even though she was the wife of his brother Philip. 18John the Baptist kept telling Herod, "It isn't right for you to be married to your brother's wife!"

19   So Herodias held a grudge against John and wanted to kill him, but she could not because of Herod. 20Herod was afraid of John because he knew that John was a good and holy man, and so he kept him safe. He liked to listen to him, even though he became greatly disturbed every time he heard him.

21   Finally Herodias got her chance. It was on Herod's birthday, when he gave a feast for all the chief government officials, the military commanders, and the leading citizens of Galilee. 22The daughter of Herodias[b] came in and danced, and pleased Herod and his guests. So the king said to the girl, "What would you like to have? I will give you anything you want." 23With many vows he said to her, "I swear that I will give you anything you ask for, even as much as half my kingdom!"

24   So the girl went out and asked her mother, "What shall I ask for?"

    "The head of John the Baptist," she answered.

25   The girl hurried back at once to the king and demanded, "I want you to give me here and now the head of John the Baptist on a dish!"

26   This made the king very sad, but he could not refuse her because of the vows he had made in front of all his guests. 27So he sent off a guard at once with orders to bring John's head. The guard left, went to the prison, and cut John's head off; 28then he brought it on a dish and gave it to the girl, who gave it to her mother. 29When John's disciples heard about this, they came and took away his body, and buried it.

Jesus Feeds a Great Crowd
(Mt 14.13–21; Lk 9.10–17; Jn 6.1–14)

30   The apostles returned and met with Jesus, and told him all they had done and taught. 31There were so many people coming and going that Jesus and his disciples didn't even have time to eat. So he said to them, "Let us go off by ourselves to some place where we will be alone and you can rest for a while." 32So they started out in a boat by themselves for a lonely place.

33   Many people, however, saw them leave and knew at once who they were; so they went from all the towns and ran ahead by land and arrived at the place ahead of Jesus and his disciples. 34When Jesus got out of the boat, he saw this large crowd, and his heart was filled with pity for them, because they were like sheep without a shepherd. So he began to teach them many things. 35When it was getting late, his disciples came to him and said, "It is already very late, and this is a lonely place. 36Send the people away, and let them go to the nearby farms and villages in order to buy themselves something to eat."

37   "You yourselves give them something to eat," Jesus answered.

    They asked, "Do you want us to go and spend two hundred silver coins[c] on bread in order to feed them?"

38   So Jesus asked them, "How much bread have you got? Go and see."

    When they found out, they told him, "Five loaves and also two fish."

39   Jesus then told his disciples to make all the people divide into groups and sit down on the

---

[a] **6.14** KING HEROD: *Herod Antipas, ruler of Galilee.*

[b] **6.22** The daughter of Herodias; *some manuscripts have* His daughter Herodias.

[c] **6.37** SILVER COINS: *A silver coin was the daily wage of a rural worker (see Mt 20.2).*

green grass. ⁴⁰So the people sat down in rows, in groups of a hundred and groups of fifty. ⁴¹Then Jesus took the five loaves and the two fish, looked up to heaven, and gave thanks to God. He broke the loaves and gave them to his disciples to distribute to the people. He also divided the two fish among them all. ⁴²Everyone ate and had enough. ⁴³Then the disciples took up twelve baskets full of what was left of the bread and the fish. ⁴⁴The number of men who were fed was 5,000.

Jesus Walks on the Water
(Mt 14.22–33; Jn 6.15–21)

45 At once Jesus made his disciples get into the boat and go ahead of him to Bethsaida, on the other side of the lake, while he sent the crowd away. ⁴⁶After saying goodbye to the people he went away to a hill to pray. ⁴⁷When evening came, the boat was in the middle of the lake, while Jesus was alone on land. ⁴⁸He saw that his disciples were straining at the oars, because they were rowing against the wind; so some time between three and six o'clock in the morning he came to them, walking on the water. He was going to pass them by,ᵃ ⁴⁹but they saw him walking on the water. "It's a ghost!" they thought, and screamed. ⁵⁰They were all terrified when they saw him.

Jesus spoke to them at once, "Courage!" he said. "It is I. Don't be afraid!" ⁵¹Then he got into the boat with them, and the wind died down. The disciples were completely amazed, ⁵²because they had not understood the real meaning of the feeding of the 5,000; their minds could not grasp it.

Jesus Heals the Sick in Gennesaret
(Mt 14.34–36)

53 They crossed the lake and came to land at Gennesaret, where they tied up the boat. ⁵⁴As they left the boat, people recognized Jesus at once. ⁵⁵So they ran throughout the whole region; and wherever they heard he was, they brought to him sick people lying on their mats. ⁵⁶And everywhere Jesus went, to villages, towns, or farms, people would take those who were ill to the market places and beg him to let them at least touch the edge of his cloak; and all who touched it were made well.

ᵃ **6.48** pass them by; *or* join them.

The Teaching of the Ancestors
(Mt 15.1–9)

7 Some Pharisees and teachers of the Law who had come from Jerusalem gathered round Jesus. ²They noticed that some of his disciples were eating their food with hands that were ritually unclean – that is, they had not washed them in the way the Pharisees said people should.

3 (For the Pharisees, as well as the rest of the Jews, follow the teaching they received from their ancestors: they do not eat unless they wash their hands in the proper way; ⁴nor do they eat anything that comes from the market unless they wash it first.ᵇ And they follow many other rules which they have received, such as the proper way to wash cups, pots, copper bowls, and beds.ᶜ)

5 So the Pharisees and the teachers of the Law asked Jesus, "Why is it that your disciples do not follow the teaching handed down by our ancestors, but instead eat with ritually unclean hands?"

6 Jesus answered them, "How right Isaiah was when he prophesied about you! You are hypocrites, just as he wrote:

'These people, says God, honour me with
　　their words,
　　but their heart is really far away from me.
7 It is no use for them to worship me,
　　because they teach human rules
　　as though they were God's laws!'

8 "You put aside God's command and obey human teachings."

9 And Jesus continued, "You have a clever way of rejecting God's law in order to uphold your own teaching. ¹⁰For Moses commanded, 'Respect your father and your mother,' and, 'Whoever curses his father or his mother is to be put to death.' ¹¹But you teach that if a person has something he could use to help his father or mother, but says, 'This is Corban' (which means, it belongs to God), ¹²he is excused from helping his father or mother. ¹³In this way the teaching you pass on to others cancels out the word of God. And there are many other things like this that you do."

ᵇ **7.4** anything that comes from the market unless they wash it first; *or* anything after they come from the market unless they wash themselves first.
ᶜ **7.4** *Some manuscripts do not have* and beds.

The Things that Make a Person Unclean
(Mt 15.10–20)

14 Then Jesus called the crowd to him once more and said to them, "Listen to me, all of you, and understand. ¹⁵There is nothing that goes into a person from the outside which can make him ritually unclean. Rather, it is what comes out of a person that makes him unclean."ᵃ

17 When he left the crowd and went into the house, his disciples asked him to explain this saying. ¹⁸"You are no more intelligent than the others," Jesus said to them. "Don't you understand? Nothing that goes into a person from the outside can really make him unclean, ¹⁹because it does not go into his heart but into his stomach and then goes on out of the body." (In saying this, Jesus declared that all foods are fit to be eaten.)

20 And he went on to say, "It is what comes out of a person that makes him unclean. ²¹For from the inside, from a person's heart, come the evil ideas which lead him to do immoral things, to rob, kill, ²²commit adultery, be greedy, and do all sorts of evil things; deceit, indecency, jealousy, slander, pride, and folly – ²³all these evil things come from inside a person and make him unclean."

A Woman's Faith
(Mt 15.21–28)

24 Then Jesus left and went away to the territory near the city of Tyre. He went into a house and did not want anyone to know he was there, but he could not stay hidden. ²⁵A woman, whose daughter had an evil spirit in her, heard about Jesus and came to him at once and fell at his feet. ²⁶The woman was a Gentile, born in the region of Phoenicia in Syria. She begged Jesus to drive the demon out of her daughter. ²⁷But Jesus answered, "Let us first feed the children. It isn't right to take the children's food and throw it to the dogs."

28 "Sir," she answered, "even the dogs under the table eat the children's leftovers!"

29 So Jesus said to her, "Because of that answer, go back home, where you will find that the demon has gone out of your daughter!"

30 She went home and found her child lying on the bed; the demon had indeed gone out of her.

Jesus Heals a Deaf-mute

31 Jesus then left the neighbourhood of Tyre and went on through Sidon to Lake Galilee, going by way of the territory of the Ten Towns. ³²Some people brought him a man who was deaf and could hardly speak, and they begged Jesus to place his hands on him. ³³So Jesus took him off alone, away from the crowd, put his fingers in the man's ears, spat, and touched the man's tongue. ³⁴Then Jesus looked up to heaven, gave a deep groan, and said to the man, *"Ephphatha,"* which means, "Open up!"

35 At once the man was able to hear, his speech impediment was removed, and he began to talk without any trouble. ³⁶Then Jesus ordered the people not to speak of it to anyone; but the more he ordered them not to, the more they spoke. ³⁷And all who heard were completely amazed. "How well he does everything!" they exclaimed. "He even causes the deaf to hear and the dumb to speak!"

Jesus Feeds Four Thousand People
(Mt 15.32–39)

8 Not long afterwards another large crowd came together. When the people had nothing left to eat, Jesus called the disciples to him and said, ²"I feel sorry for these people, because they have been with me for three days and now have nothing to eat. ³If I send them home without feeding them, they will faint as they go, because some of them have come a long way."

4 His disciples asked him, "Where in this desert can anyone find enough food to feed all these people?"

5 "How much bread have you got?" Jesus asked. "Seven loaves," they answered.

6 He ordered the crowd to sit down on the ground. Then he took the seven loaves, gave thanks to God, broke them, and gave them to his disciples to distribute to the crowd; and the disciples did so. ⁷They also had a few small fish. Jesus gave thanks for these and told the disciples to distribute them too. ⁸⁻⁹Everybody ate and had enough – there were about 4,000 people. Then the disciples took up seven baskets full of pieces left over. Jesus sent the people away ¹⁰and at once got into a boat with his disciples and went to the district of Dalmanutha.

ᵃ **7.15** *Some manuscripts add verse 16:* Listen, then, if you have ears! *(see 4.23).*

The Pharisees Ask for a Miracle
(Mt 12.38–42; 16.1–4)

11 Some Pharisees came to Jesus and started to argue with him. They wanted to trap him, so they asked him to perform a miracle to show that God approved of him. 12But Jesus gave a deep groan and said, "Why do the people of this day ask for a miracle? No, I tell you! No such proof will be given to these people!"

13 He left them, got back into the boat, and started across to the other side of the lake.

The Yeast of the Pharisees and of Herod
(Mt 16.5–12)

14 The disciples had forgotten to bring enough bread and had only one loaf with them in the boat. 15"Take care," Jesus warned them, "and be on your guard against the yeast of the Pharisees and the yeast of Herod."

16 They started discussing among themselves: "He says this because we haven't any bread."

17 Jesus knew what they were saying, so he asked them, "Why are you discussing about not having any bread? Don't you know or understand yet? Are your minds so dull? 18You have eyes – can't you see? You have ears – can't you hear? Don't you remember 19when I broke the five loaves for the five thousand people? How many baskets full of leftover pieces did you take up?"

"Twelve," they answered.

20 "And when I broke the seven loaves for the four thousand people," asked Jesus, "how many baskets full of leftover pieces did you take up?"

"Seven," they answered.

21 "And you still don't understand?" he asked them.

Jesus Heals a Blind Man at Bethsaida

22 They came to Bethsaida, where some people brought a blind man to Jesus and begged him to touch him. 23Jesus took the blind man by the hand and led him out of the village. After spitting on the man's eyes, Jesus placed his hands on him and asked him, "Can you see anything?"

24 The man looked up and said, "Yes, I can see people, but they look like trees walking about."

25 Jesus again placed his hands on the man's eyes. This time the man looked intently, his eyesight returned, and he saw everything clearly. 26Jesus then sent him home with the order, "Don't go back into the village."

Peter's Declaration about Jesus
(Mt 16.13–20; Lk 9.18–21)

27 Then Jesus and his disciples went away to the villages near Caesarea Philippi. On the way he asked them, "Tell me, who do people say I am?"

28 "Some say that you are John the Baptist," they answered; "others say that you are Elijah, while others say that you are one of the prophets."

29 "What about you?" he asked them. "Who do you say I am?"

Peter answered, "You are the Messiah."

30 Then Jesus ordered them, "Do not tell anyone about me."

Jesus Speaks about his Suffering and Death
(Mt 16.21–28; Lk 9.22–27)

31 Then Jesus began to teach his disciples: "The Son of Man must suffer much and be rejected by the elders, the chief priests, and the teachers of the Law. He will be put to death, but three days later he will rise to life." 32He made this very clear to them. So Peter took him aside and began to rebuke him. 33But Jesus turned round, looked at his disciples, and rebuked Peter. "Get away from me, Satan," he said. "Your thoughts don't come from God but from human nature!"

34 Then Jesus called the crowd and his disciples to him. "If anyone wants to come with me," he told them, "he must forget self, carry his cross, and follow me. 35For whoever wants to save his own life will lose it; but whoever loses his life for me and for the gospel will save it. 36Do people gain anything if they win the whole world but lose their life? Of course not! 37There is nothing they can give to regain their life. 38If a person is ashamed of me and of my teaching in this godless and wicked day, then the Son of Man will be ashamed of him when he comes in the glory of his Father with the holy angels."

9 And he went on to say, "I tell you, there are some here who will not die until they have seen the Kingdom of God come with power."

The Transfiguration
(Mt 17.1–13; Lk 9.28–36)

2 Six days later Jesus took with him Peter, James, and John, and led them up a high mountain, where they were alone. As they looked on, a change came over Jesus, 3and his clothes became shining white – whiter than anyone in the world could wash them. 4Then the three disciples saw Elijah and Moses talking with

Jesus. ⁵Peter spoke up and said to Jesus, "Teacher, how good it is that we are here! We will make three tents, one for you, one for Moses, and one for Elijah." ⁶He and the others were so frightened that he did not know what to say.

7   Then a cloud appeared and covered them with its shadow, and a voice came from the cloud, "This is my own dear Son – listen to him!" ⁸They took a quick look round but did not see anyone else; only Jesus was with them.

9   As they came down the mountain, Jesus ordered them, "Don't tell anyone what you have seen, until the Son of Man has risen from death."

10   They obeyed his order, but among themselves they started discussing the matter, "What does this 'rising from death' mean?" ¹¹And they asked Jesus, "Why do the teachers of the Law say that Elijah has to come first?"

12   His answer was, "Elijah is indeed coming first in order to get everything ready. Yet why do the Scriptures say that the Son of Man will suffer much and be rejected? ¹³I tell you, however, that Elijah has already come and that people treated him just as they pleased, as the Scriptures say about him."

Jesus Heals a Boy with an Evil Spirit
(Mt 17.14–21; Lk 9.37–43a)

14   When they joined the rest of the disciples, they saw a large crowd round them and some teachers of the Law arguing with them. ¹⁵When the people saw Jesus, they were greatly surprised, and ran to him and greeted him. ¹⁶Jesus asked his disciples, "What are you arguing with them about?"

17   A man in the crowd answered, "Teacher, I brought my son to you, because he has an evil spirit in him and cannot talk. ¹⁸Whenever the spirit attacks him, it throws him to the ground, and he foams at the mouth, grits his teeth, and becomes stiff all over. I asked your disciples to drive the spirit out, but they could not."

19   Jesus said to them, "How unbelieving you people are! How long must I stay with you? How long do I have to put up with you? Bring the boy to me!" ²⁰They brought him to Jesus.

As soon as the spirit saw Jesus, it threw the boy into a fit, so that he fell on the ground and rolled round, foaming at the mouth. ²¹"How long has he been like this?" Jesus asked the father.

"Ever since he was a child," he replied. ²²"Many times the evil spirit has tried to kill him by throwing him in the fire and into water. Have pity on us and help us, if you possibly can!"

23   "Yes," said Jesus, "if you yourself can! Everything is possible for the person who has faith."

24   The father at once cried out, "I do have faith, but not enough. Help me to have more!"

25   Jesus noticed that the crowd was closing in on them, so he gave a command to the evil spirit. "Deaf and dumb spirit," he said, "I order you to come out of the boy and never go into him again!"

26   The spirit screamed, threw the boy into a bad fit, and came out. The boy looked like a corpse, and everyone said, "He is dead!" ²⁷But Jesus took the boy by the hand and helped him to rise, and he stood up.

28   After Jesus had gone indoors, his disciples asked him privately, "Why couldn't we drive the spirit out?"

29   "Only prayer can drive this kind out," answered Jesus; "nothing else can."

Jesus Speaks Again about his Death
(Mt 17.22–23; Lk 9.43b–45)

30   Jesus and his disciples left that place and went on through Galilee. Jesus did not want anyone to know where he was, ³¹because he was teaching his disciples: "The Son of Man will be handed over to those who will kill him. Three days later, however, he will rise to life."

32   But they did not understand what this teaching meant, and they were afraid to ask him.

Who is the Greatest?
(Mt 18.1–5; Lk 9.46–48)

33   They came to Capernaum, and after going indoors Jesus asked his disciples, "What were you arguing about on the road?"

34   But they would not answer him, because on the road they had been arguing among themselves about who was the greatest. ³⁵Jesus sat down, called the twelve disciples, and said to them, "Whoever wants to be first must place himself last of all and be the servant of all." ³⁶Then he took a child and made him stand in front of them. He put his arms round him and said to them, ³⁷"Whoever welcomes in my name one of these children, welcomes me; and whoever welcomes me, welcomes not only me but also the one who sent me."

Whoever is not Against Us is For Us
(Lk 9.49–50)

38 John said to him, "Teacher, we saw a man who was driving out demons in your name, and we told him to stop, because he doesn't belong to our group."

39 "Do not try to stop him," Jesus told them, "because no one who performs a miracle in my name will be able soon afterwards to say evil things about me. ⁴⁰For whoever is not against us is for us. ⁴¹I assure you that anyone who gives you a drink of water because you belong to me will certainly receive his reward.

Temptations to Sin
(Mt 18.6–9; Lk 17.1–2)

42 "If anyone should cause one of these little ones to lose his faith in me, it would be better for that person to have a large millstone tied round his neck and be thrown into the sea. ⁴³So if your hand makes you lose your faith, cut it off! It is better for you to enter life without a hand than to keep both hands and go off to hell, to the fire that never goes out.ᵃ ⁴⁵And if your foot makes you lose your faith, cut it off! It is better for you to enter life without a foot than to keep both feet and be thrown into hell.ᵇ ⁴⁷And if your eye makes you lose your faith, take it out! It is better for you to enter the Kingdom of God with only one eye than to keep both eyes and be thrown into hell. ⁴⁸There 'the worms that eat them never die, and the fire that burns them is never put out.'

49 "Everyone will be purified by fire as a sacrifice is purified by salt.

50 "Salt is good; but if it loses its saltiness, how can you make it salty again?

"Have the salt of friendship among yourselves, and live in peace with one another."

Jesus Teaches about Divorce
(Mt 19.1–12; Lk 16.18)

10 Then Jesus left that place, went to the province of Judea, and crossed the River Jordan. Crowds came flocking to him again, and he taught them, as he always did.

2 Some Pharisees came to him and tried to trap him. "Tell us," they asked, "does our Law allow a man to divorce his wife?"

3 Jesus answered with a question, "What law did Moses give you?"

4 Their answer was, "Moses gave permission for a man to write a divorce notice and send his wife away."

5 Jesus said to them, "Moses wrote this law for you because you are so hard to teach. ⁶But in the beginning, at the time of creation, 'God made them male and female,' as the scripture says. ⁷'And for this reason a man will leave his father and mother and unite with his wife,ᶜ ⁸and the two will become one.' So they are no longer two, but one. ⁹No human being then must separate what God has joined together."

10 When they went back into the house, the disciples asked Jesus about this matter. ¹¹He said to them, "A man who divorces his wife and marries another woman commits adultery against his wife. ¹²In the same way, a woman who divorces her husband and marries another man commits adultery."

Jesus Blesses Little Children
(Mt 19.13–15; Lk 18.15–17)

13 Some people brought children to Jesus for him to place his hands on them, but the disciples scolded the people. ¹⁴When Jesus noticed this, he was angry and said to his disciples, "Let the children come to me, and do not stop them,

ᵃ **9.43** *Some manuscripts add verse 44:* There 'the worms that eat them never die, and the fire that burns them is never put out' *(see verse 48).*

ᵇ **9.45** *Some manuscripts add verse 46:* There 'the worms that eat them never die, and the fire that burns them is never put out' *(see verse 48).*

ᶜ **10.7** *Some manuscripts do not have* and unite with his wife.

because the Kingdom of God belongs to such as these. ¹⁵I assure you that whoever does not receive the Kingdom of God like a child will never enter it." ¹⁶Then he took the children in his arms, placed his hands on each of them, and blessed them.

The Rich Man
(Mt 19.16–30; Lk 18.18–30)

17 As Jesus was starting on his way again, a man ran up, knelt before him, and asked him, "Good Teacher, what must I do to receive eternal life?"

18 "Why do you call me good?" Jesus asked him. "No one is good except God alone. ¹⁹You know the commandments: 'Do not commit murder; do not commit adultery; do not steal; do not accuse anyone falsely; do not cheat; respect your father and your mother.'"

20 "Teacher," the man said, "ever since I was young, I have obeyed all these commandments."

21 Jesus looked straight at him with love and said, "You need only one thing. Go and sell all you have and give the money to the poor, and you will have riches in heaven; then come and follow me." ²²When the man heard this, gloom spread over his face, and he went away sad, because he was very rich.

23 Jesus looked round at his disciples and said to them, "How hard it will be for rich people to enter the Kingdom of God!"

24 The disciples were shocked at these words, but Jesus went on to say, "My children, how hard it is to enter the Kingdom of God! ²⁵It is much harder for a rich person to enter the Kingdom of God than for a camel to go through the eye of a needle."

26 At this the disciples were completely amazed and asked one another, "Who, then, can be saved?"

27 Jesus looked straight at them and answered, "This is impossible for human beings, but not for God; everything is possible for God."

28 Then Peter spoke up, "Look, we have left everything and followed you."

29 "Yes," Jesus said to them, "and I tell you that anyone who leaves home or brothers or sisters or mother or father or children or fields for me and for the gospel, ³⁰will receive much more in this present age. He will receive a hundred times more houses, brothers, sisters, mothers, children and fields – and persecutions as well; and in the age to come he will receive eternal life. ³¹But many who now are first will be last, and many who now are last will be first."

Jesus Speaks a Third Time about his Death
(Mt 20.17–19; Lk 18.31–34)

32 Jesus and his disciples were now on the road going up to Jerusalem. Jesus was going ahead of the disciples, who were filled with alarm; the people who followed behind were afraid. Once again Jesus took the twelve disciples aside and spoke of the things that were going to happen to him. ³³"Listen," he told them, "we are going up to Jerusalem where the Son of Man will be handed over to the chief priests and the teachers of the Law. They will condemn him to death and then hand him over to the Gentiles, ³⁴who will mock him, spit on him, whip him, and kill him; but three days later he will rise to life."

The Request of James and John
(Mt 20.20–28)

35 Then James and John, the sons of Zebedee, came to Jesus. "Teacher," they said, "there is something we want you to do for us."

36 "What is it?" Jesus asked them.

37 They answered, "When you sit on your throne in your glorious Kingdom, we want you to let us sit with you, one at your right and one at your left."

38 Jesus said to them, "You don't know what you are asking for. Can you drink the cup of suffering that I must drink? Can you be baptized in the way I must be baptized?"

39 "We can," they answered.

Jesus said to them, "You will indeed drink the cup I must drink and be baptized in the way I must be baptized. ⁴⁰But I do not have the right to choose who will sit at my right and my left. It is God who will give these places to those for whom he has prepared them."

41 When the other ten disciples heard about it, they became angry with James and John. ⁴²So Jesus called them all together to him and said, "You know that those who are considered rulers of the heathen have power over them, and the leaders have complete authority. ⁴³This, however, is not the way it is among you. If one of you wants to be great, he must be the servant of the rest; ⁴⁴and if one of you wants to be first, he must be the slave of all. ⁴⁵For even the Son of Man did not come to be served; he came to serve and to give his life to redeem many people."

Jesus Heals Blind Bartimaeus
(Mt 20.29–34; Lk 18.35–43)

46 They came to Jericho, and as Jesus was leaving with his disciples and a large crowd, a blind beggar named Bartimaeus son of Timaeus was sitting by the road. ⁴⁷When he heard that it was Jesus of Nazareth, he began to shout, "Jesus! Son of David! Take pity on me!"

48 Many of the people scolded him and told him to be quiet. But he shouted even more loudly, "Son of David, take pity on me!"

49 Jesus stopped and said, "Call him."

So they called the blind man. "Cheer up!" they said. "Get up, he is calling you."

50 He threw off his cloak, jumped up, and came to Jesus.

51 "What do you want me to do for you?" Jesus asked him.

"Teacher," the blind man answered, "I want to see again."

52 "Go," Jesus told him, "your faith has made you well."

At once he was able to see and followed Jesus on the road.

The Triumphant Entry into Jerusalem
(Mt 21.1–11; Lk 19.28–40; Jn 12.12–19)

11 As they approached Jerusalem, near the towns of Bethphage and Bethany, they came to the Mount of Olives. Jesus sent two of his disciples on ahead ²with these instructions: "Go to the village there ahead of you. As soon as you get there, you will find a colt tied up that has never been ridden. Untie it and bring it here. ³And if someone asks you why you are doing that, tell him that the Master[a] needs it and will send it back at once."

4 So they went and found a colt out in the street, tied to the door of a house. As they were untying it, ⁵some of the bystanders asked them, "What are you doing, untying that colt?"

6 They answered just as Jesus had told them, and the bystanders let them go. ⁷They brought the colt to Jesus, threw their cloaks over the animal, and Jesus got on. ⁸Many people spread their cloaks on the road, while others cut branches in the fields and spread them on the road. ⁹The people who were in front and those who followed behind began to shout, "Praise God! God bless him who comes in the name of the Lord! ¹⁰God bless the coming kingdom of King David, our father! Praise God!"

---

[a] **11.3** the Master; *or* its owner.

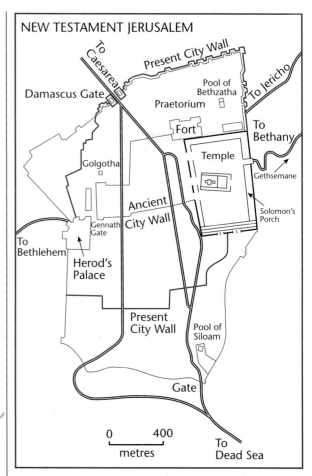

NEW TESTAMENT JERUSALEM

To Caesarea
Present City Wall
To Jericho
Pool of Bethzatha
Damascus Gate
Praetorium
Fort
To Bethany
Temple
Golgotha
Gethsemane
Ancient City Wall
Solomon's Porch
Gennath Gate
To Bethlehem
Herod's Palace
Present City Wall
Pool of Siloam
Gate
0   400 metres
To Dead Sea

11 Jesus entered Jerusalem, went into the Temple, and looked round at everything. But since it was already late in the day, he went out to Bethany with the twelve disciples.

Jesus Curses the Fig Tree
(Mt 21.18–19)

12 The next day, as they were coming back from Bethany, Jesus was hungry. ¹³He saw in the distance a fig tree covered with leaves, so he went to see if he could find any figs on it. But when he came to it, he found only leaves, because it was not the right time for figs. ¹⁴Jesus said to the fig tree, "No one shall ever eat figs from you again!"

And his disciples heard him.

Jesus Goes to the Temple
(Mt 21.12–17; Lk 19.45–48; Jn 2.13–22)

15 When they arrived in Jerusalem, Jesus went to the Temple and began to drive out all those who

were buying and selling. He overturned the tables of the money-changers and the stools of those who sold pigeons, [16]and he would not let anyone carry anything through the temple courtyards. [17]He then taught the people: "It is written in the Scriptures that God said, 'My Temple will be called a house of prayer for the people of all nations.' But you have turned it into a hideout for thieves!"

18   The chief priests and the teachers of the Law heard of this, so they began looking for some way to kill Jesus. They were afraid of him, because the whole crowd was amazed at his teaching.

19   When evening came, Jesus and his disciples left the city.

The Lesson from the Fig Tree
(Mt 21.20–22)

20   Early next morning, as they walked along the road, they saw the fig tree. It was dead all the way down to its roots. [21]Peter remembered what had happened and said to Jesus, "Look, Teacher, the fig tree you cursed has died!"

22   Jesus answered them, "Have faith in God. [23]I assure you that whoever tells this hill to get up and throw itself in the sea and does not doubt in his heart, but believes that what he says will happen, it will be done for him. [24]For this reason I tell you: when you pray and ask for something, believe that you have received it, and you will be given whatever you ask for. [25]And when you stand and pray, forgive anything you may have against anyone, so that your Father in heaven will forgive the wrongs you have done."[a]

The Question about Jesus' Authority
(Mt 21.23–27; Lk 20.1–8)

27   They arrived once again in Jerusalem. As Jesus was walking in the Temple, the chief priests, the teachers of the Law, and the elders came to him [28]and asked him, "What right have you to do these things? Who gave you this right?"

29   Jesus answered them, "I will ask you just one question, and if you give me an answer, I will tell you what right I have to do these things. [30]Tell me, where did John's right to baptize come from: was it from God or from human beings?"

31   They started to argue among themselves:

[a] **11.25** *Some manuscripts add verse 26:* If you do not forgive others, your Father in heaven will not forgive the wrongs you have done *(see Mt 6.15).*

"What shall we say? If we answer, 'From God,' he will say, 'Why, then, did you not believe John?' [32]But if we say, 'From human beings...'"(They were afraid of the people, because everyone was convinced that John had been a prophet.) [33]So their answer to Jesus was, "We don't know."

Jesus said to them, "Neither will I tell you, then, by what right I do these things."

The Parable of the Tenants in the Vineyard
(Mt 21.33–46; Lk 20.9–19)

12 Then Jesus spoke to them in parables: "Once there was a man who planted a vineyard, put a fence round it, dug a hole for the winepress, and built a watchtower. Then he let out the vineyard to tenants and left home on a journey. [2]When the time came to gather the grapes, he sent a slave to the tenants to receive from them his share of the harvest. [3]The tenants seized the slave, beat him, and sent him back without a thing. [4]Then the owner sent another slave; the tenants beat him over the head and treated him shamefully. [5]The owner sent another slave, and they killed him; and they treated many others the same way, beating some and killing others. [6]The only one left to send was the man's own dear son. Last of all, then, he sent his son to the tenants. 'I am sure they will respect my son,' he said. [7]But those tenants said to one another, 'This is the owner's son. Come on, let's kill him, and his property will be ours!' [8]So they seized the son and killed him and threw his body out of the vineyard.

9   "What, then, will the owner of the vineyard do?" asked Jesus. "He will come and kill those tenants and hand the vineyard over to others. [10]Surely you have read this scripture:

'The stone which the builders rejected as worthless
    turned out to be the most important of all.

11   This was done by the Lord;
    what a wonderful sight it is!'"

12   The Jewish leaders tried to arrest Jesus, because they knew that he had told this parable against them. But they were afraid of the crowd, so they left him and went away.

The Question about Paying Taxes
(Mt 22.15–22; Lk 20.20–26)

13   Some Pharisees and some members of Herod's party were sent to Jesus to trap him with questions. [14]They came to him and said, "Teacher, we know that you tell the

truth, without worrying about what people think. You pay no attention to anyone's status, but teach the truth about God's will for people. Tell us, is it against our Law to pay taxes to the Roman Emperor? Should we pay them or not?"

15 But Jesus saw through their trick and answered, "Why are you trying to trap me? Bring a silver coin, and let me see it."

16 They brought him one, and he asked, "Whose face and name are these?"

"The Emperor's," they answered.

17 So Jesus said, "Well, then, pay the Emperor what belongs to the Emperor, and pay God what belongs to God."

And they were amazed at Jesus.

The Question about Rising from Death
(Mt 22.23–33; Lk 20.27–40)

18 Then some Sadducees, who say that people will not rise from death, came to Jesus and said, [19]"Teacher, Moses wrote this law for us: 'If a man dies and leaves a wife but no children, that man's brother must marry the widow so that they can have children who will be considered the dead man's children.' [20]Once there were seven brothers; the eldest got married and died without having children. [21]Then the second one married the woman, and he also died without having children. The same thing happened to the third brother, [22]and then to the rest: all seven brothers married the woman and died without having children. Last of all, the woman died. [23]Now, when all the dead rise to life on the day of resurrection, whose wife will she be? All seven of them had married her."

24 Jesus answered them, "How wrong you are! And do you know why? It is because you don't know the Scriptures or God's power. [25]For when the dead rise to life, they will be like the angels in heaven and will not marry. [26]Now, as for the dead being raised: haven't you ever read in the Book of Moses the passage about the burning bush? There it is written that God said to Moses, 'I am the God of Abraham, the God of Isaac, and the God of Jacob.' [27]He is the God of the living, not of the dead. You are completely wrong!"

The Great Commandment
(Mt 22.34–40; Lk 10.25–28)

28 A teacher of the Law was there who heard the discussion. He saw that Jesus had given the Sadducees a good answer, so he came to him with a question: "Which commandment is the most important of all?"

29 Jesus replied, "The most important one is this: 'Listen, Israel! The Lord our God is the only Lord.[a] [30]Love the Lord your God with all your heart, with all your soul, with all your mind, and with all your strength.' [31]The second most important commandment is this: 'Love your neighbour as you love yourself.' There is no other commandment more important than these two."

32 The teacher of the Law said to Jesus, "Well done, Teacher! It is true, as you say, that only the Lord is God and that there is no other god but he. [33]And to love God with all your heart and with all your mind and with all your strength, and to love your neighbour as yourself, is more important than to offer animals and other sacrifices to God."

34 Jesus noticed how wise his answer was, and so he told him, "You are not far from the Kingdom of God."

After this nobody dared to ask Jesus any more questions.

The Question about the Messiah
(Mt 22.41–46; Lk 20.41–44)

35 As Jesus was teaching in the Temple, he asked the question, "How can the teachers of the Law say that the Messiah will be the descendant of David? [36]The Holy Spirit inspired David to say:

'The Lord said to my Lord:
Sit here on my right
until I put your enemies under your feet.'

37 David himself called him 'Lord'; so how can the Messiah be David's descendant?"

Jesus Warns against the Teachers of the Law
(Mt 23.1–36; Lk 20.45–47)

A large crowd was listening to Jesus gladly. [38]As he taught them, he said, "Watch out for the teachers of the Law, who like to walk around in their long robes and be greeted with respect in the market place, [39]who choose the reserved seats in the synagogues and the best places at feasts. [40]They take advantage of widows and rob them of their homes, and then make a show of saying long prayers. Their punishment will be all the worse!"

The Widow's Offering
(Lk 21.1–4)

41 As Jesus sat near the temple treasury, he

---

[a] **12.29** The Lord our God is the only Lord; or The Lord is our God, the Lord alone.

A model of Herod the Great's Temple in Jerusalem (13.1–2)

watched the people as they dropped in their money. Many rich men dropped in a lot of money; ⁴²then a poor widow came along and dropped in two little copper coins, worth about a penny. ⁴³He called his disciples together and said to them, "I tell you that this poor widow put more in the offering box than all the others. ⁴⁴For the others put in what they had to spare of their riches; but she, poor as she is, put in all she had – she gave all she had to live on."

Jesus Speaks of the Destruction of the Temple

(Mt 24.1–2; Lk 21.5–6)

13 As Jesus was leaving the Temple, one of his disciples said, "Look, Teacher! What wonderful stones and buildings!"

2 Jesus answered, "You see these great buildings? Not a single stone here will be left in its place; every one of them will be thrown down."

Troubles and Persecutions

(Mt 24.3–14; Lk 21.7–19)

3 Jesus was sitting on the Mount of Olives, across from the Temple, when Peter, James, John, and Andrew came to him in private. ⁴"Tell us when this will be," they said, "and tell us what will happen to show that the time has come for all these things to take place."

5 Jesus said to them, "Be on guard, and don't let anyone deceive you. ⁶Many men, claiming to speak for me, will come and say, 'I am he!' and they will deceive many people. ⁷And don't be troubled when you hear the noise of battles close by and news of battles far away. Such things must happen, but they do not mean that the end has come. ⁸Countries will fight each other; kingdoms will attack one another. There will be earthquakes everywhere, and there will be famines. These things are like the first pains of childbirth.

9 "You yourselves must be on guard. You will be

arrested and taken to court. You will be beaten in the synagogues; you will stand before rulers and kings for my sake to tell them the Good News. [10]But before the end comes, the gospel must be preached to all peoples. [11]And when you are arrested and taken to court, do not worry beforehand about what you are going to say; when the time comes, say whatever is then given to you. For the words you speak will not be yours; they will come from the Holy Spirit. [12]Men will hand over their own brothers to be put to death, and fathers will do the same to their children. Children will turn against their parents and have them put to death. [13]Everyone will hate you because of me. But whoever holds out to the end will be saved.

The Awful Horror
(Mt 24.15–28; Lk 21.20–24)

14   "You will see 'The Awful Horror' standing in the place where he should not be." (Note to the reader: be sure to understand what this means!) "Then those who are in Judea must run away to the hills. [15]Someone who is on the roof of his house must not lose time by going down into the house to get anything to take with him. [16]Someone who is in the field must not go back to the house for his cloak. [17]How terrible it will be in those days for women who are pregnant and for mothers with little babies! [18]Pray to God that these things will not happen in the winter! [19]For the trouble of those days will be far worse than any the world has ever known from the very beginning when God created the world until the present time. Nor will there ever be anything like it again. [20]But the Lord has reduced the number of those days; if he had not, nobody would survive. For the sake of his chosen people, however, he has reduced those days.

21   "Then, if anyone says to you, 'Look, here is the Messiah!' or, 'Look, there he is!' – do not believe him. [22]For false Messiahs and false prophets will appear. They will perform miracles and wonders in order to deceive even God's chosen people, if possible. [23]Be on your guard! I have told you everything before the time comes.

The Coming of the Son of Man
(Mt 24.29–31; Lk 21.25–28)

24   "In the days after that time of trouble the sun will grow dark, the moon will no longer shine, [25]the stars will fall from heaven, and the powers in space will be driven from their courses.

[26]Then the Son of Man will appear, coming in the clouds with great power and glory. [27]He will send the angels out to the four corners of the earth to gather God's chosen people from one end of the world to the other.

The Lesson of the Fig Tree
(Mt 24.32–35; Lk 21.29–33)

28   "Let the fig tree teach you a lesson. When its branches become green and tender and it starts putting out leaves, you know that summer is near. [29]In the same way, when you see these things happening, you will know that the time is near, ready to begin.[a] [30]Remember that all these things will happen before the people now living have all died. [31]Heaven and earth will pass away, but my words will never pass away.

No one Knows the Day or Hour
(Mt 24.36–44)

32   "No one knows, however, when that day or hour will come – neither the angels in heaven, nor the Son; only the Father knows. [33]Be on watch, be alert, for you do not know when the time will come. [34]It will be like a man who goes away from home on a journey and leaves his servants in charge, after giving to each one his own work to do and after telling the doorkeeper to keep watch. [35]Be on guard, then, because you do not know when the master of the house is coming – it might be in the evening or at midnight or before dawn or at sunrise. [36]If he comes suddenly, he must not find you asleep. [37]What I say to you, then, I say to all: watch!"

The Plot against Jesus
(Mt 26.1–5; Lk 22.1–2; Jn 11.45–53)

14 It was now two days before the Festival of Passover and Unleavened Bread. The chief priests and the teachers of the Law were looking for a way to arrest Jesus secretly and put him to death. [2]"We must not do it during the festival," they said, "or the people might riot."

Jesus is Anointed at Bethany
(Mt 26.6–13; Jn 12.1–8)

3   Jesus was in Bethany at the house of Simon, a man who had suffered from a dreaded skin disease. While Jesus was eating, a woman came

---

[a] **13.29** the time is near, ready to begin; *or* he is near, ready to come.

in with an alabaster jar full of a very expensive perfume made of pure nard. She broke the jar and poured the perfume on Jesus' head. 4Some of the people there became angry and said to one another, "What was the use of wasting the perfume? 5It could have been sold for more than three hundred silver coins[a] and the money given to the poor!" And they criticized her harshly.

6 But Jesus said, "Leave her alone! Why are you bothering her? She has done a fine and beautiful thing for me. 7You will always have poor people with you, and any time you want to, you can help them. But you will not always have me. 8She did what she could; she poured perfume on my body to prepare it ahead of time for burial. 9Now, I assure you that wherever the gospel is preached all over the world, what she has done will be told in memory of her."

Judas Agrees to Betray Jesus
(Mt 26.14–16; Lk 22.3–6)

10 Then Judas Iscariot, one of the twelve disciples, went off to the chief priests in order to betray Jesus to them. 11They were pleased to hear what he had to say, and promised to give him money. So Judas started looking for a good chance to hand Jesus over to them.

Jesus Eats the Passover Meal with his Disciples
(Mt 26.17–25; Lk 22.7–14, 21–23; Jn 13.21–30)

12 On the first day of the Festival of Unleavened Bread, the day the lambs for the Passover meal were killed, Jesus' disciples asked him, "Where do you want us to go and get the Passover meal ready for you?"

13 Then Jesus sent two of them with these instructions: "Go into the city, and a man carrying a jar of water will meet you. Follow him 14to the house he enters, and say to the owner of the house: 'The Teacher says, Where is the room where my disciples and I will eat the Passover meal?' 15Then he will show you a large upstairs room, prepared

and furnished, where you will get everything ready for us."

16 The disciples left, went to the city, and found everything just as Jesus had told them; and they prepared the Passover meal.

17 When it was evening, Jesus came with the twelve disciples. 18While they were at the table eating, Jesus said, "I tell you that one of you will betray me – one who is eating with me."

19 The disciples were upset and began to ask him, one after the other, "Surely you don't mean me, do you?"

20 Jesus answered, "It will be one of you twelve, one who dips his bread in the dish with me. 21The Son of Man will die as the Scriptures say he will; but how terrible for that man who betrays the Son of Man! It would have been better for that man if he had never been born!"

The Lord's Supper
(Mt 26.26–30; Lk 22.14–20; 1 Cor. 11.23–25)

22 While they were eating, Jesus took a piece of bread, gave a prayer of thanks, broke it, and gave it to his disciples. "Take it," he said, "this is my body."

23 Then he took a cup, gave thanks to God, and handed it to them; and they all drank from it. 24Jesus said, "This is my blood which is poured out for many, my blood which seals God's covenant. 25I tell you, I will never again drink this wine until the day I drink the new wine in the Kingdom of God."

Bread and wine used by Christians at Holy Communion (14.22–26)

a **14.5** SILVER COINS: *See 6.37.*

26   Then they sang a hymn and went out to the Mount of Olives.

Jesus Predicts Peter's Denial
(Mt 26.31–35; Lk 22.31–34; Jn 13.36–38)

27   Jesus said to them, "All of you will run away and leave me, for the scripture says, 'God will kill the shepherd, and the sheep will all be scattered.' [28]But after I am raised to life, I will go to Galilee ahead of you."

29   Peter answered, "I will never leave you, even though all the rest do!"

30   Jesus said to Peter, "I tell you that before the cock crows twice tonight, you will say three times that you do not know me."

31   Peter answered even more strongly, "I will never say that, even if I have to die with you!"

     And all the other disciples said the same thing.

Jesus Prays in Gethsemane
(Mt 26.36–46; Lk 22.39–46)

32   They came to a place called Gethsemane, and Jesus said to his disciples, "Sit here while I pray." [33]He took Peter, James, and John with him. Distress and anguish came over him, [34]and he said to them, "The sorrow in my heart is so great that it almost crushes me. Stay here and keep watch."

35   He went a little farther on, threw himself on the ground, and prayed that, if possible, he might not have to go through that time of suffering. [36]"Father," he prayed, "my Father! All things are possible for you. Take this cup of suffering away from me. Yet not what I want, but what you want."

37   Then he returned and found the three disciples asleep. He said to Peter, "Simon, are you asleep? Weren't you able to stay awake even for one hour?" [38]And he said to them, "Keep watch, and pray that you will not fall into temptation. The spirit is willing, but the flesh is weak."

39   He went away once more and prayed, saying the same words. [40]Then he came back to the disciples and found them asleep; they could not keep their eyes open. And they did not know what to say to him.

41   When he came back the third time, he said to them, "Are you still sleeping and resting? Enough! The hour has come! Look, the Son of Man is now being handed over to the power of sinners. [42]Get up, let us go. Look, here is the man who is betraying me!"

The Arrest of Jesus
(Mt 26.47–56; Lk 22.47–53; Jn 18.3–12)

43   Jesus was still speaking when Judas, one of the twelve disciples, arrived. With him was a crowd armed with swords and clubs, and sent by the chief priests, the teachers of the Law, and the elders. [44]The traitor had given the crowd a signal: "The man I kiss is the one you want. Arrest him and take him away under guard."

45   As soon as Judas arrived, he went up to Jesus and said, "Teacher!" and kissed him. [46]So they arrested Jesus and held him tight. [47]But one of those standing there drew his sword and struck at the High Priest's slave, cutting off his ear. [48]Then Jesus spoke up and said to them, "Did you have to come with swords and clubs to capture me, as though I were an outlaw? [49]Day after day I was with you teaching in the Temple, and you did not arrest me. But the Scriptures must come true."

50   Then all the disciples left him and ran away.

51   A certain young man, dressed only in a linen cloth, was following Jesus. They tried to arrest him, [52]but he ran away naked, leaving the cloth behind.

Jesus before the Council
(Mt 26.57–68; Lk 22.54–55, 63–71; Jn 18.13–14, 19–24)

53   Then Jesus was taken to the High Priest's house, where all the chief priests, the elders, and the teachers of the Law were gathering. [54]Peter followed from a distance and went into the courtyard of the High Priest's house. There he sat down with the guards, keeping himself warm by the fire. [55]The chief priests and the whole Council tried to find some evidence against Jesus in order to put him to death, but they could not find any. [56]Many witnesses told lies against Jesus, but their stories did not agree.

57   Then some men stood up and told this lie against Jesus: [58]"We heard him say, 'I will tear down this Temple which men have made, and after three days I will build one that is not made by men.'"[59]Not even they, however, could make their stories agree.

60   The High Priest stood up in front of them all and questioned Jesus, "Have you no answer to the accusation they bring against you?"

61   But Jesus kept quiet and would not say a word. Again the High Priest questioned him, "Are you the Messiah, the Son of the Blessed God?"

62   "I am," answered Jesus, "and you will all see the Son of Man seated on the right of the

Almighty and coming with the clouds of heaven!"

63 The High Priest tore his robes and said, "We don't need any more witnesses! 64You heard his blasphemy. What is your decision?"

They all voted against him: he was guilty and should be put to death.

65 Some of them began to spit on Jesus, and they blindfolded him and hit him. "Guess who hit you!" they said. And the guards took him and slapped him.

Peter Denies Jesus
(Mt 26.69–75; Lk 22.56–62; Jn 18.15–18, 25–27)

66 Peter was still down in the courtyard when one of the High Priest's servant women came by. 67When she saw Peter warming himself, she looked straight at him and said, "You, too, were with Jesus of Nazareth."

68 But he denied it. "I don't know ... I don't understand what you are talking about," he answered, and went out into the passage. Just then a cock crowed.[a]

69 The servant woman saw him there and began to repeat to the bystanders, "He is one of them!" 70But Peter denied it again.

A little while later the bystanders accused Peter again, "You can't deny that you are one of them, because you, too, are from Galilee."

71 Then Peter said, "I swear that I am telling the truth! May God punish me if I am not! I do not know the man you are talking about!"

72 Just then a cock crowed a second time, and Peter remembered how Jesus had said to him, "Before the cock crows twice, you will say three times that you do not know me." And he broke down and cried.

Jesus is Brought before Pilate
(Mt 27.1–2, 11–14; Lk 23.1–5; Jn 18.28–38)

15 Early in the morning the chief priests met hurriedly with the elders, the teachers of the Law, and the whole Council, and made their plans. They put Jesus in chains, led him away, and handed him over to Pilate. 2Pilate questioned him, "Are you the king of the Jews?"

Jesus answered, "So you say."

3 The chief priests were accusing Jesus of many things, 4so Pilate questioned him again, "Aren't you going to answer? Listen to all their accusations!"

---

[a] **14.68** *Some manuscripts do not have* Just then a cock crowed.

5 Again Jesus refused to say a word, and Pilate was amazed.

Jesus is Sentenced to Death
(Mt 27.15–26; Lk 23.13–25; Jn 18.39—19.16)

6 At every Passover Festival Pilate was in the habit of setting free any one prisoner the people asked for. 7At that time a man named Barabbas was in prison with the rebels who had committed murder in the riot. 8When the crowd gathered and began to ask Pilate for the usual favour, 9he asked them, "Do you want me to set free for you the king of the Jews?" 10He knew very well that the chief priests had handed Jesus over to him because they were jealous.

11 But the chief priests stirred up the crowd to ask, instead, for Pilate to set Barabbas free for them. 12Pilate spoke again to the crowd, "What, then, do you want me to do with the one you call the king of the Jews?"

13 They shouted back, "Crucify him!"

14 "But what crime has he committed?" Pilate asked.

They shouted all the louder, "Crucify him!"

15 Pilate wanted to please the crowd, so he set Barabbas free for them. Then he had Jesus whipped and handed him over to be crucified.

The Soldiers Mock Jesus
(Mt 27.27–31; Jn 19.2–3)

16 The soldiers took Jesus inside to the courtyard of the governor's palace and called together the rest of the company. 17They put a purple robe on Jesus, made a crown out of thorny branches, and put it on his head. 18Then they began to salute him: "Long live the King of the Jews!" 19They beat him over the head with a stick, spat on him, fell on their knees, and bowed down to him. 20When they had finished mocking him, they took off the purple robe and put his own clothes back on him. Then they led him out to crucify him.

Jesus is Crucified
(Mt 27.32–44; Lk 23.26–43; Jn 19.17–27)

21 On the way they met a man named Simon, who was coming into the city from the country, and the soldiers forced him to carry Jesus' cross. (Simon was from Cyrene and was the father of Alexander and Rufus.) 22They took Jesus to a place called Golgotha, which means "The Place of the Skull". 23There they tried to give him wine mixed with a drug called myrrh, but Jesus would

A Station of the Cross showing Simon of Cyrene carrying the cross (15.21)

not drink it. ²⁴Then they crucified him and divided his clothes among themselves, throwing dice to see who would get which piece of clothing. ²⁵It was nine o'clock in the morning when they crucified him. ²⁶The notice of the accusation against him said: "The King of the Jews". ²⁷They also crucified two bandits with Jesus, one on his right and the other on his left.[a]

29   People passing by shook their heads and hurled insults at Jesus: "Aha! You were going to tear down the Temple and build it up again in three days! ³⁰Now come down from the cross and save yourself!"

31   In the same way the chief priests and the teachers of the Law jeered at Jesus, saying to each other, "He saved others, but he cannot save himself! ³²Let us see the Messiah, the king of Israel, come down from the cross now, and we will believe in him!"

And the two who were crucified with Jesus insulted him also.

The Death of Jesus
(Mt 27.45–56; Lk 23.44–49; Jn 19.28–30)

33   At noon the whole country was covered with darkness, which lasted for three hours. ³⁴At three o'clock Jesus cried out with a loud shout, *"Eloi, Eloi, lema sabachthani?"* which means, "My God, my God, why did you abandon me?"

35   Some of the people there heard him and said, "Listen, he is calling for Elijah!" ³⁶One of them ran up with a sponge, soaked it in cheap wine, and put it on the end of a stick. Then he held it up to Jesus' lips and said, "Wait! Let us see if Elijah is coming to bring him down from the cross!"

37   With a loud cry Jesus died.

38   The curtain hanging in the Temple was torn in two, from top to bottom. ³⁹The army officer who was standing there in front of the cross saw how Jesus had died.[b] "This man was really the Son of God!" he said.

40   Some women were there, looking on from a distance. Among them were Mary Magdalene, Mary the mother of the younger James and of Joseph, and Salome. ⁴¹They had followed Jesus while he was in Galilee and had helped him. Many other women who had come to Jerusalem with him were there also.

The Burial of Jesus
(Mt 27.57–61; Lk 23.50–56; Jn 19.38–42)

42-43   It was towards evening when Joseph of Arimathea arrived. He was a respected member of the Council, who was waiting for the coming of the Kingdom of God. It was Preparation day (that is, the day before the Sabbath), so Joseph went boldly into the presence of Pilate and asked him for the body of Jesus. ⁴⁴Pilate was surprised to hear that Jesus was already dead. He called the army officer and asked him if Jesus had been dead a long time. ⁴⁵After hearing the officer's report, Pilate told Joseph he could have the body. ⁴⁶Joseph bought a linen sheet, took the body down, wrapped it in the sheet, and placed it in a tomb which had been dug out of solid rock. Then he rolled a large stone across the entrance to the tomb. ⁴⁷Mary Magdalene and Mary the mother of Joseph were watching and saw where the body of Jesus was placed.

The Resurrection
(Mt 28.1–8; Lk 24.1–12; Jn 20.1–10)

16   After the Sabbath was over, Mary Magdalene, Mary the mother of James, and Salome bought spices to go and anoint the body of Jesus. ²Very early on Sunday morning, at sunrise, they went to the

---

[a] **15.27** *Some manuscripts add verse 28:* In this way the scripture came true which says, "He shared the fate of criminals" *(see Lk 22.37).*

[b] **15.39** had died; *some manuscripts have* had cried out and died.

The body of Jesus is taken down from the cross (15.46)

tomb. ³⁻⁴On the way they said to one another, "Who will roll away the stone for us from the entrance to the tomb?" (It was a very large stone.) Then they looked up and saw that the stone had already been rolled back. ⁵So they entered the tomb, where they saw a young man sitting on the right, wearing a white robe – and they were alarmed.

6   "Don't be alarmed," he said. "I know you are looking for Jesus of Nazareth, who was crucified. He is not here – he has been raised! Look, here is the place where they put him. ⁷Now go and give this message to his disciples, including Peter: 'He is going to Galilee ahead of you; there you will see him, just as he told you.'"

8   So they went out and ran from the tomb, distressed and terrified. They said nothing to anyone, because they were afraid.

AN OLD ENDING TO THE GOSPEL[a]
16.9–20

Jesus Appears to Mary Magdalene
(Mt 28.9–10; Jn 20.11–18)

[⁹After Jesus rose from death early on Sunday, he appeared first to Mary Magdalene, from whom he had driven out seven demons. ¹⁰She went and told his companions. They were mourning and crying; ¹¹and when they heard her say that Jesus was alive and that she had seen him, they did not believe her.

Jesus Appears to Two Disciples
(Lk 24.13–35)

12   After this, Jesus appeared in a different manner to two of them while they were on their way to the country. ¹³They returned and told the others, but they would not believe it.

Jesus Appears to the Eleven
(Mt 28.16–20; Lk 24.36–49; Jn 20.19–23; Acts 1.6–8)

14   Last of all, Jesus appeared to the eleven disciples as they were eating. He scolded them, because they did not have faith and because they were too stubborn to believe those who had seen him alive. ¹⁵He said to them, "Go throughout the whole world and preach the gospel to the whole human race. ¹⁶Whoever believes and is baptized will be saved; whoever does not believe will be condemned. ¹⁷Believers will be given the power to perform miracles: they will drive out demons in my name; they will speak in strange tongues; ¹⁸if they pick up snakes or drink any poison, they will not be harmed; they will place their hands on sick people, who will get well."

Jesus is Taken Up to Heaven
(Lk 24.50–53; Acts 1.9–11)

19   After the Lord Jesus had talked with them, he was taken up to heaven and sat at the right side of God. ²⁰The disciples went and preached everywhere, and the Lord worked with them and proved that their preaching was true by the miracles that were performed.]

ANOTHER OLD ENDING[b]
16.9–10

[⁹The women went to Peter and his friends and gave them a brief account of all they had been told. ¹⁰After this, Jesus himself sent out through his disciples from the east to the west the sacred and ever-living message of eternal salvation.]

---

[a] **16.9–20** heading *Some manuscripts and ancient translations do not have this ending to the Gospel (verses 9–20).*

[b] **16.9–10** heading *Some manuscripts and ancient translations have this shorter ending to the Gospel in addition to the longer ending (verses 9–20).*

The Gospel according to LUKE

INTRODUCTION

The Gospel according to Luke presents Jesus as both the promised Saviour of Israel and as the Saviour of the whole human race. *Luke* records that Jesus was called by the Spirit of the Lord to "bring good news to the poor" (4.18), and this Gospel is filled with a concern for people with all kinds of need. The note of joy is also prominent in *Luke*, especially in the opening chapters that announce the coming of Jesus, and again at the conclusion, when Jesus ascends to heaven. The story of the growth and spread of the Christian faith after the ascension of Jesus is told by the same writer in *Acts*.

There are two sections (chapters 1–2 and 9–19) which contain much material that is found only in this Gospel, such as the stories about the song of the angels and the shepherds' visit at the birth of Jesus, Jesus in the Temple as a boy, and the parables of the Good Samaritan and the Lost Son. Throughout the Gospel great emphasis is placed on prayer, the Holy Spirit, the role of women in the ministry of Jesus, and God's forgiveness of sins.

Outline of Contents

1 Dear Theophilus:

Many people have done their best to write a report of the things that have taken place among us. ²They wrote what we have been told by those who saw these things from the beginning and who proclaimed the message. ³And so, your Excellency, because I have carefully studied all these matters from their beginning, I thought it would be good to write an orderly account for you. ⁴I do this so that you will know the full truth about everything which you have been taught.

The Birth of John the Baptist is Announced

5 During the time when Herod was king of Judea,ᵃ there was a priest named Zechariah, who belonged to the priestly order of Abijah. His wife's name was Elizabeth; she also belonged to a priestly family. ⁶They both lived good lives in God's sight and obeyed fully all the Lord's laws and commands. ⁷They had no children because Elizabeth could not have any, and she and Zechariah were both very old.

8 One day Zechariah was doing his work as a priest in the Temple, taking his turn in the daily service. ⁹According to the custom followed by the priests, he was chosen by lot to burn incense on the altar. So he went into the Temple of the Lord, ¹⁰while the crowd of people outside prayed during the hour when the incense was burnt.

11 An angel of the Lord appeared to him, standing on the right of the altar where the incense was burnt. ¹²When Zechariah saw him, he was alarmed and felt afraid. ¹³But the angel said to him, "Don't be afraid, Zechariah! God has heard

---

ᵃ **1.5** JUDEA: *The term here refers to the whole land of Palestine.*

64

your prayer, and your wife Elizabeth will bear you a son. You are to name him John. ¹⁴How glad and happy you will be, and how happy many others will be when he is born! ¹⁵He will be a great man in the Lord's sight. He must not drink any wine or strong drink. From his very birth he will be filled with the Holy Spirit, ¹⁶and he will bring back many of the people of Israel to the Lord their God. ¹⁷He will go ahead of the Lord, strong and mighty like the prophet Elijah. He will bring fathers and children together again; he will turn disobedient people back to the way of thinking of the righteous; he will get the Lord's people ready for him."

18   Zechariah said to the angel, "How shall I know if this is so? I am an old man, and my wife is old also."

19   "I am Gabriel," the angel answered. "I stand in the presence of God, who sent me to speak to you and tell you this good news. ²⁰But you have not believed my message, which will come true at the right time. Because you have not believed, you will be unable to speak; you will remain silent until the day my promise to you comes true."

21   In the meantime the people were waiting for Zechariah and wondering why he was spending such a long time in the Temple. ²²When he came out, he could not speak to them, and so they knew that he had seen a vision in the Temple. Unable to say a word, he made signs to them with his hands.

23   When his period of service in the Temple was over, Zechariah went back home. ²⁴Some time later his wife Elizabeth became pregnant and did not leave the house for five months. ²⁵"Now at last the Lord has helped me," she said. "He has taken away my public disgrace!"

The Birth of Jesus is Announced

26   In the sixth month of Elizabeth's pregnancy God sent the angel Gabriel to a town in Galilee named Nazareth. ²⁷He had a message for a young woman promised in marriage to a man named Joseph, who was a descendant of King David. Her name was Mary. ²⁸The angel came to her and said, "Peace be with you! The Lord is with you and has greatly blessed you!"

29   Mary was deeply troubled by the angel's message, and she wondered what his words meant. ³⁰The angel said to her, "Don't be afraid, Mary; God has been gracious to you. ³¹You will become pregnant and give birth to a son, and you will name him Jesus. ³²He will be great and will be called the Son of the Most High God. The

Studying
LUKE

Who wrote it? Luke, a doctor and companion of Paul, only known non-Jewish writer in New Testament. Gospel forms first part of "two-volume work" also including *The Acts of the Apostles*.

When? Probably 80–85 CE. Luke combined material from *Mark* with the sayings source "Q", adding some material of his own ("L"). One of the Synoptic Gospels, along with *Matthew* and *Mark*.

Where from? Not known.

For whom? Luke dedicated Gospel and *Acts* to Theophilus, a high-ranking Roman, showing that he had Gentiles in mind. Jews blamed for death of Jesus – Pontius Pilate protests innocence three times (23.4,14,22).

Why? *Luke* stresses that Christian message is for everyone. Gentiles figure prominently and it is often social outcasts who respond to Jesus.

KEY POINTS

- The longest book in the New Testament – only *Luke* and *Matthew* record the birth of Jesus.
- Women given a higher profile in Luke's Gospel than any other.
- Includes many well-known parables – e.g. the Good Samaritan, the Lost Son – not found elsewhere.
- Only Gospel to describe ascension of Jesus into heaven.
- Emphasizes prayer and the work of the Holy Spirit.

Lord God will make him a king, as his ancestor David was, ³³and he will be the king of the descendants of Jacob for ever; his kingdom will never end!"

34   Mary said to the angel, "I am a virgin. How, then, can this be?"

35   The angel answered, "The Holy Spirit will come on you, and God's power will rest upon you. For this reason the holy child will be called the Son of God. ³⁶Remember your relative Elizabeth. It is said that she cannot have children, but she herself is now six months pregnant, even though she is very old. ³⁷For there is nothing that God cannot do."

38   "I am the Lord's servant," said Mary; "may it happen to me as you have said." And the angel left her.

Mary Visits Elizabeth

39   Soon afterwards Mary got ready and hurried off to a town in the hill country of Judea. ⁴⁰She went into Zechariah's house and greeted Elizabeth. ⁴¹When Elizabeth heard Mary's greeting, the baby moved within her. Elizabeth was filled with the Holy Spirit ⁴²and said in a loud voice, "You are the most blessed of all women,

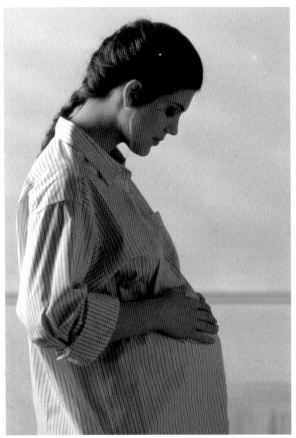

Elizabeth's child, John the Baptist, leapt within her at Mary's greeting (1.41)

and blessed is the child you will bear! 43Why should this great thing happen to me, that my Lord's mother comes to visit me? 44For as soon as I heard your greeting, the baby within me jumped with gladness. 45How happy you are to believe that the Lord's message to you will come true!"

Mary's Song of Praise

46 Mary said,

"My heart praises the Lord;
47 my soul is glad because of God my
Saviour,
48 for he has remembered me, his lowly
servant!
From now on all people will call me happy,
49 because of the great things the Mighty
God has done for me.
His name is holy;
50 from one generation to another
he shows mercy to those who honour
him.

51 He has stretched out his mighty arm
and scattered the proud with all their
plans.
52 He has brought down mighty kings from
their thrones,
and lifted up the lowly.
53 He has filled the hungry with good things,
and sent the rich away with empty hands.
54 He has kept the promise he made to our
ancestors,
and has come to the help of his servant
Israel.
55 He has remembered to show mercy to
Abraham
and to all his descendants for ever!"

56 Mary stayed about three months with Elizabeth and then went back home.

The Birth of John the Baptist

57 The time came for Elizabeth to have her baby, and she gave birth to a son. 58Her neighbours and relatives heard how wonderfully good the Lord had been to her, and they all rejoiced with her.

59 When the baby was a week old, they came to circumcise him, and they were going to name him Zechariah, after his father. 60But his mother said, "No! His name is to be John."

61 They said to her, "But you have no relatives with that name!" 62Then they made signs to his father, asking him what name he would like the boy to have.

63 Zechariah asked for a writing tablet and wrote, "His name is John." How surprised they all were! 64At that moment Zechariah was able to speak again, and he started praising God. 65The neighbours were all filled with fear, and the news about these things spread through all the hill country of Judea. 66Everyone who heard of it thought about it and asked, "What is this child going to be?" For it was plain that the Lord's power was upon him.

Zechariah's Prophecy

67 John's father Zechariah was filled with the Holy Spirit, and he spoke God's message:

68 "Let us praise the Lord, the God of Israel!
He has come to the help of his people and
has set them free.
69 He has provided for us a mighty Saviour,
a descendant of his servant David.
70 He promised through his holy prophets long
ago

71   that he would save us from our enemies,
          from the power of all those who hate us.
72   He said he would show mercy to our
             ancestors
          and remember his sacred covenant.
73–74 With a solemn oath to our ancestor Abraham
          he promised to rescue us from our
             enemies
          and allow us to serve him without fear,
75   so that we might be holy and righteous
             before him
          all the days of our life.
76   "You, my child, will be called a prophet of
             the Most High God.
          You will go ahead of the Lord
             to prepare his road for him,
77   to tell his people that they will be saved
             by having their sins forgiven.
78   Our God is merciful and tender.
          He will cause the bright dawn of salvation to
             rise on us
79   and to shine from heaven on all those
             who live in the dark shadow of death,
          to guide our steps into the path of peace."

80   The child grew and developed in body and
      spirit. He lived in the desert until the day when
      he appeared publicly to the people of Israel.

The Birth of Jesus
(Mt 1.18–25)

2 At that time the Emperor Augustus ordered a census to be taken throughout the Roman Empire. [2]When this first census took place, Quirinius was the governor of Syria. [3]Everyone, then, went to register himself, each to his own town.

4   Joseph went from the town of Nazareth in Galilee to the town of Bethlehem in Judea, the birthplace of King David. Joseph went there because he was a descendant of David. [5]He went to register with Mary, who was promised in marriage to him. She was pregnant, [6]and while they were in Bethlehem, the time came for her to have her baby. [7]She gave birth to her first son, wrapped him in strips of cloth and laid him in a manger – there was no room for them to stay in the inn.

The Shepherds and the Angels

8   There were some shepherds in that part of the country who were spending the night in the fields, taking care of their flocks. [9]An angel of the Lord appeared to them, and the glory of the Lord shone over them. They were terribly afraid,

67

[10]but the angel said to them, "Don't be afraid! I am here with good news for you, which will bring great joy to all the people. [11]This very day in David's town your Saviour was born – Christ the Lord! [12]And this is what will prove it to you: you will find a baby wrapped in strips of cloth and lying in a manger."

13 Suddenly a great army of heaven's angels appeared with the angel, singing praises to God:

14 "Glory to God in the highest heaven,
and peace on earth to those with whom he is pleased!"

15 When the angels went away from them back into heaven, the shepherds said to one another, "Let's go to Bethlehem and see this thing that has happened, which the Lord has told us."

16 So they hurried off and found Mary and Joseph and saw the baby lying in the manger. [17]When the shepherds saw him, they told them what the angel had said about the child. [18]All who heard it were amazed at what the shepherds said. [19]Mary remembered all these things and thought deeply about them. [20]The shepherds went back, singing praises to God for all they had heard and seen; it had been just as the angel had told them.

Jesus is Named

21 A week later, when the time came for the baby to be circumcised, he was named Jesus, the name which the angel had given him before he had been conceived.

Jesus is Presented in the Temple

22 The time came for Joseph and Mary to perform the ceremony of purification, as the Law of Moses commanded. So they took the child to Jerusalem to present him to the Lord, [23]as it is written in the law of the Lord: "Every firstborn male is to be dedicated to the Lord." [24]They also went to offer a sacrifice of a pair of doves or two young pigeons, as required by the law of the Lord.

25 At that time there was a man named Simeon living in Jerusalem. He was a good, God-fearing man and was waiting for Israel to be saved. The Holy Spirit was with him [26]and had assured him that he would not die before he had seen the Lord's promised Messiah. [27]Led by the Spirit, Simeon went into the Temple. When the parents brought the child Jesus into the Temple to do for him what the Law required, [28]Simeon took the child in his arms and gave thanks to God:

29 "Now, Lord, you have kept your promise,
and you may let your servant go in peace.
30 With my own eyes I have seen your salvation,
31 which you have prepared in the presence of all peoples:
32 A light to reveal your will to the Gentiles
and bring glory to your people Israel."

33 The child's father and mother were amazed at the things Simeon said about him. [34]Simeon blessed them and said to Mary, his mother, "This child is chosen by God for the destruction and the salvation of many in Israel. He will be a sign from God which many people will speak against [35]and so reveal their secret thoughts. And sorrow, like a sharp sword, will break your own heart."

36–37 There was a very old prophet, a widow named Anna, daughter of Phanuel of the tribe of Asher. She had been married for only seven years and was now 84 years old.[a] She never left the Temple; day and night she worshipped God, fasting and praying. [38]That very same hour she arrived and gave thanks to God and spoke about the child to all who were waiting for God to set Jerusalem free.

The Return to Nazareth

39 When Joseph and Mary had finished doing all that was required by the law of the Lord, they returned to their home town of Nazareth in Galilee. [40]The child grew and became strong; he was full of wisdom, and God's blessings were upon him.

The Boy Jesus in the Temple

41 Every year the parents of Jesus went to Jerusalem for the Passover Festival. [42]When Jesus was twelve years old, they went to the festival as usual. [43]When the festival was over, they started back home, but the boy Jesus stayed in Jerusalem. His parents did not know this; [44]they thought that he was with the group, so they travelled a whole day and then started looking for him among their relatives and friends. [45]They did not find him, so they went back to Jerusalem looking for him. [46]On the third day they found him in the Temple, sitting with the Jewish teachers, listening to them and asking questions. [47]All who heard him were amazed at

---

[a] **2.36–37** was now 84 years old; *or* had been a widow 84 years.

his intelligent answers. ⁴⁸His parents were astonished when they saw him, and his mother said to him, "My son, why have you done this to us? Your father and I have been terribly worried trying to find you."

49 He answered them, "Why did you have to look for me? Didn't you know that I had to be in my Father's house?" ⁵⁰But they did not understand his answer.

51 So Jesus went back with them to Nazareth, where he was obedient to them. His mother treasured all these things in her heart. ⁵²Jesus grew both in body and in wisdom, gaining favour with God and people.

The Preaching of John the Baptist
(Mt 3.1–12; Mk 1.1–8; Jn 1.19–28)

3 It was the fifteenth year of the rule of the Emperor Tiberius; Pontius Pilate was governor of Judea, Herod was ruler of Galilee, and his brother Philip was ruler of the territory of Iturea and Trachonitis; Lysanias was ruler of Abilene, ²and Annas and Caiaphas were high priests. At that time the word of God came to John son of Zechariah in the desert. ³So John went throughout the whole territory of the River Jordan, preaching, "Turn away from your sins and be baptized, and God will forgive your sins." ⁴As it is written in the book of the prophet Isaiah:

"Someone is shouting in the desert:
 'Get the road ready for the Lord;
 make a straight path for him to travel!

5 Every valley must be filled up,
 every hill and mountain levelled off.
The winding roads must be made straight,
 and the rough paths made smooth.

6 The whole human race will see God's
 salvation!'"

7 Crowds of people came out to John to be baptized by him. "You snakes!" he said to them. "Who told you that you could escape from the punishment God is about to send? ⁸Do those things that will show that you have turned from your sins. And don't start saying among yourselves that Abraham is your ancestor. I tell you that God can take these stones and make descendants for Abraham! ⁹The axe is ready to cut down the trees at the roots; every tree that does not bear good fruit will be cut down and thrown in the fire."

10 The people asked him, "What are we to do, then?"

11 He answered, "Whoever has two shirts must

KEY PLACES IN LUKE

Sidon
Iturea
Abilene
Tyre
Phoenicia
Caesarea Philippi
Trachonitis
Galilee
Chorazin
Capernaum
Bethsaida
Lake Galilee
(Lake Gennesaret)
Mediterranean Sea
Nazareth
Nain
Gadara
Samaria
Samaria
Gerasa
River Jordan
Decapolis
(The Ten Towns)
Bethphage
Bethany
Emmaus
Jerusalem
Jericho
Perea
Bethlehem
Judea
Dead Sea
Idumea

0   30 km

give one to the man who has none, and whoever has food must share it."

12 Some tax collectors came to be baptized, and they asked him, "Teacher, what are we to do?"

13 "Don't collect more than is legal," he told them.

14 Some soldiers also asked him, "What about us? What are we to do?"

He said to them, "Don't take money from anyone by force or accuse anyone falsely. Be content with your pay."

15 People's hopes began to rise, and they began to wonder whether John perhaps might be the Messiah. ¹⁶So John said to all of them, "I baptize you with water, but someone is coming who is much greater than I am. I am not good enough even to untie his sandals. He will baptize you with the Holy Spirit and fire. ¹⁷He has his winnowing shovel with him, to thresh out all the grain and gather the wheat into his barn; but he

will burn the chaff in a fire that never goes out."

18   In many different ways John preached the Good News to the people and urged them to change their ways. ¹⁹But John reprimanded Herod, the governor, because he had married Herodias, his brother's wife, and had done many other evil things. ²⁰Then Herod did an even worse thing by putting John in prison.

The Baptism of Jesus
(Mt 3.13–17; Mk 1.9–11)

21   After all the people had been baptized, Jesus also was baptized. While he was praying, heaven was opened, ²²and the Holy Spirit came down upon him in bodily form like a dove. And a voice came from heaven, "You are my own dear Son. I am pleased with you."

A mural from Haiti depicting the baptism of Jesus

The Ancestors of Jesus
(Mt 1.1–17)

23   When Jesus began his work, he was about 30 years old. He was the son, so people thought, of Joseph, who was the son of Heli, ²⁴the son of Matthat, the son of Levi, the son of Melchi, the son of Jannai, the son of Joseph, ²⁵the son of Mattathias, the son of Amos, the son of Nahum,

the son of Esli, the son of Naggai, ²⁶the son of Maath, the son of Mattathias, the son of Semein, the son of Josech, the son of Joda, ²⁷the son of Joanan, the son of Rhesa, the son of Zerubbabel, the son of Shealtiel, the son of Neri, ²⁸the son of Melchi, the son of Addi, the son of Cosam, the son of Elmadam, the son of Er, ²⁹the son of Joshua, the son of Eliezer, the son of Jorim, the son of Matthat, the son of Levi, ³⁰the son of Simeon, the son of Judah, the son of Joseph, the son of Jonam, the son of Eliakim, ³¹the son of Melea, the son of Menna, the son of Mattatha, the son of Nathan, the son of David, ³²the son of Jesse, the son of Obed, the son of Boaz, the son of Salmon, the son of Nahshon, ³³the son of Amminadab, the son of Admin, the son of Arni, the son of Hezron, the son of Perez, the son of Judah, ³⁴the son of Jacob, the son of Isaac, the son of Abraham, the son of Terah, the son of Nahor, ³⁵the son of Serug, the son of Reu, the son of Peleg, the son of Eber, the son of Shelah, ³⁶the son of Cainan, the son of Arphaxad, the son of Shem, the son of Noah, the son of Lamech, ³⁷the son of Methuselah, the son of Enoch, the son of Jared, the son of Mahalaleel, the son of Kenan, ³⁸the son of Enosh, the son of Seth, the son of Adam, the son of God.

The Temptation of Jesus
(Mt 4.1–11; Mk 1.12–13)

4 Jesus returned from the Jordan full of the Holy Spirit and was led by the Spirit into the desert, ²where he was tempted by the Devil for 40 days. In all that time he ate nothing, so that he was hungry when it was over.

3   The Devil said to him, "If you are God's Son, order this stone to turn into bread."

4   But Jesus answered, "The scripture says, 'Human beings cannot live on bread alone.'"

5   Then the Devil took him up and showed him in a second all the kingdoms of the world. ⁶"I will give you all this power and all this wealth," the Devil told him. "It has all been handed over to me, and I can give it to anyone I choose. ⁷All this will be yours, then, if you worship me."

8   Jesus answered, "The scripture says, 'Worship the Lord your God and serve only him!'"

9   Then the Devil took him to Jerusalem and set him on the highest point of the Temple, and said to him, "If you are God's Son, throw yourself down from here. ¹⁰For the scripture says, 'God will order his angels to take good care of you.' ¹¹It also says, 'They will hold you up with their hands so that not even your feet will be hurt on the stones.'"

12 But Jesus answered, "The scripture says, 'Do not put the Lord your God to the test.'"

13 When the Devil finished tempting Jesus in every way, he left him for a while.

Jesus Begins his Work in Galilee
(Mt 4.12–17; Mk 1.14–15)

14 Then Jesus returned to Galilee, and the power of the Holy Spirit was with him. The news about him spread throughout all that territory. ¹⁵He taught in the synagogues and was praised by everyone.

Jesus is Rejected at Nazareth
(Mt 13.53–58; Mk 6.1–6)

16 Then Jesus went to Nazareth, where he had been brought up, and on the Sabbath he went as usual to the synagogue. He stood up to read the Scriptures ¹⁷and was handed the book of the prophet Isaiah. He unrolled the scroll and found the place where it is written:

18 "The Spirit of the Lord is upon me,
  because he has chosen me to bring good
    news to the poor.
  He has sent me to proclaim liberty to the
    captives
    and recovery of sight to the blind;
  to set free the oppressed
19   and announce that the time has come
    when the Lord will save his people."

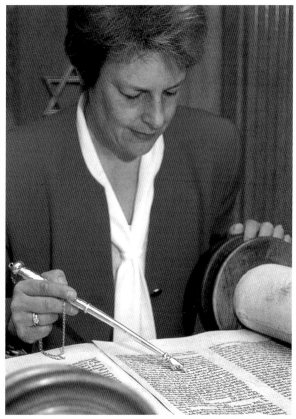

A person reads the text in the scroll with the help of a yad (4.16–17)

20 Jesus rolled up the scroll, gave it back to the attendant, and sat down. All the people in the synagogue had their eyes fixed on him, ²¹as he said to them, "This passage of scripture has come true today, as you heard it being read."

22 They were all well impressed with him and marvelled at the eloquent words that he spoke. They said, "Isn't he the son of Joseph?"

23 He said to them, "I am sure that you will quote this proverb to me, 'Doctor, heal yourself.' You will also tell me to do here in my home town the same things you heard were done in Capernaum. ²⁴I tell you this," Jesus added, "prophets are never welcomed in their home town.

25 "Listen to me: it is true that there were many widows in Israel during the time of Elijah, when there was no rain for three and a half years and a severe famine spread throughout the whole land. ²⁶Yet Elijah was not sent to anyone in Israel, but only to a widow living in Zarephath in the territory of Sidon. ²⁷And there were many people suffering from a dreaded skin disease who lived in Israel during the time of the prophet Elisha; yet not one of them was healed, but only Naaman the Syrian."

28 When the people in the synagogue heard this, they were filled with anger. ²⁹They rose up, dragged Jesus out of the town, and took him to the top of the hill on which their town was built. They meant to throw him over the cliff, ³⁰but he walked through the middle of the crowd and went his way.

A Man with an Evil Spirit
(Mk 1.21–28)

31 Then Jesus went to Capernaum, a town in Galilee, where he taught the people on the Sabbath. ³²They were all amazed at the way he taught, because he spoke with authority. ³³In the synagogue was a man who had the spirit of an evil demon in him; he screamed out in a loud voice, ³⁴"Ah! What do you want with us, Jesus of Nazareth? Are you here to destroy us? I know who you are: you are God's holy messenger!"

35 Jesus ordered the spirit, "Be quiet and come out of the man!" The demon threw the man down in front of them and went out of him without doing him any harm.

36 The people were all amazed and said to one another, "What kind of words are these? With authority and power this man gives orders to the evil spirits, and they come out!" ³⁷And the report about Jesus spread everywhere in that region.

Jesus Heals Many People
(Mt 8.14–17; Mk 1.29–34)

38 Jesus left the synagogue and went to Simon's house. Simon's mother-in-law was sick with a high fever, and they spoke to Jesus about her. ³⁹He went and stood at her bedside and ordered the fever to leave her. The fever left her, and she got up at once and began to wait on them.

40 After sunset all who had friends who were sick with various diseases brought them to Jesus; he placed his hands on every one of them and healed them all. ⁴¹Demons also went out from many people, screaming, "You are the Son of God!"

Jesus gave the demons an order and would not let them speak, because they knew that he was the Messiah.

Jesus Preaches in the Synagogues
(Mk 1.35–39)

42 At daybreak Jesus left the town and went off to a lonely place. The people started looking for him, and when they found him, they tried to keep him from leaving. ⁴³But he said to them, "I must preach the Good News about the Kingdom of God in other towns also, because that is what God sent me to do."

44 So he preached in the synagogues throughout the country.

Jesus Calls the First Disciples
(Mt 4.18–22; Mk 1.16–20)

5 One day Jesus was standing on the shore of Lake Gennesaret while the people pushed their way up to him to listen to the word of God. ²He saw two boats pulled up on the beach; the fishermen had left them and were washing the nets. ³Jesus got into one of the boats – it belonged to Simon – and asked him to push off a little from the shore. Jesus sat in the boat and taught the crowd.

4 When he finished speaking, he said to Simon, "Push the boat out further to the deep water, and you and your partners let down your nets for a catch."

5 "Master," Simon answered, "we worked hard all night long and caught nothing. But if you say so, I will let down the nets." ⁶They let them down and caught such a large number of fish that the nets were about to break. ⁷So they motioned to their partners in the other boat to come and help them. They came and filled both boats so full of fish that the boats were about to sink. ⁸When Simon Peter saw what had happened, he fell on his knees before Jesus and said, "Go away from me, Lord! I am a sinful man!"

9 He and the others with him were all amazed at the large number of fish they had caught. ¹⁰The same was true of Simon's partners, James and John, the sons of Zebedee. Jesus said to Simon, "Don't be afraid; from now on you will be catching people."

11 They pulled the boats up on the beach, left everything, and followed Jesus.

People being treated for the skin disease, leprosy, in India (5.12)

Jesus Heals a Man
(Mt 8.1–4; Mk 1.40–45)

12 Once Jesus was in a town where there was a man who was suffering from a dreaded skin disease. When he saw Jesus, he threw himself down and begged him, "Sir, if you want to, you can make me clean!"ᵃ

ᵃ **5.12** MAKE ME CLEAN: *This disease was considered to make a person ritually unclean.*

13   Jesus stretched out his hand and touched him. "I do want to," he answered. "Be clean!" At once the disease left the man. ¹⁴Jesus ordered him, "Don't tell anyone, but go straight to the priest and let him examine you; then to prove to everyone that you are cured, offer the sacrifice as Moses ordered."

15   But the news about Jesus spread all the more widely, and crowds of people came to hear him and be healed from their diseases. ¹⁶But he would go away to lonely places, where he prayed.

Jesus Heals a Paralysed Man
(Mt 9.1–8; Mk 2.1–12)

17   One day when Jesus was teaching, some Pharisees and teachers of the Law were sitting there who had come from every town in Galilee and Judea and from Jerusalem. The power of the Lord was present for Jesus to heal the sick. ¹⁸Some men came carrying a paralysed man on a bed, and they tried to take him into the house and put him in front of Jesus. ¹⁹Because of the crowd, however, they could find no way to take him in. So they carried him up on the roof, made an opening in the tiles, and let him down on his bed into the middle of the group in front of Jesus. ²⁰When Jesus saw how much faith they had, he said to the man, "Your sins are forgiven, my friend."

21   The teachers of the Law and the Pharisees began to say to themselves, "Who is this man who speaks such blasphemy! God is the only one who can forgive sins!"

22   Jesus knew their thoughts and said to them, "Why do you think such things? ²³Is it easier to say, 'Your sins are forgiven you,' or to say, 'Get up and walk'? ²⁴I will prove to you, then, that the Son of Man has authority on earth to forgive sins." So he said to the paralysed man, "I tell you, get up, pick up your bed, and go home!"

25   At once the man got up in front of them all, took the bed he had been lying on, and went home, praising God. ²⁶They were all completely amazed! Full of fear, they praised God, saying, "What marvellous things we have seen today!"

Jesus Calls Levi
(Mt 9.9–13; Mk 2.13–17)

27   After this, Jesus went out and saw a tax collector named Levi, sitting in his office. Jesus said to him, "Follow me." ²⁸Levi got up, left everything, and followed him.

29   Then Levi had a big feast in his house for Jesus, and among the guests was a large number of tax collectors and other people. ³⁰Some Pharisees and some teachers of the Law who belonged to their group complained to Jesus' disciples. "Why do you eat and drink with tax collectors and other outcasts?" they asked.

31   Jesus answered them, "People who are well do not need a doctor, but only those who are sick. ³²I have not come to call respectable people to repent, but outcasts."

The Question about Fasting
(Mt 9.14–17; Mk 2.18–22)

33   Some people said to Jesus, "The disciples of John fast frequently and offer prayers, and the disciples of the Pharisees do the same; but your disciples eat and drink."

34   Jesus answered, "Do you think you can make the guests at a wedding party go without food as long as the bridegroom is with them? Of course not! ³⁵But the day will come when the bridegroom will be taken away from them, and then they will fast."

36   Jesus also told them this parable: "No one tears a piece off a new coat to patch up an old coat. If he does, he will have torn the new coat, and the piece of new cloth will not match the old. ³⁷Nor does anyone pour new wine into used wine skins, because the new wine will burst the skins, the wine will pour out, and the skins will be ruined. ³⁸Instead, new wine must be poured into fresh wineskins! ³⁹And no one wants new wine after drinking old wine. 'The old is better,' he says."

The Question about the Sabbath
(Mt 12.1–8; Mk 2.23–28)

6 Jesus was walking through some cornfields on the Sabbath. His disciples began to pick the ears of corn, rub them in their hands, and eat the grain. ²Some Pharisees asked, "Why are you doing what our Law says you cannot do on the Sabbath?"

3   Jesus answered them, "Haven't you read what David did when he and his men were hungry? ⁴He went into the house of God, took the bread offered to God, ate it, and gave it also to his men. Yet it is against our Law for anyone except the priests to eat that bread."

5   And Jesus concluded, "The Son of Man is Lord of the Sabbath."

The Man with a Paralysed Hand
(Mt 12.9–14; Mk 3.1–6)

6 On another Sabbath Jesus went into a synagogue and taught. A man was there whose right hand was paralysed. [7]Some teachers of the Law and some Pharisees wanted a reason to accuse Jesus of doing wrong, so they watched him closely to see if he would heal on the Sabbath. [8]But Jesus knew their thoughts and said to the man, "Stand up and come here to the front." The man got up and stood there. [9]Then Jesus said to them, "I ask you: what does our Law allow us to do on the Sabbath? To help or to harm? To save someone's life or destroy it?" [10]He looked around at them all; then he said[a] to the man, "Stretch out your hand." He did so, and his hand became well again.

11 They were filled with rage and began to discuss among themselves what they could do to Jesus.

Jesus Chooses the Twelve Apostles
(Mt 10.1–4; Mk 3.13–19)

12 At that time Jesus went up a hill to pray and spent the whole night there praying to God. [13]When day came, he called his disciples to him and chose twelve of them, whom he named apostles: [14]Simon (whom he named Peter) and his brother Andrew; James and John, Philip and Bartholomew, [15]Matthew and Thomas, James son of Alphaeus, and Simon (who was called the Patriot), [16]Judas son of James, and Judas Iscariot, who became the traitor.

Jesus Teaches and Heals
(Mt 4.23–25)

17 When Jesus had come down from the hill with the apostles, he stood on a level place with a large number of his disciples. A large crowd of people was there from all over Judea and from Jerusalem and from the coastal cities of Tyre and Sidon; [18]they had come to hear him and to be healed of their diseases. Those who were troubled by evil spirits also came and were healed. [19]All the people tried to touch him, for power was going out from him and healing them all.

Happiness and Sorrow
(Mt 5.1–12)

20 Jesus looked at his disciples and said,

"Happy are you poor;
the Kingdom of God is yours!
21 Happy are you who are hungry now;
you will be filled!
Happy are you who weep now;
you will laugh!

22 "Happy are you when people hate you, reject you, insult you, and say that you are evil, all because of the Son of Man! [23]Be glad when that happens, and dance for joy, because a great reward is kept for you in heaven. For their ancestors did the very same things to the prophets.

24 "But how terrible for you who are rich now;
you have had your easy life!
25 How terrible for you who are full now;
you will go hungry!
How terrible for you who laugh now;
you will mourn and weep!

26 "How terrible when all people speak well of you; their ancestors said the very same things about the false prophets.

Love for Enemies
(Mt 5.38–48; 7.12a)

27 "But I tell you who hear me: love your enemies, do good to those who hate you, [28]bless those who curse you, and pray for those who ill-treat you. [29]If anyone hits you on one cheek, let him hit the other one too; if someone takes your coat, let him have your shirt as well. [30]Give to everyone who asks you for something, and when someone takes what is yours, do not ask for it back. [31]Do for others just what you want them to do for you.

32 "If you love only the people who love you, why should you receive a blessing? Even sinners love those who love them! [33]And if you do good only to those who do good to you, why should you receive a blessing? Even sinners do that! [34]And if you lend only to those from whom you hope to get it back, why should you receive a blessing? Even sinners lend to sinners, to get back the same amount! [35]No! Love your enemies and do good to them; lend and expect nothing back. You will then have a great reward, and you will be children of the Most High God. For he is good to the ungrateful and the wicked. [36]Be merciful just as your Father is merciful.

[a] **6.10** said; *some manuscripts have* said angrily.

Judging Others

(Mt 7.1–5)

37 "Do not judge others, and God will not judge you; do not condemn others, and God will not condemn you; forgive others, and God will forgive you. [38]Give to others, and God will give to you. Indeed, you will receive a full measure, a generous helping, poured into your hands – all that you can hold. The measure you use for others is the one that God will use for you."

39 And Jesus told them this parable: "One blind man cannot lead another one; if he does, both will fall into a ditch. [40]No pupil is greater than his teacher; but every pupil, when he has completed his training, will be like his teacher.

41 "Why do you look at the speck in your brother's eye, but pay no attention to the log in your own eye? [42]How can you say to your brother, 'Please, brother, let me take that speck out of your eye,' yet cannot even see the log in your own eye? You hypocrite! First take the log out of your own eye, and then you will be able to see clearly to take the speck out of your brother's eye.

A Tree and its Fruit

(Mt 7.16–20; 12.33–35)

43 "A healthy tree does not bear bad fruit, nor does a poor tree bear good fruit. [44]Every tree is known by the fruit it bears; you do not pick figs from thorn bushes or gather grapes from bramble bushes. [45]A good person brings good out of the treasure of good things in his heart; a bad person brings bad out of his treasure of bad things. For the mouth speaks what the heart is full of.

The Two House Builders

(Mt 7.24–27)

46 "Why do you call me, 'Lord, Lord,' and yet don't do what I tell you? [47]Anyone who comes to me and listens to my words and obeys them – I will show you what he is like. [48]He is like a man who, in building his house, dug deep and laid the foundation on rock. The river overflowed and hit that house but could not shake it, because it was well built. [49]But anyone who hears my words and does not obey them is like a man who built his house without laying a foundation; when the flood hit that house it fell at once – and what a terrible crash that was!"

Jesus Heals a Roman Officer's Servant

(Mt 8.5–13)

 When Jesus had finished saying all these things to the people, he went to Capernaum. [2]A Roman officer there had a servant who was very dear to him; the man was sick and about to die. [3]When the officer heard about Jesus, he sent some Jewish elders to ask him to come and heal his servant. [4]They came to Jesus and begged him earnestly, "This man really deserves your help. [5]He loves our people and he himself built a synagogue for us."

6 So Jesus went with them. He was not far from the house when the officer sent friends to tell him, "Sir, don't trouble yourself. I do not deserve to have you come into my house, [7]neither do I consider myself worthy to come to you in person. Just give the order, and my servant will get well. [8]I, too, am a man placed under the authority of superior officers, and I have soldiers under me. I order this one, 'Go!' and he goes; I order that one, 'Come!' and he comes; and I order my slave, 'Do this!' and he does it."

9 Jesus was surprised when he heard this; he turned round and said to the crowd following him, "I tell you, I have never found faith like this, not even in Israel!"

10 The messengers went back to the officer's house and found his servant well.

Jesus Raises a Widow's Son

11 Soon afterwards[a] Jesus went to a town called Nain, accompanied by his disciples and a large crowd. [12]Just as he arrived at the gate of the town, a funeral procession was coming out. The dead man was the only son of a woman who was a widow, and a large crowd from the town was with her. [13]When the Lord saw her, his heart was filled with pity for her, and he said to her, "Don't cry." [14]Then he walked over and touched the coffin, and the men carrying it stopped. Jesus said, "Young man! Get up, I tell you!" [15]The dead man sat up and began to talk, and Jesus gave him back to his mother.

16 They all were filled with fear and praised God. "A great prophet has appeared among us!" they said; "God has come to save his people!"

17 This news about Jesus went out through all the country and the surrounding territory.

[a] **7.11** Soon afterwards; *some manuscripts have* The next day.

The Messengers from John the Baptist

(Mt 11.2–19)

18 When John's disciples told him about all these things, he called two of them 19and sent them to the Lord to ask him, "Are you the one John said was going to come, or should we expect someone else?"

20 When they came to Jesus, they said, "John the Baptist sent us to ask if you are the one he said was going to come, or if we should expect someone else."

21 At that very time Jesus cured many people of their sicknesses, diseases, and evil spirits, and gave sight to many blind people. 22He answered John's messengers, "Go back and tell John what you have seen and heard: the blind can see, the lame can walk, those who suffer from dreaded skin diseases are made clean,ᵃ the deaf can hear, the dead are raised to life, and the Good News is preached to the poor. 23How happy are those who have no doubts about me!"

24 After John's messengers had left, Jesus began to speak about him to the crowds: "When you went out to John in the desert, what did you expect to see? A blade of grass bending in the wind? 25What did you go out to see? A man dressed up in fancy clothes? People who dress like that and live in luxury are found in palaces! 26Tell me, what did you go out to see? A prophet? Yes indeed, but you saw much more than a prophet. 27For John is the one of whom the scripture says: 'God said, I will send my messenger ahead of you to open the way for you.' 28I tell you," Jesus added, "John is greater than anyone who has ever lived. But the one who is least in the Kingdom of God is greater than John."

29 All the people heard him; they and especially the tax collectors were the ones who had obeyed God's righteous demands and had been baptized by John. 30But the Pharisees and the teachers of the Law rejected God's purpose for themselves and refused to be baptized by John.

31 Jesus continued, "Now to what can I compare the people of this day? What are they like? 32They are like children sitting in the market place. One group shouts to the other, 'We played wedding music for you, but you wouldn't dance! We sang funeral songs, but you wouldn't cry!' 33John the Baptist came, and he fasted and drank no wine, and you said, 'He has a demon in him!' 34The Son of Man came, and he ate and drank, and you said, 'Look at this man! He is a glutton and a drinker, a friend of tax collectors and other outcasts!' 35God's wisdom, however, is shown to be true by all who accept it."

Jesus at the Home of Simon the Pharisee

36 A Pharisee invited Jesus to have dinner with him, and Jesus went to his house and sat down to eat. 37In that town was a woman who lived a sinful life. She heard that Jesus was eating in the Pharisee's house, so she brought an alabaster jar full of perfume 38and stood behind Jesus, by his feet, crying and wetting his feet with her tears. Then she dried his feet with her hair, kissed them, and poured the perfume on them. 39When the Pharisee saw this, he said to himself, "If this man really were a prophet, he would know who this woman is who is touching him; he would know what kind of sinful life she lives!"

40 Jesus spoke up and said to him, "Simon, I have something to tell you."

"Yes, Teacher," he said, "tell me."

41 "There were two men who owed money to a money-lender," Jesus began. "One owed him five hundred silver coins, and the other owed him fifty. 42Neither of them could pay him back, so he cancelled the debts of both. Which one, then, will love him more?"

43 "I suppose," answered Simon, "that it would be the one who was forgiven more."

"You are right," said Jesus. 44Then he turned to the woman and said to Simon, "Do you see this woman? I came into your home, and you gave me no water for my feet, but she has washed my feet with her tears and dried them with her hair. 45You did not welcome me with a kiss, but she has not stopped kissing my feet since I came. 46You provided no olive oil for my head, but she has covered my feet with perfume. 47I tell you, then, the great love she has shown proves that her many sins have been forgiven. But whoever has been forgiven little shows only a little love."

48 Then Jesus said to the woman, "Your sins are forgiven."

49 The others sitting at the table began to say to themselves, "Who is this, who even forgives sins?"

50 But Jesus said to the woman, "Your faith has saved you; go in peace."

Women who Accompanied Jesus

8 Some time later Jesus travelled through towns and villages, preaching the Good News about the Kingdom of God. The

---

ᵃ **7.22** MADE CLEAN: *See 5.12.*

twelve disciples went with him, [2]and so did some women who had been healed of evil spirits and diseases: Mary (who was called Magdalene), from whom seven demons had been driven out; [3]Joanna, whose husband Chuza was an officer in Herod's court; and Susanna, and many other women who used their own resources to help Jesus and his disciples.

The Parable of the Sower
(Mt 13.1–9; Mk 4.1–9)

4 People kept coming to Jesus from one town after another; and when a great crowd gathered, Jesus told this parable:

5 "Once there was a man who went out to sow corn. As he scattered the seed in the field, some of it fell along the path, where it was stepped on, and the birds ate it up. [6]Some of it fell on rocky ground, and when the plants sprouted, they dried up because the soil had no moisture. [7]Some of the seed fell among thorn bushes, which grew up with the plants and choked them. [8]And some seeds fell in good soil; the plants grew and produced corn, a hundred grains each."

And Jesus concluded, "Listen, then, if you have ears!"

The Purpose of the Parables
(Mt 13.10–17; Mk 4.10–12)

9 His disciples asked Jesus what this parable meant, [10]and he answered, "The knowledge of the secrets of the Kingdom of God has been given to you, but to the rest it comes by means of parables, so that they may look but not see, and listen but not understand.

Jesus Explains the Parable of the Sower
(Mt 13.18–23; Mk 4.13–20)

11 "This is what the parable means: the seed is the word of God. [12]The seeds that fell along the path stand for those who hear; but the Devil comes and takes the message away from their hearts in order to keep them from believing and being saved. [13]The seeds that fell on rocky ground stand for those who hear the message and receive it gladly. But it does not sink deep into them; they believe only for a while but when the time of testing comes, they fall away. [14]The seeds that fell among thorn bushes stand for those who hear; but the worries and riches and pleasures of this life crowd in and choke them, and their fruit never ripens. [15]The seeds

that fell in good soil stand for those who hear the message and retain it in a good and obedient heart, and they persist until they bear fruit.

A Lamp under a Bowl
(Mk 4.21–25)

16 "People do not light a lamp and cover it with a bowl or put it under a bed. Instead, they put it on the lampstand, so that people will see the light as they come in.

17 "Whatever is hidden away will be brought out into the open, and whatever is covered up will be found and brought to light.

18 "Be careful, then, how you listen; because those who have something will be given more, but those who have nothing will have taken away from them even the little they think they have."

Jesus' Mother and Brothers
(Mt 12.46–50; Mk 3.31–35)

19 Jesus' mother and brothers came to him, but were unable to join him because of the crowd. [20]Someone said to Jesus, "Your mother and brothers are standing outside and want to see you."

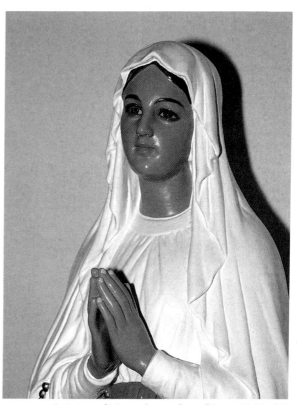

A statue of Mary, the mother of Jesus (8.19–20)

21 Jesus said to them all, "My mother and brothers are those who hear the word of God and obey it."

Jesus Calms a Storm
(Mt 8.23–27; Mk 4.35–41)

22 One day Jesus got into a boat with his disciples and said to them, "Let us go across to the other side of the lake." So they started out. [23]As they were sailing, Jesus fell asleep. Suddenly a strong wind blew down on the lake, and the boat began to fill with water, so that they were all in great danger. [24]The disciples went to Jesus and woke him up, saying, "Master, Master! We are about to die!"

Jesus got up and gave an order to the wind and the stormy water; they died down, and there was a great calm. [25]Then he said to the disciples, "Where is your faith?"

But they were amazed and afraid, and said to one another, "Who is this man? He gives orders to the winds and waves, and they obey him!"

Jesus Heals a Man with Demons
(Mt 8.28–34; Mk 5.1–20)

26 Jesus and his disciples sailed on over to the territory of Gerasa,[a] which is across the lake from Galilee. [27]As Jesus stepped ashore, he was met by a man from the town who had demons in him. For a long time this man had gone without clothes and would not stay at home, but spent his time in the burial caves. [28]When he saw Jesus, he gave a loud cry, threw himself down at his feet, and shouted, "Jesus, Son of the Most High God! What do you want with me? I beg you, don't punish me!" [29]He said this because Jesus had ordered the evil spirit to go out of him. Many times it had seized him, and even though he was kept a prisoner, his hands and feet fastened with chains, he would break the chains and be driven by the demon out into the desert.

30 Jesus asked him, "What is your name?"

"My name is 'Mob'," he answered – because many demons had gone into him. [31]The demons begged Jesus not to send them into the abyss.[b]

32 There was a large herd of pigs near by, feeding on a hillside. So the demons begged Jesus to let

them go into the pigs, and he let them. [33]They went out of the man and into the pigs. The whole herd rushed down the side of the cliff into the lake and was drowned.

34 The men who had been taking care of the pigs saw what happened, so they ran off and spread the news in the town and among the farms. [35]People went out to see what had happened, and when they came to Jesus, they found the man from whom the demons had gone out sitting at the feet of Jesus, clothed and in his right mind; and they were all afraid. [36]Those who had seen it told the people how the man had been cured. [37]Then all the people from that territory asked Jesus to go away, because they were terribly afraid. So Jesus got into the boat and left. [38]The man from whom the demons had gone out begged Jesus, "Let me go with you."

But Jesus sent him away, saying, [39]"Go back home and tell what God has done for you."

The man went through the town, telling what Jesus had done for him.

Jairus' Daughter and the Woman who Touched Jesus' Cloak
(Mt 9.18–26; Mk 5.21–43)

40 When Jesus returned to the other side of the lake, the people welcomed him, because they had all been waiting for him. [41]Then a man named Jairus arrived; he was an official in the local synagogue. He threw himself down at Jesus' feet and begged him to go to his home, [42]because his only daughter, who was twelve years old, was dying.

As Jesus went along, the people were crowding him from every side. [43]Among them was a woman who had suffered from severe bleeding for twelve years; she had spent all she had on doctors,[c] but no one had been able to cure her. [44]She came up in the crowd behind Jesus and touched the edge of his cloak, and her bleeding stopped at once. [45]Jesus asked, "Who touched me?"

Everyone denied it, and Peter said, "Master, the people are all round you and crowding in on you."

46 But Jesus said, "Someone touched me, for I knew it when power went out of me." [47]The woman saw that she had been found out, so she came trembling and threw herself at Jesus' feet. There in front of everybody, she told him why she had touched him and how she had been

[a] **8.26** Gerasa; *some manuscripts have* Gadara (*see Mt 8.28*); *others have* Gergesa.
[b] **8.31** ABYSS: *It was thought that the demons were to be imprisoned in the depths of the earth until their final punishment.*

[c] **8.43** *Some manuscripts do not have* she had spent all she had on doctors.

78

healed at once. [48]Jesus said to her, "My daughter, your faith has made you well. Go in peace."

49   While Jesus was saying this, a messenger came from the official's house. "Your daughter has died," he told Jairus; "don't bother the Teacher any longer."

50   But Jesus heard it and said to Jairus, "Don't be afraid; only believe, and she will be well."

51   When he arrived at the house, he would not let anyone go in with him except Peter, John, and James, and the child's father and mother. [52]Everyone there was crying and mourning for the child. Jesus said, "Don't cry; the child is not dead – she is only sleeping!"

53   They all laughed at him, because they knew that she was dead. [54]But Jesus took her by the hand and called out, "Get up, my child!" [55]Her life returned, and she got up at once, and Jesus ordered them to give her something to eat. [56]Her parents were astounded, but Jesus commanded them not to tell anyone what had happened.

Jesus Sends Out the Twelve Disciples
(Mt 10.5–15; Mk 6.7–13)

9 Jesus called the twelve disciples together and gave them power and authority to drive out all demons and to cure diseases. [2]Then he sent them out to preach the Kingdom of God and to heal the sick, [3]after saying to them, "Take nothing with you for the journey: no stick, no beggar's bag, no food, no money, not even an extra shirt. [4]Wherever you are welcomed, stay in the same house until you leave that town; [5]wherever people don't welcome you, leave that town and shake the dust off your feet as a warning to them."

The disciples left and travelled through all the villages, preaching the Good News and healing people everywhere.

Herod's Confusion
(Mt 14.1–12; Mk 6.14–29)

7   When Herod, the ruler of Galilee, heard about all the things that were happening, he was very confused, because some people were saying that John the Baptist had come back to life. [8]Others were saying that Elijah had appeared, and still others that one of the prophets of long ago had come back to life. [9]Herod said, "I had John's head cut off; but who is this man I hear these things about?" And he kept trying to see Jesus.

Jesus Feeds a Great Crowd
(Mt 14.13–21; Mk 6.30–44; Jn 6.1–14)

10   The apostles came back and told Jesus everything they had done. He took them with him, and they went off by themselves to a town called Bethsaida. [11]When the crowds heard about it, they followed him. He welcomed them, spoke to them about the Kingdom of God, and healed those who needed it.

12   When the sun was beginning to set, the twelve disciples came to him and said, "Send the people away so that they can go to the villages and farms round here and find food and lodging, because this is a lonely place."

13   But Jesus said to them, "You yourselves give them something to eat."

They answered, "All we have are five loaves and two fish. Do you want us to go and buy food for this whole crowd?" [14](There were about 5,000 men there.)

Jesus said to his disciples, "Make the people sit down in groups of about fifty each."

15   After the disciples had done so, [16]Jesus took the five loaves and two fish, looked up to heaven, thanked God for them, broke them, and gave them to the disciples to distribute to the people. [17]They all ate and had enough, and the disciples took up twelve baskets of what was left over.

Peter's Declaration about Jesus
(Mt 16.13–19; Mk 8.27–29)

18   One day when Jesus was praying alone, the disciples came to him. "Who do the crowds say I am?" he asked them.

19   "Some say that you are John the Baptist," they answered. "Others say that you are Elijah, while others say that one of the prophets of long ago has come back to life."

20   "What about you?" he asked them. "Who do you say I am?"

Peter answered, "You are God's Messiah."

Jesus Speaks about his Suffering and Death
(Mt 16.20–28; Mk 8.30—9.1)

21   Then Jesus gave them strict orders not to tell this to anyone. [22]He also said to them, "The Son of Man must suffer much and be rejected by the elders, the chief priests, and the teachers of the Law. He will be put to death, but three days later he will be raised to life."

23   And he said to them all, "Anyone who wants to come with me must forget self, take up their cross every day, and follow me. [24]For whoever wants to save their own life will lose it, but

whoever loses their life for my sake will save it. [25]Will people gain anything if they win the whole world but are themselves lost or defeated? Of course not! [26]If people are ashamed of me and of my teaching, then the Son of Man will be ashamed of them when he comes in his glory and in the glory of the Father and of the holy angels. [27]I assure you that there are some here who will not die until they have seen the Kingdom of God."

The Transfiguration
(Mt 17.1–8; Mk 9.2–8)

28   About a week after he had said these things, Jesus took Peter, John, and James with him and went up a hill to pray. [29]While he was praying, his face changed its appearance, and his clothes became dazzling white. [30]Suddenly two men were there talking with him. They were Moses and Elijah, [31]who appeared in heavenly glory and talked with Jesus about the way in which he would soon fulfil God's purpose by dying in Jerusalem. [32]Peter and his companions were sound asleep, but they woke up and saw Jesus' glory and the two men who were standing with him. [33]As the men were leaving Jesus, Peter said to him, "Master, how good it is that we are here! We will make three tents, one for you, one for Moses, and one for Elijah." (He did not really know what he was saying.)

34   While he was still speaking, a cloud appeared and covered them with its shadow; and the disciples were afraid as the cloud came over them. [35]A voice said from the cloud, "This is my Son, whom I have chosen – listen to him!"

36   When the voice stopped, there was Jesus all alone. The disciples kept quiet about all this, and told no one at that time anything they had seen.

Jesus Heals a Boy with an Evil Spirit
(Mt 17.14–18; Mk 9.14–27)

37   The next day Jesus and the three disciples went down from the hill, and a large crowd met Jesus. [38]A man shouted from the crowd, "Teacher! I beg you, look at my son – my only son! [39]A spirit attacks him with a sudden shout and throws him into a fit, so that he foams at the mouth; it keeps on hurting him and will hardly let him go! [40]I begged your disciples to drive it out, but they couldn't."

41   Jesus answered, "How unbelieving and wrong you people are! How long must I stay with you? How long do I have to put up with you?" Then he said to the man, "Bring your son here."

42   As the boy was coming, the demon knocked him to the ground and threw him into a fit. Jesus gave a command to the evil spirit, healed the boy, and gave him back to his father. [43]All the people were amazed at the mighty power of God.

Jesus Speaks Again about his Death
(Mt 17.22–23; Mk 9.30–32)

The people were still marvelling at everything Jesus was doing, when he said to his disciples, [44]"Don't forget what I am about to tell you! The Son of Man is going to be handed over to the power of human beings." [45]But the disciples did not know what this meant. It had been hidden from them so that they could not understand it, and they were afraid to ask him about the matter.

Who is the Greatest?
(Mt 18.1–5; Mk 9.33–37)

46   An argument broke out among the disciples as to which one of them was the greatest. [47]Jesus knew what they were thinking, so he took a child, stood him by his side, [48]and said to them, "Whoever welcomes this child in my name, welcomes me; and whoever welcomes me, also welcomes the one who sent me. For the one who is least among you all is the greatest."

Whoever is not Against You is For You
(Mk 9.38–40)

49   John spoke up, "Master, we saw a man driving out demons in your name, and we told him to stop, because he doesn't belong to our group."

50   "Do not try to stop him," Jesus said to him and to the other disciples, "because whoever is not against you is for you."

A Samaritan Village Refuses to Receive Jesus

51   As the time drew near when Jesus would be taken up to heaven, he made up his mind and set out on his way to Jerusalem. [52]He sent messengers ahead of him, who went into a village in Samaria to get everything ready for him. [53]But the people there would not receive him, because it was clear that he was on his way to Jerusalem. [54]When the disciples James and John saw this, they said, "Lord, do you want us to call fire down from heaven to destroy them?"[a]

[a] **9.54** *Some manuscripts add* as Elijah did.

55   Jesus turned and rebuked them.[a] [56]Then Jesus and his disciples went on to another village.

The Would-be Followers of Jesus
(Mt 8.19–22)

57   As they went on their way, a man said to Jesus, "I will follow you wherever you go."

58   Jesus said to him, "Foxes have holes, and birds have nests, but the Son of Man has nowhere to lie down and rest."

59   He said to another man, "Follow me."
But that man said, "Sir, first let me go back and bury my father."

60   Jesus answered, "Let the dead bury their own dead. You go and proclaim the Kingdom of God."

61   Someone else said, "I will follow you, sir; but first let me go and say goodbye to my family."

62   Jesus said to him, "Anyone who starts to plough and then keeps looking back is of no use to the Kingdom of God."

Jesus Sends Out the Seventy-two

10 After this the Lord chose another 72[b] men and sent them out two by two, to go ahead of him to every town and place where he himself was about to go. [2]He said to them, "There is a large harvest, but few workers to gather it in. Pray to the owner of the harvest that he will send out workers to gather in his harvest. [3]Go! I am sending you like lambs among wolves. [4]Don't take a purse or a beggar's bag or shoes; don't stop to greet anyone on the road. [5]Whenever you go into a house, first say, 'Peace be with this house.' [6]If a peace-loving person lives there, let your greeting of peace remain on him; if not, take back your greeting of peace. [7]Stay in that same house, eating and drinking whatever they offer you, for workers should be given their pay. Don't move round from one house to another. [8]Whenever you go into a town and are made welcome, eat what is set before you, [9]heal the sick in that town, and say to the people there, 'The Kingdom of God has come near you.' [10]But whenever you go into a town and are not welcomed, go out in the streets and say, [11]'Even the dust from your town that sticks to our feet we wipe off against you. But remember that the Kingdom of God has come near you!' [12]I assure you that on Judgement Day God will show more mercy to Sodom than to that town!

The Unbelieving Towns
(Mt 11.20–24)

13   "How terrible it will be for you, Chorazin! How terrible for you too, Bethsaida! If the miracles which were performed in you had been performed in Tyre and Sidon, the people there would long ago have sat down, put on sackcloth, and sprinkled ashes on themselves, to show that they had turned from their sins! [14]God will show more mercy on Judgement Day to Tyre and Sidon than to you. [15]And as for you, Capernaum! Did you want to lift yourself up to heaven? You will be thrown down to hell!"

16   Jesus said to his disciples, "Whoever listens to you listens to me; whoever rejects you rejects me; and whoever rejects me rejects the one who sent me."

The Return of the Seventy-two

17   The 72[c] men came back in great joy. "Lord," they said, "even the demons obeyed us when we gave them a command in your name!"

18   Jesus answered them, "I saw Satan fall like lightning from heaven. [19]Listen! I have given you authority, so that you can walk on snakes and scorpions and overcome all the power of the Enemy, and nothing will hurt you. [20]But don't be glad because the evil spirits obey you; rather be glad because your names are written in heaven."

Jesus Rejoices
(Mt 11.25–27; 13.16–17)

21   At that time Jesus was filled with joy by the Holy Spirit[d] and said, "Father, Lord of heaven and earth! I thank you because you have shown to the unlearned what you have hidden from the wise and learned. Yes, Father, this was how you wanted it to happen.

22   "My Father has given me all things. No one knows who the Son is except the Father, and no one knows who the Father is except the Son and those to whom the Son chooses to reveal him."

23   Then Jesus turned to the disciples and said to

---

[a] **9.55** *Some manuscripts add* and said, "You don't know what kind of a Spirit you belong to; for the Son of Man did not come to destroy people's lives, but to save them."
[b] **10.1** 72; *some manuscripts have* 70.

[c] **10.17** 72; *some manuscripts have* 70 (see verse 1).
[d] **10.21** by the Holy Spirit; *some manuscripts have* by the Spirit; *others have* in his spirit.

them privately, "How fortunate you are to see the things you see! ²⁴I tell you that many prophets and kings wanted to see what you see, but they could not, and to hear what you hear, but they did not."

The Parable of the Good Samaritan

25 A teacher of the Law came up and tried to trap Jesus. "Teacher," he asked, "what must I do to receive eternal life?"

26 Jesus answered him, "What do the Scriptures say? How do you interpret them?"

27 The man answered, " 'Love the Lord your God with all your heart, with all your soul, with all your strength, and with all your mind'; and 'Love your neighbour as you love yourself.' "

28 "You are right," Jesus replied; "do this and you will live."

29 But the teacher of the Law wanted to justify himself, so he asked Jesus, "Who is my neighbour?"

A church window illustrating the parable of the Good Samaritan

30 Jesus answered, "There was once a man who was going down from Jerusalem to Jericho when robbers attacked him, stripped him, and beat him up, leaving him half dead. ³¹It so happened that a priest was going down that road; but when he saw the man, he walked on by, on the other side. ³²In the same way a Levite also came along, went over and looked at the man, and then walked on by, on the other side. ³³But a Samaritan who was travelling that way came upon the man, and when he saw him, his heart was filled with pity. ³⁴He went over to him, poured oil and wine on his wounds and bandaged them; then he put the man on his own animal and took him to an inn, where he took care of him. ³⁵The next day he took out two silver coins and gave them to the innkeeper. 'Take care of him,' he told the innkeeper, 'and when I come back this way, I will pay you whatever else you spend on him.' "

36 And Jesus concluded, "In your opinion, which one of these three acted like a neighbour towards the man attacked by the robbers?"

37 The teacher of the Law answered, "The one who was kind to him."

Jesus replied, "You go, then, and do the same."

Jesus Visits Martha and Mary

38 As Jesus and his disciples went on their way, he came to a village where a woman named Martha welcomed him in her home. ³⁹She had a sister named Mary, who sat down at the feet of the Lord and listened to his teaching. ⁴⁰Martha was upset over all the work she had to do, so she came and said, "Lord, don't you care that my sister has left me to do all the work by myself? Tell her to come and help me!"

41 The Lord answered her, "Martha, Martha! You are worried and troubled over so many things, ⁴²but just one is needed. Mary has chosen the right thing, and it will not be taken away from her."

Jesus' Teaching on Prayer
(Mt 6.9–13; 7.7–11)

11 One day Jesus was praying in a certain place. When he had finished, one of his disciples said to him, "Lord, teach us to pray, just as John taught his disciples."

2 Jesus said to them, "When you pray, say this:

'Father:
May your holy name be honoured;
may your Kingdom come.

Christians praying together in church

9 "And so I say to you: ask, and you will receive; seek, and you will find; knock, and the door will be opened to you. ¹⁰For all those who ask will receive, and those who seek will find, and the door will be opened to anyone who knocks. ¹¹Would any of you who are fathers give your son a snake when he asks for fish? ¹²Or would you give him a scorpion when he asks for an egg? ¹³Bad as you are, you know how to give good things to your children. How much more, then, will the Father in heaven give the Holy Spirit to those who ask him!"

Jesus and Beelzebul
(Mt 12.22–30; Mk 3.20–27)

14 Jesus was driving out a demon that could not talk; and when the demon went out, the man began to talk. The crowds were amazed, ¹⁵but some of the people said, "It is Beelzebul, the chief of the demons, who gives him the power to drive them out."

16 Others wanted to trap Jesus, so they asked him to perform a miracle to show that God approved of him. ¹⁷But Jesus knew what they were thinking, so he said to them, "Any country that divides itself into groups which fight each other will not last very long; a family divided against itself falls apart. ¹⁸So if Satan's kingdom has groups fighting each other, how can it last? You say that I drive out demons because Beelzebul gives me the power to do so. ¹⁹If this is how I drive them out, how do your followers drive them out? Your own followers prove that you are wrong! ²⁰No, it is rather by means of God's power that I drive out demons, and this proves that the Kingdom of God has already come to you.

21 "When a strong man, with all his weapons ready, guards his own house, all his belongings are safe. ²²But when a stronger man attacks him and defeats him, he carries away all the weapons the owner was depending on and divides up what he stole.

23 "Anyone who is not for me is really against me; anyone who does not help me gather is really scattering.

The Return of the Evil Spirit
(Mt 12.43–45)

24 "When an evil spirit goes out of a person, it travels over dry country looking for a place to rest. If it can't find one, it says to itself, 'I will go back to my house.' ²⁵So it goes back and finds the house clean and tidy. ²⁶Then it goes out and

3 Give us day by day the food we need.ᵃ
4 Forgive us our sins,
   for we forgive everyone who does us
      wrong.
   And do not bring us to hard testing.' "

5 And Jesus said to his disciples, "Suppose one of you should go to a friend's house at midnight and say, 'Friend, let me borrow three loaves of bread. ⁶A friend of mine who is on a journey has just come to my house, and I haven't got any food for him!' ⁷And suppose your friend should answer from inside, 'Don't bother me! The door is already locked, and my children and I are in bed. I can't get up and give you anything.' ⁸Well, what then? I tell you that even if he will not get up and give you the bread because you are his friend, yet he will get up and give you everything you need because you are not ashamed to keep on asking.

ᵃ **11.3** the food we need; *or* food for the next day.

brings seven other spirits even worse than itself, and they come and live there. So when it is all over, that person is in a worse state than he was at the beginning."

True Happiness

27 When Jesus had said this, a woman spoke up from the crowd and said to him, "How happy is the woman who bore you and nursed you!"

28 But Jesus answered, "Rather, how happy are those who hear the word of God and obey it!"

The Demand for a Miracle
(Mt 12.38–42)

29 As the people crowded round Jesus, he went on to say, "How evil are the people of this day! They ask for a miracle, but none will be given them except the miracle of Jonah. ³⁰In the same way that the prophet Jonah was a sign for the people of Nineveh, so the Son of Man will be a sign for the people of this day. ³¹On Judgement Day the Queen of Sheba will stand up and accuse the people of today, because she travelled all the way from her country to listen to King Solomon's wise teaching; and I tell you there is something here greater than Solomon. ³²On Judgement Day the people of Nineveh will stand up and accuse you, because they turned from their sins when they heard Jonah preach; and I assure you that there is something here greater than Jonah!

The Light of the Body
(Mt 5.15; 6.22–23)

33 "No one lights a lamp and then hides it or puts it under a bowl;ᵃ instead, he puts it on the lampstand, so that people may see the light as they come in. ³⁴Your eyes are like a lamp for the body. When your eyes are sound, your whole body is full of light; but when your eyes are no good, your whole body will be in darkness. ³⁵Make certain, then, that the light in you is not darkness. ³⁶If your whole body is full of light, with no part of it in darkness, it will be bright all over, as when a lamp shines on you with its brightness."

ᵃ **11.33** *Some manuscripts do not have* or puts it under a bowl.

Jesus Accuses the Pharisees and the Teachers of the Law
(Mt 23.1–36; Mk 12.38–40)

37 When Jesus finished speaking, a Pharisee invited him to eat with him; so he went in and sat down to eat. ³⁸The Pharisee was surprised when he noticed that Jesus had not washed before eating. ³⁹So the Lord said to him, "Now then, you Pharisees clean the outside of your cup and plate, but inside you are full of violence and evil. ⁴⁰Fools! Did not God, who made the outside, also make the inside? ⁴¹But give what is in your cups and plates to the poor, and everything will be ritually clean for you.

42 "How terrible for you Pharisees! You give God a tenth of the seasoning herbs, such as mint and rue and all the other herbs, but you neglect justice and love for God. These you should practise, without neglecting the others.

43 "How terrible for you Pharisees! You love the reserved seats in the synagogues and to be greeted with respect in the market places. ⁴⁴How terrible for you! You are like unmarked graves which people walk on without knowing it."

45 One of the teachers of the Law said to him, "Teacher, when you say this, you insult us too!"

46 Jesus answered, "How terrible also for you teachers of the Law! You put loads on people's backs which are hard to carry, but you yourselves will not stretch out a finger to help them carry those loads. ⁴⁷How terrible for you! You make fine tombs for the prophets – the very prophets your ancestors murdered. ⁴⁸You yourselves admit, then, that you approve of what your ancestors did; they murdered the prophets, and you build their tombs. ⁴⁹For this reason the Wisdom of God said, 'I will send them prophets and messengers; they will kill some of them and persecute others.' ⁵⁰So the people of this time will be punished for the murder of all the prophets killed since the creation of the world, ⁵¹from the murder of Abel to the murder of Zechariah, who was killed between the altar and the Holy Place. Yes, I tell you, the people of this time will be punished for them all!

52 "How terrible for you teachers of the Law! You have kept the key that opens the door to the house of knowledge; you yourselves will not go in, and you stop those who are trying to go in!"

53 When Jesus left that place, the teachers of the Law and the Pharisees began to criticize him bitterly and ask him questions about many things, ⁵⁴trying to lay traps for him and catch him saying something wrong.

A Warning against Hypocrisy
(Mt 10.26–27)

12 As thousands of people crowded together, so that they were stepping on each other, Jesus said first to his disciples, "Be on guard against the yeast of the Pharisees – I mean their hypocrisy. ²Whatever is covered up will be uncovered, and every secret will be made known. ³So then, whatever you have said in the dark will be heard in broad daylight, and whatever you have whispered in private in a closed room will be shouted from the housetops.

Whom to Fear
(Mt 10.28–31)

4 "I tell you, my friends, do not be afraid of those who kill the body but cannot afterwards do anything worse. ⁵I will show you whom to fear: fear God, who, after killing, has the authority to throw into hell. Believe me, he is the one you must fear!

6 "Aren't five sparrows sold for two pennies? Yet not one sparrow is forgotten by God. ⁷Even the hairs of your head have all been counted. So do not be afraid; you are worth much more than many sparrows!

Confessing and Rejecting Christ
(Mt 10.32–33; 12.32; 10.19–20)

8 "I assure you that for those who declare publicly that they belong to me, the Son of Man will do the same before the angels of God. ⁹But those who reject me publicly, the Son of Man will also reject before the angels of God.

10 "Whoever says a word against the Son of Man can be forgiven; but those who say evil things against the Holy Spirit will not be forgiven.

11 "When they bring you to be tried in the synagogues or before governors or rulers, do not be worried about how you will defend yourself or what you will say. ¹²For the Holy Spirit will teach you at that time what you should say."

The Parable of the Rich Fool

13 A man in the crowd said to Jesus, "Teacher, tell my brother to divide with me the property our father left us."

14 Jesus answered him, "My friend, who gave me the right to judge or to divide the property between you two?" ¹⁵And he went on to say to them all, "Watch out and guard yourselves from every kind of greed; because a person's true life is not made up of the things he owns, no matter how rich he may be."

16 Then Jesus told them this parable: "There was once a rich man who had land which bore good crops. ¹⁷He began to think to himself, 'I haven't anywhere to keep all my crops. What can I do? ¹⁸This is what I will do,' he told himself; 'I will tear down my barns and build bigger ones, where I will store my corn and all my other goods. ¹⁹Then I will say to myself, Lucky man! You have all the good things you need for many years. Take life easy, eat, drink, and enjoy yourself!' ²⁰But God said to him, 'You fool! This very night you will have to give up your life; then who will get all these things you have kept for yourself?'"

21 And Jesus concluded, "This is how it is with those who pile up riches for themselves but are not rich in God's sight."

Trust in God
(Mt 6.25–34)

22 Then Jesus said to the disciples, "And so I tell you not to worry about the food you need to stay alive or about the clothes you need for your body. ²³Life is much more important than food, and the body much more important than clothes. ²⁴Look at the crows: they don't sow seeds or gather a harvest; they don't have store-rooms or barns; God feeds them! You are worth so much more than birds! ²⁵Can any of you live a bit longer[a] by worrying about it? ²⁶If you can't manage even such a small thing, why worry about the other things? ²⁷Look how the wild flowers grow: they don't work or make clothes for themselves. But I tell you that not even King Solomon with all his wealth had clothes as beautiful as one of these flowers. ²⁸It is God who clothes the wild grass – grass that is here today and gone tomorrow, burnt up in the oven. Won't he be all the more sure to clothe you? How little faith you have!

29 "So don't be all upset, always concerned about what you will eat and drink. ³⁰(For the pagans of this world are always concerned about all these things.) Your Father knows that you need these things. ³¹Instead, be concerned with his Kingdom, and he will provide you with these things.

---

[a] **12.25** live a bit longer; *or* grow a bit taller.

Riches in Heaven
(Mt 6.19–21)

32 "Do not be afraid, little flock, for your Father is pleased to give you the Kingdom. 33Sell all your belongings and give the money to the poor. Provide for yourselves purses that don't wear out, and save your riches in heaven, where they will never decrease, because no thief can get to them, and no moth can destroy them. 34For your heart will always be where your riches are.

Watchful Servants

35 "Be ready for whatever comes, dressed for action and with your lamps lit, 36like servants who are waiting for their master to come back from a wedding feast. When he comes and knocks, they will open the door for him at once. 37How happy are those servants whose master finds them awake and ready when he returns! I tell you, he will take off his coat, ask them to sit down, and will wait on them. 38How happy they are if he finds them ready, even if he should come at midnight or even later! 39And you can be sure that if the owner of a house knew the time when the thief would come, he would not let the thief break into his house. 40And you, too, must be ready, because the Son of Man will come at an hour when you are not expecting him."

The Faithful or the Unfaithful Servant
(Mt 24.45–51)

41 Peter said, "Lord, does this parable apply to us, or do you mean it for everyone?"

42 The Lord answered, "Who, then, is the faithful and wise servant? He is the one that his master will put in charge, to run the household and give the other servants their share of the food at the proper time. 43How happy that servant is if his master finds him doing this when he comes home! 44Indeed, I tell you, the master will put that servant in charge of all his property. 45But if that servant says to himself that his master is taking a long time to come back and if he begins to beat the other servants, both the men and the women, and eats and drinks and gets drunk, 46then the master will come back one day when the servant does not expect him and at a time he does not know. The master will cut him in pieces[a] and make him share the fate of the disobedient.

47 "The servant who knows what his master wants him to do, but does not get himself ready

---

[a] **12.46** cut him in pieces; *or* throw him out.

and do it, will be punished with a heavy whipping. 48But the servant who does not know what his master wants, and yet does something for which he deserves a whipping, will be punished with a light whipping. Much is required from the person to whom much is given; much more is required from the person to whom much more is given.

Jesus the Cause of Division
(Mt 10.34–36)

49 "I came to set the earth on fire, and how I wish it were already kindled! 50I have a baptism to receive, and how distressed I am until it is over! 51Do you suppose that I came to bring peace to the world? No, not peace, but division. 52From now on a family of five will be divided, three against two and two against three. 53Fathers will be against their sons, and sons against their fathers; mothers will be against their daughters, and daughters against their mothers; mothers-in-law will be against their daughters-in-law, and daughters-in-law against their mothers-in-law."

Understanding the Time
(Mt 16.2–3)

54 Jesus said also to the people, "When you see a cloud coming up in the west, at once you say that it is going to rain – and it does. 55And when you feel the south wind blowing, you say that it is going to get hot – and it does. 56Hypocrites! You can look at the earth and the sky and predict the weather; why, then, don't you know the meaning of this present time?

Settle with your Opponent
(Mt 5.25–26)

57 "Why do you not judge for yourselves the right thing to do? 58If someone brings a lawsuit against you and takes you to court, do your best to settle the dispute with them before you get to court. If you don't, they will drag you before the judge, who will hand you over to the police, and you will be put in jail. 59There you will stay, I tell you, until you pay the last penny of your fine."

Turn from your Sins or Die

13 At that time some people were there who told Jesus about the Galileans whom Pilate had killed while they were offering sacrifices to God. ²Jesus answered them, "Because those Galileans were killed in that way, do you think it proves that they were worse sinners than all the other Galileans? ³No indeed! And I tell you that if you do not turn from your sins, you will all die as they did. ⁴What about those eighteen people in Siloam who were killed when the tower fell on them? Do you suppose this proves that they were worse than all the other people living in Jerusalem? ⁵No indeed! And I tell you that if you do not turn from your sins, you will all die as they did."

The Parable of the Unfruitful Fig Tree

6 Then Jesus told them this parable: "There was once a man who had a fig tree growing in his vineyard. He went looking for figs on it but found none. ⁷So he said to his gardener, 'Look, for three years I have been coming here looking for figs on this fig tree, and I haven't found any. Cut it down! Why should it go on using up the soil?' ⁸But the gardener answered, 'Leave it alone, sir, just one more year; I will dig round it and put in some manure. ⁹Then if the tree bears figs next year, so much the better; if not, then you can have it cut down.'"

Jesus Heals a Crippled Woman on the Sabbath

10 One Sabbath Jesus was teaching in a synagogue. ¹¹A woman there had an evil spirit that had made her ill for eighteen years; she was bent over and could not straighten up at all. ¹²When Jesus saw her, he called out to her, "Woman, you are free from your illness!" ¹³He placed his hands on her, and at once she straightened herself up and praised God.

14 The official of the synagogue was angry that Jesus had healed on the Sabbath, so he spoke up and said to the people, "There are six days in which we should work; so come during those days and be healed, but not on the Sabbath!"

15 The Lord answered him, "You hypocrites! Any one of you would untie your ox or your donkey from the stall and take it out to give it water on the Sabbath. ¹⁶Now here is this descendant of Abraham whom Satan has kept bound up for eighteen years; should she not be released on the Sabbath?" ¹⁷His answer made his enemies ashamed of themselves, while the people rejoiced over all the wonderful things that he did.

The Parable of the Mustard Seed
(Mt 13.31–32; Mk 4.30–32)

18 Jesus asked, "What is the Kingdom of God like? What shall I compare it with? ¹⁹It is like this. A man takes a mustard seed and sows it in his field. The plant grows and becomes a tree, and the birds make their nests in its branches."

The Parable of the Yeast
(Mt 13.33)

20 Again Jesus asked, "What shall I compare the Kingdom of God with? ²¹It is like this. A woman takes some yeast and mixes it with forty litres of flour until the whole batch of dough rises."

The Narrow Door
(Mt 7.13–14, 21–23)

22 Jesus went through towns and villages, teaching the people and making his way towards Jerusalem. ²³Someone asked him, "Sir, will just a few people be saved?"

Jesus answered them, ²⁴"Do your best to go in through the narrow door; because many people will surely try to go in but will not be able. ²⁵The master of the house will get up and close the door; then when you stand outside and begin to knock on the door and say, 'Open the door for us, sir!' he will answer you, 'I don't know where you come from!' ²⁶Then you will answer, 'We ate and drank with you; you taught in our town!' ²⁷But he will say again, 'I don't know where you come from. Get away from me, all you wicked people!' ²⁸How you will cry and grind your teeth when you see Abraham, Isaac, and Jacob, and all the prophets in the Kingdom of God, while you are thrown out! ²⁹People will come from the east and the west, from the north and the south, and sit down at the feast in the Kingdom of God. ³⁰Then those who are now last will be first, and those who are now first will be last."

Jesus' Love for Jerusalem
(Mt 23.37–39)

31 At that same time some Pharisees came to Jesus and said to him, "You must get out of here and go somewhere else, because Herod wants to kill you."

32 Jesus answered them, "Go and tell that fox: 'I am driving out demons and performing cures today and tomorrow, and on the third day I shall finish my work.' ³³Yet I must be on my way

today, tomorrow, and the next day; it is not right for a prophet to be killed anywhere except in Jerusalem.

34   "Jerusalem, Jerusalem! You kill the prophets, you stone the messengers God has sent you! How many times have I wanted to put my arms round all your people, just as a hen gathers her chicks under her wings, but you would not let me! ³⁵And so your Temple will be abandoned. I assure you that you will not see me until the time comes when you say, 'God bless him who comes in the name of the Lord.'"

Jews praying at the Wailing Wall in Jerusalem, the only part of the old Temple in Jerusalem still standing (13.34–35)

Jesus Heals a Sick Man

14 One Sabbath Jesus went to eat a meal at the home of one of the leading Pharisees; and people were watching Jesus closely. ²A man whose legs and arms were swollen came to Jesus, ³and Jesus asked the teachers of the Law and the Pharisees, "Does our Law allow healing on the Sabbath or not?"

4   But they would not say anything. Jesus took the man, healed him, and sent him away. ⁵Then he said to them, "If any one of you had a son or an ox that happened to fall in a well on a Sabbath, would you not pull them out at once on the Sabbath itself?"

6   But they were not able to answer him about this.

Humility and Hospitality

7   Jesus noticed how some of the guests were choosing the best places, so he told this parable to all of them: ⁸"When someone invites you to a wedding feast, do not sit down in the best place. It could happen that someone more important than you has been invited, ⁹and your host, who invited both of you, would have to come and say to you, 'Let him have this place.' Then you would be embarrassed and have to sit in the lowest place. ¹⁰Instead, when you are invited, go and sit in the lowest place, so that your host will come to you and say, 'Come on up, my friend, to a better place.' This will bring you honour in the presence of all the other guests. ¹¹For all those who make themselves great will be humbled, and those who humble themselves will be made great."

12   Then Jesus said to his host, "When you give a lunch or a dinner, do not invite your friends or your brothers or your relatives or your rich neighbours – for they will invite you back, and in this way you will be paid for what you did. ¹³When you give a feast, invite the poor, the crippled, the lame, and the blind; ¹⁴and you will be blessed, because they are not able to pay you back. God will repay you on the day the good people rise from death."

The Parable of the Great Feast
(Mt 22.1–10)

15   When one of the men sitting at table heard this, he said to Jesus, "How happy are those who will sit down at the feast in the Kingdom of God!"

16   Jesus said to him, "There was once a man who was giving a great feast to which he invited many people. ¹⁷When it was time for the feast, he sent his servant to tell his guests, 'Come, everything is ready!' ¹⁸But they all began, one after another, to make excuses. The first one told the servant, 'I have bought a field and must go and look at it; please accept my apologies.' ¹⁹Another one said, 'I have bought five pairs of oxen and am on my way to try them out; please accept my apologies.' ²⁰Another one said, 'I have just got married, and for that reason I cannot come.'

21   "The servant went back and told all this to his master. The master was furious and said to his servant, 'Hurry out to the streets and alleys of the town, and bring back the poor, the crippled,

the blind, and the lame.' ²²Soon the servant said, 'Your order has been carried out, sir, but there is room for more.' ²³So the master said to the servant, 'Go out to the country roads and lanes and make people come in, so that my house will be full. ²⁴I tell you all that none of those who were invited will taste my dinner!'"

The Cost of Being a Disciple
(Mt 10.37–38)

25 Once when large crowds of people were going along with Jesus, he turned and said to them, ²⁶"Those who come to me cannot be my disciples unless they love me more than they love father and mother, wife and children, brothers and sisters, and themselves as well. ²⁷Those who do not carry their own cross and come after me cannot be my disciples.

28 "If one of you is planning to build a tower, you sit down first and work out what it will cost, to see if you have enough money to finish the job. ²⁹If you don't, you will not be able to finish the tower after laying the foundation; and all who see what happened will laugh at you. ³⁰'This man began to build but can't finish the job!' they will say.

31 "If a king goes out with ten thousand men to fight another king who comes against him with twenty thousand men, he will sit down first and decide if he is strong enough to face that other king. ³²If he isn't, he will send messengers to meet the other king, to ask for terms of peace while he is still a long way off. ³³In the same way," concluded Jesus, "none of you can be my disciple unless you give up everything you have.

Worthless Salt
(Mt 5.13; Mk 9.50)

34 "Salt is good, but if it loses its saltiness, there is no way to make it salty again. ³⁵It is no good for the soil or for the manure heap; it is thrown away. Listen, then, if you have ears!"

The Lost Sheep
(Mt 18.12–14)

15 One day when many tax collectors and other outcasts came to listen to Jesus, ²the Pharisees and the teachers of the Law started grumbling, "This man welcomes outcasts and even eats with them!" ³So Jesus told them this parable:

4 "Suppose one of you has a hundred sheep and loses one of them – what do you do? You leave the other ninety-nine sheep in the pasture and go looking for the one that got lost until you find it. ⁵When you find it, you are so happy that you put it on your shoulders ⁶and carry it back home. Then you call your friends and neighbours together and say to them, 'I am so happy I found my lost sheep. Let us celebrate!' ⁷In the same way, I tell you, there will be more joy in heaven over one sinner who repents than over ninety-nine respectable people who do not need to repent.

The Lost Coin

8 "Or suppose a woman who has ten silver coins loses one of them – what does she do? She lights a lamp, sweeps her house, and looks carefully everywhere until she finds it. ⁹When she finds it, she calls her friends and neighbours together, and says to them, 'I am so happy I found the coin I lost. Let us celebrate!' ¹⁰In the same way, I tell you, the angels of God rejoice over one sinner who repents."

The Lost Son

11 Jesus went on to say, "There was once a man who had two sons. ¹²The younger one said to him, 'Father, give me my share of the property now.' So the man divided his property between his two sons. ¹³After a few days the younger son sold his part of the property and left home with the money. He went to a country far away, where he wasted his money in reckless living. ¹⁴He spent everything he had. Then a severe famine spread over that country, and he was left without a thing. ¹⁵So he went to work for one of the citizens of that country, who sent him out to his farm to take care of the pigs. ¹⁶He wished he could fill himself with the bean pods the pigs ate, but no one gave him anything to eat. ¹⁷At last he came to his senses and said, 'All my father's hired workers have more than they can eat, and here I am about to starve! ¹⁸I will get up and go to my father and say, Father, I have sinned against God and against you. ¹⁹I am no longer fit to be called your son; treat me as one of your hired workers.' ²⁰So he got up and started back to his father.

"He was still a long way from home when his father saw him; his heart was filled with pity, and he ran, threw his arms round his son, and kissed him. ²¹'Father,' the son said, 'I have sinned against God and against you. I am no longer fit to be called your son.' ²²But the father called his servants. 'Hurry!' he said. 'Bring the best robe and put it on him. Put a ring on his finger and shoes on his feet. ²³Then go and get the prize calf and kill it, and let us celebrate with a feast! ²⁴For this son of mine was dead, but now he is alive; he was lost, but now he has been found.' And so the feasting began.

25 "In the meantime the elder son was out in the field. On his way back, when he came close to the house, he heard the music and dancing. ²⁶So he called one of the servants and asked him, 'What's going on?' ²⁷'Your brother has come back home,' the servant answered, 'and your father has killed the prize calf, because he got him back safe and sound.'

28 "The elder brother was so angry that he would not go into the house; so his father came out and begged him to come in. ²⁹But he answered his father, 'Look, all these years I have worked for you like a slave, and I have never disobeyed your orders. What have you given me? Not even a goat for me to have a feast with my friends! ³⁰But this son of yours wasted all your property on prostitutes, and when he comes back home, you kill the prize calf for him!' ³¹'My son,' the father answered, 'you are always here with me, and everything I have is yours. ³²But we had to celebrate and be happy, because your brother was dead, but now he is alive; he was lost, but now he has been found.'"

The Shrewd Manager

16 **p** Jesus said to his disciples, "There was once a rich man who had a servant who managed his property. The rich man was told that the manager was wasting his master's money, ²so he called him in and said, 'What is this I hear about you? Hand in a complete account of your handling of my property, because you cannot be my manager any longer.' ³The servant said to himself, 'My master is going to dismiss me from my job. What shall I do? I am not strong enough to dig ditches, and I am ashamed to beg. ⁴Now I know what I will do! Then when my job is gone, I shall have friends who will welcome me in their homes.'

5 "So he called in all the people who were in debt to his master. He asked the first one, 'How much do you owe my master?' ⁶'One hundred barrels of olive oil,' he answered. 'Here is your account,' the manager told him; 'sit down and write fifty.' ⁷Then he asked another one, 'And you – how much do you owe?' 'A thousand sacks of wheat,' he answered. 'Here is your account,' the manager told him; 'write eight hundred.'

8 "As a result the master of this dishonest manager praised him for doing such a shrewd thing; because the people of this world are much more shrewd in handling their affairs than the people who belong to the light."

9 And Jesus went on to say, "And so I tell you: make friends for yourselves with worldly wealth, so that when it gives out, you will be welcomed in the eternal home. ¹⁰Whoever is faithful in small matters will be faithful in large ones; whoever is dishonest in small matters will be dishonest in large ones. ¹¹If, then, you have not been faithful in handling worldly wealth, how can you be trusted with true wealth? ¹²And if you have not been faithful with what belongs to someone else, who will give you what belongs to you?

13 "No servant can be the slave of two masters; such a servant will hate one and love the other or will be loyal to one and despise the other. You cannot serve both God and money."

Some Sayings of Jesus
(Mt 11.12–13; 5.31–32; Mk 10.11–12)

14 When the Pharisees heard all this, they sneered at Jesus, because they loved money. ¹⁵Jesus said to them, "You are the ones who make yourselves look right in other people's sight, but God knows your hearts. For the things that are considered of great value by human beings are worth nothing in God's sight.

16 "The Law of Moses and the writings of the prophets were in effect up to the time of John the Baptist; since then the Good News about the Kingdom of God is being told, and everyone forces their way in. ¹⁷But it is easier for heaven and earth to disappear than for the smallest detail of the Law to be done away with.

18 "Any man who divorces his wife and marries another woman commits adultery; and the man who marries a divorced woman commits adultery.

The Rich Man and Lazarus

19 **p** "There was once a rich man who dressed in the most expensive clothes and lived in great luxury every day. ²⁰There was also a poor man named Lazarus, covered with sores, who used to be brought to the rich man's door, ²¹hoping to eat the bits of food that fell from the rich man's table. Even the dogs would come and lick his sores.

22 "The poor man died and was carried by the angels to sit beside Abraham at the feast in

heaven. The rich man died and was buried, [23]and in Hades,[a] where he was in great pain, he looked up and saw Abraham, far away, with Lazarus at his side. [24]So he called out, 'Father Abraham! Take pity on me, and send Lazarus to dip his finger in some water and cool my tongue, because I am in great pain in this fire!'

25 "But Abraham said, 'Remember, my son, that in your lifetime you were given all the good things, while Lazarus got all the bad things. But now he is enjoying himself here, while you are in pain. [26]Besides all that, there is a deep pit lying between us, so that those who want to cross over from here to you cannot do so, nor can anyone cross over to us from where you are.' [27]The rich man said, 'Then I beg you, father Abraham, send Lazarus to my father's house, [28]where I have five brothers. Let him go and warn them so that they, at least, will not come to this place of pain.'

29 "Abraham said, 'Your brothers have Moses and the prophets to warn them; your brothers should listen to what they say.' [30]The rich man answered, 'That is not enough, father Abraham! But if someone were to rise from death and go to them, then they would turn from their sins.' [31]But Abraham said, 'If they will not listen to Moses and the prophets, they will not be convinced even if someone were to rise from death.'"

Sin
(Mt 18.6–7, 21–22; Mk 9.42)

17 Jesus said to his disciples, "Things that make people fall into sin are bound to happen, but how terrible for the one who makes them happen! [2]It would be better for him if a large millstone were tied round his neck and he were thrown into the sea than for him to cause one of these little ones to sin. [3]So watch what you do!

"If your brother sins, rebuke him, and if he repents, forgive him. [4]If he sins against you seven times in one day, and each time he comes to you saying, 'I repent,' you must forgive him."

Faith

5 The apostles said to the Lord, "Make our faith greater."

6 The Lord answered, "If you had faith as big as a mustard seed, you could say to this mulberry tree, 'Pull yourself up by the roots and plant yourself in the sea!' and it would obey you.

A Servant's Duty

7 "Suppose one of you has a servant who is ploughing or looking after the sheep. When he comes in from the field, do you tell him to hurry and eat his meal? [8]Of course not! Instead, you say to him, 'Get my supper ready, then put on your apron and wait on me while I eat and drink; after that you may have your meal.' [9]The servant does not deserve thanks for obeying orders, does he? [10]It is the same with you; when you have done all you have been told to do, say, 'We are ordinary servants; we have only done our duty.'"

Jesus Heals Ten Men

11 As Jesus made his way to Jerusalem, he went along the border between Samaria and Galilee. [12]He was going into a village when he was met by ten men suffering from a dreaded skin disease. They stood at a distance [13]and shouted, "Jesus! Master! Take pity on us!"

14 Jesus saw them and said to them, "Go and let the priests examine you."

On the way they were made clean.[b] [15]When one of them saw that he was healed, he came back, praising God in a loud voice. [16]He threw himself to the ground at Jesus' feet and thanked him. The man was a Samaritan. [17]Jesus said, "There were ten men who were healed; where are the other nine? [18]Why is this foreigner the only one who came back to give thanks to God?" [19]And Jesus said to him, "Get up and go; your faith has made you well."

The Coming of the Kingdom
(Mt 24.23–28, 37–41)

20 Some Pharisees asked Jesus when the Kingdom of God would come. His answer was, "The Kingdom of God does not come in such a way as to be seen. [21]No one will say, 'Look, here it is!' or, 'There it is!'; because the Kingdom of God is within you."[c]

22 Then he said to the disciples, "The time will come when you will wish you could see one of the days of the Son of Man, but you will not see it. [23]There will be those who will say to you, 'Look, over there!' or, 'Look, over here!' But don't go out looking for it. [24]As the lightning

[b] **17.14** MADE CLEAN: *See 5.12.*

[c] **17.21** is within you; *or* is among you, *or* will suddenly appear among you.

[a] **16.23** HADES: *The world of the dead.*

flashes across the sky and lights it up from one side to the other, so will the Son of Man be in his day. ²⁵But first he must suffer much and be rejected by the people of this day. ²⁶As it was in the time of Noah so shall it be in the days of the Son of Man. ²⁷Everybody kept on eating and drinking, and men and women married, up to the very day Noah went into the boat and the flood came and killed them all. ²⁸It will be as it was in the time of Lot. Everybody kept on eating and drinking, buying and selling, planting and building. ²⁹On the day Lot left Sodom, fire and sulphur rained down from heaven and killed them all. ³⁰That is how it will be on the day the Son of Man is revealed.

31 "On that day someone who is on the roof of his house must not go down into the house to get any belongings; in the same way anyone who is out in the field must not go back to the house. ³²Remember Lot's wife! ³³Whoever tries to save his own life will lose it; whoever loses his life will save it. ³⁴On that night, I tell you, there will be two people sleeping in the same bed: one will be taken away, the other will be left behind. ³⁵Two women will be grinding corn together: one will be taken away, the other will be left behind."ᵃ

37 The disciples asked him, "Where, Lord?"

Jesus answered, "Wherever there is a dead body, the vultures will gather."

The Parable of the Widow and the Judge

18 Then Jesus told his disciples a parable to teach them that they should always pray and never become discouraged. ²"In a certain town there was a judge who neither feared God nor respected people. ³And there was a widow in that same town who kept coming to him and pleading for her rights, saying, 'Help me against my opponent!' ⁴For a long time the judge refused to act, but at last he said to himself, 'Even though I don't fear God or respect people, ⁵yet because of all the trouble this widow is giving me, I will see to it that she gets her rights. If I don't, she will keep on coming and finally wear me out!' "

6 And the Lord continued, "Listen to what that corrupt judge said. ⁷Now, will God not judge in favour of his own people who cry to him day and night for help? Will he be slow to help them? ⁸I tell you, he will judge in their favour

and do it quickly. But will the Son of Man find faith on earth when he comes?"

The Parable of the Pharisee and the Tax Collector

9 Jesus also told this parable to people who were sure of their own goodness and despised everybody else. ¹⁰"Once there were two men who went up to the Temple to pray: one was a Pharisee, the other a tax collector.

11 "The Pharisee stood apart by himself and prayed,ᵇ 'I thank you, God, that I am not greedy, dishonest, or an adulterer, like everybody else. I thank you that I am not like that tax collector over there. ¹²I fast two days a week, and I give you a tenth of all my income.'

13 "But the tax collector stood at a distance and would not even raise his face to heaven, but beat on his breast and said, 'God, have pity on me, a sinner!' ¹⁴I tell you," said Jesus, "the tax collector, and not the Pharisee, was in the right with God when he went home. For all who make themselves great will be humbled, and all who humble themselves will be made great."

Jesus Blesses Little Children
(Mt 19.13–15; Mk 10.13–16)

15 Some people brought their babies to Jesus for him to place his hands on them. The disciples saw them and scolded them for doing so, ¹⁶but Jesus called the children to him and said, "Let the children come to me and do not stop them, because the Kingdom of God belongs to such as these. ¹⁷Remember this! Whoever does not receive the Kingdom of God like a child will never enter it."

The Rich Man
(Mt 19.16–30; Mk 10.17–31)

18 A Jewish leader asked Jesus, "Good Teacher, what must I do to receive eternal life?"

19 "Why do you call me good?" Jesus asked him. "No one is good except God alone. ²⁰You know the commandments: 'Do not commit adultery; do not commit murder; do not steal; do not accuse anyone falsely; respect your father and your mother.'"

21 The man replied, "Ever since I was young, I have obeyed all these commandments."

ᵃ **17.35** *Some manuscripts add verse 36:* Two men will be working in a field: one will be taken away, the other will be left behind *(see Mt 24.40).*

ᵇ **18.11** stood apart by himself and prayed; *some manuscripts have* stood up and prayed to himself.

22 When Jesus heard this, he said to him, "There is still one more thing you need to do. Sell all you have and give the money to the poor, and you will have riches in heaven; then come and follow me." ²³But when the man heard this, he became very sad, because he was very rich.

24 Jesus saw that he was sad and said, "How hard it is for rich people to enter the Kingdom of God! ²⁵It is much harder for a rich person to enter the Kingdom of God than for a camel to go through the eye of a needle."

26 The people who heard him asked, "Who, then, can be saved?"

27 Jesus answered, "What is humanly impossible is possible for God."

28 Then Peter said, "Look! We have left our homes to follow you."

29 "Yes," Jesus said to them, "and I assure you that anyone who leaves home or wife or brothers or parents or children for the sake of the Kingdom of God ³⁰will receive much more in this present age and eternal life in the age to come."

Jesus Speaks a Third Time about his Death
(Mt 20.17–19; Mk 10.32–34)

31 Jesus took the twelve disciples aside and said to them, "Listen! We are going to Jerusalem where everything the prophets wrote about the Son of Man will come true. ³²He will be handed over to the Gentiles, who will mock him, insult him, and spit on him. ³³They will whip him and kill him, but three days later he will rise to life."

34 But the disciples did not understand any of these things; the meaning of the words was hidden from them, and they did not know what Jesus was talking about.

Jesus Heals a Blind Beggar
(Mt 20.29–34; Mk 10.46–52)

35 As Jesus was coming near Jericho, there was a blind man sitting by the road, begging. ³⁶When he heard the crowd passing by, he asked, "What is this?"

37 "Jesus of Nazareth is passing by," they told him.

38 He cried out, "Jesus! Son of David! Take pity on me!"

39 The people in front scolded him and told him to be quiet. But he shouted even more loudly, "Son of David! Take pity on me!"

40 So Jesus stopped and ordered the blind man to be brought to him. When he came near, Jesus asked him, ⁴¹"What do you want me to do for you?"

A blind person assisted by a guide dog

"Sir," he answered, "I want to see again."

42 Jesus said to him, "Then see! Your faith has made you well."

43 At once he was able to see, and he followed Jesus, giving thanks to God. When the crowd saw it, they all praised God.

Jesus and Zacchaeus

19 Jesus went on into Jericho and was passing through. ²There was a chief tax collector there named Zacchaeus, who was rich. ³He was trying to see who Jesus was, but he was a little man and could not see Jesus because of the crowd. ⁴So he ran ahead of the crowd and climbed a sycamore tree to see Jesus, who was going to pass that way. ⁵When Jesus came to that place, he looked up and said to Zacchaeus, "Hurry down, Zacchaeus, because I must stay in your house today."

6 Zacchaeus hurried down and welcomed him with great joy. ⁷All the people who saw it started grumbling, "This man has gone as a guest to the home of a sinner!"

8   Zacchaeus stood up and said to the Lord, "Listen, sir! I will give half my belongings to the poor, and if I have cheated anyone, I will pay back four times as much."

9   Jesus said to him, "Salvation has come to this house today, for this man, also, is a descendant of Abraham. ¹⁰The Son of Man came to seek and to save the lost."

The Parable of the Gold Coins
(Mt 25.14–30)

11   ☩p While the people were listening to this, Jesus continued and told them a parable. He was now almost at Jerusalem, and they supposed that the Kingdom of God was just about to appear. ¹²So he said, "There was once a man of high rank who was going to a country far away to be made king, after which he planned to come back home. ¹³Before he left, he called his ten servants and gave them each a gold coin and told them, 'See what you can earn with this while I am gone.' ¹⁴Now, his own people hated him, and so they sent messengers after him to say, 'We don't want this man to be our king.'

15   "The man was made king and came back. At once he ordered his servants to appear before him, in order to find out how much they had earned. ¹⁶The first one came and said, 'Sir, I have earned ten gold coins with the one you gave me.' ¹⁷'Well done,' he said; 'you are a good servant! Since you were faithful in small matters, I will put you in charge of ten cities.' ¹⁸The second servant came and said, 'Sir, I have earned five gold coins with the one you gave me.' ¹⁹To this one he said, 'You will be in charge of five cities.'

20   "Another servant came and said, 'Sir, here is your gold coin; I kept it hidden in a handkerchief. ²¹I was afraid of you, because you are a hard man. You take what is not yours and reap what you did not sow.' ²²He said to him, 'You bad servant! I will use your own words to condemn you! You know that I am a hard man, taking what is not mine and reaping what I have not sown. ²³Well, then, why didn't you put my money in the bank? Then I would have received it back with interest when I returned.'

24   "Then he said to those who were standing there, 'Take the gold coin away from him and give it to the servant who has ten coins.' ²⁵But they said to him, 'Sir, he already has ten coins!' ²⁶'I tell you,' he replied, 'that to all those who have something, even more will be given; but those who have nothing, even the little that they have will be taken away from them. ²⁷Now, as for those enemies of mine who did not want me to be their king, bring them here and kill them in my presence!' "

The Triumphant Approach to Jerusalem
(Mt 21.1–11; Mk 11.1–11; Jn 12.12–19)

28   After Jesus said this, he went on ahead of them to Jerusalem. ²⁹As he came near Bethphage and Bethany at the Mount of Olives, he sent two disciples ahead ³⁰with these instructions: "Go to the village there ahead of you; as you go in, you will find a colt tied up that has never been ridden. Untie it and bring it here. ³¹If someone asks you why you are untying it, tell him that the Master[a] needs it."

32   They went on their way and found everything just as Jesus had told them. ³³As they were untying the colt, its owners said to them, "Why are you untying it?"

34   "The Master[a] needs it," they answered, ³⁵and they took the colt to Jesus. Then they threw their cloaks over the animal and helped Jesus get on. ³⁶As he rode on, people spread their cloaks on the road.

37   When he came near Jerusalem, at the place where the road went down the Mount of Olives, the large crowd of his disciples began to thank God and praise him in loud voices for all the great things that they had seen: ³⁸"God bless the king who comes in the name of the Lord! Peace in heaven and glory to God!"

39   Then some of the Pharisees in the crowd spoke to Jesus. "Teacher," they said, "command your disciples to be quiet!"

40   Jesus answered, "I tell you that if they keep quiet, the stones themselves will start shouting."

Jesus Weeps over Jerusalem

41   He came closer to the city, and when he saw it, he wept over it, ⁴²saying, "If you only knew today what is needed for peace! But now you cannot see it! ⁴³The time will come when your enemies will surround you with barricades, blockade you, and close in on you from every side. ⁴⁴They will completely destroy you and the people within your walls; not a single stone will they leave in its place, because you did not recognize the time when God came to save you!"

---

[a] **19.31, 19.34** the Master; *or* its owner.

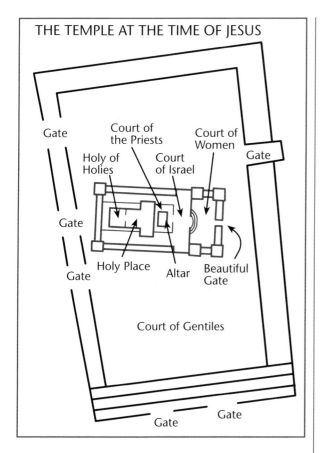

THE TEMPLE AT THE TIME OF JESUS

Gate

Court of
the Priests

Court of
Women

Gate

Holy of
Holies

Court
of Israel

Gate

Gate

Holy Place

Altar

Beautiful
Gate

Court of Gentiles

Gate

Gate

Gate

Jesus Goes to the Temple
(Mt 21.12–17; Mk 11.15–19; Jn 2.13–22)

45 Then Jesus went into the Temple and began to drive out the merchants, [46]saying to them, "It is written in the Scriptures that God said, 'My Temple will be a house of prayer.' But you have turned it into a hideout for thieves!"

47 Every day Jesus taught in the Temple. The chief priests, the teachers of the Law, and the leaders of the people wanted to kill him, [48]but they could not find a way to do it, because all the people kept listening to him, not wanting to miss a single word.

The Question about Jesus' Authority
(Mt 21.23–27; Mk 11.27–33)

20 One day when Jesus was in the Temple teaching the people and preaching the Good News, the chief priests and the teachers of the Law, together with the elders, came [2]and said to him, "Tell us, what right have you to do these things? Who gave you this right?"

3 Jesus answered them, "Now let me ask you a question. Tell me, [4]did John's right to baptize come from God or from human beings?"

5 They started to argue among themselves, "What shall we say? If we say, 'From God,' he will say, 'Why, then, did you not believe John?' [6]But if we say 'From human beings,' this whole crowd here will stone us, because they are convinced that John was a prophet." [7]So they answered, "We don't know where it came from."

8 And Jesus said to them, "Neither will I tell you, then, by what right I do these things."

The Parable of the Tenants in the Vineyard
(Mt 21.33–46; Mk 12.1–12)

9 Then Jesus told the people this parable: "There was once a man who planted a vineyard, let it out to tenants, and then left home for a long time. [10]When the time came to gather the grapes, he sent a slave to the tenants to receive from them his share of the harvest. But the tenants beat the slave and sent him back without a thing. [11]So he sent another slave; but the tenants beat him also, treated him shamefully, and sent him back without a thing. [12]Then he sent a third slave; the tenants wounded him, too, and threw him out. [13]Then the owner of the vineyard said, 'What shall I do? I will send my own dear son; surely they will respect him!' [14]But when the tenants saw him, they said to one another, 'This is the owner's son. Let's kill him, and his property will be ours!' [15]So they threw him out of the vineyard and killed him.

"What, then, will the owner of the vineyard do to the tenants?" Jesus asked. [16]"He will come and kill those men, and hand the vineyard over to other tenants."

When the people heard this, they said, "Surely not!"

17 Jesus looked at them and asked, "What, then, does this scripture mean?

'The stone which the builders rejected as
    worthless
turned out to be the most important of all.'

18 Everyone who falls on that stone will be cut to pieces; and if that stone falls on someone, it will crush him to dust."

The Question about Paying Taxes
(Mt 22.15–22; Mk 12.13–17)

19 The teachers of the Law and the chief priests tried to arrest Jesus on the spot, because they knew that he had told this

parable against them; but they were afraid of the people. ²⁰So they looked for an opportunity. They bribed some men to pretend they were sincere, and they sent them to trap Jesus with questions, so that they could hand him over to the authority and power of the Roman Governor. ²¹These spies said to Jesus, "Teacher, we know that what you say and teach is right. We know that you pay no attention to anyone's status, but teach the truth about God's will for people. ²²Tell us, is it against our Law for us to pay taxes to the Roman Emperor, or not?"

23   But Jesus saw through their trick and said to them, ²⁴"Show me a silver coin. Whose face and name are these on it?"

"The Emperor's," they answered.

25   So Jesus said, "Well, then, pay the Emperor what belongs to the Emperor, and pay God what belongs to God."

26   There before the people they could not catch him out in anything, so they kept quiet, amazed at his answer.

The Question about Rising from Death
(Mt 22.23–33; Mk 12.18–27)

27   Then some Sadducees, who say that people will not rise from death, came to Jesus and said, ²⁸"Teacher, Moses wrote this law for us: 'If a man dies and leaves a wife but no children, that man's brother must marry the widow so that they can have children who will be considered the dead man's children.' ²⁹Once there were seven brothers; the eldest got married and died without having children. ³⁰Then the second one married the woman, ³¹and then the third. The same thing happened to all seven – they died without having children. ³²Last of all, the woman died. ³³Now, on the day when the dead rise to life, whose wife will she be? All seven of them had married her."

34   Jesus answered them, "The men and women of this age marry, ³⁵but the men and women who are worthy to rise from death and live in the age to come will not then marry. ³⁶They will be like angels and cannot die. They are the children of God, because they have risen from death. ³⁷And Moses clearly proves that the dead are raised to life. In the passage about the burning bush he speaks of the Lord as 'the God of Abraham, the God of Isaac, and the God of Jacob.' ³⁸He is the God of the living, not of the dead, for to him all are alive."

39   Some of the teachers of the Law spoke up, "A good answer, Teacher!" ⁴⁰For they did not dare ask him any more questions.

The Question about the Messiah
(Mt 22.41–46; Mk 12.35–37)

41   Jesus asked them, "How can it be said that the Messiah will be the descendant of David? ⁴²For David himself says in the book of Psalms,

'The Lord said to my Lord:
    Sit here on my right
43   until I put your enemies as a footstool
        under your feet.'

⁴⁴David called him 'Lord'; how, then, can the Messiah be David's descendant?"

Jesus Warns against the Teachers of the Law
(Mt 23.1–36; Mk 12.38–40)

45   As all the people listened to him, Jesus said to his disciples, ⁴⁶"Be on your guard against the teachers of the Law, who like to walk about in their long robes and love to be greeted with respect in the market place; who choose the reserved seats in the synagogues and the best places at feasts; ⁴⁷who take advantage of widows and rob them of their homes, and then make a show of saying long prayers! Their punishment will be all the worse!"

The Widow's Offering
(Mk 12.41–44)

21 Jesus looked round and saw rich people dropping their gifts in the temple treasury, ²and he also saw a very poor widow dropping in two little copper coins. ³He said, "I tell you that this poor widow put in more than all the others. ⁴For the others offered their gifts from what they had to spare of their riches; but she, poor as she is, gave all she had to live on."

Jesus Speaks of the Destruction of the Temple
(Mt 24.1–2; Mk 13.1–2)

5   Some of the disciples were talking about the Temple, how beautiful it looked with its fine stones and the gifts offered to God. Jesus said, ⁶"All this you see – the time will come when not a single stone here will be left in its place; every one will be thrown down."

Troubles and Persecutions
(Mt 24.3–14; Mk 13.3–13)

7   "Teacher," they asked, "when will this be? And what will happen in order to show that the time has come for it to take place?"

8️⃣

ᅠᅠᅠᅠ

ᅠᅠᅠᅠᅠᅠᅠ

8 Jesus said, "Be on guard; don't be deceived. Many men, claiming to speak for me, will come and say, 'I am he!' and, 'The time has come!' But don't follow them. ⁹Don't be afraid when you hear of wars and revolutions; such things must happen first, but they do not mean that the end is near."

10 He went on to say, "Countries will fight each other; kingdoms will attack one another. ¹¹There will be terrible earthquakes, famines, and plagues everywhere; there will be strange and terrifying things coming from the sky. ¹²Before all these things take place, however, you will be arrested and persecuted; you will be handed over to be tried in synagogues and be put in prison; you will be brought before kings and rulers for my sake. ¹³This will be your chance to tell the Good News. ¹⁴Make up your minds beforehand not to worry about how you will defend yourselves, ¹⁵because I will give you such words and wisdom that none of your enemies will be able to refute or contradict what you say. ¹⁶You will be handed over by your parents, your brothers, your relatives, and your friends; and some of you will be put to death. ¹⁷Everyone will hate you because of me. ¹⁸But not a single hair from your heads will be lost. ¹⁹Stand firm, and you will save yourselves.

Jesus Speaks of the Destruction of Jerusalem
(Mt 24.15–21; Mk 13.14–19)

20 "When you see Jerusalem surrounded by armies, then you will know that it will soon be destroyed. ²¹Then those who are in Judea must run away to the hills; those who are in the city must leave, and those who are out in the country must not go into the city. ²²For those will be 'The Days of Punishment', to make all that the Scriptures say come true. ²³How terrible it will be in those days for women who are pregnant and for mothers with little babies! Terrible distress will come upon this land, and God's punishment will fall on this people. ²⁴Some will be killed by the sword, and others will be taken as prisoners to all countries; and the heathen will trample over Jerusalem until their time is up.

The Coming of the Son of Man
(Mt 24.29–31; Mk 13.24–27)

25 "There will be strange things happening to the sun, the moon, and the stars. On earth whole countries will be in despair, afraid of the roar of the sea and the raging tides. ²⁶People will faint from fear as they wait for what is coming over the whole earth, for the powers in space will be driven from their courses. ²⁷Then the Son of Man will appear, coming in a cloud with great power and glory. ²⁸When these things begin to happen, stand up and raise your heads, because your salvation is near."

The Lesson of the Fig Tree
(Mt 24.32–35; Mk 13.28–31)

29 Then Jesus told them this parable: "Think of the fig tree and all the other trees. ³⁰When you see their leaves beginning to appear, you know that summer is near. ³¹In the same way, when you see these things happening, you will know that the Kingdom of God is about to come.

32 "Remember that all these things will take place before the people now living have all died. ³³Heaven and earth will pass away, but my words will never pass away.

The Need to Watch

34 "Be on your guard! Don't let yourselves become occupied with too much feasting and drinking and with the worries of this life, or that Day may suddenly catch you ³⁵like a trap. For it will come upon all people everywhere on earth. ³⁶Be on the alert and pray always that you will have the strength to go safely through all those things that will happen and to stand before the Son of Man."

37 Jesus spent those days teaching in the Temple, and when evening came, he would go out and spend the night on the Mount of Olives. ³⁸Early each morning all the people went to the Temple to listen to him.

The Plot against Jesus
(Mt 26.1–5; Mk 14.1–2; Jn 11.45–53)

22 The time was near for the Festival of Unleavened Bread, which is called the Passover. ²The chief priests and the teachers of the Law were afraid of the people, and so they were trying to find a way of putting Jesus to death secretly.

Judas Agrees to Betray Jesus
(Mt 26.14–16; Mk 14.10–11)

3 Then Satan entered Judas, called Iscariot, who was one of the twelve disciples. ⁴So Judas went off and spoke with the chief priests and the officers of the temple guard about how he could betray Jesus to them. ⁵They were pleased and offered to pay him money. ⁶Judas agreed to it and started

looking for a good chance to hand Jesus over to them without the people knowing about it.

Jesus Prepares to Eat the Passover Meal
(Mt 26.17–25; Mk 14.12–21; Jn 13.21–30)

7   The day came during the Festival of Unleavened Bread when the lambs for the Passover meal were to be killed. [8]Jesus sent off Peter and John with these instructions: "Go and get the Passover meal ready for us to eat."

9   "Where do you want us to get it ready?" they asked him.

10   He answered, "As you go into the city, a man carrying a jar of water will meet you. Follow him into the house that he enters, [11]and say to the owner of the house: 'The Teacher says to you, Where is the room where my disciples and I will eat the Passover meal?' [12]He will show you a large furnished room upstairs, where you will get everything ready."

13   They went off and found everything just as Jesus had told them, and they prepared the Passover meal.

The Lord's Supper
(Mt 26.26–30; Mk 14.22–26; 1 Cor. 11.23–25)

14   When the hour came, Jesus took his place at the table with the apostles. [15]He said to them, "I have wanted so much to eat this Passover meal with you before I suffer! [16]For I tell you, I will never eat it until it is given its full meaning in the Kingdom of God."

17   Then Jesus took a cup, gave thanks to God, and said, "Take this and share it among yourselves. [18]I tell you that from now on I will not drink this wine until the Kingdom of God comes."

19   Then he took a piece of bread, gave thanks to God, broke it, and gave it to them, saying, "This is my body, which is given for you. Do this in memory of me." [20]In the same way, he gave them the cup after the supper, saying, "This cup is God's new covenant sealed with my blood, which is poured out for you.[a]

21   "But, look! The one who betrays me is here at the table with me! [22]The Son of Man will die as God has decided, but how terrible for that man who betrays him!"

23   Then they began to ask among themselves which one of them it could be who was going to do this.

The Argument about Greatness

24   An argument broke out among the disciples as to which one of them should be thought of as the greatest. [25]Jesus said to them, "The kings of the pagans have power over their people, and the rulers claim the title 'Friends of the People'. [26]But this is not the way it is with you; rather, the greatest one among you must be like the youngest, and the leader must be like the servant. [27]Who is greater, the one who sits down to eat or the one who serves? The one who sits down, of course. But I am among you as one who serves.

28   "You have stayed with me all through my trials; [29]and just as my Father has given me the right to rule, so I will give you the same right. [30]You will eat and drink at my table in my Kingdom, and you will sit on thrones to rule over the twelve tribes of Israel.

Jesus Predicts Peter's Denial
(Mt 26.31–35; Mk 14.27–31; Jn 13.36–38)

31   "Simon, Simon! Listen! Satan has received permission to test all of you, to separate the good from the bad, as a farmer separates the wheat from the chaff. [32]But I have prayed for you, Simon, that your faith will not fail. And when you turn back to me, you must strengthen your brothers."

33   Peter answered, "Lord, I am ready to go to prison with you and to die with you!"

34   "I tell you, Peter," Jesus said, "the cock will not crow tonight until you have said three times that you do not know me."

Purse, Bag, and Sword

35   Then Jesus asked his disciples, "When I sent you out that time without purse, bag, or shoes, did you lack anything?"

"Not a thing," they answered.

36   "But now," Jesus said, "whoever has a purse or a bag must take it; and whoever has no sword must sell his coat and buy one. [37]For I tell you that the scripture which says, 'He shared the fate of criminals,' must come true about me, because what was written about me is coming true."

38   The disciples said, "Look! Here are two swords, Lord!"

"That is enough!"[b] he replied.

---

[a] **22.20** Some manuscripts do not have the words of Jesus after This is my body *in verse 19, and all of verse 20.*

[b] **22.38** That is enough; *or* Enough of this.

A statue in the Garden of Gethsemane at the place where Jesus traditionally prayed

Jesus Prays on the Mount of Olives
(Mt 26.36–46; Mk 14.32–42)

39 Jesus left the city and went, as he usually did, to the Mount of Olives; and the disciples went with him. ⁴⁰When he arrived at the place, he said to them, "Pray that you will not fall into temptation."

41 Then he went off from them about the distance of a stone's throw and knelt down and prayed. ⁴²"Father," he said, "if you will, take this cup of suffering away from me. Not my will, however, but your will be done." ⁴³An angel from heaven appeared to him and strengthened him. ⁴⁴In great anguish he prayed even more fervently; his sweat was like drops of blood falling to the ground.ᵃ

45 Rising from his prayer, he went back to the disciples and found them asleep, worn out by their grief. ⁴⁶He said to them, "Why are you sleeping? Get up and pray that you will not fall into temptation."

The Arrest of Jesus
(Mt 26.47–56; Mk 14.43–50; Jn 18.3–11)

47 Jesus was still speaking when a crowd arrived, led by Judas, one of the twelve disciples. He came up to Jesus to kiss him. ⁴⁸But Jesus said, "Judas, is it with a kiss that you betray the Son of Man?"

49 When the disciples who were with Jesus saw what was going to happen, they asked, "Shall we use our swords, Lord?" ⁵⁰And one of them struck the High Priest's slave and cut off his right ear.

51 But Jesus said, "Enough of this!" He touched the man's ear and healed him.

52 Then Jesus said to the chief priests and the officers of the temple guard and the elders who had come there to get him, "Did you have to come with swords and clubs, as though I were an outlaw? ⁵³I was with you in the Temple every day, and you did not try to arrest me. But this is your hour to act, when the power of darkness rules."

Peter Denies Jesus
(Mt 26.57–58, 69–75; Mk 14.53–54, 66–72; Jn 18.12–18, 25–27)

54 They arrested Jesus and took him away into the house of the High Priest; and Peter followed at a distance. ⁵⁵A fire had been lit in the centre of the courtyard, and Peter joined those who were sitting round it. ⁵⁶When one of the servant women saw him sitting there at the fire, she looked straight at him and said, "This man too was with Jesus!"

57 But Peter denied it, "Woman, I don't even know him!"

58 After a little while a man noticed Peter and said, "You are one of them, too!"

But Peter answered, "Man, I am not!"

59 And about an hour later another man insisted strongly, "There isn't any doubt that this man was with Jesus, because he also is a Galilean!"

60 But Peter answered, "Man, I don't know what you are talking about!"

At once, while he was still speaking, a cock crowed. ⁶¹The Lord turned round and looked straight at Peter, and Peter remembered that the Lord had said to him, "Before the cock crows tonight, you will say three times that you do not know me." ⁶²Peter went out and wept bitterly.

Jesus is Mocked and Beaten
(Mt 26.67–68; Mk 14.65)

63 The men who were guarding Jesus mocked him and beat him. ⁶⁴They blindfolded him and asked him, "Who hit you? Guess!" ⁶⁵And they said many other insulting things to him.

ᵃ **22.44** *Some manuscripts do not have verses 43–44.*

Jesus is Brought before the Council
(Mt 26.59–66; Mk 14.55–64; Jn 18.19–24)

66 When day came, the elders, the chief priests, and the teachers of the Law met together, and Jesus was brought before the Council. [67]"Tell us," they said, "are you the Messiah?"

He answered, "If I tell you, you will not believe me; [68]and if I ask you a question, you will not answer. [69]But from now on the Son of Man will be seated on the right of Almighty God."

70 They all said, "Are you, then, the Son of God?"

He answered them, "You say that I am."

71 And they said, "We don't need any witnesses! We ourselves have heard what he said!"

Jesus is Brought before Pilate
(Mt 27.1–2, 11–14; Mk 15.1–5; Jn 18.28–38)

23 The whole group rose up and took Jesus before Pilate, [2]where they began to accuse him: "We caught this man misleading our people, telling them not to pay taxes to the Emperor and claiming that he himself is the Messiah, a king."

3 Pilate asked him, "Are you the king of the Jews?"

"So you say," answered Jesus.

4 Then Pilate said to the chief priests and the crowds, "I find no reason to condemn this man."

5 But they insisted even more strongly, "With his teaching he is starting a riot among the people all through Judea. He began in Galilee and now has come here."

Jesus is Sent to Herod

6 When Pilate heard this, he asked, "Is this man a Galilean?" [7]When he learnt that Jesus was from the region ruled by Herod, he sent him to Herod, who was also in Jerusalem at that time. [8]Herod was very pleased when he saw Jesus, because he had heard about him and had been wanting to see him for a long time. He was hoping to see Jesus perform some miracle. [9]So Herod asked Jesus many questions, but Jesus made no answer. [10]The chief priests and the teachers of the Law stepped forward and made strong accusations against Jesus. [11]Herod and his soldiers mocked Jesus and treated him with contempt; then they put a fine robe on him and sent him back to Pilate. [12]On that very day Herod and Pilate became friends; before this they had been enemies.

Jesus is Sentenced to Death
(Mt 27.15–26; Mk 15.6–15; Jn 18.39—19.16)

13 Pilate called together the chief priests, the leaders, and the people, [14]and said to them, "You brought this man to me and said that he was misleading the people. Now, I have examined him here in your presence, and I have not found him guilty of any of the crimes you accuse him of. [15]Nor did Herod find him guilty, for he sent him back to us. There is nothing this man has done to deserve death. [16]So I will have him whipped and let him go."[a]

18 The whole crowd cried out, "Kill him! Set Barabbas free for us!" [19](Barabbas had been put in prison for a riot that had taken place in the city, and for murder.)

20 Pilate wanted to set Jesus free, so he appealed to the crowd again. [21]But they shouted back, "Crucify him! Crucify him!"

22 Pilate said to them the third time, "But what crime has he committed? I cannot find anything he has done to deserve death! I will have him whipped and set him free."

23 But they kept on shouting at the top of their voices that Jesus should be crucified, and finally their shouting succeeded. [24]So Pilate passed the sentence on Jesus that they were asking for. [25]He set free the man they wanted, the one who had been put in prison for riot and murder, and he handed Jesus over for them to do as they wished.

Jesus is Crucified
(Mt 27.32–44; Mk 15.21–32; Jn 19.17–27)

26 The soldiers led Jesus away, and as they were going, they met a man from Cyrene named Simon who was coming into the city from the country. They seized him, put the cross on him, and made him carry it behind Jesus.

27 A large crowd of people followed him; among them were some women who were weeping and wailing for him. [28]Jesus turned to them and said, "Women of Jerusalem! Don't cry for me, but for yourselves and your children. [29]For the days are coming when people will say, 'How lucky are the women who never had children, who never bore babies, who never nursed them!' [30]That will be the time when people will say to the mountains, 'Fall on us!' and to the hills, 'Hide us!' [31]For if such things as these are done when the wood is green, what will happen when it is dry?"

32 Two other men, both of them criminals, were

[a] **23.16** *Some manuscripts add verse 17:* At every Passover Festival Pilate had to set free one prisoner for them (*see Mk 15.6*).

A Station of the Cross showing Jesus carrying his cross

38 Above him were written these words: "This is the King of the Jews."

39 One of the criminals hanging there hurled insults at him: "Aren't you the Messiah? Save yourself and us!"

40 The other one, however, rebuked him, saying, "Don't you fear God? You received the same sentence he did. ⁴¹Ours, however, is only right, because we are getting what we deserve for what we did; but he has done no wrong." ⁴²And he said to Jesus, "Remember me, Jesus, when you come as King!"

43 Jesus said to him, "I promise you that today you will be in Paradise with me."

The Death of Jesus
(Mt 27.45–56; Mk 15.33–41; Jn 19.28–30)

44–45 It was about twelve o'clock when the sun stopped shining and darkness covered the whole country until three o'clock; and the curtain hanging in the Temple was torn in two. ⁴⁶Jesus cried out in a loud voice, "Father! In your hands I place my spirit!" He said this and died.

47 The army officer saw what had happened, and he praised God, saying, "Certainly he was a good man!"

48 When the people who had gathered there to watch the spectacle saw what happened, they all went back home, beating their breasts in sorrow. ⁴⁹All those who knew Jesus personally, including the women who had followed him from Galilee, stood at a distance to watch.

The Burial of Jesus
(Mt 27.57–61; Mk 15.42–47; Jn 19.38–42)

50–51 There was a man named Joseph from Arimathea, a town in Judea. He was a good and honourable man, who was waiting for the coming of the Kingdom of God. Although he was a member of the Council, he had not agreed with their decision and action. ⁵²He went into the presence of Pilate and asked for the body of Jesus. ⁵³Then he took the body down, wrapped it in a linen sheet, and placed it in a tomb which had been dug out of solid rock and which had never been used. ⁵⁴It was Friday, and the Sabbath was about to begin.

55 The women who had followed Jesus from Galilee went with Joseph and saw the tomb and how Jesus' body was placed in it. ⁵⁶Then they went back home and prepared the spices and perfumes for the body.

On the Sabbath they rested, as the Law commanded.

also led out to be put to death with Jesus. ³³When they came to the place called "The Skull", they crucified Jesus there, and the two criminals, one on his right and the other on his left. ³⁴Jesus said, "Forgive them, Father! They don't know what they are doing."ᵃ

They divided his clothes among themselves by throwing dice. ³⁵The people stood there watching while the Jewish leaders jeered at him: "He saved others; let him save himself if he is the Messiah whom God has chosen!"

36 The soldiers also mocked him: they came up to him and offered him cheap wine, ³⁷and said, "Save yourself if you are the king of the Jews!"

ᵃ **23.34** *Some manuscripts do not have* Jesus said, "Forgive them, Father! They don't know what they are doing."

The Resurrection
(Mt 28.1–10; Mk 16.1–8; Jn 20.1–10)

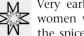 **24** Very early on Sunday morning the women went to the tomb, carrying the spices they had prepared. ²They found the stone rolled away from the entrance to the tomb, ³so they went in; but they did not find the body of the Lord Jesus. ⁴They stood there puzzled about this, when suddenly two men in bright shining clothes stood by them. ⁵Full of fear, the women bowed down to the ground, as the men said to them, "Why are you looking among the dead for one who is alive? ⁶He is not here; he has been raised. Remember what he said to you while he was in Galilee: ⁷'The Son of Man must be handed over to sinners, be crucified, and three days later rise to life.'"

8 Then the women remembered his words, ⁹returned from the tomb, and told all these things to the eleven disciples and all the rest. ¹⁰The women were Mary Magdalene, Joanna, and Mary the mother of James; they and the other women with them told these things to the apostles. ¹¹But the apostles thought that what the women said was nonsense, and they did not believe them. ¹²But Peter got up and ran to the tomb; he bent down and saw the linen wrappings but nothing else. Then he went back home amazed at what had happened.ᵃ

The Walk to Emmaus
(Mk 16.12–13)

13 On that same day two of Jesus' followers were going to a village named Emmaus, about 11 kilometres from Jerusalem, ¹⁴and they were talking to each other about all the things that had happened. ¹⁵As they talked and discussed, Jesus himself drew near and walked along with them; ¹⁶they saw him, but somehow did not recognize him. ¹⁷Jesus said to them, "What are you talking about to each other, as you walk along?"

They stood still, with sad faces. ¹⁸One of them, named Cleopas, asked him, "Are you the only visitor in Jerusalem who doesn't know the things that have been happening there these last few days?"

19 "What things?" he asked.

"The things that happened to Jesus of Nazareth," they answered. "This man was a prophet and was considered by God and by all the people to be powerful in everything he said and did. ²⁰Our chief priests and rulers handed him over to be sentenced to death, and he was crucified. ²¹And we had hoped that he would be the one who was going to set Israel free! Besides all that, this is now the third day since it happened. ²²Some of the women of our group surprised us; they went at dawn to the tomb, ²³but could not find his body. They came back saying they had seen a vision of angels who told them that he is alive. ²⁴Some of our group went to the tomb and found it exactly as the women had said, but they did not see him."

25 Then Jesus said to them, "How foolish you are, how slow you are to believe everything the prophets said! ²⁶Was it not necessary for the Messiah to suffer these things and then to enter his glory?" ²⁷And Jesus explained to them what was said about himself in all the Scriptures, beginning with the books of Moses and the writings of all the prophets.

28 As they came near the village to which they were going, Jesus acted as if he were going farther; ²⁹but they held him back, saying, "Stay with us; the day is almost over and it is getting dark." So he went in to stay with them. ³⁰He sat down to eat with them, took the bread, and said the blessing; then he broke the bread and gave it to them. ³¹Then their eyes were opened and they recognized him, but he disappeared from their sight. ³²They said to each other, "Wasn't it like a fire burning in us when he talked to us on the road and explained the Scriptures to us?"

33 They got up at once and went back to Jerusalem, where they found the eleven disciples gathered together with the others ³⁴and saying, "The Lord is risen indeed! He has appeared to Simon!"

35 The two then explained to them what had happened on the road, and how they had recognized the Lord when he broke the bread.

Jesus Appears to his Disciples
(Mt 28.16–20; Mk 16.14–18; Jn 20.19–23; Acts 1.6–8)

36 While the two were telling them this, suddenly the Lord himself stood among them and said to them, "Peace be with you."ᵇ

37 They were terrified, thinking that they were seeing a ghost. ³⁸But he said to them, "Why are you alarmed? Why are these doubts coming up in your minds? ³⁹Look at my hands and my feet, and see that it is I myself. Feel me, and you will know, for a ghost doesn't have flesh and bones, as you can see I have."

ᵃ **24.12** *Some manuscripts do not have verse 12.*

ᵇ **24.36** *Some manuscripts do not have* and said to them, "Peace be with you."

40 He said this and showed them his hands and his feet.[a] [41]They still could not believe, they were so full of joy and wonder; so he asked them, "Have you anything here to eat?" [42]They gave him a piece of cooked fish, [43]which he took and ate in their presence.

44 Then he said to them, "These are the very things I told you about while I was still with you: everything written about me in the Law of Moses, the writings of the prophets, and the Psalms had to come true."

45 Then he opened their minds to understand the Scriptures, [46]and said to them, "This is what is written: the Messiah must suffer and must rise from death three days later, [47]and in his name the message about repentance and the forgiveness of sins must be preached to all nations, beginning in Jerusalem. [48]You are witnesses of these things. [49]And I myself will send upon you what my Father has promised. But you must wait in the city until the power from above comes down upon you."

Jesus is Taken Up to Heaven
(Mk 16.19–20; Acts 1.9–11)

50 Then he led them out of the city as far as Bethany, where he raised his hands and blessed them. [51]As he was blessing them, he departed from them and was taken up into heaven.[b] [52]They worshipped him and went back into Jerusalem, filled with great joy, [53]and spent all their time in the Temple giving thanks to God.

[a] **24.40** *Some manuscripts do not have verse 40.*
[b] **24.51** *Some manuscripts do not have* and was taken up into heaven.

The Gospel according to
JOHN

INTRODUCTION

The Gospel according to John presents Jesus as the eternal Word of God, who "became a human being and lived among us" (1.14). As the book itself says, this Gospel was written so that its readers might believe that Jesus is the promised Saviour, the Son of God, and that through their faith in him they might have life (20.31).

After an introduction that identifies the eternal Word of God with Jesus, the first part of the Gospel presents various miracles which show that Jesus is the promised Saviour, the Son of God. These are followed by discourses that explain what is revealed by the miracles. This part of the book tells how some people believed in Jesus and became his followers, while others opposed him and refused to believe. Chapters 13–17 record at length the close fellowship of Jesus with his disciples on the night of his arrest, and his words of preparation and encouragement to them on the eve of his crucifixion. The closing chapters tell of Jesus' arrest and trial, his crucifixion and resurrection, and his appearances to his disciples after the resurrection.

The story of the woman caught in adultery (8.1–11) is placed in brackets because many manuscripts and early translations omit it, while others include it in other places.

John emphasizes the gift of eternal life through Christ, a gift which begins now and which comes to those who respond to Jesus as the way, the truth, and the life. A striking feature of *John* is the symbolic use of common things from everyday life to point to spiritual realities, such as water, bread, light, the shepherd and his sheep, and the grapevine and its fruit.

Outline of Contents

The Word of Life

1 In the beginning the Word already existed; the Word was with God, and the Word was God. ²From the very beginning the Word was with God. ³Through him God made all things; not one thing in all creation was made without him. ⁴The Word was the source of life,ᵃ and this life brought light to humanity. ⁵The light shines in the darkness, and the darkness has never put it out.

ᵃ **1.4** The Word was the source of life; *or* What was made had life in union with the Word.

6 God sent his messenger, a man named John, ⁷who came to tell people about the light, so that all should hear the message and believe. ⁸He himself was not the light; he came to tell about the light. ⁹This was the real light – the light that comes into the world and shines on everyone.

10 The Word was in the world, and though God made the world through him, yet the world did not recognize him. ¹¹He came to his own country, but his own people did not receive him. ¹²Some, however, did receive him and believed in him; so he gave them the right to become God's children. ¹³They did not become God's children by natural means, that is, by being born

as the children of a human father; God himself was their Father.

14   The Word became a human being and, full of grace and truth, lived among us. We saw his glory, the glory which he received as the Father's only Son.

15   John spoke about him. He cried out, "This is the one I was talking about when I said, 'He comes after me, but he is greater than I am, because he existed before I was born.'"

16   Out of the fullness of his grace he has blessed us all, giving us one blessing after another. ¹⁷God gave the Law through Moses, but grace and truth came through Jesus Christ. ¹⁸No one has ever seen God. The only Son, who is the same as God and is at the Father's side, he has made him known.

John the Baptist's Message
(Mt 3.1–12; Mk 1.1–8; Lk 3.1–18)

19   The Jewish authorities in Jerusalem sent some priests and Levites to John, to ask him, "Who are you?"

20   John did not refuse to answer, but spoke out openly and clearly, saying: "I am not the Messiah."

21   "Who are you, then?" they asked. "Are you Elijah?"

"No, I am not," John answered.

"Are you the Prophet?"ᵃ they asked.

"No," he replied.

22   "Then tell us who you are," they said. "We have to take an answer back to those who sent us. What do you say about yourself?"

23   John answered by quoting the prophet Isaiah:

"I am 'the voice of someone shouting in the desert:
    Make a straight path for the Lord to travel!'"

24   The messengers, who had been sent by the Pharisees, ²⁵thenᵇ asked John, "If you are not the Messiah nor Elijah nor the Prophet, why do you baptize?"

26   John answered, "I baptize with water, but among you stands the one you do not know. ²⁷He is coming after me, but I am not good enough even to untie his sandals."

28   All this happened in Bethany on the east side of the River Jordan, where John was baptizing.

ᵃ **1.21** THE PROPHET: *The one who was expected to appear and announce the coming of the Messiah.*
ᵇ **1.25** The messengers, who had been sent by the Pharisees, then; *or* Those who had been sent were Pharisees; they.

Studying
JOHN

Who wrote it? According to tradition, John the Apostle, but most people today think author was an unknown disciple of John.
When? Around 95 CE, the last Gospel to be written.
Where from? Most likely to have been written in Ephesus, in Asia Minor, a city long associated with John.
For whom? With both Gentile and Jewish readers in mind. The author shows a good knowledge of Jewish customs, yet Gospel also uses many Greek ideas.
Why? The writer states his aim in 20.31. He hopes that readers will be confirmed in their belief that Jesus (the Messiah) is God on earth. Clement of Alexandria (2nd century) remarked that, after the Synoptic Gospels, John wrote a "spiritual Gospel".

KEY POINTS
- Gospel is one of believing and life. True life comes through believing in Jesus.
- John does not include any parables of Jesus.
- John has distinctive ways of referring to Jesus – as the Word of God, the Light of the World, the Bread of Life; the Good Shepherd, etc. – not found in the Synoptics.
- The Holy Spirit – the Helper, the Counsellor and the Advocate – more prominent than in other Gospels.

The Lamb of God

29   The next day John saw Jesus coming to him, and said, "There is the Lamb of God, who takes away the sin of the world! ³⁰This is the one I was talking about when I said, 'A man is coming after me, but he is greater than I am, because he existed before I was born.' ³¹I did not know who he would be, but I came baptizing with water in order to make him known to the people of Israel."

32   And John gave this testimony: "I saw the Spirit come down like a dove from heaven and stay on him. ³³I still did not know that he was the one, but God, who sent me to baptize with water, had said to me, 'You will see the Spirit come down and stay on a man; he is the one who baptizes with the Holy Spirit.' ³⁴I have seen it," said John, "and I tell you that he is the Son of God."

The First Disciples of Jesus

35   The next day John was standing there again with two of his disciples, ³⁶when he saw Jesus walking by. "There is the Lamb of God!" he said.

37   The two disciples heard him say this and went with Jesus. ³⁸Jesus turned, saw them following him, and asked, "What are you looking for?"

A 13th-century sculpture of John the Baptist pointing at the Lamb of God (1.35)

They answered, "Where do you live, Rabbi?" (This word means "Teacher".)

39 "Come and see," he answered. (It was then about four o'clock in the afternoon.) So they went with him and saw where he lived, and spent the rest of that day with him.

40 One of them was Andrew, Simon Peter's brother. ⁴¹At once he found his brother Simon and told him, "We have found the Messiah." (This word means "Christ".) ⁴²Then he took Simon to Jesus.

Jesus looked at him and said, "Your name is Simon son of John, but you will be called Cephas." (This is the same as Peter and means "a rock".)

Jesus Calls Philip and Nathanael

43 The next day Jesus decided to go to Galilee. He found Philip and said to him, "Come with me!" ⁴⁴(Philip was from Bethsaida, the town where Andrew and Peter lived.) ⁴⁵Philip found Nathanael and told him, "We have found the one whom Moses wrote about in the book of the Law and whom the prophets also wrote about. He is Jesus son of Joseph, from Nazareth."

46 "Can anything good come from Nazareth?" Nathanael asked.

"Come and see," answered Philip.

47 When Jesus saw Nathanael coming to him, he said about him, "Here is a real Israelite; there is nothing false in him!"

48 Nathanael asked him, "How do you know me?"

Jesus answered, "I saw you when you were under the fig tree before Philip called you."

49 "Teacher," answered Nathanael, "you are the Son of God! You are the King of Israel!"

50 Jesus said, "Do you believe just because I told you I saw you when you were under the fig tree? You will see much greater things than this!" ⁵¹And he said to them, "I am telling you the truth: you will see heaven open and God's angels going up and coming down on the Son of Man."

The Wedding in Cana

2 Two days later there was a wedding in the town of Cana in Galilee. Jesus' mother was there, ²and Jesus and his disciples had also been invited to the wedding. ³When the wine had given out, Jesus' mother said to him, "They have no wine left."

4 "You must not tell me what to do," Jesus replied. "My time has not yet come."

5 Jesus' mother then told the servants, "Do whatever he tells you."

6 The Jews have rules about ritual washing, and for this purpose six stone water jars were there, each one large enough to hold about a hundred litres. ⁷Jesus said to the servants, "Fill these jars with water." They filled them to the brim, ⁸and then he told them, "Now draw some water out and take it to the man in charge of the feast." They took him the water, ⁹which now had turned into wine, and he tasted it. He did not know where this wine had come from (but, of course, the servants who had drawn out the water knew); so he called the bridegroom ¹⁰and said to him, "Everyone else serves the best wine first, and after the guests have had plenty to drink, he serves the ordinary wine. But you have kept the best wine until now!"

11 Jesus performed this first miracle in Cana in Galilee; there he revealed his glory, and his disciples believed in him.

12 After this, Jesus and his mother, brothers, and disciples went to Capernaum and stayed there a few days.

Jesus Goes to the Temple
(Mt 21.12–13; Mk 11.15–17; Lk 19.45–46)

13 It was almost time for the Passover Festival, so Jesus went to Jerusalem. ¹⁴There in the Temple

he found people selling cattle, sheep, and pigeons, and also the moneychangers sitting at their tables. ¹⁵So he made a whip from cords and drove all the animals out of the Temple, both the sheep and the cattle; he overturned the tables of the moneychangers and scattered their coins; ¹⁶and he ordered those who sold the pigeons, "Take them out of here! Stop making my Father's house a market place!" ¹⁷His disciples remembered that the scripture says, "My devotion to your house, O God, burns in me like a fire."

18 The Jewish authorities replied with a question, "What miracle can you perform to show us that you have the right to do this?"

19 Jesus answered, "Tear down this Temple, and in three days I will build it again."

20 "Are you going to build it again in three days?" they asked him. "It has taken forty-six years to build this Temple!"

21 But the temple Jesus was speaking about was his body. ²²So when he was raised from death, his disciples remembered that he had said this, and they believed the scripture and what Jesus had said.

Jesus' Knowledge of Human Nature

23 While Jesus was in Jerusalem during the Passover Festival, many believed in him as they saw the miracles he performed. ²⁴But Jesus did not trust himself to them, because he knew them all. ²⁵There was no need for anyone to tell him about them, because he himself knew what was in their hearts.

Jesus and Nicodemus

3 There was a Jewish leader named Nicodemus, who belonged to the party of the Pharisees. ²One night he went to Jesus and said to him, "Rabbi, we know that you are a teacher sent by God. No one could perform the miracles you are doing unless God were with him."

3 Jesus answered, "I am telling you the truth: no one can see the Kingdom of God without being born again."ᵃ

4 "How can a grown man be born again?" Nicodemus asked. "He certainly cannot enter his mother's womb and be born a second time!"

5 "I am telling you the truth," replied Jesus. "No one can enter the Kingdom of God without being born of water and the Spirit. ⁶A person is born physically of human parents, but is born spiritually of the Spirit. ⁷Do not be surprised because I tell you that you must all be born again.ᵃ ⁸The wind blows wherever it wishes; you hear the sound it makes, but you do not know where it comes from or where it is going. It is like that with everyone who is born of the Spirit."

9 "How can this be?" asked Nicodemus.

10 Jesus answered, "You are a great teacher in Israel, and you don't know this? ¹¹I am telling you the truth: we speak of what we know and report what we have seen, yet none of you is willing to accept our message. ¹²You do not believe me when I tell you about the things of this world; how will you ever believe me, then, when I tell you about the things of heaven? ¹³And no one has ever gone up to heaven except the Son of Man, who came down from heaven."ᵇ

14 As Moses lifted up the bronze snake on a pole in the desert, in the same way the Son of Man must be lifted up, ¹⁵so that everyone who believes in him may have eternal life. ¹⁶For God loved the world so much that he gave his only Son, so that everyone who believes in him may not die but have eternal life. ¹⁷For God did not send his Son into the world to be its judge, but to be its saviour.

18 Those who believe in the Son are not judged; but those who do not believe have already been judged, because they have not believed in God's only Son. ¹⁹This is how the judgement works: the light has come into the world, but people love the darkness rather than the light, because their deeds are evil. ²⁰All those who do evil things hate the light and will not come to the light, because they do not want their evil deeds to be shown up. ²¹But those who do what is true come to the light in order that the light may show that what they did was in obedience to God.

Jesus and John

22 After this, Jesus and his disciples went to the province of Judea, where he spent some time with them and baptized. ²³John also was baptizing in Aenon, not far from Salim, because there was plenty of water in that place. People were going to him, and he was baptizing them. ²⁴(This was before John had been put in prison.)

25 Some of John's disciples began arguing with a Jewᶜ about the matter of ritual washing. ²⁶So they went to John and said, "Teacher, you remember the man who was with you on the east side of the Jordan, the one you spoke about?

ᵃ **3.3, 3.7** again; *or* from above.

ᵇ **3.13** *The quotation may continue through verse 21.*

ᶜ **3.25** a Jew; *some manuscripts have* some Jews.

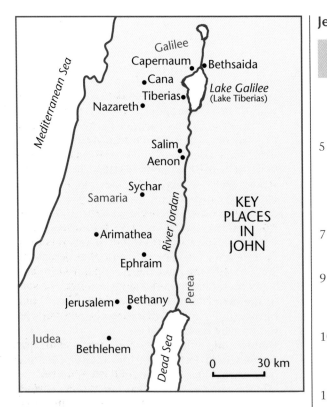

Well, he is baptizing now, and everyone is going to him!"

27   John answered, "No one can have anything unless God gives it to him. [28]You yourselves are my witnesses that I said, 'I am not the Messiah, but I have been sent ahead of him.' [29]The bridegroom is the one to whom the bride belongs; but the bridegroom's friend, who stands by and listens, is glad when he hears the bridegroom's voice. This is how my own happiness is made complete. [30]He must become more important while I become less important."

He who Comes from Heaven

31   He who comes from above is greater than all. He who is from the earth belongs to the earth and speaks about earthly matters, but he who comes from heaven is above all. [32]He tells what he has seen and heard, yet no one accepts his message. [33]But whoever accepts his message confirms by this that God is truthful. [34]The one whom God has sent speaks God's words, because God gives him the fullness of his Spirit. [35]The Father loves his Son and has put everything in his power. [36]Whoever believes in the Son has eternal life; whoever disobeys the Son will not have life, but will remain under God's punishment.

Jesus and the Samaritan Woman

4   The Pharisees heard that Jesus was winning and baptizing more disciples than John. [2](Actually, Jesus himself did not baptize anyone; only his disciples did.) [3]So when Jesus heard what was being said, he left Judea and went back to Galilee; [4]on his way there he had to go through Samaria.

5   In Samaria he came to a town named Sychar, which was not far from the field that Jacob had given to his son Joseph. [6]Jacob's well was there, and Jesus, tired out by the journey, sat down by the well. It was about noon.

7   A Samaritan woman came to draw some water, and Jesus said to her, "Give me a drink of water." [8](His disciples had gone into town to buy food.)

9   The woman answered, "You are a Jew, and I am a Samaritan – so how can you ask me for a drink?" (Jews will not use the same cups and bowls that Samaritans use.)[a]

10   Jesus answered, "If only you knew what God gives and who it is that is asking you for a drink, you would ask him, and he would give you life-giving water."

11   "Sir," the woman said, "you haven't got a bucket, and the well is deep. Where would you get that life-giving water? [12]It was our ancestor Jacob who gave us this well; he and his sons and his flocks all drank from it. You don't claim to be greater than Jacob, do you?"

13   Jesus answered, "All those who drink this water will be thirsty again, [14]but whoever drinks the water that I will give him will never be thirsty again. The water that I will give him will become in him a spring which will provide him with life-giving water and give him eternal life."

15   "Sir," the woman said, "give me that water! Then I will never be thirsty again, nor will I have to come here to draw water."

16   "Go and call your husband," Jesus told her, "and come back."

17   "I haven't got a husband," she answered.
Jesus replied, "You are right when you say you haven't got a husband. [18]You have been married to five men, and the man you live with now is not really your husband. You have told me the truth."

19   "I see you are a prophet, sir," the woman said. [20]"My Samaritan ancestors worshipped God on this mountain, but you Jews say that Jerusalem is the place where we should worship God."

---

[a] **4.9** Jews will not use the same cups and bowls that Samaritans use; *or* Jews will have nothing to do with Samaritans.

21 Jesus said to her, "Believe me, woman, the time will come when people will not worship the Father either on this mountain or in Jerusalem. 22You Samaritans do not really know whom you worship; but we Jews know whom we worship, because it is from the Jews that salvation comes. 23But the time is coming and is already here, when by the power of God's Spirit people will worship the Father as he really is, offering him the true worship that he wants. 24God is Spirit, and only by the power of his Spirit can people worship him as he really is."

25 The woman said to him, "I know that the Messiah will come, and when he comes, he will tell us everything."

26 Jesus answered, "I am he, I who am talking with you."

27 At that moment Jesus' disciples returned, and they were greatly surprised to find him talking with a woman. But none of them said to her, "What do you want?" or asked him, "Why are you talking with her?"

28 Then the woman left her water jar, went back to the town, and said to the people there, 29"Come and see the man who told me everything I have ever done. Could he be the Messiah?" 30So they left the town and went to Jesus.

31 In the meantime the disciples were begging Jesus, "Teacher, have something to eat!"

32 But he answered, "I have food to eat that you know nothing about."

33 So the disciples started asking among themselves, "Could somebody have brought him food?"

34 "My food," Jesus said to them, "is to obey the will of the one who sent me and to finish the work he gave me to do. 35You have a saying, 'Four more months and then the harvest.' But I tell you, take a good look at the fields; the crops are now ripe and ready to be harvested! 36The one who reaps the harvest is being paid and gathers the crops for eternal life; so another who sows and the one who reaps will be glad together. 37The saying is true, 'One sows, another reaps.' 38I have sent you to reap a harvest in a field where you did not work; others worked there, and you profit from their work."

39 Many of the Samaritans in that town believed in Jesus because the woman had said, "He told me everything I have ever done." 40So when the Samaritans came to him, they begged him to stay with them, and Jesus stayed there two days.

41 Many more believed because of his message, 42and they said to the woman, "We believe now, not because of what you said, but because we ourselves have heard him, and we know that he really is the Saviour of the world."

Jesus Heals an Official's Son

43 After spending two days there, Jesus left and went to Galilee. 44For he himself had said, "A prophet is not respected in his own country." 45When he arrived in Galilee, the people there welcomed him, because they had gone to the Passover Festival in Jerusalem and had seen everything that he had done during the festival.

46 Then Jesus went back to Cana in Galilee, where he had turned the water into wine. A government official was there whose son was ill in Capernaum. 47When he heard that Jesus had come from Judea to Galilee, he went to him and asked him to go to Capernaum and heal his son, who was about to die. 48Jesus said to him, "None of you will ever believe unless you see miracles and wonders."

49 "Sir," replied the official, "come with me before my child dies."

50 Jesus said to him, "Go, your son will live!"

The man believed Jesus' words and went. 51On his way home his servants met him with the news, "Your boy is going to live!"

52 He asked them what time it was when his son got better, and they answered, "It was one o'clock yesterday afternoon when the fever left him." 53Then the father remembered it was at that very hour that Jesus had told him, "Your son will live." So he and all his family believed.

54 This was the second miracle that Jesus performed after coming from Judea to Galilee.

The Healing at the Pool

5 After this, Jesus went to Jerusalem for a religious festival. 2Near the Sheep Gate in Jerusalem there is a poolª with five porches; in Hebrew it is called Bethzatha.b 3A large crowd of sick people were lying in the porches – the blind, the lame, and the paralysed.c 5A man was there who had been ill for 38 years. 6Jesus saw him lying there, and

ª **5.2** Near the Sheep Gate ... a pool; *or* Near the Sheep Pool ... a place.
b **5.2** Bethzatha; *some manuscripts have* Bethesda.
c **5.3** *Some manuscripts add verses 3b–4:* They were waiting for the water to move, 4because every now and then an angel of the Lord went down into the pool and stirred up the water. The first sick person to go into the pool after the water was stirred up was healed from whatever disease he had.

he knew that the man had been ill for such a long time; so he asked him, "Do you want to get well?"

7 The sick man answered, "Sir, I have no one here to put me in the pool when the water is stirred up; while I am trying to get in, somebody else gets there first."

8 Jesus said to him, "Get up, pick up your mat, and walk." [9]Immediately the man got well; he picked up his mat and started walking.

The day this happened was a Sabbath, [10]so the Jewish authorities told the man who had been healed, "This is a Sabbath, and it is against our Law for you to carry your mat."

11 He answered, "The man who made me well told me to pick up my mat and walk."

12 They asked him, "Who is the man who told you to do this?"

13 But the man who had been healed did not know who Jesus was, for there was a crowd in that place, and Jesus had slipped away.

14 Afterwards, Jesus found him in the Temple and said, "Listen, you are well now; so stop sinning or something worse may happen to you."

15 Then the man left and told the Jewish authorities that it was Jesus who had healed him. [16]So they began to persecute Jesus, because he had done this healing on a Sabbath. [17]Jesus answered them, "My Father is always working, and I too must work."

18 This saying made the Jewish authorities all the more determined to kill him; not only had he broken the Sabbath law, but he had said that God was his own Father and in this way had made himself equal with God.

The Authority of the Son

19 So Jesus answered them, "I am telling you the truth: the Son can do nothing on his own; he does only what he sees his Father doing. What the Father does, the Son also does. [20]For the Father loves the Son and shows him all that he himself is doing. He will show him even greater things to do than this, and you will all be amazed. [21]Just as the Father raises the dead and gives them life, in the same way the Son gives life to those he wants to. [22]Nor does the Father himself judge anyone. He has given his Son the full right to judge, [23]so that all will honour the Son in the same way as they honour the Father. Whoever does not honour the Son does not honour the Father who sent him.

24 "I am telling you the truth: those who hear my words and believe in him who sent me have eternal life. They will not be judged, but have already passed from death to life. [25]I am telling you the truth: the time is coming – the time has already come – when the dead will hear the voice of the Son of God, and those who hear it will come to life. [26]Just as the Father is himself the source of life, in the same way he has made his Son to be the source of life. [27]And he has given the Son the right to judge, because he is the Son of Man. [28]Do not be surprised at this; the time is coming when all the dead will hear his voice [29]and come out of their graves: those who have done good will rise and live, and those who have done evil will rise and be condemned.

Witnesses to Jesus

30 "I can do nothing on my own authority; I judge only as God tells me, so my judgement is right, because I am not trying to do what I want, but only what he who sent me wants.

31 "If I testify on my own behalf, what I say is not to be accepted as real proof. [32]But there is someone else who testifies on my behalf, and I know that what he says about me is true. [33]John is the one to whom you sent your messengers, and he spoke on behalf of the truth. [34]It is not that I must have a human witness; I say this only in order that you may be saved. [35]John was like a lamp, burning and shining, and you were willing for a while to enjoy his light. [36]But I have a witness on my behalf which is even greater than the witness that John gave: what I do, that is, the deeds my Father gave me to do, these speak on my behalf and show that the Father has sent me. [37]And the Father, who sent me, also testifies on my behalf. You have never heard his voice or seen his face, [38]and you do not keep his message in your hearts, for you do not believe in the one whom he sent. [39]You study the Scriptures, because you think that in them you will find eternal life. And these very Scriptures speak about me! [40]Yet you are not willing to come to me in order to have life.

41 "I am not looking for human praise. [42]But I know what kind of people you are, and I know that you have no love for God in your hearts. [43]I have come with my Father's authority, but you have not received me; when, however, someone comes with his own authority, you will receive him. [44]You like to receive praise from one another, but you do not try to win praise from the one who alone is God; how, then, can you believe me? [45]Do not think, however, that I am

the one who will accuse you to my Father. Moses, in whom you have put your hope, is the very one who will accuse you. [46]If you had really believed Moses, you would have believed me, because he wrote about me. [47]But since you do not believe what he wrote, how can you believe what I say?"

Jesus Feeds a Great Crowd
(Mt 14.13–21; Mk 6.30–44; Lk 9.10–17)

6 After this, Jesus went across Lake Galilee (or, Lake Tiberias, as it is also called). [2]A large crowd followed him, because they had seen his miracles of healing those who were ill. [3]Jesus went up a hill and sat down with his disciples. [4]The time for the Passover Festival was near. [5]Jesus looked round and saw that a large crowd was coming to him, so he asked Philip, "Where can we buy enough food to feed all these people?" [6](He said this to test Philip; actually he already knew what he would do.)

[7] Philip answered, "For everyone to have even a little, it would take more than two hundred silver coins[a] to buy enough bread."

[8] Another of his disciples, Andrew, who was Simon Peter's brother, said, [9]"There is a boy here who has five loaves of barley bread and two fish. But they will certainly not be enough for all these people."

[10] "Make the people sit down," Jesus told them. (There was a lot of grass there.) So all the people sat down; there were about 5,000 men. [11]Jesus took the bread, gave thanks to God, and distributed it to the people who were sitting there. He did the same with the fish, and they all had as much as they wanted. [12]When they were all full, he said to his disciples, "Gather the pieces left over; let us not waste any." [13]So they gathered them all up and filled twelve baskets with the pieces left over from the five barley loaves which the people had eaten.

[14] Seeing this miracle that Jesus had performed, the people there said, "Surely this is the Prophet[b] who was to come into the world!" [15]Jesus knew that they were about to come and seize him in order to make him king by force; so he went off again to the hills by himself.

Jesus Walks on the Water
(Mt 14.22–33; Mk 6.45–52)

[16] When evening came, Jesus' disciples went down to the lake, [17]got into a boat, and went back across the lake towards Capernaum. Night came on, and Jesus still had not come to them. [18]By then a strong wind was blowing and stirring up the water. [19]The disciples had rowed about five or six kilometres when they saw Jesus walking on the water, coming near the boat, and they were terrified. [20]"Don't be afraid," Jesus told them, "it is I!" [21]Then they willingly took him into the boat, and immediately the boat reached land at the place they were heading for.

The People Seek Jesus

[22] Next day the crowd which had stayed on the other side of the lake realized that there had been only one boat there. They knew that Jesus had not gone in it with his disciples, but that they had left without him. [23]Other boats, which were from Tiberias, came to shore near the place where the crowd had eaten the bread after the Lord had given thanks. [24]When the crowd saw that Jesus was not there, nor his disciples, they got into those boats and went to Capernaum, looking for him.

Jesus the Bread of Life

[25] When the people found Jesus on the other side of the lake, they said to him, "Teacher, when did you get here?"

[26] Jesus answered, "I am telling you the truth: you are looking for me because you ate the bread and had all you wanted, not because you understood my miracles. [27]Do not work for food that goes bad; instead, work for the food that lasts for eternal life. This is the food which the Son of Man will give you, because God, the Father, has put his mark of approval on him."

[28] So they asked him, "What can we do in order to do what God wants us to do?"

[29] Jesus answered, "What God wants you to do is to believe in the one he sent."

[30] They replied, "What miracle will you perform so that we may see it and believe you? What will you do? [31]Our ancestors ate manna in the desert, just as the scripture says, 'He gave them bread from heaven to eat.'"

[32] "I am telling you the truth," Jesus said. "What Moses gave you was not[c] the bread from heaven;

---

[a] **6.7** SILVER COINS: *A silver coin was the daily wage of a rural worker (see Mt 20.2).*
[b] **6.14** THE PROPHET: *See 1.21.*

[c] **6.32** What Moses gave you was not; *or* It was not Moses who gave you.

it is my Father who gives you the real bread from heaven. ³³For the bread that God gives is he who comes down from heaven and gives life to the world."

34 "Sir," they asked him, "give us this bread always."

35 "I am the bread of life," Jesus told them. "Those who come to me will never be hungry; those who believe in me will never be thirsty. ³⁶Now, I told you that you have seen me but will not believe. ³⁷Everyone whom my Father gives me will come to me. I will never turn away anyone who comes to me, ³⁸because I have come down from heaven to do not my own will but the will of him who sent me. ³⁹And it is the will of him who sent me that I should not lose any of all those he has given me, but that I should raise them all to life on the last day. ⁴⁰For what my Father wants is that all who see the Son and believe in him should have eternal life. And I will raise them to life on the last day."

A priest blesses the bread and wine at Holy Communion (6.53)

41 The people started grumbling about him, because he said, "I am the bread that came down from heaven." ⁴²So they said, "This man is Jesus son of Joseph, isn't he? We know his father and mother. How, then, does he now say he came down from heaven?"

43 Jesus answered, "Stop grumbling among yourselves. ⁴⁴No one can come to me unless the Father who sent me draws him to me; and I will raise him to life on the last day. ⁴⁵The prophets wrote, 'Everyone will be taught by God.' Anyone who hears the Father and learns from him comes to me. ⁴⁶This does not mean that anyone has seen the Father; he who is from God is the only one who has seen the Father. ⁴⁷I am telling you the truth: he who believes has eternal life. ⁴⁸I am the bread of life. ⁴⁹Your ancestors ate manna in the desert, but they died. ⁵⁰But the bread that comes down from heaven is of such a kind that whoever eats it will not die. ⁵¹I am the living bread that came down from heaven. If anyone eats this bread, he will live for ever. The bread that I will give him is my flesh, which I give so that the world may live."

52 This started an angry argument among them. "How can this man give us his flesh to eat?" they asked.

53 Jesus said to them, "I am telling you the truth: if you do not eat the flesh of the Son of Man and drink his blood, you will not have life in yourselves. ⁵⁴Those who eat my flesh and drink my blood have eternal life, and I will raise them to life on the last day. ⁵⁵For my flesh is the real food; my blood is the real drink. ⁵⁶Those who eat my flesh and drink my blood live in me, and I live in them. ⁵⁷The living Father sent me, and because of him I live also. In the same way whoever eats me will live because of me. ⁵⁸This, then, is the bread that came down from heaven; it is not like the bread that your ancestors ate. They later died, but those who eat this bread will live for ever."

59 Jesus said this as he taught in the synagogue in Capernaum.

The Words of Eternal Life

60 Many of his followers heard this and said, "This teaching is too hard. Who can listen to it?"

61 Without being told, Jesus knew that they were grumbling about this, so he said to them, "Does this make you want to give up? ⁶²Suppose, then, that you should see the Son of Man go back up to the place where he was before? ⁶³What gives life is God's Spirit; human power is of no use at all. The words I have spoken to you bring God's life-giving Spirit. ⁶⁴Yet some of you do not believe." (Jesus knew from the very beginning who were the ones that would not believe and which one would betray him.) ⁶⁵And he added, "This is the very reason I told you that no one can come to me unless the Father makes it possible for him to do so."

66 Because of this, many of Jesus' followers turned back and would not go with him any

more. [67]So he asked the twelve disciples, "And you – would you also like to leave?"

68   Simon Peter answered him, "Lord, to whom would we go? You have the words that give eternal life. [69]And now we believe and know that you are the Holy One who has come from God."

70   Jesus replied, "I chose the twelve of you, didn't I? Yet one of you is a devil!" [71]He was talking about Judas, the son of Simon Iscariot. For Judas, even though he was one of the twelve disciples, was going to betray him.

Jesus and his Brothers

7 After this, Jesus travelled in Galilee; he did not want to travel in Judea, because the Jewish authorities there were wanting to kill him. [2]The time for the Festival of Shelters was near, [3]so Jesus' brothers said to him, "Leave this place and go to Judea, so that your followers will see the things that you are doing. [4]No one hides what he is doing if he wants to be well known. Since you are doing these things, let the whole world know about you!" [5](Not even his brothers believed in him.)

6   Jesus said to them, "The right time for me has not yet come. Any time is right for you. [7]The world cannot hate you, but it hates me, because I keep telling it that its ways are bad. [8]You go on to the festival. I am not going[a] to this festival, because the right time has not come for me." [9]He said this, and then stayed on in Galilee.

Jesus at the Festival of Shelters

10   After his brothers had gone to the festival, Jesus also went; however, he did not go openly, but secretly. [11]The Jewish authorities were looking for him at the festival. "Where is he?" they asked.

12   There was much whispering about him in the crowd. "He is a good man," some people said. "No," others said, "he is misleading the people." [13]But no one talked about him openly, because they were afraid of the Jewish authorities.

14   The festival was nearly half over when Jesus went to the Temple and began teaching. [15]The Jewish authorities were greatly surprised and said, "How does this man know so much when he has never had any training?"

16   Jesus answered, "What I teach is not my own teaching, but it comes from God, who sent me.

[17]Whoever is willing to do what God wants will know whether what I teach comes from God or whether I speak on my own authority. [18]A person who speaks on his own authority is trying to gain glory for himself. But he who wants glory for the one who sent him is honest, and there is nothing false in him. [19]Moses gave you the Law, didn't he? But not one of you obeys the Law. Why are you trying to kill me?"

20   "You have a demon in you!" the crowd answered. "Who is trying to kill you?"

21   Jesus answered, "I performed one miracle, and you were all surprised. [22]Moses ordered you to circumcise your sons (although it was not Moses but your ancestors who started it), and so you circumcise a boy on the Sabbath. [23]If a boy is circumcised on the Sabbath so that Moses' Law is not broken, why are you angry with me because I made a man completely well on the Sabbath? [24]Stop judging by external standards, and judge by true standards."

Is he the Messiah?

25   Some of the people of Jerusalem said, "Isn't this the man the authorities are trying to kill? [26]Look! He is talking in public, and they say nothing against him! Can it be that they really know that he is the Messiah? [27]But when the Messiah comes, no one will know where he is from. And we all know where this man comes from."

28   As Jesus taught in the Temple, he said in a loud voice, "Do you really know me and know where I am from? I have not come on my own authority. He who sent me, however, is truthful. You do not know him, [29]but I know him, because I come from him and he sent me."

30   Then they tried to seize him, but no one laid a hand on him, because his hour had not yet come. [31]But many in the crowd believed in him and said, "When the Messiah comes, will he perform more miracles than this man has?"

Guards are Sent to Arrest Jesus

32   The Pharisees heard the crowd whispering these things about Jesus, so they and the chief priests sent some guards to arrest him. [33]Jesus said, "I shall be with you a little while longer, and then I shall go away to him who sent me. [34]You will look for me, but you will not find me, because you cannot go where I will be."

35   The Jewish authorities said among themselves, "Where is he about to go so that we shall not find him? Will he go to the Greek cities

---

[a] **7.8** I am not going; *some manuscripts have* I am not yet going.

where our people live, and teach the Greeks? 36He says that we will look for him but will not find him, and that we cannot go where he will be. What does he mean?"

Streams of Life-giving Water

37   On the last and most important day of the festival Jesus stood up and said in a loud voice, "Whoever is thirsty should come to me, and 38whoever believes in me should drink. As the scripture says, 'Streams of life-giving water will pour out from his side.'"a 39Jesus said this about the Spirit, which those who believed in him were going to receive. At that time the Spirit had not yet been given, because Jesus had not been raised to glory.

Division among the People

40   Some of the people in the crowd heard him say this and said, "This man is really the Prophet!"b

41   Others said, "He is the Messiah!"

But others said, "The Messiah will not come from Galilee! 42The scripture says that the Messiah will be a descendant of King David and will be born in Bethlehem, the town where David lived." 43So there was a division in the crowd because of Jesus. 44Some wanted to seize him, but no one laid a hand on him.

The Unbelief of the Jewish Authorities

45   When the guards went back, the chief priests and Pharisees asked them, "Why did you not bring him?"

46   The guards answered, "Nobody has ever talked like this man!"

47   "Did he fool you, too?" the Pharisees asked them. 48"Have you ever known one of the authorities or one Pharisee to believe in him? 49This crowd does not know the Law of Moses, so they are under God's curse!"

50   One of the Pharisees there was Nicodemus, the man who had gone to see Jesus before. He said to the others, 51"According to our Law we cannot condemn anyone before hearing him and finding out what he has done."

52   "Well," they answered, "are you also from Galilee? Study the Scriptures and you will learn that no prophet ever comesc from Galilee."

The Woman Caught in Adultery

8 [Then everyone went home, but Jesus went to the Mount of Olives. 2Early the next morning he went back to the Temple. All the people gathered round him, and he sat down and began to teach them. 3The teachers of the Law and the Pharisees brought in a woman who had been caught committing adultery, and they made her stand before them all. 4"Teacher," they said to Jesus, "this woman was caught in the very act of committing adultery. 5In our Law Moses commanded that such a woman must be stoned to death. Now, what do you say?" 6They said this to trap Jesus, so that they could accuse him. But he bent over and wrote on the ground with his finger.

7   As they stood there asking him questions, he straightened himself up and said to them, "Whichever one of you has committed no sin may throw the first stone at her." 8Then he bent over again and wrote on the ground. 9When they heard this, they all left, one by one, the older ones first. Jesus was left alone, with the woman still standing there. 10He straightened himself up and said to her, "Where are they? Is there no one left to condemn you?"

11   "No one, sir," she answered.

"Well, then," Jesus said, "I do not condemn you either. Go, but do not sin again."]d

Jesus the Light of the World

12   Jesus spoke to the Pharisees again. "I am the light of the world," he said. "Whoever follows me will have the light of life and will never walk in darkness."

13   The Pharisees said to him, "Now you are testifying on your own behalf; what you say proves nothing."

14   "No," Jesus answered, "even though I do testify on my own behalf, what I say is true, because I know where I came from and where I am going. You do not know where I came from or where I am going. 15You make judgements in a purely human way; I pass judgement on no

---

a **7.38** *Jesus' words in verses 37–38 may be translated:* "Whoever is thirsty should come to me and drink. 38As the scripture says, 'Streams of life-giving water will pour out from within anyone who believes in me.'"
b **7.40** THE PROPHET: *See 1.21.*

c **7.52** no prophet ever comes; *one manuscript has the* Prophet will not come.
d **8.11** *Many manuscripts and early translations do not have this passage (8.1–11); others have it after Jn 21.24; others have it after Lk 21.38; one manuscript has it after Jn 7.36.*

Orthodox Christians hold lighted candles symbolizing Jesus the light of the world (8.12)

25 "Who are you?" they asked him.

Jesus answered, "What I have told you from the very beginning.[a] 26I have much to say about you, much to condemn you for. The one who sent me, however, is truthful, and I tell the world only what I have heard from him."

27 They did not understand that Jesus was talking to them about the Father. 28So he said to them, "When you lift up the Son of Man, you will know that 'I Am Who I Am'; then you will know that I do nothing on my own authority, but I say only what the Father has instructed me to say. 29And he who sent me is with me; he has not left me alone, because I always do what pleases him."

30 Many who heard Jesus say these things believed in him.

The Truth will Set you Free

31 So Jesus said to those who believed in him, "If you obey my teaching, you are really my disciples; 32you will know the truth, and the truth will set you free."

33 "We are the descendants of Abraham," they answered, "and we have never been anybody's slaves. What do you mean, then, by saying, 'You will be free'?"

34 Jesus said to them, "I am telling you the truth: everyone who sins is a slave of sin. 35A slave does not belong to a family permanently, but a son belongs there for ever. 36If the Son sets you free, then you will be really free. 37I know you are Abraham's descendants. Yet you are trying to kill me, because you will not accept my teaching. 38I talk about what my Father has shown me, but you do what your father has told you."

39 They answered him, "Our father is Abraham."

"If you really were Abraham's children," Jesus replied, "you would do[b] the same things that he did. 40All I have ever done is to tell you the truth I heard from God, yet you are trying to kill me. Abraham did nothing like this! 41You are doing what your father did."

"God himself is the only Father we have," they answered, "and we are his true children."

42 Jesus said to them, "If God really were your Father, you would love me, because I came from God and now I am here. I did not come on my own authority, but he sent me. 43Why do you

one. 16But if I were to do so, my judgement would be true, because I am not alone in this; the Father who sent me is with me. 17It is written in your Law that when two witnesses agree, what they say is true. 18I testify on my own behalf, and the Father who sent me also testifies on my behalf."

19 "Where is your father?" they asked him.

"You know neither me nor my Father," Jesus answered. "If you knew me, you would know my Father also."

20 Jesus said all this as he taught in the Temple, in the room where the offering boxes were placed. And no one arrested him, because his hour had not come.

You cannot Go Where I am Going

21 Again Jesus said to them, "I will go away; you will look for me, but you will die in your sins. You cannot go where I am going."

22 So the Jewish authorities said, "He says that we cannot go where he is going. Does this mean that he will kill himself?"

23 Jesus answered, "You belong to this world here below, but I come from above. You are from this world, but I am not from this world. 24That is why I told you that you will die in your sins. And you will die in your sins if you do not believe that 'I Am Who I Am'."

[a] **8.25** What I have told you from the very beginning; *or* Why should I speak to you at all?
[b] **8.39** If you really were ... you would do; *some manuscripts have* If you are ... do.

not understand what I say? It is because you cannot bear to listen to my message. [44]You are the children of your father, the Devil, and you want to follow your father's desires. From the very beginning he was a murderer and has never been on the side of truth, because there is no truth in him. When he tells a lie, he is only doing what is natural to him, because he is a liar and the father of all lies. [45]But I tell the truth, and that is why you do not believe me. [46]Which one of you can prove that I am guilty of sin? If I tell the truth, then why do you not believe me? [47]He who comes from God listens to God's words. You, however, are not from God, and that is why you will not listen."

Jesus and Abraham

48   They asked Jesus, "Were we not right in saying that you are a Samaritan and have a demon in you?"

49   "I have no demon," Jesus answered. "I honour my Father, but you dishonour me. [50]I am not seeking honour for myself. But there is one who is seeking it and who judges in my favour. [51]I am telling you the truth: whoever obeys my teaching will never die."

52   They said to him, "Now we are certain that you have a demon! Abraham died, and the prophets died, yet you say that whoever obeys your teaching will never die. [53]Our father Abraham died; you do not claim to be greater than Abraham, do you? And the prophets also died. Who do you think you are?"

54   Jesus answered, "If I were to honour myself, that honour would be worth nothing. The one who honours me is my Father – the very one you say is your God. [55]You have never known him, but I know him. If I were to say that I do not know him, I would be a liar like you. But I do know him, and I obey his word. [56]Your father Abraham rejoiced that he was to see the time of my coming; he saw it and was glad."

57   They said to him, "You are not even fifty years old – and you have seen Abraham?"[a]

58   "I am telling you the truth," Jesus replied. "Before Abraham was born, 'I Am'."

59   Then they picked up stones to throw at him, but Jesus hid himself and left the Temple.

---

[a] **8.57** you have seen Abraham?; *some manuscripts have* has Abraham seen you?

Jesus Heals a Man Born Blind

9 As Jesus was walking along, he saw a man who had been born blind. [2]His disciples asked him, "Teacher, whose sin caused him to be born blind? Was it his own or his parents' sin?"

3   Jesus answered, "His blindness has nothing to do with his sins or his parents' sins. He is blind so that God's power might be seen at work in him. [4]As long as it is day, we must keep on doing the work of him who sent me; night is coming when no one can work. [5]While I am in the world, I am the light for the world."

6   After he said this, Jesus spat on the ground and made some mud with the spittle; he rubbed the mud on the man's eyes [7]and said, "Go and wash your face in the Pool of Siloam." (This name means "Sent".) So the man went, washed his face, and came back seeing.

8   His neighbours, then, and the people who had seen him begging before this, asked, "Isn't this the man who used to sit and beg?"

9   Some said, "He is the one," but others said, "No he isn't; he just looks like him."

So the man himself said, "I am the man."

10   "How is it that you can now see?" they asked him.

11   He answered, "The man called Jesus made some mud, rubbed it on my eyes, and told me to go to Siloam and wash my face. So I went, and as soon as I washed, I could see."

12   "Where is he?" they asked.

"I don't know," he answered.

The Pharisees Investigate the Healing

13   Then they took to the Pharisees the man who had been blind. [14]The day that Jesus made the mud and cured him of his blindness was a Sabbath. [15]The Pharisees, then, asked the man again how he had received his sight. He told them, "He put some mud on my eyes; I washed my face, and now I can see."

16   Some of the Pharisees said, "The man who did this cannot be from God, for he does not obey the Sabbath law."

Others, however, said, "How could a man who is a sinner perform such miracles as these?" And there was a division among them.

17   So the Pharisees asked the man once more, "You say he cured you of your blindness – well, what do you say about him?"

"He is a prophet," the man answered.

18   The Jewish authorities, however, were not willing to believe that he had been blind and could now see, until they called his parents [19]and

asked them, "Is this your son? You say that he was born blind; how is it, then, that he can now see?"

20 His parents answered, "We know that he is our son, and we know that he was born blind. ²¹But we do not know how it is that he is now able to see, nor do we know who cured him of his blindness. Ask him; he is old enough, and he can answer for himself!" ²²His parents said this because they were afraid of the Jewish authorities, who had already agreed that anyone who said he believed that Jesus was the Messiah would be expelled from the synagogue. ²³That is why his parents said, "He is old enough; ask him!"

24 A second time they called back the man who had been born blind, and said to him, "Promise before God that you will tell the truth! We know that this man who cured you is a sinner."

25 "I do not know if he is a sinner or not," the man replied. "One thing I do know: I was blind, and now I see."

26 "What did he do to you?" they asked. "How did he cure you of your blindness?"

27 "I have already told you," he answered, "and you would not listen. Why do you want to hear it again? Maybe you, too, would like to be his disciples?"

28 They cursed him and said, "You are that fellow's disciple; but we are Moses' disciples. ²⁹We know that God spoke to Moses; as for that fellow, however, we do not even know where he comes from!"

30 The man answered, "What a strange thing that is! You do not know where he comes from, but he cured me of my blindness! ³¹We know that God does not listen to sinners; he does listen to people who respect him and do what he wants them to do. ³²Since the beginning of the world nobody has ever heard of anyone giving sight to a person born blind. ³³Unless this man came from God, he would not be able to do a thing."

34 They answered, "You were born and brought up in sin – and you are trying to teach us?" And they expelled him from the synagogue.

Spiritual Blindness

35 When Jesus heard what had happened, he found the man and asked him, "Do you believe in the Son of Man?"

36 The man answered, "Tell me who he is, sir, so that I can believe in him!"

37 Jesus said to him, "You have already seen him, and he is the one who is talking with you now."

38 "I believe, Lord!" the man said, and knelt down before Jesus.

39 Jesus said, "I came to this world to judge, so that the blind should see and those who see should become blind."

40 Some Pharisees who were there with him heard him say this and asked him, "Surely you don't mean that we are blind, too?"

41 Jesus answered, "If you were blind, then you would not be guilty; but since you claim that you can see, this means that you are still guilty."

The Parable of the Shepherd

10 Jesus said, "I am telling you the truth: the man who does not enter the sheepfold by the gate, but climbs in some other way, is a thief and a robber. ²The man who goes in through the gate is the shepherd of the sheep. ³The gatekeeper opens the gate for him; the sheep hear his voice as he calls his own sheep by name, and he leads them out. ⁴When he has brought them out, he goes ahead of them, and the sheep follow him, because they know his voice. ⁵They will not follow someone else; instead, they will run away from such a person, because they do not know his voice."

6 Jesus told them this parable, but they did not understand what he meant.

Jesus the Good Shepherd

7 So Jesus said again, "I am telling you the truth: I am the gate for the sheep. ⁸All others who came before me are thieves and robbers, but the sheep did not listen to them. ⁹I am the gate. Whoever comes in by me will be saved; they will come in and go out and find pasture. ¹⁰The thief comes only in order to steal, kill, and destroy. I have come in order that you might have life – life in all its fullness.

11 "I am the good shepherd, who is willing to die for the sheep. ¹²When the hired man, who is not a shepherd and does not own the sheep, sees a wolf coming, he leaves the sheep and runs away; so the wolf snatches the sheep and scatters them. ¹³The hired man runs away because he is only a hired man and does not care about the sheep. ¹⁴⁻¹⁵I am the good shepherd. As the Father knows me and I know the Father, in the same way I know my sheep and they know me. And I am willing to die for them. ¹⁶There are other sheep which belong to me that are not in this sheepfold. I must bring them, too; they will listen to my voice, and they will become[a] one flock with one shepherd.

---

[a] **10.16** they will become; *some manuscripts have* there will be.

25 Jesus answered, "I have already told you, but you would not believe me. The things I do by my Father's authority speak on my behalf; ²⁶but you will not believe, for you are not my sheep. ²⁷My sheep listen to my voice; I know them, and they follow me. ²⁸I give them eternal life, and they shall never die. No one can snatch them away from me. ²⁹What my Father has given me is greater[a] than everything, and no one can snatch them away from the Father's care. ³⁰The Father and I are one."

31 Then the people again picked up stones to throw at him. ³²Jesus said to them, "I have done many good deeds in your presence which the Father gave me to do; for which one of these do you want to stone me?"

33 They replied, "We do not want to stone you because of any good deeds, but because of your blasphemy! You are only a man, but you are trying to make yourself God!"

34 Jesus answered, "It is written in your own Law that God said, 'You are gods.' ³⁵We know that what the scripture says is true for ever; and God called those people gods, the people to whom his message was given. ³⁶As for me, the Father chose me and sent me into the world. How, then, can you say that I blaspheme because I said that I am the Son of God? ³⁷Do not believe me, then, if I am not doing the things my Father wants me to do. ³⁸But if I do them, even though you do not believe me, you should at least believe my deeds, in order that you may know once and for all that the Father is in me and that I am in the Father."

39 Once more they tried to seize Jesus, but he slipped out of their hands.

40 Jesus then went back again across the River Jordan to the place where John had been baptizing, and he stayed there. ⁴¹Many people came to him. "John performed no miracles," they said, "but everything he said about this man was true." ⁴²And many people there believed in him.

The Death of Lazarus

11 A man named Lazarus, who lived in Bethany, was ill. Bethany was the town where Mary and her sister Martha lived. ²(This Mary was the one who poured the perfume on the Lord's feet and wiped them with her hair; it was her brother Lazarus who was ill.) ³The sisters sent Jesus a message: "Lord, your dear friend is ill."

17 "The Father loves me because I am willing to give up my life, in order that I may receive it back again. ¹⁸No one takes my life away from me. I give it up of my own free will. I have the right to give it up, and I have the right to take it back. This is what my Father has commanded me to do."

19 Again there was a division among the people because of these words. ²⁰Many of them were saying, "He has a demon! He is mad! Why do you listen to him?"

21 But others were saying, "A man with a demon could not talk like this! How could a demon give sight to blind people?"

Jesus is Rejected

22 It was winter, and the Festival of the Dedication of the Temple was being celebrated in Jerusalem. ²³Jesus was walking in Solomon's Porch in the Temple, ²⁴when the people gathered round him and asked, "How long are you going to keep us in suspense? Tell us the plain truth: are you the Messiah?"

[a] **10.29** What my Father has given me is greater; *some manuscripts have* My Father, who gave them to me, *greater*.

118

4   When Jesus heard it, he said, "The final result of this illness will not be the death of Lazarus; this has happened in order to bring glory to God, and it will be the means by which the Son of God will receive glory."

5   Jesus loved Martha and her sister and Lazarus. ⁶Yet when he received the news that Lazarus was ill, he stayed where he was for two more days. ⁷Then he said to the disciples, "Let us go back to Judea."

8   "Teacher," the disciples answered, "just a short time ago the people there wanted to stone you; and are you planning to go back?"

9   Jesus said, "A day has twelve hours, hasn't it? So whoever walks in broad daylight does not stumble, for they see the light of this world. ¹⁰But if they walk during the night they stumble, because they have no light." ¹¹Jesus said this and then added, "Our friend Lazarus has fallen asleep, but I will go and wake him up."

12   The disciples answered, "If he is asleep, Lord, he will get well."

13   Jesus meant that Lazarus had died, but they thought he meant natural sleep. ¹⁴So Jesus told them plainly, "Lazarus is dead, ¹⁵but for your sake I am glad that I was not with him, so that you will believe. Let us go to him."

16   Thomas (called the Twin) said to his fellow-disciples, "Let us all go with the Teacher, so that we may die with him!"

Jesus the Resurrection and the Life

17   When Jesus arrived, he found that Lazarus had been buried four days before. ¹⁸Bethany was less than three kilometres from Jerusalem, ¹⁹and many Judeans had come to see Martha and Mary to comfort them over their brother's death.

20   When Martha heard that Jesus was coming, she went out to meet him, but Mary stayed in the house. ²¹Martha said to Jesus, "If you had been here, Lord, my brother would not have died! ²²But I know that even now God will give you whatever you ask him for."

23   "Your brother will rise to life," Jesus told her.

24   "I know," she replied, "that he will rise to life on the last day."

25   Jesus said to her, "I am the resurrection and the life. Those who believe in me will live, even though they die; ²⁶and all those who live and believe in me will never die. Do you believe this?"

27   "Yes, Lord!" she answered. "I do believe that you are the Messiah, the Son of God, who was to come into the world."

Jesus Weeps

28   After Martha said this, she went back and called her sister Mary privately. "The Teacher is here," she told her, "and is asking for you." ²⁹When Mary heard this, she got up and hurried out to meet him. ³⁰(Jesus had not yet arrived in the village, but was still in the place where Martha had met him.) ³¹The people who were in the house with Mary, comforting her, followed her when they saw her get up and hurry out. They thought that she was going to the grave to weep there.

32   Mary arrived where Jesus was, and as soon as she saw him, she fell at his feet. "Lord," she said, "if you had been here, my brother would not have died!"

33   Jesus saw her weeping, and he saw how the people who were with her were weeping also; his heart was touched, and he was deeply moved. ³⁴"Where have you buried him?" he asked them.
    "Come and see, Lord," they answered.

35   Jesus wept. ³⁶"See how much he loved him!" the people said.

37   But some of them said, "He gave sight to the blind man, didn't he? Could he not have kept Lazarus from dying?"

Lazarus is Brought to Life

38   Deeply moved once more, Jesus went to the tomb, which was a cave with a stone placed at the entrance. ³⁹"Take the stone away!" Jesus ordered.
    Martha, the dead man's sister, answered, "There will be a bad smell, Lord. He has been buried four days!"

40   Jesus said to her, "Didn't I tell you that you would see God's glory if you believed?" ⁴¹They took the stone away. Jesus looked up and said, "I thank you, Father, that you listen to me. ⁴²I know that you always listen to me, but I say this for the sake of the people here, so that they will believe that you sent me." ⁴³After he had said this, he called out in a loud voice, "Lazarus, come out!" ⁴⁴He came out, his hands and feet wrapped in grave clothes, and with a cloth round his face. "Untie him," Jesus told them, "and let him go."

The Plot against Jesus
(Mt 26.1–5; Mk 14.1–2; Lk 22.1–2)

45   Many of the people who had come to visit Mary saw what Jesus did, and they believed in him. ⁴⁶But some of them returned to the Pharisees and told them what Jesus had done.

47So the Pharisees and the chief priests met with the Council and said, "What shall we do? Look at all the miracles this man is performing! 48If we let him go on in this way, everyone will believe in him, and the Roman authorities will take action and destroy our Temple and our nation!"

49 One of them, named Caiaphas, who was High Priest that year, said, "What fools you are! 50Don't you realize that it is better for you to let one man die for the people, instead of having the whole nation destroyed?" 51Actually, he did not say this of his own accord; rather, as he was High Priest that year, he was prophesying that Jesus was going to die for the Jewish people, 52and not only for them, but also to bring together into one body all the scattered people of God.

53 From that day on the Jewish authorities made plans to kill Jesus. 54So Jesus did not travel openly in Judea, but left and went to a place near the desert, to a town named Ephraim, where he stayed with the disciples.

55 The time for the Passover Festival was near, and many people went up from the country to Jerusalem to perform the ritual of purification before the festival. 56They were looking for Jesus, and as they gathered in the Temple, they asked one another, "What do you think? Surely he will not come to the festival, will he?" 57The chief priests and the Pharisees had given orders that if anyone knew where Jesus was, he must report it, so that they could arrest him.

Jesus is Anointed at Bethany
(Mt 26.6–13; Mk 14.3–9)

12 Six days before the Passover, Jesus went to Bethany, the home of Lazarus, the man he had raised from death. 2They prepared a dinner for him there, which Martha helped to serve; Lazarus was one of those who were sitting at the table with Jesus. 3Then Mary took half a litre of a very expensive perfume made of pure nard, poured it on Jesus' feet, and wiped them with her hair. The sweet smell of the perfume filled the whole house. 4One of Jesus' disciples, Judas Iscariot – the one who was going to betray him – said, 5"Why wasn't this perfume sold for three hundred silver coinsa and the money given to the poor?" 6He said this, not because he cared about the poor, but because he was a thief. He carried the money bag and would help himself from it.

7 But Jesus said, "Leave her alone! Let her keep

---
a **12.5** SILVER COINS: *See 6.7.*

what she has for the day of my burial. 8You will always have poor people with you, but you will not always have me."

The Plot against Lazarus

9 A large number of people heard that Jesus was in Bethany, so they went there, not only because of Jesus but also to see Lazarus, whom Jesus had raised from death. 10So the chief priests made plans to kill Lazarus too, 11because on his account many Jews were rejecting them and believing in Jesus.

The Triumphant Entry into Jerusalem
(Mt 21.1–11; Mk 11.1–11; Lk 19.28–40)

12 The next day the large crowd that had come to the Passover Festival heard that Jesus was coming to Jerusalem. 13So they took branches of palm trees and went out to meet him, shouting, "Praise God! God bless him who comes in the name of the Lord! God bless the King of Israel!"

14 Jesus found a donkey and rode on it, just as the scripture says,

15 "Do not be afraid, city of Zion!
   Here comes your king,
      riding on a young donkey."

16 His disciples did not understand this at the time; but when Jesus had been raised to glory, they remembered that the scripture said this about him and that they had done this for him.

17 The people who had been with Jesus when he called Lazarus out of the grave and raised him from death had reported what had happened. 18That was why the crowd met him – because they heard that he had performed this miracle. 19The Pharisees then said to one another, "You see, we are not succeeding at all! Look, the whole world is following him!"

Some Greeks Seek Jesus

20 Some Greeks were among those who had gone to Jerusalem to worship during the festival. 21They went to Philip (he was from Bethsaida in Galilee) and said, "Sir, we want to see Jesus."

22 Philip went and told Andrew, and the two of them went and told Jesus. 23Jesus answered them, "The hour has now come for the Son of Man to receive great glory. 24I am telling you the truth: a grain of wheat remains no more than a single grain unless it is dropped into the ground and dies. If it does die, then it produces many grains. 25Those who love their own life will lose

it; those who hate their own life in this world will keep it for life eternal. ²⁶Whoever wants to serve me must follow me, so that my servant will be with me where I am. And my Father will honour anyone who serves me.

Jesus Speaks about his Death

27 "Now my heart is troubled – and what shall I say? Shall I say, 'Father, do not let this hour come upon me'? But that is why I came – so that I might go through this hour of suffering. ²⁸Father, bring glory to your name!"

Then a voice spoke from heaven, "I have brought glory to it, and I will do so again."

29 The crowd standing there heard the voice, and some of them said it was thunder, while others said, "An angel spoke to him!"

30 But Jesus said to them, "It was not for my sake that this voice spoke, but for yours. ³¹Now is the time for this world to be judged; now the ruler of this world will be overthrown. ³²When I am lifted up from the earth, I will draw everyone to me." ³³(In saying this he indicated the kind of death he was going to suffer.)

34 The crowd answered, "Our Law tells us that the Messiah will live for ever. How, then, can you say that the Son of Man must be lifted up? Who is this Son of Man?"

35 Jesus answered, "The light will be among you a little longer. Continue on your way while you have the light, so that the darkness will not come upon you; for the one who walks in the dark does not know where he is going. ³⁶Believe in the light, then, while you have it, so that you will be the people of the light."

The Unbelief of the People

After Jesus said this, he went off and hid himself from them. ³⁷Even though he had performed all these miracles in their presence, they did not believe in him, ³⁸so that what the prophet Isaiah had said might come true:

"Lord, who believed the message we told?
To whom did the Lord reveal his power?"

39 And so they were not able to believe, because Isaiah also said:

40 "God has blinded their eyes
and closed their minds,
so that their eyes would not see,
and their minds would not understand,
and they would not turn to me, says God,
for me to heal them."

41 Isaiah said this because he saw Jesus' glory and spoke about him.

42 Even then, many of the Jewish authorities believed in Jesus; but because of the Pharisees they did not talk about it openly, so as not to be expelled from the synagogue. ⁴³They loved human approval rather than the approval of God.

Judgement by Jesus' Words

44 Jesus said in a loud voice, "Whoever believes in me believes not only in me but also in him who sent me. ⁴⁵Whoever sees me sees also him who sent me. ⁴⁶I have come into the world as light, so that everyone who believes in me should not remain in the darkness. ⁴⁷If anyone hears my message and does not obey it, I will not judge him. I came, not to judge the world, but to save it. ⁴⁸Those who reject me and do not accept my message have one who will judge them. The words I have spoken will be their judge on the last day! ⁴⁹This is true, because I have not spoken on my own authority, but the Father who sent me has commanded me what I must say and speak. ⁵⁰And I know that his command brings eternal life. What I say, then, is what the Father has told me to say."

Jesus Washes his Disciples' Feet

13 It was now the day before the Passover Festival. Jesus knew that the hour had come for him to leave this world and go to the Father. He had always loved those in the world who were his own, and he loved them to the very end.

2 Jesus and his disciples were at supper. The Devil had already put into the heart of Judas, the son of Simon Iscariot, the thought of betraying Jesus.ᵃ ³Jesus knew that the Father had given him complete power; he knew that he had come from God and was going to God. ⁴So he rose from the table, took off his outer garment, and tied a towel round his waist. ⁵Then he poured some water into a basin and began to wash the disciples' feet and dry them with the towel round his waist. ⁶He came to Simon Peter, who said to him, "Are you going to wash my feet, Lord?"

7 Jesus answered him, "You do not understand now what I am doing, but you will understand later."

ᵃ **13.2** The Devil ... betraying Jesus; *or* The Devil had already decided that Judas, the son of Simon Iscariot, would betray Jesus.

8 Peter declared, "Never at any time will you wash my feet!"

"If I do not wash your feet," Jesus answered, "you will no longer be my disciple."

9 Simon Peter answered, "Lord, do not wash only my feet, then! Wash my hands and head, too!"

10 Jesus said, "Those who have had a bath are completely clean and do not have to wash themselves, except for their feet.[a] All of you are clean – all except one." [11](Jesus already knew who was going to betray him; that is why he said, "All of you, except one, are clean.")

12 After Jesus had washed their feet, he put his outer garment back on and returned to his place at the table. "Do you understand what I have just done to you?" he asked. [13]"You call me Teacher and Lord, and it is right that you do so, because that is what I am. [14]I, your Lord and Teacher, have just washed your feet. You, then, should wash one another's feet. [15]I have set an example for you, so that you will do just what I have done for you. [16]I am telling you the truth: slaves are never greater than their master, and messengers are never greater than the one who sent them. [17]Now that you know this truth, how happy you will be if you put it into practice!

Feet being washed (13.1–20)

18 "I am not talking about all of you; I know those I have chosen. But the scripture must come true that says, 'The man who shared my food turned against me.' [19]I tell you this now before it happens, so that when it does happen, you will believe that 'I Am Who I Am.' [20]I am telling you the truth: whoever receives anyone I send receives me also; and whoever receives me receives him who sent me."

Jesus Predicts his Betrayal
(Mt 26.20–25; Mk 14.17–21; Lk 22.21–23)

21 After Jesus had said this, he was deeply troubled and declared openly, "I am telling you the truth: one of you is going to betray me."

22 The disciples looked at one another, completely puzzled about whom he meant. [23]One of the disciples, the one whom Jesus loved, was sitting next to Jesus. [24]Simon Peter motioned to him and said, "Ask him whom he is talking about."

25 So that disciple moved closer to Jesus' side and asked, "Who is it, Lord?"

26 Jesus answered, "I will dip some bread in the sauce and give it to him; he is the man." So he took a piece of bread, dipped it, and gave it to Judas, the son of Simon Iscariot. [27]As soon as Judas took the bread, Satan entered him. Jesus said to him, "Be quick about what you are doing!" [28]None of the others at the table understood why Jesus said this to him. [29]Since Judas was in charge of the money bag, some of the disciples thought that Jesus had told him to go and buy what they needed for the festival, or to give something to the poor.

30 Judas accepted the bread and went out at once. It was night.

The New Commandment

31 After Judas had left, Jesus said, "Now the Son of Man's glory is revealed; now God's glory is revealed through him. [32]And if God's glory is revealed through him, then God will reveal the glory of the Son of Man in himself, and he will do so at once. [33]My children, I shall not be with you very much longer. You will look for me; but I tell you now what I told the Jewish authorities, 'You cannot go where I am going.' [34]And now I give you a new commandment: love one another. As I have loved you, so you must love one another. [35]If you have love for one another, then everyone will know that you are my disciples."

Jesus Predicts Peter's Denial
(Mt 26.31–35; Mk 14.27–31; Lk 22.31–34)

36 "Where are you going, Lord?" Simon Peter asked him.

"You cannot follow me now where I am going," answered Jesus; "but later you will follow me."

[a] **13.10** *Some manuscripts do not have* except for their feet.

37   "Lord, why can't I follow you now?" asked Peter. "I am ready to die for you!"

38   Jesus answered, "Are you really ready to die for me? I am telling you the truth: before the cock crows you will say three times that you do not know me.

Jesus the Way to the Father

14 "Do not be worried and upset," Jesus told them. "Believe[a] in God and believe also in me. [2]There are many rooms in my Father's house, and I am going to prepare a place for you. I would not tell you this if it were not so.[b] [3]And after I go and prepare a place for you, I will come back and take you to myself, so that you will be where I am. [4]You know the way that leads to the place where I am going."

5   Thomas said to him, "Lord, we do not know where you are going; so how can we know the way to get there?"

6   Jesus answered him, "I am the way, the truth, and the life; no one goes to the Father except by me. [7]Now that you have known me," he said to them, "you will know[c] my Father also, and from now on you do know him and you have seen him."

8   Philip said to him, "Lord, show us the Father; that is all we need."

9   Jesus answered, "For a long time I have been with you all; yet you do not know me, Philip? Whoever has seen me has seen the Father. Why, then, do you say, 'Show us the Father'? [10]Do you not believe, Philip, that I am in the Father and the Father is in me? The words that I have spoken to you," Jesus said to his disciples, "do not come from me. The Father, who remains in me, does his own work. [11]Believe me when I say that I am in the Father and the Father is in me. If not, believe because of the things I do. [12]I am telling you the truth: those who believe in me will do what I do – yes, they will do even greater things, because I am going to the Father. [13]And I will do whatever you ask for in my name, so that the Father's glory will be shown through the Son. [14]If you ask me[d] for anything in my name, I will do it.

---

[a] **14.1** Believe; *or* You believe.
[b] **14.2** There are ... were not so; *or* There are many rooms in my Father's house; if it were not so, would I tell you that I am going to prepare a place for you?
[c] **14.7** Now that you have known me ... you will know; *some manuscripts have* If you had known me ... you would know.
[d] **14.14** *Some manuscripts do not have* me.

The Promise of the Holy Spirit

15   "If you love me, you will obey my commandments. [16]I will ask the Father, and he will give you another Helper, who will stay with you for ever. [17]He is the Spirit who reveals the truth about God. The world cannot receive him, because it cannot see him or know him. But you know him, because he remains with you and is[e] in you.

18   "When I go, you will not be left all alone; I will come back to you. [19]In a little while the world will see me no more, but you will see me; and because I live, you also will live. [20]When that day comes, you will know that I am in my Father and that you are in me, just as I am in you.

21   "Those who accept my commandments and obey them are the ones who love me. My Father will love those who love me; I too will love them and reveal myself to them."

22   Judas (not Judas Iscariot) said, "Lord, how can it be that you will reveal yourself to us and not to the world?"

23   Jesus answered him, "Whoever loves me will obey my teaching. My Father will love him, and my Father and I will come to him and live with him. [24]Whoever does not love me does not obey my teaching. And the teaching you have heard is not mine, but comes from the Father, who sent me.

25   "I have told you this while I am still with you. [26]The Helper, the Holy Spirit, whom the Father will send in my name, will teach you everything and make you remember all that I have told you.

27   "Peace is what I leave with you; it is my own peace that I give you. I do not give it as the world does. Do not be worried and upset; do not be afraid. [28]You heard me say to you, 'I am leaving, but I will come back to you.' If you loved me, you would be glad that I am going to the Father; for he is greater than I. [29]I have told you this now before it all happens, so that when it does happen, you will believe. [30]I cannot talk with you much longer, because the ruler of this world is coming. He has no power over me, [31]but the world must know that I love the Father; that is why I do everything as he commands me.

"Come, let us go from this place.

Jesus the Real Vine

15 "I am the real vine, and my Father is the gardener. [2]He breaks off every branch in me that does not bear fruit, and he prunes every branch that does bear

---

[e] **14.17** is; *some manuscripts have* will be.

fruit, so that it will be clean and bear more fruit. ³You have been made clean already by the teaching I have given you. ⁴Remain united to me, and I will remain united to you. A branch cannot bear fruit by itself; it can do so only if it remains in the vine. In the same way you cannot bear fruit unless you remain in me.

5 "I am the vine, and you are the branches. Those who remain in me, and I in them, will bear much fruit; for you can do nothing without me. ⁶Whoever does not remain in me is thrown out like a branch and dries up; such branches are gathered up and thrown into the fire, where they are burnt. ⁷If you remain in me and my words remain in you, then you will ask for anything you wish, and you shall have it. ⁸My Father's glory is shown by your bearing much fruit; and in this way you become my disciples. ⁹I love you just as the Father loves me; remain in my love. ¹⁰If you obey my commands, you will remain in my love, just as I have obeyed my Father's commands and remain in his love.

11 "I have told you this so that my joy may be in you and that your joy may be complete. ¹²My commandment is this: love one another, just as I love you. ¹³The greatest love a person can have for his friends is to give his life for them. ¹⁴And you are my friends if you do what I command you. ¹⁵I do not call you servants any longer, because servants do not know what their master is doing. Instead, I call you friends, because I have told you everything I have heard from my Father. ¹⁶You did not choose me; I chose you and appointed you to go and bear much fruit, the kind of fruit that endures. And so the Father will give you whatever you ask of him in my name. ¹⁷This, then, is what I command you: love one another.

The World's Hatred

18 "If the world hates you, just remember that it has hated me first. ¹⁹If you belonged to the world, then the world would love you as its own. But I chose you from this world, and you do not belong to it; that is why the world hates you. ²⁰Remember what I told you: 'Slaves are not greater than their master.' If people persecuted me, they will persecute you too; if they obeyed my teaching, they will obey yours too. ²¹But they will do all this to you because you are mine; for they do not know the one who sent me. ²²They would not have been guilty of sin if I had not come and spoken to them; as it is, they no longer have any excuse for their sin.

²³Whoever hates me hates my Father also. ²⁴They would not have been guilty of sin if I had not done among them the things that no one else ever did; as it is, they have seen what I did, and they hate both me and my Father. ²⁵This, however, was bound to happen so that what is written in their Law may come true: 'They hated me for no reason at all.'

26 "The Helper will come – the Spirit, who reveals the truth about God and who comes from the Father. I will send him to you from the Father, and he will speak about me. ²⁷And you, too, will speak about me, because you have been with me from the very beginning.

16 **t** "I have told you this, so that you will not give up your faith. ²You will be expelled from the synagogues, and the time will come when anyone who kills you will think that by doing this he is serving God. ³People will do these things to you because they have not known either the Father or me. ⁴But I have told you this, so that when the time comes for them to do these things, you will remember that I told you.

The Work of the Holy Spirit

"I did not tell you these things at the beginning, for I was with you. ⁵But now I am going to him who sent me, yet none of you asks me where I am going. ⁶And now that I have told you, your hearts are full of sadness. ⁷But I am telling you the truth: it is better for you that I go away, because if I do not go, the Helper will not come to you. But if I do go away, then I will send him to you. ⁸And when he comes, he will prove to the people of the world that they are wrong about sin and about what is right and about God's judgement. ⁹They are wrong about sin, because they do not believe in me; ¹⁰they are wrong about what is right, because I am going to the Father and you will not see me any more; ¹¹and they are wrong about judgement, because the ruler of this world has already been judged.

12 "I have much more to tell you, but now it would be too much for you to bear. ¹³When, however, the Spirit comes, who reveals the truth about God, he will lead you into all the truth. He will not speak on his own authority, but he will speak of what he hears, and will tell you of things to come. ¹⁴He will give me glory, because he will take what I say and tell it to you. ¹⁵All that my Father has is mine; that is why I said that the Spirit will take what I give him and tell it to you.

Sadness and Gladness

16   "In a little while you will not see me any more, and then a little while later you will see me."

17   Some of his disciples asked among themselves, "What does this mean? He tells us that in a little while we will not see him, and then a little while later we will see him; and he also says, 'It is because I am going to the Father.' ¹⁸What does this 'a little while' mean? We don't know what he is talking about!"

19   Jesus knew that they wanted to question him, so he said to them, "I said, 'In a little while you will not see me, and then a little while later you will see me.' Is this what you are asking about among yourselves? ²⁰I am telling you the truth: you will cry and weep, but the world will be glad; you will be sad, but your sadness will turn into gladness. ²¹When a woman is about to give birth, she is sad because her hour of suffering has come; but when the baby is born, she forgets her suffering, because she is happy that a baby has been born into the world. ²²That is how it is with you: now you are sad, but I will see you again, and your hearts will be filled with gladness, the kind of gladness that no one can take away from you.

23   "When that day comes, you will not ask me for anything. I am telling you the truth: the Father will give you whatever you ask him for in my name.ᵃ ²⁴Until now you have not asked for anything in my name; ask and you will receive, so that your happiness may be complete.

Victory over the World

25   "I have used figures of speech to tell you these things. But the time will come when I will not use figures of speech, but will speak to you plainly about the Father. ²⁶When that day comes, you will ask him in my name; and I do not say that I will ask him on your behalf, ²⁷for the Father himself loves you. He loves you because you love me and have believed that I came from God. ²⁸I did come from the Father, and I came into the world; and now I am leaving the world and going to the Father."

29   Then his disciples said to him, "Now you are speaking plainly, without using figures of speech. ³⁰We know now that you know everything; you do not need someone to ask you questions. This makes us believe that you came from God."

ᵃ **16.23** the Father will give you whatever you ask him for in my name; *some manuscripts have* if you ask the Father for anything, he will give it to you in my name.

31   Jesus answered them, "Do you believe now? ³²The time is coming, and is already here, when all of you will be scattered, each of you to your own home, and I will be left all alone. But I am not really alone, because the Father is with me. ³³I have told you this so that you will have peace by being united to me. The world will make you suffer. But be brave! I have defeated the world!"

Jesus Prays for his Disciples

17 ⟨t⟩ After Jesus finished saying this, he looked up to heaven and said, "Father, the hour has come. Give glory to your Son, so that the Son may give glory to you. ²For you gave him authority over all humanity, so that he might give eternal life to all those you gave him. ³And eternal life means knowing you, the only true God, and knowing Jesus Christ, whom you sent. ⁴I have shown your glory on earth; I have finished the work you gave me to do. ⁵Father! Give me glory in your presence now, the same glory I had with you before the world was made.

6   "I have made you known to those you gave me out of the world. They belonged to you, and you gave them to me. They have obeyed your word, ⁷and now they know that everything you gave me comes from you. ⁸I gave them the message that you gave me, and they received it; they know that it is true that I came from you, and they believe that you sent me.

9   "I pray for them. I do not pray for the world but for those you gave me, for they belong to you. ¹⁰All I have is yours, and all you have is mine; and my glory is shown through them. ¹¹And now I am coming to you; I am no longer in the world, but they are in the world. Holy Father! Keep them safe by the power of your name, the name you gave me,ᵇ so that they may be one just as you and I are one. ¹²While I was with them, I kept them safe by the power of your name, the name you gave me.ᶜ I protected them, and not one of them was lost, except the man who was bound to be lost – so that the scripture might come true. ¹³And now I am coming to you, and I say these things in the world so that they might have my joy in their

ᵇ **17.11** Keep them safe by the power of your name, the name you gave me; *some manuscripts have* By the power of your name keep safe those you have given me.

ᶜ **17.12** I kept them safe by the power of your name, the name you gave me; *some manuscripts have* By the power of your name I kept safe those you have given me.

hearts in all its fullness. ¹⁴I gave them your message, and the world hated them, because they do not belong to the world, just as I do not belong to the world. ¹⁵I do not ask you to take them out of the world, but I do ask you to keep them safe from the Evil One. ¹⁶Just as I do not belong to the world, they do not belong to the world. ¹⁷Dedicate them to yourself by means of the truth; your word is truth. ¹⁸I sent them into the world, just as you sent me into the world. ¹⁹And for their sake I dedicate myself to you, in order that they, too, may be truly dedicated to you.

20 "I pray not only for them, but also for those who believe in me because of their message. ²¹I pray that they may all be one. Father! May they be in us, just as you are in me and I am in you. May they be one, so that the world will believe that you sent me. ²²I gave them the same glory you gave me, so that they may be one, just as you and I are one: ²³I in them and you in me, so that they may be completely one, in order that the world may know that you sent me and that you love them as you love me.

24 "Father! You have given them to me, and I want them to be with me where I am, so that they may see my glory, the glory you gave me; for you loved me before the world was made. ²⁵Righteous Father! The world does not know you, but I know you, and these know that you sent me. ²⁶I made you known to them, and I will continue to do so, in order that the love you have for me may be in them, and so that I also may be in them."

The Arrest of Jesus
(Mt 26.47–56; Mk 14.43–50; Lk 22.47–53)

18 After Jesus had said this prayer, he left with his disciples and went across the brook called Kidron. There was a garden in that place, and Jesus and his disciples went in. ²Judas, the traitor, knew where it was, because many times Jesus had met there with his disciples. ³So Judas went to the garden, taking with him a group of Roman soldiers, and some temple guards sent by the chief priests and the Pharisees; they were armed and carried lanterns and torches. ⁴Jesus knew everything that was going to happen to him, so he stepped forward and asked them, "Who is it you are looking for?"

5 "Jesus of Nazareth," they answered.
"I am he," he said.
Judas, the traitor, was standing there with them. ⁶When Jesus said to them, "I am he," they moved back and fell to the ground. ⁷Again Jesus asked them, "Who is it you are looking for?"
"Jesus of Nazareth," they said.

8 "I have already told you that I am he," Jesus said. "If, then, you are looking for me, let these others go." ⁹(He said this so that what he had said might come true: "Father, I have not lost even one of those you gave me.")

10 Simon Peter, who had a sword, drew it and struck the High Priest's slave, cutting off his right ear. The name of the slave was Malchus. ¹¹Jesus said to Peter, "Put your sword back in its place! Do you think that I will not drink the cup of suffering which my Father has given me?"

Jesus before Annas

12 Then the Roman soldiers with their commanding officer and the Jewish guards arrested Jesus, bound him, ¹³and took him first to Annas. He was the father-in-law of Caiaphas, who was High Priest that year. ¹⁴It was Caiaphas who had advised the Jewish authorities that it was better that one man should die for all the people.

Peter Denies Jesus
(Mt 26.69–70; Mk 14.66–68; Lk 22.55–57)

15 Simon Peter and another disciple followed Jesus. That other disciple was well known to the High Priest, so he went with Jesus into the courtyard of the High Priest's house, ¹⁶while Peter stayed outside by the gate. Then the other disciple went back out, spoke to the girl at the gate, and brought Peter inside. ¹⁷The girl at the gate said to Peter, "Aren't you also one of the disciples of that man?"
"No, I am not," answered Peter.

18 It was cold, so the servants and guards had built a charcoal fire and were standing round it, warming themselves. So Peter went over and stood with them, warming himself.

The High Priest Questions Jesus
(Mt 26.59–66; Mk 14.55–64; Lk 22.66–71)

19 The High Priest questioned Jesus about his disciples and about his teaching. ²⁰Jesus answered, "I have always spoken publicly to everyone; all my teaching was done in the synagogues and in the Temple, where all the people come together. I have never said anything in secret. ²¹Why, then, do you question me? Question the people who heard me. Ask them what I told them – they know what I said."

22 When Jesus said this, one of the guards there

slapped him and said, "How dare you talk like that to the High Priest!"

23   Jesus answered him, "If I have said anything wrong, tell everyone here what it was. But if I am right in what I have said, why do you hit me?"

24   Then Annas sent him, still bound, to Caiaphas the High Priest.

Peter Denies Jesus Again
(Mt 26.71–75; Mk 14.69–72; Lk 22.58–62)

25   Peter was still standing there keeping himself warm. So the others said to him, "Aren't you also one of the disciples of that man?"

But Peter denied it. "No, I am not," he said.

26   One of the High Priest's slaves, a relative of the man whose ear Peter had cut off, spoke up. "Didn't I see you with him in the garden?" he asked.

27   Again Peter said "No" – and at once a cock crowed.

Jesus is Brought before Pilate
(Mt 27.1–2, 11–14; Mk 15.1–5; Lk 23.1–5)

28   Early in the morning Jesus was taken from Caiaphas' house to the governor's palace. The Jewish authorities did not go inside the palace, for they wanted to keep themselves ritually clean, in order to be able to eat the Passover meal. ²⁹So Pilate went outside to them and asked, "What do you accuse this man of?"

30   Their answer was, "We would not have brought him to you if he had not committed a crime."

31   Pilate said to them, "Then you yourselves take him and try him according to your own law."

They replied, "We are not allowed to put anyone to death." ³²(This happened in order to make the words of Jesus come true, the words he used when he indicated the kind of death he would die.)

33   Pilate went back into the palace and called Jesus. "Are you the King of the Jews?" he asked him.

34   Jesus answered, "Does this question come from you or have others told you about me?"

35   Pilate replied, "Do you think I am a Jew? It was your own people and the chief priests who handed you over to me. What have you done?"

36   Jesus said, "My kingdom does not belong to this world; if my kingdom belonged to this world, my followers would fight to keep me from being handed over to the Jewish authorities. No, my kingdom does not belong here!"

Jesus' appearance before Pilate is depicted in this Station of the Cross

37   So Pilate asked him, "Are you a king, then?"

Jesus answered, "You say that I am a king. I was born and came into the world for this one purpose, to speak about the truth. Whoever belongs to the truth listens to me."

38   "And what is truth?" Pilate asked.

Jesus is Sentenced to Death
(Mt 27.15–31; Mk 15.6–20; Lk 23.13–25)

Then Pilate went back outside to the people and said to them, "I cannot find any reason to condemn him. ³⁹But according to the custom you have, I always set free a prisoner for you during the Passover. Do you want me to set free for you the King of the Jews?"

40   They answered him with a shout, "No, not him! We want Barabbas!" (Barabbas was a bandit.)

19 Then Pilate took Jesus and had him whipped. ²The soldiers made a crown out of thorny branches and put it on his head; then they put a purple robe on him ³and came to him and said, "Long live the King of the Jews!" And they went up and slapped him.

4   Pilate went out once more and said to the crowd, "Look, I will bring him out here to you to let you see that I cannot find any reason to

condemn him." ⁵So Jesus came out, wearing the crown of thorns and the purple robe. Pilate said to them, "Look! Here is the man!"

6   When the chief priests and the temple guards saw him, they shouted, "Crucify him! Crucify him!"

Pilate said to them, "You take him, then, and crucify him. I find no reason to condemn him."

7   The crowd answered back, "We have a law that says he ought to die, because he claimed to be the Son of God."

8   When Pilate heard this, he was even more afraid. ⁹He went back into the palace and asked Jesus, "Where do you come from?"

But Jesus did not answer. ¹⁰Pilate said to him, "You will not speak to me? Remember, I have the authority to set you free and also to have you crucified."

11   Jesus answered, "You have authority over me only because it was given to you by God. So the man who handed me over to you is guilty of a worse sin."

12   When Pilate heard this, he tried to find a way to set Jesus free. But the crowd shouted back, "If you set him free, that means that you are not the Emperor's friend! Anyone who claims to be a king is a rebel against the Emperor!"

13   When Pilate heard these words, he took Jesus outside and sat down on the judge's seat in the place called "The Stone Pavement". (In Hebrew the name is "Gabbatha".) ¹⁴It was then almost noon of the day before the Passover. Pilate said to the people, "Here is your king!"

15   They shouted back, "Kill him! Kill him! Crucify him!"

Pilate asked them, "Do you want me to crucify your king?"

The chief priests answered, "The only king we have is the Emperor!"

16   Then Pilate handed Jesus over to them to be crucified.

Jesus is Crucified
(Mt 27.32–44; Mk 15.21–32; Lk 23.26–43)

So they took charge of Jesus. ¹⁷He went out, carrying his cross, and came to "The Place of the Skull", as it is called. (In Hebrew it is called "Golgotha".) ¹⁸There they crucified him; and they also crucified two other men, one on each side, with Jesus between them. ¹⁹Pilate wrote a notice and had it put on the cross. "Jesus of Nazareth, the King of the Jews", is what he wrote. ²⁰Many people read it, because the place where Jesus was crucified was not far from the city. The notice was written in Hebrew, Latin, and Greek. ²¹The chief priests said to Pilate, "Do not write 'The King of the Jews', but rather, 'This man said, I am the King of the Jews.'"

22   Pilate answered, "What I have written stays written."

23   After the soldiers had crucified Jesus, they took his clothes and divided them into four parts, one part for each soldier. They also took the robe, which was made of one piece of woven cloth without any seams in it. ²⁴The soldiers said to one another, "Let's not tear it; let's throw dice to see who will get it." This happened in order to make the scripture come true:

"They divided my clothes among themselves
    and gambled for my robe."

And this is what the soldiers did.

25   Standing close to Jesus' cross were his mother, his mother's sister, Mary the wife of Clopas, and Mary Magdalene. ²⁶Jesus saw his mother and the disciple he loved standing there; so he said to his mother, "He is your son."

27   Then he said to the disciple, "She is your mother." From that time the disciple took her to live in his home.

This crown of thorns reminds Christians of what happened to Jesus shortly before he died (19.5)

The Death of Jesus
(Mt 27.45–56; Mk 15.33–41; Lk 23.44–49)

28   Jesus knew that by now everything had been completed; and in order to make the scripture come true, he said, "I am thirsty."

29   A bowl was there, full of cheap wine; so a sponge was soaked in the wine, put on a stalk of hyssop, and lifted up to his lips. ³⁰Jesus drank the wine and said, "It is finished!"

Then he bowed his head and died.

Jesus' Side is Pierced

31   Then the Jewish authorities asked Pilate to allow them to break the legs of the men who had been crucified, and to take the bodies down from the crosses. They requested this because it was Friday, and they did not want the bodies to stay on the crosses on the Sabbath, since the coming Sabbath was especially holy. ³²So the soldiers went and broke the legs of the first man and then of the other man who had been crucified with Jesus. ³³But when they came to Jesus, they saw that he was already dead, so they did not break his legs. ³⁴One of the soldiers, however, plunged his spear into Jesus' side, and at once blood and water poured out. ³⁵(The one who saw this happen has spoken of it, so that you also may believe.ᵃ What he said is true, and he knows that he speaks the truth.) ³⁶This was done to make the scripture come true: "Not one of his bones will be broken." ³⁷And there is another scripture that says, "People will look at him whom they pierced."

The Burial of Jesus
(Mt 27.57–61; Mk 15.42–47; Lk 23.50–56)

38   After this, Joseph, who was from the town of Arimathea, asked Pilate if he could take Jesus' body. (Joseph was a follower of Jesus, but in secret, because he was afraid of the Jewish authorities.) Pilate told him he could have the body, so Joseph went and took it away. ³⁹Nicodemus, who at first had gone to see Jesus at night, went with Joseph, taking with him about 30 kilogrammes of spices, a mixture of myrrh and aloes. ⁴⁰The two men took Jesus' body and wrapped it in linen with the spices according to the Jewish custom of preparing a body for burial. ⁴¹There was a garden in the place where Jesus had been put to death, and in it there was a new tomb where no one had ever

ᵃ **19.35** believe; *some manuscripts have* continue to believe.

been buried. ⁴²Since it was the day before the Sabbath and because the tomb was close by, they placed Jesus' body there.

The Empty Tomb
(Mt 28.1–8; Mk 16.1–8; Lk 24.1–12)

20   Early on Sunday morning, while it was still dark, Mary Magdalene went to the tomb and saw that the stone had been taken away from the entrance. ²She went running to Simon Peter and the other disciple, whom Jesus loved, and told them, "They have taken the Lord from the tomb, and we don't know where they have put him!"

3   Then Peter and the other disciple went to the tomb. ⁴The two of them were running, but the other disciple ran faster than Peter and reached the tomb first. ⁵He bent over and saw the linen wrappings, but he did not go in. ⁶Behind him came Simon Peter, and he went straight into the tomb. He saw the linen wrappings lying there ⁷and the cloth which had been round Jesus' head. It was not lying with the linen wrappings but was rolled up by itself. ⁸Then the other disciple, who had reached the tomb first, also went in; he saw and believed. ⁹(They still did not understand the scripture which said that he must rise from death.) ¹⁰Then the disciples went back home.

Jesus Appears to Mary Magdalene
(Mt 28.9–10; Mk 16.9–11)

11   Mary stood crying outside the tomb. While she was still crying, she bent over and looked in the tomb ¹²and saw two angels there dressed in white, sitting where the body of Jesus had been, one at the head and the other at the feet. ¹³"Woman, why are you crying?" they asked her.

She answered, "They have taken my Lord away, and I do not know where they have put him!"

14   Then she turned round and saw Jesus standing there; but she did not know that it was Jesus. ¹⁵"Woman, why are you crying?" Jesus asked her. "Who is it that you are looking for?"

She thought he was the gardener, so she said to him, "If you took him away, sir, tell me where you have put him, and I will go and get him."

16   Jesus said to her, "Mary!"

She turned towards him and said in Hebrew, "Rabboni!" (This means "Teacher".)

17   "Do not hold on to me," Jesus told her, "because I have not yet gone back up to the Father. But go to my brothers and tell them that

I am returning to him who is my Father and their Father, my God and their God."

18 So Mary Magdalene went and told the disciples that she had seen the Lord and related to them what he had told her.

Jesus Appears to his Disciples
(Mt 28.16–20; Mk 16.14–18; Lk 24.36–49)

19 It was late that Sunday evening, and the disciples were gathered together behind locked doors, because they were afraid of the Jewish authorities. Then Jesus came and stood among them. "Peace be with you," he said. [20]After saying this, he showed them his hands and his side. The disciples were filled with joy at seeing the Lord. [21]Jesus said to them again, "Peace be with you. As the Father sent me, so I send you." [22]Then he breathed on them and said, "Receive the Holy Spirit. [23]If you forgive people's sins, they are forgiven; if you do not forgive them, they are not forgiven."

Jesus and Thomas

24 One of the twelve disciples, Thomas (called the Twin), was not with them when Jesus came. [25]So the other disciples told him, "We have seen the Lord!"

Thomas said to them, "Unless I see the scars of the nails in his hands and put my finger on those scars and my hand in his side, I will not believe."

26 A week later the disciples were together again indoors, and Thomas was with them. The doors were locked, but Jesus came and stood among them and said, "Peace be with you." [27]Then he said to Thomas, "Put your finger here, and look at my hands; then stretch out your hand and put it in my side. Stop your doubting, and believe!"

28 Thomas answered him, "My Lord and my God!"

29 Jesus said to him, "Do you believe because you see me? How happy are those who believe without seeing me!"

The Purpose of this Book

30 In his disciples' presence Jesus performed many other miracles which are not written down in this book. [31]But these have been written in order that you may believe[a] that Jesus

---

a **20.31** believe; *some manuscripts have* continue to believe.

is the Messiah, the Son of God, and that through your faith in him you may have life.

Jesus Appears to Seven Disciples

21 After this, Jesus appeared once more to his disciples at Lake Tiberias. This is how it happened. [2]Simon Peter, Thomas (called the Twin), Nathanael (the one from Cana in Galilee), the sons of Zebedee, and two other disciples of Jesus were all together. [3]Simon Peter said to the others, "I am going fishing."

"We will come with you," they told him. So they went out in a boat, but all that night they did not catch a thing. [4]As the sun was rising, Jesus stood at the water's edge, but the disciples did not know that it was Jesus. [5]Then he asked them, "Young men, haven't you caught anything?"

"Not a thing," they answered.

6 He said to them, "Throw your net out on the right side of the boat, and you will catch some." So they threw the net out and could not pull it back in, because they had caught so many fish.

7 The disciple whom Jesus loved said to Peter, "It is the Lord!" When Peter heard that it was the Lord, he wrapped his outer garment round him (for he had taken his clothes off) and jumped into the water. [8]The other disciples came to shore in the boat, pulling the net full of fish. They were not very far from land, about a hundred metres away. [9]When they stepped ashore, they saw a charcoal fire there with fish on it and some bread. [10]Then Jesus said to them, "Bring some of the fish you have just caught."

11 Simon Peter went aboard and dragged the net ashore full of big fish, 153 in all; even though there were so many, still the net did not tear. [12]Jesus said to them, "Come and eat." None of the disciples dared ask him, "Who are you?" because they knew it was the Lord. [13]So Jesus went over, took the bread, and gave it to them; he did the same with the fish.

14 This, then, was the third time Jesus appeared to the disciples after he was raised from death.

Jesus and Peter

15 After they had eaten, Jesus said to Simon Peter, "Simon son of John, do you love me more than these others do?"

"Yes, Lord," he answered, "you know that I love you."

Jesus said to him, "Take care of my lambs." [16]A second time Jesus said to him, "Simon son of John, do you love me?"

A window depicting the risen Jesus and Simon Peter (21.15–19)

third time, "Do you love me?" so he said to him, "Lord, you know everything; you know that I love you!"

Jesus said to him, "Take care of my sheep. [18]I am telling you the truth: when you were young, you used to get ready and go anywhere you wanted to; but when you are old, you will stretch out your hands and someone else will bind you and take you where you don't want to go." [19](In saying this, Jesus was indicating the way in which Peter would die and bring glory to God.) Then Jesus said to him, "Follow me!"

Jesus and the Other Disciple

20 Peter turned round and saw behind him that other disciple, whom Jesus loved – the one who had leaned close to Jesus at the meal and had asked, "Lord, who is going to betray you?" [21]When Peter saw him, he asked Jesus, "Lord, what about this man?"

22 Jesus answered him, "If I want him to live until I come, what is that to you? Follow me!"

23 So a report spread among the followers of Jesus that this disciple would not die. But Jesus did not say that he would not die; he said, "If I want him to live until I come, what is that to you?"

24 He is the disciple who spoke of these things, the one who also wrote them down; and we know that what he said is true.

Conclusion

25 Now, there are many other things that Jesus did. If they were all written down one by one, I suppose that the whole world could not hold the books that would be written.

"Yes, Lord," he answered, "you know that I love you."

Jesus said to him, "Take care of my sheep." [17]A third time Jesus said, "Simon son of John, do you love me?"

Peter was sad because Jesus asked him the

THE ACTS
of the Apostles

INTRODUCTION

The Acts of the Apostles is a continuation of *Luke*. Its chief purpose is to tell how Jesus' early followers, led by the Holy Spirit, spread the Good News about him "in Jerusalem, in all Judea and Samaria, and to the ends of the earth" (1.8). It is the story of the Christian movement as it began among the Jewish people and went on to become a faith for the whole world. The writer was also concerned to reassure his readers that the Christians were not a subversive political threat to the Roman Empire, and that the Christian faith was the fulfilment of the Jewish religion.

Acts may be divided into three principal parts, reflecting the ever widening area in which the Good News about Jesus was proclaimed and the Church established: (1) The beginning of the Christian movement in Jerusalem following the ascension of Jesus; (2) Expansion into other parts of Palestine; (3) Further expansion, into the Mediterranean world as far as Rome.

An important feature of *Acts* is the activity of the Holy Spirit, who comes with power upon the believers in Jerusalem on the day of Pentecost and continues to guide and strengthen the Church and its leaders throughout the events reported in the book. The early Christian message is summarized in a number of sermons, and the events recorded in *Acts* show the power of this message in the lives of the believers and in the fellowship of the Church.

Outline of Contents

1 Dear Theophilus:
In my first book I wrote about all the things that Jesus did and taught from the time he began his work [2]until the day he was taken up to heaven. Before he was taken up, he gave instructions by the power of the Holy Spirit to the men he had chosen as his apostles. [3]For 40 days after his death he appeared to them many times in ways that proved beyond doubt that he was alive. They saw him, and he talked with them about the Kingdom of God.

[4]And when they came together,[a] he gave them this order: "Do not leave Jerusalem, but wait for the gift I told you about, the gift my Father promised. [5]John baptized with water, but in a few days you will be baptized with the Holy Spirit."

---

[a] **1.4** when they came together; *or* while he was staying with them; *or* while he was eating with them.

Jesus is Taken Up to Heaven
(Mk 16.19–20; Lk 24.50–53)

6   When the apostles met together with Jesus, they asked him, "Lord, will you at this time give the Kingdom back to Israel?"

7   Jesus said to them, "The times and occasions are set by my Father's own authority, and it is not for you to know when they will be. ⁸But when the Holy Spirit comes upon you, you will be filled with power, and you will be witnesses for me in Jerusalem, in all Judea and Samaria, and to the ends of the earth." ⁹After saying this, he was taken up to heaven as they watched him, and a cloud hid him from their sight.

10   They still had their eyes fixed on the sky as he went away, when two men dressed in white suddenly stood beside them ¹¹and said, "Galileans, why are you standing there looking up at the sky? This Jesus, who was taken from you into heaven, will come back in the same way that you saw him go to heaven."

Judas' Successor
(Mt 27.3–10)

12   Then the apostles went back to Jerusalem from the Mount of Olives, which is about a kilometre away from the city. ¹³They entered the city and went up to the room where they were staying: Peter, John, James and Andrew, Philip and Thomas, Bartholomew and Matthew, James son of Alphaeus, Simon the Patriot, and Judas son of James. ¹⁴They gathered frequently to pray as a group, together with the women and with Mary the mother of Jesus and with his brothers.

15   A few days later there was a meeting of the believers, about 120 in all, and Peter stood up to speak. ¹⁶"My fellow-believers," he said, "the scripture had to come true in which the Holy Spirit, speaking through David, made a prediction about Judas, who was the guide for those who arrested Jesus. ¹⁷Judas was a member of our group, for he had been chosen to have a part in our work."

18   (With the money that Judas got for his evil act he bought a field, where he fell to his death; he burst open and all his bowels spilt out. ¹⁹All the people living in Jerusalem heard about it, and so in their own language they call that field Akeldama, which means "Field of Blood".)

20   "For it is written in the book of Psalms:

'May his house become empty;
  may no one live in it.'

Studying
ACTS

Who wrote it? Luke, author of the third Gospel. Both books dedicated to Theophilus. Luke accompanied Paul on his journeys.
When? Probably 80–85 CE. *Luke* and *Acts* intended to form a two-part history, from birth of Jesus to death of Paul.
Where from? Unknown.
For whom? Dedication to Theophilus – possibly a recent convert asking for information or an important person whose protection was sought for the Church.
Why? Many possible aims – to show the unity of the early Christians; to defend Christianity against political charges; to show parts played by Peter and Paul in early Church's expansion, or simply how the Church began.

KEY POINTS

- Impact of the giving of the Holy Spirit to the early Church.
- First Christian martyr – Stephen (chapter 7). This began the first persecution of the Church under the instigation of Saul.
- Conversion of Saul to Christianity, leading to Paul's tireless travels to spread the Christian message.
- Welcoming of Gentiles (non-Jews) as well as Jews into the Church.
- Paul's three missionary journeys, leading to final visit to Rome.

It is also written:

'May someone else take his place of service.'

21–22 "So then, someone must join us as a witness to the resurrection of the Lord Jesus. He must be one of the men who were in our group during the whole time that the Lord Jesus travelled about with us, beginning from the time John preached his message of baptism[a] until the day Jesus was taken up from us to heaven."

23   So they proposed two men: Joseph, who was called Barsabbas (also known as Justus), and Matthias. ²⁴Then they prayed, "Lord, you know the thoughts of everyone, so show us which of these two you have chosen ²⁵to serve as an apostle in the place of Judas, who left to go to the place where he belongs." ²⁶Then they drew lots to choose between the two men, and the one chosen was Matthias, who was added to the group of eleven apostles.

[a] **1.21–22** John preached his message of baptism; *or* John baptized him.

ACTS 2

The Coming of the Holy Spirit

2 When the day of Pentecost came, all the believers were gathered together in one place. ²Suddenly there was a noise from the sky which sounded like a strong wind blowing, and it filled the whole house where they were sitting. ³Then they saw what looked like tongues of fire which spread out and touched each person there. ⁴They were all filled with the Holy Spirit and began to talk in other languages, as the Spirit enabled them to speak.

5 There were Jews living in Jerusalem, religious people who had come from every country in the world. ⁶When they heard this noise, a large crowd gathered. They were all excited, because each one of them heard the believers speaking in his or her own language. ⁷In amazement and wonder they exclaimed, "These people who are talking like this are Galileans! ⁸How is it, then, that all of us hear them speaking in our own native languages? ⁹We are from Parthia, Media, and Elam; from Mesopotamia, Judea, and Cappadocia; from Pontus and Asia, ¹⁰from Phrygia and Pamphylia, from Egypt and the regions of Libya near Cyrene. Some of us are from Rome, ¹¹both Jews and Gentiles converted to Judaism, and some of us are from Crete and Arabia – yet all of us hear them speaking in our own languages about the great things that God has done!" ¹²Amazed and confused, they kept asking each other, "What does this mean?"

13 But others made fun of the believers, saying, "These people are drunk!"

Peter's Message

14 Then Peter stood up with the other eleven apostles and in a loud voice began to speak to the crowd: "Fellow-Jews and all of you who live in Jerusalem, listen to me and let me tell you what this means. ¹⁵These people are not drunk, as you suppose; it is only nine o'clock in the morning. ¹⁶Instead, this is what the prophet Joel spoke about:

17 'This is what I will do in the last days, God says:
I will pour out my Spirit on everyone.
Your sons and daughters will proclaim my message;
your young men will see visions,
and your old men will have dreams.

18 Yes, even on my servants, both men and women,
I will pour out my Spirit in those days,
and they will proclaim my message.

19 I will perform miracles in the sky above
and wonders on the earth below.
There will be blood, fire, and thick smoke;
20 the sun will be darkened,
and the moon will turn red as blood,
before the great and glorious Day of the Lord comes.

21 And then, whoever calls out to the Lord for help will be saved.'

22 "Listen to these words, fellow-Israelites! Jesus of Nazareth was a man whose divine authority was clearly proven to you by all the miracles and wonders which God performed through him. You yourselves know this, for it happened here among you. ²³In accordance with his own plan God had already decided that Jesus would be handed over to you; and you killed him by letting sinful men crucify him. ²⁴But God raised him from death, setting him free from its power, because it was impossible that death should hold him prisoner. ²⁵For David said about him:

'I saw the Lord before me at all times;
he is near me, and I will not be troubled.
26 And so I am filled with gladness,
and my words are full of joy.
And I, mortal though I am,
will rest assured in hope,
27 because you will not abandon me in the world of the dead;
you will not allow your faithful servant to rot in the grave.
28 You have shown me the paths that lead to life,
and your presence will fill me with joy.'

29 "My fellow-Israelites, I must speak to you plainly about our famous ancestor King David. He died and was buried, and his grave is here with us to this very day. ³⁰He was a prophet, and he knew what God had promised him: God had made a vow that he would make one of David's descendants a king, just as David was. ³¹David saw what God was going to do in the future, and so he spoke about the resurrection of the Messiah when he said:

'He was not abandoned in the world of the dead;
his body did not rot in the grave.'

³²God has raised this very Jesus from death, and we are all witnesses to this fact. ³³He has been raised to the right-hand side of God, his Father, and has received from him the Holy Spirit, as he had promised. What you now see and hear is his gift that he has poured out on us. ³⁴For it was not David who went up into heaven; rather he said:

'The Lord said to my Lord:
Sit here at my right

35   until I put your enemies as a footstool under
       your feet.'

36   "All the people of Israel, then, are to know for
sure that this Jesus, whom you crucified, is the
one that God has made Lord and Messiah!"

37   When the people heard this, they were deeply
troubled and said to Peter and the other apostles, "What shall we do, brothers?"

38   Peter said to them, "Each one of you must
turn away from your sins and be baptized in the
name of Jesus Christ, so that your sins will be
forgiven; and you will receive God's gift, the
Holy Spirit. [39]For God's promise was made to
you and your children, and to all who are far
away – all whom the Lord our God calls to
himself."

40   Peter made his appeal to them and with
many other words he urged them, saying, "Save
yourselves from the punishment coming on this
wicked people!" [41]Many of them believed his
message and were baptized, and about 3,000
people were added to the group that day. [42]They
spent their time in learning from the apostles,
taking part in the fellowship, and sharing in the
fellowship meals and the prayers.

Life among the Believers

43   Many miracles and wonders were being done
through the apostles, and everyone was filled
with awe. [44]All the believers continued together

Bread being broken and shared by Christians (3.43–47)

in close fellowship and shared their belongings
with one another. [45]They would sell their property and possessions, and distribute the money
among all, according to what each one needed.
[46]Day after day they met as a group in the
Temple, and they had their meals together in
their homes, eating with glad and humble
hearts, [47]praising God, and enjoying the good
will of all the people. And every day the Lord
added to their group those who were being
saved.

A Lame Man is Healed

3 One day Peter and John went to the Temple
at three o'clock in the afternoon, the hour
for prayer. [2]There at the Beautiful Gate, as it
was called, was a man who had been lame all his
life. Every day he was carried to the gate to beg
for money from the people who were going into
the Temple. [3]When he saw Peter and John going
in, he begged them to give him something.
[4]They looked straight at him, and Peter said,
"Look at us!" [5]So he looked at them, expecting
to get something from them. [6]But Peter said to
him, "I have no money at all, but I give you
what I have: in the name of Jesus Christ of
Nazareth I order you to get up and walk!" [7]Then
he took him by his right hand and helped him
up. At once the man's feet and ankles became
strong; [8]he jumped up, stood on his feet, and
started walking around. Then he went into the
Temple with them, walking and jumping and
praising God. [9]The people there saw him
walking and praising God, [10]and when they recognized him as the beggar who had sat at the
Beautiful Gate, they were all surprised and
amazed at what had happened to him.

Peter's Message in the Temple

11   As the man held on to Peter and John in
Solomon's Porch, as it was called, the people
were amazed and ran to them. [12]When Peter
saw the people, he said to them, "Fellow-Israelites, why are you surprised at this, and
why do you stare at us? Do you think that it was
by means of our own power or godliness that
we made this man walk? [13]The God of
Abraham, Isaac, and Jacob, the God of our
ancestors, has given divine glory to his Servant
Jesus. But you handed him over to the authorities, and you rejected him in Pilate's presence,
even after Pilate had decided to set him free.
[14]He was holy and good, but you rejected him,
and instead you asked Pilate to do you the

favour of turning loose a murderer. ¹⁵You killed the one who leads to life, but God raised him from death – and we are witnesses to this. ¹⁶It was the power of his name that gave strength to this lame man. What you see and know was done by faith in his name; it was faith in Jesus that has made him well, as you can all see.

¹⁷ "And now, my fellow-Israelites, I know that what you and your leaders did to Jesus was due to your ignorance. ¹⁸God announced long ago through all the prophets that his Messiah had to suffer; and he made it come true in this way. ¹⁹Repent, then, and turn to God, so that he will forgive your sins. If you do, ²⁰times of spiritual strength will come from the Lord, and he will send Jesus, who is the Messiah he has already chosen for you. ²¹He must remain in heaven until the time comes for all things to be made new, as God announced through his holy prophets who lived long ago. ²²For Moses said, 'The Lord your God will send you a prophet, just as he sent me,ᵃ and he will be one of your own people. You are to obey everything that he tells you to do. ²³Anyone who does not obey that prophet shall be separated from God's people and destroyed.' ²⁴And all the prophets who had a message, including Samuel and those who came after him, also announced what has been happening these days. ²⁵The promises of God through his prophets are for you, and you share in the covenant which God made with your ancestors. As he said to Abraham, 'Through your descendants I will bless all the people on earth.' ²⁶And so God chose his Servant and sent him first to you, to bless you by making every one of you turn away from your wicked ways."

Peter and John before the Council

4 Peter and John were still speaking to the people when some priests,ᵇ the officer in charge of the temple guards, and some Sadducees arrived. ²They were annoyed because the two apostles were teaching the people that Jesus had risen from death, which proved that the dead will rise to life. ³So they arrested them and put them in jail until the next day, since it was already late. ⁴But many who heard the message believed; and the number of men grew to about 5,000.

⁵ The next day the Jewish leaders, the elders, and the teachers of the Law gathered in Jerusalem. ⁶They met with the High Priest Annas and with Caiaphas, John, Alexander, and the others who belonged to the High Priest's family. ⁷They made the apostles stand before them and asked them, "How did you do this? What power have you got or whose name did you use?"

⁸ Peter, full of the Holy Spirit, answered them, "Leaders of the people and elders: ⁹if we are being questioned today about the good deed done to the lame man and how he was healed, ¹⁰then you should all know, and all the people of Israel should know, that this man stands here before you completely well through the power of the name of Jesus Christ of Nazareth – whom you crucified and whom God raised from death. ¹¹Jesus is the one of whom the scripture says:

'The stone that you the builders despised turned out to be the most important of all.'

¹²Salvation is to be found through him alone; in all the world there is no one else whom God has given who can save us."

¹³ The members of the Council were amazed to see how bold Peter and John were and to learn that they were ordinary men of no education. They realized then that they had been companions of Jesus. ¹⁴But there was nothing that they could say, because they saw the man who had been healed standing there with Peter and John. ¹⁵So they told them to leave the Council room, and then they started discussing among themselves. ¹⁶"What shall we do with these men?" they asked. "Everyone in Jerusalem knows that this extraordinary miracle has been performed by them, and we cannot deny it. ¹⁷But to keep this matter from spreading any further among the people, let us warn these men never again to speak to anyone in the name of Jesus."

¹⁸ So they called them back in and told them that on no condition were they to speak or to teach in the name of Jesus. ¹⁹But Peter and John answered them, "You yourselves judge which is right in God's sight – to obey you or to obey God. ²⁰For we cannot stop speaking of what we ourselves have seen and heard." ²¹So the Council warned them even more strongly and then set them free. They saw that it was impossible to punish them, because the people were all praising God for what had happened. ²²The man on whom this miracle of healing had been performed was over 40 years old.

The Believers Pray for Boldness

²³ As soon as Peter and John were set free, they returned to their group and told them what the

---

ᵃ **3.22** just as he sent me; *or* like me.
ᵇ **4.1** priests; *some manuscripts have* chief priests.

chief priests and the elders had said. [24]When the believers heard it, they all joined together in prayer to God: "Master and Creator of heaven, earth, and sea, and all that is in them! [25]By means of the Holy Spirit you spoke through our ancestor David, your servant, when he said:

> 'Why were the Gentiles furious;
>> why did people make their useless plots?
> 26   The kings of the earth prepared themselves,
>> and the rulers met together
>> against the Lord and his Messiah.'

[27]For indeed Herod and Pontius Pilate met together in this city with the Gentiles and the people of Israel against Jesus, your holy Servant, whom you made Messiah. [28]They gathered to do everything that you by your power and will had already decided would happen. [29]And now, Lord, take notice of the threats they have made, and allow us, your servants, to speak your message with all boldness. [30]Stretch out your hand to heal, and grant that wonders and miracles may be performed through the name of your holy Servant Jesus."

31   When they finished praying, the place where they were meeting was shaken. They were all filled with the Holy Spirit and began to proclaim God's message with boldness.

The Believers Share their Possessions

32   The group of believers was one in mind and heart. None of them said that any of their belongings were their own, but they all shared with one another everything they had. [33]With great power the apostles gave witness to the resurrection of the Lord Jesus, and God poured rich blessings on them all. [34]There was no one in the group who was in need. Those who owned fields or houses would sell them, bring the money received from the sale, [35]and hand it over to the apostles; and the money was distributed to each one according to his need.

36   And so it was that Joseph, a Levite born in Cyprus, whom the apostles called Barnabas (which means "One who Encourages"), [37]sold a field he owned, brought the money, and handed it over to the apostles.

Ananias and Sapphira

5 But there was a man named Ananias, who with his wife Sapphira sold some property that belonged to them. [2]But with his wife's agreement he kept part of the money for himself and handed the rest over to the apostles. [3]Peter said to him, "Ananias, why did you let Satan take control of you and make you lie to the Holy Spirit by keeping part of the money you received for the property? [4]Before you sold the property, it belonged to you; and after you sold it, the money was yours. Why, then, did you decide to do such a thing? You have not lied to human beings – you have lied to God!" [5]As soon as Ananias heard this, he fell down dead; and all who heard about it were terrified. [6]The young men came in, wrapped up his body, carried him out, and buried him.

7   About three hours later his wife, not knowing what had happened, came in. [8]Peter asked her, "Tell me, was this the full amount you and your husband received for your property?"

"Yes," she answered, "the full amount."

9   So Peter said to her, "Why did you and your husband decide to put the Lord's Spirit to the test? The men who buried your husband are now at the door, and they will carry you out too!" [10]At once she fell down at his feet and died. The young men came in and saw that she was dead, so they carried her out and buried her beside her husband. [11]The whole church and all the others who heard of this were terrified.

Miracles and Wonders

12   Many miracles and wonders were being performed among the people by the apostles. All the believers met together in Solomon's Porch. [13]Nobody outside the group dared to join them, even though the people spoke highly of them. [14]But more and more people were added to the group – a crowd of men and women who believed in the Lord. [15]As a result of what the apostles were doing, sick people were carried out into the streets and placed on beds and mats so that at least Peter's shadow might fall on some of them as he passed by. [16]And crowds of people came in from the towns around Jerusalem, bringing those who were ill or who had evil spirits in them; and they were all healed.

The Apostles are Persecuted

17   Then the High Priest and all his companions, members of the local party of the Sadducees, became extremely jealous of the apostles; so they decided to take action. [18]They arrested the apostles and put them in the public jail. [19]But that night an angel of the Lord opened the prison gates, led the apostles out, and said to them, [20]"Go and stand in the Temple, and tell the people all about this new life." [21]The

apostles obeyed, and at dawn they entered the Temple and started teaching.

The High Priest and his companions called together all the Jewish elders for a full meeting of the Council; then they sent orders to the prison to have the apostles brought before them. ²²But when the officials arrived, they did not find the apostles in prison, so they returned to the Council and reported, ²³"When we arrived at the jail, we found it locked up tight and all the guards on watch at the gates;

The Salvation Army preaching the Gospel in the open air (5.42)

but when we opened the gates, we found no one inside!" ²⁴When the chief priests and the officer in charge of the temple guards heard this, they wondered what had happened to the apostles. ²⁵Then a man came in and said to them, "Listen! The men you put in prison are in the Temple teaching the people!" ²⁶So the officer went off with his men and brought the apostles back. They did not use force, however, because they were afraid that the people might stone them.

27   They brought the apostles in, made them stand before the Council, and the High Priest questioned them. ²⁸"We gave you strict orders not to teach in the name of this man," he said; "but see what you have done! You have spread your teaching all over Jerusalem, and you want to make us responsible for his death!"

29   Peter and the other apostles replied, "We must obey God, not men. ³⁰The God of our ancestors raised Jesus from death, after you had killed him by nailing him to a cross. ³¹God raised him to his right-hand side as Leader and Saviour, to give the people of Israel the opportunity to repent and have their sins forgiven. ³²We are witnesses to these things – we and the Holy Spirit, who is God's gift to those who obey him."

33   When the members of the Council heard this, they were so furious that they wanted to have the apostles put to death. ³⁴But one of them, a Pharisee named Gamaliel, who was a teacher of the Law and was highly respected by all the people, stood up in the Council. He ordered the apostles to be taken out for a while, ³⁵and then he said to the Council, "Fellow-Israelites, be careful what you do to these men. ³⁶You remember that Theudas appeared some time ago, claiming to be somebody great, and about four hundred men joined him. But he was killed, all his followers were scattered, and his movement

died out. ³⁷After that, Judas the Galilean appeared during the time of the census; he drew a crowd after him, but he also was killed, and all his followers were scattered. ³⁸And so in this case, I tell you, do not take any action against these men. Leave them alone! If what they have planned and done is of human origin, it will disappear, ³⁹but if it comes from God, you cannot possibly defeat them. You could find yourselves fighting against God!"

The Council followed Gamaliel's advice. ⁴⁰They called the apostles in, had them whipped, and ordered them never again to speak in the name of Jesus; and then they set them free. ⁴¹As the apostles left the Council, they were happy, because God had considered them worthy to suffer disgrace for the sake of Jesus. ⁴²And every day in the Temple and in people's homes they continued to teach and preach the Good News about Jesus the Messiah.

The Seven Helpers

6   Some time later, as the number of disciples kept growing, there was a quarrel between the Greek-speaking Jews and the native Jews. The Greek-speaking Jews claimed that their widows were being neglected in the daily distribution of funds. ²So the twelve apostles called the whole group of believers together and said, "It is not right for us to neglect the preaching of God's word in order to handle finances. ³So then, brothers and sisters, choose seven men among you who are known to be full of the Holy Spirit and wisdom, and we will put them in charge of this matter. ⁴We ourselves, then, will give our full time to prayer and the work of preaching."

5   The whole group was pleased with the apostles' proposal, so they chose Stephen, a man full

of faith and the Holy Spirit, and Philip, Prochorus, Nicanor, Timon, Parmenas, and Nicolaus, a Gentile from Antioch who had earlier been converted to Judaism. 6The group presented them to the apostles, who prayed and placed their hands on them.

7   And so the word of God continued to spread. The number of disciples in Jerusalem grew larger and larger, and a great number of priests accepted the faith.

The Arrest of Stephen

8   Stephen, a man richly blessed by God and full of power, performed great miracles and wonders among the people. 9But he was opposed by some men who were members of the synagogue of the Freedmen[a] (as it was called), which included Jews from Cyrene and Alexandria. They and other Jews from the provinces of Cilicia and Asia started arguing with Stephen. 10But the Spirit gave Stephen such wisdom that when he spoke, they could not refute him. 11So they bribed some men to say, "We heard him speaking against Moses and against God!" 12In this way they stirred up the people, the elders, and the teachers of the Law. They seized Stephen and took him before the Council. 13Then they brought in some men to tell lies about him. "This man," they said, "is always talking against our sacred Temple and the Law of Moses. 14We heard him say that this Jesus of Nazareth will tear down the Temple and change all the customs which have come down to us from Moses!" 15All those sitting in the Council fixed their eyes on Stephen and saw that his face looked like the face of an angel.

Stephen's Speech

7   The High Priest asked Stephen, "Is this true?" Stephen answered, "Brothers and fathers, listen to me! Before our ancestor Abraham had gone to live in Haran, the God of glory appeared to him in Mesopotamia 3and said to him, 'Leave your family and country and go to the land that I will show you.' 4And so he left his country and went to live in Haran. After Abraham's father died, God made him move to this land where you now live. 5God did not then give Abraham any part of it as his own, not even a square metre of ground, but God promised to give it to him, and that it would belong to him

and to his descendants. At the time God made this promise, Abraham had no children. 6This is what God said to him: 'Your descendants will live in a foreign country, where they will be slaves and will be badly treated for four hundred years. 7But I will pass judgement on the people that they will serve, and afterwards your descendants will come out of that country and will worship me in this place.' 8Then God gave Abraham the ceremony of circumcision as a sign of the covenant. So Abraham circumcised Isaac a week after he was born; Isaac circumcised his son Jacob, and Jacob circumcised his twelve sons, the famous ancestors of our race.

9   "Jacob's sons became jealous of their brother Joseph and sold him to be a slave in Egypt. But God was with him 10and brought him safely through all his troubles. When Joseph appeared before the king of Egypt, God gave him a pleasing manner and wisdom, and the king made Joseph governor over the country and the royal household. 11Then there was a famine all over Egypt and Canaan, which caused much suffering. Our ancestors could not find any food, 12and when Jacob heard that there was corn in Egypt, he sent his sons, our ancestors, on their first visit there. 13On the second visit Joseph made himself known to his brothers, and the king of Egypt came to know about Joseph's family. 14So Joseph sent a message to his father Jacob, telling him and the whole family, seventy-five people in all, to come to Egypt. 15Then Jacob went to Egypt, where he and his sons died. 16Their bodies were taken to Shechem, where they were buried in the grave which Abraham had bought from the clan of Hamor for a sum of money.

17   "When the time drew near for God to keep the promise he had made to Abraham, the number of our people in Egypt had grown much larger. 18At last a king who did not know about Joseph began to rule in Egypt. 19He tricked our ancestors and was cruel to them, forcing them to put their babies out of their homes, so that they would die. 20It was at this time that Moses was born, a very beautiful child. He was cared for at home for three months, 21and when he was put out of his home, the king's daughter adopted him and brought him up as her own son. 22He was taught all the wisdom of the Egyptians and became a great man in words and deeds.

23   "When Moses was forty years old, he decided to find out how his fellow-Israelites were being treated. 24He saw one of them being ill-treated by an Egyptian, so he went to his help and took revenge on the Egyptian by killing him. 25(He

a **6.9** FREEDMEN: *These were Jews who had been slaves, but had bought or been given their freedom.*

thought that his own people would understand that God was going to use him to set them free, but they did not understand.) 26The next day he saw two Israelites fighting, and he tried to make peace between them. 'Listen, men,' he said, 'you are fellow-Israelites; why are you fighting like this?' 27But the one who was ill-treating the other pushed Moses aside. 'Who made you ruler and judge over us?' he asked. 28'Do you want to kill me, just as you killed that Egyptian yesterday?' 29When Moses heard this, he fled from Egypt and went to live in the land of Midian. There he had two sons.

30 "After forty years had passed, an angel appeared to Moses in the flames of a burning bush in the desert near Mount Sinai. 31Moses was amazed by what he saw, and went near the bush to get a better look. But he heard the Lord's voice: 32'I am the God of your ancestors, the God of Abraham, Isaac, and Jacob.' Moses trembled with fear and dared not look. 33The Lord said to him, 'Take your sandals off, for the place where you are standing is holy ground. 34I have seen the cruel suffering of my people in Egypt. I have heard their groans, and I have come down to set them free. Come now; I will send you to Egypt.'

35 "Moses is the one who was rejected by the people of Israel. 'Who made you ruler and judge over us?' they asked. He is the one whom God sent to rule the people and set them free with the help of the angel who appeared to him in the burning bush. 36He led the people out of Egypt, performing miracles and wonders in Egypt and at the Red Sea and for forty years in the desert. 37Moses is the one who said to the people of Israel, 'God will send you a prophet, just as he sent me,a and he will be one of your own people.' 38He is the one who was with the people of Israel assembled in the desert; he was there with our ancestors and with the angel who spoke to him on Mount Sinai, and he received God's living messages to pass on to us.

39 "But our ancestors refused to obey him; they pushed him aside and wished that they could go back to Egypt. 40So they said to Aaron, 'Make us some gods who will lead us. We do not know what has happened to that man Moses, who brought us out of Egypt.' 41It was then that they made an idol in the shape of a bull, offered sacrifice to it, and had a feast in honour of what they themselves had made. 42So God turned away from them and gave them over to worship the stars of heaven, as it is written in the book of the prophets:

'People of Israel! It was not to me
  that you slaughtered and sacrificed animals
  for forty years in the desert.
43 It was the tent of the god Molech that you carried,
  and the image of Rephan, your star god;
  they were idols that you had made to worship.
And so I will send you into exile beyond Babylon.'

44 "Our ancestors had the Tent of God's presence with them in the desert. It had been made as God had told Moses to make it, according to the pattern that Moses had been shown. 45Later on, our ancestors who received the tent from their fathers carried it with them when they went with Joshua and took over the land from the nations that God drove out as they advanced. And it stayed there until the time of David. 46He won God's favour and asked God to allow him to provide a dwelling place for the God of Jacob.b 47But it was Solomon who built him a house.

48 "But the Most High God does not live in houses built by human hands; as the prophet says:

49 'Heaven is my throne, says the Lord,
  and the earth is my footstool.
What kind of house would you build for me?
  Where is the place for me to live in?
50 Did not I myself make all these things?'

51 "How stubborn you are!" Stephen went on to say. "How heathen your hearts, how deaf you are to God's message! You are just like your ancestors: you too have always resisted the Holy Spirit! 52Was there any prophet that your ancestors did not persecute? They killed God's messengers, who long ago announced the coming of his righteous Servant. And now you have betrayed and murdered him. 53You are the ones who received God's law, that was handed down by angels – yet you have not obeyed it!"

The Stoning of Stephen

54 As the members of the Council listened to Stephen, they became furious and ground their teeth at him in anger. 55But Stephen, full of the Holy Spirit, looked up to heaven and saw God's glory and Jesus standing at the right-hand side of God. 56"Look!" he said. "I see heaven opened

---

a **7.37** just as he sent me; *or* like me.

b **7.46** the God of Jacob; *some manuscripts have* the people of Israel.

and the Son of Man standing at the right-hand side of God!"

57 With a loud cry the members of the Council covered their ears with their hands. Then they all rushed at him at once, [58]threw him out of the city, and stoned him. The witnesses left their cloaks in the care of a young man named Saul. [59]They kept on stoning Stephen as he called out to the Lord, "Lord Jesus, receive my spirit!" [60]He knelt down and cried out in a loud voice, "Lord! Do not remember this sin against them!" He said this and died.

8

And Saul approved of his murder.

Saul Persecutes the Church

That very day the church in Jerusalem began to suffer cruel persecution. All the believers, except the apostles, were scattered throughout the provinces of Judea and Samaria. [2]Some devout men buried Stephen, mourning for him with loud cries.

3 But Saul tried to destroy the church; going from house to house, he dragged out the believers, both men and women, and threw them into jail.

The Gospel is Preached in Samaria

4 The believers who were scattered went everywhere, preaching the message. [5]Philip went to the principal city[a] in Samaria and preached the Messiah to the people there. [6]The crowds paid close attention to what Philip said, as they listened to him and saw the miracles that he performed. [7]Evil spirits came out from many people with a loud cry, and many paralysed and lame people were healed. [8]So there was great joy in that city.

9 A man named Simon lived there, who for some time had astounded the Samaritans with his magic. He claimed that he was someone great, [10]and everyone in the city, from all classes of society, paid close attention to him. "He is that power of God known as 'The Great Power'," they said. [11]They paid this attention to him because for such a long time he had astonished them with his magic. [12]But when they believed Philip's message about the good news of the Kingdom of God and about Jesus Christ, they were baptized, both men and women. [13]Simon himself also believed; and after being baptized, he stayed close to Philip and was astounded

when he saw the great wonders and miracles that were being performed.

14 The apostles in Jerusalem heard that the people of Samaria had received the word of God, so they sent Peter and John to them. [15]When they arrived, they prayed for the believers that they might receive the Holy Spirit. [16]For the Holy Spirit had not yet come down on any of them; they had only been baptized in the name of the Lord Jesus. [17]Then Peter and John placed their hands on them, and they received the Holy Spirit.

18 Simon saw that the Spirit had been given to the believers when the apostles placed their hands on them. So he offered money to Peter and John, [19]and said, "Give this power to me too, so that anyone I place my hands on will receive the Holy Spirit."

20 But Peter answered him, "May you and your money go to hell, for thinking that you can buy God's gift with money! [21]You have no part or share in our work, because your heart is not right in God's sight. [22]Repent, then, of this evil plan of yours, and pray to the Lord that he will forgive you for thinking such a thing as this. [23]For I see that you are full of bitter envy and are a prisoner of sin."

24 Simon said to Peter and John, "Please pray to the Lord for me, so that none of these things you spoke of will happen to me."

25 After they had given their testimony and proclaimed the Lord's message, Peter and John went back to Jerusalem. On their way they preached the Good News in many villages of Samaria.

An Anglican priest preaching in church (8.4)

---

[a] **8.5** the principal city; *some manuscripts have* a city.

Philip and the Ethiopian Official

26 An angel of the Lord said to Philip, "Get ready and go south[a] to the road that goes from Jerusalem to Gaza." (This road is not used nowadays.)[b] 27-28So Philip got ready and went. Now an Ethiopian eunuch, who was an important official in charge of the treasury of the queen of Ethiopia, was on his way home. He had been to Jerusalem to worship God and was going back home in his carriage. As he rode along, he was reading from the book of the prophet Isaiah. 29The Holy Spirit said to Philip, "Go over to that carriage and stay close to it." 30Philip ran over and heard him reading from the book of the prophet Isaiah. He asked him, "Do you understand what you are reading?"

31 The official replied, "How can I understand unless someone explains it to me?" And he invited Philip to climb up and sit in the carriage with him. 32The passage of scripture which he was reading was this:

"Like a sheep that is taken to be slaughtered,
    like a lamb that makes no sound when its
        wool is cut off,
    he did not say a word.

33 He was humiliated, and justice was denied
        him.
    No one will be able to tell about his
        descendants,
    because his life on earth has come to an
        end."

34 The official asked Philip, "Tell me, of whom is the prophet saying this? Of himself or of someone else?" 35Then Philip began to speak; starting from this passage of scripture, he told him the Good News about Jesus. 36As they travelled down the road, they came to a place where there was some water, and the official said, "Here is some water. What is to keep me from being baptized?"[c]

38 The official ordered the carriage to stop, and both Philip and the official went down into the water, and Philip baptized him. 39When they came up out of the water, the Spirit of the Lord took Philip away. The official did not see him again, but continued on his way, full of joy. 40Philip found himself in Azotus; he went on to Caesarea, and on the way he preached the Good News in every town.

The Conversion of Saul
(Acts 22.6–16; 26.12–18)

9 In the meantime Saul kept up his violent threats of murder against the followers of the Lord. He went to the High Priest 2and asked for letters of introduction to the synagogues in Damascus, so that if he should find there any followers of the Way of the Lord, he would be able to arrest them, both men and women, and bring them back to Jerusalem.

3 As Saul was coming near the city of Damascus, suddenly a light from the sky flashed round him. 4He fell to the ground and heard a voice saying to him, "Saul, Saul! Why do you persecute me?"

5 "Who are you, Lord?" he asked.

"I am Jesus, whom you persecute," the voice said. 6"But get up and go into the city, where you will be told what you must do."

7 The men who were travelling with Saul had stopped, not saying a word; they heard the voice but could not see anyone. 8Saul got up from the ground and opened his eyes, but could not see a thing. So they took him by the hand and led him into Damascus. 9For three days he was not able to see, and during that time he did not eat or drink anything.

10 There was a believer in Damascus named Ananias. He had a vision, in which the Lord said to him, "Ananias!"

"Here I am, Lord," he answered.

11 The Lord said to him, "Get ready and go to Straight Street, and at the house of Judas ask for a man from Tarsus named Saul. He is praying, 12and in a vision he has seen a man named Ananias come in and place his hands on him so that he might see again."

13 Ananias answered, "Lord, many people have told me about this man and about all the terrible things he has done to your people in Jerusalem. 14And he has come to Damascus with authority from the chief priests to arrest all who worship you."

15 The Lord said to him, "Go, because I have chosen him to serve me, to make my name known to Gentiles and kings and to the people of Israel. 16And I myself will show him all that he must suffer for my sake."

17 So Ananias went, entered the house where Saul was, and placed his hands on him. "Brother Saul," he said, "the Lord has sent me – Jesus himself, who appeared to you on the road as you

---

[a] **8.26** south; *or* at midday.
[b] **8.26** This road is not used nowadays; *or* This is the desert road.
[c] **8.36** *Some manuscripts add verse 37:* Philip said to him, "You may be baptized if you believe with all your heart." "I do," he answered; "I believe that Jesus Christ is the Son of God."

Saul's vision, his meeting with Ananias and preaching at Damascus are depicted in this 8th-century illustration (9.1–23)

were coming here. He sent me so that you might see again and be filled with the Holy Spirit." [18]At once something like fish scales fell from Saul's eyes, and he was able to see again. He stood up and was baptized; [19]and after he had eaten, his strength came back.

Saul Preaches in Damascus

Saul stayed for a few days with the believers in Damascus. [20]He went straight to the synagogues and began to preach that Jesus was the Son of God.

21 All who heard him were amazed and asked, "Isn't he the one who in Jerusalem was killing those who worship that man Jesus? And didn't he come here for the very purpose of arresting those people and taking them back to the chief priests?"

22 But Saul's preaching became even more powerful, and his proofs that Jesus was the Messiah were so convincing that the Jews who lived in Damascus could not answer him.

23 After many days had gone by, the Jews met together and made plans to kill Saul, [24]but he was told of their plan. Day and night they watched the city gates in order to kill him. [25]But one night Saul's followers took him and let him down through an opening in the wall, lowering him in a basket.

Saul in Jerusalem

26 Saul went to Jerusalem and tried to join the disciples. But they would not believe that he was a disciple, and they were all afraid of him. [27]Then Barnabas came to his help and took him to the apostles. He explained to them how Saul had seen the Lord on the road and that the Lord had spoken to him. He also told them how boldly Saul had preached in the name of Jesus in Damascus. [28]And so Saul stayed with them and went all over Jerusalem, preaching boldly in the name of the Lord. [29]He also talked and disputed with the Greek-speaking Jews, but they tried to kill him. [30]When the believers found out about this, they took Saul to Caesarea and sent him away to Tarsus.

31 And so it was that the church throughout Judea, Galilee, and Samaria had a time of peace. Through the help of the Holy Spirit it was strengthened and grew in numbers, as it lived in reverence for the Lord.

Peter in Lydda and Joppa

32 Peter travelled everywhere, and on one occasion he went to visit God's people who lived in Lydda. [33]There he met a man named Aeneas, who was paralysed and had not been able to get out of bed for eight years. [34]"Aeneas," Peter said to him, "Jesus Christ makes you well. Get up and make your bed." At once Aeneas got up. [35]All the people living in Lydda and Sharon saw him, and they turned to the Lord.

36 In Joppa there was a woman named Tabitha, who was a believer. (Her name in Greek is Dorcas, meaning "a deer".) She spent all her time doing good and helping the poor. [37]At that time she became ill and died. Her body was washed and laid in a room upstairs. [38]Joppa was not very far from Lydda, and when the believers in Joppa heard that Peter was in Lydda, they sent two men to him with the message, "Please hurry and come to us." [39]So Peter got ready and went with them. When he arrived, he was taken to the room upstairs, where all the widows crowded round him, crying and showing him all the shirts and coats that Dorcas had made while

she was alive. [40]Peter put them all out of the room, and knelt down and prayed; then he turned to the body and said, "Tabitha, get up!" She opened her eyes, and when she saw Peter, she sat up. [41]Peter reached over and helped her get up. Then he called all the believers, including the widows, and presented her alive to them. [42]The news about this spread all over Joppa, and many people believed in the Lord. [43]Peter stayed on in Joppa for many days with a tanner of leather named Simon.

Peter and Cornelius

10 There was a man in Caesarea named Cornelius, who was a captain in the Roman regiment called "The Italian Regiment". [2]He was a religious man; he and his whole family worshipped God. He also did much to help the Jewish poor people and was constantly praying to God. [3]It was about three o'clock one afternoon when he had a vision, in which he clearly saw an angel of God come in and say to him, "Cornelius!"

4 He stared at the angel in fear and said, "What is it, sir?"

The angel answered, "God is pleased with your prayers and works of charity, and is ready to answer you. [5]And now send some men to Joppa for a certain man whose full name is Simon Peter. [6]He is a guest in the home of a tanner of leather named Simon, who lives by the sea." [7]Then the angel went away, and Cornelius called two of his house servants and a soldier, a religious man who was one of his personal attendants. [8]He told them what had happened and sent them off to Joppa.

9 The next day, as they were on their way and coming near Joppa, Peter went up on the roof of the house about noon in order to pray. [10]He became hungry and wanted something to eat; while the food was being prepared, he had a vision. [11]He saw heaven opened and something coming down that looked like a large sheet being lowered by its four corners to the earth. [12]In it were all kinds of animals, reptiles, and wild birds. [13]A voice said to him, "Get up, Peter; kill and eat!"

14 But Peter said, "Certainly not, Lord! I have never eaten anything ritually unclean or defiled."

15 The voice spoke to him again, "Do not consider anything unclean that God has declared clean." [16]This happened three times, and then the thing was taken back up into heaven.

17 While Peter was wondering about the meaning of this vision, the men sent by Cornelius had learnt where Simon's house was, and they were now standing in front of the gate. [18]They called out and asked, "Is there a guest here by the name of Simon Peter?"

19 Peter was still trying to understand what the vision meant, when the Spirit said, "Listen! Three[a] men are here looking for you. [20]So get ready and go down, and do not hesitate to go with them, for I have sent them." [21]So Peter went down and said to the men, "I am the man you are looking for. Why have you come?"

22 "Captain Cornelius sent us," they answered. "He is a good man who worships God and is highly respected by all the Jewish people. An angel of God told him to invite you to his house, so that he could hear what you have to say." [23]Peter invited the men in and persuaded them to spend the night there.

The next day he got ready and went with them; and some of the believers from Joppa went along with him. [24]The following day he arrived in Caesarea, where Cornelius was waiting for him, together with relatives and close friends that he had invited. [25]As Peter was about to go in, Cornelius met him, fell at his feet, and bowed down before him. [26]But Peter made him rise. "Stand up," he said; "I myself am only a man." [27]Peter kept on talking to Cornelius as he went into the house, where he found many people gathered. [28]He said to them, "You yourselves know very well that a Jew is not allowed by his religion to visit or associate with Gentiles. But God has shown me that I must not consider any person ritually unclean or defiled. [29]And so when you sent for me, I came without any objection. I ask you, then, why did you send for me?"

30 Cornelius said, "It was about this time three days ago that I was praying[b] in my house at three o'clock in the afternoon. Suddenly a man dressed in shining clothes stood in front of me [31]and said: 'Cornelius! God has heard your prayer and has taken notice of your works of charity. [32]Send someone to Joppa for a man whose full name is Simon Peter. He is a guest in the home of Simon the tanner of leather, who lives by the sea.' [33]And so I sent for you at once, and you have been good enough to come. Now we are all here in the presence of God, waiting to hear anything that the Lord has instructed you to say."

[a] **10.19** Three; *some manuscripts have* Some; *one manuscript has* Two.
[b] **10.30** praying; *some manuscripts have* fasting and praying.

Peter's Speech

34 Peter began to speak: "I now realize that it is true that God treats everyone on the same basis. [35]Those who worship him and do what is right are acceptable to him, no matter what race they belong to. [36]You know the message he sent to the people of Israel, proclaiming the Good News of peace through Jesus Christ, who is Lord of all. [37]You know of the great event that took place throughout the land of Israel, beginning in Galilee after John preached his message of baptism. [38]You know about Jesus of Nazareth and how God poured out on him the Holy Spirit and power. He went everywhere, doing good and healing all who were under the power of the Devil, for God was with him. [39]We are witnesses of everything that he did in the land of Israel and in Jerusalem. Then they put him to death by nailing him to a cross. [40]But God raised him from death three days later and caused him to appear, [41]not to everyone, but only to the witnesses that God had already chosen, that is, to us who ate and drank with him after he rose from death. [42]And he commanded us to preach the gospel to the people and to testify that he is the one whom God has appointed judge of the living and the dead. [43]All the prophets spoke about him, saying that all who believe in him will have their sins forgiven through the power of his name."

The Gentiles Receive the Holy Spirit

44 While Peter was still speaking, the Holy Spirit came down on all those who were listening to his message. [45]The Jewish believers who had come from Joppa with Peter were amazed that God had poured out his gift of the Holy Spirit on the Gentiles also. [46]For they heard them speaking in strange tongues and praising God's greatness. Peter spoke up: [47]"These people have received the Holy Spirit, just as we also did. Can anyone, then, stop them from being baptized with water?" [48]So he ordered them to be baptized in the name of Jesus Christ. Then they asked him to stay with them for a few days.

Peter's Report to the Church at Jerusalem

11 The apostles and the other believers throughout Judea heard that the Gentiles also had received the word of God. [2]When Peter went to Jerusalem, those who were in favour of circumcising Gentiles criticized him, saying, [3]"You were a guest in the home of uncircumcised Gentiles, and you even ate with them!" [4]So Peter gave them a complete account of what had happened from the very beginning:

5 "While I was praying in the city of Joppa, I had a vision. I saw something coming down that looked like a large sheet being lowered by its four corners from heaven, and it stopped next to me. [6]I looked closely inside and saw domesticated and wild animals, reptiles, and wild birds. [7]Then I heard a voice saying to me, 'Get up, Peter; kill and eat!' [8]But I said, 'Certainly not, Lord! No ritually unclean or defiled food has ever entered my mouth.' [9]The voice spoke again from heaven, 'Do not consider anything unclean that God has declared clean.' [10]This happened three times, and finally the whole thing was drawn back up into heaven. [11]At that very moment three men who had been sent to me from Caesarea arrived at the house where I was[a] staying. [12]The Spirit told me to go with them without hesitation. These six fellow-believers from Joppa accompanied me to Caesarea, and we all went into the house of Cornelius. [13]He told us how he had seen an angel standing in his house, who said to him, 'Send someone to Joppa for a man whose full name is Simon Peter. [14]He will speak words to you by which you and all your family will be saved.' [15]And when I began to speak, the Holy Spirit came down on them just as on us at the beginning. [16]Then I remembered what the Lord had said: 'John baptized with water, but you will be baptized with the Holy Spirit.' [17]It is clear that God gave those Gentiles the same gift that he gave us when we believed in the Lord Jesus Christ; who was I, then, to try to stop God!"

18 When they heard this, they stopped their criticism and praised God, saying, "Then God has given to the Gentiles also the opportunity to repent and live!"

The Church at Antioch

19 Some of the believers who were scattered by the persecution which took place when Stephen was killed went as far as Phoenicia, Cyprus, and Antioch, telling the message to Jews only. [20]But other believers, who were from Cyprus and Cyrene, went to Antioch and proclaimed the message to Gentiles[b] also, telling them the Good News about the Lord Jesus. [21]The Lord's power was with them, and a great number of people believed and turned to the Lord.

---

[a] **11.11** I was; *some manuscripts have* we were.
[b] **11.20** Gentiles; *some manuscripts have* Greek-speaking Jews *or* Greek-speaking people.

22 The news about this reached the church in Jerusalem, so they sent Barnabas to Antioch. [23]When he arrived and saw how God had blessed the people, he was glad and urged them all to be faithful and true to the Lord with all their hearts. [24]Barnabas was a good man, full of the Holy Spirit and faith, and many people were brought to the Lord.

25 Then Barnabas went to Tarsus to look for Saul. [26]When he found him, he took him to Antioch, and for a whole year the two met with the people of the church and taught a large group. It was at Antioch that the believers were first called Christians.

27 About that time some prophets went from Jerusalem to Antioch. [28]One of them, named Agabus, stood up and by the power of the Spirit predicted that a severe famine was about to come over all the earth. (It came when Claudius was emperor.) [29]The disciples decided that they would each send as much as they could to help their fellow-believers who lived in Judea. [30]They did this, then, and sent the money to the church elders by Barnabas and Saul.

More Persecution

12 About this time King Herod[a] began to persecute some members of the church. [2]He had James, the brother of John, put to death by the sword. [3]When he saw that this pleased the Jews, he went on to arrest Peter. (This happened during the time of the Festival of Unleavened Bread.) [4]After his arrest Peter was put in jail, where he was handed over to be guarded by four groups of four soldiers each. Herod planned to put him on trial in public after Passover. [5]So Peter was kept in jail, but the people of the church were praying earnestly to God for him.

Peter is Set Free from Prison

6 The night before Herod was going to bring him out to the people, Peter was sleeping between two guards. He was tied with two chains, and there were guards on duty at the prison gate. [7]Suddenly an angel of the Lord stood there, and a light shone in the cell. The angel shook Peter by the shoulder, woke him up, and said, "Hurry! Get up!" At once the chains fell off Peter's hands. [8]Then the angel said, "Fasten your belt and put on your sandals." Peter did so, and the angel said, "Put your cloak

<hr>

[a] **12.1** KING HEROD: *Herod Agrippa I, ruler of all Palestine.*

round you and come with me." [9]Peter followed him out of the prison, not knowing, however, if what the angel was doing was real; he thought he was seeing a vision. [10]They passed by the first guard post and then the second, and came at last to the iron gate leading into the city. The gate opened for them by itself, and they went out. They walked down a street, and suddenly the angel left Peter.

11 Then Peter realized what had happened to him, and said, "Now I know that it is really true! The Lord sent his angel to rescue me from Herod's power and from everything the Jewish people expected to happen."

12 Aware of his situation, he went to the home of Mary, the mother of John Mark, where many people had gathered and were praying. [13]Peter knocked at the outside door, and a servant named Rhoda came to answer it. [14]She recognized Peter's voice and was so happy that she ran back in without opening the door, and announced that Peter was standing outside. [15]"You are mad!" they told her. But she insisted that it was true. So they answered, "It is his angel."

16 Meanwhile Peter kept on knocking. At last they opened the door, and when they saw him, they were amazed. [17]He motioned with his hand for them to be quiet, and he explained to them how the Lord had brought him out of prison. "Tell this to James and the rest of the believers," he said; then he left and went somewhere else.

18 When morning came, there was a tremendous confusion among the guards – what had happened to Peter? [19]Herod gave orders to search for him, but they could not find him. So he had the guards questioned and ordered them to be put to death.

After this, Herod left Judea and spent some time in Caesarea.

The Death of Herod

20 Herod was very angry with the people of Tyre and Sidon, so they went in a group to see him. First they convinced Blastus, the man in charge of the palace, that he should help them. Then they went to Herod and asked him for peace, because their country got its food supplies from the king's country.

21 On a chosen day Herod put on his royal robes, sat on his throne, and made a speech to the people. [22]"It isn't a man speaking, but a god!" they shouted. [23]At once the angel of the Lord struck Herod down, because he did not give honour to God. He was eaten by worms and died.

PAUL'S MISSIONARY JOURNEYS

——————▶	Paul's first journey
– – – – –▶	Paul's second journey
· · · · · ·▶	Paul's third journey

0   500km

24   Meanwhile the word of God continued to spread and grow.

25   Barnabas and Saul finished their mission and returned from[a] Jerusalem, taking John Mark with them.

Barnabas and Saul are Chosen and Sent

13 In the church at Antioch there were some prophets and teachers: Barnabas, Simeon (called the Black), Lucius (from Cyrene), Manaen (who had been brought up with Herod[b] the governor), and Saul. [2]While they were serving the Lord and fasting, the Holy Spirit said to them, "Set apart for me Barnabas and Saul, to do the work to which I have called them."

---

[a] **12.25** from; *some manuscripts have to.*
[b] **13.1** HEROD: *Herod Antipas, ruler of Galilee (see Lk 3.1).*

3   They fasted and prayed, placed their hands on them, and sent them off.

In Cyprus

4   Having been sent by the Holy Spirit, Barnabas and Saul went to Seleucia and sailed from there to the island of Cyprus. [5]When they arrived at Salamis, they preached the word of God in the synagogues. They had John Mark with them to help in the work.

6   They went all the way across the island to Paphos, where they met a certain magician named Bar-Jesus, a Jew who claimed to be a prophet. [7]He was a friend of the governor of the island, Sergius Paulus, who was an intelligent man. The governor called Barnabas and Saul before him because he wanted to hear the word of God. [8]But they were opposed by the magician Elymas (that is his name in Greek), who tried to

turn the governor away from the faith. [9]Then Saul – also known as Paul – was filled with the Holy Spirit; he looked straight at the magician [10]and said, "You son of the Devil! You are the enemy of everything that is good. You are full of all kinds of evil tricks, and you always keep trying to turn the Lord's truths into lies! [11]The Lord's hand will come down on you now; you will be blind and will not see the light of day for a time."

At once Elymas felt a dark mist cover his eyes, and he walked about trying to find someone to lead him by the hand. [12]When the governor saw what had happened, he believed; for he was greatly amazed at the teaching about the Lord.

In Antioch in Pisidia

13 Paul and his companions sailed from Paphos and came to Perga, a city in Pamphylia, where John Mark left them and went back to Jerusalem. [14]They went on from Perga and arrived in Antioch in Pisidia, and on the Sabbath they went into the synagogue and sat down. [15]After the reading from the Law of Moses and from the writings of the prophets, the officials of the synagogue sent them a message: "Brothers and sisters, we want you to speak to the people if you have a message of encouragement for them." [16]Paul stood up, motioned with his hand, and began to speak:

"Fellow-Israelites and all Gentiles here who worship God: hear me! [17]The God of the people of Israel chose our ancestors and made the people a great nation during the time they lived as foreigners in Egypt. God brought them out of Egypt by his great power, [18]and for forty years he endured[a] them in the desert. [19]He destroyed seven nations in the land of Canaan and made his people the owners of the land. [20]All this took about four hundred and fifty years.

"After this[b] he gave them judges until the time of the prophet Samuel. [21]And when they asked for a king, God gave them Saul son of Kish from the tribe of Benjamin, to be their king for forty years. [22]After removing him, God made David their king. This is what God said about him: 'I have found that David son of Jesse is the kind of man I like, a man who will do all I want him to do.' [23]It was Jesus, a descendant of David, whom God made the Saviour of the people of Israel, as he had promised. [24]Before Jesus began his work, John preached to all the people of Israel that they should turn from their sins and be baptized. [25]And as John was about to finish his mission, he said to the people, 'Who do you think I am? I am not the one you are waiting for. But listen! He is coming after me, and I am not good enough to take his sandals off his feet.'

26 "My fellow-Israelites, descendants of Abraham, and all Gentiles here who worship God: it is to us that this message of salvation has been sent! [27]For the people who live in Jerusalem and their leaders did not know that he is the Saviour, nor did they understand the words of the prophets that are read every Sabbath. Yet they made the prophets' words come true by condemning Jesus. [28]And even though they could find no reason to pass the death sentence on him, they asked Pilate to have him put to death. [29]And after they had done everything that the Scriptures say about him, they took him down from the cross and placed him in a tomb. [30]But God raised him from death, [31]and for many days he appeared to those who had travelled with him from Galilee to Jerusalem. They are now witnesses for him to the people of Israel. [32-33]And we are here to bring the Good News to you: what God promised our ancestors he would do, he has now done for us, who are their descendants, by raising Jesus to life. As it is written in the second Psalm:

'You are my Son;
    today I have become your Father.'

[34]And this is what God said about raising him from death, never to rot away in the grave:

'I will give you the sacred and sure blessings
    that I promised to David.'

[35]As indeed he says in another passage:

'You will not allow your faithful servant to
    rot in the grave.'

[36]For David served God's purposes in his own time, and then he died, was buried with his ancestors, and his body rotted in the grave. [37]But this did not happen to the one whom God raised from death. [38-39]We want you to know, my fellow-Israelites, that it is through Jesus that the message about forgiveness of sins is preached to you; and that everyone who believes in him is set free from all the sins from which the Law of Moses could not set you free. [40]Take care, then, so that what the prophets said may not happen to you:[c]

---

[a] **13.18** he endured; *some manuscripts have* he took care of.

[b] **13.20** All this took about four hundred and fifty years. After this; *or* Some four hundred and fifty years later.

[c] **13.40** *Some manuscripts do not have* to you.

41   'Look, you scoffers! Be astonished and die!
       For what I am doing today
              is something that you will not believe,
              even when someone explains it to you!' "

42   As Paul and Barnabas were leaving the synagogue, the people invited them to come back the next Sabbath and tell them more about these things. ⁴³After the people had left the meeting, Paul and Barnabas were followed by many Jews and by many Gentiles who had been converted to Judaism. The apostles spoke to them and encouraged them to keep on living in the grace of God.

44   The next Sabbath nearly everyone in the town came to hear the word of the Lord. ⁴⁵When the Jews saw the crowds, they were filled with jealousy; they disputed what Paul was saying and insulted him. ⁴⁶But Paul and Barnabas spoke out even more boldly: "It was necessary that the word of God should be spoken first to you. But since you reject it and do not consider yourselves worthy of eternal life, we will leave you and go to the Gentiles. ⁴⁷For this is the commandment that the Lord has given us:

       'I have made you a light for the Gentiles,
              so that all the world may be saved.' "

48   When the Gentiles heard this, they were glad and praised the Lord's message; and those who had been chosen for eternal life became believers.

49   The word of the Lord spread everywhere in that region. ⁵⁰But the Jews stirred up the leading men of the city and the Gentile women of high social standing who worshipped God. They started a persecution against Paul and Barnabas and threw them out of their region. ⁵¹The apostles shook the dust off their feet in protest against them and went on to Iconium. ⁵²The believers in Antioch were full of joy and the Holy Spirit.

In Iconium

14 The same thing happened in Iconium: Paul and Barnabas went to the synagogue and spoke in such a way that a great number of Jews and Gentiles became believers. ²But the Jews who would not believe stirred up the Gentiles and turned them against the believers. ³The apostles stayed there for a long time, speaking boldly about the Lord, who proved that their message about his grace was true by giving them the power to perform miracles and wonders. ⁴The people of the city were divided: some were for the Jews, others for the apostles.

*Reading the Gospel (which means "Good News")
in church (14.7)*

5   Then some Gentiles and Jews, together with their leaders, decided to ill-treat the apostles and stone them. ⁶When the apostles learnt about it, they fled to the cities of Lystra and Derbe in Lycaonia and to the surrounding territory. ⁷There they preached the Good News.

In Lystra and Derbe

8   In Lystra there was a man who had been lame from birth and had never been able to walk. ⁹He sat there and listened to Paul's words. Paul saw that he believed and could be healed, so he looked straight at him ¹⁰and said in a loud voice, "Stand up straight on your feet!" The man jumped up and started walking around. ¹¹When the crowds saw what Paul had done, they started shouting in their own Lycaonian language, "The gods have become like men and have come down to us!" ¹²They gave Barnabas the name Zeus, and Paul the name Hermes, because he was the chief speaker. ¹³The priest of the god Zeus, whose temple stood just outside the town, brought bulls and flowers to the gate, for he and the crowds wanted to offer sacrifice to the apostles.

14   When Barnabas and Paul heard what they were about to do, they tore their clothes and ran into the middle of the crowd, shouting, ¹⁵"Why are you doing this? We ourselves are only human beings like you! We are here to announce the Good News, to turn you away from these worthless things to the living God, who made heaven, earth, sea, and all that is in them. ¹⁶In the past he allowed all people to go

their own way. 17But he has always given evidence of his existence by the good things he does: he gives you rain from heaven and crops at the right times; he gives you food and fills your hearts with happiness." 18Even with these words the apostles could hardly keep the crowd from offering a sacrifice to them.

19 Some Jews came from Antioch in Pisidia and from Iconium; they won the crowd over to their side, stoned Paul and dragged him out of the town, thinking that he was dead. 20But when the believers gathered round him, he got up and went back into the town. The next day he and Barnabas went to Derbe.

The Return to Antioch in Syria

21 Paul and Barnabas preached the Good News in Derbe and won many disciples. Then they went back to Lystra, to Iconium, and on to Antioch in Pisidia. 22They strengthened the believers and encouraged them to remain true to the faith. "We must pass through many troubles to enter the Kingdom of God," they taught. 23In each church they appointed elders, and with prayers and fasting they commended them to the Lord, in whom they had put their trust.

24 After going through the territory of Pisidia, they came to Pamphylia. 25There they preached the message in Perga and then went to Attalia, 26and from there they sailed back to Antioch, the place where they had been commended to the care of God's grace for the work they had now completed.

27 When they arrived in Antioch, they gathered the people of the church together and told them about all that God had done with them and how he had opened the way for the Gentiles to believe. 28And they stayed a long time there with the believers.

The Meeting at Jerusalem

15 Some men came from Judea to Antioch and started teaching the believers, "You cannot be saved unless you are circumcised as the Law of Moses requires." 2Paul and Barnabas got into a fierce argument with them about this, so it was decided that Paul and Barnabas and some of the others in Antioch should go to Jerusalem and see the apostles and elders about this matter.

3 They were sent on their way by the church; and as they went through Phoenicia and Samaria, they reported how the Gentiles had turned to God; this news brought great joy to all the believers. 4When they arrived in Jerusalem,

they were welcomed by the church, the apostles, and the elders, to whom they told all that God had done through them. 5But some of the believers who belonged to the party of the Pharisees stood up and said, "The Gentiles must be circumcised and told to obey the Law of Moses."

6 The apostles and the elders met together to consider this question. 7After a long debate Peter stood up and said, "My brothers and sisters, you know that a long time ago God chose me from among you to preach the Good News to the Gentiles, so that they could hear and believe. 8And God, who knows the thoughts of everyone, showed his approval of the Gentiles by giving the Holy Spirit to them, just as he had to us. 9He made no difference between us and them; he forgave their sins because they believed. 10So then, why do you now want to put God to the test by laying a load on the backs of the believers which neither our ancestors nor we ourselves were able to carry? 11No! We believe and are saved by the grace of the Lord Jesus, just as they are."

12 The whole group was silent as they heard Barnabas and Paul report all the miracles and wonders that God had performed through them among the Gentiles. 13When they had finished speaking, James spoke up: "Listen to me, my brothers and sisters! 14Simon has just explained how God first showed his care for the Gentiles by taking from among them a people to belong to him. 15The words of the prophets agree completely with this. As the scripture says:

16 'After this I will return, says the Lord,
  and restore the kingdom of David.
I will rebuild its ruins
  and make it strong again.

17 And so all the rest of the human race will
    come to me,
  all the Gentiles whom I have called to be
  my own.

18 So says the Lord, who made this known long
  ago.'

19 "It is my opinion," James went on, "that we should not trouble the Gentiles who are turning to God. 20Instead, we should write a letter telling them not to eat any food that is ritually unclean because it has been offered to idols; to keep themselves from sexual immorality; and not to eat any animal that has been strangled, or any blood. 21For the Law of Moses has been read for a very long time in the synagogues every Sabbath, and his words are preached in every town."

The Letter to the Gentile Believers

22 Then the apostles and the elders, together with the whole church, decided to choose some men from the group and send them to Antioch with Paul and Barnabas. They chose two men who were highly respected by the believers, Judas, called Barsabbas, and Silas, [23]and they sent the following letter by them:

"We, the apostles and the elders, your brothers, send greetings to all our brothers of Gentile birth who live in Antioch, Syria, and Cilicia. [24]We have heard that some who went from our group have troubled and upset you by what they said; they had not, however, received any instruction from us. [25]And so we have met together and have all agreed to choose some messengers and send them to you. They will go with our dear friends Barnabas and Paul, [26]who have risked their lives in the service of our Lord Jesus Christ. [27]We send you, then, Judas and Silas, who will tell you in person the same things we are writing. [28]The Holy Spirit and we have agreed not to put any other burden on you besides these necessary rules: [29]eat no food that has been offered to idols; eat no blood; eat no animal that has been strangled; and keep yourselves from sexual immorality. You will do well if you take care not to do these things. With our best wishes."

30 The messengers were sent off and went to Antioch, where they gathered the whole group of believers and gave them the letter. [31]When the people read it, they were filled with joy by the message of encouragement. [32]Judas and Silas, who were themselves prophets, spoke a long time with them, giving them courage and strength. [33]After spending some time there, they were sent off in peace by the believers and went back to those who had sent them.[a]

35 Paul and Barnabas spent some time in Antioch, and together with many others they taught and preached the word of the Lord.

Paul and Barnabas Separate

36 Some time later Paul said to Barnabas, "Let us go back and visit our brothers and sisters in every town where we preached the word of the Lord, and let us find out how they are getting on." [37]Barnabas wanted to take John Mark with them, [38]but Paul did not think it was right to take him, because he had not stayed with them to the end of their mission, but had turned back

and left them in Pamphylia. [39]There was a sharp argument, and they separated: Barnabas took Mark and sailed off for Cyprus, [40]while Paul chose Silas and left, commended by the believers to the care of the Lord's grace. [41]He went through Syria and Cilicia, strengthening the churches.

Timothy Goes with Paul and Silas

16 Paul travelled on to Derbe and Lystra, where a Christian named Timothy lived. His mother, who was also a Christian, was Jewish, but his father was a Greek. [2]All the believers in Lystra and Iconium spoke well of Timothy. [3]Paul wanted to take Timothy along with him, so he circumcised him. He did so because all the Jews who lived in those places knew that Timothy's father was Greek. [4]As they went through the towns, they delivered to the believers the rules decided upon by the apostles and elders in Jerusalem, and told them to obey those rules. [5]So the churches were made stronger in the faith and grew in numbers every day.

In Troas: Paul's Vision

6 They travelled through the region of Phrygia and Galatia because the Holy Spirit did not let them preach the message in the province of Asia. [7]When they reached the border of Mysia, they tried to go into the province of Bithynia, but the Spirit of Jesus did not allow them. [8]So they travelled right on through[b] Mysia and went to Troas. [9]That night Paul had a vision in which he saw a Macedonian standing and begging him, "Come over to Macedonia and help us!" [10]As soon as Paul had this vision, we got ready to leave for Macedonia, because we decided that God had called us to preach the Good News to the people there.

In Philippi: the Conversion of Lydia

11 We left by ship from Troas and sailed straight across to Samothrace, and the next day to Neapolis. [12]From there we went inland to Philippi, a city of the first district of Macedonia;[c] it is also a Roman colony. We spent several days there. [13]On the Sabbath we went out of the city to the riverside, where we thought there would

[a] **15.33** *Some manuscripts add verse 34:* But Silas decided to stay there.

[b] **16.8** travelled right on through; *or* passed by.
[c] **16.12** a city of the first district of Macedonia; *some manuscripts have* a leading city of the district of Macedonia; *or* a leading city of that district in Macedonia.

be a place where Jews gathered for prayer. We sat down and talked to the women who gathered there. ¹⁴One of those who heard us was Lydia from Thyatira, who was a dealer in purple cloth. She was a woman who worshipped God, and the Lord opened her mind to pay attention to what Paul was saying. ¹⁵After she and the people of her house had been baptized, she invited us, "Come and stay in my house if you have decided that I am a true believer in the Lord." And she persuaded us to go.

In Prison at Philippi

16 One day as we were going to the place of prayer, we were met by a young servant woman who had an evil spirit that enabled her to predict the future. She earned a lot of money for her owners by telling fortunes. ¹⁷She followed Paul and us, shouting, "These men are servants of the Most High God! They announce to you how you can be saved!" ¹⁸She did this for many days, until Paul became so upset that he turned round and said to the spirit, "In the name of Jesus Christ I order you to come out of her!" The spirit went out of her that very moment.

19 When her owners realized that their chance of making money was gone, they seized Paul and Silas and dragged them to the authorities in the public square. ²⁰They brought them before the Roman officials and said, "These men are Jews, and they are causing trouble in our city. ²¹They are teaching customs that are against our law; we are Roman citizens, and we cannot accept these customs or practise them." ²²And the crowd joined in the attack against Paul and Silas.

Then the officials tore the clothes off Paul and Silas and ordered them to be whipped. ²³After a severe beating, they were thrown into jail, and the jailer was ordered to lock them up tight. ²⁴Upon receiving this order, the jailer threw them into the inner cell and fastened their feet between heavy blocks of wood.

25 About midnight Paul and Silas were praying and singing hymns to God, and the other prisoners were listening to them. ²⁶Suddenly there was a violent earthquake, which shook the prison to its foundations. At once all the doors opened, and the chains fell off all the prisoners. ²⁷The jailer woke up, and when he saw the prison doors open, he thought that the prisoners had escaped; so he pulled out his sword and was about to kill himself. ²⁸But Paul shouted at the top of his voice, "Don't harm yourself! We are all here!"

29 The jailer called for a light, rushed in, and fell trembling at the feet of Paul and Silas. ³⁰Then he led them out and asked, "Sirs, what must I do to be saved?"

31 They answered, "Believe in the Lord Jesus, and you will be saved – you and your family." ³²Then they preached the word of the Lord to him and to all the others in his house. ³³At that very hour of the night the jailer took them and washed their wounds; and he and all his family were baptized at once. ³⁴Then he took Paul and Silas up into his house and gave them some food to eat. He and his family were filled with joy, because they now believed in God.

35 The next morning the Roman authorities sent police officers with the order, "Let those men go."

36 So the jailer told Paul, "The officials have sent an order for you and Silas to be released. You may leave, then, and go in peace."

37 But Paul said to the police officers, "We were not found guilty of any crime, yet they whipped us in public – and we are Roman citizens! Then they threw us in prison. And now they want to send us away secretly. Not likely! The Roman officials themselves must come here and let us out."

38 The police officers reported these words to the Roman officials; and when they heard that Paul and Silas were Roman citizens, they were afraid. ³⁹So they went and apologized to them; then they led them out of the prison and asked them to leave the city. ⁴⁰Paul and Silas left the prison and went to Lydia's house. There they met the believers, spoke words of encouragement to them, and left.

In Thessalonica

17 Paul and Silas travelled on through Amphipolis and Apollonia and came to Thessalonica, where there was a synagogue. ²According to his usual habit Paul went to the synagogue. There during three Sabbaths he held discussions with the people, quoting ³and explaining the Scriptures and proving from them that the Messiah had to suffer and rise from death. "This Jesus whom I announce to you," Paul said, "is the Messiah." ⁴Some of them were convinced and joined Paul and Silas; so did many of the leading women and a large group of Greeks who worshipped God.

5 But some Jews were jealous and gathered worthless loafers from the streets and formed a mob. They set the whole city in an uproar and attacked the home of a man called Jason, in an

attempt to find Paul and Silas and bring them out to the people. ⁶But when they did not find them, they dragged Jason and some other believers before the city authorities and shouted, "These men have caused trouble everywhere! Now they have come to our city, ⁷and Jason has kept them in his house. They are all breaking the laws of the Emperor, saying that there is another king, whose name is Jesus." ⁸With these words they threw the crowd and the city authorities into an uproar. ⁹The authorities made Jason and the others pay the required amount of money to be released, and then let them go.

In Berea

10 As soon as night came, the believers sent Paul and Silas to Berea. When they arrived, they went to the synagogue. ¹¹The people there were more open-minded than the people in Thessalonica. They listened to the message with great eagerness, and every day they studied the Scriptures to see if what Paul said was really true. ¹²Many of them believed; and many Greek women of high social standing and many Greek men also believed. ¹³But when the Jews in Thessalonica heard that Paul had preached the word of God in Berea also, they came there and started exciting and stirring up the mob. ¹⁴At once the believers sent Paul away to the coast; but both Silas and Timothy stayed in Berea. ¹⁵The men who were taking Paul went with him as far as Athens and then returned to Berea with instructions from Paul that Silas and Timothy should join him as soon as possible.

In Athens

16 While Paul was waiting in Athens for Silas and Timothy, he was greatly upset when he noticed how full of idols the city was. ¹⁷So he held discussions in the synagogue with the Jews and with the Gentiles who worshipped God, and also in the public square every day with the people who happened to pass by. ¹⁸Certain Epicurean and Stoic teachers also debated with him. Some of them asked, "What is this ignorant show-off trying to say?"

Others answered, "He seems to be talking about foreign gods." They said this because Paul was preaching about Jesus and the resurrection.ᵃ ¹⁹So they took Paul, brought him

before the city council, the Areopagus, and said, "We would like to know what this new teaching is that you are talking about. ²⁰Some of the things we hear you say sound strange to us, and we would like to know what they mean." ²¹(For all the citizens of Athens and the foreigners who lived there liked to spend all their time telling and hearing the latest new thing.)

22 Paul stood up in front of the city council and said, "I see that in every way you Athenians are very religious. ²³For as I walked through your city and looked at the places where you worship, I found an altar on which is written, 'To an Unknown God'. That which you worship, then, even though you do not know it, is what I now proclaim to you. ²⁴God, who made the world and everything in it, is Lord of heaven and earth and does not live in temples made by human hands. ²⁵Nor does he need anything that we can supply by working for him, since it is he himself who gives life and breath and everything else to everyone. ²⁶From one human being he created all races on earth and made them live throughout the whole earth. He himself fixed beforehand the exact times and the limits of the places where they would live. ²⁷He did this so that they would look for him, and perhaps find him as they felt about for him. Yet God is actually not far from any one of us; ²⁸as someone has said,

'In him we live and move and exist.'

It is as some of your poets have said,

'We too are his children.'

29 Since we are God's children, we should not suppose that his nature is anything like an image of gold or silver or stone, shaped by human art and skill. ³⁰God has overlooked the times when people did not know him, but now he commands all of them everywhere to turn away from their evil ways. ³¹For he has fixed a day in which he will judge the whole world with justice by means of a man he has chosen. He has given proof of this to everyone by raising that man from death!"

32 When they heard Paul speak about a raising from death, some of them made fun of him, but others said, "We want to hear you speak about this again." ³³And so Paul left the meeting. ³⁴Some men joined him and believed, among whom was Dionysius, a member of the council; there was also a woman named Damaris, and some other people.

ᵃ **17.18** JESUS AND THE RESURRECTION: *In Greek, the feminine noun "resurrection" could be understood to be the name of a goddess.*

In Corinth

18 After this, Paul left Athens and went on to Corinth. ²There he met a Jew named Aquila, born in Pontus, who had recently come from Italy with his wife Priscilla, for the Emperor Claudius had ordered all the Jews to leave Rome. Paul went to see them, ³and stayed and worked with them, because he earned his living by making tents, just as they did. ⁴He held discussions in the synagogue every Sabbath, trying to convince both Jews and Greeks.

5 When Silas and Timothy arrived from Macedonia, Paul gave his whole time to preaching the message, testifying to the Jews that Jesus is the Messiah. ⁶When they opposed him and said evil things about him, he protested by shaking the dust from his clothes and saying to them, "If you are lost, you yourselves must take the blame for it! I am not responsible. From now on I will go to the Gentiles." ⁷So he left them and went to live in the house of a Gentile named Titius Justus, who worshipped God; his house was next to the synagogue. ⁸Crispus, who was the leader of the synagogue, believed in the Lord, together with all his family; and many other people in Corinth heard the message, believed, and were baptized.

9 One night Paul had a vision in which the Lord said to him, "Do not be afraid, but keep on speaking and do not give up, ¹⁰for I am with you. No one will be able to harm you, for many in this city are my people." ¹¹So Paul stayed there for a year and a half, teaching the people the word of God.

12 When Gallio was made the Roman governor of Achaia, Jews there got together, seized Paul, and took him into court. ¹³"This man," they said, "is trying to persuade people to worship God in a way that is against the law!"

14 Paul was about to speak when Gallio said to the Jews, "If this were a matter of some evil crime or wrong that has been committed, it would be reasonable for me to be patient with you Jews. ¹⁵But since it is an argument about words and names and your own law, you yourselves must settle it. I will not be the judge of such things!" ¹⁶And he drove them out of the court. ¹⁷They all seized Sosthenes, the leader of the synagogue, and beat him in front of the court. But that did not bother Gallio a bit.

The Return to Antioch

18 Paul stayed on with the believers in Corinth for many days, then left them and sailed off with Priscilla and Aquila for Syria. Before sailing from Cenchreae he had his head shaved because of a vow he had taken.[a] ¹⁹They arrived in Ephesus, where Paul left Priscilla and Aquila. He went into the synagogue and held discussions with the Jews. ²⁰The people asked him to stay longer, but he would not consent. ²¹Instead, he told them as he left, "If it is the will of God, I will come back to you." And so he sailed from Ephesus.

22 When he arrived at Caesarea, he went to Jerusalem and greeted the church, and then went to Antioch. ²³After spending some time there, he left and went through the region of Galatia and Phrygia, strengthening all the believers.

Apollos in Ephesus and Corinth

24 At that time a Jew named Apollos, who had been born in Alexandria, came to Ephesus. He was an eloquent speaker and had a thorough knowledge of the Scriptures. ²⁵He had been instructed in the Way of the Lord, and with great enthusiasm he proclaimed and taught correctly the facts about Jesus. However, he knew only the baptism of John. ²⁶He began to speak boldly in the synagogue. When Priscilla and Aquila heard him, they took him home with them and explained to him more correctly the Way of God. ²⁷Apollos then decided to go to Achaia, so the believers in Ephesus helped him by writing to the believers in Achaia, urging them to welcome him. When he arrived, he was a great help to those who through God's grace had become believers. ²⁸For with his strong arguments he defeated the Jews in public debates by proving from the Scriptures that Jesus is the Messiah.

Paul in Ephesus

19 While Apollos was in Corinth, Paul travelled through the interior of the province and arrived in Ephesus. There he found some disciples ²and asked them, "Did you receive the Holy Spirit when you became believers?"

"We have not even heard that there is a Holy Spirit," they answered.

3 "Well, then, what kind of baptism did you receive?" Paul asked.

ᵃ **18.18** A VOW HE HAD TAKEN: *This refers to the Jewish custom of shaving the head as a sign that a vow has been kept.*

"The baptism of John," they answered.

4   Paul said, "The baptism of John was for those who turned from their sins; and he told the people of Israel to believe in the one who was coming after him – that is, in Jesus."

5   When they heard this, they were baptized in the name of the Lord Jesus. ⁶Paul placed his hands on them, and the Holy Spirit came upon them; they spoke in strange tongues and also proclaimed God's message. ⁷They were about twelve men in all.

8   Paul went into the synagogue and during three months spoke boldly with the people, holding discussions with them and trying to convince them about the Kingdom of God. ⁹But some of them were stubborn and would not believe, and before the whole group they said evil things about the Way of the Lord. So Paul left them and took the believers with him, and every dayᵃ he held discussions in the lecture hall of Tyrannus. ¹⁰This went on for two years, so that all the people who lived in the province of Asia, both Jews and Gentiles, heard the word of the Lord.

The Sons of Sceva

11   God was performing unusual miracles through Paul. ¹²Even handkerchiefs and aprons he had used were taken to those who were ill, and their diseases were driven away, and the evil spirits would go out of them. ¹³Some Jews who travelled round and drove out evil spirits also tried to use the name of the Lord Jesus to do this. They said to the evil spirits, "I command you in the name of Jesus, whom Paul preaches." ¹⁴Seven brothers, who were the sons of a Jewish High Priest named Sceva, were doing this.

15   But the evil spirit said to them, "I know Jesus, and I know about Paul; but you – who are you?"

16   The man who had the evil spirit in him attacked them with such violence that he overpowered them all. They ran away from his house, wounded and with their clothes torn off. ¹⁷All the Jews and Gentiles who lived in Ephesus heard about this; they were all filled with fear, and the name of the Lord Jesus was given greater honour. ¹⁸Many of the believers came, publicly admitting and revealing what they had done. ¹⁹Many of those who had practised magic brought their books together and burnt them in public. They added up the price of the books, and the total came to 50,000 silver coins.ᵇ ²⁰In this powerful way the word of the Lordᶜ kept spreading and growing stronger.

The Riot in Ephesus

21   After these things had happened, Paul made up his mindᵈ to travel through Macedonia and Achaia and go on to Jerusalem. "After I go there," he said, "I must also see Rome." ²²So he sent Timothy and Erastus, two of his helpers, to Macedonia, while he spent more time in the province of Asia.

23   It was at this time that there was serious trouble in Ephesus because of the Way of the Lord. ²⁴A certain silversmith named Demetrius made silver models of the temple of the goddess Artemis, and his business brought a great deal of profit to the workers. ²⁵So he called them all together with others whose work was like theirs and said to them, "Men, you know that our prosperity comes from this work. ²⁶Now, you can see and hear for yourselves what this fellow Paul is doing. He says that gods made by human hands are not gods at all, and he has succeeded in convincing many people, both here in Ephesus and in nearly the whole province of Asia. ²⁷There is the danger, then, that this business of ours will get a bad name. Not only that, but there is also the danger that the temple of the great goddess Artemis will come to mean nothing and that her greatness will be destroyed – the goddess worshipped by everyone in Asia and in all the world!"

28   As the crowd heard these words, they became furious and started shouting, "Great is Artemis of Ephesus!" ²⁹The uproar spread throughout the whole city. The mob seized Gaius and Aristarchus, two Macedonians who were travelling with Paul, and rushed with them to the theatre. ³⁰Paul himself wanted to go before the crowd, but the believers would not let him. ³¹Some of the provincial authorities, who were his friends, also sent him a message begging him not to show himself in the theatre. ³²Meanwhile the whole meeting was in an uproar: some people were shouting one thing, others were shouting something else, because most of them did not even know why they had come together. ³³Some of the people concluded that Alexander

---

ᵃ **19.9** *Some manuscripts add* from 11 a.m. until 4 p.m.

ᵇ **19.19** SILVER COINS: *A silver coin was the daily wage of a rural worker (see Mt 20.2).*

ᶜ **19.20** In this ... Lord; *or* And so, by the power of the Lord, the message.

ᵈ **19.21** Paul made up his mind; *or* Paul, led by the Spirit, decided.

was responsible, since the Jews made him go up to the front. Then Alexander motioned with his hand for the people to be silent, and he tried to make a speech of defence. [34]But when they recognized that he was a Jew, they all shouted together the same thing for two hours: "Great is Artemis of Ephesus!"

35 At last the town clerk was able to calm the crowd. "Fellow-Ephesians!" he said. "Everyone knows that the city of Ephesus is the keeper of the temple of the great Artemis and of the sacred stone that fell down from heaven. [36]Nobody can deny these things. So then, you must calm down and not do anything reckless. [37]You have brought these men here even though they have not robbed temples or said evil things about our goddess. [38]If Demetrius and his workers have an accusation against anyone, we have the authorities and the regular days for court; charges can be made there. [39]But if there is something more that you want, it will have to be settled in a legal meeting of citizens. [40]For after what has happened today, there is the danger that we will be accused of a riot. There is no excuse for all this uproar, and we would not be able to give a good reason for it." [41]After saying this, he dismissed the meeting.

To Macedonia and Achaia

20 After the uproar died down, Paul called together the believers and with words of encouragement said goodbye to them. Then he left and went on to Macedonia. [2]He went through those regions and encouraged the people with many messages. Then he came to Achaia, [3]where he stayed three months. He was getting ready to go to Syria when he discovered that there were Jews plotting against him; so he decided to go back through Macedonia. [4]Sopater son of Pyrrhus, from Berea, went with him; so did Aristarchus and Secundus, from Thessalonica; Gaius, from Derbe; Tychicus and Trophimus, from the province of Asia; and Timothy. [5]They went ahead and waited for us in Troas. [6]We sailed from Philippi after the Festival of Unleavened Bread, and five days later we joined them in Troas, where we spent a week.

Paul's Last Visit to Troas

7 On Saturday[a] evening we gathered together for the fellowship meal. Paul spoke to the people and kept on speaking until midnight,

Christians celebrate Holy Communion, a fellowship meal for all believers (20.7)

since he was going to leave the next day. [8]Many lamps were burning in the upstairs room where we were meeting. [9]A young man named Eutychus was sitting in the window, and as Paul kept on talking, Eutychus got sleepier and sleepier, until he finally went sound asleep and fell from the third storey to the ground. When they picked him up, he was dead. [10]But Paul went down and threw himself on him and hugged him. "Don't worry," he said, "he is still alive!" [11]Then he went back upstairs, broke bread, and ate. After talking with them for a long time, even until sunrise, Paul left. [12]They took the young man home alive and were greatly comforted.

From Troas to Miletus

13 We went on ahead to the ship and sailed off to Assos, where we were going to take Paul aboard. He had told us to do this, because he was going there by land. [14]When he met us in Assos, we took him aboard and went on to Mitylene. [15]We sailed from there and arrived off Chios the next day. A day later we came to Samos, and the following day we reached Miletus. [16]Paul had decided to sail on past Ephesus, so as not to lose any time in the province of Asia. He was in a hurry to arrive in Jerusalem by the day of Pentecost, if at all possible.

---

[a] **20.7** Saturday; *or* Sunday.

Paul's Farewell Speech to the Elders of Ephesus

17 From Miletus Paul sent a message to Ephesus, asking the elders of the church to meet him. ¹⁸When they arrived, he said to them, "You know how I spent the whole time I was with you, from the first day I arrived in the province of Asia. ¹⁹With all humility and many tears I did my work as the Lord's servant during the hard times that came to me because of the plots of some Jews. ²⁰You know that I did not hold back anything that would be of help to you as I preached and taught in public and in your homes. ²¹To Jews and Gentiles alike I gave solemn warning that they should turn from their sins to God and believe in our Lord Jesus. ²²And now, in obedience to the Holy Spirit I am going to Jerusalem, not knowing what will happen to me there. ²³I only know that in every city the Holy Spirit has warned me that prison and troubles wait for me. ²⁴But I reckon my own life to be worth nothing to me; I only want to complete my mission and finish the work that the Lord Jesus gave me to do, which is to declare the Good News about the grace of God.

25 "I have gone about among all of you, preaching the Kingdom of God. And now I know that none of you will ever see me again. ²⁶So I solemnly declare to you this very day: if any of you should be lost, I am not responsible. ²⁷For I have not held back from announcing to you the whole purpose of God. ²⁸So keep watch over yourselves and over all the flock which the Holy Spirit has placed in your care. Be shepherds of the church of God,^a which he made his own through the blood of his Son.^b ²⁹I know that after I leave, fierce wolves will come among you, and they will not spare the flock. ³⁰The time will come when some men from your own group will tell lies to lead the believers away after them. ³¹Watch, then, and remember that with many tears, day and night, I taught every one of you for three years.

32 "And now I commend you to the care of God and to the message of his grace, which is able to build you up and give you the blessings God has for all his people. ³³I have not wanted anyone's silver or gold or clothing. ³⁴You yourselves know that I have worked with these hands of mine to provide everything that my companions and I have needed. ³⁵I have shown you in all things that by working hard in this way we must help the weak, remembering the words that the Lord Jesus himself said, 'There is more happiness in giving than in receiving.'"

36 When Paul finished, he knelt down with them and prayed. ³⁷They were all crying as they hugged him and kissed him goodbye. ³⁸They were especially sad because he had said that they would never see him again. And so they went with him to the ship.

Paul Goes to Jerusalem

21 We said goodbye to them and left. After sailing straight across, we came to Cos; the next day we reached Rhodes, and from there we went on to Patara. ²There we found a ship that was going to Phoenicia, so we went aboard and sailed away. ³We came to where we could see Cyprus, and then sailed south of it on to Syria. We went ashore at Tyre, where the ship was going to unload its cargo. ⁴There we found some believers and stayed with them a week. By the power of the Spirit they told Paul not to go to Jerusalem. ⁵But when our time with them was over, we left and went on our way. All of them, together with their wives and children, went with us out of the city to the beach, where we all knelt and prayed. ⁶Then we said goodbye to one another, and we went on board the ship while they went back home.

7 We continued our voyage, sailing from Tyre to Ptolemais, where we greeted the believers and stayed with them for a day. ⁸On the following day we left and arrived in Caesarea. There we stayed at the house of Philip the evangelist, one of the seven men who had been chosen as helpers in Jerusalem. ⁹He had four unmarried daughters who proclaimed God's message. ¹⁰We had been there for several days when a prophet named Agabus arrived from Judea. ¹¹He came to us, took Paul's belt, tied up his own feet and hands with it, and said, "This is what the Holy Spirit says: The owner of this belt will be tied up in this way by the Jews in Jerusalem, and they will hand him over to the Gentiles."

12 When we heard this, we and the others there begged Paul not to go to Jerusalem. ¹³But he answered, "What are you doing, crying like this and breaking my heart? I am ready not only to be tied up in Jerusalem but even to die there for the sake of the Lord Jesus."

14 We could not convince him, so we gave up and said, "May the Lord's will be done."

15 After spending some time there, we got our things ready and left for Jerusalem. ¹⁶Some of the disciples from Caesarea also went with us

---

^a **20.28** God; *some manuscripts have* the Lord.
^b **20.28** through the blood of his Son; *or* through the sacrificial death of his Son; *or* through his own blood.

and took us to the house of the man we were going to stay with[a] – Mnason, from Cyprus, who had been a believer since the early days.

Paul Visits James

17 When we arrived in Jerusalem, the believers welcomed us warmly. [18]The next day Paul went with us to see James; and all the church elders were present. [19]Paul greeted them and gave a complete report of everything that God had done among the Gentiles through his work. [20]After hearing him, they all praised God. Then they said, "Brother Paul, you can see how many thousands of Jews have become believers, and how devoted they all are to the Law. [21]They have been told that you have been teaching all the Jews who live in Gentile countries to abandon the Law of Moses, telling them not to circumcise their children or follow the Jewish customs. [22]They are sure to hear that you have arrived. What should be done, then? [23]This is what we want you to do. There are four men here who have taken a vow. [24]Go along with them and join them in the ceremony of purification and pay their expenses; then they will be able to shave their heads.[b] In this way everyone will know that there is no truth in any of the things that they have been told about you, but that you yourself live in accordance with the Law of Moses. [25]But as for the Gentiles who have become believers, we have sent them a letter telling them we decided that they must not eat any food that has been offered to idols, or any blood, or any animal that has been strangled, and that they must keep themselves from sexual immorality."

26 So Paul took the men and the next day performed the ceremony of purification with them. Then he went into the Temple and gave notice of how many days it would be until the end of the period of purification, when a sacrifice would be offered for each one of them.

Paul is Arrested in the Temple

27 But just when the seven days were about to come to an end, some Jews from the province of Asia saw Paul in the Temple. They stirred up the whole crowd and seized Paul. [28]"Men of Israel!" they shouted. "Help! This is the man who goes

everywhere teaching everyone against the people of Israel, the Law of Moses, and this Temple. And now he has even brought some Gentiles into the Temple and defiled this holy place!" [29](They said this because they had seen Trophimus from Ephesus with Paul in the city, and they thought that Paul had taken him into the Temple.)

30 Confusion spread through the whole city, and the people all ran together, seized Paul, and dragged him out of the Temple. At once the Temple doors were closed. [31]The mob was trying to kill Paul, when a report was sent up to the commander of the Roman troops that all Jerusalem was rioting. [32]At once the commander took some officers and soldiers and rushed down to the crowd. When the people saw him with the soldiers, they stopped beating Paul. [33]The commander went over to Paul, arrested him, and ordered him to be bound with two chains. Then he asked, "Who is this man, and what has he done?" [34]Some in the crowd shouted one thing, others something else. There was such confusion that the commander could not find out exactly what had happened, so he ordered his men to take Paul up into the fort. [35]They got as far as the steps with him, and then the soldiers had to carry him because the mob was so wild. [36]They were all coming after him and screaming, "Kill him!"

Paul Defends Himself

37 As the soldiers were about to take Paul into the fort, he spoke to the commander: "May I say something to you?"

"You speak Greek, do you?" the commander asked. [38]"Then you are not that Egyptian fellow who some time ago started a revolution and led four thousand armed terrorists out into the desert?"

39 Paul answered, "I am a Jew, born in Tarsus in Cilicia, a citizen of an important city. Please let me speak to the people."

40 The commander gave him permission, so Paul stood on the steps and motioned with his hand for the people to be silent. When they were quiet, Paul spoke to them in Hebrew:

22 "My fellow-Jews, listen to me as I make my defence before you!" [2]When they heard him speaking to them in Hebrew, they became even quieter; and Paul went on:

3 "I am a Jew, born in Tarsus in Cilicia, but brought up here in Jerusalem as a student of Gamaliel. I received strict instruction in the Law of our ancestors and was just as dedicated to

[a] **21.16** and took us to the house of the man we were going to stay with; *or* bringing with them the man at whose house we were going to stay.
[b] **21.24** SHAVE THEIR HEADS: *See 18.18.*

God as are all of you who are here today. ⁴I persecuted to the death the people who followed this Way. I arrested men and women and threw them into prison. ⁵The High Priest and the whole Council can prove that I am telling the truth. I received from them letters written to fellow-Jews in Damascus, so I went there to arrest these people and bring them back in chains to Jerusalem to be punished.

Paul Tells of his Conversion
(Acts 9.1–19; 26.12–18)

6   "As I was travelling and coming near Damascus, about midday a bright light from the sky flashed suddenly round me. ⁷I fell to the ground and heard a voice saying to me, 'Saul, Saul! Why do you persecute me?' ⁸'Who are you, Lord?' I asked. 'I am Jesus of Nazareth, whom you persecute,' he said to me. ⁹The men with me saw the light, but did not hear the voice of the one who was speaking to me. ¹⁰I asked, 'What shall I do, Lord?' and the Lord said to me, 'Get up and go into Damascus, and there you will be told everything that God has determined for you to do.' ¹¹I was blind because of the bright light, and so my companions took me by the hand and led me into Damascus.

12   "In that city was a man named Ananias, a religious man who obeyed our Law and was highly respected by all the Jews living there. ¹³He came to me, stood by me, and said, 'Brother Saul, see again!' At that very moment I saw again and looked at him. ¹⁴He said, 'The God of our ancestors has chosen you to know his will, to see his righteous Servant, and to hear him speaking with his own voice. ¹⁵For you will be a witness for him to tell everyone what you have seen and heard. ¹⁶And now, why wait any longer? Get up and be baptized and have your sins washed away by praying to him.'

Paul's Call to Preach to the Gentiles

17   "I went back to Jerusalem, and while I was praying in the Temple, I had a vision, ¹⁸in which I saw the Lord, as he said to me, 'Hurry and leave Jerusalem quickly, because the people here will not accept your witness about me.' ¹⁹'Lord,' I answered, 'they know very well that I went to the synagogues and arrested and beat those who believe in you. ²⁰And when your witness Stephen was put to death, I myself was there, approving of his murder and taking care of the cloaks of his murderers.' ²¹'Go,' the Lord said to me, 'for I will send you far away to the Gentiles.'"

22   The people listened to Paul until he said this; but then they started shouting at the top of their voices, "Away with him! Kill him! He's not fit to live!" ²³They were screaming, waving their clothes, and throwing dust up in the air. ²⁴The Roman commander ordered his men to take Paul into the fort, and he told them to whip him in order to find out why the Jews were screaming like this against him. ²⁵But when they had tied him up to be whipped, Paul said to the officer standing there, "Is it lawful for you to whip a Roman citizen who hasn't even been tried for any crime?"

26   When the officer heard this, he went to the commander and asked him, "What are you doing? That man is a Roman citizen!"

27   So the commander went to Paul and asked him, "Tell me, are you a Roman citizen?"

"Yes," answered Paul.

28   The commander said, "I became one by paying a large amount of money."

"But I am one by birth," Paul answered.

29   At once the men who were going to question Paul drew back from him; and the commander was frightened when he realized that Paul was a Roman citizen and that he had put him in chains.

Paul before the Council

30   The commander wanted to find out for certain what the Jews were accusing Paul of; so the next day he had Paul's chains taken off and ordered the chief priests and the whole Council to meet. Then he took Paul and made him stand before them.

23 Paul looked straight at the Council and said, "My fellow-Israelites! My conscience is perfectly clear about the way in which I have lived before God to this very day." ²The High Priest Ananias ordered those who were standing close to Paul to strike him on the mouth. ³Paul said to him, "God will certainly strike you – you whitewashed wall! You sit there to judge me according to the Law, yet you break the Law by ordering them to strike me!"

4   The men close to Paul said to him, "You are insulting God's High Priest!"

5   Paul answered, "My fellow-Israelites, I did not know that he was the High Priest. The scripture says, 'You must not speak evil of the ruler of your people.'"

6   When Paul saw that some of the group were Sadducees and the others were Pharisees, he called out in the Council, "Fellow-Israelites! I am a Pharisee, the son of Pharisees. I am on trial

here because of the hope I have that the dead will rise to life!"

7   As soon as he said this, the Pharisees and Sadducees started to quarrel, and the group was divided. ⁸(For the Sadducees say that people will not rise from death and that there are no angels or spirits; but the Pharisees believe in all three.) ⁹The shouting became louder, and some of the teachers of the Law who belonged to the party of the Pharisees stood up and protested strongly: "We cannot find anything wrong with this man! Perhaps a spirit or an angel really did speak to him!"

10   The argument became so violent that the commander was afraid that Paul would be torn to pieces. So he ordered his soldiers to go down into the group, get Paul away from them, and take him into the fort.

11   That night the Lord stood by Paul and said, "Don't be afraid! You have given your witness for me here in Jerusalem, and you must also do the same in Rome."

The Plot against Paul's Life

12   The next morning some Jews met together and made a plan. They took a vow that they would not eat or drink anything until they had killed Paul. ¹³There were more than 40 who planned this together. ¹⁴Then they went to the chief priests and elders and said, "We have taken a solemn vow together not to eat a thing until we have killed Paul. ¹⁵Now then, you and the Council send word to the Roman commander to bring Paul down to you, pretending that you want to get more accurate information about him. But we will be ready to kill him before he ever gets here."

16   But the son of Paul's sister heard about the plot; so he went to the fort and told Paul. ¹⁷Then Paul called one of the officers and said to him, "Take this young man to the commander; he has something to tell him." ¹⁸The officer took him, led him to the commander, and said, "The prisoner Paul called me and asked me to bring this young man to you, because he has something to say to you."

19   The commander took him by the hand, led him off by himself, and asked him, "What have you got to tell me?"

20   He said, "The Jewish authorities have agreed to ask you tomorrow to take Paul down to the Council, pretending that the Council wants to get more accurate information about him. ²¹But don't listen to them, because there are more than forty men who will be hiding and waiting for him. They have taken a vow not to eat or drink until they have killed him. They are now ready to do it and are waiting for your decision."

22   The commander said, "Don't tell anyone that you have reported this to me." And he sent the young man away.

Paul is Sent to Governor Felix

23   Then the commander called two of his officers and said, "Get two hundred soldiers ready to go to Caesarea, together with seventy horsemen and two hundred spearmen, and be ready to leave by nine o'clock tonight. ²⁴Provide some horses for Paul to ride and get him safely through to the governor Felix." ²⁵Then the commander wrote a letter that went like this:

26   "Claudius Lysias to His Excellency, the governor Felix: Greetings. ²⁷The Jews seized this man and were about to kill him. I learnt that he was a Roman citizen, so I went with my soldiers and rescued him. ²⁸I wanted to know what they were accusing him of, so I took him down to their Council. ²⁹I found out that he had not done anything for which he deserved to die or be put in prison; the accusation against him had to do with questions about their own law. ³⁰And when I was informed that there was a plot against him, at once I decided to send him to you. I have told his accusers to make their charges against him before you."

31   The soldiers carried out their orders. They got Paul and took him that night as far as Antipatris. ³²The next day the foot soldiers returned to the fort and left the horsemen to go on with him. ³³They took him to Caesarea, delivered the letter to the governor, and handed Paul over to him. ³⁴The governor read the letter and asked Paul what province he was from. When he found out that he was from Cilicia, ³⁵he said, "I will hear you when your accusers arrive." Then he gave orders for Paul to be kept under guard in the governor's headquarters.

The Case Against Paul

24 Five days later the High Priest Ananias went to Caesarea with some elders and a lawyer named Tertullus. They appeared before Felix and made their charges against Paul. ²Then Paul was called in, and Tertullus began to make his accusation, as follows:

"Your Excellency! Your wise leadership has brought us a long period of peace, and many necessary reforms are being made for the good of our country. ³We welcome this everywhere and at all times, and we are deeply grateful to you. ⁴I do not want to take up too much of your time, however, so I beg you to be kind and listen to our brief account. ⁵We found this man to be a dangerous nuisance; he starts riots among Jews all over the world and is a leader of the party of the Nazarenes. ⁶He also tried to defile the Temple, and we arrested him.ᵃ ⁸If you question this man, you yourself will be able to learn from him all the things that we are accusing him of." ⁹The Jews joined in the accusation and said that all this was true.

Paul's Defence before Felix

10   The governor then motioned to Paul to speak, and Paul said,

"I know that you have been a judge over this nation for many years, and so I am happy to defend myself before you. ¹¹As you can find out for yourself, it was no more than twelve days ago that I went to Jerusalem to worship. ¹²The Jews did not find me arguing with anyone in the Temple, nor did they find me stirring up the people, either in the synagogues or anywhere else in the city. ¹³Nor can they give you proof of the accusations they now bring against me. ¹⁴I do admit this to you: I worship the God of our ancestors by following that Way which they say is false. But I also believe in everything written in the Law of Moses and the books of the prophets. ¹⁵I have the same hope in God that these themselves have, namely, that all people, both the good and the bad, will rise from death. ¹⁶And so I do my best always to have a clear conscience before God and human beings.

17   "After being away from Jerusalem for several years, I went there to take some money to my own people and to offer sacrifices. ¹⁸It was while I was doing this that they found me in the Temple after I had completed the ceremony of purification. There was no crowd with me and no disorder. ¹⁹But some Jews from the province of Asia were there; they themselves ought to come before you and make their accusations if they have anything against me. ²⁰Or let these who are here tell what crime they found me guilty of when I stood before the Council – ²¹except for the one thing I called out when I stood before them: 'I am being tried by you

today for believing that the dead will rise to life.'"

22   Then Felix, who was well informed about the Way, brought the hearing to a close. "When Lysias the commander arrives," he told them, "I will decide your case." ²³He ordered the officer in charge of Paul to keep him under guard, but to give him some freedom and allow his friends to provide for his needs.

Paul before Felix and Drusilla

24   After some days Felix came with his wife Drusilla, who was Jewish. He sent for Paul and listened to him as he talked about faith in Christ Jesus. ²⁵But as Paul went on discussing about goodness, self-control, and the coming Day of Judgement, Felix was afraid and said, "You may leave now. I will call you again when I get the chance." ²⁶At the same time he was hoping that Paul would give him some money; and for this reason he would often send for him and talk with him.

27   After two years had passed, Porcius Festus succeeded Felix as governor. Felix wanted to gain favour with the Jews so he left Paul in prison.

Paul Appeals to the Emperor

25   Three days after Festus arrived in the province, he went from Caesarea to Jerusalem, ²where the chief priests and the Jewish leaders brought their charges against Paul. They begged Festus ³to do them the favour of bringing Paul to Jerusalem, for they had made a plot to kill him on the way. ⁴Festus answered, "Paul is being kept a prisoner in Caesarea, and I myself will be going back there soon. ⁵Let your leaders go to Caesarea with me and accuse the man if he has done anything wrong."

6   Festus spent another eight or ten days with them and then went to Caesarea. On the next day he sat down in the court of judgement and ordered Paul to be brought in. ⁷When Paul arrived, the Jews who had come from Jerusalem stood round him and started making many serious charges against him, which they were not able to prove. ⁸But Paul defended himself: "I have done nothing wrong against the Law of the Jews or against the Temple or against the Roman Emperor."

9   But Festus wanted to gain favour with the Jews, so he asked Paul, "Would you be willing to go to Jerusalem and be tried on these charges before me there?"

10   Paul said, "I am standing before the Emperor's

ᵃ **24.6** *Some manuscripts add verses 6b–8a:* We planned to judge him according to our own law, ⁷but Lysias the commander came, and with great violence took him from us. ⁸Then Lysias gave orders that his accusers should come before you.

own court of judgement, where I should be tried. I have done no wrong to the Jews, as you yourself well know. [11]If I have broken the law and done something for which I deserve the death penalty, I do not ask to escape it. But if there is no truth in the charges they bring against me, no one can hand me over to them. I appeal to the Emperor."

12   Then Festus, after conferring with his advisers, answered, "You have appealed to the Emperor, so to the Emperor you will go."

Paul before Agrippa and Bernice

13   Some time later King Agrippa and Bernice came to Caesarea to pay a visit of welcome to Festus. [14]After they had been there several days, Festus explained Paul's situation to the king: "There is a man here who was left a prisoner by Felix; [15]and when I went to Jerusalem, the Jewish chief priests and elders brought charges against him and asked me to condemn him. [16]But I told them that we Romans are not in the habit of handing over anyone accused of a crime before he has met his accusers face to face and has had the chance of defending himself against the accusation. [17]When they came here, then, I lost no time, but on the very next day I sat in the court and ordered the man to be brought in. [18]His opponents stood up, but they did not accuse him of any of the evil crimes that I thought they would. [19]All they had were some arguments with him about their own religion and about a man named Jesus, who has died; but Paul claims that he is alive. [20]I was undecided about how I could get information on these matters, so I asked Paul if he would be willing to go to Jerusalem and be tried there on these charges. [21]But Paul appealed; he asked to be kept under guard and to let the Emperor decide his case. So I gave orders for him to be kept under guard until I could send him to the Emperor."

22   Agrippa said to Festus, "I would like to hear this man myself."

"You will hear him tomorrow," Festus answered.

23   The next day Agrippa and Bernice came with great pomp and ceremony and entered the audience hall with the military chiefs and the leading men of the city. Festus gave the order, and Paul was brought in. [24]Festus said, "King Agrippa and all who are here with us: You see this man against whom all the Jewish people, both here and in Jerusalem, have brought complaints to me. They scream that he should not live any longer. [25]But I could not find that he had done anything for which he deserved the death sentence. And since he himself made an appeal to the Emperor, I have decided to send him. [26]But I have nothing definite about him to write to the Emperor. So I have brought him here before you – and especially before you, King Agrippa! – so that, after investigating his case, I may have something to write. [27]For it seems unreasonable to me to send a prisoner without clearly indicating the charges against him."

Paul Defends Himself before Agrippa

26 Agrippa said to Paul, "You have permission to speak on your own behalf." Paul stretched out his hand and defended himself as follows:

2   "King Agrippa! I consider myself fortunate that today I am to defend myself before you from all the things these Jews accuse me of, [3]particularly since you know so well all the Jewish customs and disputes. I ask you, then, to listen to me with patience.

4   "All the Jews know how I have lived ever since I was young. They know how I have spent my whole life, at first in my own country and then in Jerusalem. [5]They have always known, if they are willing to testify, that from the very first I have lived as a member of the strictest party of our religion, the Pharisees. [6]And now I stand here to be tried because of the hope I have in the promise that God made to our ancestors – [7]the very thing that the twelve tribes of our people hope to receive, as they worship God day and night. And it is because of this hope, Your Majesty, that I am being accused by these Jews! [8]Why do you who are here find it impossible to believe that God raises the dead?

9   "I myself thought that I should do everything I could against the cause of Jesus of Nazareth. [10]That is what I did in Jerusalem. I received authority from the chief priests and put many of God's people in prison; and when they were sentenced to death, I also voted against them. [11]Many times I had them punished in the synagogues and tried to make them deny their faith. I was so furious with them that I even went to foreign cities to persecute them.

Paul Tells of his Conversion
(Acts 9.1–19; 22.6–16)

12   "It was for this purpose that I went to Damascus with authority and orders from the chief priests. [13]It was on the road at midday, Your Majesty, that I saw a light much brighter

than the sun, coming from the sky and shining round me and the men travelling with me. [14]All of us fell to the ground, and I heard a voice say to me in Hebrew, 'Saul, Saul! Why are you persecuting me? You are hurting yourself by hitting back, like an ox kicking against its owner's stick.' [15]'Who are you, Lord?' I asked. And the Lord answered, 'I am Jesus, whom you persecute. [16]But get up and stand on your feet. I have appeared to you to appoint you as my servant. You are to tell others what you have seen of me[a] today and what I will show you in the future. [17]I will rescue you from the people of Israel and from the Gentiles to whom I will send you. [18]You are to open their eyes and turn them from the darkness to the light and from the power of Satan to God, so that through their faith in me they will have their sins forgiven and receive their place among God's chosen people.'

Paul Tells of his Work

19   "And so, King Agrippa, I did not disobey the vision I had from heaven. [20]First in Damascus and in Jerusalem and then in all Judea and among the Gentiles, I preached that they must repent of their sins and turn to God and do the things that would show they had repented. [21]It was for this reason that these Jews seized me while I was in the Temple, and they tried to kill me. [22]But to this very day I have been helped by God, and so I stand here giving my witness to all, to small and great alike. What I say is the very same thing which the prophets and Moses said was going to happen: [23]that the Messiah must suffer and be the first one to rise from death, to announce the light of salvation to the Jews and to the Gentiles."

24   As Paul defended himself in this way, Festus shouted at him, "You are mad, Paul! Your great learning is driving you mad!"

25   Paul answered, "I am not mad, Your Excellency! I am speaking the sober truth. [26]King Agrippa! I can speak to you with all boldness, because you know about these things. I am sure that you have taken notice of every one of them, for this thing has not happened hidden away in a corner. [27]King Agrippa, do you believe the prophets? I know that you do!"

28   Agrippa said to Paul, "In this short time do you think you will make me a Christian?"

29   "Whether a short time or a long time," Paul answered, "my prayer to God is that you and all

the rest of you who are listening to me today might become what I am – except, of course, for these chains!"

30   Then the king, the governor, Bernice, and all the others got up, [31]and after leaving they said to each other, "This man has not done anything for which he should die or be put in prison." [32]And Agrippa said to Festus, "This man could have been released if he had not appealed to the Emperor."

Paul Sails for Rome

27 When it was decided that we should sail to Italy, they handed Paul and some other prisoners over to Julius, an officer in the Roman regiment called "The Emperor's Regiment". [2]We went aboard a ship from Adramyttium, which was ready to leave for the seaports of the province of Asia, and we sailed away. Aristarchus, a Macedonian from Thessalonica, was with us. [3]The next day we arrived at Sidon. Julius was kind to Paul and allowed him to go and see his friends, to be given what he needed. [4]We went on from there, and because the winds were blowing against us, we sailed on the sheltered side of the island of Cyprus. [5]We crossed over the sea off Cilicia and Pamphylia and came to Myra in Lycia. [6]There the officer found a ship from Alexandria that was going to sail for Italy, so he put us aboard.

7   We sailed slowly for several days and with great difficulty finally arrived off the town of Cnidus. The wind would not let us go any further in that direction, so we sailed down the sheltered side of the island of Crete, passing by Cape Salmone. [8]We kept close to the coast and with great difficulty came to a place called Safe Harbours, not far from the town of Lasea.

9   We spent a long time there, until it became dangerous to continue the voyage, for by now the Day of Atonement[b] was already past. So Paul gave them this advice: [10]"Men, I see that our voyage from here on will be dangerous; there will be great damage to the cargo and to the ship, and loss of life as well." [11]But the army officer was convinced by what the captain and the owner of the ship said, and not by what Paul said. [12]The harbour was not a good one to spend the winter in; so most people were in favour of putting out to sea and trying to reach Phoenix, if possible, in order to spend the winter there.

---

[a] **26.16** *Some manuscripts do not have* of me.

[b] **27.9** DAY OF ATONEMENT: This was celebrated towards the end of September or beginning of October, at which time bad weather made sailing dangerous.

PAUL'S FINAL JOURNEY

Mediterranean Sea

Phoenix is a harbour in Crete that faces south-west and north-west.[a]

The Storm at Sea

13 A soft wind from the south began to blow, and the men thought that they could carry out their plan, so they pulled up the anchor and sailed as close as possible along the coast of Crete. [14]But soon a very strong wind – the one called "North-easter" – blew down from the island. [15]It hit the ship, and since it was impossible to keep the ship headed into the wind, we gave up trying and let it be carried along by the wind. [16]We got some shelter when we passed to the south of the little island of Cauda. There, with some difficulty, we managed to make the ship's boat secure. [17]They pulled it aboard and then fastened some ropes tight round the ship. They were afraid that they might run into the sandbanks off the coast of Libya, so they lowered the sail and let the ship be carried by the wind. [18]The violent storm continued, so on the next day they began to throw some of the ship's cargo overboard, [19]and on the following day they threw part of the ship's equipment overboard. [20]For many days we could not see the sun or the stars, and the wind kept on blowing very hard. We finally gave up all hope of being saved.

21 After those on board had gone a long time without food, Paul stood before them and said, "Men, you should have listened to me and not have sailed from Crete; then we would have avoided all this damage and loss. [22]But now I beg you, take heart! Not one of you will lose your life; only the ship will be lost. [23]For last night an angel of the God to whom I belong and whom I worship came to me [24]and said, 'Don't be afraid, Paul! You must stand before the Emperor. And God in his goodness to you has spared the lives of all those who are sailing with you.' [25]So take heart, men! For I trust in God that it will be just as I was told. [26]But we will be driven ashore on some island."

27 It was the fourteenth night, and we were being driven about in the Mediterranean by the storm. About midnight the sailors suspected that we were getting close to land. [28]So they dropped a line with a weight tied to it and found that the water was 40 metres deep; a little later they did the same and found that it was 30 metres deep. [29]They were afraid that the ship would go on the rocks, so they lowered four anchors from the back of the ship and prayed for daylight. [30]Then the sailors tried to escape from the ship; they lowered the boat into the water and pretended that they were going to put out some anchors

---

[a] **27.12** south-west and north-west; *or* north-east and south-east.

from the front of the ship. ³¹But Paul said to the army officer and soldiers, "If the sailors don't stay on board, you have no hope of being saved." ³²So the soldiers cut the ropes that held the boat and let it go.

33   Just before dawn, Paul begged them all to eat some food: "You have been waiting for fourteen days now, and all this time you have not eaten anything. ³⁴I beg you, then, eat some food; you need it in order to survive. Not even a hair of your heads will be lost." ³⁵After saying this, Paul took some bread, gave thanks to God before them all, broke it, and began to eat. ³⁶They took heart, and every one of them also ate some food. ³⁷There was a total of 276ᵃ of us on board. ³⁸After everyone had eaten enough, they lightened the ship by throwing all the wheat into the sea.

The Shipwreck

39   When day came, the sailors did not recognize the coast, but they noticed a bay with a beach and decided that, if possible, they would run the ship aground there. ⁴⁰So they cut off the anchors and let them sink in the sea, and at the same time they untied the ropes that held the steering oars. Then they raised the sail at the front of the ship so that the wind would blow the ship forward, and we headed for shore. ⁴¹But the ship hit a sandbank and went aground; the front part of the ship got stuck and could not move, while the back part was being broken to pieces by the violence of the waves.

42   The soldiers made a plan to kill all the prisoners, in order to keep them from swimming ashore and escaping. ⁴³But the army officer wanted to save Paul, so he stopped them from doing this. Instead, he ordered those who could swim to jump overboard first and swim ashore; ⁴⁴the rest were to follow, holding on to the planks or to some broken pieces of the ship. And this was how we all got safely ashore.

In Malta

28 When we were safely ashore, we learnt that the island was called Malta. ²The natives there were very friendly to us. It had started to rain and was cold, so they lit a fire and made us all welcome. ³Paul gathered up a bundle of sticks and was putting them on the fire when a snake came out on account of the heat and fastened itself to his hand. ⁴The natives saw the snake hanging on Paul's hand and said to one another, "This man must be a murderer, but Fate will not let him live, even though he escaped from the sea." ⁵But Paul shook the snake off into the fire without being harmed at all. ⁶They were waiting for him to swell up or suddenly fall down dead. But after waiting for a long time and not seeing anything unusual happening to him, they changed their minds and said, "He is a god!"

7   Not far from that place were some fields that belonged to Publius, the chief official of the island. He welcomed us kindly and for three days we were his guests. ⁸Publius' father was in bed, sick with fever and dysentery. Paul went into his room, prayed, placed his hands on him, and healed him. ⁹When this happened, all the other sick people on the island came and were healed. ¹⁰They gave us many gifts, and when we sailed, they put on board what we needed for the voyage.

From Malta to Rome

11   After three months we sailed away on a ship from Alexandria, called "The Twin Gods", which had spent the winter in the island. ¹²We arrived in the city of Syracuse and stayed there for three days. ¹³From there we sailed on and arrived in the city of Rhegium. The next day a wind began to blow from the south, and in two days we came to the town of Puteoli. ¹⁴We found some believers there who asked us to stay with them a week. And so we came to Rome. ¹⁵The believers in Rome heard about us and came as far as the towns of Market of Appius and Three Inns to meet us. When Paul saw them, he thanked God and was greatly encouraged.

In Rome

16   When we arrived in Rome, Paul was allowed to live by himself with a soldier guarding him.

17   After three days Paul called the local Jewish leaders to a meeting. When they had gathered, he said to them, "My fellow-Israelites, even though I did nothing against our people or the customs that we received from our ancestors, I was made a prisoner in Jerusalem and handed over to the Romans. ¹⁸After questioning me, the Romans wanted to release me, because they found that I had done nothing for which I deserved to die. ¹⁹But when the Jews opposed this, I was forced to appeal to the Emperor, even though I had no accusation to make against my own people. ²⁰That is why I asked to see you and

---

ᵃ **27.37** 276; *some manuscripts have* 275; *others have* about 76.

talk with you. As a matter of fact, I am bound in chains like this for the sake of him for whom the people of Israel hope."

21 They said to him, "We have not received any letters from Judea about you, nor have any of our people come from there with any news or anything bad to say about you. 22But we would like to hear your ideas, because we know that everywhere people speak against this party to which you belong."

23 So they fixed a date with Paul, and a large number of them came that day to the place where Paul was staying. From morning till night he explained to them his message about the Kingdom of God, and he tried to convince them about Jesus by quoting from the Law of Moses and the writings of the prophets. 24Some of them were convinced by his words, but others would not believe. 25So they left, disagreeing among themselves, after Paul had said this one thing: "How well the Holy Spirit spoke through the prophet Isaiah to your ancestors! 26For he said,

'Go and say to this people:
You will listen and listen, but not
    understand;
    you will look and look, but not see,
27 because this people's minds are dull,
    and they have stopped up their ears
    and closed their eyes.
Otherwise, their eyes would see,
    their ears would hear,
    their minds would understand,
    and they would turn to me, says God,
    and I would heal them.'"

28 And Paul concluded: "You are to know, then, that God's message of salvation has been sent to the Gentiles. They will listen!"[a]

30 For two years Paul lived in a place he rented for himself, and there he welcomed all who came to see him. 31He preached about the Kingdom of God and taught about the Lord Jesus Christ, speaking with all boldness and freedom.

---

[a] **28.28** *Some manuscripts add verse 29:* After Paul said this, the Jews left, arguing violently among themselves.

Paul's Letter to the ROMANS

INTRODUCTION

Paul's Letter to the Romans was written to prepare the way for a visit Paul planned to make to the church at Rome. His plan was to work among the Christians there for a while and then, with their support, to go on to Spain. He wrote to explain his understanding of the Christian faith and its practical implications for the lives of Christians. The book contains Paul's most complete statement of his message.

After greeting the people of the church at Rome and telling them of his prayers for them, Paul states the theme of the letter: "The gospel reveals how God puts people right with himself: it is through faith from beginning to end." (1.17)

Paul then develops this theme. The whole human race, both Jew and Gentile, needs to be put right with God, for all alike are under the power of sin. People are put right with God through faith in Jesus Christ. Next Paul describes the new life in union with Christ that results from this new relation with God. The believer has peace with God and is set free by God's Spirit from the power of sin and death. In chapters 5–8 Paul also discusses the purpose of the Law of God and the power of God's Spirit in the believer's life. Then the apostle wrestles with the question of how Jews and Gentiles fit into the plan of God for humanity. He concludes that the Jewish rejection of Jesus is part of God's plan for bringing the whole human race within the reach of God's grace in Jesus Christ, and he believes that the Jews will not always reject Jesus. Finally Paul writes about how the Christian life should be lived, especially about the way of love in relations with others. He takes up such themes as service to God, the duty of Christians to the state and to one another, and questions of conscience. He ends the letter with personal messages and with words of praise to God.

Outline of Contents

1 From Paul, a servant of Christ Jesus and an apostle chosen and called by God to preach his Good News.

2 The Good News was promised long ago by God through his prophets, as written in the Holy Scriptures. [3]It is about his Son, our Lord Jesus Christ: as to his humanity, he was born a descendant of David; [4]as to his divine holiness, he was shown with great power to be the Son of God by being raised from death. [5]Through him God gave me the privilege of being an apostle for the sake of Christ, in order to lead people of all nations to believe and obey. [6]This also includes you who are in Rome, whom God has called to belong to Jesus Christ.

7 And so I write to all of you in Rome whom God loves and has called to be his own people:

May God our Father and the Lord Jesus Christ give you grace and peace.

Prayer of Thanksgiving

8 First, I thank my God through Jesus Christ for all of you, because the whole world is hearing

167

Studying
ROMANS

Who wrote it? Paul.
When? 57–58 CE.
Where from? Probably Corinth or Cenchreae.
For whom? The mainly Gentile community of Christians in Rome. Letter later sent to many other Christian communities.
Why? To prepare the church in Rome for his coming and to lay out the most important Christian beliefs.

KEY POINTS

- Romans is the longest and most important of Paul's letters.
- Describes the Christian Gospel – everyone has sinned and needs salvation; Jew and Gentile can only be saved through the death of Jesus on cross.
- People receive God's salvation by faith. After being saved, people enter into new life through the Holy Spirit.
- In the end "all Israel will be saved" (11.26).

about your faith. [9]God is my witness that what I say is true – the God whom I serve with all my heart by preaching the Good News about his Son. God knows that I remember you [10]every time I pray. I ask that God in his good will may at last make it possible for me to visit you now. [11]For I want very much to see you, in order to share a spiritual blessing with you to make you strong. [12]What I mean is that both you and I will be helped at the same time, you by my faith and I by yours.

13   You must remember, my brothers and sisters, that many times I have planned to visit you, but something has always kept me from doing so. I want to win converts among you also, as I have among other Gentiles. [14]For I have an obligation to all peoples, to the civilized and to the savage, to the educated and to the ignorant. [15]So then, I am eager to preach the Good News to you also who live in Rome.

The Power of the Gospel

16   I have complete confidence in the gospel; it is God's power to save all who believe, first the Jews and also the Gentiles. [17]For the gospel reveals how God puts people right with himself: it is through faith from beginning to end. As the scripture says, "The person who is put right with God through faith shall live."[a]

[a] **1.17** put right with God through faith shall live; *or* put right with God shall live through faith.

The Guilt of the Human Race

18   God's anger is revealed from heaven against all the sin and evil of the people whose evil ways prevent the truth from being known. [19]God punishes them, because what can be known about God is plain to them, for God himself made it plain. [20]Ever since God created the world, his invisible qualities, both his eternal power and his divine nature, have been clearly seen; they are perceived in the things that God has made. So those people have no excuse at all! [21]They know God, but they do not give him the honour that belongs to him, nor do they thank him. Instead, their thoughts have become complete nonsense, and their empty minds are filled with darkness. [22]They say they are wise, but they are fools; [23]instead of worshipping the immortal God, they worship images made to look like mortal human beings or birds or animals or reptiles.

24   And so God has given those people over to do the filthy things their hearts desire, and they do shameful things with each other. [25]They exchange the truth about God for a lie; they worship and serve what God has created instead of the Creator himself, who is to be praised for ever! Amen.

26   Because they do this, God has given them over to shameful passions. Even the women pervert the natural use of their sex by unnatural acts. [27]In the same way the men give up natural sexual relations with women and burn with passion for each other. Men do shameful things with each other, and as a result they bring upon themselves the punishment they deserve for their wrongdoing.

28   Because those people refuse to keep in mind the true knowledge about God, he has given them over to corrupted minds, so that they do the things that they should not do. [29]They are filled with all kinds of wickedness, evil, greed, and vice; they are full of jealousy, murder, fighting, deceit, and malice. They gossip [30]and speak evil of one another; they are hateful to God, insolent,[b] proud, and boastful; they think of more ways to do evil; they disobey their parents; [31]they have no conscience; they do not keep their promises, and they show no kindness or pity for others. [32]They know that God's law says that people who live in this way deserve death. Yet, not only do they continue to do these very things, but they even approve of others who do them.

[b] **1.30** are hateful to God, insolent; *or* hate God, and are insolent.

God's Judgement

2 Do you, my friend, pass judgement on others? You have no excuse at all, whoever you are. For when you judge others and then do the same things which they do, you condemn yourself. [2]We know that God is right when he judges the people who do such things as these. [3]But you, my friend, do those very things for which you pass judgement on others! Do you think you will escape God's judgement? [4]Or perhaps you despise his great kindness, tolerance, and patience. Surely you know that God is kind, because he is trying to lead you to repent. [5]But you have a hard and stubborn heart, and so you are making your own punishment even greater on the Day when God's anger and righteous judgements will be revealed. [6]For God will reward every person according to what each has done. [7]Some people keep on doing good, and seek glory, honour, and immortal life; to them God will give eternal life. [8]Other people are selfish and reject what is right, in order to follow what is wrong; on them God will pour out his anger and fury. [9]There will be suffering and pain for all those who do what is evil, for the Jews first and also for the Gentiles. [10]But God will give glory, honour, and peace to all who do what is good, to the Jews first and also to the Gentiles. [11]For God judges everyone by the same standard.

[12] The Gentiles do not have the Law of Moses; they sin and are lost apart from the Law. The Jews have the Law; they sin and are judged by the Law. [13]For it is not by hearing the Law that people are put right with God, but by doing what the Law commands. [14]The Gentiles do not have the Law; but whenever they do by instinct what the Law commands, they are their own law, even though they do not have the Law. [15]Their conduct shows that what the Law commands is written in their hearts. Their consciences also show that this is true, since their thoughts sometimes accuse them and sometimes defend them. [16]And so, according to the Good News I preach, this is how it will be on that Day when God through Jesus Christ will judge the secret thoughts of all.

The Jews and the Law

[17] What about you? You call yourself a Jew; you depend on the Law and boast about God; [18]you know what God wants you to do, and you have learnt from the Law to choose what is right; [19]you are sure that you are a guide for the blind, a light for those who are in darkness, [20]an instructor for the foolish, and a teacher for the ignorant. You are certain that in the Law you have the full content of knowledge and of truth. [21]You teach others – why don't you teach yourself? You preach, "Do not steal" – but do you yourself steal? [22]You say, "Do not commit adultery" – but do you commit adultery? You detest idols – but do you rob temples? [23]You boast about having God's law – but do you bring shame on God by breaking his law? [24]The scripture says, "Because of you Jews, the Gentiles speak evil of God."

[25] If you obey the Law, your circumcision is of value; but if you disobey the Law, you might as well never have been circumcised. [26]If the Gentile, who is not circumcised, obeys the commands of the Law, will God not regard him as though he were circumcised? [27]And so you Jews will be condemned by the Gentiles because you break the Law, even though you have it written down and are circumcised; but they obey the Law, even though they are not physically circumcised. [28]After all, who is a real Jew, truly circumcised? It is not the man who is a Jew on the outside, whose circumcision is a physical thing. [29]Rather, the real Jew is the person who is a Jew on the inside, that is, whose heart has been circumcised, and this is the work of God's Spirit, not of the written Law. Such a person receives praise from God, not from human beings.

A Jewish boy is circumcised (2.29)

3

Have the Jews then any advantage over the Gentiles? Or is there any value in being circumcised? [2]Much, indeed, in every way! In the first place, God trusted his message to the Jews. [3]But what if some of them were not faithful? Does this mean that God will not be faithful? [4]Certainly not! God must be true, even though every human being is a liar. As the scripture says,

> "You must be shown to be right when you speak;
> you must win your case when you are being tried."

5 But what if our doing wrong serves to show up more clearly God's doing right? Can we say that God does wrong when he punishes us? (This would be the natural question to ask.) [6]By no means! If God is not just, how can he judge the world?

7 But what if my untruth serves God's glory by making his truth stand out more clearly? Why should I still be condemned as a sinner? Why not say, then, "Let us do evil so that good may come"? Some people, indeed, have insulted me by accusing me of saying this very thing! They will be condemned, as they should be.

No one is Righteous

9 Well then, are we Jews in any better condition than the Gentiles? Not at all![a] I have already shown that Jews and Gentiles alike are all under the power of sin. [10]As the Scriptures say:

> "There is no one who is righteous,
11 no one who is wise
> or who worships God.
12 All have turned away from God;
> they have all gone wrong;
> no one does what is right, not even one.
13 Their words are full of deadly deceit;
> wicked lies roll off their tongues,
> and dangerous threats, like snake's poison,
> from their lips;
14 their speech is filled with bitter curses.
15 They are quick to hurt and kill;
16 they leave ruin and destruction wherever
> they go.
17 They have not known the path of peace,
18 nor have they learnt reverence for God."

19 Now we know that everything in the Law applies to those who live under the Law, in order to stop all human excuses and bring the whole world under God's judgement. [20]For no one is put right in God's sight by doing what the Law requires; what the Law does is to make people know that they have sinned.

How We are Put Right with God

21 But now God's way of putting people right with himself has been revealed. It has nothing to do with law, even though the Law of Moses and the prophets gave their witness to it. [22]God puts people right through their faith in Jesus Christ. God does this to all who believe in Christ, because there is no difference at all: [23]everyone has sinned and is far away from God's saving presence. [24]But by the free gift of God's grace all are put right with him through Christ Jesus, who sets them free. [25-26]God offered him, so that by his blood[b] he should become the means by which people's sins are forgiven through their faith in him. God did this in order to demonstrate that he is righteous. In the past he was patient and overlooked people's sins; but in the present time he deals with their sins, in order to demonstrate his righteousness. In this way God shows that he himself is righteous and that he puts right everyone who believes in Jesus.

27 What, then, can we boast about? Nothing! And what is the reason for this? Is it that we obey the Law? No, but that we believe. [28]For we conclude that a person is put right with God only through faith, and not by doing what the Law commands. [29]Or is God the God of the Jews only? Is he not the God of the Gentiles also? Of course he is. [30]God is one, and he will put the Jews right with himself on the basis of their faith, and will put the Gentiles right through their faith. [31]Does this mean that by this faith we do away with the Law? No, not at all; instead, we uphold the Law.

The Example of Abraham

4

What shall we say, then, of Abraham, the father of our race? What was his experience? [2]If he was put right with God by the things he did, he would have something to boast about – but not in God's sight. [3]The scripture says, "Abraham believed God, and because of his faith God accepted him as righteous." [4]Those who work are paid wages, but they are not regarded

---

[a] **3.9** any better condition than the Gentiles? Not at all!; *or* any worse condition than the Gentiles? Not altogether.

[b] **3.25–26** by his blood; *or* by his sacrificial death.

as a gift; they are something that has been earned. ⁵But those who depend on faith, not on deeds, and who believe in the God who declares the guilty to be innocent, it is this faith that God takes into account in order to put them right with himself. ⁶This is what David meant when he spoke of the happiness of the person whom God accepts as righteous, apart from anything that person does:

7   "Happy are those whose wrongs are forgiven,
     whose sins are pardoned!

8   Happy is the person whose sins the Lord will
     not keep account of!"

9   Does this happiness that David spoke of belong only to those who are circumcised? No indeed! It belongs also to those who are not circumcised. For we have quoted the scripture, "Abraham believed God, and because of his faith God accepted him as righteous." ¹⁰When did this take place? Was it before or after Abraham was circumcised? It was before, not after. ¹¹He was circumcised later, and his circumcision was a sign to show that because of his faith God had accepted him as righteous before he had been circumcised. And so Abraham is the spiritual father of all who believe in God and are accepted as righteous by him, even though they are not circumcised. ¹²He is also the father of those who are circumcised, that is, of those who, in addition to being circumcised, also live the same life of faith that our father Abraham lived before he was circumcised.

God's Promise is Received through Faith

13   When God promised Abraham and his descendants that the world would belong to him, he did so, not because Abraham obeyed the Law, but because he believed and was accepted as righteous by God. ¹⁴For if what God promises is to be given to those who obey the Law, then faith means nothing and God's promise is worthless. ¹⁵The Law brings down God's anger; but where there is no law, there is no disobeying of the law.

16   And so the promise was based on faith, in order that the promise should be guaranteed as God's free gift to all of Abraham's descendants – not just to those who obey the Law, but also to those who believe as Abraham did. For Abraham is the spiritual father of us all; ¹⁷as the scripture says, "I have made you father of many nations." So the promise is good in the sight of God, in whom Abraham believed – the God who brings the dead to life and whose command brings into being what did not exist. ¹⁸Abraham believed and

hoped, even when there was no reason for hoping, and so became "the father of many nations." Just as the scripture says, "Your descendants will be as many as the stars." ¹⁹He was then almost one hundred years old; but his faith did not weaken when he thought of his body, which was already practically dead, or of the fact that Sarah could not have children. ²⁰His faith did not leave him, and he did not doubt God's promise; his faith filled him with power, and he gave praise to God. ²¹He was absolutely sure that God would be able to do what he had promised. ²²That is why Abraham, through faith, "was accepted as righteous by God". ²³The words "he was accepted as righteous" were not written for him alone. ²⁴They were written also for us who are to be accepted as righteous, who believe in him who raised Jesus our Lord from death. ²⁵Because of our sins he was handed over to die, and he was raised to life in order to put us right with God.

Right with God

5 Now that we have been put right with God through faith, we have[a] peace with God through our Lord Jesus Christ. ²He has brought us by faith into this experience of God's grace, in which we now live. And so we boast[b] of the hope we have of sharing God's glory! ³We also boast[c] of our troubles, because we know that trouble produces endurance, ⁴endurance brings God's approval, and his approval creates hope. ⁵This hope does not disappoint us, for God has poured out his love into our hearts by means of the Holy Spirit, who is God's gift to us.

6   For when we were still helpless, Christ died for the wicked at the time that God chose. ⁷It is a difficult thing for someone to die for a righteous person. It may even be that someone might dare to die for a good person. ⁸But God has shown us how much he loves us – it was while we were still sinners that Christ died for us! ⁹By his blood[d] we are now put right with God; how much more, then, will we be saved by him from God's anger! ¹⁰We were God's enemies, but he made us his friends through the death of his Son. Now that we are God's friends, how much more will we be saved by Christ's life! ¹¹But that is not all; we rejoice because of what God has done through our Lord Jesus Christ, who has now made us God's friends.

---

[a] **5.1** we have; *some manuscripts have* let us have.
[b] **5.2** we boast; *or* let us boast.
[c] **5.3** We also boast; *or* Let us also boast.
[d] **5.9** By his blood; *or* By his sacrificial death.

Adam and Christ

12   Sin came into the world through one man, and his sin brought death with it. As a result, death has spread to the whole human race because everyone has sinned. [13]There was sin in the world before the Law was given; but where there is no law, no account is kept of sins. [14]But from the time of Adam to the time of Moses death ruled over the whole human race, even over those who did not sin in the same way that Adam did when he disobeyed God's command.

Adam was a figure of the one who was to come. [15]But the two are not the same, because God's free gift is not like Adam's sin. It is true that many people died because of the sin of that one man. But God's grace is much greater, and so is his free gift to so many people through the grace of the one man, Jesus Christ. [16]And there is a difference between God's gift and the sin of one man. After the one sin, came the judgement of "Guilty"; but after so many sins, comes the undeserved gift of "Not guilty!" [17]It is true that through the sin of one man death began to rule because of that one man. But how much greater is the result of what was done by the one man, Jesus Christ! All who receive God's abundant grace and are freely put right with him will rule in life through Christ.

18   So then, as the one sin condemned all people, in the same way the one righteous act sets all people free and gives them life. [19]And just as the mass of people were made sinners as the result of the disobedience of one man, in the same way the mass of people will all be put right with God as the result of the obedience of the one man.

20   Law was introduced in order to increase wrongdoing; but where sin increased, God's grace increased much more. [21]So then, just as sin ruled by means of death, so also God's grace rules by means of righteousness, leading us to eternal life through Jesus Christ our Lord.

Dead to Sin but Alive in Union with Christ

6 What shall we say, then? Should we continue to live in sin so that God's grace will increase? [2]Certainly not! We have died to sin – how then can we go on living in it? [3]For surely you know that when we were baptized into union with Christ Jesus, we were baptized into union with his death. [4]By our baptism, then, we were buried with him and shared his death, in order that, just as Christ was raised from death by the glorious power of the Father, so also we might live a new life.

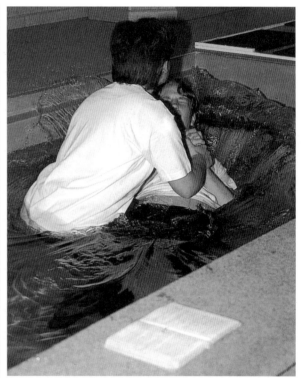

An adult is baptized by immersion in a Baptist church (6.4)

5   For since we have become one with him in dying as he did, in the same way we shall be one with him by being raised to life as he was. [6]And we know that our old being has been put to death with Christ on his cross, in order that the power of the sinful self might be destroyed, so that we should no longer be the slaves of sin. [7]For when people die, they are set free from the power of sin. [8]Since we have died with Christ, we believe that we will also live with him. [9]For we know that Christ has been raised from death and will never die again – death will no longer rule over him. [10]And so, because he died, sin has no power over him; and now he lives his life in fellowship with God. [11]In the same way you are to think of yourselves as dead, so far as sin is concerned, but living in fellowship with God through Christ Jesus.

12   Sin must no longer rule in your mortal bodies, so that you obey the desires of your natural self. [13]Nor must you surrender any part of yourselves to sin to be used for wicked purposes. Instead, give yourselves to God, as those who have been brought from death to life, and surrender your whole being to him to be used for righteous purposes. [14]Sin must not be your master; for you do not live under law but under God's grace.

A person leaves a baptismal pool after being baptised to symbolize their new life in Jesus (6.10)

Slaves of Righteousness

15 What, then? Shall we sin, because we are not under law but under God's grace? By no means! ¹⁶Surely you know that when you surrender yourselves as slaves to obey someone, you are in fact the slaves of the master you obey – either of sin, which results in death, or of obedience, which results in being put right with God. ¹⁷But thanks be to God! For though at one time you were slaves to sin, you have obeyed with all your heart the truths found in the teaching you received. ¹⁸You were set free from sin and became the slaves of righteousness. ¹⁹(I use everyday language because of the weakness of your natural selves.) At one time you surrendered yourselves entirely as slaves to impurity and wickedness for wicked purposes. In the same way you must now surrender yourselves entirely as slaves of righteousness for holy purposes.

20 When you were the slaves of sin, you were free from righteousness. ²¹What did you gain from doing the things that you are now ashamed of? The result of those things is death! ²²But now you have been set free from sin and are the slaves of God. Your gain is a life fully dedicated to him, and the result is eternal life.

²³For sin pays its wage – death; but God's free gift is eternal life in union with Christ Jesus our Lord.

An Illustration from Marriage

7 Certainly you will understand what I am about to say, my brothers and sisters, because all of you know about law. The law rules over people only as long as they live. ²A married woman, for example, is bound by the law to her husband as long as he lives; but if he dies, then she is free from the law that bound her to him. ³So then, if she lives with another man while her husband is alive, she will be called an adulteress; but if her husband dies, she is legally a free woman and does not commit adultery if she marries another man. ⁴That is how it is with you, my sisters and brothers. As far as the Law is concerned, you also have died because you are part of the body of Christ; and now you belong to him who was raised from death in order that we might be useful in the service of God. ⁵For when we lived according to our human nature, the sinful desires stirred up by the Law were at work in our bodies, and all we did ended in death. ⁶Now, however, we are free from the Law, because we died to that which once held us prisoners. No longer do we serve in the old way of a written law, but in the new way of the Spirit.

Law and Sin

7 Shall we say, then, that the Law itself is sinful? Of course not! But it was the Law that made me know what sin is. If the Law had not said, "Do not desire what belongs to someone else," I would not have known such a desire. ⁸But by means of that commandment sin found its chance to stir up all kinds of selfish desires in me. Apart from law, sin is a dead thing. ⁹I myself was once alive apart from law; but when the commandment came, sin sprang to life, ¹⁰and I died. And the commandment which was meant to bring life, in my case brought death. ¹¹Sin found its chance, and by means of the commandment it deceived me and killed me.

12 So then, the Law itself is holy, and the commandment is holy, right, and good. ¹³But does this mean that what is good caused my death? By no means! It was sin that did it; by using what is good, sin brought death to me, in order that its true nature as sin might be revealed. And so, by means of the commandment sin is shown to be even more terribly sinful.

The Conflict within Us

14 We know that the Law is spiritual; but I am unspiritual, sold as a slave to sin. [15]I do not understand what I do; for I don't do what I would like to do, but instead I do what I hate. [16]Since what I do is what I don't want to do, this shows that I agree that the Law is right. [17]So I am not really the one who does this thing; rather it is the sin that lives in me. [18]I know that good does not live in me – that is, in my human nature. For even though the desire to do good is in me, I am not able to do it. [19]I don't do the good I want to do; instead, I do the evil that I do not want to do. [20]If I do what I don't want to do, this means that I am no longer the one who does it; instead, it is the sin that lives in me.

21 So I find that this law is at work: when I want to do what is good, what is evil is the only choice I have. [22]My inner being delights in the law of God. [23]But I see a different law at work in my body – a law that fights against the law which my mind approves of. It makes me a prisoner to the law of sin which is at work in my body. [24]What an unhappy man I am! Who will rescue me from this body that is taking me to death? [25]Thanks be to God, who does this through our Lord Jesus Christ!

This, then, is my condition: on my own I can serve God's law only with my mind, while my human nature serves the law of sin.

Life in the Spirit

8 There is no condemnation now for those who live in union with Christ Jesus. [2]For the law of the Spirit, which brings us life in union with Christ Jesus, has set me[a] free from the law of sin and death. [3]What the Law could not do, because human nature was weak, God did. He condemned sin in human nature by sending his own Son, who came with a nature like sinful human nature, to do away with sin. [4]God did this so that the righteous demands of the Law might be fully satisfied in us who live according to the Spirit, and not according to human nature. [5]Those who live as their human nature tells them to, have their minds controlled by what human nature wants. Those who live as the Spirit tells them to, have their minds controlled by what the Spirit wants. [6]To be controlled by human nature results in death; to be controlled by the Spirit results in life and peace. [7]And so people become enemies of God when they are controlled by their human

An Orthodox icon showing Mary with her child, Jesus (8.3)

nature; for they do not obey God's law, and in fact they cannot obey it. [8]Those who obey their human nature cannot please God.

9 But you do not live as your human nature tells you to; instead, you live as the Spirit tells you to – if, in fact, God's Spirit lives in you. Whoever does not have the Spirit of Christ does not belong to him. [10]But if Christ lives in you, the Spirit is life for you[b] because you have been put right with God, even though your bodies are going to die because of sin. [11]If the Spirit of God, who raised Jesus from death, lives in you, then he who raised Christ from death will also give life to your mortal bodies by the presence of his Spirit in you.

12 So then, my brothers and sisters, we have an obligation, but it is not to live as our human nature wants us to. [13]For if you live according to your human nature, you are going to die; but if by the Spirit you put to death your sinful actions, you will live. [14]Those who are led by God's Spirit are God's children. [15]For the Spirit that God has given you does not make you slaves and cause

---

[a] **8.2** me; *some manuscripts have* you; *others have* us.

[b] **8.10** the Spirit is life for you; *or* your spirit is alive.

you to be afraid; instead, the Spirit makes you God's children, and by the Spirit's power we cry out to God, "Father! my Father!" [16]God's Spirit joins himself to our spirits to declare that we are God's children. [17]Since we are his children, we will possess the blessings he keeps for his people, and we will also possess with Christ what God has kept for him; for if we share Christ's suffering, we will also share his glory.

The Future Glory

18   I consider that what we suffer at this present time cannot be compared at all with the glory that is going to be revealed to us. [19]All of creation waits with eager longing for God to reveal his children. [20]For creation was condemned to lose its purpose, not of its own will, but because God willed it to be so. Yet there was the hope [21]that creation itself would one day be set free from its slavery to decay and would share the glorious freedom of the children of God. [22]For we know that up to the present time all of creation groans with pain, like the pain of childbirth. [23]But it is not just creation alone which groans; we who have the Spirit as the first of God's gifts also groan within ourselves, as we wait for God to make us his children and[a] set our whole being free. [24]For it was by hope that we were saved; but if we see what we hope for, then it is not really hope. For which of us hopes for something we see? [25]But if we hope for what we do not see, we wait for it with patience.

26   In the same way the Spirit also comes to help us, weak as we are. For we do not know how we ought to pray; the Spirit himself pleads with God for us in groans that words cannot express. [27]And God, who sees into our hearts, knows what the thought of the Spirit is; because the Spirit pleads with God on behalf of his people and in accordance with his will.

28   We know that in all things God works for good with those who love him,[b] those whom he has called according to his purpose. [29]Those whom God had already chosen he also set apart to become like his Son, so that the Son would be the eldest brother in a large family. [30]And so those whom God set apart, he called; and those he called, he put right with himself, and he shared his glory with them.

---

[a] **8.23** *Some manuscripts do not have* make us his children and.
[b] **8.28** in all things God works for good with those who love him; *some manuscripts have* all things work for good for those who love God.

God's Love in Christ Jesus

31   In view of all this, what can we say? If God is for us, who can be against us? [32]Certainly not God, who did not even keep back his own Son, but offered him for us all! He gave us his Son – will he not also freely give us all things? [33]Who will accuse God's chosen people? God himself declares them not guilty! [34]Who, then, will condemn them? Not Christ Jesus, who died, or rather, who was raised to life and is at the right-hand side of God, pleading with him for us! [35]Who, then, can separate us from the love of Christ? Can trouble do it, or hardship or persecution or hunger or poverty or danger or death? [36]As the scripture says,

> "For your sake we are in danger of death at
>   all times;
>   we are treated like sheep that are going to
>   be slaughtered."

[37]No, in all these things we have complete victory through him who loved us! [38]For I am certain that nothing can separate us from his love: neither death nor life, neither angels nor other heavenly rulers or powers, neither the present nor the future, [39]neither the world above nor the world below – there is nothing in all creation that will ever be able to separate us from the love of God which is ours through Christ Jesus our Lord.

God and his People

9   I am speaking the truth; I belong to Christ and I do not lie. My conscience, ruled by the Holy Spirit, also assures me that I am not lying [2]when I say how great is my sorrow, how endless the pain in my heart [3]for my people, my own flesh and blood! For their sake I could wish that I myself were under God's curse and separated from Christ. [4]They are God's people; he made them his children and revealed his glory to them; he made his covenants[c] with them and gave them the Law; they have the true worship; they have received God's promises; [5]they are descended from the famous Hebrew ancestors; and Christ, as a human being, belongs to their race. May God, who rules over all, be praised for ever![d] Amen.

6   I am not saying that the promise of God has failed; for not all the people of Israel are the

---

[c] **9.4** covenants; *some manuscripts have* covenant.
[d] **9.5** May God, who rules over all, be praised for ever!; *or* And may he, who is God ruling over all, be praised for ever!

people of God. [7]Nor are all Abraham's descendants the children of God. God said to Abraham, "It is through Isaac that you will have the descendants I promised you." [8]This means that the children born in the usual way[a] are not the children of God; instead, the children born as a result of God's promise are regarded as the true descendants. [9]For God's promise was made in these words: "At the right time[b] I will come back, and Sarah will have a son."

10 And this is not all. For Rebecca's two sons had the same father, our ancestor Isaac. [11-12]But in order that the choice of one son might be completely the result of God's own purpose, God said to her, "The elder will serve the younger." He said this before they were born, before they had done anything either good or bad; so God's choice was based on his call, and not on anything they had done. [13]As the scripture says, "I loved Jacob, but I hated Esau."

14 Shall we say, then, that God is unjust? Not at all. [15]For he said to Moses, "I will have mercy on anyone I wish; I will take pity on anyone I wish." [16]So then, everything depends, not on what human beings want or do, but only on God's mercy. [17]For the scripture says to the king of Egypt, "I made you king in order to use you to show my power and to spread my fame over the whole world." [18]So then, God has mercy on anyone he wishes, and he makes stubborn anyone he wishes.

God's Anger and Mercy

19 But one of you will say to me, "If this is so, how can God find fault with anyone? Who can resist God's will?" [20]But who are you, my friend, to answer God back? A clay pot does not ask the man who made it, "Why did you make me like this?" [21]After all, the man who makes the pots has the right to use the clay as he wishes, and to make two pots from the same lump of clay, one for special occasions and the other for ordinary use.

22 And the same is true of what God has done. He wanted to show his anger and to make his power known. But he was very patient in enduring those who were the objects of his anger, who were doomed to destruction. [23]And he also wanted to reveal his abundant glory, which was poured out on us who are the objects of his

mercy, those of us whom he has prepared to receive his glory. [24]For we are the people he called, not only from among the Jews but also from among the Gentiles. [25]This is what he says in the book of Hosea:

> "The people who were not mine
>   I will call 'My People'.
> The nation that I did not love
>   I will call 'My Beloved'.

26 And in the very place where they were told,
>   'You are not my people,'
>   there they will be called the children of
>   the living God."

27 And Isaiah exclaims about Israel: "Even if the people of Israel are as many as the grains of sand by the sea, yet only a few of them will be saved; [28]for the Lord will quickly settle his full account with the world." [29]It is as Isaiah had said before, "If the Lord Almighty had not left us some descendants, we would have become like Sodom, we would have been like Gomorrah."

Paul's Prayer for Israel

30 So we say that the Gentiles, who were not trying to put themselves right with God, were put right with him through faith; [31]while God's people, who were seeking a law that would put them right with God, did not find it. [32]And why not? Because they did not depend on faith but on what they did. And so they stumbled over the "stumbling stone" [33]that the scripture speaks of:

> "Look, I place in Zion a stone
>   that will make people stumble,
>   a rock that will make them fall.
> But whoever believes in him will not be
>   disappointed."

10 My brothers and sisters, how I wish with all my heart that my own people might be saved! How I pray to God for them! [2]I can assure you that they are deeply devoted to God; but their devotion is not based on true knowledge. [3]They have not known the way in which God puts people right with himself, and instead, they have tried to set up their own way; and so they did not submit themselves to God's way of putting people right. [4]For Christ has brought the Law to an end, so that everyone who believes is put right with God.

Salvation is for All

5 Moses wrote this about being put right with God by obeying the Law: "Whoever obeys the

---

[a] **9.8** CHILDREN BORN IN THE USUAL WAY: *This refers to the descendants Abraham had through Ishmael, his son by Hagar (see Gal 4.22–23).*
[b] **9.9** At the right time; *or* At this time next year.

commands of the Law will live." [6]But what the scripture says about being put right with God through faith is this: "You are not to ask yourself, Who will go up into heaven?" (that is, to bring Christ down). [7]"Nor are you to ask, Who will go down into the world below?" (that is, to bring Christ up from death). [8]What it says is this: "God's message is near you, on your lips and in your heart" – that is, the message of faith that we preach. [9]If you confess that Jesus is Lord and believe that God raised him from death, you will be saved. [10]For it is by our faith that we are put right with God; it is by our confession that we are saved. [11]The scripture says, "Whoever believes in him will not be disappointed." [12]This includes everyone, because there is no difference between Jews and Gentiles; God is the same Lord of all and richly blesses all who call to him. [13]As the scripture says, "Everyone who calls out to the Lord for help will be saved."

[14]But how can they call to him for help if they have not believed? And how can they believe if they have not heard the message? And how can they hear if the message is not proclaimed? [15]And how can the message be proclaimed if the messengers are not sent out? As the scripture says, "How wonderful is the coming of messengers who bring good news!" [16]But not all have accepted the Good News. Isaiah himself said, "Lord, who believed our message?" [17]So then, faith comes from hearing the message, and the message comes through preaching Christ.

[18]But I ask: is it true that they did not hear the message? Of course they did – for as the scripture says:

"The sound of their voice went out to all the
world;
their words reached the ends of the earth."

[19]Again I ask: did the people of Israel not understand? Moses himself is the first one to answer:

"I will use a so-called nation
to make my people jealous;
and by means of a nation of fools
I will make my people angry."

[20]And Isaiah is even bolder when he says,

"I was found by those who were not looking
for me;
I appeared to those who were not asking
for me."

[21]But concerning Israel he says, "All day long I held out my hands to welcome a disobedient and rebellious people."

God's Mercy on Israel

11 I ask, then: did God reject his own people? Certainly not! I myself am an Israelite, a descendant of Abraham, a member of the tribe of Benjamin. [2]God has not rejected his people, whom he chose from the beginning. You know what the scripture says in the passage where Elijah pleads with God against Israel: [3]"Lord, they have killed your prophets and torn down your altars; I am the only one left, and they are trying to kill me." [4]What answer did God give him? "I have kept for myself seven thousand men who have not worshipped the false god Baal." [5]It is the same way now: there is a small number left of those whom God has chosen because of his grace. [6]His choice is based on his grace, not on what they have done. For if God's choice were based on what people do, then his grace would not be real grace.

[7]What then? The people of Israel did not find what they were looking for. It was only the small group that God chose who found it; the rest grew deaf to God's call. [8]As the scripture says, "God made their minds and hearts dull; to this very day they cannot see or hear." [9]And David says:

"May they be caught and trapped at their
feasts;
may they fall, may they be punished!
[10]May their eyes be blinded so that they
cannot see;
and make them bend under their troubles
at all times."

[11]I ask, then: when the Jews stumbled, did they fall to their ruin? By no means! Because they sinned, salvation has come to the Gentiles, to make the Jews jealous of them. [12]The sin of the Jews brought rich blessings to the world, and their spiritual poverty brought rich blessings to the Gentiles. Then, how much greater the blessings will be when the complete number of Jews is included!

The Salvation of the Gentiles

[13]I am speaking now to you Gentiles: as long as I am an apostle to the Gentiles, I will take pride in my work. [14]Perhaps I can make the people of my own race jealous, and so be able to save some of them. [15]For when they were rejected, the human race was changed from God's enemies into his friends. What will it be, then, when they are accepted? It will be life for the dead!

[16]If the first piece of bread is given to God, then the whole loaf is his also; and if the roots of a

tree are offered to God, the branches are his also. [17]Some of the branches of the cultivated olive tree have been broken off, and a branch of a wild olive tree has been joined to it. You Gentiles are like that wild olive tree, and now you share the strong spiritual life of the Jews. [18]So then, you must not despise those who were broken off like branches. How can you be proud? You are just a branch; you don't support the roots – the roots support you.

19 But you will say, "Yes, but the branches were broken off to make room for me." [20]That is true. They were broken off because they did not believe, while you remain in place because you do believe. But do not be proud of it; instead, be afraid. [21]God did not spare the Jews, who are like natural branches; do you think he will spare you? [22]Here we see how kind and how severe God is. He is severe towards those who have fallen, but kind to you – if you continue in his kindness. But if you do not, you too will be broken off. [23]And if the Jews abandon their unbelief, they will be put back in the place where they were; for God is able to do that. [24]You Gentiles are like the branch of a wild olive tree that is broken off and then, contrary to nature, is joined to a cultivated olive tree. The Jews are like this cultivated tree; and it will be much easier for God to join these broken-off branches to their own tree again.

God's Mercy on All

25 There is a secret truth, my brothers and sisters, which I want you to know, for it will keep you from thinking how wise you are. It is that the stubbornness of the people of Israel is not permanent, but will last only until the complete number of Gentiles comes to God. [26]And this is how all Israel will be saved. As the scripture says:

"The Saviour will come from Zion
and remove all wickedness from the descendants of Jacob.

27 I will make this covenant with them
when I take away their sins."

[28]Because they reject the Good News, the Jews are God's enemies for the sake of you Gentiles. But because of God's choice, they are his friends because of their ancestors. [29]For God does not change his mind about whom he chooses and blesses. [30]As for you Gentiles, you disobeyed God in the past; but now you have received God's mercy because the Jews were disobedient. [31]In the same way, because of the mercy that you have received, the Jews now disobey God, in order that they also may now[a] receive God's mercy. [32]For God has made all people prisoners of disobedience, so that he might show mercy to them all.

Praise to God

33 How great are God's riches! How deep are his wisdom and knowledge! Who can explain his decisions? Who can understand his ways? [34]As the scripture says:

"Who knows the mind of the Lord?
Who is able to give him advice?
35 Who has ever given him anything,
so that he had to pay it back?"

[36]For all things were created by him, and all things exist through him and for him. To God be the glory for ever! Amen.

Life in God's Service

12 So then, my brothers and sisters, because of God's great mercy to us I appeal to you: offer yourselves as a living sacrifice to God, dedicated to his service and pleasing to him. This is the true worship that you should offer. [2]Do not conform yourselves to the standards of this world, but let God transform you inwardly by a complete change of your mind. Then you will be able to know the will of God – what is good and is pleasing to him and is perfect.

3 And because of God's gracious gift to me I say to every one of you: do not think of yourself more highly than you should. Instead, be modest in your thinking, and judge yourself according to the amount of faith that God has given you. [4]We have many parts in the one body, and all these parts have different functions. [5]In the same way, though we are many, we are one body in union with Christ, and we are all joined to each other as different parts of one body. [6]So we are to use our different gifts in accordance with the grace that God has given us. If our gift is to speak God's message, we should do it according to the faith that we have; [7]if it is to serve, we should serve; if it is to teach, we should teach; [8]if it is to encourage others, we should do so. Whoever shares with others should do it generously; whoever has authority should work hard; whoever shows kindness to others should do it cheerfully.

9 Love must be completely sincere. Hate what is evil, hold on to what is good. [10]Love one

---

[a] **11.31** *Some manuscripts do not have* now.

another warmly as Christian brothers and sisters, and be eager to show respect for one another. ¹¹Work hard and do not be lazy. Serve the Lord with a heart full of devotion. ¹²Let your hope keep you joyful, be patient in your troubles, and pray at all times. ¹³Share your belongings with your needy fellow-Christians, and open your homes to strangers.

14 Ask God to bless those who persecute you – yes, ask him to bless, not to curse. ¹⁵Be happy with those who are happy, weep with those who weep. ¹⁶Have the same concern for everyone. Do not be proud, but accept humble duties.ᵃ Do not think of yourselves as wise.

17 If someone has done you wrong, do not repay him with a wrong. Try to do what everyone considers to be good. ¹⁸Do everything possible on your part to live in peace with everybody. ¹⁹Never take revenge, my friends, but instead let God's anger do it. For the scripture says, "I will take revenge, I will pay back, says the Lord." ²⁰Instead, as the scripture says: "If your enemies are hungry, feed them; if they are thirsty, give them a drink; for by doing this you will make them burn with shame." ²¹Do not let evil defeat you; instead, conquer evil with good.

Duties towards the State Authorities

13 Everyone must obey the state authorities, because no authority exists without God's permission, and the existing authorities have been put there by God. ²Whoever opposes the existing authority opposes what God has ordered; and anyone who does so will bring judgement on himself. ³For rulers are not to be feared by those who do good, but by those who do evil. Would you like to be unafraid of those in authority? Then do what is good, and they will praise you, ⁴because they are God's servants working for your own good. But if you do evil, then be afraid of them, because their power to punish is real. They are God's servants and carry out God's punishment on those who do evil. ⁵For this reason you must obey the authorities – not just because of God's punishment, but also as a matter of conscience.

6 That is also why you pay taxes, because the authorities are working for God when they fulfil their duties. ⁷Pay, then, what you owe them; pay them your personal and property taxes, and show respect and honour for them all.

ᵃ **12.16** accept humble duties; *or* make friends with humble people.

The Ten Sayings (Commandments) on the wall of a synagogue (13.8–10)

Duties towards One Another

8 Be under obligation to no one – the only obligation you have is to love one another. Whoever does this has obeyed the Law. ⁹The commandments, "Do not commit adultery; do not commit murder; do not steal; do not desire what belongs to someone else" – all these, and any others besides, are summed up in the one command, "Love your neighbour as you love yourself." ¹⁰If you love someone, you will never do them wrong; to love, then, is to obey the whole Law.

11 You must do this, because you know that the time has come for you to wake up from your sleep. For the moment when we will be saved is closer now than it was when we first believed. ¹²The night is nearly over, day is almost here. Let us stop doing the things that belong to the dark, and let us take up weapons for fighting in the light. ¹³Let us conduct ourselves properly, as people who live in the light of day – no orgies or drunkenness, no immorality or indecency, no fighting or jealousy. ¹⁴But take up the weapons of the Lord Jesus Christ, and stop paying attention to your sinful nature and satisfying its desires.

Do not Judge One Another

14 Welcome those who are weak in faith, but do not argue with them about their personal opinions. ²Some people's faith allows them to eat anything, but the person who is weak in the faith eats only vegetables. ³Those who will eat anything are not to despise those who don't; while those who eat only vegetables are not to pass judgement on those who will eat anything; for God has accepted them. [4]Who are you to judge someone else's servants? It is their own Master who will decide whether they succeed or fail. And they will succeed, because the Lord is able to make them succeed.

[5] Some people think that a certain day is more important than other days, while others think that all days are the same. We should each firmly make up our own minds. [6]Those who think highly of a certain day do so in honour of the Lord; those who will eat anything do so in honour of the Lord, because they give thanks to God for the food. Those who refuse to eat certain things do so in honour of the Lord, and they give thanks to God. [7]None of us lives for himself only, none of us dies for himself only. [8]If we live, it is for the Lord that we live, and if we die, it is for the Lord that we die. So whether we live or die, we belong to the Lord. [9]For Christ died and rose to life in order to be the Lord of the living and of the dead. [10]You then, who eat only vegetables – why do you pass judgement on others? And you who eat anything – why do you despise other believers? All of us will stand before God to be judged by him. [11]For the scripture says:

> "As surely as I am the living God, says the
>   Lord,
>   everyone will kneel before me,
>   and everyone will confess that I am God."

[12]Every one of us, then, will have to give an account of ourselves to God.

Do not Make One Another Fall

[13] So then, let us stop judging one another. Instead, you should decide never to do anything that would make another stumble or fall into sin. [14]My union with the Lord Jesus makes me certain that no food is of itself ritually unclean; but if a person believes that some food is unclean, then it becomes unclean for that person. [15]If you hurt your brother or sister because of something you eat, then you are no longer acting from love. Do not let the food that you eat ruin the person for whom Christ died! [16]Do not let what you regard as good get a bad name. [17]For God's Kingdom is not a matter of eating and drinking, but of the righteousness, peace, and joy which the Holy Spirit gives. [18]And when people serve Christ in this way, they please God and are approved by others.

[19] So then, we must always aim[a] at those things that bring peace and that help to strengthen one another. [20]Do not, because of food, destroy what God has done. All foods may be eaten, but it is wrong to eat anything that will cause someone else to fall into sin. [21]The right thing to do is to keep from eating meat, drinking wine, or doing anything else that will make your brother or sister fall. [22]Keep what you believe about this matter, then, between yourself and God. Happy are those who do not feel guilty when they do something they judge is right! [23]But if they have doubts about what they eat, God condemns them when they eat it, because their action is not based on faith. And anything that is not based on faith is sin.

Please Others, not Yourselves

15 We who are strong in the faith ought to help the weak to carry their burdens. We should not please ourselves. [2]Instead, we should all please our brothers and sisters for their own good, in order to build them up in the faith. [3]For Christ did not please himself. Instead, as the scripture says, "The insults which are hurled at you have fallen on me." [4]Everything written in the Scriptures was written to teach us, in order that we might have hope through the patience and encouragement which the Scriptures give us. [5]And may God, the source of patience and encouragement, enable you to have the same point of view among yourselves by following the example of Christ Jesus, [6]so that all of you together may praise with one voice the God and Father of our Lord Jesus Christ.

Good News for the Gentiles

[7] Accept one another, then, for the glory of God, as Christ has accepted you. [8]For I tell you that Christ's life of service was on behalf of the Jews, to show that God is faithful, to make his promises to their ancestors come true, [9]and to enable even the Gentiles to praise God for his mercy. As the scripture says:

> "And so I will praise you among the Gentiles;
>   I will sing praises to you."

[10]Again it says,

> "Rejoice, Gentiles, with God's people!"

[11]And again,

---

[a] **14.19** we must always aim; *some manuscripts have* we always aim.

"Praise the Lord, all Gentiles;
    praise him, all peoples!"

¹²And again, Isaiah says,

"A descendant of Jesse will appear;
    he will come to rule the Gentiles,
    and they will put their hope in him."

13   May God, the source of hope, fill you with all joy and peace by means of your faith in him, so that your hope will continue to grow by the power of the Holy Spirit.

Paul's Reason for Writing so Boldly

14   My brothers and sisters, I myself feel sure that you are full of goodness, that you have all knowledge, and that you are able to teach one another. ¹⁵But in this letter I have been quite bold about certain subjects of which I have reminded you. I have been bold because of the privilege God has given me ¹⁶of being a servant of Christ Jesus to work for the Gentiles. I serve like a priest in preaching the Good News from God, in order that the Gentiles may be an offering acceptable to God, dedicated to him by the Holy Spirit. ¹⁷In union with Christ Jesus, then, I can be proud of my service for God. ¹⁸I will be bold and speak only about what Christ has done through me to lead the Gentiles to obey God. He has done this by means of words and deeds, ¹⁹by the power of miracles and wonders, and by the power of the Spirit of God. And so, in travelling all the way from Jerusalem to Illyricum, I have proclaimed fully the Good News about Christ. ²⁰My ambition has always been to proclaim the Good News in places where Christ has not been heard of, so as not to build on a foundation laid by someone else. ²¹As the scripture says:

"Those who were not told about him will see,
    and those who have not heard will
        understand."

Paul's Plan to Visit Rome

22   And so I have been prevented many times from coming to you. ²³But now that I have finished my work in these regions and since I have been wanting for so many years to come to see you, ²⁴I hope to do so now. I would like to see you on my way to Spain, and be helped by you to go there, after I have enjoyed visiting you for a while. ²⁵Just now, however, I am going to Jerusalem in the service of God's people there. ²⁶For the churches in Macedonia and Achaia have freely decided to give an offering to help the poor among God's people in Jerusalem. ²⁷That decision was their own; but, as a matter of fact, they have an obligation to help them. Since the Jews shared their spiritual blessings with the Gentiles, the Gentiles ought to use their material blessings to help the Jews. ²⁸When I have finished this task and have handed over to them all the money that has been raised for them, I shall leave for Spain and visit you on my way there. ²⁹When I come to you, I know that I shall come with a full measure of the blessing of Christ.

30   I urge you, brothers and sisters, by our Lord Jesus Christ and by the love that the Spirit gives: join me in praying fervently to God for me. ³¹Pray that I may be kept safe from the unbelievers in Judea and that my service in Jerusalem may be acceptable to God's people there. ³²And so I will come to you full of joy, if it is God's will, and enjoy a refreshing visit to you. ³³May God, our source of peace, be with all of you. Amen.

Personal Greetings

16 I recommend to you our sister Phoebe, who serves the church at Cenchreae. ²Receive her in the Lord's name, as God's people should, and give her any help she may need from you; for she herself has been a good friend to many people and also to me.

3   I send greetings to Priscilla and Aquila, my fellow-workers in the service of Christ Jesus; ⁴they risked their lives for me. I am grateful to them – not only I, but all the Gentile churches as well. ⁵Greetings also to the church that meets in their house.

Greetings to my dear friend Epaenetus, who was the first in the province of Asia to believe in Christ. ⁶Greetings to Mary, who has worked so hard for you. ⁷Greetings also to Andronicus and Junia,ᵃ fellow-Jews who were in prison with me; they are well known among the apostles, and they became Christians before I did.

8   My greetings to Ampliatus, my dear friend in the fellowship of the Lord. ⁹Greetings also to Urbanus, our fellow-worker in Christ's service, and to Stachys, my dear friend. ¹⁰Greetings to Apelles, whose loyalty to Christ has been proved. Greetings to those who belong to the family of Aristobulus. ¹¹Greetings to Herodion, a fellow-Jew, and to the Christians in the family of Narcissus.

12   My greetings to Tryphaena and Tryphosa, who work in the Lord's service, and to my dear

---

ᵃ **16.7** Junia; *or* Junias; *some manuscripts have* Julia.

friend Persis, who has done so much work for the Lord. [13]I send greetings to Rufus, that outstanding worker in the Lord's service, and to his mother, who has always treated me like a son. [14]My greetings to Asyncritus, Phlegon, Hermes, Patrobas, Hermas, and all the other Christian brothers and sisters with them. [15]Greetings to Philologus and Julia, to Nereus and his sister, to Olympas and to all of God's people who are with them.

16   Greet one another with a holy kiss. All the churches of Christ send you their greetings.

Final Instructions

17   I urge you, my brothers and sisters: watch out for those who cause divisions and upset people's faith and go against the teaching which you have received. Keep away from them! [18]For those who do such things are not serving Christ our Lord, but their own appetites. By their fine words and flattering speech they deceive innocent people. [19]Everyone has heard of your loyalty to the gospel, and for this reason I am happy about you. I want you to be wise about what is good, but innocent in what is evil. [20]And God, our source of peace, will soon crush Satan under your feet.

The grace of our Lord Jesus be with you.[a]

21   Timothy, my fellow-worker, sends you his greetings; and so do Lucius, Jason, and Sosipater, fellow-Jews.

22   I, Tertius, the writer of this letter, send you Christian greetings.

23   My host Gaius, in whose house the church meets, sends you his greetings; Erastus, the city treasurer, and our brother Quartus send you their greetings.[b]

Concluding Prayer of Praise

25   Let us give glory to God! He is able to make you stand firm in your faith, according to the Good News I preach about Jesus Christ and according to the revelation of the secret truth which was hidden for long ages in the past. [26]Now, however, that truth has been brought out into the open through the writings of the prophets; and by the command of the eternal God it is made known to all nations, so that all may believe and obey.

27   To the only God, who alone is all-wise, be glory through Jesus Christ for ever! Amen.[c]

[a] **16.20** *Some manuscripts omit this sentence.*
[b] **16.23** *Some manuscripts add verse 24:* The grace of our Lord Jesus Christ be with you all. Amen; *others add this after verse 27.*
[c] **16.27** *Some manuscripts have verses 25–27 here and after 14.23; others have them only after 14.23; one has them after 15.33.*

Paul's First Letter to the CORINTHIANS

INTRODUCTION

Paul's First Letter to the Corinthians was written to deal with problems of Christian life and faith that had arisen in the church which Paul had established at Corinth. At that time Corinth was a great cosmopolitan Greek city, the capital of the Roman province of Achaia. It was noted for its thriving commerce, proud culture, widespread immorality, and variety of religions.

The apostle's chief concerns are with problems such as divisions and immorality in the church, and with questions about sex and marriage, matters of conscience, church order, gifts of the Holy Spirit, and the resurrection. With deep insight he shows how the Good News speaks to these questions.

Chapter 13, which presents love as the best of God's gifts to his people, is probably the most widely known passage in the book.

Outline of Contents

1 From Paul, who was called by the will of God to be an apostle of Christ Jesus, and from our brother Sosthenes –

2 To the church of God which is in Corinth, to all who are called to be God's holy people, who belong to him in union with Christ Jesus, together with all people everywhere who worship our Lord Jesus Christ, their Lord and ours:

3 May God our Father and the Lord Jesus Christ give you grace and peace.

Blessings in Christ

4 I always give thanks to my God for you because of the grace he has given you through Christ Jesus. [5]For in union with Christ you have become rich in all things, including all speech and all knowledge. [6]The message about Christ has become so firmly established in you [7]that you have not failed to receive a single blessing, as you wait for our Lord Jesus Christ to be revealed. [8]He will also keep you firm to the end, so that you will be faultless on the Day of our Lord Jesus Christ. [9]God is to be trusted, the God who called you to have fellowship with his Son Jesus Christ, our Lord.

Divisions in the Church

10 By the authority of our Lord Jesus Christ I appeal to all of you, my brothers and sisters, to agree in what you say, so that there will be no divisions among you. Be completely united, with only one thought and one purpose. [11]For some people from Chloe's family have told me quite plainly, my friends, that there are quarrels among you. [12]Let me put it this way: each one of you says something different. One says, "I follow Paul"; another, "I follow Apollos"; another, "I follow Peter"; and another, "I follow Christ". [13]Christ has been divided[a] into groups! Was it

---

[a] **1.13** Christ has been divided; *some manuscripts have* Christ cannot be divided.

Paul who died on the cross for you? Were you baptized as Paul's disciples?

14   I thank God that I did not baptize any of you except Crispus and Gaius. ¹⁵No one can say, then, that you were baptized as my disciples. ¹⁶(Oh yes, I also baptized Stephanas and his family; but I can't remember whether I baptized anyone else.) ¹⁷Christ did not send me to baptize. He sent me to tell the Good News, and to tell it without using the language of human wisdom, in order to make sure that Christ's death on the cross is not robbed of its power.

Christ the Power and the Wisdom of God

18   For the message about Christ's death on the cross is nonsense to those who are being lost; but for us who are being saved it is God's power. ¹⁹The scripture says:

"I will destroy the wisdom of the wise
    and set aside the understanding of the
        scholars."

²⁰So then, where does that leave the wise? or the scholars? or the skilful debaters of this world? God has shown that this world's wisdom is foolishness!

21   For God in his wisdom made it impossible for people to know him by means of their own wisdom. Instead, by means of the so-called "foolish" message we preach, God decided to save those who believe. ²²Jews want miracles for proof, and Greeks look for wisdom. ²³As for us, we proclaim the crucified Christ, a message that is offensive to the Jews and nonsense to the Gentiles; ²⁴but for those whom God has called, both Jews and Gentiles, this message is Christ, who is the power of God and the wisdom of God. ²⁵For what seems to be God's foolishness is wiser than human wisdom, and what seems to be God's weakness is stronger than human strength.

26   Now remember what you were, my brothers and sisters, when God called you. From the human point of view few of you were wise or powerful or of high social standing. ²⁷God purposely chose what the world considers nonsense in order to shame the wise, and he chose what the world considers weak in order to shame the powerful. ²⁸He chose what the world looks down on and despises, and thinks is nothing, in order to destroy what the world thinks is important. ²⁹This means that no one can boast in God's presence. ³⁰But God has brought you into union with Christ Jesus, and God has made Christ to be our wisdom. By him we are put right with God; we become God's holy people and are set free. ³¹So then, as the scripture says, "Whoever wants to boast must boast of what the Lord has done."

The Message about the Crucified Christ

2   When I came to you, my brothers and sisters, to preach God's secret truth,ᵃ I did not use big words and great learning. ²For while I was with you, I made up my mind to forget everything except Jesus Christ and especially his death on the cross. ³So when I came to you, I was weak and trembled all over with fear, ⁴and my teaching and message were not delivered with skilful words of human wisdom, but with convincing proof of the power of God's Spirit. ⁵Your faith, then, does not rest on human wisdom but on God's power.

God's Wisdom

6   Yet I do proclaim a message of wisdom to those who are spiritually mature. But it is not the wisdom that belongs to this world or to the powers that rule this world – powers that are losing their power. ⁷The wisdom I proclaim is God's hidden wisdom, which he had already chosen for our glory even before the world was made. ⁸None of the rulers of this world knew this wisdom. If they had known it, they would not have crucified the Lord of glory. ⁹However, as the scripture says:

A woven Station of the Cross showing Jesus collapsing under the cross (1.25)

ᵃ **2.1** God's secret truth; *some manuscripts have* the testimony about God.

"What no one ever saw or heard,
what no one ever thought could happen,
is the very thing God prepared for those
who love him."

[10]But[a] it was to us that God made known his secret by means of his Spirit. The Spirit searches everything, even the hidden depths of God's purposes. [11]It is only the spirit within people that knows all about them; in the same way, only God's Spirit knows all about God. [12]We have not received this world's spirit; instead, we have received the Spirit sent by God, so that we may know all that God has given us.

13 So then, we do not speak in words taught by human wisdom, but in words taught by the Spirit, as we explain spiritual truths to those who have the Spirit.[b] [14]Whoever does not have the Spirit cannot receive the gifts that come from God's Spirit. Such people really do not understand them; they are nonsense to them, because their value can be judged only on a spiritual basis. [15]Whoever has the Spirit, however, is able to judge the value of everything, but no one is able to judge him. [16]As the scripture says:

"Who knows the mind of the Lord?
Who is able to give him advice?"

We, however, have the mind of Christ.

Servants of God

3 As a matter of fact, my brothers and sisters, I could not talk to you as I talk to people who have the Spirit; I had to talk to you as though you belonged to this world, as children in the Christian faith. [2]I had to feed you with milk, not solid food, because you were not ready for it. And even now you are not ready for it, [3]because you still live as the people of this world live. When there is jealousy among you and you quarrel with one another, doesn't this prove that you belong to this world, living by its standards? [4]When one of you says, "I follow Paul", and another, "I follow Apollos" – aren't you acting like worldly people?

5 After all, who is Apollos? And who is Paul? We are simply God's servants, by whom you were led to believe. Each one of us does the work which the Lord gave him to do: [6]I sowed the seed, Apollos watered the plant, but it was God who made the plant grow. [7]The one who sows and the one who waters really do not matter. It

---

[a] **2.10** But; *some manuscripts have* For.
[b] **2.13** to those who have the Spirit; *or* with words given by the Spirit.

Studying
1 CORINTHIANS

Who wrote it? Paul.
When? About 54 CE.
Where from? From Ephesus during his third missionary journey.
For whom? The Christian community in Corinth. Paul arrived in the city in 49 CE and made many converts. The church was made up of Jews and Gentiles.
Why? To deal with problems in the Corinth church – including sexual immorality and misuse of worship. Sought to establish his own authority as an apostle – which many questioned.

KEY POINTS

- Christians should live bearing in mind the return of Christ to the world. Celibacy is the ideal state. If impossible, then marriage is best.
- "Spiritual gifts" such as prophecy and speaking in tongues are important, but other things more vital – unity and love.
- Highlights the importance of the Lord's Supper and the danger that it was being ruined by some in the church.
- Proclaims the resurrection of Jesus as most important Christian belief.

---

is God who matters, because he makes the plant grow. [8]There is no difference between the one who sows and the one who waters; God will reward each one according to the work each has done. [9]For we are partners working together for God, and you are God's field.

You are also God's building. [10]Using the gift that God gave me, I did the work of an expert builder and laid the foundation, and someone else is building on it. But each one must be careful how he builds. [11]For God has already placed Jesus Christ as the one and only foundation, and no other foundation can be laid. [12]Some will use gold or silver or precious stones in building on the foundation; others will use wood or grass or straw. [13]And the quality of each person's work will be seen when the Day of Christ exposes it. For on that Day fire will reveal everyone's work; the fire will test it and show its real quality. [14]If what was built on the foundation survives the fire, the builder will receive a reward. [15]But if anyone's work is burnt up, then he will lose it; but he himself will be saved, as if he had escaped through the fire.

16 Surely you know that you are God's temple and that God's Spirit lives in you! [17]So if anyone destroys God's temple, God will destroy him. For God's temple is holy, and you yourselves are his temple.

18 No one should fool himself. If anyone among

you thinks that he is wise by this world's standards, he should become a fool, in order to be really wise. [19]For what this world considers to be wisdom is nonsense in God's sight. As the scripture says, "God traps the wise in their cleverness"; [20]and another scripture says, "The Lord knows that the thoughts of the wise are worthless." [21]No one, then, should boast about what human beings can do. Actually everything belongs to you: [22]Paul, Apollos, and Peter; this world, life and death, the present and the future – all these are yours, [23]and you belong to Christ, and Christ belongs to God.

Apostles of Christ

4 You should think of us as Christ's servants, who have been put in charge of God's secret truths. [2]The one thing required of such servants is that they be faithful to their master. [3]Now, I am not at all concerned about being judged by you or by any human standard; I don't even pass judgement on myself. [4]My conscience is clear, but that does not prove that I am really innocent. The Lord is the one who passes judgement on me. [5]So you should not pass judgement on anyone before the right time comes. Final judgement must wait until the Lord comes; he will bring to light the dark secrets and expose the hidden purposes of people's minds. And then all will receive from God the praise they deserve.

[6]For your sake, my brothers and sisters, I have applied all this to Apollos and me, using the two of us as an example, so that you may learn what the saying means, "Observe the proper rules." None of you should be proud of one person and despise another. [7]Who made you superior to others? Didn't God give you everything you have? Well, then, how can you boast, as if what you have were not a gift?

[8]Do you already have everything you need? Are you already rich? Have you become kings, even though we are not? Well, I wish you really were kings, so that we could be kings together with you. [9]For it seems to me that God has given the very last place to us apostles, like people condemned to die in public as a spectacle for the whole world of angels and of humanity. [10]For Christ's sake we are fools; but you are wise in union with Christ! We are weak, but you are strong! We are despised, but you are honoured! [11]To this very moment we go hungry and thirsty; we are clothed in rags; we are beaten; we wander from place to place; [12]we wear ourselves out with hard work. When we are cursed, we

bless; when we are persecuted, we endure; [13]when we are insulted, we answer with kind words. We are no more than this world's refuse; we are the scum of the earth to this very moment!

[14]I write this to you, not because I want to make you feel ashamed, but to instruct you as my own dear children. [15]For even if you have ten thousand guardians in your Christian life, you have only one father. For in your life in union with Christ Jesus I have become your father by bringing the Good News to you. [16]I beg you, then, to follow my example. [17]For this purpose I am sending to you Timothy, who is my own dear and faithful son in the Christian life. He will remind you of the principles which I follow in the new life in union with Christ Jesus and which I teach in all the churches everywhere.

[18]Some of you have become proud because you have thought that I would not be coming to visit you. [19]If the Lord is willing, however, I will come to you soon, and then I will find out for myself the power which these proud people have, and not just what they say. [20]For the Kingdom of God is not a matter of words but of power. [21]Which do you prefer? Shall I come to you with a whip, or in a spirit of love and gentleness?

Immorality in the Church

5 Now, it is actually being said that there is sexual immorality among you so terrible that not even the heathen would be guilty of it. I am told that a man is sleeping with his stepmother! [2]How, then, can you be proud? On the contrary, you should be filled with sadness, and the man who has done such a thing should be expelled from your fellowship. [3-4]And even though I am far away from you in body, still I am there with you in spirit; and as though I were there with you, I have in the name of our Lord Jesus already passed judgement on the man who has done this terrible thing. As you meet together, and I meet with you in my spirit, by the power of our Lord Jesus present with us, [5]you are to hand this man over to Satan for his body to be destroyed, so that his spirit may be saved in the Day of the Lord.

[6]It is not right for you to be proud! You know the saying, "A little bit of yeast makes the whole batch of dough rise." [7]You must remove the old yeast of sin so that you will be entirely pure. Then you will be like a new batch of dough without any yeast, as indeed I know you actually are. For our Passover Festival is ready, now that

Christ, our Passover lamb, has been sacrificed. [8]Let us celebrate our Passover, then, not with bread having the old yeast of sin and wickedness, but with the bread that has no yeast, the bread of purity and truth.

9 In the letter that I wrote you I told you not to associate with immoral people. [10]Now I did not mean pagans who are immoral or greedy or are thieves or who worship idols. To avoid them you would have to get out of the world completely. [11]What I meant was that you should not associate with a person who calls himself a believer but is immoral or greedy or worships idols or is a slanderer or a drunkard or a thief. Don't even sit down to eat with such a person.

12–13 After all, it is none of my business to judge outsiders. God will judge them. But should you not judge the members of your own fellowship? As the scripture says, "Remove the evil person from your group."

Lawsuits against Fellow-Christians

6 If any of you have a dispute with another Christian, how dare you go before heathen judges instead of letting God's people settle the matter? [2]Don't you know that God's people will judge the world? Well, then, if you are to judge the world, aren't you capable of judging small matters? [3]Do you not know that we shall judge the angels? How much more, then, the things of this life! [4]If such matters come up, are you going to take them to be settled by people who have no standing in the church? [5]Shame on you! Surely there is at least one wise person in your fellowship who can settle a dispute between fellow-Christians. [6]Instead, one Christian goes to court against another and lets unbelievers judge the case!

7 The very fact that you have legal disputes among yourselves shows that you have failed completely. Would it not be better for you to be wronged? Would it not be better for you to be robbed? [8]Instead, you yourselves wrong one another and rob one another, even your own brothers and sisters! [9]Surely you know that the wicked will not possess God's Kingdom. Do not fool yourselves; people who are immoral or who worship idols or are adulterers or homosexual perverts [10]or who steal or are greedy or are drunkards or who slander others or are thieves – none of these will possess God's Kingdom. [11]Some of you were like that. But you have been purified from sin; you have been dedicated to God; you have been put right with God by the Lord Jesus Christ and by the Spirit of our God.

Use your Bodies for God's Glory

12 Someone will say, "I am allowed to do anything." Yes; but not everything is good for you. I could say that I am allowed to do anything, but I am not going to let anything make me its slave. [13]Someone else will say, "Food is for the stomach, and the stomach is for food." Yes; but God will put an end to both. The body is not to be used for sexual immorality, but to serve the Lord; and the Lord provides for the body. [14]God raised the Lord from death, and he will also raise us by his power.

15 You know that your bodies are parts of the body of Christ. Shall I take a part of Christ's body and make it part of the body of a prostitute? Impossible! [16]Or perhaps you don't know that the man who joins his body to a prostitute becomes physically one with her? The scripture says quite plainly, "The two will become one body." [17]But he who joins himself to the Lord becomes spiritually one with him.

18 Avoid immorality. Any other sin a man commits does not affect his body; but the man who is guilty of sexual immorality sins against his own body. [19]Don't you know that your body is the temple of the Holy Spirit, who lives in you and who was given to you by God? You do not belong to yourselves but to God; [20]he bought you for a price. So use your bodies for God's glory.

Questions about Marriage

7 Now, to deal with the matters you wrote about.
A man does well not to marry.[a] [2]But because there is so much immorality, every man should have his own wife, and every woman should have her own husband. [3]A man should fulfil his duty as a husband, and a woman should fulfil her duty as a wife, and each should satisfy the other's needs. [4]A wife is not the master of her own body, but her husband is; in the same way a husband is not the master of his own body, but his wife is. [5]Do not deny yourselves to each other, unless you first agree to do so for a while in order to spend your time in prayer; but then resume normal marital relations. In this way you will be kept from giving in to Satan's temptation because of your lack of self-control.

6 I tell you this not as an order, but simply as a concession. [7]Actually I would prefer that all of

---

[a] **7.1** A man does well not to marry; *or* You say that a man does well not to marry.

A couple, once they marry, have clear responsibilities towards each other (7.1–5)

you were as I am; but each one has a special gift from God, one person this gift, another one that gift.

8 Now, to the unmarried and to the widows I say that it would be better for you to continue to live alone as I do. ⁹But if you cannot restrain your desires, go ahead and marry – it is better to marry than to burn with passion.

10 For married people I have a command which is not my own but the Lord's: a wife must not leave her husband; ¹¹but if she does, she must remain single or else be reconciled to her husband; and a husband must not divorce his wife.

12 To the others I say (I, myself, not the Lord): if a Christian man has a wife who is an unbeliever and she agrees to go on living with him, he must not divorce her. ¹³And if a Christian woman is married to a man who is an unbeliever and he agrees to go on living with her, she must not divorce him. ¹⁴For the unbelieving husband is made acceptable to God by being united to his wife, and the unbelieving wife is made acceptable to God by being united to her Christian husband. If this were not so, their children would be like pagan children; but as it is, they are acceptable to God. ¹⁵However, if the one who is not a believer wishes to leave the Christian partner, let it be so. In such cases the Christian partner, whether husband or wife, is free to act. God has called you to live in peace. ¹⁶How can you be sure, Christian wife, that you will not save[a] your husband? Or how can you be sure, Christian husband, that you will not save[a] your wife?

Live as God Called You

17 Each of you should go on living according to the Lord's gift to you, and as you were when God called you. This is the rule I teach in all the churches. ¹⁸If a circumcised man has accepted God's call, he should not try to remove the marks of circumcision; if an uncircumcised man has accepted God's call, he should not get circumcised. ¹⁹For whether or not a man is circumcised means nothing; what matters is to obey God's commandments. ²⁰Each of you should remain as you were when you accepted God's call. ²¹Were you a slave when God called you? Well, never mind; but if you have a chance to become free, use it.[b] ²²For a slave who has been called by the Lord is free for the Lord; in the same way a free person who has been called by Christ is his slave. ²³God bought you for a price; so do not become slaves of human beings. ²⁴My friends, each of you should remain in fellowship with God in the same condition as you were when you were called.

Questions about the Unmarried and the Widows

25 Now, concerning what you wrote about unmarried people: I do not have a command from the Lord, but I give my opinion as one who by the Lord's mercy is worthy of trust.

26 Considering the present distress, I think it is better for a man to stay as he is. ²⁷Have you got a wife? Then don't try to get rid of her. Are you unmarried? Then don't look for a wife. ²⁸But if you do marry, you haven't committed a sin; and if an unmarried woman marries, she hasn't committed a sin. But I would rather spare you the everyday troubles that married people will have.

29 What I mean, my friends, is this: there is not much time left, and from now on married people should live as though they were not married; ³⁰those who weep, as though they were not sad; those who laugh, as though they were not happy; those who buy, as though they did not own what they bought; ³¹those who deal in material goods, as though they were not fully occupied with them. For this world, as it is now, will not last much longer.

---

[a] **7.16** How can you be sure … that you will not save; *or* How do you know … that you will save.

[b] **7.21** but if you have a chance to become free, use it; *or* but even if you have a chance to become free, choose rather to make the best of your condition as a slave.

1 CORINTHIANS 9

32   I would like you to be free from worry. An unmarried man concerns himself with the Lord's work, because he is trying to please the Lord. [33]But a married man concerns himself with worldly matters, because he wants to please his wife; [34]and so he is pulled in two directions. An unmarried woman or a virgin concerns herself with the Lord's work, because she wants to be dedicated both in body and spirit; but a married woman concerns herself with worldly matters, because she wants to please her husband.

35   I am saying this because I want to help you. I am not trying to put restrictions on you. Instead, I want you to do what is right and proper, and to give yourselves completely to the Lord's service without any reservation.

36   In the case of an engaged couple who have decided not to marry: if the man feels that he is not acting properly towards the young woman and if his passions are too strong and he feels that they ought to marry, then they should get married, as he wants to.[a] There is no sin in this. [37]But if a man, without being forced to do so, has firmly made up his mind not to marry,[b] and if he has his will under complete control and has already decided in his own mind what to do – then he does well not to marry the young woman.[c] [38]So the man who marries[d] does well, but the one who doesn't marry[e] does even better.

39   A married woman is not free as long as her husband lives; but if her husband dies, then she is free to be married to any man she wishes, but only if he is a Christian. [40]She will be happier, however, if she stays as she is. That is my opinion, and I think that I too have God's Spirit.

The Question about Food Offered to Idols

8 Now, concerning what you wrote about food offered to idols.

It is true, of course, that "all of us have knowledge", as they say. Such knowledge, however, puffs a person up with pride; but love builds up. [2]Those who think they know something really don't know as they ought to know.

---

[a] **7.36** an engaged couple … as he wants to; *or* a man and his unmarried daughter: if he feels that he is not acting properly towards her, and if she is at the right age to marry, then he should do as he wishes and let her get married.
[b] **7.37** not to marry; *or* not to let his daughter get married.
[c] **7.37** marry the young woman; *or* let her get married.
[d] **7.38** marries; *or* lets his daughter get married.
[e] **7.38** doesn't marry; *or* doesn't let her get married.

[3]But the person who loves God is known by him.

4   So then, about eating the food offered to idols: we know that an idol stands for something that does not really exist; we know that there is only the one God. [5]Even if there are so-called "gods", whether in heaven or on earth, and even though there are many of these "gods" and "lords", [6]yet there is for us only one God, the Father, who is the Creator of all things and for whom we live; and there is only one Lord, Jesus Christ, through whom all things were created and through whom we live.

7   But not everyone knows this truth. Some people have been so used to idols that to this day when they eat such food they still think of it as food that belongs to an idol; their conscience is weak, and they feel they are defiled by the food. [8]Food, however, will not improve our relations with God; we shall not lose anything if we do not eat, nor shall we gain anything if we do eat.

9   Be careful, however, not to let your freedom of action make those who are weak in the faith fall into sin. [10]Suppose a person whose conscience is weak in this matter sees you, who have so-called "knowledge", eating in the temple of an idol; will not this encourage him to eat food offered to idols? [11]And so this weak person, your brother for whom Christ died, will perish because of your "knowledge"! [12]And in this way you will be sinning against Christ by sinning against your Christian brothers and sisters and wounding their weak conscience. [13]So then, if food makes my brother or sister sin, I will never eat meat again, so as not to make my brother or sister fall into sin.

Rights and Duties of an Apostle

9 Am I not a free man? Am I not an apostle? Haven't I seen Jesus our Lord? And aren't you the result of my work for the Lord? [2]Even if others do not accept me as an apostle, surely you do! Because of your life in union with the Lord you yourselves are proof of the fact that I am an apostle.

3   When people criticize me, this is how I defend myself: [4]Haven't I the right to be given food and drink for my work? [5]Haven't I the right to follow the example of the other apostles and the Lord's brothers and Peter, by taking a Christian wife with me on my travels? [6]Or are Barnabas and I the only ones who have to work for our living? [7]What soldier ever has to pay his own expenses in the army? What farmer does

189

not eat the grapes from his own vineyard? What shepherd does not use the milk from his own sheep?

8 I don't have to limit myself to these everyday examples, because the Law says the same thing. ⁹We read in the Law of Moses, "Do not muzzle an ox when you are using it to thresh corn." Now, is God concerned about oxen? ¹⁰Didn't he really mean us when he said that? Of course that was written for us. The one who ploughs and the one who reaps should do their work in the hope of getting a share of the crop. ¹¹We have sown spiritual seed among you. Is it too much if we reap material benefits from you? ¹²If others have the right to expect this from you, haven't we an even greater right?

But we haven't made use of this right. Instead, we have endured everything in order not to put any obstacle in the way of the Good News about Christ. ¹³Surely you know that the men who work in the Temple get their food from the Temple and that those who offer the sacrifices on the altar get a share of the sacrifices. ¹⁴In the same way, the Lord has ordered that those who preach the gospel should get their living from it.

15 But I haven't made use of any of these rights, nor am I writing this now in order to claim such rights for myself. I would rather die first! Nobody is going to turn my rightful boast into empty words! ¹⁶I have no right to boast just because I preach the gospel. After all, I am under orders to do so. And how terrible it would be for me if I did not preach the gospel! ¹⁷If I did my work as a matter of free choice, then I could expect to be paid; but I do it as a matter of duty, because God has entrusted me with this task. ¹⁸What pay do I get, then? It is the privilege of preaching the Good News without charging for it, without claiming my rights in my work for the gospel.

19 I am a free man, nobody's slave; but I make myself everybody's slave in order to win as many people as possible. ²⁰While working with the Jews, I live like a Jew in order to win them; and even though I myself am not subject to the Law of Moses, I live as though I were when working with those who are, in order to win them. ²¹In the same way, when working with Gentiles, I live like a Gentile, outside the Jewish Law, in order to win Gentiles. This does not mean that I don't obey God's law; I am really under Christ's law. ²²Among the weak in faith I become weak like one of them, in order to win them. So I become all things to all people, that I may save some of them by whatever means are possible.

23 All this I do for the gospel's sake, in order to share in its blessings. ²⁴Surely you know that many runners take part in a race, but only one of them wins the prize. Run, then, in such a way as to win the prize. ²⁵Every athlete in training submits to strict discipline, in order to be crowned with a wreath that will not last; but we do it for one that will last for ever. ²⁶That is why I run straight for the finishing line; that is why I am like a boxer who does not waste his punches. ²⁷I harden my body with blows and bring it under complete control, to keep myself from being disqualified after having called others to the contest.

Christians meet together in the open air on Good Friday to remember the death of Jesus (9.18)

Warnings against Idols

10 I want you to remember, my brothers and sisters, what happened to our ancestors who followed Moses. They were all under the protection of the cloud, and all passed safely through the Red Sea. [2]In the cloud and in the sea they were all baptized as followers of Moses. [3]All ate the same spiritual bread [4]and drank the same spiritual drink. They drank from the spiritual rock that went with them; and that rock was Christ himself. [5]But even then God was not pleased with most of them, and so their dead bodies were scattered over the desert.

6 Now, all this is an example for us, to warn us not to desire evil things, as they did, [7]nor to worship idols, as some of them did. As the scripture says, "The people sat down to a feast which turned into an orgy of drinking and sex." [8]We must not be guilty of sexual immorality, as some of them were – and in one day 23,000 of them fell dead. [9]We must not put the Lord[a] to the test, as some of them did – and they were killed by snakes. [10]We must not complain, as some of them did – and they were destroyed by the Angel of Death.

11 All these things happened to them as examples for others, and they were written down as a warning for us. For we live at a time when the end is about to come.

12 Those who think they are standing firm had better be careful that they do not fall. [13]Every test that you have experienced is the kind that normally comes to people. But God keeps his promise, and he will not allow you to be tested beyond your power to remain firm; at the time you are put to the test, he will give you the strength to endure it, and so provide you with a way out.

14 So then, my dear friends, keep away from the worship of idols. [15]I speak to you as sensible people; judge for yourselves what I say. [16]The cup we use in the Lord's Supper and for which we give thanks to God: when we drink from it, we are sharing in the blood of Christ. And the bread we break: when we eat it, we are sharing in the body of Christ. [17]Because there is the one loaf of bread, all of us, though many, are one body, for we all share the same loaf.

18 Consider the people of Israel; those who eat what is offered in sacrifice share in the altar's service to God. [19]Do I imply, then, that an idol or the food offered to it really amounts to anything? [20]No! What I am saying is that what is sacrificed on pagan altars is offered to demons,

---

[a] **10.9** the Lord; *some manuscripts have* Christ.

not to God. And I do not want you to be partners with demons. [21]You cannot drink from the Lord's cup and also from the cup of demons; you cannot eat at the Lord's table and also at the table of demons. [22]Or do we want to make the Lord jealous? Do we think that we are stronger than he?

23 "We are allowed to do anything," so they say. That is true, but not everything is good. "We are allowed to do anything" – but not everything is helpful. [24]None of you should be looking to your own interests, but to the interests of others.

25 You are free to eat anything sold in the meat market, without asking any questions because of your conscience. [26]For, as the scripture says, "The earth and everything in it belong to the Lord."

27 If an unbeliever invites you to a meal and you decide to go, eat what is set before you, without asking any questions because of your conscience. [28]But if someone says to you, "This food was offered to idols," then do not eat that food, for the sake of the one who told you and for conscience' sake – [29]that is, not your own conscience, but the other person's conscience.

"Well, then," someone asks, "why should my freedom to act be limited by another person's conscience? [30]If I thank God for my food, why should anyone criticize me about food for which I give thanks?"

31 Well, whatever you do, whether you eat or drink, do it all for God's glory. [32]Live in such a way as to cause no trouble either to Jews or Gentiles or to the church of God. [33]Just do as I do; I try to please everyone in all that I do, not thinking of my own good, but of the good of all, so that they might be saved.

11 Imitate me, then, just as I imitate Christ.

Covering the Head in Worship

2 I praise you because you always remember me and follow the teachings that I have handed on to you. [3]But I want you to understand that Christ is supreme over every man, the husband is supreme over his wife, and God is supreme over Christ. [4]So a man who prays or proclaims God's message in public worship with his head covered disgraces Christ. [5]And any woman who prays or proclaims God's message in public worship with nothing on her head disgraces her husband; there is no difference between her and a woman whose head has been shaved. [6]If the woman does not cover her head, she might as well cut her hair. And since it is a shameful thing

for a woman to shave her head or cut her hair, she should cover her head. [7]A man has no need to cover his head, because he reflects the image and glory of God. But woman reflects the glory of man; [8]for man was not created from woman, but woman from man. [9]Nor was man created for woman's sake, but woman was created for man's sake. [10]On account of the angels, then, a woman should have a covering over her head to show that she is under her husband's authority. [11]In our life in the Lord, however, woman is not independent of man, nor is man independent of woman. [12]For as woman was made from man, in the same way man is born of woman; and it is God who brings everything into existence.

13 Judge for yourselves whether it is proper for a woman to pray to God in public worship with nothing on her head. [14]Why, nature itself teaches you that long hair on a man is a disgrace, [15]but on a woman it is a thing of beauty. Her long hair has been given her to serve as a covering. [16]But if anyone wants to argue about it, all I have to say is that neither we nor the churches of God have any other custom in worship.

The Lord's Supper
(Mt 26.26–29; Mk 14.22–25; Lk 22.14–20)

17 In the following instructions, however, I do not praise you, because your meetings for worship actually do more harm than good. [18]In the first place, I have been told that there are opposing groups in your meetings; and this I believe is partly true. [19](No doubt there must be divisions among you so that the ones who are in the right may be clearly seen.) [20]When you meet together as a group, it is not the Lord's Supper that you eat. [21]For as you eat, you each go ahead with your own meal, so that some are hungry while others get drunk. [22]Haven't you got your own homes in which to eat and drink? Or would you rather despise the church of God and put to shame the people who are in need? What do you expect me to say to you about this? Shall I praise you? Of course I don't!

23 For I received from the Lord the teaching that I passed on to you: that the Lord Jesus, on the night he was betrayed, took a piece of bread, [24]gave thanks to God, broke it, and said, "This is my body, which is for you. Do this in memory of me." [25]In the same way, after the supper he took the cup and said, "This cup is God's new covenant, sealed with my blood. Whenever you drink it, do so in memory of me."

26 This means that every time you eat this bread and drink from this cup you proclaim the Lord's death until he comes. [27]It follows that if anyone eats the Lord's bread or drinks from his cup in a way that dishonours him, he or she is guilty of sin against the Lord's body and blood. [28]So then, you should all examine yourselves first, and then eat the bread and drink from the cup. [29]For if people do not recognize the meaning of the Lord's body when they eat the bread and drink from the cup, they bring judgement on themselves as they eat and drink. [30]That is why many of you are weak and ill, and several have died. [31]If we would examine ourselves first, we would not come under God's judgement. [32]But we are judged and punished by the Lord, so that we shall not be condemned together with the world.

33 So then, my brothers and sisters, when you gather together to eat the Lord's Supper, wait for one another. [34]Anyone who is hungry should eat at home, so that you will not come under God's judgement as you meet together. As for the other matters, I will settle them when I come.

Gifts from the Holy Spirit

12 Now, concerning what you wrote about the gifts from the Holy Spirit.

I want you to know the truth about them,

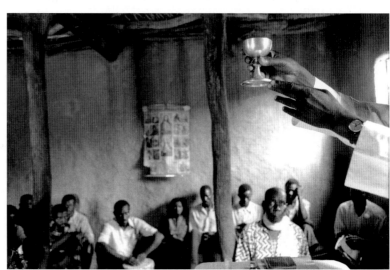

When Christians share Holy Communion they are remembering the death of Jesus (11.26)

my brothers and sisters. ²You know that while you were still heathen, you were led astray in many ways to the worship of lifeless idols. ³I want you to know that no one who is led by God's Spirit can say "A curse on Jesus!" and no one can confess "Jesus is Lord", without being guided by the Holy Spirit.

4 There are different kinds of spiritual gifts, but the same Spirit gives them. ⁵There are different ways of serving, but the same Lord is served. ⁶There are different abilities to perform service, but the same God gives ability to all for their particular service. ⁷The Spirit's presence is shown in some way in each person for the good of all. ⁸The Spirit gives one person a message full of wisdom, while to another person the same Spirit gives a message full of knowledge. ⁹One and the same Spirit gives faith to one person, while to another person he gives the power to heal. ¹⁰The Spirit gives one person the power to work miracles; to another, the gift of speaking God's message; and to yet another, the ability to tell the difference between gifts that come from the Spirit and those that do not. To one person he gives the ability to speak in strange tongues, and to another he gives the ability to explain what is said. ¹¹But it is one and the same Spirit who does all this; as he wishes, he gives a different gift to each person.

One Body with Many Parts

12 Christ is like a single body, which has many parts; it is still one body, even though it is made up of different parts. ¹³In the same way, all of us, whether Jews or Gentiles, whether slaves or free, have been baptized into the one body by the same Spirit, and we have all been given the one Spirit to drink.

14 For the body itself is not made up of only one part, but of many parts. ¹⁵If the foot were to say, "Because I am not a hand, I don't belong to the body," that would not keep it from being a part of the body. ¹⁶And if the ear were to say, "Because I am not an eye, I don't belong to the body," that would not keep it from being a part of the body. ¹⁷If the whole body were just an eye, how could it hear? And if it were only an ear, how could it smell? ¹⁸As it is, however, God put every different part in the body just as he wanted it to be. ¹⁹There would not be a body if it were all only one part! ²⁰As it is, there are many parts but one body.

21 So then, the eye cannot say to the hand, "I don't need you!" Nor can the head say to the feet, "Well, I don't need you!" ²²On the contrary, we cannot do without the parts of the body that seem to be weaker; ²³and those parts that we think aren't worth very much are the ones which we treat with greater care; while the parts of the body which don't look very nice are treated with special modesty, ²⁴which the more beautiful parts do not need. God himself has put the body together in such a way as to give greater honour to those parts that need it. ²⁵And so there is no division in the body, but all its different parts have the same concern for one another. ²⁶If one part of the body suffers, all the other parts suffer with it; if one part is praised, all the other parts share its happiness.

27 All of you are Christ's body, and each one is a part of it. ²⁸In the church God has put all in place: in the first place apostles, in the second place prophets, and in the third place teachers; then those who perform miracles, followed by those who are given the power to heal or to help others or to direct them or to speak in strange tongues. ²⁹They are not all apostles or prophets or teachers. Not everyone has the power to work miracles ³⁰or to heal diseases or to speak in strange tongues or to explain what is said. ³¹Set your hearts, then, on the more important gifts.

Best of all, however, is the following way.

Love

13 I may be able to speak the languages of human beings and even of angels, but if I have no love, my speech is no more than a noisy gong or a clanging bell. ²I may have the gift of inspired preaching; I may have all knowledge and understand all secrets; I may have all the faith needed to move mountains – but if I have no love, I am nothing. ³I may give away everything I have, and even give up my body to be burnt[a] – but if I have no love, this does me no good.

4 Love is patient and kind; it is not jealous or conceited or proud; ⁵love is not ill-mannered or selfish or irritable; love does not keep a record of wrongs; ⁶love is not happy with evil, but is happy with the truth. ⁷Love never gives up; and its faith, hope, and patience never fail.

8 Love is eternal. There are inspired messages, but they are temporary; there are gifts of speaking in strange tongues, but they will cease; there is knowledge, but it will pass. ⁹For our gifts of knowledge and of inspired messages are only partial; ¹⁰but when what is perfect comes, then what is partial will disappear.

---

[a] **13.3** to be burnt; *some manuscripts have* in order to boast.

11   When I was a child, my speech, feelings, and thinking were all those of a child; now that I have grown up, I have no more use for childish ways. [12]What we see now is like a dim image in a mirror; then we shall see face to face. What I know now is only partial; then it will be complete – as complete as God's knowledge of me.

13   Meanwhile these three remain: faith, hope, and love; and the greatest of these is love.

More about Gifts from the Spirit

14 It is love, then, that you should strive for. Set your hearts on spiritual gifts, especially the gift of proclaiming God's message. [2]Those who speak in strange tongues do not speak to others but to God, because no one understands them. They are speaking secret truths by the power of the Spirit. [3]But those who proclaim God's message speak to people and give them help, encouragement, and comfort. [4]Those who speak in strange tongues help only themselves, but those who proclaim God's message help the whole church.

5   I would like all of you to speak in strange tongues; but I would rather that you had the gift of proclaiming God's message. For the person who proclaims God's message is of greater value than the one who speaks in strange tongues – unless there is someone present who can explain what is said, so that the whole church may be helped. [6]So when I come to you, my brothers and sisters, what use will I be to you if I speak in strange tongues? Not a bit, unless I bring you some revelation from God or some knowledge or some inspired message, or some teaching.

7   Take such lifeless musical instruments as the flute or the harp – how will anyone know the tune that is being played unless the notes are sounded distinctly? [8]And if the one who plays the bugle does not sound a clear call, who will prepare for battle? [9]In the same way, how will anyone understand what you are talking about if your message given in strange tongues is not clear? Your words will vanish in the air! [10]There are many different languages in the world, yet none of them is without meaning. [11]But if I do not know the language being spoken, those who use it will be foreigners to me and I will be a foreigner to them. [12]Since you are eager to have the gifts of the Spirit, you must try above everything else to make greater use of those which help to build up the church.

13   The person who speaks in strange tongues, then, must pray for the gift to explain what is said. [14]For if I pray in this way, my spirit prays indeed, but my mind has no part in it. [15]What should I do, then? I will pray with my spirit, but I will pray also with my mind; I will sing with my spirit, but I will sing also with my mind. [16]When you give thanks to God in spirit only, how can ordinary people taking part in the meeting say "Amen" to your prayer of thanksgiving? They have no way of knowing what you are saying. [17]Even if your prayer of thanks to God is quite good, other people are not helped at all.

18   I thank God that I speak in strange tongues much more than any of you. [19]But in church worship I would rather speak five words that can be understood, in order to teach others, than speak thousands of words in strange tongues.

20   Do not be like children in your thinking, my brothers and sisters; be children so far as evil is concerned, but be grown-up in your thinking. [21]In the Scriptures it is written:

"By means of people speaking strange
    languages
    I will speak to my people, says the Lord.
I will speak through lips of foreigners,
    but even then my people will not listen to
    me."

[22]So then, the gift of speaking in strange tongues is proof for unbelievers, not for believers, while the gift of proclaiming God's message is proof for believers, not for unbelievers.

23   If, then, the whole church meets together and everyone starts speaking in strange tongues – and if some ordinary people or unbelievers come in, won't they say that you are all crazy? [24]But if everyone is proclaiming God's message when some unbelievers or ordinary people come in, they will be convinced of their sin by what they hear. They will be judged by all they hear, [25]their secret thoughts will be brought into the open, and they will bow down and worship God, confessing, "Truly God is here among you!"

Order in the Church

26   This is what I mean, my brothers and sisters. When you meet for worship, one person has a hymn, another a teaching, another a revelation from God, another a message in strange tongues, and still another the explanation of what is said. Everything must be of help to the church. [27]If someone is going to speak in strange tongues, two or three at the most should speak, one after the other, and someone else must explain what is being said. [28]But if no one is there who can explain, then the one who speaks in strange tongues must be quiet and speak only to himself

and to God. ²⁹Two or three who are given God's message should speak, while the others are to judge what they say. ³⁰But if someone sitting in the meeting receives a message from God, the one who is speaking should stop. ³¹All of you may proclaim God's message, one by one, so that everyone will learn and be encouraged. ³²The gift of proclaiming God's message should be under the speaker's control, ³³because God does not want us to be in disorder but in harmony and peace.

As in all the churches of God's people, ³⁴the women should keep quiet in the meetings. They are not allowed to speak; as the Jewish Law says, they must not be in charge. ³⁵If they want to find out about something, they should ask their husbands at home. It is a disgraceful thing for a woman to speak in church.

36   Or could it be that the word of God came from you? Or are you the only ones to whom it came? ³⁷If anyone supposes he is God's messenger or has a spiritual gift, he must realize that what I am writing to you is the Lord's command. ³⁸But if he does not pay attention to this, pay no attention to him.

39   So then, my brothers and sisters, set your hearts on proclaiming God's message, but do not forbid the speaking in strange tongues. ⁴⁰Everything must be done in a proper and orderly way.

The Resurrection of Christ

15 And now I want to remind you, my brothers and sisters, of the Good News which I preached to you, which you received, and on which your faith stands firm. ²That is the gospel, the message that I preached to you. You are saved by the gospel if you hold firmly to it – unless it was for nothing that you believed.

3   I passed on to you what I received, which is of the greatest importance: that Christ died for our sins, as written in the Scriptures; ⁴that he was buried and that he was raised to life three days later, as written in the Scriptures; ⁵that he appeared to Peter and then to all twelve apostles. ⁶Then he appeared to more than 500 of his followers at once, most of whom are still alive, although some have died. ⁷Then he appeared to James, and afterwards to all the apostles.

8   Last of all he appeared also to me – even though I am like someone whose birth was abnormal.ᵃ ⁹For I am the least of all the apostles – I do not even deserve to be called an apostle, because I persecuted God's church. ¹⁰But by God's grace I am what I am, and the grace that he gave me was not without effect. On the contrary, I have worked harder than any of the other apostles, although it was not really my own doing, but God's grace working with me. ¹¹So then, whether it came from me or from them, this is what we all preach, and this is what you believe.

Our Resurrection

12   Now, since our message is that Christ has been raised from death, how can some of you say that the dead will not be raised to life? ¹³If that is true, it means that Christ was not raised; ¹⁴and if Christ has not been raised from death, then we have nothing to preach and you have nothing to believe. ¹⁵More than that, we are shown to be lying about God, because we said that he raised Christ from death – but if it is true that the dead are not raised to life, then he did not raise Christ. ¹⁶For if the dead are not raised, neither has Christ been raised. ¹⁷And if Christ has not been raised, then your faith is a delusion and you are still lost in your sins. ¹⁸It would also mean that the believers in Christ who have died are lost. ¹⁹If our hope in Christ is good for this life only and no more,ᵇ then we deserve more pity than anyone else in all the world.

20   But the truth is that Christ has been raised from death, as the guarantee that those who sleep in death will also be raised. ²¹For just as death came by means of a man, in the same way the rising from death comes by means of a man. ²²For just as all people die because of their union with Adam, in the same way all will be raised to life because of their union with Christ. ²³But each one will be raised in the right order: Christ, first of all; then, at the time of his coming, those who belong to him. ²⁴Then the end will come; Christ will overcome all spiritual rulers, authorities, and powers, and will hand over the Kingdom to God the Father. ²⁵For Christ must rule until God defeats all enemies and puts them under his feet. ²⁶The last enemy to be defeated will be death. ²⁷For the scripture says, "God put *all* things under his feet." It is clear, of course, that the words "all things" do not include God himself, who puts all things under Christ. ²⁸But when all things have been placed under Christ's

---

ᵃ **15.8** whose birth was abnormal; *or* who was born at the wrong time.

ᵇ **15.19** If our hope in Christ is good for this life only and no more; *or* If all we have in this life is our hope in Christ.

rule, then he himself, the Son, will place himself under God, who placed all things under him; and God will rule completely over all.

29 Now, what about those people who are baptized for the dead? What do they hope to accomplish? If it is true, as some claim, that the dead are not raised to life, why are those people being baptized for the dead? [30]And as for us – why would we run the risk of danger every hour? [31]My brothers and sisters, I face death every day! The pride I have in you, in our life in union with Christ Jesus our Lord, makes me declare this. [32]If I have, as it were, fought "wild beasts" here in Ephesus simply from human motives, what have I gained? But if the dead are not raised to life, then, as the saying goes, "Let us eat and drink, for tomorrow we will die."

33 Do not be fooled. "Bad companions ruin good character." [34]Come back to your right senses and stop your sinful ways. I declare to your shame that some of you do not know God.

The Resurrection Body

35 Someone will ask, "How can the dead be raised to life? What kind of body will they have?" [36]You fool! When you sow a seed in the ground, it does not sprout to life unless it dies. [37]And what you sow is a bare seed, perhaps a grain of wheat or some other grain, not the full-bodied plant that will later grow up. [38]God provides that seed with the body he wishes; he gives each seed its own proper body.

39 And the flesh of living beings is not all the same kind of flesh; human beings have one kind of flesh, animals another, birds another, and fish another.

40 And there are heavenly bodies and earthly bodies; the beauty that belongs to heavenly bodies is different from the beauty that belongs to earthly bodies. [41]The sun has its own beauty, the moon another beauty, and the stars a different beauty; and even among stars there are different kinds of beauty.

42 This is how it will be when the dead are raised to life. When the body is buried, it is mortal; when raised, it will be immortal. [43]When buried, it is ugly and weak; when raised, it will be beautiful and strong. [44]When buried, it is a physical body; when raised, it will be a spiritual body. There is, of course, a physical body, so there has to be a spiritual body. [45]For the scripture says, "The first man, Adam, was created a living being"; but the last Adam is the life-giving Spirit. [46]It is not the spiritual that comes first, but the physical, and then the spiritual. [47]The first Adam, made of earth, came from the earth; the second Adam came from heaven. [48]Those who belong to the earth are like the one who was made of earth; those who are of heaven are like the one who came from heaven. [49]Just as we wear the likeness of the man made of earth, so we will wear[a] the likeness of the Man from heaven.

50 What I mean, brothers and sisters, is that what is made of flesh and blood cannot share in God's Kingdom, and what is mortal cannot possess immortality.

51–52 Listen to this secret truth: we shall not all die, but when the last trumpet sounds, we shall all be changed in an instant, as quickly as the blinking of an eye. For when the trumpet sounds, the dead will be raised, never to die again, and we shall all be changed. [53]For what is mortal must be changed into what is immortal; what will die must be changed into what cannot die. [54]So when this takes place, and the mortal has been changed into the immortal, then the scripture will come true: "Death is destroyed; victory is complete!"

55 "Where, Death, is your victory?
Where, Death, is your power to hurt?"

[56]Death gets its power to hurt from sin, and sin gets its power from the Law. [57]But thanks be to God who gives us the victory through our Lord Jesus Christ!

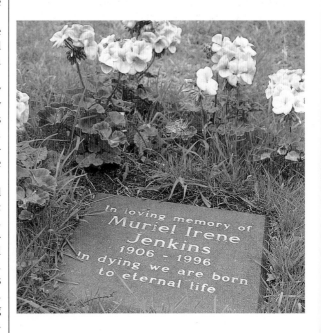

---

[a] **15.49** we will wear; *some manuscripts have* let us wear.

58 So then, my dear brothers and sisters, stand firm and steady. Keep busy always in your work for the Lord, since you know that nothing you do in the Lord's service is ever useless.

The Offering for Fellow-believers

16 Now, concerning what you wrote about the money to be raised to help God's people in Judea. You must do what I told the churches in Galatia to do. ²Every Sunday each of you must put aside some money, in proportion to what you have earned, and save it up, so that there will be no need to collect money when I come. ³After I come, I shall give letters of introduction to those you have approved, and send them to take your gift to Jerusalem. ⁴If it seems worthwhile for me to go, then they can go along with me.

Paul's Plans

5 I shall come to you after I have gone through Macedonia – for I have to go through Macedonia. ⁶I shall probably spend some time with you, perhaps the whole winter, and then you can help me to continue my journey, wherever it is I shall go next. ⁷I want to see you more than just briefly in passing; I hope to spend quite a long time with you, if the Lord allows.

8 I will stay here in Ephesus until the day of Pentecost. ⁹There is a real opportunity here for great and worthwhile work, even though there are many opponents.

10 If Timothy comes your way, be sure to make him feel welcome among you, because he is working for the Lord, just as I am. ¹¹No one should look down on him, but you must help him to continue his trip in peace, so that he will come back to me; for I am expecting him back with the brothers and sisters.

12 Now, about brother Apollos. I have often encouraged him to visit you with the other believers, but he is not completely convinced[a] that he should go at this time. When he gets the chance, however, he will go.

Final Words

13 Be alert, stand firm in the faith, be brave, be strong. ¹⁴Do all your work in love.

15 You know about Stephanas and his family; they are the first Christian converts in Achaia and have given themselves to the service of God's people. I beg you, my brothers and sisters, ¹⁶to follow the leadership of such people as these, and of anyone else who works and serves with them.

17 I am happy about the coming of Stephanas, Fortunatus, and Achaicus; they have made up for your absence ¹⁸and have cheered me up, just as they cheered you up. Such men as these deserve notice.

19 The churches in the province of Asia send you their greetings; Aquila and Priscilla and the church that meets in their house send warm Christian greetings. ²⁰All the believers here send greetings.

Greet one another with a holy kiss.

21 With my own hand I write this: *Greetings from Paul.*

22 Whoever does not love the Lord – a curse on him!

Marana tha – Our Lord, come!

23 The grace of the Lord Jesus be with you.

24 My love be with you all in Christ Jesus.

---

a **16.12** he is not completely convinced; *or* it is not at all God's will.

Paul's Second Letter to the CORINTHIANS

INTRODUCTION

Paul's Second Letter to the Corinthians was written during a difficult period in his relations with the church at Corinth. Some members of the church had evidently made strong attacks against Paul, but he shows his deep longing for reconciliation and expresses his great joy when this is brought about.

In the first part of the letter Paul discusses his relationship with the church at Corinth, explaining why he had responded with severity to insult and opposition in the church and expressing his joy that this severity had resulted in repentance and reconciliation. Then he appeals to the church for a generous offering to help the needy Christians in Judea. In the final chapters Paul defends his apostleship against a few people at Corinth who had set themselves up as true apostles, while accusing Paul of being a false one.

Outline of Contents

Introduction 1.1–11
Paul and the church at Corinth 1.12—7.16
The offering for the Christians in Judea 8.1—9.15
Paul's defence of his authority as an apostle 10.1—13.10
Conclusion 13.11–13

1 From Paul, an apostle of Christ Jesus by God's will, and from our brother Timothy – To the church of God in Corinth, and to all God's people throughout Achaia:

2 May God our Father and the Lord Jesus Christ give you grace and peace.

Paul Gives Thanks to God

3 Let us give thanks to the God and Father of our Lord Jesus Christ, the merciful Father, the God from whom all help comes! ⁴He helps us in all our troubles, so that we are able to help others who have all kinds of troubles, using the same help that we ourselves have received from God. ⁵Just as we have a share in Christ's many sufferings, so also through Christ we share in God's great help. ⁶If we suffer, it is for your help and salvation; if we are helped, then you too are helped and given the strength to endure with patience the same sufferings that we also endure. ⁷So our hope in you is never shaken; we know that just as you share in our sufferings, you also share in the help we receive.

8 We want to remind you, brothers and sisters, of the trouble we had in the province of Asia. The burdens laid upon us were so great and so heavy that we gave up all hope of staying alive. ⁹We felt that the death sentence had been passed on us. But this happened so that we should rely, not on ourselves, but only on God, who raises the dead. ¹⁰From such terrible dangers of death[a] he saved us, and will save us; and we have placed our hope in him that he will save us again, ¹¹as you help us by means of your prayers for us. So it will be that the many prayers for us will be answered, and God will bless us; and many will raise their voices to him in thanksgiving for us.

The Change in Paul's Plans

12 We are proud that our conscience assures us that our lives in this world, and especially our relations with you, have been ruled by God-given frankness[b] and sincerity, by the power of God's grace, and not by human wisdom. ¹³⁻¹⁴We

---

[a] **1.10** terrible dangers of death; *some manuscripts have* terrible death.
[b] **1.12** frankness; *some manuscripts have* holiness.

write to you only what you can read and understand. But even though you now understand us only in part, I hope that you will come to understand us completely, so that in the Day of our Lord Jesus you can be as proud of us as we shall be of you.

15 I was so sure of all this that I made plans at first to visit you, in order that you might be blessed twice. ¹⁶For I planned to visit you on my way to Macedonia and again on my way back, in order to get help from you for my journey to Judea. ¹⁷In planning this, did I appear fickle? When I make my plans, do I make them from selfish motives, ready to say "Yes, yes" and "No, no" at the same time? ¹⁸As surely as God speaks the truth, my promise to you was not a "Yes" and a "No". ¹⁹For Jesus Christ, the Son of God, who was preached among you by Silas, Timothy, and myself, is not one who is "Yes" and "No". On the contrary, he is God's "Yes"; ²⁰for it is he who is the "Yes" to all God's promises. This is why through Jesus Christ our "Amen" is said to the glory of God. ²¹It is God himself who makes us, together with you, sure of our life in union with Christ; it is God himself who has set us apart, ²²who has placed his mark of ownership upon us, and who has given us the Holy Spirit in our hearts as the guarantee of all that he has in store for us.

23 I call God as my witness – he knows my heart! It was in order to spare you that I decided not to go to Corinth. ²⁴We are not trying to dictate to you what you must believe; we know that you stand firm in the faith. Instead, we are working with you for your own happiness.

2 So I made up my mind not to come to you again to make you sad. ²For if I were to make you sad, who would be left to cheer me up? Only the very persons I had made sad. ³That is why I wrote that letter to you – I did not want to come to you and be made sad by the very people who should make me glad. For I am convinced that when I am happy, then all of you are happy too. ⁴I wrote to you with a greatly troubled and distressed heart and with many tears; my purpose was not to make you sad, but to make you realize how much I love you all.

Forgiveness for the Offender

5 Now, if anyone has made somebody sad, he has not done it to me but to all of you – in part at least. (I say this because I do not want to be too hard on him.) ⁶It is enough that this person

has been punished in this way by most of you. ⁷Now, however, you should forgive him and encourage him, in order to keep him from becoming so sad as to give up completely. ⁸And so I beg you to let him know that you really do love him. ⁹I wrote you that letter because I wanted to find out how well you had stood the test and whether you are always ready to obey my instructions. ¹⁰When you forgive someone for what he or she has done, I forgive them too. For when I forgive – if, indeed, I need to forgive anything – I do it in Christ's presence because of you, ¹¹in order to keep Satan from getting the upper hand of us; for we know what his plans are.

Paul's Anxiety in Troas

12 When I arrived in Troas to preach the Good News about Christ, I found that the Lord had opened the way for the work there. ¹³But I was deeply worried, because I could not find our brother Titus. So I said goodbye to the people there and went on to Macedonia.

Victory through Christ

14 But thanks be to God! For in union with Christ we are always led by God as prisoners in Christ's victory procession. God uses us to make the knowledge about Christ spread everywhere

---

Studying
2 CORINTHIANS

Who wrote it? Paul.
When? 54–56 CE.
Where from? Ephesus.
For whom? The Christians in Corinth.
Why? Many of Paul's opponents had arrived in Corinth. Paul had made a disastrous second visit to the city. The relationship between Paul and the church in Corinth had deteriorated since his first letter. Paul wrote to set the record straight on his own work and authority.

KEY POINTS

- The Christian Gospel is superior in every way over the Law of Moses (1.1—3.3).
- Paul claims that he is utterly faithful in preaching this Gospel even if his work is inadequate.
- The church in Corinth is encouraged to be generous in supporting churches elsewhere – especially in Jerusalem. The Corinthians may need the support of others some day.
- Accused of being a coward when he was in Corinth, Paul reminds readers that meekness is a sign of true spirituality.

like a sweet fragrance. [15]For we are like a sweet-smelling incense offered by Christ to God, which spreads among those who are being saved and those who are being lost. [16]For those who are being lost, it is a deadly stench that kills; but for those who are being saved, it is a fragrance that brings life. Who, then, is capable of such a task? [17]We are not like so many others, who handle God's message as if it were cheap merchandise; but because God has sent us, we speak with sincerity in his presence, as servants of Christ.

Servants of the New Covenant

3 Does this sound as if we were again boasting about ourselves? Could it be that, like some other people, we need letters of recommendation to you or from you? [2]You yourselves are the letter we have, written on our hearts for everyone to know and read. [3]It is clear that Christ himself wrote this letter and sent it by us. It is written, not with ink but with the Spirit of the living God, and not on stone tablets but on human hearts.

4 We say this because we have confidence in God through Christ. [5]There is nothing in us that allows us to claim that we are capable of doing this work. The capacity we have comes from God; [6]it is he who made us capable of serving the new covenant, which consists not of a written law but of the Spirit. The written law brings death, but the Spirit gives life.

7 The Law was carved in letters on stone tablets, and God's glory appeared when it was given. Even though the brightness on Moses' face was fading, it was so strong that the people of Israel could not keep their eyes fixed on him. If the Law, which brings death when it is in force, came with such glory, [8]how much greater is the glory that belongs to the activity of the Spirit! [9]The system which brings condemnation was glorious; how much more glorious is the activity which brings salvation! [10]We may say that because of the far brighter glory now the glory that was so bright in the past is gone. [11]For if there was glory in that which lasted for a while, how much more glory is there in that which lasts for ever!

12 Because we have this hope, we are very bold. [13]We are not like Moses, who had to put a veil over his face so that the people of Israel would not see the brightness fade and disappear. [14]Their minds, indeed, were closed; and to this very day their minds are covered with the same veil as they read the books of the old covenant.

The veil is removed only when a person is joined to Christ. [15]Even today, whenever they read the Law of Moses, the veil still covers their minds. [16]But it can be removed, as the scripture says about Moses: "His veil was removed when he turned to the Lord."[a] [17]Now, "the Lord" in this passage is the Spirit; and where the Spirit of the Lord is present, there is freedom. [18]All of us, then, reflect the glory of the Lord with uncovered faces; and that same glory, coming from the Lord, who is the Spirit, transforms us into his likeness in an ever greater degree of glory.

Spiritual Treasure in Clay Pots

4 God in his mercy has given us this work to do, and so we are not discouraged. [2]We put aside all secret and shameful deeds; we do not act with deceit, nor do we falsify the word of God. In the full light of truth we live in God's sight and try to commend ourselves to everyone's good conscience. [3]For if the gospel we preach is hidden, it is hidden only from those who are being lost. [4]They do not believe, because their minds have been kept in the dark by the evil god of this world. He keeps them from seeing the light shining on them, the light that comes from the Good News about the glory of Christ, who is the exact likeness of God. [5]For it is not ourselves that we preach; we preach Jesus Christ as Lord, and ourselves as your servants for Jesus' sake. [6]The God who said, "Out of darkness the light shall shine!" is the same God who made his light shine in our hearts, to bring us the knowledge of God's glory shining in the face of Christ.

7 Yet we who have this spiritual treasure are like common clay pots, in order to show that the supreme power belongs to God, not to us. [8]We are often troubled, but not crushed; sometimes in doubt, but never in despair; [9]there are many enemies, but we are never without a friend; and though badly hurt at times, we are not destroyed. [10]At all times we carry in our mortal bodies the death of Jesus, so that his life also may be seen in our bodies. [11]Throughout our lives we are always in danger of death for Jesus' sake, in order that his life may be seen in this mortal body of ours. [12]This means that death is at work in us, but life is at work in you.

13 The scripture says, "I spoke because I believed." In the same spirit of faith, we also speak because we believe. [14]We know that God, who raised the Lord Jesus to life, will also raise us

---

[a] **3.16** *Verse 16 may be translated:* But the veil is removed whenever someone turns to the Lord.

Paul reminds his readers that they share in the death of Jesus

this earthly tent, we groan with a feeling of oppression; it is not that we want to get rid of our earthly body, but that we want to have the heavenly one put on over us, so that what is mortal will be transformed by life. [5]God is the one who has prepared us for this change, and he gave us his Spirit as the guarantee of all that he has in store for us.

6 So we are always full of courage. We know that as long as we are at home in the body we are away from the Lord's home. [7]For our life is a matter of faith, not of sight. [8]We are full of courage and would much prefer to leave our home in the body and be at home with the Lord. [9]More than anything else, however, we want to please him, whether in our home here or there. [10]For all of us must appear before Christ, to be judged by him. We will each receive what we deserve, according to everything we have done, good or bad, in our bodily life.

Friendship with God through Christ

11 We know what it means to fear the Lord, and so we try to persuade others. God knows us completely, and I hope that in your hearts you know me as well. [12]We are not trying again to recommend ourselves to you; rather, we are trying to give you a good reason to be proud of us, so that you will be able to answer those who boast about people's appearance and not about their character. [13]Are we really insane? It is for God's sake. Or are we sane? Then it is for your sake. [14]We are ruled by the love of Christ, now that we recognize that one man died for everyone, which means that all share in his death. [15]He died for all, so that those who live should no longer live for themselves, but only for him who died and was raised to life for their sake.

up with Jesus and take us, together with you, into his presence. [15]All this is for your sake; and as God's grace reaches more and more people, they will offer to the glory of God more prayers of thanksgiving.

Living by Faith

16 For this reason we never become discouraged. Even though our physical being is gradually decaying, yet our spiritual being is renewed day after day. [17]And this small and temporary trouble we suffer will bring us a tremendous and eternal glory, much greater than the trouble. [18]For we fix our attention, not on things that are seen, but on things that are unseen. What can be seen lasts only for a time, but what cannot be seen lasts for ever.

5 For we know that when this tent we live in – our body here on earth – is torn down, God will have a house in heaven for us to live in, a home he himself has made, which will last for ever. [2]And now we sigh, so great is our desire that our home which comes from heaven should be put on over us; [3]by being clothed with it we shall not be without a body. [4]While we live in

16 No longer, then, do we judge anyone by human standards. Even if at one time we judged Christ according to human standards, we no longer do so. [17]Anyone who is joined to Christ is a new being; the old is gone, the new has come. [18]All this is done by God, who through Christ changed us from enemies into his friends and gave us the task of making others his friends also. [19]Our message is that God was making the whole human race his friends through Christ.[a] God did not keep an account of their sins, and he has given us the message which tells how he makes them his friends.

[a] **5.19** God was making the whole human race his friends through Christ; *or* God was in Christ making the whole human race his friends.

20 Here we are, then, speaking for Christ, as though God himself were making his appeal through us. We plead on Christ's behalf: let God change you from enemies into his friends! ²¹Christ was without sin, but for our sake God made him share our sin in order that in union with him we might share the righteousness of God.

6 In our work together with God, then, we beg you who have received God's grace not to let it be wasted. ²Hear what God says:

"When the time came for me to show you favour
I heard you;
when the day arrived for me to save you,
I helped you."

Listen! This is the hour to receive God's favour; today is the day to be saved!

3 We do not want anyone to find fault with our work, so we try not to put obstacles in anyone's way. ⁴Instead, in everything we do we show that we are God's servants by patiently enduring troubles, hardships, and difficulties. ⁵We have been beaten, imprisoned, and mobbed; we have been overworked and have gone without sleep or food. ⁶By our purity, knowledge, patience, and kindness we have shown ourselves to be God's servants – by the Holy Spirit, by our true love, ⁷by our message of truth, and by the power of God. We have righteousness as our weapon, both to attack and to defend ourselves. ⁸We are honoured and disgraced; we are insulted and praised. We are treated as liars, yet we speak the truth; ⁹as unknown, yet we are known by all; as though we were dead, but, as you see, we live on. Although punished, we are not killed; ¹⁰although saddened, we are always glad; we seem poor, but we make many people rich; we seem to have nothing, yet we really possess everything.

11 Dear friends in Corinth! We have spoken frankly to you; we have opened our hearts wide. ¹²It is not we who have closed our hearts to you; it is you who have closed your hearts to us. ¹³I speak now as though you were my children: show us the same feelings that we have for you. Open your hearts wide!

Warning against Pagan Influences

14 Do not try to work together as equals with unbelievers, for it cannot be done. How can right and wrong be partners? How can light and darkness live together? ¹⁵How can Christ and the Devil agree? What does a believer have in common with an unbeliever? ¹⁶How can God's

temple come to terms with pagan idols? For we are the temple of the living God! As God himself has said:

"I will make my home with my people
and live among them;
I will be their God,
and they shall be my people."

¹⁷And so the Lord says,

"You must leave them
and separate yourselves from them.
Have nothing to do with what is unclean,
and I will accept you.
18 I will be your father,
and you shall be my sons and daughters,
says the Lord Almighty."

7 All these promises are made to us, my dear friends. So then, let us purify ourselves from everything that makes body or soul unclean, and let us be completely holy by living in awe of God.

Paul's Joy

2 Make room for us in your hearts. We have wronged no one; we have ruined no one, nor tried to take advantage of anyone. ³I do not say this to condemn you; for, as I have said before, you are so dear to us that we are always together, whether we live or die. ⁴I am so sure of you; I take such pride in you! In all our troubles I am still full of courage; I am running over with joy.

5 Even after we arrived in Macedonia, we had no rest. There were troubles everywhere, quarrels with others, fears in our hearts. ⁶But God, who encourages the downhearted, encouraged us with the coming of Titus. ⁷It was not only his coming that cheered us, but also his report of how you encouraged him. He told us how much you want to see me, how sorry you are, how ready you are to defend me; and so I am even happier now.

8 For even if that letter of mine made you sad, I am not sorry I wrote it. I could have been sorry when I saw that it made you sad for a while. ⁹But now I am happy – not because I made you sad, but because your sadness made you change your ways. That sadness was used by God, and so we caused you no harm. ¹⁰For the sadness that is used by God brings a change of heart that leads to salvation – and there is no regret in that! But sadness that is merely human causes death. ¹¹See what God did with this sadness of yours: how earnest it has made you, how eager to prove

Christians today look upon giving as a central part of their worship (8.1–7)

your innocence! Such indignation, such alarm, such feelings, such devotion, such readiness to punish wrongdoing! You have shown yourselves to be without fault in the whole matter.

12 So, even though I wrote that letter, it was not because of the one who did wrong or the one who was wronged. Instead, I wrote it to make plain to you, in God's sight, how deep your devotion to us really is. [13]That is why we were encouraged.

Not only were we encouraged; how happy Titus made us with his happiness over the way in which all of you helped to cheer him up! [14]I did boast of you to him, and you have not disappointed me. We have always spoken the truth to you, and in the same way the boast we made to Titus has proved true. [15]And so his love for you grows stronger, as he remembers how all of you were ready to obey his instructions, how you welcomed him with fear and trembling. [16]How happy I am that I can depend on you completely!

Christian Giving

8 Our brothers and sisters, we want you to know what God's grace has accomplished in the churches in Macedonia. [2]They have been severely tested by the troubles they went through; but their joy was so great that they were extremely generous in their giving, even though they are very poor. [3]I can assure you that they gave as much as they could, and even more than they could. Of their own free will [4]they begged us and pleaded for the privilege of having a part in helping God's people in Judea. [5]It was more than we could have hoped for! First they gave themselves to the Lord; and then, by God's will they gave themselves to us as well. [6]So we urged Titus, who began this work, to continue it and help you complete this special service of love. [7]You are so rich in all you have: in faith, speech, and knowledge, in your eagerness to help and in your love for us.[a] And so we want you to be generous also in this service of love.

8 I am not laying down any rules. But by showing how eager others are to help, I am trying to find out how real your own love is. [9]You know the grace of our Lord Jesus Christ; rich as he was, he made himself poor for your sake, in order to make you rich by means of his poverty.

10 My opinion is that it is better for you to finish now what you began last year. You were the first, not only to act, but also to be willing to act. [11]On with it, then, and finish the job! Be as eager to finish it as you were to plan it, and do it with

[a] **8.7** your love for us; *some manuscripts have* our love for you.

what you now have. [12]If you are eager to give, God will accept your gift on the basis of what you have to give, not on what you haven't.

13–14   I am not trying to relieve others by putting a burden on you; but since you have plenty at this time, it is only fair that you should help those who are in need. Then, when you are in need and they have plenty, they will help you. In this way both are treated equally. [15]As the scripture says, "The one who gathered much did not have too much, and the one who gathered little did not have too little."

Titus and his Companions

16   How we thank God for making Titus as eager as we are to help you! [17]Not only did he welcome our request; he was so eager to help that of his own free will he decided to go to you. [18]With him we are sending the brother who is highly respected in all the churches for his work in preaching the gospel. [19]And besides that, he has been chosen and appointed by the churches to travel with us as we carry out this service of love for the sake of the Lord's glory, and in order to show that we want to help.

20   We are taking care not to stir up any complaints about the way we handle this generous gift. [21]Our purpose is to do what is right, not only in the sight of the Lord, but also in the sight of others.

22   So we are sending our brother with them; we have tested him many times and found him always very eager to help. And now that he has so much confidence in you, he is all the more eager to help. [23]As for Titus, he is my partner and works with me to help you; as for the other brothers who are going with him, they represent the churches and bring glory to Christ. [24]Show your love to them, so that all the churches will be sure of it and know that we are right in boasting about you.

Help for Fellow-Christians

9 There is really no need for me to write to you about the help being sent to God's people in Judea. [2]I know that you are willing to help, and I have boasted of you to the people in Macedonia. "The brothers and sisters in Achaia," I said, "have been ready to help since last year." Your eagerness has stirred up most of them. [3]Now I am sending these brothers and sisters, so that our boasting about you in this matter may not turn out to be empty words. But, just as I said, you will be ready with your help.

[4]However, if the people from Macedonia should come with me and find out that you are not ready, how ashamed we would be – not to speak of your shame – for feeling so sure of you! [5]So I thought it was necessary to urge these brothers and sisters to go to you ahead of me and get ready in advance the gift you promised to make. Then it will be ready when I arrive, and it will show that you give because you want to, not because you have to.

6   Remember that the person who sows few seeds will have a small crop; the one who sows many seeds will have a large crop. [7]You should each give, then, as you have decided, not with regret or out of a sense of duty; for God loves the one who gives gladly. [8]And God is able to give you more than you need, so that you will always have all you need for yourselves and more than enough for every good cause. [9]As the scripture says:

"He gives generously to the needy;
  his kindness lasts for ever."

10   And God, who supplies seed to sow and bread to eat, will also supply you with all the seed you need and will make it grow and produce a rich harvest from your generosity. [11]He will always make you rich enough to be generous at all times, so that many will thank God for your gifts which they receive from us. [12]For this service you perform not only meets the needs of God's people, but also produces an outpouring of gratitude to God. [13]And because of the proof which this service of yours brings, many will give glory to God for your loyalty to the gospel of Christ, which you profess, and for your generosity in sharing with them and everyone else. [14]And so with deep affection they will pray for you because of the extraordinary grace God has shown you. [15]Let us thank God for his priceless gift!

Paul Defends his Ministry

10 I, Paul, make a personal appeal to you – I who am said to be meek and mild when I am with you, but harsh with you when I am away. By the gentleness and kindness of Christ [2]I beg you not to force me to be harsh when I come; for I am sure I can deal harshly with those who say that we act from worldly motives. [3]It is true that we live in the world, but we do not fight from worldly motives. [4]The weapons we use in our fight are not the world's weapons but God's powerful weapons, which we use to destroy strongholds. We destroy false arguments; [5]we pull down every proud obstacle that is raised against the knowledge of God; we take every thought captive and make it obey Christ. [6]And after you have proved your complete loyalty, we will be ready to punish any act of disloyalty.

[7] You are looking at the outward appearance of things. Is there someone there who reckons himself or herself to belong to Christ? Well, let them think again about themselves, because we belong to Christ just as much as they do. [8]For I am not ashamed, even if I have boasted somewhat too much about the authority that the Lord has given us – authority to build you up, not to tear you down. [9]I do not want it to appear that I am trying to frighten you with my letters. [10]Someone will say, "Paul's letters are severe and strong, but when he is with us in person, he is weak, and his words are nothing!" [11]Such a person must understand that there is no difference between what we write in our letters when we are away and what we will do when we are there with you.

[12] Of course we would not dare to classify ourselves or compare ourselves with those who rate themselves so highly. How stupid they are! They make up their own standards to measure themselves by, and they judge themselves by their own standards! [13]As for us, however, our boasting will not go beyond certain limits; it will stay within the limits of the work which God has set for us, and this includes our work among you. [14]And since you are within those limits, we were not going beyond them when we came to you, bringing the Good News about Christ. [15]So we do not boast about the work that others have done beyond the limits God set for us. Instead, we hope that your faith may grow and that we may be able to do a much greater work among you, always within the limits that God has set. [16]Then we can preach the Good News in other countries beyond you and shall not have to boast about work already done in someone else's field.

[17] But as the scripture says, "Whoever wants to boast must boast about what the Lord has done." [18]For it is people of whom the Lord thinks well who are really approved, not people who think well of themselves.

Paul and the False Apostles

11 I wish you would tolerate me, even when I am a bit foolish. Please do! [2]I am jealous for you, just as God is; you are like a pure virgin whom I have promised in marriage to one man only, Christ himself. [3]I am afraid that your minds will be corrupted and that you will abandon your full and pure devotion to Christ – in the same way that Eve was deceived by the snake's clever lies. [4]For you gladly tolerate anyone who comes to you and preaches a different Jesus, not the one we preached; and you accept a spirit and a gospel completely different from the Spirit and the gospel you received from us!

[5] I do not think that I am the least bit inferior to those very special so-called "apostles" of yours! [6]Perhaps I am an amateur in speaking, but certainly not in knowledge; we have made this clear to you at all times and in all conditions.

[7] I did not charge you a thing when I preached the Good News of God to you; I humbled myself in order to make you important. Was that wrong of me? [8]While I was working among you, I was paid by other churches. I was robbing them, so to speak, in order to help you. [9]And during the time I was with you I did not bother you for help when I needed money; the brothers and sisters who came from Macedonia brought me everything I needed. As in the past, so in the future: I will never be a burden to you! [10]By Christ's truth in me, I promise that this boast of mine will not be silenced anywhere in all Achaia. [11]Do I say this because I don't love you? God knows I love you!

[12] I will go on doing what I am doing now, in order to keep those other "apostles" from having any reason for boasting and saying that they work in the same way that we do. [13]Those men are not true apostles – they are false apostles, who lie about their work and disguise themselves to look like real apostles of Christ. [14]Well, no wonder! Even Satan can disguise himself to look like an angel of light! [15]So it is no great thing if his servants disguise themselves to look like servants of righteousness. In the end they will get exactly what their actions deserve.

Paul's Sufferings as an Apostle

[16] I repeat: no one should think that I am a fool. But if you do, at least accept me as a fool, so that I will have a little to boast of. [17]Of course what I am saying now is not what the Lord would like me to say; in this matter of boasting I am really talking like a fool. [18]But since there are so many who boast for merely human reasons, I will do the same. [19]You yourselves are so wise, and so you gladly tolerate fools! [20]You tolerate anyone who orders you about or takes advantage of you or traps you or looks down on you or slaps you

in the face. [21]I am ashamed to admit that we were too timid to do those things!

But if anyone dares to boast about something – I am talking like a fool – I will be just as daring. [22]Are they Hebrews? So am I. Are they Israelites? So am I. Are they Abraham's descendants? So am I. [23]Are they Christ's servants? I sound like a madman – but I am a better servant than they are! I have worked much harder, I have been in prison more times, I have been whipped much more, and I have been near death more often. [24]Five times I was given the thirty-nine lashes by the Jews; [25]three times I was whipped by the Romans; and once I was stoned. I have been in three shipwrecks, and once I spent twenty-four hours in the water. [26]In my many travels I have been in danger from floods and from robbers, in danger from fellow-Jews and from Gentiles; there have been dangers in the cities, dangers in the wilds, dangers on the high seas, and dangers from false friends. [27]There has been work and toil; often I have gone without sleep; I have been hungry and thirsty; I have often been without enough food, shelter, or clothing. [28]And not to mention other things, every day I am under the pressure of my concern for all the churches. [29]When someone is weak, then I feel weak too; when someone is led into sin, I am filled with distress.

30 If I must boast, I will boast about things that show how weak I am. [31]The God and Father of the Lord Jesus – blessed be his name for ever! – knows that I am not lying. [32]When I was in Damascus, the governor under King Aretas placed guards at the city gates to arrest me. [33]But I was let down in a basket through an opening in the wall and escaped from him.

Paul's Visions and Revelations

12 I have to boast, even though it doesn't do any good. But I will now talk about visions and revelations given me by the Lord. [2]I know a certain Christian man who fourteen years ago was snatched up to the highest heaven (I do not know whether this actually happened or whether he had a vision – only God knows). [3-4]I repeat, I know that this man was snatched to Paradise (again, I do not know whether this actually happened or whether it was a vision – only God knows), and there he heard things which cannot be put into words, things that human lips may not speak. [5]So I will boast about this man – but I will not boast about myself, except the things that show how weak I am. [6]If I wanted to boast, I would not be a fool, because I would be telling the truth. But I will not boast, because I do not want anyone to have a higher opinion of me than he has as a result of what he has seen me do and heard me say.

7 But to keep me from being puffed up with pride because of the many wonderful things I saw, I was given a painful physical ailment, which acts as Satan's messenger to beat me and keep me from being proud. [8]Three times I prayed to the Lord about this and asked him to take it away. [9]But his answer was: "My grace is all you need, for my power is greatest when you are weak." I am most happy, then, to be proud of my weaknesses, in order to feel the protection of Christ's power over me. [10]I am content with weaknesses, insults, hardships, persecutions, and difficulties for Christ's sake. For when I am weak, then I am strong.

Paul's Concern for the Corinthians

11 I am acting like a fool – but you have made me do it. You are the ones who ought to show your approval of me. For even if I am nothing, I am in no way inferior to those very special "apostles" of yours. [12]The many miracles and wonders that prove that I am an apostle were performed among you with much patience. [13]How were you treated any worse than the other churches, except that I did not bother you for financial help? Please forgive me for being so unfair!

14 This is now the third time that I am ready to come to visit you – and I will not make any demands on you. It is you I want, not your money. After all, children should not have to provide for their parents, but parents should provide for their children. [15]I will be glad to spend all I have, and myself as well, in order to help you. Will you love me less because I love you so much?

16 You will agree, then, that I was not a burden to you. But someone will say that I was crafty, and trapped you with lies. [17]How? Did I take advantage of you through any of the messengers I sent? [18]I begged Titus to go, and I sent the other Christian brother with him. Would you say that Titus took advantage of you? Do he and I not act from the very same motives and behave in the same way?

19 Perhaps you think that all along we have been trying to defend ourselves before you. No! We speak as Christ would wish us to speak in the presence of God, and everything we do, dear friends, is done to help you. [20]I am afraid that when I get there I will find you different from what I would like you to be and you will find me

different from what you would like me to be. I am afraid that I will find quarrelling and jealousy, hot tempers and selfishness, insults and gossip, pride and disorder. [21]I am afraid that the next time I come my God will humiliate me in your presence, and I shall weep over many who sinned in the past and have not repented of the immoral things they have done – their lust and their sexual sins.

Final Warnings and Greetings

13 This is now the third time that I am coming to visit you. "Any accusation must be upheld by the evidence of two or more witnesses" – as the scripture says. [2]I want to say to those of you who have sinned in the past, and to all the others; I said it before during my second visit to you, but I will say it again now that I am away: the next time I come nobody will escape punishment. [3]You will have all the proof you want that Christ speaks through me. When he deals with you, he is not weak; instead, he shows his power among you. [4]For even though it was in weakness that he was put to death on the cross, it is by God's power that he lives. In union with him we also are weak; but in our relations with you we shall share God's power in his life.

[5] Put yourselves to the test and judge yourselves, to find out whether you are living in faith. Surely you know that Christ Jesus is in you? – unless you have completely failed. [6]I trust you will know that we are not failures. [7]We pray to God that you will do no wrong – not in order to show that we are a success, but so that you may do what is right, even though we may seem to be failures. [8]For we cannot do a thing against the truth, but only for it. [9]We are glad when we are weak but you are strong. And so we also pray that you will become perfect. [10]That is why I write this while I am away from you; it is so that when I arrive I will not have to deal harshly with you in using the authority that the Lord has given me – authority to build you up, not to tear you down.

[11] And now, my brothers and sisters, goodbye! Strive for perfection; listen to my appeals; agree with one another; live in peace. And the God of love and peace will be with you.

[12] Greet one another with a holy kiss.

All God's people send you their greetings.

[13] The grace of the Lord Jesus Christ, the love of God, and the fellowship of the Holy Spirit be with you all.

Paul's Letter to the GALATIANS

INTRODUCTION

As the good news about Jesus began to be preached and welcomed among people who were not Jews, the question arose as to whether a person must obey the Law of Moses in order to be a true Christian. Paul had argued that this was not necessary – that in fact, the only sound basis for life in Christ was faith, by which all are put right with God. But among the churches of Galatia, a Roman province in Asia Minor, there had come people who opposed Paul and claimed that one must also observe the Law of Moses in order to be right with God.

Paul's Letter to the Galatians was written in order to bring back to true faith and practice those people who were being misled by this false teaching. Paul begins by defending his right to be called an apostle of Jesus Christ. He insists that his call to be an apostle came from God, not from any human authority, and that his mission was especially to the non-Jews. Then he develops the argument that it is by faith alone that people are put right with God. In the concluding chapters Paul shows that Christian conduct flows naturally from the love that results from faith in Christ.

Outline of Contents

Introduction 1.1–10
Paul's authority as an apostle 1.11—2.21
The gospel of God's grace 3.1—4.31
Christian freedom and responsibility 5.1—6.10
Conclusion 6.11–18

1 From Paul, whose call to be an apostle did not come from human beings or by human means, but from Jesus Christ and God the Father, who raised him from death. ²All the brothers and sisters who are here join me in sending greetings to the churches of Galatia:

3 May God our Father and the Lord Jesus Christ give you grace and peace.

4 In order to set us free from this present evil age, Christ gave himself for our sins, in obedience to the will of our God and Father. ⁵To God be the glory for ever and ever! Amen.

The One Gospel

6 I am surprised at you! In no time at all you are deserting the one who called you by the grace of Christ,ᵃ and are accepting another gospel. ⁷Actually, there is no "other gospel", but I say

---

ᵃ **1.6** by the grace of Christ; *some manuscripts have* by his grace.

---

this because there are some people who are upsetting you and trying to change the gospel of Christ. ⁸But even if we or an angel from heaven should preach to you a gospel that is different from the one we preached to you, may he be condemned to hell! ⁹We have said it before, and now I say it again: if anyone preaches to you a gospel that is different from the one you accepted, may he be condemned to hell!

10 Does this sound as if I am trying to win human approval? No indeed! What I want is God's approval! Am I trying to be popular with people? If I were still trying to do so, I would not be a servant of Christ.

How Paul Became an Apostle

11 Let me tell you, my brothers and sisters, that the gospel I preach is not of human origin. ¹²I did not receive it from any human being, nor did anyone teach it to me. It was Jesus Christ himself who revealed it to me.

13   You have been told how I used to live when I was devoted to the Jewish religion, how I persecuted without mercy the church of God and did my best to destroy it. [14]I was ahead of most fellow-Jews of my age in my practice of the Jewish religion, and was much more devoted to the traditions of our ancestors.

15   But God in his grace chose me even before I was born, and called me to serve him. And when he decided [16]to reveal his Son to me, so that I might preach the Good News about him to the Gentiles, I did not go to anyone for advice, [17]nor did I go to Jerusalem to see those who were apostles before me. Instead, I went at once to Arabia, and then I returned to Damascus. [18]It was three years later that I went to Jerusalem to obtain information from Peter, and I stayed with him for two weeks. [19]I did not see any other apostle except James,[a] the Lord's brother.

20   What I write is true. God knows that I am not lying!

21   Afterwards I went to places in Syria and Cilicia. [22]At that time the members of the churches in Judea did not know me personally. [23]They knew only what others were saying: "The man who used to persecute us is now preaching the faith that he once tried to destroy!" [24]And so they praised God because of me.

Paul and the Other Apostles

2   Fourteen years later I went back to Jerusalem with Barnabas, taking Titus along with me. [2]I went because God revealed to me that I should go. In a private meeting with the leaders I explained the gospel message that I preach to the Gentiles. I did not want my work in the past or in the present to be a failure. [3]My companion Titus, even though he is Greek, was not forced to be circumcised, [4]although some wanted it done. Pretending to be fellow-believers, these men slipped into our group as spies, in order to find out about the freedom we have through our union with Christ Jesus. They wanted to make slaves of us, [5]but in order to keep the truth of the gospel safe for you, we did not give in to them for a minute.

6   But those who seemed to be the leaders – I say this because it makes no difference to me what they were; God does not judge by outward appearances – those leaders, I say, made no new suggestions to me. [7]On the contrary, they saw that God had given me the task of preaching the

---

a **1.19** any other apostle except James; *or* any other apostle; the only other person I saw was James.

Studying
GALATIANS

Who wrote it? Paul.
When? Written either 48–49 CE, making it Paul's earliest letter, or around 55 CE. The later date is most likely.
Where from? From Ephesus or Macedonia.
For whom? Paul founded one of several churches in Galatia. Scholars not sure whether letter was sent to churches in north or south Galatia.
Why? Epistle is concerned with activity of "Judaizers" in Galatia, i.e. people who wanted to impose Jewish religious practices on young Christians. To counter such teaching Paul wrote a stern and uncompromising letter.

KEY POINTS

- Christians are "justified" (forgiven by God) because of their faith in Christ – not through keeping the Jewish Law.
- The death of Jesus marks the end of the old age, based on the Jewish Law, and the beginning of the new, based on faith in Christ.
- Those who preach another message are not offering the people good news. Paul received his authority directly from God.

---

gospel to the Gentiles, just as he had given Peter the task of preaching the gospel to the Jews. [8]For by God's power I was made an apostle to the Gentiles, just as Peter was made an apostle to the Jews. [9]James, Peter, and John, who seemed to be the leaders, recognized that God had given me this special task; so they shook hands with Barnabas and me, as a sign that we were all partners. We agreed that Barnabas and I would work among the Gentiles and they among the Jews. [10]All they asked was that we should remember the needy in their group, which is the very thing I have[b] been eager to do.

Paul Rebukes Peter at Antioch

11   But when Peter came to Antioch, I opposed him in public, because he was clearly wrong. [12]Before some men who had been sent by James arrived there, Peter had been eating with the Gentile brothers and sisters. But after these men arrived, he drew back and would not eat with the Gentiles, because he was afraid of those who were in favour of circumcising them. [13]The other Jewish brothers and sisters also started acting like cowards along with Peter; and even Barnabas was swept along by their cowardly action. [14]When I saw that they were not walking

---

b **2.10** have; *or* had.

---

a straight path in line with the truth of the gospel, I said to Peter in front of them all, "You are a Jew, yet you have been living like a Gentile, not like a Jew. How, then, can you try to force Gentiles to live like Jews?"

Jews and Gentiles are Saved by Faith

15 Indeed, we are Jews by birth and not "Gentile sinners", as they are called. [16]Yet we know that a person is put right with God only through faith in Jesus Christ, never by doing what the Law requires. We, too, have believed in Christ Jesus in order to be put right with God through our faith in Christ, and not by doing what the Law requires. For no one is put right with God by doing what the Law requires. [17]If, then, as we try to be put right with God by our union with Christ, we are found to be sinners as much as the Gentiles are – does this mean that Christ is serving the cause of sin? By no means! [18]If I start to rebuild the system of Law that I tore down, then I show myself to be someone who breaks the Law. [19]So far as the Law is concerned, however, I am dead – killed by the Law itself – in order that I might live for God. I have been put to death with Christ on his cross, [20]so that it is no longer I who live, but it is Christ who lives in me. This life that I live now, I live by faith in the Son of God, who loved me and gave his life for me. [21]I refuse to reject the grace of God. But if a person is put right with God through the Law, it means that Christ died for nothing!

Law or Faith

3 You foolish Galatians! Who put a spell on you? Before your very eyes you had a clear description of the death of Jesus Christ on the cross! [2]Tell me this one thing: did you receive God's Spirit by doing what the Law requires or by hearing the gospel and believing it? [3]How can you be so foolish! You began by God's Spirit; do you now want to finish by your own power? [4]Did all your experience mean nothing at all? Surely it meant something! [5]Does God give you the Spirit and work miracles among you because you do what the Law requires or because you hear the gospel and believe it?

6 Consider the experience of Abraham; as the scripture says, "He believed God, and because of his faith God accepted him as righteous." [7]You should realize then, that the real descendants of Abraham are the people who have faith. [8]The scripture predicted that God would put the Gentiles right with himself through faith. And so the scripture announced the Good News to Abraham: "Through you God will bless the whole human race." [9]Abraham believed and was blessed; so all who believe are blessed as he was.

10 Those who depend on obeying the Law live under a curse. For the scripture says, "Whoever does not always obey everything that is written in the book of the Law is under God's curse!" [11]Now, it is clear that no one is put right with God by means of the Law, because the scripture says, "Only the person who is put right with God through faith shall live."[a] [12]But the Law has nothing to do with faith. Instead, as the scripture says, "Whoever *does* everything the Law requires will live."

13 But by becoming a curse for us Christ has redeemed us from the curse that the Law brings; for the scripture says, "Anyone who is hanged on a tree is under God's curse." [14]Christ did this in order that the blessing which God promised to Abraham might be given to the Gentiles by means of Christ Jesus, so that through faith we might receive the Spirit promised by God.

The Law and the Promise

15 My brothers and sisters, I am going to use an everyday example: when two people agree on a matter and sign an agreement, no one can break it or add anything to it. [16]Now, God made his promises to Abraham and to his descendant. The scripture does not use the plural "descendants", meaning many people, but the singular "descendant", meaning one person only, namely, Christ. [17]What I mean is that God made a covenant with Abraham and promised to keep it. The Law, which was given 430 years later, cannot break that covenant and cancel God's promise. [18]For if God's gift depends on the Law, then it no longer depends on his promise. However, it was because of his promise that God gave that gift to Abraham.

19 What, then, was the purpose of the Law? It was added in order to show what wrongdoing is, and it was meant to last until the coming of Abraham's descendant, to whom the promise was made. The Law was handed down by angels, with a man acting as a go-between. [20]But a go-between is not needed when only one person is involved; and God is one.[b]

[a] **3.11** put right with God through faith shall live; *or* put right with God shall live through faith.
[b] **3.20** and God is one; *or* and God acts alone.

(3.28)

union with Christ Jesus. [29]If you belong to Christ, then you are the descendants of Abraham and will receive what God has promised.

4 But now to continue – the son who will receive his father's property is treated just like a slave while he is young, even though he really owns everything. [2]While he is young, there are men who take care of him and manage his affairs until the time set by his father. [3]In the same way, we too were slaves of the ruling spirits of the universe before we reached spiritual maturity. [4]But when the right time finally came, God sent his own Son. He came as the son of a human mother and lived under the Jewish Law, [5]to redeem those who were under the Law, so that we might become God's sons and daughters.

6 To show that you are[a] his sons and daughters, God sent the Spirit of his Son into our hearts, the Spirit who cries out, "Father, my Father." [7]So then, you are no longer a slave but a son or daughter. And since that is what you are, God will give you all that he has for his heirs.

The Purpose of the Law

21 Does this mean that the Law is against God's promises? No, not at all! For if human beings had received a law that could bring life, then everyone could be put right with God by obeying it. [22]But the scripture says that the whole world is under the power of sin; and so the gift which is promised on the basis of faith in Jesus Christ is given to those who believe.

23 But before the time for faith came, the Law kept us all locked up as prisoners until this coming faith should be revealed. [24]And so the Law was in charge of us until Christ came, in order that we might then be put right with God through faith. [25]Now that the time for faith is here, the Law is no longer in charge of us.

26 It is through faith that all of you are God's children in union with Christ Jesus. [27]You were baptized into union with Christ, and now you are clothed, so to speak, with the life of Christ himself. [28]So there is no difference between Jews and Gentiles, between slaves and free people, between men and women; you are all one in

An Orthodox icon showing Mary and her child, Jesus (4.4)

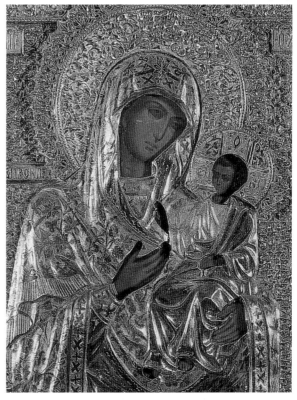

[a] **4.6** To show that you are; *or* Because you are.

Paul's Concern for the Galatians

8   In the past you did not know God, and so you were slaves of beings who are not gods. [9]But now that you know God – or, I should say, now that God knows you – how is it that you want to turn back to those weak and pitiful ruling spirits? Why do you want to become their slaves all over again? [10]You pay special attention to certain days, months, seasons, and years. [11]I am worried about you! Can it be that all my work for you has been for nothing?

12   I beg you, my brothers and sisters, be like me. After all, I am like you. You have not done me any wrong. [13]You remember why I preached the gospel to you the first time; it was because I was ill. [14]But even though my physical condition was a great trial to you, you did not despise or reject me. Instead, you received me as you would an angel from heaven; you received me as you would Christ Jesus. [15]You were so happy! What has happened? I myself can say that you would have taken out your own eyes, if you could, and given them to me. [16]Have I now become your enemy by telling you the truth?

17   Those other people show a deep interest in you, but their intentions are not good. All they want is to separate you from me, so that you will have the same interest in them as they have in you. [18]Now, it is good to have such a deep interest if the purpose is good – this is true always, and not merely when I am with you. [19]My dear children! Once again, just like a mother in childbirth, I feel the same kind of pain for you until Christ's nature is formed in you. [20]How I wish I were with you now, so that I could take a different attitude towards you. I am so worried about you!

The Example of Hagar and Sarah

21   Let me ask those of you who want to be subject to the Law: do you not hear what the Law says? [22]It says that Abraham had two sons, one by a slave woman, the other by a free woman. [23]His son by the slave woman was born in the usual way, but his son by the free woman was born as a result of God's promise. [24]These things can be understood as a figure: the two women represent two covenants. The one whose children are born in slavery is Hagar, and she represents the covenant made at Mount Sinai. [25]Hagar, who stands for Mount Sinai in Arabia, is[a] a figure of the present city of Jerusalem, in

---

[a] **4.25** Hagar … is; *some manuscripts have* Sinai is a mountain in Arabia, and it is.

slavery with all its people. [26]But the heavenly Jerusalem is free, and she is our mother. [27]For the scripture says:

> "Be happy, you childless woman!
>   Shout and cry with joy, you who never felt
>   the pains of childbirth!
> For the woman who was deserted will have
>   more children
>   than the woman whose husband never
>   left her."

28   Now, you, my brothers and sisters, are God's children as a result of his promise, just as Isaac was. [29]At that time the son who was born in the usual way persecuted the one who was born because of God's Spirit; and it is the same now. [30]But what does the scripture say? It says, "Send the slave woman and her son away; for the son of the slave woman will not have a part of the father's property along with the son of the free woman." [31]So then, my brothers and sisters, we are not the children of a slave woman but of a free woman.

Preserve your Freedom

5   Freedom is what we have – Christ has set us free! Stand, then, as free people, and do not allow yourselves to become slaves again.

2   Listen! I, Paul, tell you that if you allow yourselves to be circumcised, it means that Christ is of no use to you at all. [3]Once more I warn any man who allows himself to be circumcised that he is obliged to obey the whole Law. [4]Those of you who try to be put right with God by obeying the Law have cut yourselves off from Christ. You are outside God's grace. [5]As for us, our hope is that God will put us right with him; and this is what we wait for by the power of God's Spirit working through our faith. [6]For when we are in union with Christ Jesus, neither circumcision nor the lack of it makes any difference at all; what matters is faith that works through love.

7   You were doing so well! Who made you stop obeying the truth? How did he persuade you? [8]It was not done by God, who calls you. [9]"It takes only a little yeast to make the whole batch of dough rise," as they say. [10]But I still feel confident about you. Our life in union with the Lord makes me confident that you will not take a different view and that the man who is upsetting you, whoever he is, will be punished by God.

11   But as for me, my brothers and sisters, if I continue to preach that circumcision is necessary, why am I still being persecuted? If that were true, then my preaching about the cross of

Christ would cause no trouble. ¹²I wish that the people who are upsetting you would go all the way; let them go on and castrate themselves!

13   As for you, my brothers and sisters, you were called to be free. But do not let this freedom become an excuse for letting your physical desires control you. Instead, let love make you serve one another. ¹⁴For the whole Law is summed up in one commandment: "Love your neighbour as you love yourself." ¹⁵But if you act like wild animals, hurting and harming each other, then watch out, or you will completely destroy one another.

The Spirit and Human Nature

16   What I say is this: let the Spirit direct your lives, and you will not satisfy the desires of the human nature. ¹⁷For what our human nature wants is opposed to what the Spirit wants, and what the Spirit wants is opposed to what our human nature wants. These two are enemies, and this means that you cannot do what you want to do. ¹⁸If the Spirit leads you, then you are not subject to the Law.

19   What human nature does is quite plain. It shows itself in immoral, filthy, and indecent actions; ²⁰in worship of idols and witchcraft. People become enemies and they fight; they become jealous, angry, and ambitious. They separate into parties and groups; ²¹they are envious, get drunk, have orgies, and do other things like these. I warn you now as I have before: those who do these things will not possess the Kingdom of God.

22   But the Spirit produces love, joy, peace, patience, kindness, goodness, faithfulness, ²³humility, and self-control. There is no law against such things as these. ²⁴And those who belong to Christ Jesus have put to death their human nature with all its passions and desires. ²⁵The Spirit has given us life; he must also control our lives. ²⁶We must not be proud or irritate one another or be jealous of one another.

Bear One Another's Burdens

6   My brothers and sisters, if someone is caught in any kind of wrongdoing, those of you who are spiritual should set him right; but you must do it in a gentle way. And keep an eye on yourselves, so that you will not be tempted, too. ²Help to carry one another's burdens, and in this way you will obey[a] the law of Christ. ³If someone thinks he or she is somebody when really they are nobody, they are only deceiving themselves. ⁴You should each judge your own conduct. If it is good, then you can be proud of what you yourself have done, without having to compare it with what someone else has done. ⁵For we each have our own load to carry.

6   Those who are being taught the Christian message should share all the good things they have with their teachers.

7   Do not deceive yourselves; no one makes a fool of God. People will reap exactly what they sow. ⁸If they sow in the field of their natural desires, from it they will gather the harvest of death; if they sow in the field of the Spirit, from the Spirit they will gather the harvest of eternal life. ⁹So let us not become tired of doing good; for if we do not give up, the time will come when we will reap the harvest. ¹⁰So then, as often as we have the chance, we should do good to everyone, and especially to those who belong to our family in the faith.

Final Warning and Greeting

11   See what big letters I make as I write to you now with my own hand! ¹²The people who are trying to force you to be circumcised are the ones who want to show off and boast about external matters. They do it, however, only so that they may not be persecuted for the cross of Christ. ¹³Even those who practise circumcision do not obey the Law; they want you to be circumcised so that they can boast that you submitted to this physical ceremony. ¹⁴As for me, however, I will boast only about the cross of our Lord Jesus Christ; for by means of his cross the world is dead to me, and I am dead to the world. ¹⁵It does not matter at all whether or not one is circumcised; what does matter is being a new creature. ¹⁶As for those who follow this rule in their lives, may peace and mercy be with them – with them and with all God's people!

17   To conclude: let no one give me any more trouble, because the scars I have on my body show that I am the slave of Jesus.

18   May the grace of our Lord Jesus Christ be with you all, my brothers and sisters. Amen.

---

a **6.2** you will obey; *some manuscripts have* obey.

Paul's Letter to the EPHESIANS

INTRODUCTION

Paul's Letter to the Ephesians is concerned first of all with "God's plan ... to bring all creation together, everything in heaven and on earth, with Christ as head". (1.10) It is also an appeal to God's people to live out the meaning of this great plan for the unity of the human race through oneness with Jesus Christ.

In the first part of *Ephesians* the writer develops the theme of unity by speaking of the way in which God the Father has chosen his people, how they are forgiven and set free from their sins through Jesus Christ the Son, and how God's great promise is guaranteed by the Holy Spirit. In the second part he appeals to the readers to live in such a way that their oneness in Christ may become real in their life together.

Several figures of speech are used to show the oneness of God's people in union with Christ: the church is like a body, with Christ as the head; or like a building, with Christ as the cornerstone; or like a wife, with Christ as the husband. This letter rises to great heights of expression as the writer is moved by the thought of God's grace in Christ. Everything is seen in the light of Christ's love, sacrifice, forgiveness, grace, and purity.

Outline of Contents

1 From Paul, who by God's will is an apostle of Christ Jesus –
To God's people in Ephesus,[a] who are faithful in their life in union with Christ Jesus:

2 May God our Father and the Lord Jesus Christ give you grace and peace.

Spiritual Blessings in Christ

3 Let us give thanks to the God and Father of our Lord Jesus Christ! For in our union with Christ he has blessed us by giving us every spiritual blessing in the heavenly world. [4]Even before the world was made, God had already chosen us to be his through our union with Christ, so that we would be holy and without fault before him.

Because of his love [5]God[b] had already decided that through Jesus Christ he would make us his sons and daughters – this was his pleasure and purpose. [6]Let us praise God for his glorious grace, for the free gift he gave us in his dear Son! [7]For by the blood[c] of Christ we are set free, that is, our sins are forgiven. How great is the grace of God, [8]which he gave to us in such large measure!

In all his wisdom and insight [9]God did what he had purposed, and made known to us the secret plan he had already decided to complete by means of Christ. [10]This plan, which God will complete when the time is right, is to bring all creation together, everything in heaven and on earth, with Christ as head.

11 All things are done according to God's plan and decision; and God chose us to be his own people in union with Christ because of his own purpose, based on what he had decided from the very beginning. [12]Let us, then, who were the first to hope in Christ, praise God's glory!

13 And you also became God's people when you

---

[a] **1.1** *Some manuscripts do not have* in Ephesus.
[b] **1.5** before him. Because of his love God; *or* before him, and to live in love. God.
[c] **1.7** by the blood; *or* by the sacrificial death.

heard the true message, the Good News that brought you salvation. You believed in Christ, and God put his stamp of ownership on you by giving you the Holy Spirit he had promised. [14]The Spirit is the guarantee that we shall receive what God has promised his people, and this assures us that God will give complete freedom to those who are his. Let us praise his glory!

Paul's Prayer

15 For this reason, ever since I heard of your faith in the Lord Jesus and your love for all God's people, [16]I have not

As the body of Christ, the Church brings together worshippers (1.23)

stopped giving thanks to God for you. I remember you in my prayers [17]and ask the God of our Lord Jesus Christ, the glorious Father, to give you the Spirit, who will make you wise and reveal God to you, so that you will know him. [18]I ask that your minds may be opened to see his light, so that you will know what is the hope to which he has called you, how rich are the wonderful blessings he promises his people, [19]and how very great is his power at work in us who believe. This power working in us is the same as the mighty strength [20]which he used when he raised Christ from death and seated him at his right side in the heavenly world. [21]Christ rules there above all heavenly rulers, authorities, powers, and lords; he has a title superior to all titles of authority in this world and in the next. [22]God put all things under Christ's feet and gave him to the church as supreme Lord over all things. [23]The church is Christ's body, the completion of him who himself completes all things everywhere.[a]

From Death to Life

2 In the past you were spiritually dead because of your disobedience and sins. [2]At that time you followed the world's evil way; you obeyed the ruler of the spiritual powers in space, the spirit who now controls the people who disobey God. [3]Actually all of us were like them and lived according to our natural desires, doing whatever suited the wishes of our own bodies and minds. In our natural condition we, like everyone else, were destined to suffer God's anger.

4 But God's mercy is so abundant, and his love for us is so great, [5]that while we were spiritually dead in our disobedience he brought us to life with Christ. It is by God's grace that you have been saved. [6]In our union with Christ Jesus he raised us up with him to rule with him in the heavenly world. [7]He did this to demonstrate for all time to come the extraordinary greatness of his grace in the love he showed us in Christ Jesus. [8-9]For it is by God's grace that you have been saved through faith. It is not the result of your own efforts, but God's gift, so that no one can boast about it. [10]God has made us what we are, and in our union with Christ Jesus he has created us for a life of good deeds, which he has already prepared for us to do.

One in Christ

11 You Gentiles by birth – called "the uncircumcised" by the Jews, who call themselves "the circumcised" (which refers to what men do to their bodies) – remember what you were in the past. [12]At that time you were apart from Christ. You were foreigners and did not belong to God's chosen people. You had no part in the covenants, which were based on God's promises to his people, and you lived in this world without hope and without God. [13]But now, in union with Christ Jesus, you who used to be far away have been brought near by the blood[b] of

---

[a] **1.23** who himself completes all things everywhere; *or* who is himself completely filled with God's fullness.

[b] **2.13** by the blood of Christ; *or* by the sacrificial death of Christ.

A cathedral is the central church of the diocese (2.21–22)

Christ. ¹⁴For Christ himself has brought us peace by making Jews and Gentiles one people. With his own body he broke down the wall that separated them and kept them enemies. ¹⁵He abolished the Jewish Law with its commandments and rules, in order to create out of the two races one new people in union with himself, in this way making peace. ¹⁶By his death on the cross Christ destroyed their enmity; by means of the cross he united both races into one body and brought them back to God. ¹⁷So Christ came and preached the Good News of peace to all – to you Gentiles, who were far away from God, and to the Jews, who were near to him. ¹⁸It is through Christ that all of us, Jews and Gentiles, are able to come in the one Spirit into the presence of the Father.

19 So then, you Gentiles are not foreigners or strangers any longer; you are now fellow-citizens with God's people and members of the family of God. ²⁰You, too, are built upon the foundation laid by the apostles and prophets,^a the cornerstone being Christ Jesus himself. ²¹He is the one

---

^a **2.20** the foundation laid by the apostles and prophets; *or* the foundation, that is, the apostles and prophets.

who holds the whole building together and makes it grow into a sacred temple dedicated to the Lord. ²²In union with him you too are being built together with all the others into a place where God lives through his Spirit.

Paul's Work for the Gentiles

3 For this reason I, Paul, the prisoner of Christ Jesus for the sake of you Gentiles, pray to God. ²Surely you have heard that God in his grace has given me this work to do for your good. ³God revealed his secret plan and made it known to me. (I have written briefly about this, ⁴and if you will read what I have written, you can learn about my understanding of the secret of Christ.) ⁵In past times human beings were not told this secret, but God has revealed it now by the Spirit to his holy apostles and prophets. ⁶The secret is that by means of the gospel the Gentiles have a part with the Jews in God's blessings; they are members of the same body and share in the promise that God made through Christ Jesus.

7 I was made a servant of the gospel by God's special gift, which he gave me through the working of his power. ⁸I am less than the least of

all God's people; yet God gave me this privilege of taking to the Gentiles the Good News about the infinite riches of Christ, ⁹and of making all people see how God's secret plan is to be put into effect. God, who is the Creator of all things, kept his secret hidden through all the past ages, ¹⁰in order that at the present time, by means of the church, the angelic rulers and powers in the heavenly world might learn of his wisdom in all its different forms. ¹¹God did this according to his eternal purpose, which he achieved through Christ Jesus our Lord. ¹²In union with Christ and through our faith in him we have the boldness to go into God's presence with all confidence. ¹³I beg you, then, not to be discouraged because I am suffering for you; it is all for your benefit.

The Love of Christ

14   For this reason I fall on my knees before the Father, ¹⁵from whom every family in heaven and on earth receives its true name. ¹⁶I ask God from the wealth of his glory to give you power through his Spirit to be strong in your inner selves, ¹⁷and I pray that Christ will make his home in your hearts through faith. I pray that you may have your roots and foundation in love, ¹⁸so that you, together with all God's people, may have the power to understand how broad and long, how high and deep, is Christ's love. ¹⁹Yes, may you come to know his love – although it can never be fully known – and so be completely filled with the very nature of God.

20   To him who by means of his power working in us is able to do so much more than we can ever ask for, or even think of: ²¹to God be the glory in the church and in Christ Jesus for all time, for ever and ever! Amen.

The Unity of the Body

4 I urge you, then – I who am a prisoner because I serve the Lord: live a life that measures up to the standard God set when he called you. ²Be always humble, gentle, and patient. Show your love by being tolerant with one another. ³Do your best to preserve the unity which the Spirit gives by means of the peace that binds you together. ⁴There is one body and one Spirit, just as there is one hope to which God has called you. ⁵There is one Lord, one faith, one baptism; ⁶there is one God and Father of all, who is Lord of all, works through all, and is in all.

7   Each one of us has received a special gift in proportion to what Christ has given. ⁸As the scripture says:

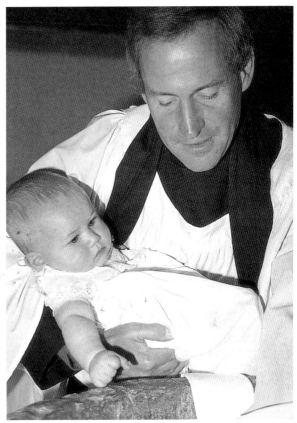

A baby is baptized by an Anglican vicar (4.5)

"When he went up to the very heights,
     he took many captives with him;
     he gave gifts to people."

⁹Now, what does "he went up" mean? It means that first he came down to the lowest depths of the earth.ᵃ ¹⁰So the one who came down is the same one who went up, above and beyond the heavens, to fill the whole universe with his presence. ¹¹It was he who "gave gifts"; he appointed some to be apostles, others to be prophets, others to be evangelists, others to be pastors and teachers. ¹²He did this to prepare all God's people for the work of Christian service, in order to build up the body of Christ. ¹³And so we shall all come together to that oneness in our faith and in our knowledge of the Son of God; we shall become mature people, reaching to the very height of Christ's full stature. ¹⁴Then we shall no longer be children, carried by the waves and blown about by every shifting wind of the teaching of deceitful people, who lead others into error by the tricks they invent. ¹⁵Instead, by

ᵃ **4.9** the lowest depths of the earth; *or* the lower depths, the earth itself.

Studying
EPHESIANS

Who wrote it? Tradition says Paul, but this is unlikely. Probably a follower of Paul, and it was linked to the apostle to give it authority.
When? Probably 65–75 CE.
Where from? No clues in book.
For whom? Probably began as a general letter circulated among many churches.
Why? The readers are Gentiles but they are told not to live as the Gentiles do. Writer reminds them they are now members of God's kingdom – and must live as such.

KEY POINTS

- God has a long-term plan for the human race – to save both Jews and Gentiles. Christians have become members of the Church of which Jesus is the cornerstone and which is built on the foundations of the prophets and the apostles (1.3—2.22).
- The responsibilities of parents and children, husbands and wives, slaves and owners (5.22—6.9).
- Each believer is encouraged to put on "the whole armour of God" in their struggle against the forces of darkness (6.10–20).

speaking the truth in a spirit of love, we must grow up in every way to Christ, who is the head. [16]Under his control all the different parts of the body fit together, and the whole body is held together by every joint with which it is provided. So when each separate part works as it should, the whole body grows and builds itself up through love.

The New Life in Christ

17 In the Lord's name, then, I warn you: do not continue to live like the heathen, whose thoughts are worthless [18]and whose minds are in the dark. They have no part in the life that God gives, for they are completely ignorant and stubborn. [19]They have lost all feeling of shame; they give themselves over to vice and do all sorts of indecent things without restraint.

20 That was not what you learnt about Christ! [21]You certainly heard about him, and as his followers you were taught the truth that is in Jesus. [22]So get rid of your old self, which made you live as you used to – the old self that was being destroyed by its deceitful desires. [23]Your hearts and minds must be made completely new, [24]and you must put on the new self, which is created in God's likeness and reveals itself in the true life that is upright and holy.

25 No more lying, then! Each of you must tell the truth to one another, because we are all members together in the body of Christ. [26]If you become angry, do not let your anger lead you into sin, and do not stay angry all day. [27]Don't give the Devil a chance. [28]Those who used to rob must stop robbing and start working, in order to earn an honest living for themselves and to be able to help the poor. [29]Do not use harmful words, but only helpful words, the kind that build up and provide what is needed, so that what you say will do good to those who hear you. [30]And do not make God's Holy Spirit sad; for the Spirit is God's mark of ownership on you, a guarantee that the Day will come when God will set you free. [31]Get rid of all bitterness, passion, and anger. No more shouting or insults, no more hateful feelings of any sort. [32]Instead, be kind and tender-hearted to one another, and forgive one another, as God has forgiven you through Christ.

Living in the Light

5 Since you are God's dear children, you must try to be like him. [2]Your life must be controlled by love, just as Christ loved us and gave his life for us as a sweet-smelling offering and sacrifice that pleases God.

3 Since you are God's people, it is not right that any matters of sexual immorality or indecency or greed should even be mentioned among you. [4]Nor is it fitting for you to use language which is obscene, profane, or vulgar. Rather you should give thanks to God. [5]You may be sure that no one who is immoral, indecent, or greedy (for greed is a form of idolatry) will ever receive a share in the Kingdom of Christ and of God.

6 Do not let anyone deceive you with foolish words; it is because of these very things that God's anger will come upon those who do not obey him. [7]So have nothing at all to do with such people. [8]You yourselves used to be in the darkness, but since you have become the Lord's people, you are in the light. So you must live like people who belong to the light, [9]for it is the light[a] that brings a rich harvest of every kind of goodness, righteousness, and truth. [10]Try to learn what pleases the Lord. [11]Have nothing to do with the worthless things that people do, things that belong to the darkness. Instead, bring them out to the light. [12](It is really too shameful even to talk about the things they do in secret.) [13]And when all things are brought out

---

[a] **5.9** the light; *some manuscripts have* the Spirit.

to the light, then their true nature is clearly revealed; [14]for anything that is clearly revealed becomes light.[a] That is why it is said:

"Wake up, sleeper,
    and rise from death,
and Christ will shine on you."

15 So be careful how you live. Don't live like ignorant people, but like wise people. [16]Make good use of every opportunity you have, because these are evil days. [17]Don't be fools, then, but try to find out what the Lord wants you to do.

18 Do not get drunk with wine, which will only ruin you; instead, be filled with the Spirit. [19]Speak to one another with the words of psalms, hymns, and sacred songs; sing hymns and psalms to the Lord with praise in your hearts. [20]In the name of our Lord Jesus Christ, always give thanks for everything to God the Father.

Wives and Husbands

21 Submit yourselves to one another because of your reverence for Christ.

22 Wives, submit to your husbands as to the Lord. [23]For a husband has authority over his wife just as Christ has authority over the church; and Christ is himself the Saviour of the church, his body. [24]And so wives must submit completely to their husbands just as the church submits itself to Christ.

25 Husbands, love your wives just as Christ loved the church and gave his life for it. [26]He did this to dedicate the church to God by his word, after making it clean by washing it in water, [27]in order to present the church to himself in all its beauty – pure and faultless, without spot or wrinkle or any other imperfection. [28]Men ought to love their wives just as they love their own bodies. A man who loves his wife loves himself. [29](People never hate their own bodies. Instead, they feed them and take care of them, just as Christ does the church; [30]for we are members of his body.) [31]As the scripture says, "For this reason a man will leave his father and mother and unite with his wife, and the two will become one." [32]There is a deep secret truth revealed in this scripture, which I understand as applying to Christ and the church. [33]But it also applies to you: every husband must love his wife as himself, and every wife must respect her husband.

Children and Parents

 Children, it is your Christian duty to[b] obey your parents, for this is the right thing to do. [2]"Respect your father and mother" is the first commandment that has a promise added: [3]"so that all may go well with you, and you may live a long time in the land."

4 Parents, do not treat your children in such a way as to make them angry. Instead, bring them up with Christian discipline and instruction.

Slaves and Masters

5 Slaves, obey your human masters with fear and trembling; and do it with a sincere heart, as though you were serving Christ. [6]Do this not only when they are watching you, because you want to gain their approval; but with all your heart do what God wants, as slaves of Christ. [7]Do your work as slaves cheerfully, as though you served the Lord, and not merely human beings. [8]Remember that the Lord will reward everyone, whether slave or free, for the good work they do.

9 Masters, behave in the same way towards your slaves and stop using threats. Remember that you and your slaves belong to the same Master in heaven, who judges everyone by the same standard.

The Whole Armour of God

10 Finally, build up your strength in union with the Lord and by means of his mighty power. [11]Put on all the armour that God gives you, so that you will be able to stand up against the Devil's evil tricks. [12]For we are not fighting against human beings but against the wicked spiritual forces in the heavenly world, the rulers, authorities, and cosmic powers of this dark age. [13]So put on God's armour now! Then when the evil day comes, you will be able to resist the enemy's attacks; and after fighting to the end, you will still hold your ground.

14 So stand ready, with truth as a belt tight round your waist, with righteousness as your breastplate, [15]and as your shoes the readiness to announce the Good News of peace. [16]At all times carry faith as a shield; for with it you will be able to put out all the burning arrows shot by the Evil One. [17]And accept salvation as a helmet, and the word of God as the sword which the Spirit gives you. [18]Do all this in

---

[a] **5.14** anything that is clearly revealed becomes light; *or* it is light that clearly reveals everything.

[b] **6.1** *Some manuscripts do not have* it is your Christian duty to.

prayer, asking for God's help. Pray on every occasion, as the Spirit leads. For this reason keep alert and never give up; pray always for all God's people. [19]And pray also for me, that God will give me a message when I am ready to speak, so that I may speak boldly and make known the gospel's secret. [20]For the sake of this gospel I am an ambassador, though now I am in prison. Pray that I may be bold in speaking about the gospel as I should.

Final Greetings

21 Tychicus, our dear brother and faithful servant in the Lord's work, will give you all the news about me, so that you may know how I am getting on. [22]That is why I am sending him to you – to tell you how all of us are getting on, and to encourage you.

23 May God the Father and the Lord Jesus Christ give to all Christian brothers and sisters peace and love with faith. [24]May God's grace be with all those who love our Lord Jesus Christ with undying love.

Paul's Letter to the
PHILIPPIANS

INTRODUCTION

Paul's Letter to the Philippians was written to the first church that Paul established on European soil, in the Roman province of Macedonia. It was written while the apostle was in prison, and at a time when he was troubled by the opposition of other Christian workers towards himself and was distressed by false teaching in the church at Philippi. Yet this letter breathes a joy and confidence that can be explained only by Paul's deep faith in Jesus Christ.

The immediate reason for writing the letter was to thank the Philippian Christians for the gift which they had sent to help him in his time of need. He uses this opportunity to reassure them, so that they may have courage and confidence in spite of all his troubles and their own as well. He pleads with them to have the humble attitude of Jesus, rather than to be controlled by selfish ambition and pride. He reminds them that their life in union with Christ is a gift of God's grace which they have received through faith, not through obedience to the ceremonies of the Jewish Law. He writes of the joy and peace that God gives to those who live in union with Christ.

This letter is marked by its emphasis on joy, confidence, unity, and perseverance in the Christian faith and life. It also reveals the deep affection Paul had for the church at Philippi.

1 From Paul and Timothy, servants of Christ Jesus –

To all God's people in Philippi who are in union with Christ Jesus, including the church leaders and helpers:

2 May God our Father and the Lord Jesus Christ give you grace and peace.

Paul's Prayer for his Readers

3 I thank my God for you every time I think of you; 4and every time I pray for you all, I pray with joy 5because of the way in which you have helped me in the work of the gospel from the very first day until now. 6And so I am sure that God, who began this good work in you, will carry it on until it is finished on the Day of Christ Jesus. 7You are always in my heart! And so it is only right for me to feel as I do about you. For you have all shared with me in this privilege that God has given me, both now that I am in prison and also while I was free to defend the gospel and establish it firmly. 8God is my witness that I am telling the truth when I say that my deep feeling for you all comes from the heart of Christ Jesus himself.

9 I pray that your love will keep on growing more and more, together with true knowledge and perfect judgement, 10so that you will be able to choose what is best. Then you will be free from all impurity and blame on the Day of Christ. 11Your lives will be filled with the truly good qualities which only Jesus Christ can produce, for the glory and praise of God.

Studying
PHILIPPIANS

Who wrote it? Paul.
When? Evident that it was written from prison. Likely date is 61 CE.
Where from? Could have been written from Ephesus or Caesarea but most likely that Paul was in Rome. Probably written when Paul was under house-arrest (Acts 28.14–31).
For whom? For the Christians in Philippi – a prosperous city in which inhabitants were Roman citizens. There was a very small Jewish presence in the city.
Why? Main purpose was to thank the Philippians for the gift they had sent him while he was in prison. They also prayed for him.

KEY POINTS

- The Philippians are encouraged to stand firm during persecution – and to rejoice in their circumstances. This was what Paul did (1.27–30).
- The Philippians are encouraged to be both humble and united (2.1–11). In this way they are following the example of Jesus.
- The Philippians are told to resist the Judaizers who would encourage them to follow Jewish traditions.

To Live is Christ

12 I want you to know, my brothers and sisters, that the things that have happened to me have really helped the progress of the gospel. [13]As a result, the whole palace guard and all the others here know that I am in prison because I am a servant of Christ. [14]And my being in prison has given most of the brothers and sisters more confidence in the Lord, so that they grow bolder all the time to preach the message[a] fearlessly.

15 Of course some of them preach Christ because they are jealous and quarrelsome, but others from genuine goodwill. [16]These do so from love, because they know that God has given me the work of defending the gospel. [17]The others do not proclaim Christ sincerely, but from a spirit of selfish ambition; they think that they will make more trouble for me while I am in prison.

18 It does not matter! I am happy about it – so long as Christ is preached in every way possible, whether from wrong or right motives. And I will continue to be happy, [19]because I know that by means of your prayers and the help which comes from the Spirit of Jesus Christ I shall be set free. [20]My deep desire and hope is that I shall never fail in my duty, but that at all times, and

---

[a] **1.14** the message; *some manuscripts have* God's message.

especially just now, I shall be full of courage, so that with my whole being I shall bring honour to Christ, whether I live or die. [21]For what is life? To me, it is Christ. Death, then, will bring more. [22]But if by continuing to live I can do more worthwhile work, then I am not sure which I should choose. [23]I am pulled in two directions. I want very much to leave this life and be with Christ, which is a far better thing; [24]but for your sake it is much more important that I remain alive. [25]I am sure of this, and so I know that I will stay. I will stay on with you all, to add to your progress and joy in the faith, [26]so that when I am with you again, you will have even more reason to be proud of me in your life in union with Christ Jesus.

27 Now, the important thing is that your way of life should be as the gospel of Christ requires, so that, whether or not I am able to go and see you, I will hear that you are standing firm with one common purpose and that with only one desire you are fighting together for the faith of the gospel. [28]Don't be afraid of your enemies; always be courageous, and this will prove to them that they will lose and that you will win, because it is God who gives you the victory. [29]For you have been given the privilege of serving Christ, not only by believing in him, but also by suffering for him. [30]Now you can take part with me in the battle. It is the same battle you saw me fighting in the past, and as you hear, the one I am fighting still.

Christ's Humility and Greatness

2 Your life in Christ makes you strong, and his love comforts you. You have fellowship with the Spirit,[b] and you have kindness and compassion for one another. [2]I urge you, then, to make me completely happy by having the same thoughts, sharing the same love, and being one in soul and mind. [3]Don't do anything from selfish ambition or from a cheap desire to boast, but be humble towards one another, always considering others better than yourselves. [4]And look out for one another's interests, not just for your own. [5]The attitude you should have is the one that Christ Jesus had:

6 He always had the nature of God,
but he did not think that by force he
should try to remain[c] equal with God.

---

[b] **2.1** You have fellowship with the Spirit; *or* The Spirit has brought you into fellowship with one another.
[c] **2.6** remain; *or* become.

7   Instead of this, of his own free will he gave
       up all he had,
       and took the nature of a servant.
       He became like a human being
       and appeared in human likeness.

8   He was humble and walked the path of
       obedience all the way to death –
       his death on the cross.

9   For this reason God raised him to the highest
       place above
       and gave him the name that is greater
       than any other name.

10   And so, in honour of the name of Jesus
       all beings in heaven, on earth, and in the
       world below[a]
       will fall on their knees,

11   and all will openly proclaim that Jesus Christ
       is Lord,
       to the glory of God the Father.

Shining as Lights in the World

12   So then, dear friends, as you always obeyed me when I was with you, it is even more important that you obey me now while I am away from you. Keep on working with fear and trembling to complete your salvation, [13]because God is always at work in you to make you willing and able to obey his own purpose.

14   Do everything without complaining or arguing, [15]so that you may be innocent and pure as God's perfect children, who live in a world of corrupt and sinful people. You must shine among them like stars lighting up the sky, [16]as you offer them the message of life. If you do so, I shall have reason to be proud of you on the Day of Christ, because it will show that all my effort and work have not been wasted.

17   Perhaps my life's blood is to be poured out like an offering on the sacrifice that your faith offers to God. If that is so, I am glad and share my joy with you all. [18]In the same way, you too must be glad and share your joy with me.

Timothy and Epaphroditus

19   If it is the Lord's will, I hope that I will be able to send Timothy to you soon, so that I may be encouraged by news about you. [20]He is the only one who shares my feelings and who really cares about you. [21]All the others are concerned only with their own affairs, not with the cause of Jesus Christ. [22]And you yourselves know how he has proved his worth, how he and I, like a son and his father, have worked together for the sake of the gospel. [23]So I hope to send him to you as soon as I know how things are going to turn out for me. [24]And I trust in the Lord that I myself will be able to come to you soon.

25   I have thought it necessary to send you our brother Epaphroditus, who has worked and fought by my side and who has served as your messenger in helping me. [26]He is anxious to see you all and is very upset because you had heard that he was ill. [27]Indeed he was ill and almost died. But God had pity on him, and not only on him but on me, too, and spared me an even greater sorrow. [28]I am all the more eager, then, to send him to you, so that you will be glad again when you see him, and my own sorrow will disappear. [29]Receive him, then, with joy, as a brother in the Lord. Show respect to all such people as he, [30]because he risked his life and nearly died for the sake of the work of Christ, in order to give me the help that you yourselves could not give.

The True Righteousness

3 In conclusion, my brothers and sisters, be joyful in your union with the Lord. I don't mind repeating what I have written before, and you will be safer if I do so. [2]Watch out for those who do evil things, those dogs, those who insist on cutting the body. [3]It is we, not they, who have received the true circumcision, for we worship God by means of his Spirit and rejoice in our life in union with Christ Jesus. We do not put any trust in external ceremonies. [4]I could, of course, put my trust in such things. If anyone thinks they can trust in external ceremonies, I have even more reason to feel that way. [5]I was circumcised when I was a week old. I am an Israelite by birth, of the tribe of Benjamin, a pure-blooded Hebrew. As far as keeping the Jewish Law is concerned, I was a Pharisee, [6]and I was so zealous that I persecuted the church. As far as a person can be righteous by obeying the commands of the Law, I was without fault. [7]But all those things that I might count as profit I now reckon as loss for Christ's sake. [8]Not only those things; I reckon everything as complete loss for the sake of what is so much more valuable, the knowledge of Christ Jesus my Lord. For his sake I have thrown everything away; I consider it all as mere refuse, so that I may gain Christ [9]and be completely united with him. I no longer have a righteousness of my own, the kind that is

---

[a] **2.10** WORLD BELOW: *It was thought that the dead continued to exist in a dark world under the ground.*

gained by obeying the Law. I now have the righteousness that is given through faith in Christ, the righteousness that comes from God and is based on faith. [10]All I want is to know Christ and to experience the power of his resurrection, to share in his sufferings and become like him in his death, [11]in the hope that I myself will be raised from death to life.

Running towards the Goal

12   I do not claim that I have already succeeded or have already become perfect. I keep striving to win the prize for which Christ Jesus has already won me to himself. [13]Of course, my brothers and sisters, I really do not[a] think that I have already won it; the one thing I do, however, is to forget what is behind me and do my best to reach what is ahead. [14]So I run straight towards the goal in order to win the prize, which is God's call through Christ Jesus to the life above.

15   All of us who are spiritually mature should have this same attitude. But if some of you have a different attitude, God will make this clear to you. [16]However that may be, let us go forward according to the same rules we have followed until now.

17   Keep on imitating me, my brothers and sisters. Pay attention to those who follow the right example that we have set for you. [18]I have told you this many times before, and now I repeat it with tears: there are many whose lives make them enemies of Christ's death on the cross. [19]They are going to end up in hell, because their god is their bodily desires. They are proud of what they should be ashamed of, and they think only of things that belong to this world. [20]We, however, are citizens of heaven, and we eagerly wait for our Saviour, the Lord Jesus Christ, to come from heaven. [21]He will change our weak mortal bodies and make them like his own glorious body, using that power by which he is able to bring all things under his rule.

Instructions

4   So then, my brothers and sisters, how dear you are to me and how I miss you! How happy you make me, and how proud I am of you! This then, dear brothers and sisters, is how you should stand firm in your life in the Lord.

2   Euodia and Syntyche, please, I beg you, try to agree as sisters in the Lord. [3]And you too, my faithful partner, I want you to help these women; for they have worked hard with me to spread the gospel, together with Clement and all my other fellow-workers, whose names are in God's book of the living.

4   May you always be joyful in your union with the Lord. I say it again: rejoice!

5   Show a gentle attitude towards everyone. The Lord is coming soon. [6]Don't worry about anything, but in all your prayers ask God for what you need, always asking him with a thankful heart. [7]And God's peace, which is far beyond human understanding, will keep your hearts and minds safe in union with Christ Jesus.

8   In conclusion, my brothers and sisters, fill your minds with those things that are good and that deserve praise: things that are true, noble, right, pure, lovely, and honourable. [9]Put into practice what you learnt and received from me, both from my words and from my actions. And the God who gives us peace will be with you.

Prayer is a very important part of Christian worship (4.6)

---

[a] **3.13** not; *some manuscripts have* not yet.

Thanks for the Gift

10   In my life in union with the Lord it is a great joy to me that after so long a time you once more had the chance of showing that you care for me. I don't mean that you had stopped caring for me – you just had no chance to show it. [11]And I am not saying this because I feel neglected, for I have learnt to be satisfied with what I have. [12]I know what it is to be in need and what it is to have more than enough. I have learnt this secret, so that anywhere, at any time, I am content, whether I am full or hungry, whether I have too much or too little. [13]I have the strength to face all conditions by the power that Christ gives me.

14   But it was very good of you to help me in my troubles. [15]You Philippians know very well that when I left Macedonia in the early days of preaching the Good News, you were the only church to help me; you were the only ones who shared my profits and losses. [16]More than once when I needed help in Thessalonica, you sent it to me. [17]It is not that I just want to receive gifts; rather, I want to see profit added to your account. [18]Here, then, is my receipt for everything you have given me – and it has been more than enough! I have all I need now that Epaphroditus has brought me all your gifts. They are like a sweet-smelling offering to God, a sacrifice which is acceptable and pleasing to him. [19]And with all his abundant wealth through Christ Jesus, my God will supply all your needs. [20]To our God and Father be the glory for ever and ever! Amen.

Final Greetings

21   Greetings to each one of God's people who belong to Christ Jesus. The brothers and sisters here with me send you their greetings. [22]All God's people here send greetings, especially those who belong to the Emperor's palace.

23   May the grace of the Lord Jesus Christ be with you all.

Paul's Letter to the
COLOSSIANS

INTRODUCTION

Paul's Letter to the Colossians was written to the church at Colossae, a town in Asia Minor east of Ephesus. This church had not been established by Paul, but was in an area for which Paul felt responsible, as he sent out workers from Ephesus, the capital of the Roman province of Asia. Paul had learnt that there were false teachers in the church at Colossae who insisted that in order to know God and have full salvation one must worship certain "spiritual rulers and authorities". In addition, these teachers said, one must submit to special rites such as circumcision and must observe strict rules about foods and other matters.

Paul writes to oppose these teachings with the true Christian message. The heart of his reply is that Jesus Christ is able to give full salvation and that these other beliefs and practices actually lead away from him. Through Christ, God created the world and through him he is bringing it back to himself. Only in union with Christ is there hope of salvation for the world. Paul then spells out the implications of this great teaching for the lives of believers.

It is noteworthy that Tychicus, who took this letter to Colossae for Paul, was accompanied by Onesimus, the slave on whose behalf Paul wrote his letter to Philemon.

Outline of Contents

1 From Paul, who by God's will is an apostle of Christ Jesus, and from our brother Timothy –

2 To God's people in Colossae, who are our faithful brothers and sisters in union with Christ:
May God our Father give you grace and peace.

Prayer of Thanksgiving

3 We always give thanks to God, the Father of our Lord Jesus Christ, when we pray for you. [4]For we have heard of your faith in Christ Jesus and of your love for all God's people. [5]When the true message, the Good News, first came to you, you heard about the hope it offers. So your faith and love are based on what you hope for, which is kept safe for you in heaven. [6]The gospel keeps bringing blessings and is spreading throughout the world, just as it has among you ever since the day you first heard about the grace of God and came to know it as it really is. [7]You learnt of God's grace from Epaphras, our dear fellow-servant, who is Christ's faithful worker on our[a] behalf. [8]He has told us of the love that the Spirit has given you.

9 For this reason we have always prayed for you, ever since we heard about you. We ask God to fill you with the knowledge of his will, with all the wisdom and understanding that his Spirit gives. [10]Then you will be able to live as the Lord wants and will always do what pleases him. Your lives will produce all kinds of good deeds, and you will grow in your knowledge of God. [11-12]May you be made strong with all the strength which comes from his glorious power, so that you may be able to endure everything

---

[a] **1.7** our; *some manuscripts have* your.

226

with patience. And with joy give thanks to[a] the Father, who has made you fit to have your share of what God has reserved for his people in the kingdom of light. [13]He rescued us from the power of darkness and brought us safe into the kingdom of his dear Son, [14]by whom we are set free, that is, our sins are forgiven.

The Person and Work of Christ

15   Christ is the visible likeness of the invisible God. He is the firstborn Son, superior to all created things. [16]For through him God created everything in heaven and on earth, the seen and the unseen things, including spiritual powers, lords, rulers, and authorities. God created the whole universe through him and for him. [17]Christ existed before all things, and in union with him all things have their proper place. [18]He is the head of his body, the church; he is the source of the body's life. He is the firstborn Son, who was raised from death, in order that he alone might have the first place in all things. [19]For it was by God's own decision that the Son has in himself the full nature of God. [20]Through

Christians drinking wine from a chalice at Holy Communion, a reminder of the death of Jesus (1.20)

the Son, then, God decided to bring the whole universe back to himself. God made peace through his Son's blood[b] on the cross and so brought back to himself all things, both on earth and in heaven.

21   At one time you were far away from God and were his enemies because of the evil things you did and thought. [22]But now, by means of the physical death of his Son, God has made you his friends, in order to bring you, holy, pure, and faultless, into his presence. [23]You must, of course, continue faithful on a firm and sure foundation, and must not allow yourselves to be shaken from the hope you gained when you heard the gospel. It is of this gospel that I, Paul, became a servant – this gospel which has been preached to everybody in the world.

Paul's Work as a Servant of the Church

24   And now I am happy about my sufferings for you, for by means of my physical sufferings I am helping to complete what still remains of Christ's sufferings on behalf of his body, the church. [25]And I have been made a servant of the church by God, who gave me this task to perform for your good. It is the task of fully proclaiming his message, [26]which is the secret he hid through all past ages from all the human race but has now revealed to his people. [27]God's plan is to make known his secret to his people, this rich and glorious secret which he has for all peoples. And the secret is that Christ is in you, which means that you will share in the glory of God. [28]So we preach Christ to everyone. With all possible wisdom we warn and teach them in order to bring each one into God's presence as a mature individual in union with Christ. [29]To get this done I toil and struggle, using the mighty strength which Christ supplies and which is at work in me.

2 Let me tell you how hard I have worked for you and for the people in Laodicea and for all others who do not know me personally. [2]I do this in order that they may be filled with courage and may be drawn together in love, and so have the full wealth of assurance which true understanding brings. In this way they will know God's secret, which is Christ himself.[c] [3]He is the key that opens all the hidden treasures of God's wisdom and knowledge.

[b] **1.20** his Son's blood; *or* his Son's sacrificial death.
[c] **2.2** God's secret, which is Christ himself; *some manuscripts have* God's secret; *others have* the secret of God the Father of Christ; *others have* the secret of the God and Father, and of Christ.

[a] **1.11–12** with patience. And with joy give thanks to; *or* with patience and joy. And give thanks to.

Studying
COLOSSIANS

Who wrote it? Almost certainly written by Paul during his first imprisonment when he was under house arrest (Acts 28.16–31).
When? About 60–61 CE.
Where from? Almost certainly Rome but just possibly Ephesus.
For whom? The Christians in Colossae. Paul had not founded the church in Colossae. Most of its members were Gentiles.
Why? There was false teaching in the church at Colossae which greatly worried the writer. We do not know exactly what it was. It had strict rules, worshipped angels, encouraged "secret knowledge" and relied on human wisdom. The writer opposed these teachings strongly.

KEY POINTS

- Jesus Christ is foremost. He is the image of God; supreme over creation; head of the Church – the new creation – and has risen from the dead never to die again (1.15–18).
- Jewish traditions are not important when placed alongside Christ. The worship of angels only leads to human pride.
- Christians are joined with Christ in his death, resurrection and ascension. They have died to their old life so that they live in God.

4   I tell you, then, do not let anyone deceive you with false arguments, no matter how good they seem to be. ⁵For even though I am absent in body, yet I am with you in spirit, and I am glad as I see the resolute firmness with which you stand together in your faith in Christ.

Fullness of Life in Christ

6   Since you have accepted Christ Jesus as Lord, live in union with him. ⁷Keep your roots deep in him, build your lives on him, and become stronger in your faith, as you were taught. And be filled with thanksgiving.

8   See to it, then, that no one enslaves you by means of the worthless deceit of human wisdom, which comes from the teachings handed down by human beings and from the ruling spirits of the universe, and not from Christ. ⁹For the full content of divine nature lives in Christ, in his humanity, ¹⁰and you have been given full life in union with him. He is supreme over every spiritual ruler and authority.

11   In union with Christ you were circumcised, not with the circumcision that is made by human beings, but with the circumcision made by Christ, which consists of being freed from the power of this sinful self. ¹²For when you were baptized, you were buried with Christ, and in baptism you were also raised with Christ through your faith in the active power of God, who raised him from death. ¹³You were at one time spiritually dead because of your sins and because you were Gentiles without the Law. But God has now brought you to life with Christ. God forgave us all our sins; ¹⁴he cancelled the unfavourable record of our debts with its binding rules and did away with it completely by nailing it to the cross. ¹⁵And on that cross Christ freed himself from the power of the spiritual rulers and authorities;ᵃ he made a public spectacle of them by leading them as captives in his victory procession.

16   So let no one make rules about what you eat or drink or about holy days or the New Moon Festival or the Sabbath. ¹⁷All such things are only a shadow of things in the future; the reality is Christ. ¹⁸Do not allow yourselves to be condemned by anyone who claims to be superior because of special visions and who insists on false humility and the worship of angels. For no reason at all, such people are all puffed up by their human way of thinking ¹⁹and have stopped holding on to Christ, who is the head of the body. Under Christ's control the whole body is nourished and held together by its joints and ligaments, and it grows as God wants it to grow.

Dying and Living with Christ

20   You have died with Christ and are set free from the ruling spirits of the universe. Why, then, do you live as though you belonged to this world? Why do you obey such rules as ²¹"Don't handle this," "Don't taste that," "Don't touch the other"? ²²All these refer to things which become useless once they are used; they are only human rules and teachings. ²³Of course such rules appear to be based on wisdom in their forced worship of angels, and false humility, and severe treatment of the body; but they have no real value in controlling physical passions.

3   You have been raised to life with Christ, so set your hearts on the things that are in heaven, where Christ sits on his throne at the right-hand side of God. ²Keep your minds fixed on things there, not on things here on earth. ³For you have died, and your life is hidden

---

ᵃ **2.15** Christ freed himself from the power of the spiritual rulers and authorities; *or* Christ stripped the spiritual rulers and authorities of their power.

with Christ in God. [4]Your real life is Christ and when he appears, then you too will appear with him and share his glory!

The Old Life and the New

5 You must put to death, then, the earthly desires at work in you, such as sexual immorality, indecency, lust, evil passions, and greed (for greed is a form of idolatry). [6]Because of such things God's anger will come upon those who do not obey him.[a] [7]At one time you yourselves used to live according to such desires, when your life was dominated by them.

8 But now you must get rid of all these things: anger, passion, and hateful feelings. No insults or obscene talk must ever come from your lips. [9]Do not lie to one another, for you have taken off the old self with its habits [10]and have put on the new self. This is the new being which God, its Creator, is constantly renewing in his own image, in order to bring you to a full knowledge of himself. [11]As a result, there is no longer any distinction between Gentiles and Jews, circumcised and uncircumcised, barbarians, savages, slaves, and free, but Christ is all, Christ is in all.

12 You are the people of God; he loved you and chose you for his own. So then, you must clothe yourselves with compassion, kindness, humility, gentleness, and patience. [13]Be tolerant with one another and forgive one another whenever any of you has a complaint against someone else. You must forgive one another just as the Lord has forgiven you. [14]And to all these qualities add love, which binds all things together in perfect unity. [15]The peace that Christ gives is to guide you in the decisions you make; for it is to this peace that God has called you together in the one body. And be thankful. [16]Christ's message in all its richness must live in your hearts. Teach and instruct each other with all wisdom. Sing psalms, hymns, and sacred songs; sing to God with thanksgiving in your hearts. [17]Everything you do or say, then, should be done in the name of the Lord Jesus, as you give thanks through him to God the Father.

Personal Relations in the New Life

18 Wives, submit to your husbands, for that is what you should do as Christians.

19 Husbands, love your wives and do not be harsh with them.

---

[a] **3.6** *Some manuscripts do not have* upon those who do not obey him.

20 Children, it is your Christian duty to obey your parents always, for that is what pleases God.

21 Parents, do not irritate your children, or they will become discouraged.

22 Slaves, obey your human masters in all things, not only when they are watching you because you want to gain their approval; but do it with a sincere heart because of your reverence for the Lord. [23]Whatever you do, work at it with all your heart, as though you were working for the Lord and not for human beings. [24]Remember that the Lord will give you as a reward what he has kept for his people. For Christ is the real Master you serve. [25]And wrongdoers will be repaid for the wrong things they do, because God judges everyone by the same standard.

 4 Masters, be fair and just in the way you treat your slaves. Remember that you too have a Master in heaven.

Instructions

2 Be persistent in prayer, and keep alert as you pray, giving thanks to God. [3]At the same time pray also for us, so that God will give us a good opportunity to preach his message about the secret of Christ. For that is why I am now in prison. [4]Pray, then, that I may speak, as I should, in such a way as to make it clear.

5 Be wise in the way you act towards those who are not believers, making good use of every opportunity you have. [6]Your speech should always be pleasant and interesting, and you should know how to give the right answer to everyone.

Paul encouraged Christians to be persistent and alert in their praying (4.2)

Final Greetings

7 Our dear brother Tychicus, who is a faithful worker and fellow-servant in the Lord's work, will give you all the news about me. [8]That is why I am sending him to you, in order to cheer you up by telling you how all of us are getting on. [9]With him goes Onesimus, that dear and faithful brother, who belongs to your group. They will tell you everything that is happening here.

10 Aristarchus, who is in prison with me, sends you greetings, and so does Mark, the cousin of Barnabas. (You have already received instructions to welcome Mark if he comes your way.) [11]Joshua, also called Justus, sends greetings too. These three are the only Jewish believers who work with me for the Kingdom of God, and they have been a great help to me.

12 Greetings from Epaphras, another member of your group and a servant of Christ Jesus. He always prays fervently for you, asking God to make you stand firm, as mature and fully convinced Christians, in complete obedience to God's will. [13]I can personally testify to his hard work for you and for the people in Laodicea and Hierapolis. [14]Luke, our dear doctor, and Demas send you their greetings.

15 Give our best wishes to the brothers and sisters in Laodicea and to Nympha and the church that meets in her house.[a] [16]After you read this letter, make sure that it is read also in the church at Laodicea. At the same time, you are to read the letter that the brothers and sisters in Laodicea will send you. [17]And say to Archippus, "Be sure to finish the task you were given in the Lord's service."

18 With my own hand I write this: *Greetings from Paul*. Do not forget my chains!

May God's grace be with you.

---

[a] **4.15** Nympha ... her house; *some manuscripts have* Nymphas ... his house.

Paul's First Letter to the THESSALONIANS

INTRODUCTION

Thessalonica was the capital city of the Roman province of Macedonia. Paul established a church there after he left Philippi. Soon, however, there was opposition from Jews who were jealous of Paul's success in preaching the Christian message among the non-Jews who had become interested in Judaism. Paul was forced to leave Thessalonica and go on to Berea. Later on, after he reached Corinth, Paul received a personal report from his companion and fellow-worker Timothy about the situation in the church at Thessalonica.

Paul's First Letter to the Thessalonians was then written to encourage and reassure the Christians there. He gives thanks for the news about their faith and love; he reminds them of the kind of life he had lived while he was with them, and then answers questions that had arisen in the church about the return of Christ: could a believer who died before Christ's return still share in the eternal life that his return will bring? And when will Christ come again? Paul takes this occasion to tell them to go on working quietly while waiting in hope for Christ's return.

Outline of Contents

1 From Paul, Silas, and Timothy –
To the people of the church in Thessalonica, who belong to God the Father and the Lord Jesus Christ:
May grace and peace be yours.

The Life and Faith of the Thessalonians

2 We always thank God for you all and always mention you in our prayers. ³For we remember before our God and Father how you put your faith into practice, how your love made you work so hard, and how your hope in our Lord Jesus Christ is firm. ⁴Our brothers and sisters, we know that God loves you and has chosen you to be his own. ⁵For we brought the Good News to you, not with words only, but also with power and the Holy Spirit, and with complete conviction of its truth. You know how we lived when we were with you; it was for your own good. ⁶You imitated us and the Lord; and even though you suffered much, you received the message with the joy that comes from the Holy Spirit. ⁷So you became an example to all believers in Macedonia and Achaia. ⁸For not only did the message about the Lord go out from you throughout Macedonia and Achaia, but the news about your faith in God has gone everywhere. There is nothing, then, that we need to say. ⁹All those people speak about how you received us when we visited you, and how you turned away from idols to God, to serve the true and living God ¹⁰and to wait for his Son to come from heaven – his Son Jesus, whom he raised from death and who rescues us from God's anger that is coming.

Paul's Work in Thessalonica

 Our brothers and sisters, you yourselves know that our visit to you was not a failure. ²You know how we had already been

231

Studying
1 THESSALONIANS

Who wrote it? Paul.
When? Probably 51 CE, making it the oldest book in the New Testament and Paul's first letter.
Where from? Corinth.
For whom? The church in Thessalonica, a port on the northern shore of the Aegean Sea.
Why? Paul founded the church in Thessalonica but they were forced to leave the city after Jewish opposition. Timothy returned to city and brought Paul news that church was wondering why he had not returned.

KEY POINTS

- Paul makes little reference to the Jewish Scriptures.
- Christians should live their lives knowing that Jesus could return to earth at any time (4.1—5.11)
- The importance of the Christian community strengthening one another in their Christian lives (5.12–22).

ill-treated and insulted in Philippi before we came to you in Thessalonica. And even though there was much opposition, our God gave us courage to tell you the Good News that comes from him. ³Our appeal to you is not based on error or impure motives, nor do we try to trick anyone. ⁴Instead, we always speak as God wants us to, because he has judged us worthy to be entrusted with the Good News. We do not try to please people, but to please God, who tests our motives. ⁵You know very well that we did not come to you with flattering talk, nor did we use words to cover up greed – God is our witness! ⁶We did not try to get praise from anyone, either from you or from others, ⁷even though as apostles of Christ we could have made demands on you. But we were gentle when we were with you, like a mother[a] taking care of her children. ⁸Because of our love for you we were ready to share with you not only the Good News from God but even our own lives. You were so dear to us! ⁹Surely you remember, our brothers and sisters, how we worked and toiled! We worked day and night so that we would not be any trouble to you as we preached to you the Good News from God.

10   You are our witnesses, and so is God, that our conduct towards you who believe was pure, right, and without fault. ¹¹You know that we treated each one of you just as a father treats his own children. ¹²We encouraged you, we

---

[a] **2.7** we were gentle when we were with you, like a mother; *some manuscripts have* we were like children when we were with you; we were like a mother.

comforted you, and we kept urging you to live the kind of life that pleases God, who calls you to share in his own Kingdom and glory.

13   And there is another reason why we always give thanks to God. When we brought you God's message, you heard it and accepted it, not as a message from human beings but as God's message, which indeed it is. For God is at work in you who believe. ¹⁴Our brothers and sisters, the same things happened to you that happened to the churches of God in Judea, to the people there who belong to Christ Jesus. You suffered the same persecutions from your own people that they suffered from the Jews, ¹⁵who killed the Lord Jesus and the prophets, and persecuted us. How displeasing they are to God! How hostile they are to everyone! ¹⁶They even tried to stop us from preaching to the Gentiles the message that would bring them salvation. In this way they have brought to completion all the sins they have always committed. And now God's anger has at last come down on them!

Paul's Desire to Visit them Again

17   As for us, brothers and sisters, when we were separated from you for a little while – not in our thoughts, of course, but only in body – how we missed you and how hard we tried to see you again! ¹⁸We wanted to return to you. I myself tried to go back more than once, but Satan would not let us. ¹⁹After all, it is you – you, no less than others! – who are our hope, our joy, and our reason for boasting of our victory in the presence of our Lord Jesus when he comes. ²⁰Indeed, you are our pride and our joy!

3 Finally, we could not bear it any longer. So we decided to stay on alone in Athens ²while we sent Timothy, our brother who works with us for God in preaching the Good News about Christ. We sent him to strengthen you and help your faith, ³so that none of you should turn back because of these persecutions. You yourselves know that such persecutions are part of God's will for us. ⁴For while we were still with you, we told you beforehand that we were going to be persecuted; and as you well know, that is exactly what happened. ⁵That is why I had to send Timothy. I could not bear it any longer, so I sent him to find out about your faith. Surely it could not be that the Devil had tempted you and all our work had been for nothing!

6   Now Timothy has come back, and he has brought us the welcome news about your faith and love. He has told us that you always think well of us and that you want to see us just as

much as we want to see you. [7]So, in all our trouble and suffering we have been encouraged about you, brothers and sisters. It was your faith that encouraged us, [8]because now we really live if you stand firm in your life in union with the Lord. [9]Now we can give thanks to our God for you. We thank him for the joy we have in his presence because of you. [10]Day and night we ask him with all our heart to let us see you personally and supply what is needed in your faith.

11 May our God and Father himself and our Lord Jesus prepare the way for us to come to you! [12]May the Lord make your love for one another and for all people grow more and more and become as great as our love for you. [13]In this way he will strengthen you, and you will be perfect and holy in the presence of our God and Father when our Lord Jesus comes with all who belong to him.[a]

Paul encouraged the Christians in Thessalonica to earn their own living (4.11)

A Life that Pleases God

4 Finally, our brothers and sisters, you learnt from us how you should live in order to please God. This is, of course, how you have been living. And now we beg and urge you in the name of the Lord Jesus to do even more. [2]For you know the instructions we gave you by the authority of the Lord Jesus. [3]God wants you to be holy and completely free from sexual immorality. [4]Each of you men should know how to live with his wife[b] in a holy and honourable way, [5]not with a lustful desire, like the heathen who do not know God. [6]In this matter, then, no man should do wrong to his fellow-Christian or take advantage of him. We have told you this before, and we strongly warned you that the Lord will punish those who do that. [7]God did not call us to live in immorality, but in holiness. [8]So then, whoever rejects this teaching is not rejecting a human being, but God, who gives you his Holy Spirit.

9 There is no need to write to you about love for your fellow-believers. You yourselves have been taught by God how you should love one another. [10]And you have, in fact, behaved like this towards all the brothers and sisters in all Macedonia. So we beg you, our brothers and sisters, to do even more. [11]Make it your aim to live a quiet life, to mind your own business, and to earn your own living, just as we told you before. [12]In this way you will win the respect of those who are not believers, and you will not have to depend on anyone for what you need.

The Lord's Coming

13 Our brothers and sisters, we want you to know the truth about those who have died, so that you will not be sad, as are those who have no hope. [14]We believe that Jesus died and rose again, and so we believe that God will take back with Jesus those who have died believing in him.

15 What we are teaching you now is the Lord's teaching: we who are alive on the day the Lord comes will not go ahead of those who have died. [16]There will be the shout of command, the archangel's voice, the sound of God's trumpet, and the Lord himself will come down from heaven. Those who have died believing in Christ will rise to life first; [17]then we who are living at that time will be gathered up along with them in the clouds to meet the Lord in the air. And so we will always be with the Lord. [18]So then, encourage one another with these words.

Be Ready for the Lord's Coming

5 There is no need to write to you, brothers and sisters, about the times and occasions when these things will happen. [2]For you yourselves know very well that the Day of the Lord will come as a thief comes at night. [3]When

[a] **3.13** all who belong to him; *or* all his angels.
[b] **4.4** live with his wife; *or* control his body.

people say, "Everything is quiet and safe," then suddenly destruction will hit them! It will come as suddenly as the pains that come upon a woman in labour, and people will not escape. [4]But you, brothers and sisters, are not in the darkness, and the Day should not take you by surprise like a thief. [5]All of you are people who belong to the light, who belong to the day. We do not belong to the night or to the darkness. [6]So then, we should not be sleeping like the others; we should be awake and sober. [7]It is at night that people sleep; it is at night that they get drunk. [8]But we belong to the day, and we should be sober. We must wear faith and love as a breastplate, and our hope of salvation as a helmet. [9]God did not choose us to suffer his anger, but to possess salvation through our Lord Jesus Christ, [10]who died for us in order that we might live together with him, whether we are alive or dead when he comes. [11]And so encourage one another and help one another, just as you are now doing.

Final Instructions and Greetings

12 We beg you, our brothers and sisters, to pay proper respect to those who work among you, who guide and instruct you in the Christian life. [13]Treat them with the greatest respect and love because of the work they do. Be at peace among yourselves.

14 We urge you, our brothers and sisters, to warn the idle, encourage the timid, help the weak, be patient with everyone. [15]See that no one pays back wrong for wrong, but at all times make it your aim to do good to one another and to all people.

16 Be joyful always, [17]pray at all times, [18]be thankful in all circumstances. This is what God wants from you in your life in union with Christ Jesus.

19 Do not restrain the Holy Spirit; [20]do not despise inspired messages. [21]Put all things to the test: keep what is good [22]and avoid every kind of evil.

23 May the God who gives us peace make you holy in every way and keep your whole being – spirit, soul, and body – free from every fault at the coming of our Lord Jesus Christ. [24]He who calls you will do it, because he is faithful.

25 Pray also for us, brothers and sisters.

26 Greet all the believers with a holy kiss.

27 I urge you by the authority of the Lord to read this letter to all the believers.

28 The grace of our Lord Jesus Christ be with you.

Paul's Second Letter to the
THESSALONIANS

INTRODUCTION

Confusion over the expected return of Christ continued to cause disturbances in the church at Thessalonica. *Paul's Second Letter to the Thessalonians* deals with the belief that the day of the Lord's coming had already arrived. Paul corrects this idea, pointing out that before Christ returns, evil and wickedness will reach a climax under the leadership of a mysterious figure called "the Wicked One" (2.3), who would be opposed to Christ.

The apostle emphasizes the need for his readers to remain steady in their faith in spite of trouble and suffering, to work for a living as did Paul and his fellow-workers, and to persevere in doing good.

Outline of Contents

1 From Paul, Silas, and Timothy –
To the people of the church in Thessalonica, who belong to God our Father and the Lord Jesus Christ:

2 May God our Father and the Lord Jesus Christ give you grace and peace.

The Judgement at Christ's Coming

3 Our brothers and sisters, we must thank God at all times for you. It is right for us to do so, because your faith is growing so much and the love each of you has for the others is becoming greater. ⁴That is why we ourselves boast about you in the churches of God. We boast about the way you continue to endure and believe through all the persecutions and sufferings you are experiencing.

5 All of this proves that God's judgement is just and as a result you will become worthy of his Kingdom, for which you are suffering. ⁶God will do what is right: he will bring suffering on those who make you suffer, ⁷and he will give relief to you who suffer and to us as well. He will do this when the Lord Jesus appears from heaven with his mighty angels, ⁸with a flaming fire, to

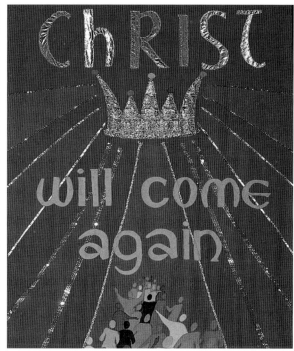

Paul encouraged the Christians in Thessalonica to look for the return of Christ from heaven (1.7)

Studying
2 THESSALONIANS

Who wrote it? Paul.
When? Probably 52–53 CE.
Where from? Corinth.
For whom? The church in Thessalonica, as
  1 Thessalonians.
Why? In his first letter to them Paul had said that Jesus
  could return at any time. Now he wanted to tell them
  that certain things must happen first.

KEY POINTS

- The church is still suffering in Thessalonica but Paul says that God will judge those who are persecuting it (1.3–12).
- Satan will oppose God on earth before Jesus returns.
- The Christians in Thessalonica are asked to pray for Paul.
- Paul attacks those who have given up work, and are living off others, because they are expecting Jesus to return at any time (3.1–16).

punish those who reject God and who do not obey the Good News about our Lord Jesus. [9]They will suffer the punishment of eternal destruction, separated from the presence of the Lord and from his glorious might, [10]when he comes on that Day to receive glory from all his people and honour from all who believe. You too will be among them, because you have believed the message that we told you.

11 That is why we always pray for you. We ask our God to make you worthy of the life he has called you to live. May he fulfil by his power all your desire for goodness and complete your work of faith. [12]In this way the name of our Lord Jesus will receive glory from you, and you from him, by the grace of our God and of the Lord[a] Jesus Christ.

The Wicked One

2 Concerning the coming of our Lord Jesus Christ and our being gathered together to be with him: I beg you, my brothers and sisters, [2]not to be so easily confused in your thinking or upset by the claim that the Day of the Lord has come. Perhaps it is thought that we said this while prophesying or preaching, or that we wrote it in a letter. [3]Do not let anyone deceive you in any way. For the Day will not come until the final Rebellion takes place and the Wicked One appears, who is destined for hell. [4]He will oppose every so-called god or object of worship

---

[a] **1.12** our God and of the Lord; *or* our God and Lord.

and will put himself above them all. He will even go in and sit down in God's Temple and claim to be God.

5 Don't you remember? I told you all this while I was with you. [6]Yet there is something that keeps this from happening now, and you know what it is. At the proper time, then, the Wicked One will appear. [7]The Mysterious Wickedness is already at work, but what is going to happen will not happen until the one who holds it back is taken out of the way. [8]Then the Wicked One will be revealed, but when the Lord Jesus comes, he will kill him with the breath from his mouth and destroy him with his dazzling presence. [9]The Wicked One will come with the power of Satan and perform all kinds of false miracles and wonders, [10]and use every kind of wicked deceit on those who will perish. They will perish because they did not welcome and love the truth so as to be saved. [11]And so God sends the power of error to work in them so that they believe what is false. [12]The result is that all who have not believed the truth, but have taken pleasure in sin, will be condemned.

You are Chosen for Salvation

13 We must thank God at all times for you, brothers and sisters, you whom the Lord loves. For God chose you as the first[b] to be saved by the Spirit's power to make you his holy people and by your faith in the truth. [14]God called you to this through the Good News we preached to you; he called you to possess your share of the glory of our Lord Jesus Christ. [15]So then, our brothers and sisters, stand firm and hold on to those truths which we taught you, both in our preaching and in our letter.

16 May our Lord Jesus Christ himself and God our Father, who loved us and in his grace gave us unfailing courage and a firm hope, [17]encourage you and strengthen you always to do and say what is good.

Pray for Us

3 Finally, our brothers and sisters, pray for us, that the Lord's message may continue to spread rapidly and be received with honour, just as it was among you. [2]Pray also that God will rescue us from wicked and evil people; for not everyone believes the message.

3 But the Lord is faithful, and he will strengthen

---

[b] **2.13** as the first; *some manuscripts have* from the beginning.

you and keep you safe from the Evil One. [4]And the Lord gives us confidence in you, and we are sure that you are doing and will continue to do what we tell you.

5   May the Lord lead you into a greater understanding of God's love and the endurance that is given by Christ.

The Obligation to Work

6   Our brothers and sisters, we command you in the name of our Lord Jesus Christ to keep away from all believers who are living a lazy life and who do not follow the instructions that we gave them. [7]You yourselves know very well that you should do just what we did. We were not lazy when we were with you. [8]We did not accept anyone's support without paying for it. Instead, we worked and toiled; we kept working day and night so as not to be an expense to any of you. [9]We did this, not because we have no right to demand our support; we did it to be an example for you to follow. [10]While we were with you, we used to say to you, "Whoever refuses to work is not allowed to eat."

11   We say this because we hear that there are some people among you who live lazy lives and who do nothing except meddle in other people's business. [12]In the name of the Lord Jesus Christ we command these people and warn them to lead orderly lives and work to earn their own living.

13   But you, brothers and sisters, must not get tired of doing good. [14]It may be that someone there will not obey the message we send you in this letter. If so, take note of that person and have nothing to do with him or her, so that they will be ashamed. [15]But do not treat them as an enemy; instead, warn them as a fellow-believer.

Final Words

16   May the Lord himself, who is our source of peace, give you peace at all times and in every way. The Lord be with you all.

17   With my own hand I write this: *Greetings from Paul*. This is the way I sign every letter; this is how I write.

18   May the grace of our Lord Jesus Christ be with you all.

Paul's First Letter to TIMOTHY

INTRODUCTION

Timothy, a young Christian from Asia Minor, was the son of a Jewish mother and a Greek father. He became a companion and assistant to Paul in his missionary work. *Paul's First Letter to Timothy* deals with three main concerns.

The letter is first of all a warning against false teaching in the church. This teaching, a mixture of Jewish and non-Jewish ideas, was based on the belief that the physical world is evil and that one can attain salvation only by special secret knowledge and by practices such as avoiding certain foods and not marrying. The letter also contains instructions about church administration and worship, with a description of the kind of character that church leaders and helpers should have. Finally, Timothy is advised how to be a good servant of Jesus Christ and about the responsibilities that he has towards various groups of believers.

Outline of Contents

1 From Paul, an apostle of Christ Jesus by order of God our Saviour and Christ Jesus our hope –

2 To Timothy, my true son in the faith:

May God the Father and Christ Jesus our Lord give you grace, mercy, and peace.

Warnings against False Teaching

3 I want you to stay in Ephesus, just as I urged you when I was on my way to Macedonia. Some people there are teaching false doctrines, and you must order them to stop. [4]Tell them to give up those legends and those long lists of ancestors, which only produce arguments; they do not serve God's plan, which is known by faith. [5]The purpose of this order is to arouse the love that comes from a pure heart, a clear conscience, and a genuine faith. [6]Some people have turned away from these and have lost their way in foolish discussions. [7]They want to be teachers of God's law, but they do not understand their own words or the matters about which they speak with so much confidence.

8 We know that the Law is good if it is used as it should be used. [9]It must be remembered, of course, that laws are made, not for good people, but for lawbreakers and criminals, for the godless and sinful, for those who are not religious or spiritual, for those who kill their fathers or mothers, for murderers, [10]for the immoral, for sexual perverts, for kidnappers, for those who lie and give false testimony or who do anything else contrary to sound doctrine. [11]That teaching is found in the gospel that was entrusted to me to announce, the Good News from the glorious and blessed God.

Gratitude for God's Mercy

12 I give thanks to Christ Jesus our Lord, who has given me strength for my work. I thank him for considering me worthy and appointing me to serve him, [13]even though in the past I spoke evil of him and persecuted and insulted him. But God was merciful to me because I did not yet have faith and so did not know what I was doing. [14]And our Lord poured out his abundant grace on me and gave me the faith and love which are ours in union with Christ Jesus. [15]This is a true saying, to be completely accepted and believed: Christ Jesus came into the world to save sinners. I am the worst of them, [16]but God

was merciful to me in order that Christ Jesus might show his full patience in dealing with me, the worst of sinners, as an example for all those who would later believe in him and receive eternal life. [17]To the eternal King, immortal and invisible, the only God – to him be honour and glory for ever and ever! Amen.

18 Timothy, my child, I entrust to you this command, which is in accordance with the words of prophecy spoken in the past about you. Use those words as weapons in order to fight well, [19]and keep your faith and a clear conscience. Some people have not listened to their conscience and have made a ruin of their faith. [20]Among them are Hymenaeus and Alexander, whom I have punished by handing them over to the power of Satan; this will teach them to stop their blasphemy.

Church Worship

2 First of all, then, I urge that petitions, prayers, requests, and thanksgivings be offered to God for all people; [2]for kings and all others who are in authority, that we may live a quiet and peaceful life with all reverence towards God and with proper conduct. [3]This is good and it pleases God our Saviour, [4]who wants everyone to be saved and to come to know the truth. [5]For there is one God, and there is one who brings God and human beings together, the man Christ Jesus, [6]who gave himself to redeem everyone. That was the proof at the right time that God wants everyone to be saved, [7]and that is why I was sent as an apostle and teacher of the Gentiles, to proclaim the message of faith and truth. I am not lying; I am telling the truth!

8 In every church service I want the men to pray, men who are dedicated to God and can lift up their hands in prayer without anger or argument. [9]I also want the women to be modest and sensible about their clothes and to dress properly; not with fancy hair styles or with gold ornaments or pearls or expensive dresses, [10]but with good deeds, as is proper for women who claim to be religious. [11]Women should learn in silence and all humility. [12]I do not allow them to teach or to have authority over men; they must keep quiet. [13]For Adam was created first, and then Eve. [14]And it was not Adam who was deceived; it was the woman who was deceived and broke God's law. [15]But a woman will be saved through having children,[a]

Studying
1 TIMOTHY

Who wrote it? Unknown. Probably not Paul, despite the inscription in 1.1. More likely a disciple after his death.
When? 80–85 CE.
Where from? Not known.
For whom? Timothy, a church leader, who is held up as the almost perfect example of what a church leader should be like.
Why? The Church had entered the time following Paul's departure. There were many teachers who were passing on false messages. The author writes to one of Paul's most trusted co-workers and, through him, to the Church generally. It must remain faithful to the teaching and example of Paul – and others.

KEY POINTS

- There is false teaching in the Church which the author attacks.
- The Church should follow the example of Paul – especially in his willingness to suffer for the faith (1.8).
- Everything that God has created is good – marriage, food, wine, possessions and everyday life.

if she perseveres[b] in faith and love and holiness, with modesty.

Leaders in the Church

3 This is a true saying: if a man is eager to be a church leader, he desires an excellent work. [2]A church leader must be without fault; he must have only one wife,[c] be sober, self-controlled, and orderly; he must welcome strangers in his home; he must be able to teach; [3]he must not be a drunkard or a violent man, but gentle and peaceful; he must not love money; [4]he must be able to manage his own family well and make his children obey him with all respect. [5]For if a man does not know how to manage his own family, how can he take care of the church of God? [6]He must be mature in the faith, so that he will not swell up with pride and be condemned, as the Devil was. [7]He should be a man who is respected by the people outside the church, so that he will not be disgraced and fall into the Devil's trap.

Helpers in the Church

8 Church helpers must also have a good character and be sincere; they must not drink too much wine or be greedy for money; [9]they

[a] **2.15** will be saved through having children; *or* will be kept safe through childbirth.

[b] **2.15** if she perseveres; *or* if they persevere.
[c] **3.2** have only one wife; *or* be married only once.

The deacons in a Baptist Church during a Breaking of Bread service (3.8)

should hold to the revealed truth of the faith with a clear conscience. [10]They should be tested first, and then, if they pass the test, they are to serve. [11]Their wives[a] also must be of good character and must not gossip; they must be sober and honest in everything. [12]A church helper must have only one wife,[b] and be able to manage his children and family well. [13]Those helpers who do their work well win for themselves a good standing and are able to speak boldly about their faith in Christ Jesus.

The Great Secret

14   As I write this letter to you, I hope to come and see you soon. [15]But if I am delayed, this letter will let you know how we should conduct ourselves in God's household, which is the church of the living God, the pillar and support of the truth. [16]No one can deny how great is the secret of our religion:

> He appeared in human form,
>   was shown to be right by the Spirit,[c]
>   and was seen by angels.

[a] **3.11** Their wives; *or* Women helpers.
[b] **3.12** have only one wife; *or* be married only once.
[c] **3.16** was shown to be right by the Spirit; *or* and, in spiritual form, was shown to be right.

> He was preached among the nations,
>   was believed in throughout the world,
>   and was taken up to heaven.

False Teachers

4   The Spirit says clearly that some people will abandon the faith in later times; they will obey lying spirits and follow the teachings of demons. [2]Such teachings are spread by deceitful liars, whose consciences are dead, as if burnt with a hot iron. [3]Such people teach that it is wrong to marry and to eat certain foods. But God created those foods to be eaten, after a prayer of thanks, by those who are believers and have come to know the truth. [4]Everything that God has created is good; nothing is to be rejected, but everything is to be received with a prayer of thanks, [5]because the word of God and the prayer make it acceptable to God.

A Good Servant of Christ Jesus

6   If you give these instructions to the believers, you will be a good servant of Christ Jesus, as you feed yourself spiritually on the words of faith and of the true teaching which you have followed. [7]But keep away from those godless legends, which are not worth telling. Keep

Reading the Bible in public is a very important part of Christian worship (4.13)

yourself in training for a godly life. [8]Physical exercise has some value, but spiritual exercise is valuable in every way, because it promises life both for the present and for the future. [9]This is a true saying, to be completely accepted and believed. [10]We struggle[a] and work hard, because we have placed our hope in the living God, who is the Saviour of all and especially of those who believe.

11 Give them these instructions and these teachings. [12]Do not let anyone look down on you because you are young, but be an example for the believers in your speech, your conduct, your love, faith, and purity. [13]Until I come, give your time and effort to the public reading of the Scriptures and to preaching and teaching. [14]Do not neglect the spiritual gift that is in you, which was given to you when the prophets spoke and the elders laid their hands on you. [15]Practise these things and devote yourself to them, in order that your progress may be seen by all. [16]Watch yourself and watch your teaching. Keep on doing these things, because if you do, you will save both yourself and those who hear you.

Responsibilities towards Believers

5 Do not rebuke an older man, but appeal to him as if he were your father. Treat the younger men as your brothers, [2]the older women as mothers, and the younger women as sisters, with all purity.

3 Show respect for widows who really are all alone. [4]But if a widow has children or grandchildren, they should learn first to carry out their religious duties towards their own family and in this way repay their parents and grandparents, because that is what pleases God. [5]A widow who is all alone, with no one to take care of her, has placed her hope in God and continues to pray and ask him for his help night and day. [6]But a widow who gives herself to pleasure has already died, even though she lives. [7]Give them these instructions, so that no one will find fault with them. [8]But if anyone does not take care of his relatives, especially the members of his own family, he has denied the faith and is worse than an unbeliever.

9 Do not add any widow to the list of widows unless she is over 60 years of age. In addition, she must have been married only once[b] [10]and have a reputation for good deeds: a woman who brought up her children well, received strangers in her home, performed humble duties for fellow-Christians, helped people in trouble, and devoted herself to doing good.

11 But do not include younger widows in the list; because when their desires make them want to marry, they turn away from Christ, [12]and so become guilty of breaking their earlier promise to him. [13]They also learn to waste their time in going round from house to house; but even worse, they learn to be gossips and busybodies, talking of things they should not. [14]So I would prefer that the younger widows get married, have children, and take care of their homes, so as to give our enemies no chance of speaking evil of us. [15]For some widows have already turned away to follow Satan. [16]But if any Christian woman has widows in her family, she must take care of them and not put the burden on the church, so that it may take care of the widows who are all alone.

17 The elders who do good work as leaders should be considered worthy of receiving double pay, especially those who work hard at preaching and teaching. [18]For the scripture says, "Do not muzzle an ox when you are using it to thresh corn" and "Workers should be given their pay." [19]Do not listen to an accusation against an

---

[a] **4.10** struggle; *some manuscripts have* are reviled.

[b] **5.9** married only once; *or* faithful to her husband.

elder unless it is brought by two or more witnesses. [20]Rebuke publicly all those who commit sins, so that the rest may be afraid.

21 In the presence of God and of Christ Jesus and of the holy angels I solemnly call upon you to obey these instructions without showing any prejudice or favour to anyone in anything you do. [22]Be in no hurry to lay hands on anyone in dedication to the Lord's service. Take no part in the sins of others; keep yourself pure.

23 Do not drink water only, but take a little wine to help your digestion, since you are ill so often.

24 The sins of some people are plain to see, and their sins go ahead of them to judgement; but the sins of others are seen only later. [25]In the same way good deeds are plainly seen, and even those that are not so plain cannot be hidden.

6 Those who are slaves must consider their masters worthy of all respect, so that no one will speak evil of the name of God and of our teaching. [2]Slaves belonging to Christian masters must not despise them, for they are their brothers and sisters. Instead, they are to serve them even better, because those who benefit from their work are believers whom they love.

False Teaching and True Riches

You must teach and preach these things. [3]Whoever teaches a different doctrine and does not agree with the true words of our Lord Jesus Christ and with the teaching of our religion [4]is swollen with pride and knows nothing. He has an unhealthy desire to argue and quarrel about words, and this brings on jealousy, disputes, insults, evil suspicions, [5]and constant arguments from people whose minds do not function and who no longer have the truth. They think that religion is a way to become rich.

6 Well, religion does make a person very rich, if he is satisfied with what he has. [7]What did we bring into the world? Nothing! What can we take out of the world? Nothing! [8]So then, if we have food and clothes, that should be enough for us. [9]But those who want to get rich fall into temptation and are caught in the trap of many foolish and harmful desires, which pull them down to ruin and destruction. [10]For the love of money is a source of all kinds of evil. Some have been so eager to have it that they have wandered away from the faith and have broken their hearts with many sorrows.

Personal Instructions

11 But you, man of God, avoid all these things. Strive for righteousness, godliness, faith, love, endurance, and gentleness. [12]Run your best in the race of faith, and win eternal life for yourself; for it was to this life that God called you when you firmly professed your faith before many witnesses. [13]Before God, who gives life to all things, and before Christ Jesus, who firmly professed his faith before Pontius Pilate, I command you [14]to obey your orders and keep them faithfully until the Day when our Lord Jesus Christ will appear. [15]His appearing will be brought about at the right time by God, the blessed and only Ruler, the King of kings and the Lord of lords. [16]He alone is immortal; he lives in the light that no one can approach. No one has ever seen him; no one can ever see him. To him be honour and eternal dominion! Amen.

17 Command those who are rich in the things of this life not to be proud, but to place their hope, not in such an uncertain thing as riches, but in God, who generously gives us everything for our enjoyment. [18]Command them to do good, to be rich in good works, to be generous and ready to share with others. [19]In this way they will store up for themselves a treasure which will be a solid foundation for the future. And then they will be able to win the life which is true life.

20 Timothy, keep safe what has been entrusted to your care. Avoid the profane talk and foolish arguments of what some people wrongly call "Knowledge". [21]For some have claimed to possess it, and as a result they have lost the way of faith.

God's grace be with you all.

Paul's Second Letter to TIMOTHY

INTRODUCTION

Paul's Second Letter to Timothy consists largely of personal advice to Timothy, as a younger colleague and assistant. The main theme is endurance. Timothy is advised and encouraged to keep on witnessing faithfully to Jesus Christ, to hold to the true teaching of the Good News and the Old Testament, and to do his duty as teacher and evangelist, all in the face of suffering and opposition.

Timothy is especially warned about the dangers of becoming involved in "foolish and ignorant arguments" (2.23) that do no good, but only ruin the people who listen to them.

In all this, Timothy is reminded of the example of the writer's own life and purpose – his faith, patience, love, endurance, and suffering in persecution.

Outline of Contents

1 From Paul, an apostle of Christ Jesus by God's will, sent to proclaim the promised life which we have in union with Christ Jesus –

2 To Timothy, my dear son:

May God the Father and Christ Jesus our Lord give you grace, mercy, and peace.

Thanksgiving and Encouragement

3 I give thanks to God, whom I serve with a clear conscience, as my ancestors did. I thank him as I remember you always in my prayers night and day. ⁴I remember your tears, and I want to see you very much, so that I may be filled with joy. ⁵I remember the sincere faith you have, the kind of faith that your grandmother Lois and your mother Eunice also had. I am sure that you have it also. ⁶For this reason I remind you to keep alive the gift that God gave you when I laid my hands on you. ⁷For the Spirit that God has given us does not make us timid; instead, his Spirit fills us with power, love, and self-control.

8 Do not be ashamed, then, of witnessing for our Lord; nor be ashamed of me, a prisoner for Christ's sake. Instead, take your part in suffering for the Good News, as God gives you the strength to do it. ⁹He saved us and called us to be his own people, not because of what we have done, but because of his own purpose and grace. He gave us this grace by means of Christ Jesus before the beginning of time, ¹⁰but now it has been revealed to us through the coming of our Saviour, Christ Jesus. He has ended the power of death and through the gospel has revealed immortal life.

11 God has appointed me as an apostle and teacher to proclaim the Good News, ¹²and it is for this reason that I suffer these things. But I am still full of confidence, because I know whom I have trusted, and I am sure that he is able to keep safe until that Day what he has entrusted to me.[a] ¹³Hold firmly to the true words that I taught you, as the example for you to follow, and remain in the faith and love that are ours in union with Christ Jesus. ¹⁴Through the power of the Holy Spirit, who lives in us, keep the good things that have been entrusted to you.

15 You know that everyone in the province of

---

[a] **1.12** what he has entrusted to me; *or* what I have entrusted to him.

Studying
2 TIMOTHY

Who wrote it? Probably a follower of Paul, like *1 Timothy*.
When? Date similar to *1 Timothy* – 80–85 CE.
Where from? Not known.
For whom? For Timothy, a church leader, and through him to the Church generally.
Why? Christians had realized that Jesus was not going to return at any moment. Now the Church needed to be organized in the best possible way and remain true to the teaching of Paul. It needed to be warned of the activities of false teachers.

KEY POINTS

- The imprisonment of Paul runs through the letter – his imminent death seems likely (4.6–8). Reads like a "last will and testament".
- The sufferings of Paul are used to encourage Timothy – and through him all Christians – to similar endurance.

they too may obtain the salvation that comes through Christ Jesus and brings eternal glory. ¹¹This is a true saying:

"If we have died with him,
we shall also live with him.
12 If we continue to endure,
we shall also rule with him.
If we deny him,
he also will deny us.
13 If we are not faithful,
he remains faithful,
because he cannot be false to himself."

An Approved Worker

14 Remind your people of this, and give them a solemn warning in God's presence not to fight over words. It does no good, but only ruins the people who listen. ¹⁵Do your best to win full approval in God's sight, as a worker who is not ashamed of his work, one who correctly teaches the message of God's truth. ¹⁶Keep away from profane and foolish discussions, which only drive people further away from God. ¹⁷Such teaching is like an open sore that eats away the flesh. Two men who have taught such things are Hymenaeus and Philetus. ¹⁸They have left the way of truth and are upsetting the faith of some believers by saying that our resurrection has already taken place. ¹⁹But the solid foundation that God has laid cannot be shaken; and on it are written these words: "The Lord knows those who are his" and "All who say that they belong to the Lord must turn away from wrongdoing."

20 In a large house there are dishes and bowls of all kinds: some are made of silver and gold, others of wood and clay; some are for special occasions, others for ordinary use. ²¹If anyone makes himself or herself clean from all those evil things, they will be used for special purposes, because they are dedicated and useful to their Master, ready to be used for every good deed. ²²Avoid the passions of youth, and strive for righteousness, faith, love, and peace, together with those who with a pure heart call out to the Lord for help. ²³But keep away from foolish and ignorant arguments; you know that they end up in quarrels. ²⁴As the Lord's servant, you must not quarrel. You must be kind towards all, a good and patient teacher, ²⁵gentle as you correct your opponents, for it may be that God will give them the opportunity to repent and come to know the truth. ²⁶And then they will come to their senses and escape from the trap of the Devil, who had caught them and made them obey his will.

Asia, including Phygelus and Hermogenes, has deserted me. ¹⁶May the Lord show mercy to the family of Onesiphorus, because he cheered me up many times. He was not ashamed that I am in prison, ¹⁷but as soon as he arrived in Rome, he started looking for me until he found me. ¹⁸May the Lord grant him his mercy on that Day! And you know very well how much he did for me in Ephesus.

A Loyal Soldier of Christ Jesus

2 As for you, my son, be strong through the grace that is ours in union with Christ Jesus. ²Take the teachings that you heard me proclaim in the presence of many witnesses, and entrust them to reliable people, who will be able to teach others also.

3 Take your part in suffering, as a loyal soldier of Christ Jesus. ⁴A soldier on active service wants to please his commanding officer and so does not get mixed up in the affairs of civilian life. ⁵An athlete who runs in a race cannot win the prize unless he obeys the rules. ⁶The farmer who has done the hard work should have the first share of the harvest. ⁷Think about what I am saying, because the Lord will enable you to understand it all.

8 Remember Jesus Christ, who was raised from death, who was a descendant of David, as is taught in the Good News I preach. ⁹Because I preach the Good News, I suffer and I am even chained like a criminal. But the word of God is not in chains, ¹⁰and so I endure everything for the sake of God's chosen people, in order that

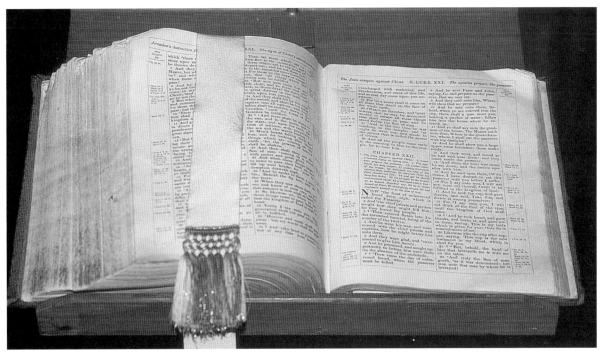

Paul commended Timothy for knowing the teaching of Scripture since he was a child (3.15)

The Last Days

3 Remember that there will be difficult times in the last days. [2]People will be selfish, greedy, boastful, and conceited; they will be insulting, disobedient to their parents, ungrateful, and irreligious; [3]they will be unkind, merciless, slanderers, violent, and fierce; they will hate the good; [4]they will be treacherous, reckless, and swollen with pride; they will love pleasure rather than God; [5]they will hold to the outward form of our religion, but reject its real power. Keep away from such people. [6]Some of them go into people's houses and gain control over weak women who are burdened by the guilt of their sins and driven by all kinds of desires, [7]women who are always trying to learn but who can never come to know the truth. [8]As Jannes and Jambres were opposed to Moses, so also these people are opposed to the truth – people whose minds do not function and who are failures in the faith. [9]But they will not get very far, because everyone will see how stupid they are. That is just what happened to Jannes and Jambres.

Last Instructions

10 But you have followed my teaching, my conduct, and my purpose in life; you have observed my faith, my patience, my love, my endurance, [11]my persecutions, and my sufferings. You know all that happened to me in Antioch, Iconium, and Lystra, the terrible persecutions I endured! But the Lord rescued me from them all. [12]Everyone who wants to live a godly life in union with Christ Jesus will be persecuted; [13]and evil persons and impostors will keep on going from bad to worse, deceiving others and being deceived themselves. [14]But as for you, continue in the truths that you were taught and firmly believe. You know who your teachers were, [15]and you remember that ever since you were a child, you have known the Holy Scriptures, which are able to give you the wisdom that leads to salvation through faith in Christ Jesus. [16]All Scripture is inspired by God and is useful[a] for teaching the truth, rebuking error, correcting faults, and giving instruction for right living, [17]so that the person who serves God may be fully qualified and equipped to do every kind of good deed.

4 In the presence of God and of Christ Jesus, who will judge the living and the dead, and because he is coming to rule as King, I solemnly urge you [2]to preach the message, to insist upon proclaiming it (whether the time is right or not), to convince, reproach, and encourage, as you teach with all patience. [3]The time

[a] **3.16** All Scripture is inspired by God and is useful; *or* Every scripture inspired by God is also useful.

will come when people will not listen to sound doctrine, but will follow their own desires and will collect for themselves more and more teachers who will tell them what they are itching to hear. ⁴They will turn away from listening to the truth and give their attention to legends. ⁵But you must keep control of yourself in all circumstances; endure suffering, do the work of a preacher of the Good News, and perform your whole duty as a servant of God.

6 As for me, the hour has come for me to be sacrificed; the time is here for me to leave this life. ⁷I have done my best in the race, I have run the full distance, and I have kept the faith.ᵃ ⁸And now there is waiting for me the victory prize of being put right with God, which the Lord, the righteous Judge, will give me on that Day – and not only to me, but to all those who wait with love for him to appear.

Personal Words

9 Do your best to come to me soon. ¹⁰Demas fell in love with this present world and has deserted me, going off to Thessalonica. Crescens went to Galatia, and Titus to Dalmatia. ¹¹Only Luke is with me. Get Mark and bring him with you, because he can help me in the work. ¹²I sent Tychicus to Ephesus. ¹³When you come, bring my coat that I left in Troas with Carpus;

bring the books too, and especially the ones made of parchment.

14 Alexander the metalworker did me much harm; the Lord will reward him according to what he has done. ¹⁵Be on your guard against him yourself, because he was violently opposed to our message.

16 No one stood by me the first time I defended myself; all deserted me. May God not count it against them! ¹⁷But the Lord stayed with me and gave me strength, so that I was able to proclaim the full message for all the Gentiles to hear; and I was rescued from being sentenced to death. ¹⁸And the Lord will rescue me from all evil and take me safely into his heavenly Kingdom. To him be the glory for ever and ever! Amen.

Final Greetings

19 I send greetings to Priscilla and Aquila and to the family of Onesiphorus. ²⁰Erastus stayed in Corinth, and I left Trophimus in Miletus, because he was ill. ²¹Do your best to come before winter.

Eubulus, Pudens, Linus, and Claudia send their greetings, and so do all the other Christians.

22 The Lord be with your spirit.
God's grace be with you all.

ᵃ **4.7** kept the faith; *or* been true to my promise.

Paul's Letter to
TITUS

INTRODUCTION

Titus was a Gentile convert to Christianity who became a fellow-worker and assistant to Paul in his missionary work. *Paul's Letter to Titus* is addressed to his young helper in Crete, who had been left there to supervise the work of the church. The letter expresses three main concerns.

First, Titus is reminded of the kind of character that church leaders should have, especially in view of the bad character of many Cretans. Next, Titus is advised how to teach the various groups in the church, the older men, the older women (who are, in turn, to teach the younger women), the young men, and the slaves. Finally, the writer gives Titus advice regarding Christian conduct, especially the need to be peaceful and friendly, and to avoid hatred, argument, and division in the church.

1 From Paul, a servant of God and an apostle of Jesus Christ.

I was chosen and sent to help the faith of God's chosen people and to lead them to the truth taught by our religion, ²which is based on the hope for eternal life. God, who does not lie, promised us this life before the beginning of time, ³and at the right time he revealed it in his message. This was entrusted to me, and I proclaim it by order of God our Saviour.

4 I write to Titus, my true son in the faith that we have in common.

May God the Father and Christ Jesus our Saviour give you grace and peace.

Titus' Work in Crete

5 I left you in Crete, so that you could put in order the things that still needed doing and appoint church elders in every town. Remember my instructions: ⁶an elder must be blameless; he must have only one wife,ᵃ and his children must be believers and not have the reputation of being wild or disobedient. ⁷For since a church

ᵃ **1.6** have only one wife; *or* be married only once.

leader is in charge of God's work, he should be blameless. He must not be arrogant or quick-tempered, or a drunkard or violent or greedy for money. ⁸He must be hospitable and love what is good. He must be self-controlled, upright, holy, and disciplined. ⁹He must hold firmly to the message which can be trusted and which agrees with the doctrine. In this way he will be able to encourage others with the true teaching and also to show the error of those who are opposed to it.

10 For there are many, especially converts from Judaism, who rebel and deceive others with their nonsense. ¹¹It is necessary to stop their talk, because they are upsetting whole families by teaching what they should not, and all for the shameful purpose of making money. ¹²⁻¹³It was a Cretan himself, one of their own prophets, who spoke the truth when he said, "Cretans are always liars, wicked beasts, and lazy gluttons." For this reason you must rebuke them sharply, so that they may have a healthy faith ¹⁴and no longer hold on to Jewish legends and to human commandments which come from people who have rejected the truth. ¹⁵Everything is pure to those who are themselves pure; but nothing is pure to those who are defiled and unbelieving,

Studying
TITUS

Who wrote it? Probably not Paul. More likely to have been a disciple of his.
When? 80–85 CE is likely.
Where from? Not known.
For whom? Titus, Paul's Gentile assistant. Accompanied Paul on journeys.
Why? Titus appears to have been the leader of a church. The author writes giving details of how the church should be organized and what should be the qualities of its leaders.

KEY POINTS

- The appointment and qualifications expected of bishops (1.5–9).
- Dealing with false teachers (1.10–16).
- The teaching of good conduct in the church (2.1—3.8).

for their minds and consciences have been defiled. [16]They claim that they know God, but their actions deny it. They are hateful and disobedient, not fit to do anything good.

Sound Doctrine

2 But you must teach what agrees with sound doctrine. [2]Instruct the older men to be sober, sensible, and self-controlled; to be sound in their faith, love, and endurance. [3]In the same way instruct the older women to behave as women should who live a holy life. They must not be slanderers or slaves to wine. They must teach what is good, [4]in order to train the younger women to love their husbands and children, [5]to be self-controlled and pure, and to be good housewives who submit to their husbands, so that no one will speak evil of the message that comes from God.

[6] In the same way urge the young men to be self-controlled. [7]In all things you yourself must be an example of good behaviour. Be sincere and serious in your teaching. [8]Use sound words that cannot be criticized, so that your enemies may be put to shame by not having anything bad to say about us.

[9] Slaves are to submit to their masters and please them in all things. They must not answer them back [10]or steal from them. Instead, they must show that they are always good and faithful, so as to bring credit to the teaching about God our Saviour in all they do.

[11] For God has revealed his grace for the salvation of the whole human race. [12]That grace instructs us to give up ungodly living and worldly passions, and to live self-controlled, upright, and godly lives in this world, [13]as we wait for the blessed Day we hope for, when the glory of our great God and Saviour Jesus Christ[a] will appear. [14]He gave himself for us, to rescue us from all wickedness and to make us a pure people who belong to him alone and are eager to do good.

[15] Teach these things and use your full authority as you encourage and rebuke your hearers. Let none of them look down on you.

Christian Conduct

3 Remind your people to submit to rulers and authorities, to obey them, and to be ready to do good in every way. [2]Tell them not to speak evil of anyone, but to be peaceful and friendly, and always to show a gentle attitude towards everyone. [3]For we ourselves were once foolish, disobedient, and wrong. We were slaves to passions and pleasures of all kinds. We spent our lives in malice and envy; others hated us and we hated them. [4]But when the kindness and love of God our Saviour was revealed, [5]he saved us. It was not because of any good deeds that we ourselves had done, but because of his own mercy that he saved us, through the Holy Spirit, who gives us new birth and new life by washing us. [6]God poured out the Holy Spirit abundantly on us through Jesus Christ our Saviour, [7]so that by his grace we might be put right with God and come into possession of the eternal life we hope for. [8]This is a true saying.

I want you to give special emphasis to these matters, so that those who believe in God may be concerned with giving their time to doing good deeds, which are good and useful for everyone. [9]But avoid stupid arguments, long lists of ancestors, quarrels, and fights about the Law. They are useless and worthless. [10]Give at least two warnings to those who cause divisions, and then have nothing more to do with them. [11]You know that such people are corrupt, and their sins prove that they are wrong.

Final Instructions

[12] When I send Artemas or Tychicus to you, do your best to come to me in Nicopolis, because I have decided to spend the winter there. [13]Do your best to help Zenas the lawyer and Apollos

[a] **2.13** our great God and Saviour Jesus Christ; *or* the great God and our Saviour Jesus Christ.

to get started on their travels, and see to it that they have everything they need. [14]Our people must learn to spend their time doing good, in order to provide for real needs; they should not live useless lives.

15   All who are with me send you greetings. Give our greetings to our friends in the faith.
    God's grace be with you all.

Paul's Letter to
PHILEMON

INTRODUCTION

Philemon was a prominent Christian, probably a member of the church at Colossae and the owner of a slave named Onesimus. This slave had run away from his master, and then somehow he had come in contact with Paul, who was then in prison. Through Paul, Onesimus became a Christian. *Paul's Letter to Philemon* is an appeal to Philemon to be reconciled to his slave, whom Paul is sending back to him, and to welcome him not only as a forgiven slave but as a Christian brother.

Outline of Contents

Introduction 1–3
Praise for Philemon 4–7
Appeal for Onesimus 8–22
Conclusion 23–25

1   From Paul, a prisoner for the sake of Christ Jesus, and from our brother Timothy –

To our friend and fellow-worker Philemon, [2]and the church that meets in your house, and our sister Apphia, and our fellow-soldier Archippus:

3   May God our Father and the Lord Jesus Christ give you grace and peace.

Philemon's Love and Faith

4   Brother Philemon, every time I pray, I mention you and give thanks to my God. [5]For I hear of your love for all God's people and the faith you have in the Lord Jesus. [6]My prayer is that our fellowship with you as believers will bring about a deeper understanding of every blessing which we have in our life in union with Christ. [7]Your love, dear brother, has brought me great joy and much encouragement! You have cheered the hearts of all God's people.

A Request for Onesimus

8   For this reason I could be bold enough, as your brother in Christ, to order you to do what should be done. [9]But because I love you, I make a request instead. I do this even though I am Paul, the ambassador of Christ Jesus, and at present also a prisoner for his sake.[a] [10]So I make a request to you on behalf of Onesimus, who is my own son in Christ; for while in prison I have become his spiritual father. [11]At one time he was of no use to you, but now he is useful[b] both to you and to me.

12   I am sending him back to you now, and with him goes my heart. [13]I would like to keep him here with me, while I am in prison for the gospel's sake, so that he could help me in your place. [14]However, I do not want to force you to help me; rather, I would like you to do it of your own free will. So I will not do anything unless you agree.

15   It may be that Onesimus was away from you for a short time so that you might have him back for all time. [16]And now he is not just a slave, but much more than a slave: he is a dear brother in Christ. How much he means to me! And how much more he will mean to you, both as a slave and as a brother in the Lord!

17   So, if you think of me as your partner, welcome him back just as you would welcome me. [18]If he has done you any wrong or owes you anything, charge it to my account. [19]Here,

---

[a] **v.9** the ambassador of Christ Jesus, and at present also a prisoner for his sake; *or* an old man, and at present a prisoner for the sake of Christ Jesus.
[b] **v.11** *The Greek name Onesimus means "useful".*

PHILEMON

I will write this with my own hand: *I, Paul, will pay you back.* (I should not have to remind you, of course, that you owe your very self to me.) 20So, my brother, please do me this favour for the Lord's sake; as a brother in Christ, cheer me up!

21   I am sure, as I write this, that you will do what I ask – in fact I know that you will do even more. 22At the same time, get a room ready for me, because I hope that God will answer the prayers of all of you and give me back to you.

Final Greetings

23   Epaphras, who is in prison with me for the sake of Christ Jesus, sends you his greetings, 24and so do my fellow-workers Mark, Aristarchus, Demas, and Luke.

25   May the grace of the Lord Jesus Christ be with you all.

Studying
PHILEMON

Who wrote it? Paul.
When? Probably 57–58 CE.
Where from? Paul was in prison when he wrote the epistle – not clear where. Could have been Rome which would make letter later than date suggested.
For whom? The letter is written to Philemon asking him to receive a runaway slave, Onesimus, back.
Why? Philemon is asked not to exact the punishment which, under Roman law, he was entitled to demand.

KEY POINTS

- Philemon is the shortest letter known to have been written by Paul.
- Paul claims the support of others when he asks Philemon to be lenient in treatment of Onesimus.
- Paul does not condemn slavery but asks the slave-owner to treat his slave as a fellow-Christian (verse 16).

The Letter to the HEBREWS

INTRODUCTION

The Letter to the Hebrews was written to a group of Christians who, faced with increasing opposition, were in danger of abandoning the Christian faith. The writer encourages them in their faith primarily by showing that Jesus Christ is the true and final revelation of God. In doing this he emphasizes three truths: first, Jesus is the eternal Son of God, who learnt true obedience to the Father through the suffering that he endured. As the Son of God, Jesus is superior to the prophets of the Old Testament, to the angels, and to Moses himself. Secondly, Jesus has been declared by God to be an eternal priest, superior to the priests of the Old Testament, and thirdly, through Jesus the believer is saved from sin, fear, and death; and Jesus, as High Priest, provides the true salvation, which was only foreshadowed by the rituals and animal sacrifices of the Hebrew religion.

By citing the example of the faith of some famous persons in Israel's history (chapter 11), the writer appeals to his readers to remain faithful, and in chapter 12 he urges his readers to continue faithful to the end, with eyes fixed on Jesus, and to endure whatever suffering and persecution may come to them. The book closes with words of advice and warning.

Outline of Contents

God's Word through his Son

1 In the past, God spoke to our ancestors many times and in many ways through the prophets, ²but in these last days he has spoken to us through his Son. He is the one through whom God created the universe, the one whom God has chosen to possess all things at the end. ³He reflects the brightness of God's glory and is the exact likeness of God's own being, sustaining the universe with his powerful word. After achieving forgiveness for human sins, he sat down in heaven at the right-hand side of God, the Supreme Power.

The Greatness of God's Son

4   The Son was made greater than the angels, just as the name that God gave him is greater than theirs. ⁵For God never said to any of his angels:

"You are my Son;
    today I have become your Father."

Nor did God say about any angel,

"I will be his Father,
    and he will be my Son."

⁶But when God was about to send his firstborn Son into the world, he said:

"All God's angels must worship him."

[7]But about the angels God said,

"God makes his angels winds,
and his servants flames of fire."

[8]About the Son, however, God said:

"Your kingdom, O God, will last[a] for ever and
ever!
You rule over your[b] people with justice.
9   You love what is right and hate what is
wrong.
That is why God, your God, has chosen you
and has given you the joy of an honour
far greater
than he gave to your companions."

[10]He also said:

"You, Lord, in the beginning created the
earth,
and with your own hands you made the
heavens.
11 They will disappear, but you will remain;
they will all wear out like clothes.
12 You will fold them up like a coat,
and they will be changed like clothes.
But you are always the same,
and your life never ends."

[13]God never said to any of his angels:

"Sit here on my right
until I put your enemies
as a footstool under your feet."

14   What are the angels, then? They are spirits
who serve God and are sent by him to help those
who are to receive salvation.

The Great Salvation

2 That is why we must hold on all the more
firmly to the truths we have heard, so that we
will not be carried away. [2]The message given
to our ancestors by the angels was shown to be
true, and all who did not follow it or obey it
received the punishment they deserved. [3]How,
then, shall we escape if we pay no attention to
such a great salvation? The Lord himself first
announced this salvation, and those who heard
him proved to us that it is true. [4]At the same time
God added his witness to theirs by performing all
kinds of miracles and wonders and by distributing
the gifts of the Holy Spirit according to his will.

[a] **1.8** Your kingdom, O God, will last; *or* God is your
kingdom.
[b] **1.8** your; *some manuscripts have* his.

Studying
HEBREWS

Who wrote it? Unknown. Certainly not Paul.
When? Written before the destruction of the Temple in
Jerusalem in 70 CE.
Where from? Not known.
For whom? The content of the letter makes it clear that it
was sent to Jewish Christians, i.e. those who had
recognized Jesus as the Messiah.
Why? These Jewish Christians may have been tempted to
return to their old religion. In highly technical
language, and drawing heavily on the Old Testament,
the author tries to show the superiority of the new
Christianity to the old Judaism.

KEY POINTS

● Jesus is superior not only to the Jewish religion but also
to prophets of old, angels, Moses, Joshua and Aaron.
Warnings are issued against leaving the true faith
(apostasy).
● Encouragement can be drawn from following the
example of Christ (12.1–11) and the faith of all the
heroes and heroines in the Jewish Scriptures
(chapter 11).

The One who Leads us to Salvation

5   God has not placed the angels as rulers over
the new world to come – the world of which we
speak. [6]Instead, as it is said somewhere in the
Scriptures:

"What are human beings, O God, that you
should think of them;
mere human beings, that you should care
for them?
7   You made them for a little while lower than
the angels;
you crowned them with glory and
honour,[c]
8   and made them rulers over all things."

It says that God made them "rulers over all
things"; this clearly includes everything. We do
not, however, see human beings ruling over all
things now. [9]But we do see Jesus, who for a little
while was made lower than the angels, so that
through God's grace he should die for everyone.
We see him now crowned with glory and
honour because of the death he suffered. [10]It was
only right that God, who creates and preserves
all things, should make Jesus perfect through
suffering, in order to bring many children to
share his glory. For Jesus is the one who leads
them to salvation.

[c] **2.7** *Many manuscripts add:* You made them rulers over
everything you made *(see Ps 8.6).*

11 He purifies people from their sins, and both he and those who are made pure all have the same Father. That is why Jesus is not ashamed to call them his family. [12]He says to God:

> "I will tell my people what you have done;
> I will praise you in their meeting."

[13]He also says, "I will put my trust in God." And he also says, "Here I am with the children that God has given me."

14 Since the children, as he calls them, are people of flesh and blood, Jesus himself became like them and shared their human nature. He did this so that through his death he might destroy the Devil, who has the power over death, [15]and in this way set free those who were slaves all their lives because of their fear of death. [16]For it is clear that it is not the angels that he helps. Instead, he helps the descendants of Abraham. [17]This means that he had to become like his brothers and sisters in every way, in order to be their faithful and merciful High Priest in his service to God, so that the people's sins would be forgiven. [18]And now he can help those who are tempted, because he himself was tempted and suffered.

Jesus is Greater than Moses

3 My Christian brothers and sisters, who also have been called by God! Think of Jesus, whom God sent to be the High Priest of the faith we profess. [2]He was faithful to God, who chose him to do this work, just as Moses was faithful in his work in God's house. [3]A man who builds a house receives more honour than the house itself. In the same way Jesus is worthy of much greater honour than Moses. [4]Every house, of course, is built by someone – and God is the one who has built all things. [5]Moses was faithful in God's house as a servant, and he spoke of the things that God would say in the future. [6]But Christ is faithful as the Son in charge of God's house. We are his house if we keep up our courage and our confidence in what we hope for.

A Rest for God's People

7 So then, as the Holy Spirit says:

> "If you hear God's voice today,
8 > do not be stubborn, as your ancestors were
> when they rebelled against God,
> as they were that day in the desert
> when they put him to the test.
9 There they put me to the test and tried me,
> says God,

although they had seen what I did for
> forty years.
10 And so I was angry with those people and
> said,
> 'They are always disloyal
> and refuse to obey my commands.'
11 I was angry and made a solemn promise:
> 'They will never enter the land where I
> would have given them rest!'"

12 My fellow-believers, be careful that no one among you has a heart so evil and unbelieving as to turn away from the living God. [13]Instead, in order that none of you be deceived by sin and become stubborn, you must help one another every day, as long as the word "Today" in the scripture applies to us. [14]For we are all partners with Christ if we hold firmly to the end the confidence we had at the beginning.

15 This is what the scripture says:

> "If you hear God's voice today,
> do not be stubborn, as your ancestors were
> when they rebelled against God."

16 Who were the people who heard God's voice and rebelled against him? All those who were led out of Egypt by Moses. [17]With whom was God angry for forty years? With the people who sinned, who fell down dead in the desert. [18]When God made his solemn promise, "They will never enter the land where I would have given them rest" – of whom was he speaking? Of those who rebelled. [19]We see, then, that they were not able to enter the land, because they did not believe.

4 Now, God has offered us the promise that we may receive that rest he spoke about. Let us take care, then, that none of you will be found to have failed to receive that promised rest. [2]For we have heard the Good News, just as they did. They heard the message, but it did them no good, because when they heard it, they did not accept it with faith. [3]We who believe, then, do receive that rest which God promised. It is just as he said:

> "I was angry and made a solemn promise:
> 'They will never enter the land where I
> would have given them rest!'"

He said this even though his work had been finished from the time he created the world. [4]For somewhere in the Scriptures this is said about the seventh day: "God rested on the seventh day from all his work." [5]This same matter is spoken of again: "They will never enter that land where I would have given them rest." [6]Those who first heard the Good News did not receive that rest, because they did not believe. There are, then, others who are allowed to receive it. [7]This is shown by the fact that God sets another day, which is called "Today". Many years later he spoke of it through David in the scripture already quoted:

"If you hear God's voice today,
　do not be stubborn."

[8] If Joshua had given the people the rest that God had promised, God would not have spoken later about another day. [9]As it is, however, there still remains for God's people a rest like God's resting on the seventh day. [10]For those who receive that rest which God promised will rest from their own work, just as God rested from his. [11]Let us, then, do our best to receive that rest, so that no one of us will fail as they did because of their lack of faith.

[12] The word of God is alive and active, sharper than any double-edged sword. It cuts all the way through, to where soul and spirit meet, to where joints and marrow come together. It judges the desires and thoughts of the heart. [13]There is nothing that can be hidden from God; everything in all creation is exposed and lies open before his eyes. And it is to him that we must all give an account of ourselves.

Jesus the Great High Priest

[14] Let us, then, hold firmly to the faith we profess. For we have a great High Priest who has gone into the very presence of God – Jesus, the Son of God. [15]Our High Priest is not one who cannot feel sympathy for our weaknesses. On the contrary, we have a High Priest who was tempted in every way that we are, but did not sin. [16]Let us have confidence, then, and approach God's throne, where there is grace. There we will receive mercy and find grace to help us just when we need it.

5 Every high priest is chosen from his fellow-men and appointed to serve God on their behalf, to offer sacrifices and offerings for sins. [2]Since he himself is weak in many ways, he is able to be gentle with those who are ignorant and make mistakes. [3]And because he is himself weak, he must offer sacrifices not only for the sins of the people but also for his own sins. [4]No one chooses for

himself the honour of being a high priest. It is only by God's call that a man is made a high priest – just as Aaron was.

[5] In the same way, Christ did not take upon himself the honour of being a high priest. Instead, God said to him:

"You are my Son;
　today I have become your Father."

[6]He also said in another place,

"You will be a priest for ever,
　in the priestly order of Melchizedek."[a]

[7] In his life on earth Jesus made his prayers and requests with loud cries and tears to God, who could save him from death. Because he was humble and devoted, God heard him. [8]But even though he was God's Son, he learnt through his sufferings to be obedient. [9]When he was made perfect, he became the source of eternal salvation for all those who obey him, [10]and God declared him to be high priest, in the priestly order of Melchizedek.[b]

Warning against Abandoning the Faith

[11] There is much we have to say about this matter, but it is hard to explain to you, because you are so slow to understand. [12]There has been enough time for you to be teachers – yet you still need someone to teach you the first lessons of God's message. Instead of eating solid food, you still have to drink milk. [13]Anyone who has to drink milk is still a child, without any

A Christian seeks God's forgiveness through the Sacrament of Reconciliation (4.16)

[a] **5.6** in … Melchizedek; *or* like Melchizedek; *or* in the line of succession to Melchizedek.
[b] **5.10** in … Melchizedek *(see 5.6)*

experience in the matter of right and wrong. [14]Solid food, on the other hand, is for adults, who through practice are able to distinguish between good and evil.

6 Let us go forward, then, to mature teaching and leave behind us the first lessons of the Christian message. We should not lay again the foundation of turning away from useless works and believing in God; [2]of the teaching about baptisms[a] and the laying on of hands; of the resurrection of the dead and the eternal judgement. [3]Let us go forward! And this is what we will do, if God allows.

[4] For how can those who abandon their faith be brought back to repent again? They were once in God's light; they tasted heaven's gift and received their share of the Holy Spirit; [5]they knew from experience that God's word is good, and they had felt the powers of the coming age. [6]And then they abandoned their faith! It is impossible to bring them back to repent again, because they are again crucifying the Son of God and exposing him to public shame.

[7] God blesses the soil which drinks in the rain that often falls on it and which grows plants that are useful to those for whom it is cultivated. [8]But if it grows thorns and weeds, it is worth nothing; it is in danger of being cursed by God and will be destroyed by fire.

[9] But even if we speak like this, dear friends, we feel sure about you. We know that you have the better blessings that belong to your salvation. [10]God is not unfair. He will not forget the work you did or the love you showed for him in the help you gave and are still giving to your fellow-Christians. [11]Our great desire is that each of you keep up your eagerness to the end, so that the things you hope for will come true. [12]We do not want you to become lazy, but to be like those who believe and are patient, and so receive what God has promised.

God's Sure Promise

[13] When God made his promise to Abraham, he made a vow to do what he had promised. Since there was no one greater than himself, he used his own name when he made his vow. [14]He said, "I promise you that I will bless you and give you many descendants." [15]Abraham was patient, and so he received what God had promised. [16]When people make vows, they use the name of someone greater than themselves, and the vow settles all arguments. [17]To those who were to

receive what he promised, God wanted to make it very clear that he would never change his purpose; so he added his vow to the promise. [18]There are these two things, then, that cannot change and about which God cannot lie. So we who have found safety with him are greatly encouraged to hold firmly to the hope placed before us. [19]We have this hope as an anchor for our lives. It is safe and sure, and goes through the curtain of the heavenly temple into the inner sanctuary. [20]On our behalf Jesus has gone in there before us, and has become a high priest for ever, in the priestly order of Melchizedek.[b]

The Priest Melchizedek

7 This Melchizedek was king of Salem and a priest of the Most High God. As Abraham was coming back from the battle in which he defeated the four kings, Melchizedek met him and blessed him, [2]and Abraham gave him a tenth of all he had taken. (The first meaning of Melchizedek's name is "King of Righteousness"; and because he was king of Salem, his name also means "King of Peace".) [3]There is no record of Melchizedek's father or mother or of any of his ancestors; no record of his birth or of his death. He is like the Son of God; he remains a priest for ever.

[4] You see, then, how great he was. Abraham, our famous ancestor, gave him a tenth of all he got in the battle. [5]And those descendants of Levi who are priests are commanded by the Law to collect a tenth from the people of Israel, that is, from their own people, even though they are also descendants of Abraham. [6]Melchizedek was not descended from Levi, but he collected a tenth from Abraham and blessed him, the man who received God's promises. [7]There is no doubt that the one who blesses is greater than the one who is blessed. [8]In the case of the priests the tenth is collected by men who die; but as for Melchizedek the tenth was collected by one who lives, as the scripture says. [9]And, so to speak, when Abraham paid the tenth, Levi (whose descendants collect the tenth) also paid it. [10]For Levi had not yet been born, but was, so to speak, in the body of his ancestor Abraham when Melchizedek met him.

[11] It was on the basis of the levitical priesthood that the Law was given to the people of Israel. Now, if the work of the levitical priests had been perfect, there would have been no need for a different kind of priest to appear, one who

[a] **6.2** baptisms; *or* purification ceremonies.

[b] **6.20** in ... Melchizedek (*see 5.6*).

is in the priestly order of Melchizedek,[a] not of Aaron. [12]For when the priesthood is changed, there also has to be a change in the law. [13]And our Lord, of whom these things are said, belonged to a different tribe, and no member of his tribe ever served as a priest. [14]It is well known that he was born a member of the tribe of Judah; and Moses did not mention this tribe when he spoke of priests.

Another Priest, like Melchizedek

15 The matter becomes even plainer; a different priest has appeared, who is like Melchizedek. [16]He was made a priest, not by human rules and regulations, but through the power of a life which has no end. [17]For the scripture says, "You will be a priest for ever, in the priestly order of Melchizedek."[a] [18]The old rule, then, is set aside, because it was weak and useless. [19]For the Law of Moses could not make anything perfect. And now a better hope has been provided through which we come near to God.

20 In addition, there is also God's vow. There was no such vow when the others were made priests. [21]But Jesus became a priest by means of a vow when God said to him:

> "The Lord has made a solemn promise
>   and will not take it back:
>   'You will be a priest for ever.'"

[22]This difference, then, also makes Jesus the guarantee of a better covenant.

23 There is another difference: there were many of those other priests, because they died and could not continue their work. [24]But Jesus lives on for ever, and his work as priest does not pass on to someone else. [25]And so he is able, now and always, to save those who come to God through him, because he lives for ever to plead with God for them.

26 Jesus, then, is the High Priest that meets our needs. He is holy; he has no fault or sin in him; he has been set apart from sinners and raised above the heavens. [27]He is not like other high priests; he does not need to offer sacrifices every day for his own sins first and then for the sins of the people. He offered one sacrifice, once and for all, when he offered himself. [28]The Law of Moses appoints men who are imperfect to be high priests; but God's promise made with the vow, which came later than the Law, appoints the Son, who has been made perfect for ever.

a **7.11, 7.17** in ... Melchizedek *(see 5.6).*

Jesus our High Priest

8 The whole point of what we are saying is that we have such a High Priest, who sits at the right of the throne of the Divine Majesty in heaven. [2]He serves as High Priest in the Most Holy Place, that is, in the real tent which was put up by the Lord, not by human hands.

3 Every High Priest is appointed to present offerings and animal sacrifices to God, and so our High Priest must also have something to offer. [4]If he were on earth, he would not be a priest at all, since there are priests who offer the gifts required by the Jewish Law. [5]The work they do as priests is really only a copy and a shadow of what is in heaven. It is the same as it was with Moses. When he was about to build the Sacred Tent, God said to him, "Be sure to make everything according to the pattern you were shown on the mountain." [6]But now, Jesus has been given priestly work which is superior to theirs, just as the covenant which he arranged between God and his people is a better one, because it is based on promises of better things.

7 If there had been nothing wrong with the first covenant, there would have been no need for a second one. [8]But God finds fault with his people when he says:

> "The days are coming, says the Lord,
>   when I will draw up a new covenant with
>   the people of Israel and with the people
>   of Judah.

9 It will not be like the covenant that I made
>   with their ancestors
>   on the day I took them by the hand and
>   led them out of Egypt.
> They were not faithful to the covenant I
>   made with them,
>   and so I paid no attention to them.

10 Now, this is the covenant that I will make
>   with the people of Israel
>   in the days to come, says the Lord:
> I will put my laws in their minds
>   and write them on their hearts.
> I will be their God,
>   and they will be my people.

11 None of them will have to teach their fellow-
>   citizens
>   or say to their fellow-citizens,
>   'Know the Lord.'
> For they will all know me,
>   from the least to the greatest.

12 I will forgive their sins
>   and will no longer remember their
>   wrongs."

[13]By speaking of a new covenant, God has made

the first one old; and anything that becomes old and worn out will soon disappear.

Earthly and Heavenly Worship

9 The first covenant had rules for worship and an earthly place for worship as well. [2]A Tent was put up, the outer one, which was called the Holy Place. In it were the lampstand and the table with the bread offered to God. [3]Behind the second curtain was the Tent called the Most Holy Place. [4]In it were the gold altar for the burning of incense and the Covenant Box all covered with gold and containing the gold jar with the manna in it, Aaron's stick that had sprouted leaves, and the two stone tablets with the commandments written on them. [5]Above the Box were the winged creatures representing God's presence, with their wings spread over the place where sins were forgiven. But now is not the time to explain everything in detail.

[6] This is how those things have been arranged. The priests go into the outer Tent every day to perform their duties, [7]but only the High Priest goes into the inner Tent, and he does so only once a year. He takes with him blood which he offers to God on behalf of himself and for the sins which the people have committed without knowing they were sinning. [8]The Holy Spirit clearly teaches from all these arrangements that the way into the Most Holy Place has not yet been opened as long as the outer Tent still stands. [9]This is an illustration which points to the present time. It means that the offerings and animal sacrifices presented to God cannot make the worshipper's heart perfect, [10]since they have to do only with food, drink, and various purification ceremonies. These are all outward rules, which apply only until the time when God will establish the new order.

[11] But Christ has already come as the High Priest of the good things that are already here.[a] The tent in which he serves is greater and more perfect; it is not a tent made by human hands, that is, it is not a part of this created world. [12]When Christ went through the tent and entered once and for all into the Most Holy Place, he did not take the blood of goats and bulls to offer as a sacrifice; rather, he took his own blood and obtained eternal salvation for us. [13]The blood of goats and bulls and the ashes of a burnt calf are sprinkled on the people who are ritually unclean, and this purifies them by taking away their ritual impurity. [14]Since this is

true, how much more is accomplished by the blood of Christ! Through the eternal Spirit he offered himself as a perfect sacrifice to God. His blood will purify our consciences from useless rituals, so that we may serve the living God.

[15] For this reason Christ is the one who arranges a new covenant, so that those who have been called by God may receive the eternal blessings that God has promised. This can be done because there has been a death which sets people free from the wrongs they did while the first covenant was in force.

[16] In the case of a will it is necessary to prove that the person who made it has died, [17]for a will means nothing while the person who made it is alive; it comes into effect only after his death. [18]That is why even the first covenant[b] came into effect only with the use of blood. [19]First, Moses proclaimed to the people all the commandments as set forth in the Law. Then he took the blood of bulls and goats, mixed it with water, and sprinkled it on the book of the Law and all the people, using a sprig of hyssop and some red wool. [20]He said, "This is the blood which seals the covenant that God has commanded you to obey." [21]In the same way Moses also sprinkled the blood on the Sacred Tent and over all the things used in worship. [22]Indeed, according to the Law almost everything is purified by blood, and sins are forgiven only if blood is poured out.

Christ's Sacrifice Takes Away Sins

[23] Those things, which are copies of the heavenly originals, had to be purified in that way. But the heavenly things themselves require much better sacrifices. [24]For Christ did not go into a Holy Place made by human hands, which was a copy of the real one. He went into heaven itself, where he now appears on our behalf in the presence of God. [25]The Jewish High Priest goes into the Most Holy Place every year with the blood of an animal. But Christ did not go in to offer himself many times, [26]for then he would have had to suffer many times ever since the creation of the world. Instead, now when all ages of time are nearing the end, he has appeared once and for all, to remove sin through the sacrifice of himself. [27]Everyone must die once, and after that be judged by God. [28]In the same manner Christ also was offered in sacrifice once to take away the sins of many. He will appear a second

---

[a] **9.11** already here; *some manuscripts have* coming.

[b] **9.18** COVENANT: *In Greek the same word means "will" and "covenant".*

time, not to deal with sin, but to save those who are waiting for him.

10 The Jewish Law is not a full and faithful model of the real things; it is only a faint outline of the good things to come. The same sacrifices are offered for ever, year after year. How can the Law, then, by means of these sacrifices make perfect the people who come to God? [2]If the people worshipping God had really been purified from their sins, they would not feel guilty of sin any more, and all sacrifices would stop. [3]As it is, however, the sacrifices serve year after year to remind people of their sins. [4]For the blood of bulls and goats can never take away sins.

5 For this reason, when Christ was about to come into the world, he said to God:

"You do not want sacrifices and offerings,
    but you have prepared a body for me.
6 You are not pleased with animals burnt
        whole on the altar
    or with sacrifices to take away sins.
7 Then I said, 'Here I am,
        to do your will, O God,
        just as it is written of me in the book of
            the Law.'"

[8]First he said, "You neither want nor are you pleased with sacrifices and offerings or with animals burnt on the altar and the sacrifices to take away sins." He said this even though all these sacrifices are offered according to the Law. [9]Then he said, "Here I am, O God, to do your will." So God does away with all the old sacrifices and puts the sacrifice of Christ in their place. [10]Because Jesus Christ did what God wanted him to do, we are all purified from sin by the offering that he made of his own body once and for all.

11 Every Jewish priest performs his services every day and offers the same sacrifices many times; but these sacrifices can never take away sins. [12]Christ, however, offered one sacrifice for sins, an offering that is effective for ever, and then he sat down at the right-hand side of God. [13]There he now waits until God puts his enemies as a footstool under his feet. [14]With one sacrifice, then, he has made perfect for ever those who are purified from sin.

15 And the Holy Spirit also gives us his witness. First he says:

16 "This is the covenant that I will make with
            them
        in the days to come, says the Lord:
    I will put my laws in their hearts
        and write them on their minds."

[17]And then he says, "I will not remember their sins and evil deeds any longer." [18]So when these have been forgiven, an offering to take away sins is no longer needed.

Let us Come Near to God

19 We have, then, my brothers and sisters, complete freedom to go into the Most Holy Place by means of the death of Jesus. [20]He opened for us a new way, a living way, through the curtain – that is, through his own body. [21]We have a great priest in charge of the house of God. [22]So let us come near to God with a sincere heart and a sure faith, with hearts that have been purified from a guilty conscience and with bodies washed with clean water. [23]Let us hold on firmly to the hope we profess, because we can trust God to keep his promise. [24]Let us be concerned for one another, to help one another to show love and to do good. [25]Let us not give up the habit of meeting together, as some are doing. Instead, let us encourage one another all the more, since you see that the Day of the Lord is coming nearer.

26 For there is no longer any sacrifice that will take away sins if we purposely go on sinning after the truth has been made known to us. [27]Instead, all that is left is to wait in fear for the coming Judgement and the fierce fire which will destroy those who oppose God! [28]Anyone who disobeys the Law of Moses is put to death without any mercy when judged guilty on the evidence of two or more witnesses. [29]What, then, of those who despise the Son of God? who treat as a cheap thing the blood of God's covenant which purified them from sin? who insult the Spirit of grace? Just think how much worse is the punishment they will deserve! [30]For we know who said, "I will take revenge, I will repay"; and who also said, "The Lord will judge his people." [31]It is a terrifying thing to fall into the hands of the living God!

32 Remember how it was with you in the past. In those days, after God's light had shone on you, you suffered many things, yet were not defeated by the struggle. [33]You were at times publicly insulted and ill-treated, and at other times you were ready to join those who were being treated in this way. [34]You shared the sufferings of prisoners, and when all your belongings were seized, you endured your loss gladly, because you knew that you still possessed something much better, which would last for ever. [35]Do not lose your courage, then, because it brings with it a great reward. [36]You need to be patient, in order to do the will of God and receive what he promises.

[37]For, as the scripture says:

"Just a little while longer,
    and he who is coming will come;
    he will not delay.
[38]   My righteous people, however, will believe
        and live;
    but if any of them turns back,
        I will not be pleased with him."

[39]We are not people who turn back and are lost. Instead, we have faith and are saved.

Faith

11 To have faith is to be sure of the things we hope for, to be certain of the things we cannot see. [2]It was by their faith that people of ancient times won God's approval.

[3] It is by faith that we understand that the universe was created by God's word, so that what can be seen was made out of what cannot be seen.

[4] It was faith that made Abel offer to God a better sacrifice than Cain's. Through his faith he won God's approval as a righteous man, because God himself approved of his gifts. By means of his faith Abel still speaks, even though he is dead.

[5] It was faith that kept Enoch from dying. Instead, he was taken up to God, and nobody could find him, because God had taken him up. The scripture says that before Enoch was taken up, he had pleased God. [6]No one can please God without faith, for whoever comes to God must have faith that God exists and rewards those who seek him.

[7] It was faith that made Noah hear God's warnings about things in the future that he could not see. He obeyed God and built a boat in which he and his family were saved. As a result, the world was condemned, and Noah received from God the righteousness that comes by faith.

[8] It was faith that made Abraham obey when God called him to go out to a country which God had promised to give him. He left his own country without knowing where he was going. [9]By faith he lived as a foreigner in the country that God had promised him. He lived in tents, as did Isaac and Jacob, who received the same promise from God. [10]For Abraham was waiting for the city which God has designed and built, the city with permanent foundations.

[11] It was faith that made Abraham able to become a father, even though he was too old and Sarah herself could not have children.

He[a] trusted God to keep his promise. [12]Though Abraham was practically dead, from this one man came as many descendants as there are stars in the sky, as many as the numberless grains of sand on the seashore.

[13] It was in faith that all these persons died. They did not receive the things God had promised, but from a long way off they saw them and welcomed them, and admitted openly that they were foreigners and refugees on earth. [14]Those who say such things make it clear that they are looking for a country of their own. [15]They did not keep thinking about the country they had left; if they had, they would have had the chance to return. [16]Instead, it was a better country they longed for, the heavenly country. And so God is not ashamed for them to call him their God, because he has prepared a city for them.

[17] It was faith that made Abraham offer his son Isaac as a sacrifice when God put Abraham to the test. Abraham was the one to whom God had made the promise, yet he was ready to offer his only son as a sacrifice. [18]God had said to him, "It is through Isaac that you will have the descendants I promised." [19]Abraham reckoned that God was able to raise Isaac from death – and, so to speak, Abraham did receive Isaac back from death.

[20] It was faith that made Isaac promise blessings for the future to Jacob and Esau.

[21] It was faith that made Jacob bless each of the sons of Joseph just before he died. He leaned on the top of his walking stick and worshipped God.

[22] It was faith that made Joseph, when he was about to die, speak of the departure of the Israelites from Egypt, and leave instructions about what should be done with his body.

[23] It was faith that made the parents of Moses hide him for three months after he was born. They saw that he was a beautiful child, and they were not afraid to disobey the king's order.

[24] It was faith that made Moses, when he had grown up, refuse to be called the son of the king's daughter. [25]He preferred to suffer with God's people rather than to enjoy sin for a little while. [26]He reckoned that to suffer scorn for the Messiah was worth far more than all the treasures of Egypt, for he kept his eyes on the future reward.

[a] **11.11** It was faith ... children. He; *some manuscripts have* It was faith that made Sarah herself able to conceive, even though she was too old to have children. She.

27 It was faith that made Moses leave Egypt without being afraid of the king's anger. As though he saw the invisible God, he refused to turn back. ²⁸It was faith that made him establish the Passover and order the blood to be sprinkled on the doors, so that the Angel of Death would not kill the firstborn sons of the Israelites.

29 It was faith that made the Israelites able to cross the Red Sea as if on dry land; when the Egyptians tried to do it, the water swallowed them up.

30 It was faith that made the walls of Jericho fall down after the Israelites had marched round them for seven days. ³¹It was faith that kept the prostitute Rahab from being killed with those who disobeyed God, for she gave the Israelite spies a friendly welcome.

32 Should I go on? There isn't enough time for me to speak of Gideon, Barak, Samson, Jephthah, David, Samuel, and the prophets. ³³Through faith they fought whole countries and won. They did what was right and received what God had promised. They shut the mouths of lions, ³⁴put out fierce fires, escaped being killed by the sword. They were weak, but became strong; they were mighty in battle and defeated the armies of foreigners. ³⁵Through faith women received their dead relatives raised back to life.

Others, refusing to accept freedom, died under torture in order to be raised to a better life. ³⁶Some were mocked and whipped, and others were put in chains and taken off to prison. ³⁷They were stoned, they were sawn in two, they were killed by the sword. They went round clothed in skins of sheep or goats – poor, persecuted, and ill-treated. ³⁸The world was not good enough for them! They wandered like refugees in the deserts and hills, living in caves and holes in the ground.

39 What a record all of these have won by their faith! Yet they did not receive what God had promised, ⁴⁰because God had decided on an even better plan for us. His purpose was that only in company with us would they be made perfect.

God our Father

12 As for us, we have this large crowd of witnesses round us. So then, let us rid ourselves of everything that gets in the way, and of the sin which holds on to us so tightly, and let us run with determination the race that lies before us. ²Let us keep our eyes fixed on Jesus, on whom our faith depends from beginning to end. He did not give up because of the cross! On the contrary, because of the joy that was waiting for him, he thought nothing of the disgrace of dying on the cross, and he is now seated at the right-hand side of God's throne.

3 Think of what he went through; how he put up with so much hatred from sinners! So do not let yourselves become discouraged and give up. ⁴For in your struggle against sin you have not yet had to resist to the point of being killed. ⁵Have you forgotten the encouraging words which God speaks to you as his sons and daughters?

"My child, pay attention when the Lord
    corrects you,
  and do not be discouraged when he
    rebukes you.

6 Because the Lord corrects everyone he loves,
  and punishes everyone he accepts as his
    child."

⁷Endure what you suffer as being a father's punishment; your suffering shows that God is treating you as his children. Was there ever a child who was not punished by his father? ⁸If you are not punished, as all his children are, it means you are not real children, but bastards. ⁹In the case of our human fathers, they punished us and we respected them. How much more, then, should we submit to our spiritual Father and live! ¹⁰Our human fathers punished us for a short time, as it seemed right to them; but God does it for our own good, so that we may share his holiness. ¹¹When we are punished, it seems to us at the time something to make us sad, not glad. Later, however, those who have been disciplined by such punishment reap the peaceful reward of a righteous life.

Instructions and Warnings

12 Lift up your tired hands, then, and strengthen your trembling knees! ¹³Keep walking on straight paths, so that the lame foot may not be disabled, but instead be healed.

14 Try to be at peace with everyone, and try to live a holy life, because no one will see the Lord without it. ¹⁵Guard against turning back from the grace of God. Let no one become like a bitter plant that grows up and causes many troubles with its poison. ¹⁶Let no one become immoral or unspiritual like Esau, who for a single meal sold his rights as the elder son. ¹⁷Afterwards, you know, he wanted to receive his father's blessing; but he was turned away, because he could not find any way to change

Christians exchanging a Sign of God's peace (12.14)

what he had done, even though in tears he looked for it.[a]

18 You have not come, as the people of Israel came, to what you can feel, to Mount Sinai with its blazing fire, the darkness and the gloom, the storm, [19]the blast of a trumpet, and the sound of a voice. When the people heard the voice, they begged not to hear another word, [20]because they could not bear the order which said, "If even an animal touches the mountain, it must be stoned to death." [21]The sight was so terrifying that Moses said, "I am trembling and afraid!"

22 Instead, you have come to Mount Zion and to the city of the living God, the heavenly Jerusalem, with its thousands of angels. [23]You have come to the joyful gathering of God's first-born, whose names are written in heaven. You have come to God, who is the judge of all people, and to the spirits of good people made perfect. [24]You have come to Jesus, who arranged the new covenant, and to the sprinkled blood that promises much better things than does the blood of Abel.

25 Be careful, then, and do not refuse to hear him who speaks. Those who refused to hear the one who gave the divine message on earth did not escape. How much less shall we escape, then, if we turn away from the one who speaks from heaven! [26]His voice shook the earth at that time, but now he has promised, "I will once more shake not only the earth but heaven as well." [27]The words "once more" plainly show that the created things will be shaken and removed, so that the things that cannot be shaken will remain.

28 Let us be thankful, then, because we receive a kingdom that cannot be shaken. Let us be grateful and worship God in a way that will please him, with reverence and awe; [29]because our God is indeed a destroying fire.

How to Please God

13 Keep on loving one another as Christian brothers and sisters. [2]Remember to welcome strangers in your homes. There were some who did that and welcomed angels without knowing it. [3]Remember those who are in prison, as though you were in prison with them. Remember those who are suffering, as though you were suffering as they are.

4 Marriage is to be honoured by all, and husbands and wives must be faithful to each other.

---

[a] **12.17** he looked for it; *or* he tried to get the blessing.

God will judge those who are immoral and those who commit adultery.

5 Keep your lives free from the love of money, and be satisfied with what you have. For God has said, "I will never leave you; I will never abandon you." [6]Let us be bold, then, and say:

"The Lord is my helper,
    I will not be afraid.
What can anyone do to me?"

7 Remember your former leaders, who spoke God's message to you. Think back on how they lived and died, and imitate their faith. [8]Jesus Christ is the same yesterday, today, and for ever. [9]Do not let all kinds of strange teachings lead you from the right way. It is good to receive inner strength from God's grace, and not by obeying rules about foods; those who obey these rules have not been helped by them.

10 The priests who serve in the Jewish place of worship have no right to eat any of the sacrifice on our altar. [11]The Jewish High Priest brings the blood of the animals into the Most Holy Place to offer it as a sacrifice for sins; but the bodies of the animals are burnt outside the camp. [12]For this reason Jesus also died outside the city, in order to purify the people from sin with his own blood. [13]Let us, then, go to him outside the camp and share his shame. [14]For there is no permanent city for us here on earth; we are looking for the city which is to come. [15]Let us, then, always offer praise to God as our sacrifice through Jesus, which is the offering presented by lips that confess him as Lord. [16]Do not forget to do good and to help one another, because these are the sacrifices that please God.

17 Obey your leaders and follow their orders. They watch over your souls without resting, since they must give God an account of their service. If you obey them, they will do their work gladly; if not, they will do it with sadness, and that would be of no help to you.

18 Keep on praying for us. We are sure we have a clear conscience, because we want to do the right thing at all times. [19]And I beg you even more earnestly to pray that God will send me back to you soon.

Closing Prayer

20–21 God has raised from death our Lord Jesus, who is the Great Shepherd of the sheep as the result of his blood,[a] by which the eternal covenant is sealed. May the God of peace provide you with every good thing you need in order to do his will, and may he, through Jesus Christ, do in us what pleases him. And to Christ be the glory for ever and ever! Amen.

Final Words

22 I beg you, my brothers and sisters, to listen patiently to this message of encouragement; for this letter I have written to you is not very long. [23]I want you to know that our brother Timothy has been let out of prison. If he comes soon enough, I will have him with me when I see you.

24 Give our greetings to all your leaders and to all God's people. The brothers and sisters from Italy send you their greetings.

25 May God's grace be with you all.

---

[a] **13.20–21** his blood; or his sacrificial death.

The Letter from
JAMES

INTRODUCTION

The Letter from James is a collection of practical instructions, written to "all God's people scattered over the whole world". The writer uses many vivid figures of speech to present instructions regarding practical wisdom and guidance for Christian attitudes and conduct. From the Christian perspective he deals with a variety of topics such as riches and poverty, temptation, good conduct, prejudice, faith and actions, the use of the tongue, wisdom, quarrelling, pride and humility, judging others, boasting, patience, and prayer.

The letter emphasizes the importance of actions along with faith, in the practice of the Christian religion.

1 From James, a servant of God and of the Lord Jesus Christ:

Greetings to all God's people scattered over the whole world.

Faith and Wisdom

2 My brothers and sisters, consider yourselves fortunate when all kinds of trials come your way, ³for you know that when your faith succeeds in facing such trials, the result is the ability to endure. ⁴Make sure that your endurance carries you all the way without failing, so that you may be perfect and complete, lacking nothing. ⁵But if any of you lack wisdom, you should pray to God, who will give it to you; because God gives generously and graciously to all. ⁶But when you pray, you must believe and not doubt at all. Whoever doubts is like a wave in the sea that is driven and blown about by the wind. ⁷⁻⁸People like that, unable to make up their minds and undecided in all they do, must not think that they will receive anything from the Lord.

Poverty and Riches

9 Those Christians who are poor must be glad when God lifts them up, ¹⁰and the rich Christians must be glad when God brings them down. For the rich will pass away like the flower of a wild plant. ¹¹The sun rises with its blazing heat and burns the plant; its flower falls off, and its beauty is destroyed. In the same way the rich will be destroyed while they go about their business.

Testing and Tempting

12 Happy are those who remain faithful under trials, because when they succeed in passing such a test, they will receive as their reward the life which God has promised to those who love him. ¹³If people are tempted by such trials, they

must not say, "This temptation comes from God." For God cannot be tempted by evil, and he himself tempts no one. ¹⁴But people are tempted when they are drawn away and trapped by their own evil desires. ¹⁵Then their evil desires conceive and give birth to sin; and sin, when it is full-grown, gives birth to death.

16   Do not be deceived, my dear brothers and sisters! ¹⁷Every good gift and every perfect present comes from heaven; it comes down from God, the Creator of the heavenly lights, who does not change or cause darkness by turning. ¹⁸By his own will he brought us into being through the word of truth, so that we should have first place among all his creatures.

Hearing and Doing

19   Remember this, my dear brothers and sisters! Everyone must be quick to listen, but slow to speak and slow to become angry. ²⁰Human anger does not achieve God's righteous purpose. ²¹So get rid of every filthy habit and all wicked conduct. Submit to God and accept the word that he plants in your hearts, which is able to save you.

22   Do not deceive yourselves by just listening to his word; instead, put it into practice. ²³Whoever listens to the word but does not put it into practice is like a man who looks in a mirror and sees himself as he is. ²⁴He takes a good look at himself and then goes away and at once forgets what he looks like. ²⁵But those who look closely into the perfect law that sets people free, who keep on paying attention to it and do not simply listen and then forget it, but put it into practice – they will be blessed by God in what they do.

26   Do any of you think you are religious? If you do not control your tongue, your religion is worthless and you deceive yourselves. ²⁷What God the Father considers to be pure and genuine religion is this: to take care of orphans and widows in their suffering and to keep oneself from being corrupted by the world.

Warning against Prejudice

2 My brothers and sisters, as believers in our Lord Jesus Christ, the Lord of glory, you must never treat people in different ways according to their outward appearance. ²Suppose a rich man wearing a gold ring and fine clothes comes to your meeting, and a poor man in ragged clothes also comes. ³If you show more respect to the well-dressed man and say to him, "Have this best seat here," but say to the poor

Studying
JAMES

Who wrote it? Likely to have been James, brother of Jesus, leader of the church in Jerusalem.
When? Around 59–60 CE. James was martyred in 61 CE.
Where from? Unknown.
For whom? Author had a real audience in mind which seemed to be poor (1.10–11). It may have been largely Jewish.
Why? Written to emphasize the moral side of religion – faith without works is dead. Probably there were some telling people that behaviour was unimportant as long as they believed in God.

KEY POINTS

- God offers all people wisdom to help them withstand the Devil's testing (3.13–18).
- Wealth is a gift from God – Christians should share their wealth with others (2.14–26).
- Prayer is the key to endurance (chapter 1), to the supply of real needs (chapter 4) and to healing (chapter 5).

man, "Stand over there, or sit here on the floor by my feet," ⁴then you are guilty of creating distinctions among yourselves and of making judgements based on evil motives.

5   Listen, my dear brothers and sisters! God chose the poor people of this world to be rich in faith and to possess the kingdom which he promised to those who love him. ⁶But you dishonour the poor! Who are the ones who oppress you and drag you before the judges? The rich! ⁷They are the ones who speak evil of that good name which has been given to you.

8   You will be doing the right thing if you obey the law of the Kingdom, which is found in the scripture, "Love your neighbour as you love yourself." ⁹But if you treat people according to their outward appearance, you are guilty of sin, and the Law condemns you as a lawbreaker. ¹⁰Whoever breaks one commandment is guilty of breaking them all. ¹¹For the same one who said, "Do not commit adultery," also said, "Do not commit murder." Even if you do not commit adultery, you have become a lawbreaker if you commit murder. ¹²Speak and act as people who will be judged by the law that sets us free. ¹³For God will not show mercy when he judges the person who has not been merciful; but mercy triumphs over judgement.

Faith and Actions

14   My brothers and sisters, what good is it for people to say that they have faith if their actions

do not prove it? Can that faith save them? [15]Suppose there are brothers or sisters who need clothes and don't have enough to eat. [16]What good is there in your saying to them, "God bless you! Keep warm and eat well!" – if you don't give them the necessities of life? [17]So it is with faith: if it is alone and includes no actions, then it is dead.

18   But someone will say, "One person has faith, another has actions." My answer is, "Show me how anyone can have faith without actions. I will show you my faith by my actions." [19]Do you believe that there is only one God? Good! The demons also believe – and tremble with fear. [20]You fool! Do you want to be shown that faith without actions is useless?[a] [21]How was our ancestor Abraham put right with God? It was through his actions, when he offered his son Isaac on the altar. [22]Can't you see? His faith and his actions worked together; his faith was made perfect through his actions. [23]And the scripture came true that said, "Abraham believed God, and because of his faith God accepted him as righteous." And so Abraham was called God's friend. [24]You see, then, that it is by people's actions that they are put right with God, and not by their faith alone.

25   It was the same with the prostitute Rahab. She was put right with God through her actions, by welcoming the Israelite spies and helping them to escape by a different road.

26   So then, as the body without the spirit is dead, so also faith without actions is dead.

The Tongue

3 My brothers and sisters, not many of you should become teachers. As you know, we teachers will be judged with greater strictness than others. [2]All of us often make mistakes. But if a person never makes a mistake in what he says, he is perfect and is also able to control his whole being. [3]We put a bit into the mouth of a horse to make it obey us, and we are able to make it go where we want. [4]Or think of a ship: big as it is and driven by such strong winds, it can be steered by a very small rudder, and it goes wherever the pilot wants it to go. [5]So it is with the tongue: small as it is, it can boast about great things.

Just think how large a forest can be set on fire by a tiny flame! [6]And the tongue is like a fire. It is a world of wrong, occupying its place in our bodies and spreading evil through our whole being. It sets on fire the entire course of

our existence with the fire that comes to it from hell itself. [7]Human beings can tame and have tamed all other creatures – wild animals and birds, reptiles and fish. [8]But no one has ever been able to tame the tongue. It is evil and uncontrollable, full of deadly poison. [9]We use it to give thanks to our Lord and Father and also to curse other people, who are created in the likeness of God. [10]Words of thanksgiving and cursing pour out from the same mouth. My brothers and sisters, this should not happen! [11]No spring of water pours out sweet water and bitter water from the same opening. [12]A fig tree, my brothers and sisters, cannot bear olives; a grapevine cannot bear figs, nor can a salty spring produce sweet water.

The Wisdom from Above

13   Are there people among you who are wise and understanding? They are to prove it by their good lives, by their good deeds performed with humility and wisdom. [14]But if in your heart you are jealous, bitter, and selfish, don't sin against the truth by boasting of your wisdom. [15]Such wisdom does not come down from heaven; it belongs to the world, it is unspiritual and demonic. [16]Where there is jealousy and selfishness, there is also disorder and every kind of evil. [17]But the wisdom from above is pure first of all; it is also peaceful, gentle, and friendly; it is full of compassion and produces a harvest of good deeds; it is free from prejudice and hypocrisy. [18]And goodness is the harvest that is produced from the seeds the peacemakers plant in peace.

Friendship with the World

4 Where do all the fights and quarrels among you come from? They come from your desires for pleasure, which are constantly fighting within you. [2]You want things, but you cannot have them, so you are ready to kill; you strongly desire things, but you cannot get them, so you quarrel and fight. You do not have what you want because you do not ask God for it. [3]And when you ask, you do not receive it, because your motives are bad; you ask for things to use for your own pleasures. [4]Unfaithful people! Don't you know that to be the world's friend means to be God's enemy? People who want to be the world's friends make themselves God's enemies. [5]Don't think that there is no truth in the scripture that says, "The spirit that God placed in us is filled with fierce

---

[a] **2.20** useless; *some manuscripts have* dead.

desires."[a] [6]But the grace that God gives is even stronger. As the scripture says, "God resists the proud, but gives grace to the humble."

[7] So then, submit to God. Resist the Devil, and he will run away from you. [8]Come near to God, and he will come near to you. Wash your hands, you sinners! Purify your hearts, you hypocrites! [9]Be sorrowful, cry, and weep; change your laughter into crying, your joy into gloom! [10]Humble yourselves before the Lord, and he will lift you up.

Warning against Judging a Fellow-Christian

[11] Do not criticize one another, my brothers and sisters. If you criticize fellow-Christians or judge them, you criticize the Law and judge it. If you judge the Law, then you are no longer one who obeys the Law, but one who judges it. [12]God is the only lawgiver and judge. He alone can save and destroy. Who do you think you are, to judge someone else?

Warning against Boasting

[13] Now listen to me, you that say, "Today or tomorrow we will travel to a certain city, where we will stay a year and go into business and make a lot of money." [14]You don't even know what your life tomorrow will be! You are like a puff of smoke, which appears for a moment and then disappears. [15]What you should say is this: "If the Lord is willing, we will live and do this or that." [16]But now you are proud, and you boast; all such boasting is wrong.

[17] So then, those who do not do the good they know they should do are guilty of sin.

Warning to the Rich

5 And now, you rich people, listen to me! Weep and wail over the miseries that are coming upon you! [2]Your riches have rotted away, and your clothes have been eaten by moths. [3]Your gold and silver are covered with rust, and this rust will be a witness against you and will eat up your flesh like fire. You have piled up riches in these last days. [4]You have not paid any wages to those who work in your fields. Listen to their complaints! The cries of those who gather in your crops have reached the ears of God, the Lord Almighty. [5]Your life here on earth has been full of luxury and pleasure. You have made yourselves fat for the day of slaughter. [6]You have condemned and murdered innocent people, and they do not resist you.[b]

Patience and Prayer

[7] Be patient, then, my brothers and sisters, until the Lord comes. See how patient a farmer is as he waits for his land to produce precious crops. He waits patiently for the autumn and spring rains. [8]You also must be patient. Keep your hopes high, for the day of the Lord's coming is near.

[9] Do not complain against one another, my brothers and sisters, so that God will not judge you. The Judge is near, ready to appear. [10]My brothers and sisters, remember the prophets who spoke in the name of the Lord. Take them as examples of patient endurance under suffering. [11]We call them happy because they endured. You have heard of Job's patience, and you know how the Lord provided for him in the end. For the Lord is full of mercy and compassion.

[12] Above all, my brothers and sisters, do not use an oath when you make a promise. Do not swear by heaven or by earth or by anything else. Say only "Yes" when you mean yes, and "No" when you mean no, and then you will not come under God's judgement.

[13] Are any of you in trouble? You should pray. Are any of you happy? You should sing praises. [14]Are any of you ill? You should send for the church elders, who will pray for them and rub olive oil on them in the name of the Lord. [15]This

A priest anoints a hospice patient with oil (5.14)

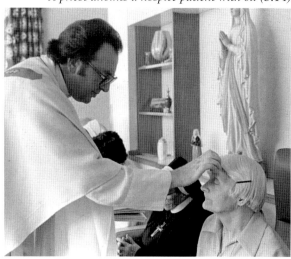

[a] **4.5** The spirit … fierce desires; *or* God yearns jealously over the spirit that he placed in us.

[b] **5.6** people, and they do not resist you; *or* people. Will God not resist you?

prayer made in faith will heal the sick; the Lord will restore them to health, and the sins they have committed will be forgiven. [16]So then, confess your sins to one another and pray for one another, so that you will be healed. The prayer of a good person has a powerful effect. [17]Elijah was the same kind of person as we are. He prayed earnestly that there would be no rain, and no rain fell on the land for three and a half years. [18]Once again he prayed, and the sky poured out its rain and the earth produced its crops.

19 My brothers and sisters, if any of you wander away from the truth and another one brings them back again, [20]remember this: whoever turns a sinner back from his or her wrong way will save that sinner's soul[a] from death and bring about the forgiveness of many sins.

---

[a] **5.20** that sinner's soul; *or* his own soul.

The First Letter from
PETER

INTRODUCTION

The First Letter from Peter was addressed to Christians, here called "God's chosen people", who were scattered throughout the northern part of Asia Minor. The main purpose of the letter is to encourage the readers, who were facing persecution and suffering for their faith. The writer does this by reminding his readers of the Good News about Jesus Christ, whose death, resurrection, and promised coming give them hope. In the light of this they are to accept and endure their suffering, confident that it is a test of the genuineness of their faith and that they will be rewarded on "the Day when Jesus Christ is revealed" (1.7).

Along with his encouragement in time of trouble, the writer also urges his readers to live as people who belong to Christ.

1 From Peter, apostle of Jesus Christ –
To God's chosen people who live as refugees scattered throughout the provinces of Pontus, Galatia, Cappadocia, Asia, and Bithynia. ²You were chosen according to the purpose of God the Father and were made a holy people by his Spirit, to obey Jesus Christ and be purified by his blood.

May grace and peace be yours in full measure.

A Living Hope

3 Let us give thanks to the God and Father of our Lord Jesus Christ! Because of his great mercy he gave us new life by raising Jesus Christ from death. This fills us with a living hope, ⁴and so we look forward to possessing the rich blessings that God keeps for his people. He keeps them for you in heaven, where they cannot decay or spoil or fade away. ⁵They are for you, who through faith are kept safe by God's power for the salvation which is ready to be revealed at the end of time.

6 Be glad about this, even though it may now be necessary for you to be sad for a while because of the many kinds of trials you suffer.

⁷Their purpose is to prove that your faith is genuine. Even gold, which can be destroyed, is tested by fire; and so your faith, which is much more precious than gold, must also be tested, so that it may endure. Then you will receive praise and glory and honour on the Day when Jesus Christ is revealed. ⁸You love him, although you have not seen him, and you believe in him, although you do not now see him. So you rejoice with a great and glorious joy which words cannot express, ⁹because you are receiving the salvation of your souls, which is the purpose of your faith in him.

10 It was concerning this salvation that the prophets made careful search and investigation, and they prophesied about this gift which God would give you. ¹¹They tried to find out when the time would be and how it would come.ᵃ This was the time to which Christ's Spirit in them was pointing, in predicting the sufferings that Christ would have to endure and the glory that

---

ᵃ **1.11** when the time would be and how it would come; *or* who the person would be and when he would come.

Studying
1 PETER

Who wrote it? Possibly the Apostle Peter, otherwise unknown.
When? If Peter then around 61–62 CE (Peter was martyred in 64 CE). If not Peter then around 80 CE.
Where from? Possibly Rome.
For whom? Several churches are mentioned in 1.1. These were all small groups of believers over a wide area who had been persecuted. The persecution had not come from the Romans but from governors, soldiers and even relations.
Why? To encourage isolated groups of believers. They are urged to stick together and not to retaliate when they are persecuted.

KEY POINTS

- All Christians can be confident in God. They have been reborn through the resurrection of Jesus (1.3–5) and so can wait in hope (1.6–9). They are called to live holy lives (1.13–21) as they are members of a holy people (2.4–10)
- Christians have a responsibility to live a holy life whether they are free citizens (2.13–17), slaves (2.18–25), wives or husbands (3.1–7).
- When Christians suffer it should be because they are doing good and not because they have committed some crime (3.13–17).

would follow. ¹²God revealed to these prophets that their work was not for their own benefit, but for yours, as they spoke about those things which you have now heard from the messengers who announced the Good News by the power of the Holy Spirit sent from heaven. These are things which even the angels would like to understand.

A Call to Holy Living

13 So then, have your minds ready for action. Keep alert and set your hope completely on the blessing which will be given you when Jesus Christ is revealed. ¹⁴Be obedient to God, and do not allow your lives to be shaped by those desires you had when you were still ignorant. ¹⁵Instead, be holy in all that you do, just as God who called you is holy. ¹⁶The scripture says, "Be holy because I am holy."

17 You call him Father, when you pray to God, who judges all people by the same standard, according to what each one has done; so then, spend the rest of your lives here on earth in reverence for him. ¹⁸For you know what was paid to set you free from the worthless manner of life handed down by your ancestors. It was not something that can be destroyed, such as

silver or gold; ¹⁹it was the costly sacrifice of Christ, who was like a lamb without defect or flaw. ²⁰He had been chosen by God before the creation of the world and was revealed in these last days for your sake. ²¹Through him you believe in God, who raised him from death and gave him glory; and so your faith and hope are fixed on God.

22 Now that by your obedience to the truth you have purified yourselves and have come to have a sincere love for your fellow-believers, love one another earnestly with all your heart.ᵃ ²³For through the living and eternal word of God you have been born again as the children of a parent who is immortal, not mortal. ²⁴As the scripture says:

"All human beings are like grass,
    and all their glory is like wild flowers.
The grass withers, and the flowers fall,
25   but the word of the Lord remains for ever."

This word is the Good News that was proclaimed to you.

The Living Stone and the Holy Nation

2 Rid yourselves, then, of all evil; no more lying or hypocrisy or jealousy or insulting language. ²Be like newborn babies, always thirsty for the pure spiritual milk, so that by drinking it you may grow up and be saved. ³As the scripture says, "You have found out for yourselves how kind the Lord is."

4 Come to the Lord, the living stone rejected by people as worthless but chosen by God as valuable. ⁵Come as living stones, and let yourselves be used in building the spiritual temple, where you will serve as holy priests to offer spiritual and acceptable sacrifices to God through Jesus Christ. ⁶For the scripture says:

"I chose a valuable stone,
    which I am placing as the cornerstone in Zion;
    and whoever believes in him will never be disappointed."

⁷This stone is of great value for you that believe; but for those who do not believe:

"The stone which the builders rejected as worthless
    turned out to be the most important of all."

ᵃ **1.22** with all your heart; *some manuscripts have* with a pure heart.

8And another scripture says:

"This is the stone that will make people
    stumble,
  the rock that will make them fall."

They stumbled because they did not believe in the word; such was God's will for them.

9 But you are the chosen race, the King's priests, the holy nation, God's own people, chosen to proclaim the wonderful acts of God, who called you out of darkness into his own marvellous light. 10At one time you were not God's people, but now you are his people; at one time you did not know God's mercy, but now you have received his mercy.

Slaves of God

11 I appeal to you, my friends, as strangers and refugees in this world! Do not give in to bodily passions, which are always at war against the soul. 12Your conduct among the heathen should be so good that when they accuse you of being evildoers, they will have to recognize your good deeds and so praise God on the Day of his coming.

13 For the sake of the Lord submit to every human authority: to the Emperor, who is the supreme authority, 14and to the governors, who have been appointed by him to punish the evildoers and to praise those who do good. 15For God wants you to silence the ignorant talk of foolish people by the good things you do. 16Live as free people; do not, however, use your freedom to cover up any evil, but live as God's slaves. 17Respect everyone, love your fellow-believers, honour God, and respect the Emperor.

The Example of Christ's Suffering

18 You servants must submit to your masters and show them complete respect, not only to those who are kind and considerate, but also to those who are harsh. 19God will bless you for this, if you endure the pain of undeserved suffering because you are conscious of his will. 20For what credit is there if you endure the beatings you deserve for having done wrong? But if you endure suffering even when you have done right, God will bless you for it. 21It was to this that God called you, for Christ himself suffered for you and left you an example, so that you would follow in his steps. 22He committed no sin, and no one ever heard a lie come from his lips. 23When he was insulted, he did not answer back with an insult; when he suffered, he did not threaten, but placed his hopes in God, the righteous Judge. 24Christ himself carried our sins in his body to the cross, so that we might die to sin and live for righteousness. It is by his wounds that you have been healed. 25You were like sheep that had lost their way, but now you have been brought back to follow the Shepherd and Keeper of your souls.

Wives and Husbands

3 In the same way you wives must submit to your husbands, so that if any of them do not believe God's word, your conduct will win them over to believe. It will not be necessary for you to say a word, 2because they will see how pure and reverent your conduct is. 3You should not use outward aids to make yourselves beautiful, such as the way you do your hair, or the jewellery you put on, or the dresses you wear. 4Instead, your beauty should consist of your true inner self, the ageless beauty of a gentle and quiet spirit, which is of the greatest value in God's sight. 5For the devout women of the past who placed their hope in God used to make themselves beautiful by submitting to their husbands. 6Sarah was like that; she obeyed Abraham and called him her master. You are now her daughters if you do good and are not afraid of anything.

7 In the same way you husbands must live with your wives with the proper understanding that they are weaker than you. Treat them with respect, because they also will receive, together with you, God's gift of life. Do this so that nothing will interfere with your prayers.

Suffering for Doing Right

8 To conclude: you must all have the same attitude and the same feelings; love one another as brothers and sisters, and be kind and humble with one another. 9Do not pay back evil with evil or cursing with cursing; instead, pay back with a blessing, because a blessing is what God promised to give you when he called you. 10As the scripture says:

"Whoever wants to enjoy life
    and wishes to see good times,
  must keep from speaking evil
    and stop telling lies.
11 They must turn away from evil and do good;
    they must strive for peace with all their
        heart.
12 For the Lord watches over the righteous
    and listens to their prayers;
  but he opposes those who do evil."

Women weeping over the crucified body of Jesus (2.24)

13 Who will harm you if you are eager to do what is good? [14]But even if you should suffer for doing what is right, how happy you are! Do not be afraid of anyone, and do not worry. [15]But have reverence for Christ in your hearts, and honour him as Lord. Be ready at all times to answer anyone who asks you to explain the hope you have in you, [16]but do it with gentleness and respect. Keep your conscience clear, so that when you are insulted, those who speak evil of your good conduct as followers of Christ will be ashamed of what they say. [17]For it is better to suffer for doing good, if this should be God's will, than for doing evil. [18]For Christ died[a] for sins once and for all, a good man on behalf of sinners, in order to lead you to God. He was put to death physically, but made alive spiritually, [19]and in his spiritual existence he went and preached to the imprisoned spirits. [20]These were the spirits of those who had not obeyed God when he waited patiently during the days that Noah was building his boat. The few people in the boat – eight in all – were saved by the water, [21]which was a symbol pointing to baptism, which now saves you. It is

not the washing away of bodily dirt, but the promise made to God from a good conscience. It saves you through the resurrection of Jesus Christ, [22]who has gone to heaven and is at the right-hand side of God, ruling over all angels and heavenly authorities and powers.

Changed Lives

4 Since Christ suffered physically, you too must strengthen yourselves with the same way of thinking that he had; because whoever suffers physically is no longer involved with sin. [2]From now on, then, you must live the rest of your earthly lives controlled by God's will and not by human desires. [3]You have spent enough time in the past doing what the heathen like to do. Your lives were spent in indecency, lust, drunkenness, orgies, drinking parties, and the disgusting worship of idols. [4]And now the heathen are surprised when you do not join them in the same wild and reckless living, and so they insult you. [5]But they will have to give an account of themselves to God, who is ready to judge the living and the dead. [6]That is why the Good News was preached also to the dead, to

---

[a] **3.18** died; *many manuscripts have* suffered.

those who had been judged in their physical existence as everyone is judged; it was preached to them so that in their spiritual existence they may live as God lives.

Good Managers of God's Gifts

7 The end of all things is near. You must be self-controlled and alert, to be able to pray. [8]Above everything, love one another earnestly, because love covers over many sins. [9]Open your homes to each other without complaining. [10]Each one, as a good manager of God's different gifts, must use for the good of others the special gift he has received from God. [11]Whoever preaches must preach God's messages; whoever serves must serve with the strength that God gives, so that in all things praise may be given to God through Jesus Christ, to whom belong glory and power for ever and ever. Amen.

Suffering as a Christian

12 My dear friends, do not be surprised at the painful test you are suffering, as though something unusual were happening to you. [13]Rather be glad that you are sharing Christ's sufferings, so that you may be full of joy when his glory is revealed. [14]Happy are you if you are insulted because you are Christ's followers; this means that the glorious Spirit, the Spirit of God, is resting on you. [15]If any of you suffer, it must not be because you are a murderer or a thief or a criminal or a meddler in other people's affairs. [16]However, if you suffer because you are a Christian, don't be ashamed of it, but thank God that you bear Christ's name.

17 The time has come for judgement to begin, and God's own people are the first to be judged. If it starts with us, how will it end with those who do not believe the Good News from God? [18]As the scripture says:

> "It is difficult for good people to be saved;
> what, then, will become of godless
> sinners?"

[19]So then, those who suffer because it is God's will for them, should by their good actions trust themselves completely to their Creator, who always keeps his promise.

The Flock of God

5 I, who am an elder myself, appeal to the church elders among you. I am a witness of Christ's sufferings, and I will share in the glory that will be revealed. I appeal to you [2]to be shepherds of the flock that God gave you and to take care of it willingly, as God wants you to, and not unwillingly. Do your work, not for mere pay, but from a real desire to serve. [3]Do not try to rule over those who have been put in your care, but be examples to the flock. [4]And when the Chief Shepherd appears, you will receive the glorious crown which will never lose its brightness.

5 In the same way you younger people must submit to your elders. And all of you must put on the apron of humility, to serve one another; for the scripture says, "God resists the proud, but shows favour to the humble." [6]Humble yourselves, then, under God's mighty hand, so that he will lift you up in his own good time. [7]Leave all your worries with him, because he cares for you.

8 Be alert, be on the watch! Your enemy, the Devil, roams round like a roaring lion, looking for someone to devour. [9]Be firm in your faith and resist him, because you know that your fellow-believers in all the world are going through the same kind of sufferings. [10]But after you have suffered for a little while, the God of all grace, who calls you to share his eternal glory in union with Christ, will himself perfect you and give you firmness, strength, and a sure foundation. [11]To him be the power for ever! Amen.

Final Greetings

12 I write you this brief letter with the help of Silas, whom I regard as a faithful fellow-Christian. I want to encourage you and give my testimony that this is the true grace of God. Stand firm in it.

13 Your sister church in Babylon,[a] also chosen by God, sends you greetings, and so does my son Mark. [14]Greet one another with the kiss of Christian love.

May peace be with all of you who belong to Christ.

---

a **5.13** BABYLON: *As in the book of Revelation, this probably refers to Rome.*

The Second Letter from PETER

INTRODUCTION

The Second Letter from Peter is addressed to a wide circle of early Christians. Its main concern is to combat the work of false teachers and the immorality which results from such teaching. The answer to these problems is found in holding to the true knowledge of God and of the Lord Jesus Christ, knowledge which has been conveyed by persons who themselves have seen Jesus and have heard him teach. The writer is especially concerned with the teaching of those who claim that Christ will not return again. He says that the apparent delay in Christ's return is due to the fact that God "does not want anyone to be destroyed, but wants all to turn away from their sins". (3.9)

Outline of Contents

1 From Simon Peter, a servant and apostle of Jesus Christ –
To those who through the righteousness of our God and Saviour Jesus Christ have been given a faith as precious as ours:
2 May grace and peace be yours in full measure through your knowledge of God and of Jesus our Lord.

God's Call and Choice

3 God's divine power has given us everything we need to live a truly religious life through our knowledge of the one who called us to share in his own[a] glory and goodness. 4In this way he has given us the very great and precious gifts he promised, so that by means of these gifts you may escape from the destructive lust that is in the world, and may come to share the divine nature. 5For this very reason do your best to add goodness to your faith; to your goodness add knowledge; 6to your knowledge add self-control; to your self-control add endurance; to your endurance add godliness; 7to your godliness add Christian affection; and to your Christian affection add love. 8These are the qualities you need, and if you have them in abundance, they will make you active and effective in your knowledge of our Lord Jesus Christ. 9But those who do not have them are so short-sighted that they cannot see and have forgotten that they have been purified from their past sins.

10 So then, my brothers and sisters, try even harder to make God's call and his choice of you a permanent experience; if you do so, you will never abandon your faith.[b] 11In this way you will be given the full right to enter the eternal Kingdom of our Lord and Saviour Jesus Christ.

12 And so I will always remind you of these matters, even though you already know them and are firmly grounded in the truth you have received. 13I think it only right for me to stir up your memory of these matters as long as I am still alive. 14I know that I shall soon put off this mortal body, as our Lord Jesus Christ plainly told me. 15I will do my best, then, to provide a way for you to remember these matters at all times after my death.

---

[a] **1.3** to share in his own; *some manuscripts have* through his.

[b] **1.10** abandon your faith; *or* fall into sin.

Eyewitnesses of Christ's Glory

16   We have not depended on made-up stories in making known to you the mighty coming of our Lord Jesus Christ. With our own eyes we saw his greatness. [17]We were there when he was given honour and glory by God the Father, when the voice came to him from the Supreme Glory, saying, "This is my own dear Son, with whom I am pleased!" [18]We ourselves heard this voice coming from heaven, when we were with him on the holy mountain.

19   So we are even more confident of the message proclaimed by the prophets. You will do well to pay attention to it, because it is like a lamp shining in a dark place until the Day dawns and the light of the morning star shines in your hearts. [20]Above all else, however, remember that no one can explain by himself or herself a prophecy in the Scriptures. [21]For no prophetic message ever came just from human will, but people were under the control of the Holy Spirit as they spoke the message that came from God.

Studying
2 PETER

Who wrote it? Presented as an account of Peter's teaching as he would wish to be remembered. Most scholars, though, think it was written after Peter's death in 64 CE by an unknown writer.
When? If Peter wrote it then shortly before martyrdom in 64 CE. If not, then probably 80–90 CE.
Where from? Possibly Rome.
For whom? Not known.
Why? Written to show how Christianity should cope with a pagan rather than Jewish society – at a time when nearly all the early Church leaders had died.

KEY POINTS

- The "opponent" in the author's mind doubted that Jesus would return – or that it mattered how people lived. The author attacks both of these beliefs.
- There would be judgement and salvation when Jesus returned to the earth.
- In the light of Christ's certain return, Christians should live holy lives.

False Teachers

2 False prophets appeared in the past among the people, and in the same way false teachers will appear among you. They will bring in destructive, untrue doctrines, and will deny the Master who redeemed them, and so they will bring upon themselves sudden destruction. [2]Even so, many will follow their immoral ways; and because of what they do, others will speak evil of the Way of truth. [3]In their greed these false teachers will make a profit out of telling you made-up stories. For a long time now their Judge has been ready, and their Destroyer has been wide awake!

4   God did not spare the angels who sinned, but threw them into hell, where they are kept chained in darkness,[a] waiting for the Day of Judgement. [5]God did not spare the ancient world, but brought the flood on the world of godless people; the only ones he saved were Noah, who preached righteousness, and seven other people. [6]God condemned the cities of Sodom and Gomorrah, destroying them with fire, and made them an example of what will happen to the godless. [7]He rescued Lot, a good man, who was distressed by the immoral conduct of lawless people. [8]That good man lived among them, and day after day he suffered agony as he saw and heard their evil actions.

---

[a] **2.4** chained in darkness; *some manuscripts have* in dark pits.

---

[9]And so the Lord knows how to rescue godly people from their trials and how to keep the wicked under punishment for the Day of Judgement, [10]especially those who follow their filthy bodily lusts and despise God's authority.

These false teachers are bold and arrogant, and show no respect for the glorious beings above; instead, they insult them. [11]Even the angels, who are so much stronger and mightier than these false teachers, do not accuse them with insults in the presence of the Lord. [12]But these people act by instinct, like wild animals born to be captured and killed; they attack with insults anything they do not understand. They will be destroyed like wild animals, [13]and they will be paid with suffering for the suffering they have caused. Pleasure for them is to do anything in broad daylight that will satisfy their bodily appetites; they are a shame and a disgrace as they join you in your meals, all the while enjoying their deceitful ways! [14]They want to look at nothing but immoral women; their appetite for sin is never satisfied. They lead weak people into a trap. Their hearts are trained to be greedy. They are under God's curse! [15]They have left the straight path and have lost their way; they have followed the path taken by Balaam son of Beor, who loved the money he would get for doing wrong [16]and was rebuked for his sin. His donkey spoke with a human voice and stopped the prophet's insane action.

17   These people are like dried-up springs, like clouds blown along by a storm; God has reserved

a place for them in the deepest darkness. [18]They make proud and stupid statements, and use immoral bodily lusts to trap those who are just beginning to escape from among people who live in error. [19]They promise them freedom while they themselves are slaves of destructive habits – for a person is a slave of anything that has conquered him. [20]If people have escaped from the corrupting forces of the world through their knowledge of our Lord and Saviour Jesus Christ, and then are again caught and conquered by them, such people are in a worse state at the end than they were at the beginning. [21]It would have been much better for them never to have known the way of righteousness than to know it and then turn away from the sacred command that was given them. [22]What happened to them shows that the proverbs are true: "A dog goes back to what it has vomited" and "A pig that has been washed goes back to roll in the mud."

The Promise of the Lord's Coming

3 My dear friends, this is now the second letter I have written to you. In both letters I have tried to arouse pure thoughts in your minds by reminding you of these things. [2]I want you to remember the words that were spoken long ago by the holy prophets, and the command from the Lord and Saviour which was given you by your apostles. [3]First of all, you must understand that in these last days some people will appear whose lives are controlled by their own lusts. They will mock you [4]and will ask, "He promised to come, didn't he? Where is he? Our ancestors have already died, but everything is still the same as it was since the creation of the world!" [5]They purposely ignore the fact that long ago God gave a command, and the heavens and earth were created. The earth was formed out of water and by water, [6]and it was also by water, the water of the flood, that the old world was destroyed. [7]But the heavens and the earth that now exist are being preserved by the same command of God, in order to be destroyed by fire. They are being kept for the day when godless people will be judged and destroyed.

8 But do not forget one thing, my dear friends! There is no difference in the Lord's sight between one day and a thousand years; to him the two are the same. [9]The Lord is not slow to do what he has promised, as some think. Instead, he is patient with you, because he does not want anyone to be destroyed, but wants all to turn away from their sins.

10 But the Day of the Lord will come like a thief. On that Day the heavens will disappear with a shrill noise, the heavenly bodies will burn up and be destroyed, and the earth with everything in it will vanish.[a] [11]Since all these things will be destroyed in this way, what kind of people should you be? Your lives should be holy and dedicated to God, [12]as you wait for the Day of God and do your best to make it come soon – the Day when the heavens will burn up and be destroyed, and the heavenly bodies will be melted by the heat. [13]But we wait for what God has promised: new heavens and a new earth, where righteousness will be at home.

14 And so, my friends, as you wait for that Day, do your best to be pure and faultless in God's sight and to be at peace with him. [15]Look on our Lord's patience as the opportunity he is giving you to be saved, just as our dear brother Paul wrote to you, using the wisdom that God gave him. [16]This is what he says in all his letters when he writes on the subject. There are some difficult things in his letters which ignorant and unstable people explain falsely, as they do with other passages of the Scriptures. So they bring on their own destruction.

17 But you, my friends, already know this. Be on your guard, then, so that you will not be led away by the errors of lawless people and fall from your safe position. [18]But continue to grow in the grace and knowledge of our Lord and Saviour Jesus Christ. To him be the glory, now and for ever! Amen.

---

[a] **3.10** vanish; *some manuscripts have* be found; *others have* be burnt up; *one has* be found destroyed.

The First Letter from
JOHN

INTRODUCTION

The First Letter from John has two main purposes: to encourage its readers to live in fellowship with God and with his Son, Jesus Christ, and to warn them against following false teaching that would destroy this fellowship. This teaching was based on the belief that evil results from contact with the physical world, and so Jesus, the Son of God, could not really have been a human being. Those teachers claimed that to be saved was to be set free from concern with life in this world; and they also taught that salvation had nothing to do with matters of morality or of love for others.

In opposition to this teaching the writer clearly states that Jesus Christ was a real human being, and he emphasizes that all who believe in Jesus and love God must also love one another.

The Word of Life

1 We write to you about the Word of life, which has existed from the very beginning. We have heard it, and we have seen it with our eyes; yes, we have seen it, and our hands have touched it. ²When this life became visible, we saw it; so we speak of it and tell you about the eternal life which was with the Father and was made known to us. ³What we have seen and heard we announce to you also, so that you will join with us in the fellowship that we have with the Father and with his Son Jesus Christ. ⁴We write this in order that our[a] joy may be complete.

God is Light

5 Now the message that we have heard from his Son and announce is this: God is light, and there is no darkness at all in him. ⁶If, then, we say that we have fellowship with him, yet at the same time live in the darkness, we are lying both in our words and in our actions. ⁷But if we live in the light – just as he is in the light – then we have fellowship with one another, and the blood of Jesus, his Son, purifies us from every sin.

8 If we say that we have no sin, we deceive ourselves, and there is no truth in us. ⁹But if we confess our sins to God, he will keep his promise and do what is right: he will forgive us our sins and purify us from all our wrongdoing. ¹⁰If we say that we have not sinned, we make God out to be a liar, and his word is not in us.

Christ our Helper

2 I am writing this to you, my children, so that you will not sin; but if anyone does sin, we have someone who pleads with the Father on our behalf – Jesus Christ, the righteous one. ²And Christ himself is the means by which our sins are forgiven, and not our sins only, but also the sins of everyone.

3 If we obey God's commands, then we are sure that we know him. ⁴Those who say that they know him, but do not obey his commands, are liars and there is no truth in them. ⁵All those

---

[a] **1.4** our; *some manuscripts have* your.

Studying
1 JOHN

Who wrote it? Likely to be the same person who wrote *The Gospel according to John* – either John, the disciple of Jesus, or an unknown follower of John.
When? Probably written after Gospel, 90–100 CE.
Where from? Most likely to have been written in Ephesus, a city long associated with John.
For whom? An unknown Christian community. Letter seeks to explain how those preaching the truth and those preaching error can be distinguished.
Why? Written to oppose the teaching of a growing number in the Church that Jesus was not both God and man.

KEY POINTS

- The writer urges readers to stay with the truth about the divine and human Jesus (2.13–14; 3.11).
- The commandment to love one another must be kept (5.2–3).
- A person cannot love God unless they love other Christians (4.8).

who obey his word are people whose love for God has really been made perfect. This is how we can be sure that we are in union with God: 6those who say that they remain in union with God should live just as Jesus Christ did.

The New Command

7 My dear friends, this command I am writing to you is not new; it is the old command, the one you have had from the very beginning. The old command is the message you have already heard. 8However, the command I am now writing to you is new, because its truth is seen in Christ and also in you. For the darkness is passing away, and the real light is already shining.

9 Those who say that they are in the light, yet hate their brothers and sisters, are in the darkness to this very hour. 10Those who love their brothers and sisters live in the light, and so there is nothing in them that will cause someone else[a] to sin. 11But those who hate their brothers and sisters are in the darkness; they walk in it and do not know where they are going, because the darkness has made them blind.

12 I am writing to you, my children, because your sins are forgiven for the sake of Christ. 13I am writing to you, fathers, because you know him who has existed from the beginning. I am writing to you, young people, because you have defeated the Evil One.

---

[a] **2.10** someone else; *or* them.

14 I am writing to you, my children, because you know the Father. I am writing to you, fathers, because you know him who has existed from the beginning. I am writing to you, young people, because you are strong; the word of God lives in you, and you have defeated the Evil One.

15 Do not love the world or anything that belongs to the world. If you love the world, you do not love the Father. 16Everything that belongs to the world – what the sinful self desires, what people see and want, and everything in this world that people are so proud of – none of this comes from the Father; it all comes from the world. 17The world and everything in it that people desire is passing away; but those who do the will of God live for ever.

The Enemy of Christ

18 My children, the end is near! You were told that the Enemy of Christ would come; and now many enemies of Christ have already appeared, and so we know that the end is near. 19These people really did not belong to our fellowship, and that is why they left us; if they had belonged to our fellowship, they would have stayed with us. But they left so that it might be clear that none of them really belonged to us.

20 But you have had the Holy Spirit poured out on you by Christ, and so all of you know the truth. 21I am writing to you, then, not because you do not know the truth; instead, it is because you do know it, and you also know that no lie ever comes from the truth.

22 Who, then, is the liar? It is those who say that Jesus is not the Messiah. Such people are the Enemies of Christ – they reject both the Father and the Son. 23For all those who reject the Son also reject the Father; those who accept the Son have the Father also.

24 Be sure, then, to keep in your hearts the message you heard from the beginning. If you keep that message, then you will always live in union with the Son and the Father. 25And this is what Christ himself promised to give us – eternal life.

26 I am writing this to you about those who are trying to deceive you. 27But as for you, Christ has poured out his Spirit on you. As long as his Spirit remains in you, you do not need anyone to teach you. For his Spirit teaches you about everything, and what he teaches is true, not false. Obey the Spirit's teaching, then, and remain in union with Christ.

28 Yes, my children, remain in union with him, so that when he appears we may be full of

courage and need not hide in shame from him on the Day he comes. ²⁹You know that Christ is righteous; you should know, then, that everyone who does what is right is God's child.

Children of God

3 See how much the Father has loved us! His love is so great that we are called God's children – and so, in fact, we are. This is why the world does not know us: it has not known God. ²My dear friends, we are now God's children, but it is not yet clear what we shall become. But we know that when Christ appears, we shall be like him, because we shall see him as he really is. ³Everyone who has this hope in Christ keeps himself pure, just as Christ is pure.

4 Whoever sins is guilty of breaking God's law, because sin is a breaking of the law. ⁵You know that Christ appeared in order to take away sins,ᵃ and that there is no sin in him. ⁶So everyone who lives in union with Christ does not continue to sin; but whoever continues to sin has never seen him or known him.

7 Let no one deceive you, my children! Whoever does what is right is righteous, just as Christ is righteous. ⁸Whoever continues to sin belongs to the Devil, because the Devil has sinned from the very beginning. The Son of God appeared for this very reason, to destroy what the Devil had done.

9 None of those who are children of God continue to sin, for God's very nature is in them; and because God is their Father, they cannot continue to sin. ¹⁰This is the clear difference between God's children and the Devil's children: all who do not do what is right or do not love others are not God's children.

Love One Another

11 The message you heard from the very beginning is this: we must love one another. ¹²We must not be like Cain; he belonged to the Evil One and murdered his own brother Abel. Why did Cain murder him? Because the things he himself did were wrong, but the things his brother did were right.

13 So do not be surprised, my brothers and sisters, if the people of the world hate you. ¹⁴We know that we have left death and come over into life; we know it because we love our brothers and sisters. Whoever does not love is still under the power of death. ¹⁵All who hate others

are murderers, and you know that murderers have not got eternal life in them. ¹⁶This is how we know what love is: Christ gave his life for us. We too, then, ought to give our lives for our brothers and sisters! ¹⁷Rich people who see a brother or sister in need, yet close their hearts against them, cannot claim that they love God. ¹⁸My children, our love should not be just words and talk; it must be true love, which shows itself in action.

Courage before God

19 This, then, is how we will know that we belong to the truth; this is how we will be confident in God's presence. ²⁰If our conscience condemns us, we know that God is greater than our conscience and that he knows everything. ²¹And so, my dear friends, if our conscience does not condemn us, we have courage in God's presence. ²²We receive from him whatever we ask, because we obey his commands and do what pleases him. ²³What he commands is that we believe in his Son Jesus Christ and love one another, just as Christ commanded us. ²⁴Those who obey God's commands live in union with God and God lives in union with them. And because of the Spirit that God has given us we know that God lives in union with us.

The True Spirit and the False

4 My dear friends, do not believe all who claim to have the Spirit, but test them to find out if the spirit they have comes from God. For many false prophets have gone out everywhere. ²This is how you will be able to know whether it is God's Spirit: anyone who acknowledges that Jesus Christ came as a human being has the Spirit who comes from God. ³But anyone who denies this about Jesus does not have the Spirit from God. The spirit that he has is from the Enemy of Christ; you heard that it would come, and now it is here in the world already.

4 But you belong to God, my children, and have defeated the false prophets, because the Spirit who is in you is more powerful than the spirit in those who belong to the world. ⁵Those false prophets speak about matters of the world, and the world listens to them because they belong to the world. ⁶But we belong to God. Whoever knows God listens to us; whoever does not belong to God does not listen to us. This, then, is how we can tell the difference between the Spirit of truth and the spirit of error.

ᵃ **3.5** sins; *some manuscripts have* our sins.

God is Love

7   Dear friends, let us love one another, because love comes from God. Whoever loves is a child of God and knows God. ⁸Whoever does not love does not know God, for God is love. ⁹And God showed his love for us by sending his only Son into the world, so that we might have life through him. ¹⁰This is what love is: it is not that we have loved God, but that he loved us and sent his Son to be the means by which our sins are forgiven.

11   Dear friends, if this is how God loved us, then we should love one another. ¹²No one has ever seen God, but if we love one another, God lives in union with us, and his love is made perfect in us.

13   We are sure that we live in union with God and that he lives in union with us, because he has given us his Spirit. ¹⁴And we have seen and tell others that the Father sent his Son to be the Saviour of the world. ¹⁵If anyone declares that Jesus is the Son of God, he lives in union with God and God lives in union with him. ¹⁶And we ourselves know and believe the love which God has for us.

God is love, and those who live in love live in union with God and God lives in union with them. ¹⁷Love is made perfect in us in order that we may have courage on Judgement Day; and we will have it because our life in this world is the same as Christ's. ¹⁸There is no fear in love; perfect love drives out all fear. So then, love has not been made perfect in anyone who is afraid, because fear has to do with punishment.

19   We love because God first loved us. ²⁰If we say we love God, but hate our brothers and sisters, we are liars. For people cannot love God, whom they have not seen, if they do not love their brothers and sisters, whom they have seen. ²¹The command that Christ has given us is this: all who love God must love their brother or sister also.

Our Victory over the World

5   Whoever believes that Jesus is the Messiah is a child of God; and whoever loves a father loves his child also. ²This is how we know that we love God's children: it is by loving God and obeying his commands. ³For our love for God means that we obey his commands. And his commands are not too hard for us, ⁴because every child of God is able to defeat the world. And we win the victory over the world by means of our faith. ⁵Who can defeat the world? Only the person who believes that Jesus is the Son of God.

Praying together is a very important part of Christian worship.

The Witness about Jesus Christ

6   Jesus Christ is the one who came with the water of his baptism and the blood of his death. He came not only with the water, but with both the water and the blood. And the Spirit himself testifies that this is true, because the Spirit is truth. ⁷There are three witnesses: ⁸the Spirit, the water, and the blood; and all three give the same testimony. ⁹We believe human testimony; but God's testimony is much stronger, and he has given this testimony about his Son. ¹⁰So all who believe in the Son of God have this testimony in their own hearts; but those who do not believe God have made him out to be a liar, because they have not believed what God has said about his Son. ¹¹The testimony is this: God has given us eternal life, and this life has its source in his Son. ¹²Whoever has the Son has this life; whoever does not have the Son of God does not have life.

Eternal Life

13   I am writing this to you so that you may know that you have eternal life – you that believe in the Son of God. ¹⁴We have courage in God's presence, because we are sure that he hears us if we ask him for anything that is according to his will. ¹⁵He hears us whenever we ask him; and since we know this is true, we know also that he gives us what we ask from him.

16   If you see your brother or sister commit a sin that does not lead to death, you should pray to God, who will give them life. This applies to those whose sins do not lead to death. But there is sin which leads to death, and I do not say that you should pray to God about that. ¹⁷All wrongdoing is sin, but there is sin which does not lead to death.

18   We know that none of God's children keep on sinning, for the Son of God keeps them safe, and the Evil One cannot harm them.

19   We know that we belong to God even though the whole world is under the rule of the Evil One.

20   We know that the Son of God has come and has given us understanding, so that we know the true God. We live in union with the true God – in union with his Son Jesus Christ. This is the true God, and this is eternal life.

21   My children, keep yourselves safe from false gods!

The Second Letter from JOHN

INTRODUCTION

The Second Letter from John was written by "the Elder" to "the dear Lady and to her children", probably meaning a local church and its members. The brief message is an appeal to love one another and a warning against false teachers and their teachings.

Outline of Contents

1 From the Elder –
To the dear Lady and to her children,[a] whom I truly love. And I am not the only one, but all who know the truth love you, [2]because the truth remains in us and will be with us for ever.

3 May God the Father and Jesus Christ, the Father's Son, give us grace, mercy, and peace; may they be ours in truth and love.

Truth and Love

4 How happy I was to find that some of your children live in the truth, just as the Father commanded us. [5]And so I ask you, dear Lady: let us all love one another. This is no new command I am writing to you; it is the command which we have had from the beginning. [6]This love I speak of means that we must live in obedience to God's commands. The command, as you have all heard from the beginning, is that you must all live in love.

7 Many deceivers have gone out all over the world, people who do not acknowledge that Jesus Christ came as a human being. Such a person is a deceiver and the Enemy of Christ. [8]Be on your guard, then, so that you will not lose what we[b] have worked for, but will receive your reward in full.

---

[a] **v.1** LADY AND … HER CHILDREN: *This probably refers to a church and its members (also in verses 4–5).*
[b] **v.8** we; *some manuscripts have* you.

> ### *Studying*
> ## 2 JOHN
>
> ***Who wrote it?*** Author calls himself "the Elder" (verse 1) suggesting he was a leader of a Christian community. Same as author of *3 John* and probably *1 John*. Likely to have written fourth Gospel. Either the Apostle John or an unknown disciple of his.
> ***When?*** Probably written after Gospel, between 90–100 CE.
> ***Where from?*** Most likely to have been written from Ephesus, a city in Asia Minor long associated with John.
> ***For whom?*** Sent to a Christian congregation addressed as "dear lady" (verse 1).
> ***Why?*** Written to oppose the "many deceivers" (verse 7) who were teaching false beliefs – especially that Jesus was not both God and man.
>
> #### KEY POINTS
>
> - The importance of Christians loving one another (4–6).
> - Conflict with group who denied that Jesus was God in human form. True Christians told to avoid any contact with them.

9 Anyone who does not stay with the teaching of Christ, but goes beyond it, does not have God. Whoever does stay with the teaching has both the Father and the Son. [10]So then, if someone comes to you who does not bring this teaching, do not welcome him or her in your homes; do not even say, "Peace be with you." [11]For anyone who wishes them peace becomes their partner in the evil things they do.

Final Words

12 I have so much to tell you, but I would rather not do it with paper and ink; instead, I hope to visit you and talk with you personally, so that we shall be completely happy.

13 The children of your dear Sister[a] send you their greetings.

---

[a] **v.13** CHILDREN OF YOUR DEAR SISTER: *This probably refers to the members of the church to which the writer belonged.*

The Third Letter from JOHN

INTRODUCTION

The Third Letter from John was written by "the Elder" to a church leader named Gaius. The writer praises Gaius because of his help to other Christians, and warns against a man named Diotrephes.

Outline of Contents

Introduction 1–4
Gaius is praised 5–8
Diotrephes is condemned 9–10
Demetrius is commended 11–12
Conclusion 13–15

1 From the Elder –
To my dear Gaius, whom I truly love.
2 My dear friend, I pray that everything may go well with you and that you may be in good health – as I know you are well in spirit. ³I was so happy when some fellow-Christians arrived and told me how faithful you are to the truth – just as you always live in the truth. ⁴Nothing makes me happier than to hear that my children live in the truth.

Gaius is Praised

5 My dear friend, you are so faithful in the work you do for your fellow-Christians, even when they are strangers. ⁶They have spoken to the church here about your love. Please help them to continue their journey in a way that will please God. ⁷For they set out on their journey in the service of Christ without accepting any help from unbelievers. ⁸We Christians, then, must help these people, so that we may share in their work for the truth.

Diotrephes and Demetrius

9 I wrote a short letter to the church; but Diotrephes, who likes to be their leader, will not pay any attention to what I say. ¹⁰When I come, then, I will call attention to everything he has done: the terrible things he says about us and the lies he tells! But that is not enough for him; he will not receive our fellow-Christians when

Studying
3 JOHN

Who wrote it? "The Elder" (verse 1), same as author of 2 John and probably 1 John as well. Likely to have been the author of John's Gospel – either the Apostle John or an unknown disciple.
When? Soon after 2 John, between 90–100 CE.
Where from? Probably from Ephesus, a city in Asia Minor long associated with John.
For whom? Addressed to "Gaius" thanking him for his hospitality.
Why? Letter opposes strongly a person called Diotrephes who was destroying the community. The author threatens to confront Diotrephes face to face (9–11).

KEY POINTS

- Letter says nothing about Christian belief.
- Author commends Gaius and Demetrius.

they come, and even stops those who want to receive them and tries to drive them out of the church!
11 My dear friend, do not imitate what is bad, but imitate what is good. Whoever does good belongs to God; whoever does what is bad has not seen God.
12 Everyone speaks well of Demetrius; truth itself speaks well of him. And we add our testimony, and you know that what we say is true.

Final Greetings

13 I have so much to tell you, but I do not want to do it with pen and ink. ¹⁴I hope to see you soon, and then we will talk personally.

15 Peace be with you.

All your friends send greetings. Greet all our friends personally.

The Letter from
JUDE

INTRODUCTION

The Letter from Jude was written to warn against false teachers who claimed to be believers. In this brief letter, which is similar in content to *2 Peter*, the writer encourages his readers "to fight on for the faith which once and for all God has given to his people".

Outline of Contents

Introduction 1–2
Character, teaching, and doom of the false teachers 3–16
Admonition to keep the faith 17–23
Benediction 24–25

1 From Jude, servant of Jesus Christ, and brother of James –

To those who have been called by God, who live in the love of God the Father and the protection of Jesus Christ:

2 May mercy, peace, and love be yours in full measure.

False Teachers

3 My dear friends, I was doing my best to write to you about the salvation we share in common, when I felt the need of writing at once to encourage you to fight on for the faith which once and for all God has given to his people. 4For some godless people have slipped in unnoticed among us, persons who distort the message about the grace of our God in order to excuse their immoral ways, and who reject Jesus Christ, our only Master and Lord. Long ago the Scriptures predicted the condemnation they have received.

5 For even though you know all this, I want to remind you of how the Lord[a] once rescued the people of Israel from Egypt, but afterwards destroyed those who did not believe. 6Remember the angels who did not stay within the limits of their proper authority, but abandoned their own dwelling place: they are bound with eternal

---

[a] **v.5** the Lord; *some manuscripts have* Jesus, *which in Greek is the same as* Joshua.

---

chains in the darkness below, where God is keeping them for that great Day on which they will be condemned. 7Remember Sodom and Gomorrah, and the nearby towns, whose people acted as those angels did and indulged in sexual immorality and perversion: they suffer the punishment of eternal fire as a plain warning to all.

8 In the same way also, these people have visions which make them sin against their own bodies; they despise God's authority and insult the glorious beings above. 9Not even the chief angel Michael did this. In his quarrel with the Devil, when they argued about who would have the body of Moses, Michael did not dare to condemn the Devil with insulting words, but said, "The Lord rebuke you!" 10But these people attack with insults anything they do not understand; and those things that they know by instinct, like wild animals, are the very things that destroy them. 11How terrible for them! They have followed the way that Cain took. For the sake of money they have given themselves over to the error that Balaam committed. They have rebelled as Korah rebelled, and like him they are destroyed. 12With their shameless carousing they are like dirty spots in your fellowship meals. They take care only of themselves. They are like clouds carried along by the wind, but bringing no rain. They are like trees that bear no fruit, even in autumn, trees that have been pulled up by the roots and are completely dead. 13They are like wild waves of the sea, with their

shameful deeds showing up like foam. They are like wandering stars, for whom God has reserved a place for ever in the deepest darkness.

14 It was Enoch, the seventh[a] direct descendant from Adam, who long ago prophesied this about them: "The Lord will come with many thousands of his holy angels [15]to bring judgement on all, to condemn them all for the godless deeds they have performed and for all the terrible words that godless sinners have spoken against him!"

16 These people are always grumbling and blaming others; they follow their own evil desires; they boast about themselves and flatter others in order to get their own way.

Warnings and Instructions

17 But remember, my friends, what you were told in the past by the apostles of our Lord Jesus Christ. [18]They said to you, "When the last days come, people will appear who will mock you, people who follow their own godless desires." [19]These are the people who cause divisions, who are controlled by their natural desires, who do not have the Spirit. [20]But you, my friends, keep on building yourselves up on your most sacred faith. Pray in the power of the Holy Spirit, [21]and keep yourselves in the love of God, as you wait for our Lord Jesus Christ in his mercy to give you eternal life.

22 Show mercy towards those who have doubts;

Studying

JUDE

Who wrote it? Jude, the brother of Jesus.
When? Probably one of the earliest books in the New Testament.
Where from? Not known.
For whom? Unknown church or group of churches.
Why? To combat a group of teachers who were saying that it did not matter how a person lived as long as they believed in God.

KEY POINTS

- Christians who live immoral lives will suffer eternal fire and punishment when Christ returns to the earth (verse 7).
- Christians should live out the Gospel in faith, hope and love. (20–21).

---

[23]save others by snatching them out of the fire; and to others show mercy mixed with fear, but hate their very clothes, stained by their sinful lusts.

Prayer of Praise

24 To him who is able to keep you from falling, and to bring you faultless and joyful before his glorious presence – [25]to the only God our Saviour, through Jesus Christ our Lord, be glory, majesty, might, and authority, from all ages past, and now, and for ever and ever! Amen.

---

[a] **v.14** Seventh: *This numbering includes both the first and the last in the series of seven names from Adam to Enoch.*

THE REVELATION
to John

INTRODUCTION

The Revelation to John was written at a time when Christians were being persecuted because of their faith in Jesus Christ as Lord. The writer's main concern is to give his readers hope and encouragement, and to urge them to remain faithful during times of suffering and persecution.

For the most part the book consists of several series of revelations and visions presented in symbolic language that would have been understood by Christians of that day, but would have remained a mystery to all others. As with the themes of a symphony, the themes of this book are repeated again and again in different ways through the various series of visions. Although there are differences of opinion regarding the details of interpretation of the book, the central theme is clear: through Christ the Lord, God will finally and totally defeat all his enemies, including Satan, and will reward his faithful people with the blessings of a new heaven and a new earth when this victory is complete.

Outline of Contents

1 This book is the record of the events that Jesus Christ revealed. God gave him this revelation in order to show his servants what must happen very soon. Christ made these things known to his servant John by sending his angel to him, [2]and John has told all that he has seen. This is his report concerning the message from God and the truth revealed by Jesus Christ. [3]Happy is the one who reads this book, and happy are those who listen to the words of this prophetic message and obey what is written in this book! For the time is near when all these things will happen.

Greetings to the Seven Churches

4 From John to the seven churches in the province of Asia:

Grace and peace be yours from God, who is, who was, and who is to come, and from the seven spirits in front of his throne, [5]and from Jesus Christ, the faithful witness, the first to be raised from death and who is also the ruler of the kings of the world.

He loves us, and by his sacrificial death he has freed us from our sins [6]and made us a kingdom of priests to serve his God and Father. To Jesus Christ be the glory and power for ever and ever! Amen.

7 Look, he is coming on the clouds! Everyone

will see him, including those who pierced him. All peoples on earth will mourn over him. So shall it be!

8   "I am the first and the last," says the Lord God Almighty, who is, who was, and who is to come.

A Vision of Christ

9   I am John, your brother, and as a follower of Jesus I am your partner in patiently enduring the suffering that comes to those who belong to his Kingdom. I was put on the island of Patmos because I had proclaimed God's word and the truth that Jesus revealed. [10]On the Lord's day the Spirit took control of me, and I heard a loud voice, that sounded like a trumpet, speaking behind me. [11]It said, "Write down what you see, and send the book to the churches in these seven cities: Ephesus, Smyrna, Pergamum, Thyatira, Sardis, Philadelphia, and Laodicea."

12   I turned round to see who was talking to me, and I saw seven gold lampstands, [13]and among them there was what looked like a human being, wearing a robe that reached to his feet, and a gold belt round his chest. [14]His hair was white as wool, or as snow, and his eyes blazed like fire; [15]his feet shone like brass that has been refined and polished, and his voice sounded like a roaring waterfall. [16]He held seven stars in his right hand, and a sharp two-edged sword came out of his mouth. His face was as bright as the midday sun. [17]When I saw him, I fell down at his feet like a dead man. He placed his right hand on me and said, "Don't be afraid! I am the first and the last. [18]I am the living one! I was dead, but now I am alive for ever and ever. I have authority over death and the world of the dead. [19]Write, then, the things you see, both the things that are now and the things that will happen afterwards. [20]This is the secret meaning of the seven stars that you see in my right hand, and of the seven gold lampstands: the seven stars are the angels of the seven churches, and the seven lampstands are the seven churches.

The Message to Ephesus

2   "To the angel of the church in Ephesus write:

"This is the message from the one who holds the seven stars in his right hand and who walks among the seven gold lampstands. [2]I know what you have done; I know how hard you have worked and how patient you have been. I know that you cannot tolerate evil

Studying
REVELATION

Who wrote it? Either John, the Apostle, or, more likely, a member of the community which gathered around John.
When? Probably towards the end of the reign of the Roman Emperor Domitian (81–96 CE).
Where from? The author is in exile on the island of Patmos "because I had proclaimed God's word and the truth that Jesus revealed" (1.9).
For whom? It seems that the author was writing for seven congregations in Asia listed in chapters 2 and 3. "Seven", though, was a symbolic number and book may have been intended for the whole Church.
Why? The theme of the persecution of Christians lies behind book. Written to assure Christians that God was in control.

KEY POINTS

● Book is an example of "apocalyptic" ("revelation") writing in which a vision of the future is described. *The Book of Daniel*, in the Old Testament, is the only other book like this in the Bible.
● There is a conflict between God and Satan on earth leading to great suffering before God intervenes. God's people are rewarded. Those who oppressed them are punished or eliminated. Satan is defeated. God sets up a new heaven and a new earth.
● An "interpreting angel" explained the meaning the visions to the author (1.1).

people and that you have tested those who say they are apostles but are not, and have found out that they are liars. [3]You are patient, you have suffered for my sake, and you have not given up. [4]But this is what I have against you: you do not love me now as you did at first. [5]Think how far you have fallen! Turn from your sins and do what you did at first. If you don't turn from your sins, I will come to you and take your lampstand from its place. [6]But this is what you have in your favour: you hate what the Nicolaitans do, as much as I do.

7   "If you have ears, then, listen to what the Spirit says to the churches!

"To those who win the victory I will give the right to eat the fruit of the tree of life that grows in the Garden of God.

The Message to Smyrna

8   "To the angel of the church in Smyrna write:

"This is the message from the one who is the first and the last, who died and lived again. [9]I know your troubles; I know that you are poor – but really you are rich! I know the evil things said against you by those who claim to be Jews but are not; they are a group that belongs to Satan! [10]Don't be afraid of anything you are about to suffer. Listen! The Devil will put you to the test by having some of you thrown into prison, and your troubles will last ten days. Be faithful to me, even if it means death, and I will give you life as your prize of victory.

11 "If you have ears, then, listen to what the Spirit says to the churches!

"Those who win the victory will not be hurt by the second death.

The Message to Pergamum

12 "To the angel of the church in Pergamum write:

"This is the message from the one who has the sharp two-edged sword. [13]I know where you live, there where Satan has his throne. You are true to me, and you did not abandon your faith in me even during the time when Antipas, my faithful witness, was killed there where Satan lives. [14]But there are a few things I have against you: there are some among you who follow the teaching of Balaam, who taught Balak how to lead the people of Israel into sin by persuading them to eat food that had been offered to idols and to practise sexual immorality. [15]In the same way you have people among you who follow the teaching of the Nicolaitans. [16]Now turn from your sins! If you don't, I will come to you soon and fight against those people with the sword that comes out of my mouth.

17 "If you have ears, then, listen to what the Spirit says to the churches!

"To those who win the victory I will give some of the hidden manna. I will also give each of them a white stone on which is written a new name that no one knows except the one who receives it.

The Message to Thyatira

18 "To the angel of the church in Thyatira write:

"This is the message from the Son of God, whose eyes blaze like fire, whose feet shine like polished brass. [19]I know what you do. I know your love, your faithfulness, your service, and your patience. I know that you are doing more now than you did at first. [20]But this is what I have against you: you tolerate that woman Jezebel, who calls herself a messenger of God. By her teaching she misleads my servants into practising sexual immorality and eating food that has been offered to idols. [21]I have given her time to repent of her sins, but she does not want to

turn from her immorality. [22]And so I will throw her on to a bed where she and those who committed adultery with her will suffer terribly. I will do this now unless they repent of the wicked things they did with her. [23]I will also kill her followers, and then all the churches will know that I am the one who knows everyone's thoughts and wishes. I will repay each of you according to what you have done.

24 "But the rest of you in Thyatira have not followed this evil teaching; you have not learnt what the others call 'the deep secrets of Satan'. I say to you that I will not put any other burden on you. [25]But until I come, you must hold firmly to what you have. [26-28]To those who win the victory, who continue to the end to do what I want, I will give the same authority that I received from my Father: I will give them authority over the nations, to rule them with an iron rod and to break them to pieces like clay pots. I will also give them the morning star.

29 "If you have ears, then, listen to what the Spirit says to the churches!

The Message to Sardis

3 "To the angel of the church in Sardis write:

"This is the message from the one who has the seven spirits of God and the seven stars. I know what you are doing; I know that you have the reputation of being alive, even though you are dead! [2]So wake up, and strengthen what you still have before it dies completely. For I find that what you have done is not yet perfect in the sight of my God. [3]Remember, then, what you were taught and what you heard; obey it and turn from your sins. If you do not wake up, I will come upon you like a thief, and you will not even know the time when I will come. [4]But a few of you there in Sardis have kept your clothes clean. You will walk with me, clothed in white, because you are worthy to do so. [5]Those who win the victory will be clothed like this in white, and I will not remove their names from the book of the living. In the presence of my Father and of his angels I will declare openly that they belong to me.

6 "If you have ears, then, listen to what the Spirit says to the churches!

The Message to Philadelphia

7 "To the angel of the church in Philadelphia write:

"This is the message from the one who is holy and true. He has the key that belonged to David, and when he opens a door, no one can close it, and when he closes it, no one can open it. [8]I know what you do; I know that you have a little power; you have followed my teaching and have been faithful to me. I have opened a door in front of you, which no one can close. [9]Listen! As for that group that belongs to Satan, those liars who claim that they are Jews but are not, I will make them come and bow down at your feet. They will all know that I love you. [10]Because you have kept my command to endure, I will also keep you safe from the time of trouble which is coming upon the world to test all the people on earth. [11]I am coming soon. Keep safe what you have, so that no one will rob you of your victory prize. [12]I will make those who are victorious pillars in the temple of my God, and they will never leave it. I will write on them the name of my God and the name of the city of my God, the new Jerusalem, which will come down out of heaven from my God. I will also write on them my new name.

13 "If you have ears, then, listen to what the Spirit says to the churches!

The Message to Laodicea

14 "To the angel of the church in Laodicea write:

"This is the message from the Amen, the faithful and true witness, who is the origin[a] of all that God has created. [15]I know what you have done; I know that you are neither cold nor hot. How I wish you were either one or the other! [16]But because you are lukewarm, neither hot nor cold, I am going to spit you out of my mouth! [17]You say, 'I am rich and well off; I have all I need.' But you do not know how miserable and pitiful you are! You are poor, naked, and blind. [18]I advise you, then, to buy gold from me, pure gold, in order to be rich. Buy also white clothing to dress yourself and cover up your shameful nakedness. Buy also some ointment to put on your eyes, so that you may see. [19]I rebuke and punish all whom I love. Be in earnest, then, and turn from your sins. [20]Listen! I stand at the door and knock; if anyone hears my voice and opens the door, I will come in and eat with them, and they will eat with me. [21]To those who win the victory I will give the right to sit beside me on my throne, just as I have been victorious and now sit by my Father on his throne.

22 "If you have ears, then, listen to what the Spirit says to the churches!"

---

[a] **3.14** origin; *or* ruler.

Worship in Heaven

4 At this point I had another vision and saw an open door in heaven. And the voice that sounded like a trumpet, which I had heard speaking to me before, said, "Come up here, and I will show you what must happen after this." [2]At once the Spirit took control of me. There in heaven was a throne with someone sitting on it. [3]His face gleamed like such precious stones as jasper and carnelian, and all round the throne there was a rainbow the colour of an emerald. [4]In a circle round the throne were twenty-four other thrones, on which were seated twenty-four elders dressed in white and wearing crowns of gold. [5]From the throne came flashes of lightning, rumblings, and peals of thunder. In front of the throne seven lighted torches were burning, which are the seven spirits of God. [6]Also in front of the throne there was what looked like a sea of glass, clear as crystal.

Surrounding the throne on each of its sides, were four living creatures covered with eyes in front and behind. [7]The first one looked like a lion; the second looked like a bull; the third had a face like a human face; and the fourth looked like an eagle in flight. [8]Each one of the four living creatures had six wings, and they were covered with eyes, inside and out. Day and night they never stop singing:

"Holy, holy, holy, is the Lord God Almighty,
who was, who is, and who is to come."

9 The four living creatures sing songs of glory and honour and thanks to the one who sits on the throne, who lives for ever and ever. When they do so, [10]the twenty-four elders fall down before the one who sits on the throne, and worship him who lives for ever and ever. They throw their crowns down in front of the throne and say:

11 "Our Lord and God! You are worthy
to receive glory, honour, and power.
For you created all things,
and by your will they were given existence
and life."

The Scroll and the Lamb

5 I saw a scroll in the right hand of the one who sits on the throne; it was covered with writing on both sides and was sealed with seven seals. [2]And I saw a mighty angel, who announced in a loud voice, "Who is worthy to break the seals and open the scroll?" [3]But there was no one in heaven or on earth or in the world below[a] who could open the scroll and look inside it. ⁴I cried bitterly because no one could be found who was worthy to open the scroll or look inside it. ⁵Then one of the elders said to me, "Don't cry. Look! The Lion from Judah's tribe, the great descendant of David, has won the victory, and he can break the seven seals and open the scroll."

6 Then I saw a Lamb standing in the centre of the throne, surrounded by the four living creatures and the elders. The Lamb appeared to have been killed. It had seven horns and seven eyes, which are the seven spirits of God that have been sent throughout the whole earth. ⁷The Lamb went and took the scroll from the right hand of the one who sits on the throne. ⁸As he did so, the four living creatures and the twenty-four elders fell down before the Lamb. Each had a harp and gold bowls filled with incense, which are the prayers of God's people. ⁹They sang a new song:

"You are worthy to take the scroll
    and to break open its seals.
For you were killed, and by your sacrificial
        death you bought for God
    people from every tribe, language, nation,
        and race.
10 You have made them a kingdom of priests to
        serve our God,
    and they shall rule on earth."

11 Again I looked, and I heard angels, thousands and millions of them! They stood round the throne, the four living creatures, and the elders, ¹²and sang in a loud voice:

"The Lamb who was killed is worthy
    to receive power, wealth, wisdom, and
        strength,
    honour, glory, and praise!"

¹³And I heard every creature in heaven, on earth, in the world below, and in the sea – all living beings in the universe – and they were singing:

"To him who sits on the throne and to the
        Lamb,
    be praise and honour, glory and might,
    for ever and ever!"

¹⁴The four living creatures answered, "Amen!" And the elders fell down and worshipped.

THE SEVEN CHURCHES IN ASIA

The Seals

6 Then I saw the Lamb break open the first of the seven seals, and I heard one of the four living creatures say in a voice that sounded like thunder, "Come!" ²I looked, and there was a white horse. Its rider held a bow, and he was given a crown. He rode out as a conqueror to conquer.

3 Then the Lamb broke open the second seal; and I heard the second living creature say, "Come!" ⁴Another horse came out, a red one. Its rider was given the power to bring war on the earth, so that people should kill each other. He was given a large sword.

5 Then the Lamb broke open the third seal; and I heard the third living creature say, "Come!" I looked, and there was a black horse. Its rider held a pair of scales in his hand. ⁶I heard what sounded like a voice coming from among the four living creatures, which said, "A litre of wheat for a day's wages, and three litres of barley for a day's wages. But do not damage the olive trees and the vineyards!"

7 Then the Lamb broke open the fourth seal; and I heard the fourth living creature say, "Come!" ⁸I looked, and there was a pale-coloured horse. Its rider was named Death, and Hades[b] followed close behind. They were given authority over a quarter of the earth, to kill by means of war, famine, disease, and wild animals.

9 Then the Lamb broke open the fifth seal. I

---

[a] **5.3** WORLD BELOW: *The world of the dead (see 1.18).*

[b] **6.8** HADES: *The world of the dead (see 1.18).*

saw underneath the altar the souls of those who had been killed because they had proclaimed God's word and had been faithful in their witnessing. [10]They shouted in a loud voice, "Almighty Lord, holy and true! How long will it be until you judge the people on earth and punish them for killing us?" [11]Each of them was given a white robe, and they were told to rest a little while longer, until the complete number of their fellow-servants and fellow-Christians had been killed, as they had been.

12 And I saw the Lamb break open the sixth seal. There was a violent earthquake, and the sun became black like coarse black cloth, and the moon turned completely red like blood. [13]The stars fell down to the earth, like unripe figs falling from the tree when a strong wind shakes it. [14]The sky disappeared like a scroll being rolled up, and every mountain and island was moved from its place. [15]Then the kings of the earth, the rulers and the military chiefs, the rich and the powerful, and all other people, slave and free, hid themselves in caves and under rocks on the mountains. [16]They called out to the mountains and to the rocks, "Fall on us and hide us from the eyes of the one who sits on the throne and from the anger of the Lamb! [17]The terrible day of their anger is here, and who can stand against it?"

The 144,000 People of Israel

7 After this I saw four angels standing at the four corners of the earth, holding back the four winds so that no wind should blow on the earth or the sea or against any tree. [2]And I saw another angel coming up from the east with the seal of the living God. He called out in a loud voice to the four angels to whom God had given the power to damage the earth and the sea. [3]The angel said, "Do not harm the earth, the sea, or the trees, until we mark the servants of our God with a seal on their foreheads." [4]And I was told that the number of those who were marked with God's seal on their foreheads was 144,000. They were from the twelve tribes of Israel, [5-8]twelve thousand from each tribe: Judah, Reuben, Gad, Asher, Naphtali, Manasseh, Simeon, Levi, Issachar, Zebulun, Joseph, and Benjamin.

The Enormous Crowd

9 After this I looked, and there was an enormous crowd – no one could count all the people! They were from every race, tribe, nation, and language, and they stood in front of the throne and of the Lamb, dressed in white robes and holding palm branches in their hands. [10]They called out in a loud voice: "Salvation comes from our God, who sits on the throne, and from the Lamb!" [11]All the angels stood round the throne, the elders, and the four living creatures. Then they threw themselves face downwards in front of the throne and worshipped God, [12]saying, "Amen! Praise, glory, wisdom, thanksgiving, honour, power, and might belong to our God for ever and ever! Amen!"

13 One of the elders asked me, "Who are these people dressed in white robes, and where do they come from?"

14 "I don't know, sir. You do," I answered.

He said to me, "These are the people who have come safely through the terrible persecution. They have washed their robes and made them white with the blood of the Lamb. [15]That is why they stand before God's throne and serve him day and night in his temple. He who sits on the throne will protect them with his presence. [16]Never again will they hunger or thirst; neither sun nor any scorching heat will burn them, [17]because the Lamb, who is in the centre of the throne, will be their shepherd, and he will guide them to springs of life-giving water. And God will wipe away every tear from their eyes."

The Seventh Seal

8 When the Lamb broke open the seventh seal, there was silence in heaven for about half an hour. [2]Then I saw the seven angels who stand before God, and they were given seven trumpets.

3 Another angel, who had a gold incense burner, came and stood at the altar. He was given a lot of incense to add to the prayers of all God's people and to offer it on the gold altar that stands before the throne. [4]The smoke of the burning incense went up with the prayers of God's people from the hands of the angel standing before God. [5]Then the angel took the incense burner, filled it with fire from the altar, and threw it on the earth. There were rumblings and peals of thunder, flashes of lightning, and an earthquake.

The Trumpets

6 Then the seven angels with the seven trumpets prepared to blow them.

7 The first angel blew his trumpet. Hail and fire, mixed with blood, came pouring down on the earth. A third of the earth was burnt up, a third of the trees, and every blade of green grass.

8 Then the second angel blew his trumpet. Something that looked like a huge mountain on fire was thrown into the sea. A third of the sea was turned into blood, 9a third of the living creatures in the sea died, and a third of the ships were destroyed.

10 Then the third angel blew his trumpet. A large star, burning like a torch, dropped from the sky and fell on a third of the rivers and on the springs of water. 11(The name of the star is "Bitterness".) A third of the water turned bitter, and many people died from drinking the water, because it had turned bitter.

12 Then the fourth angel blew his trumpet. A third of the sun was struck, and a third of the moon, and a third of the stars, so that their light lost a third of its brightness; there was no light during a third of the day and a third of the night.

13 Then I looked, and I heard an eagle that was flying high in the air say in a loud voice, "O horror! horror! How horrible it will be for all who live on earth when the sound comes from the trumpets that the other three angels must blow!"

9 Then the fifth angel blew his trumpet. I saw a star which had fallen down to the earth, and it was given the key to the abyss.ᵃ 2The star opened the abyss, and smoke poured out of it, like the smoke from a large furnace; the sunlight and the air were darkened by the smoke from the abyss. 3Locusts came down out of the smoke upon the earth, and they were given the same kind of power that scorpions have. 4They were told not to harm the grass or the trees or any other plant; they could harm only the people who did not have the mark of God's seal on their foreheads. 5The locusts were not allowed to kill these people, but only to torture them for five months. The pain caused by the torture is like the pain caused by a scorpion's sting. 6During those five months they will seek death, but will not find it; they will want to die, but death will flee from them.

7 The locusts looked like horses ready for battle; on their heads they had what seemed to be crowns of gold, and their faces were like human faces. 8Their hair was like women's hair, their teeth were like lions' teeth. 9Their chests were covered with what looked like iron breastplates, and the sound made by their wings was like the noise of many horse-drawn chariots rushing into battle. 10They have tails and stings like those of a

ᵃ **9.1** ABYSS: *The place in the depths of the earth where the demons were imprisoned until their final punishment.*

scorpion, and it is with their tails that they have the power to hurt people for five months. 11They have a king ruling over them, who is the angel in charge of the abyss. His name in Hebrew is Abaddon; in Greek the name is Apollyon (meaning "The Destroyer").

12 The first horror is over; after this there are still two more horrors to come.

13 Then the sixth angel blew his trumpet. I heard a voice coming from the four corners of the gold altar standing before God. 14The voice said to the sixth angel, "Release the four angels who are bound at the great river Euphrates!" 15The four angels were released; for this very hour of this very day of this very month and year they had been kept ready to kill a third of all humanity. 16I was told the number of the mounted troops: it was two hundred million. 17And in my vision I saw the horses and their riders: they had breastplates red as fire, blue as sapphire, and yellow as sulphur. The horses' heads were like lions' heads, and from their mouths came out fire, smoke, and sulphur. 18A third of humanity was killed by those three plagues: the fire, the smoke, and the sulphur coming out of the horses' mouths. 19For the power of the horses is in their mouths and also in their tails. Their tails are like snakes with heads, and they use them to hurt people.

20 The rest of humanity, all those who had not been killed by these plagues, did not turn away from what they themselves had made. They did not stop worshipping demons, nor the idols of gold, silver, bronze, stone, and wood, which cannot see, hear, or walk. 21Nor did they repent of their murders, their magic, their sexual immorality, or their stealing.

The Angel and the Little Scroll

10 Then I saw another mighty angel coming down out of heaven. He was wrapped in a cloud and had a rainbow round his head; his face was like the sun, and his legs were like pillars of fire. 2He had a small scroll open in his hand. He put his right foot on the sea and his left foot on the land, 3and called out in a loud voice that sounded like the roar of lions. After he had called out, the seven thunders answered with a roar. 4As soon as they spoke, I was about to write. But I heard a voice speak from heaven, "Keep secret what the seven thunders have said; do not write it down!"

5 Then the angel that I saw standing on the sea and on the land raised his right hand to heaven 6and took a vow in the name of God, who lives

for ever and ever, who created heaven, earth, and the sea, and everything in them. The angel said, "There will be no more delay! ⁷But when the seventh angel blows his trumpet, then God will accomplish his secret plan, as he announced to his servants, the prophets."

8 Then the voice that I had heard speaking from heaven spoke to me again, saying, "Go and take the open scroll which is in the hand of the angel standing on the sea and on the land."

9 I went to the angel and asked him to give me the little scroll. He said to me, "Take it and eat it; it will turn sour in your stomach, but in your mouth it will be sweet as honey."

10 I took the little scroll from his hand and ate it, and it tasted sweet as honey in my mouth. But after I swallowed it, it turned sour in my stomach. ¹¹Then I was told, "Once again you must proclaim God's message about many nations, races, languages, and kings."

The Two Witnesses

11 I was then given a stick that looked like a measuring rod, and was told, "Go and measure the temple of God and the altar, and count those who are worshipping in the temple. ²But do not measure the outer courts, because they have been given to the heathen, who will trample on the Holy City for forty-two months. ³I will send my two witnesses dressed in sackcloth, and they will proclaim God's message during those 1,260 days."

4 The two witnesses are the two olive trees and the two lamps that stand before the Lord of the earth. ⁵If anyone tries to harm them, fire comes out of their mouths and destroys their enemies; and in this way, whoever tries to harm them will be killed. ⁶They have authority to shut up the sky so that there will be no rain during the time they proclaim God's message. They have authority also over the springs of water, to turn them into blood; they have authority also to strike the earth with every kind of plague as often as they wish.

7 When they finish proclaiming their message, the beast that comes up out of the abyss will fight against them. He will defeat them and kill them, ⁸and their bodies will lie in the street of the great city, where their Lord was crucified. The symbolic name of that city is Sodom, or Egypt. ⁹People from all nations, tribes, languages, and races will look at their bodies for three and a half days and will not allow them to be buried. ¹⁰The people of the earth will be happy because of the death of these two. They will celebrate and send presents to each other,

because those two prophets brought much suffering upon the earth. ¹¹After three and a half days a life-giving breath came from God and entered them, and they stood up; and all who saw them were terrified. ¹²Then the two prophets heard a loud voice say to them from heaven, "Come up here!" As their enemies watched, they went up into heaven in a cloud. ¹³At that very moment there was a violent earthquake; a tenth of the city was destroyed, and seven thousand people were killed. The rest of the people were terrified and praised the greatness of the God of heaven.

14 The second horror is over, but the third horror will come soon!

The Seventh Trumpet

15 Then the seventh angel blew his trumpet, and there were loud voices in heaven, saying, "The power to rule over the world belongs now to our Lord and his Messiah, and he will rule for ever and ever!" ¹⁶Then the twenty-four elders who sit on their thrones in front of God threw themselves face downwards and worshipped God, ¹⁷saying:

"Lord God Almighty, the one who is and
    who was!
We thank you that you have taken your great
    power
    and have begun to rule!
18 The heathen were filled with rage,
    because the time for your anger has come,
    the time for the dead to be judged.
The time has come to reward your servants,
    the prophets,
    and all your people, all who have
    reverence for you,
    great and small alike.
The time has come to destroy those who
    destroy the earth!"

19 God's temple in heaven was opened, and the Covenant Box was seen there. Then there were flashes of lightning, rumblings and peals of thunder, an earthquake, and heavy hail.

The Woman and the Dragon

12 Then a great and mysterious sight appeared in the sky. There was a woman, whose dress was the sun and who had the moon under her feet and a crown of twelve stars on her head. ²She was soon to give birth, and the pains and suffering of childbirth made her cry out.

3 Another mysterious sight appeared in the sky.

There was a huge red dragon with seven heads and ten horns and a crown on each of his heads. [4]With his tail he dragged a third of the stars out of the sky and threw them down to the earth. He stood in front of the woman, in order to eat her child as soon as it was born. [5]Then she gave birth to a son, who will rule over all nations with an iron rod. But the child was snatched away and taken to God and his throne. [6]The woman fled to the desert, to a place God had prepared for her, where she will be taken care of for 1,260 days.

7 Then war broke out in heaven. Michael and his angels fought against the dragon, who fought back with his angels; [8]but the dragon was defeated, and he and his angels were not allowed to stay in heaven any longer. [9]The huge dragon was thrown out – that ancient serpent, called the Devil, or Satan, that deceived the whole world. He was thrown down to earth, and all his angels with him.

10 Then I heard a loud voice in heaven saying, "Now God's salvation has come! Now God has shown his power as King! Now his Messiah has shown his authority! For the one who stood before our God and accused our brothers and sisters day and night has been thrown out of heaven. [11]Our brothers and sisters won the victory over him by the blood of the Lamb and by the truth which they proclaimed; and they were willing to give up their lives and die. [12]And so be glad, you heavens, and all you that live there! But how terrible for the earth and the sea! For the Devil has come down to you, and he is filled with rage, because he knows that he has only a little time left."

13 When the dragon realized that he had been thrown down to the earth, he began to pursue the woman who had given birth to the boy. [14]She was given the two wings of a large eagle in order to fly to her place in the desert, where she will be taken care of for three and a half years, safe from the dragon's attack. [15]And then from his mouth the dragon poured out a flood of water after the woman, so that it would carry her away. [16]But the earth helped the woman; it opened its mouth and swallowed the water that had come from the dragon's mouth. [17]The dragon was furious with the woman and went off to fight against the rest of her descendants, all those who obey God's commandments and are faithful to the truth revealed by Jesus. [18]And the dragon stood[a] on the seashore.

[a] **12.18** And the dragon stood; *some manuscripts have* And I stood, *connecting this verse with what follows.*

The Two Beasts

13 Then I saw a beast coming up out of the sea. It had ten horns and seven heads; on each of its horns there was a crown, and on each of its heads there was a name that was insulting to God. [2]The beast looked like a leopard, with feet like a bear's feet and a mouth like a lion's mouth. The dragon gave the beast his own power, his throne, and his vast authority. [3]One of the heads of the beast seemed to have been fatally wounded, but the wound had healed. The whole earth was amazed and followed the beast. [4]Everyone worshipped the dragon because he had given his authority to the beast. They worshipped the beast also, saying, "Who is like the beast? Who can fight against it?"

5 The beast was allowed to make proud claims which were insulting to God, and it was permitted to have authority for forty-two months. [6]It began to curse God, his name, the place where he lives, and all those who live in heaven. [7]It was allowed to fight against God's people and to defeat them, and it was given authority over every tribe, nation, language, and race. [8]All people living on earth will worship it, except those whose names were written before the creation of the world in the book of the living which belongs to the Lamb that was killed.

9 "Listen, then, if you have ears! [10]Whoever is meant to be captured will surely be captured; whoever is meant to be killed by the sword will surely be killed by the sword. This calls for endurance and faith on the part of God's people."

11 Then I saw another beast, which came up out of the earth. It had two horns like a lamb's horns, and it spoke like a dragon. [12]It used the vast authority of the first beast in its presence. It forced the earth and all who live on it to worship the first beast, whose wound had healed. [13]This second beast performed great miracles; it made fire come down out of heaven to earth in the sight of everyone. [14]And it deceived all the people living on earth by means of the miracles which it was allowed to perform in the presence of the first beast. The beast told them to build an image in honour of the beast that had been wounded by the sword and yet lived. [15]The second beast was allowed to breathe life into the image of the first beast, so that the image could talk and put to death all those who would not worship it. [16]The beast forced all the people, small and great, rich and poor, slave and free, to have a mark placed on their right hands or on their foreheads. [17]No one could buy or sell without having this mark, that is, the beast's name or the number that stands for the name.

18   This calls for wisdom. Whoever is intelligent can work out the meaning of the number of the beast, because the number stands for a human name. Its number is 666.

The Lamb and his People

14 Then I looked, and there was the Lamb standing on Mount Zion; with him were 144,000 people who have his name and his Father's name written on their foreheads. ²And I heard a voice from heaven that sounded like a roaring waterfall, like a loud peal of thunder. It sounded like the music made by musicians playing their harps. ³The 144,000 people stood before the throne, the four living creatures, and the elders; they were singing a new song, which only they could learn. They are the only ones who have been redeemed. ⁴They are the men who have kept themselves pure by not having sexual relations with women; they are virgins. They follow the Lamb wherever he goes. They have been redeemed from the rest of the human race and are the first ones to be offered to God and to the Lamb. ⁵They have never been known to tell lies; they are faultless.

The Three Angels

6   Then I saw another angel flying high in the air, with an eternal message of Good News to announce to the peoples of the earth, to every race, tribe, language, and nation. ⁷He said in a loud voice, "Honour God and praise his greatness! For the time has come for him to judge. Worship him who made heaven, earth, sea, and the springs of water!"

8   A second angel followed the first one, saying, "She has fallen! Great Babylon has fallen! She made all peoples drink her wine – the strong wine of her immoral lust!"

9   A third angel followed the first two, saying in a loud voice, "Whoever worships the beast and its image and receives the mark on their forehead or on their hand ¹⁰will themselves drink God's wine, the wine of his fury, which he has poured at full strength into the cup of his anger! All who do this will be tormented in fire and sulphur before the holy angels and the Lamb. ¹¹The smoke of the fire that torments them goes up for ever and ever. There is no relief day or night for those who worship the beast and its image, for anyone who has the mark of its name."

12   This calls for endurance on the part of God's people, those who obey God's commandments and are faithful to Jesus.

13   Then I heard a voice from heaven saying, "Write this: happy are those who from now on die in the service of the Lord!"

"Yes indeed!" answers the Spirit. "They will enjoy rest from their hard work, because the results of their service go with them."

The Harvest of the Earth

14   Then I looked, and there was a white cloud, and sitting on the cloud was what looked like a human being, with a crown of gold on his head and a sharp sickle in his hand. ¹⁵Then another angel came out from the temple and cried out in a loud voice to the one who was sitting on the cloud, "Use your sickle and reap the harvest, because the time has come; the earth is ripe for the harvest!" ¹⁶Then the one who sat on the cloud swung his sickle on the earth, and the earth's harvest was reaped.

17   Then I saw another angel come out of the temple in heaven, and he also had a sharp sickle.

18   Then another angel, who is in charge of the fire, came from the altar. He shouted in a loud voice to the angel who had the sharp sickle, "Use your sickle, and cut the grapes from the vineyard of the earth, because the grapes are ripe!" ¹⁹So the angel swung his sickle on the earth, cut the grapes from the vine, and threw them into the winepress of God's furious anger. ²⁰The grapes were squeezed out in the winepress outside the city, and blood came out of the winepress in a flood three hundred kilometres long and nearly two metres deep.

The Angels with the Last Plagues

15 Then I saw in the sky another mysterious sight, great and amazing. There were seven angels with seven plagues, which are the last ones, because they are the final expression of God's anger.

2   Then I saw what looked like a sea of glass mixed with fire. I also saw those who had won the victory over the beast and its image and over the one whose name is represented by a number. They were standing by the sea of glass, holding harps that God had given them ³and singing the song of Moses, the servant of God, and the song of the Lamb:

"Lord God Almighty,
    how great and wonderful are your deeds!
King of the nations,ᵃ
    how right and true are your ways!

ᵃ **15.3** nations; *some manuscripts have* ages.

4 Who will not stand in awe of you, Lord?
    Who will refuse to declare your greatness?
    You alone are holy.
All the nations will come
    and worship you,
    because your just actions are seen by all."

5 After this I saw the temple in heaven open, with the Sacred Tent in it. [6]The seven angels who had the seven plagues came out of the temple, dressed in clean shining linen and with gold belts tied around their chests. [7]Then one of the four living creatures gave the seven angels seven gold bowls full of the anger of God, who lives for ever and ever. [8]The temple was filled with smoke from the glory and power of God, and no one could go into the temple until the seven plagues brought by the seven angels had come to an end.

The Bowls of God's Anger

16 Then I heard a loud voice speaking from the temple to the seven angels: "Go and pour out the seven bowls of God's anger on the earth!"

2 The first angel went and poured out his bowl on the earth. Terrible and painful sores appeared on those who had the mark of the beast and on those who had worshipped its image.

3 Then the second angel poured out his bowl on the sea. The water became like the blood of a dead person, and every living creature in the sea died.

4 Then the third angel poured out his bowl on the rivers and the springs of water, and they turned into blood. [5]I heard the angel in charge of the waters say, "The judgements you have made are just, O Holy One, you who are and who were! [6]They poured out the blood of God's people and of the prophets, and so you have given them blood to drink. They are getting what they deserve!" [7]Then I heard a voice from the altar saying, "Lord God Almighty! True and just indeed are your judgements!"

8 Then the fourth angel poured out his bowl on the sun, and it was allowed to burn people with its fiery heat. [9]They were burnt by the fierce heat, and they cursed the name of God, who has authority over these plagues. But they would not turn from their sins and praise his greatness.

10 Then the fifth angel poured out his bowl on the throne of the beast. Darkness fell over the beast's kingdom, and people bit their tongues because of their pain, [11]and they cursed the God of heaven for their pains and sores. But they did not turn from their evil ways.

12 Then the sixth angel poured out his bowl on the great river Euphrates. The river dried up, to provide a way for the kings who come from the east. [13]Then I saw three unclean spirits that looked like frogs. They were coming out of the mouth of the dragon, the mouth of the beast, and the mouth of the false prophet. [14]They are the spirits of demons that perform miracles. These three spirits go out to all the kings of the world, to bring them together for the battle on the great Day of Almighty God.

15 "Listen! I am coming like a thief! Happy is he who stays awake and guards his clothes, so that he will not walk around naked and be ashamed in public!"

16 Then the spirits brought the kings together in the place that in Hebrew is called Armageddon.

17 Then the seventh angel poured out his bowl in the air. A loud voice came from the throne in the temple, saying, "It is done!" [18]There were flashes of lightning, rumblings and peals of thunder, and a terrible earthquake. There has never been such an earthquake since the creation of the human race; this was the worst earthquake of all! [19]The great city was split into three parts, and the cities of all countries were destroyed. God remembered great Babylon and made her drink the wine from his cup – the wine of his furious anger. [20]All the islands disappeared, all the mountains vanished. [21]Huge hailstones, each weighing as much as fifty kilogrammes, fell from the sky on people, who cursed God on account of the plague of hail, because it was such a terrible plague.

The Famous Prostitute

17 Then one of the seven angels who had the seven bowls came to me and said, "Come, and I will show you how the famous prostitute is to be punished, that great city that is built near many rivers. [2]The kings of the earth practised sexual immorality with her, and the people of the world became drunk from drinking the wine of her immorality."

3 The Spirit took control of me, and the angel carried me to a desert. There I saw a woman sitting on a red beast that had names insulting to God written all over it; the beast had seven heads and ten horns. [4]The woman was dressed in purple and scarlet, and covered with gold ornaments, precious stones, and pearls. In her hand she held a gold cup full of obscene and filthy things, the result of her immorality. [5]On her forehead was written a name that has a secret meaning: "Great Babylon, the mother of

all the prostitutes and perverts in the world." [6]And I saw that the woman was drunk with the blood of God's people and the blood of those who were killed because they had been loyal to Jesus.

When I saw her, I was completely amazed. [7]"Why are you amazed?" the angel asked me. "I will tell you the secret meaning of the woman and of the beast that carries her, the beast with seven heads and ten horns. [8]That beast was once alive, but lives no longer; it is about to come up from the abyss and will go off to be destroyed. The people living on earth whose names have not been written before the creation of the world in the book of the living, will all be amazed as they look at the beast. It was once alive; now it no longer lives, but it will reappear.

9 "This calls for wisdom and understanding. The seven heads are seven hills, on which the woman sits. They are also seven kings: [10]five of them have fallen, one still rules, and the other one has not yet come; when he comes, he must rule only a little while. [11]And the beast that was once alive, but lives no longer, is itself an eighth king who is one of the seven and is going off to be destroyed.

12 "The ten horns you saw are ten kings who have not yet begun to rule, but who will be given authority to rule as kings for one hour with the beast. [13]These ten all have the same purpose, and they give their power and authority to the beast. [14]They will fight against the Lamb; but the Lamb, together with his called, chosen, and faithful followers, will defeat them, because he is Lord of lords and King of kings."

15 The angel also said to me, "The waters you saw, on which the prostitute is sitting, are nations, peoples, races, and languages. [16]The ten horns you saw, and the beast, will hate the prostitute; they will take away everything she has and leave her naked; they will eat her flesh and destroy her with fire. [17]For God has placed in their hearts the will to carry out his purpose by acting together and giving the beast their power to rule until God's words come true.

18 "The woman you saw is the great city that rules over the kings of the earth."

The Fall of Babylon

18 After this I saw another angel coming down out of heaven. He had great authority, and his splendour brightened the whole earth. [2]He cried out in a loud voice: "She has fallen! Great Babylon has fallen! She is now haunted by demons and unclean spirits; all kinds of filthy and hateful birds live in her. [3]For all the nations have drunk her wine – the strong wine of her immoral lust. The kings of the earth practised sexual immorality with her, and the merchants of the world grew rich from her unrestrained lust."

4 Then I heard another voice from heaven, saying:

"Come out, my people! Come out from her!
    You must not take part in her sins;
    you must not share in her punishment!

5 For her sins are piled up as high as heaven,
    and God remembers her wicked ways.

6 Treat her exactly as she has treated you;
    pay her back double for all she has done.
Fill her cup with a drink twice as strong
    as the drink she prepared for you.

7 Give her as much suffering and grief
    as the glory and luxury she gave herself.
For she keeps telling herself:
'Here I sit, a queen!
    I am no widow,
    I will never know grief!'

8 Because of this, in one day she will be struck
        with plagues –
    disease, grief, and famine.
And she will be burnt with fire,
    because the Lord God, who judges her, is
        mighty."

9 The kings of the earth who took part in her immorality and lust will cry and weep over the city when they see the smoke from the flames that consume her. [10]They stand a long way off, because they are afraid of sharing in her suffering. They say, "How terrible! How awful! This great and mighty city Babylon! In just one hour you have been punished!"

11 The merchants of the earth also cry and mourn for her, because no one buys their goods any longer; [12]no one buys their gold, silver, precious stones, and pearls; their goods of linen, purple cloth, silk, and scarlet cloth; all kinds of rare woods and all kinds of objects made of ivory and of expensive wood, of bronze, iron, and marble; [13]and cinnamon, spice, incense, myrrh, and frankincense; wine and oil, flour and wheat, cattle and sheep, horses and carriages, slaves, and even human lives. [14]The merchants say to her, "All the good things you longed to own have disappeared, and all your wealth and glamour are gone, and you will never find them again!" [15]The merchants, who became rich from doing business in that city, will stand a long way off, because they are afraid of sharing in her suffering. They will cry

and mourn, [16]and say, "How terrible! How awful for the great city! She used to dress herself in linen, purple, and scarlet, and cover herself with gold ornaments, precious stones, and pearls! [17]And in one hour she has lost all this wealth!"

All the ships' captains and passengers, the sailors and all others who earn their living on the sea, stood a long way off, [18]and cried out as they saw the smoke from the flames that consumed her: "There never has been another city like this great city!" [19]They threw dust on their heads, they cried and mourned, saying, "How terrible! How awful for the great city! She is the city where all who have ships sailing the seas became rich on her wealth! And in one hour she has lost everything!"

20 Be glad, heaven, because of her destruction! Be glad, God's people and the apostles and prophets! For God has condemned her for what she did to you!

21 Then a mighty angel picked up a stone the size of a large millstone and threw it into the sea, saying, "This is how the great city Babylon will be violently thrown down and will never be seen again. [22]The music of harps and of human voices, of players of the flute and the trumpet, will never be heard in you again! No workman in any trade will ever be found in you again; and the sound of the millstone will be heard no more! [23]Never again will the light of a lamp be seen in you; no more will the voices of brides and grooms be heard in you. Your merchants were the most powerful in all the world, and with your false magic you deceived all the peoples of the world!"

24 Babylon was punished because the blood of prophets and of God's people was found in the city; yes, the blood of all those who have been killed on earth.

19 After this I heard what sounded like the roar of a large crowd of people in heaven, saying, "Praise God! Salvation, glory, and power belong to our God! [2]True and just are his judgements! He has condemned the prostitute who was corrupting the earth with her immorality. God has punished her because she killed his servants." [3]Again they shouted, "Praise God! The smoke from the flames that consume the great city goes up for ever and ever!" [4]The twenty-four elders and the four living creatures fell down and worshipped God, who was seated on the throne. They said, "Amen! Praise God!"

The Wedding Feast of the Lamb

5 Then there came from the throne the sound of a voice, saying, "Praise our God, all his servants and all people, both great and small, who have reverence for him!" [6]Then I heard what sounded like a large crowd, like the sound of a roaring waterfall, like loud peals of thunder. I heard them say, "Praise God! For the Lord, our Almighty God, is King! [7]Let us rejoice and be glad; let us praise his greatness! For the time has come for the wedding of the Lamb, and his bride has prepared herself for it. [8]She has been given clean shining linen to wear." (The linen is the good deeds of God's people.)

9 Then the angel said to me, "Write this: happy are those who have been invited to the wedding feast of the Lamb." And the angel added, "These are the true words of God."

10 I fell down at his feet to worship him, but he said to me, "Don't do it! I am a servant together with you and with your fellow-believers, all those who hold to the truth that Jesus revealed. Worship God!"

For the truth that Jesus revealed is what inspires the prophets.

The Rider on the White Horse

11 Then I saw heaven open, and there was a white horse. Its rider is called Faithful and True; it is with justice that he judges and fights his battles. [12]His eyes were like a flame of fire, and he wore many crowns on his head. He had a name written on him, but no one except himself knows what it is. [13]The robe he wore was covered with blood. His name is "The Word of God". [14]The armies of heaven followed him, riding on white horses and dressed in clean white linen. [15]Out of his mouth came a sharp sword, with which he will defeat the nations. He will rule over them with a rod of iron, and he will trample out the wine in the winepress of the furious anger of the Almighty God. [16]On his robe and on his thigh was written the name: "King of kings and Lord of lords".

17 Then I saw an angel standing on the sun. He shouted in a loud voice to all the birds flying in midair: "Come and gather together for God's great feast! [18]Come and eat the flesh of kings, generals, and soldiers, the flesh of horses and their riders, the flesh of all people, slave and free, great and small!"

19 Then I saw the beast and the kings of the earth and their armies gathered to fight against the one who was riding the horse and against his army. [20]The beast was taken prisoner, together

with the false prophet who had performed miracles in his presence. (It was by those miracles that he had deceived those who had the mark of the beast and those who had worshipped the image of the beast.) The beast and the false prophet were both thrown alive into the lake of fire that burns with sulphur. ²¹Their armies were killed by the sword that comes out of the mouth of the one who was riding the horse; and all the birds ate all they could of their flesh.

The Thousand Years

20 Then I saw an angel coming down from heaven, holding in his hand the key of the abyss and a heavy chain. ²He seized the dragon, that ancient serpent – that is, the Devil, or Satan – and chained him up for a thousand years. ³The angel threw him into the abyss, locked it, and sealed it, so that he could not deceive the nations any more until the thousand years were over. After that he must be let loose for a little while.

4 Then I saw thrones, and those who sat on them were given the power to judge. I also saw the souls of those who had been executed because they had proclaimed the truth that Jesus revealed and the word of God. They had not worshipped the beast or its image, nor had they received the mark of the beast on their foreheads or their hands. They came to life and ruled as kings with Christ for a thousand years. ⁵(The rest of the dead did not come to life until the thousand years were over.) This is the first raising of the dead. ⁶Happy and greatly blessed are those who are included in this first raising of the dead. The second death has no power over them; they shall be priests of God and of Christ, and they will rule with him for a thousand years.

The Defeat of Satan

7 After the thousand years are over, Satan will be let loose from his prison, ⁸and he will go out to deceive the nations scattered over the whole world, that is, Gog and Magog. Satan will bring them all together for battle, as many as the grains of sand on the seashore. ⁹They spread out over the earth and surrounded the camp of God's people and the city that he loves. But fire came down from heaven and destroyed them. ¹⁰Then the Devil, who deceived them, was thrown into the lake of fire and sulphur, where the beast and the false prophet had already been thrown; and they will be tormented day and night for ever and ever.

The Final Judgement

11 Then I saw a great white throne and the one who sits on it. Earth and heaven fled from his presence and were seen no more. ¹²And I saw the dead, great and small alike, standing before the throne. Books were opened, and then another book was opened, the book of the living. The dead were judged according to what they had done, as recorded in the books. ¹³Then the sea gave up its dead. Death and the world of the dead also gave up the dead they held. And all were judged according to what they had done. ¹⁴Then death and the world of the dead were thrown into the lake of fire. (This lake of fire is the second death.) ¹⁵Whoever did not have their names written in the book of the living were thrown into the lake of fire.

The New Heaven and the New Earth

21 Then I saw a new heaven and a new earth. The first heaven and the first earth disappeared, and the sea vanished. ²And I saw the Holy City, the new Jerusalem, coming down out of heaven from God, prepared and ready, like a bride dressed to meet her husband. ³I heard a loud voice speaking from the throne: "Now God's home is with human beings! He will live with them, and they shall be his people. God himself will be with them, and he will be their God. ⁴He will wipe away all tears from their eyes. There will be no more death, no more grief or crying or pain. The old things have disappeared."

5 Then the one who sits on the throne said, "And now I make all things new!" He also said to me, "Write this, because these words are true and can be trusted." ⁶And he said, "It is done! I am the first and the last, the beginning and the end. To anyone who is thirsty I will give the right to drink from the spring of the water of life without paying for it. ⁷Those who win the victory will receive this from me: I will be their God, and they will be my children. ⁸But cowards, traitors, perverts, murderers, the immoral, those who practise magic, those who worship idols, and all liars – the place for them is the lake burning with fire and sulphur, which is the second death."

The New Jerusalem

9 One of the seven angels who had the seven bowls full of the seven last plagues came to me and said, "Come, and I will show you the Bride, the wife of the Lamb." ¹⁰The Spirit took control of

me, and the angel carried me to the top of a very high mountain. He showed me Jerusalem, the Holy City, coming down out of heaven from God [11]and shining with the glory of God. The city shone like a precious stone, like a jasper, clear as crystal. [12]It had a great, high wall with twelve gates and with twelve angels in charge of the gates. On the gates were written the names of the twelve tribes of the people of Israel. [13]There were three gates on each side: three on the east, three on the south, three on the north, and three on the west. [14]The city's wall was built on twelve foundation stones, on which were written the names of the twelve apostles of the Lamb. [15]The angel who spoke to me had a gold measuring rod to measure the city, its gates, and its wall. [16]The city was perfectly square, as wide as it was long. The angel measured the city with his measuring rod: it was 2,400 kilometres long and was as wide and as high as it was long. [17]The angel also measured the wall, and it was sixty metres high,[a] according to the standard unit of measure which he was using.[b] [18]The wall was made of jasper, and the city itself was made of pure gold, as clear as glass. [19]The foundation stones of the city wall were adorned with all kinds of precious stones. The first foundation stone was jasper, the second sapphire, the third agate, the fourth emerald, [20]the fifth onyx, the sixth carnelian, the seventh yellow quartz, the eighth beryl, the ninth topaz, the tenth chalcedony, the eleventh turquoise, the twelfth amethyst. [21]The twelve gates were twelve pearls; each gate was made from a single pearl. The street of the city was of pure gold, transparent as glass.

22 I did not see a temple in the city, because its temple is the Lord God Almighty and the Lamb. [23]The city has no need of the sun or the moon to shine on it, because the glory of God shines on it, and the Lamb is its lamp. [24]The peoples of the world will walk by its light, and the kings of the earth will bring their wealth into it. [25]The gates of the city will stand open all day; they will never be closed, because there will be no night there. [26]The greatness and the wealth of the nations will be brought into the city. [27]But nothing that is impure will enter the city, nor anyone who does shameful things or tells lies. Only those whose names are written in the Lamb's book of the living will enter the city.

[a] **21.17** high; *or* thick.
[b] **21.17** *In verses 16 and 17 the Greek text speaks of "12,000 furlongs" and "144 cubits" which may have symbolic significance.*

22 The angel also showed me the river of the water of life, sparkling like crystal, and coming from the throne of God and of the Lamb [2]and flowing down the middle of the city's street. On each side of the river was the tree of life, which bears fruit twelve times a year, once each month; and its leaves are for the healing of the nations. [3]Nothing that is under God's curse will be found in the city.

The throne of God and of the Lamb will be in the city, and his servants will worship him. [4]They will see his face, and his name will be written on their foreheads. [5]There shall be no more night, and they will not need lamps or sunlight, because the Lord God will be their light, and they will rule as kings for ever and ever.

The Coming of Jesus

6 Then the angel said to me, "These words are true and can be trusted. And the Lord God, who gives his Spirit to the prophets, has sent his angel to show his servants what must happen very soon."

7 "Listen!" says Jesus. "I am coming soon! Happy are those who obey the prophetic words in this book!"

8 I, John, have heard and seen all these things. And when I finished hearing and seeing them, I fell down at the feet of the angel who had shown me these things, and I was about to worship him. [9]But he said to me, "Don't do it! I am a servant together with you and with your brothers the prophets and with all those who obey the words in this book. Worship God!" [10]And he said to me, "Do not keep the prophetic words of this book a secret, because the time is near when all this will happen. [11]Whoever is evil must go on doing evil, and whoever is filthy must go on being filthy; whoever is good must go on doing good, and whoever is holy must go on being holy."

12 "Listen!" says Jesus. "I am coming soon! I will bring my rewards with me, to give to each one according to what he has done. [13]I am the first and the last, the beginning and the end."

14 Happy are those who wash their robes clean and so have the right to eat the fruit from the tree of life and to go through the gates into the city. [15]But outside the city are the perverts and those who practise magic, the immoral and the murderers, those who worship idols and those who are liars both in words and deeds.

16 "I, Jesus, have sent my angel to announce these things to you in the churches. I am

descended from the family of David; I am the bright morning star."

17   The Spirit and the Bride say, "Come!"

Everyone who hears this must also say, "Come!"

Come, whoever is thirsty; accept the water of life as a gift, whoever wants it.

Conclusion

18   I, John, solemnly warn everyone who hears the prophetic words of this book: if anyone adds anything to them, God will add to his or her punishment the plagues described in this book. [19]And if anyone takes anything away from the prophetic words of this book, God will take away from them their share of the fruit of the tree of life and of the Holy City, which are described in this book.

20   He who gives his testimony to all this says, "Yes indeed! I am coming soon!"

So be it. Come, Lord Jesus!

21   May the grace of the Lord Jesus be with everyone.[a]

---

[a] **22.21** everyone; *some manuscripts have* God's people; *others have* all God's people.

Social Issues

Abortion

In the New Testament
Matthew 18.1–6
Luke 1.39–45; 12.6–7

Abortion is "the legal termination [ending] of a pregnancy". Since 1967, abortion has been legal in Great Britain as long as two doctors agree that it is necessary. The pregnancy can only be terminated before it has reached 24 weeks. Before 1990, the limit was 28 weeks, but advances in medical care mean that some babies born at 24 weeks – 16 weeks premature – can survive. A termination is allowed if the health of the mother is at risk or there is a real risk that the baby will be born mentally or physically handicapped. It is also permitted if the mother's mental health is thought to be in danger. Before 1967, over 200,000 back-street abortions were performed illegally every year. Because these operations were carried out illegally, and therefore not subject to regulation or monitoring, the mother's life was often at great risk. Now about 150,000 abortions – 18 per cent of all pregnancies – are carried out each year in Great Britain.

The Roman Catholic Church is strongly opposed to abortion in all circumstances – even if the mother has been raped or her life is at risk. The Church of England and the Church of Scotland are opposed to abortion but accept that in extreme circumstances (i.e. when the mother's health is at serious risk) the mother's right to life overrides that of the unborn child. Other churches, notably the Free Churches, regard abortion as a matter for the conscience of each individual.

The New Testament does not, of course, refer to abortion directly, although one or two references might be applied indirectly.

Discussion Questions

1 Those against abortion argue that each baby is a unique gift from God. Do you think that this applies to every baby?

2 The Roman Catholic Church argues that the rights of the unborn child are at least equal to those of its mother – and in certain situations greater. Do you agree with this?

3 When do you think that life begins? At conception? At some time during pregnancy? At birth? How do you think the answer to this question affects one's attitude to abortion?

Capital Punishment

In the New Testament
Matthew 5.38–39
Mark 6.14–29
Luke 23.39–43
Acts 12.20–23

The death penalty is the lawful taking of a human life by the civil authorities. In the ancient world the death penalty was inflicted by almost all nations. In Palestine the usual method was stoning, but such forms as beheading, hanging and crucifixion were also common. In Great Britain the death penalty remained for most forms of murder until 1957, when it was restricted to killing a policeman, killing during an armed robbery or killing more than one person. In 1965 it was suspended for a trial period of five years and in 1970 abolished altogether.

The last execution in Great Britain was carried out in 1964. From time to time since then it has been debated by Parliament when those who wanted it restored argued that some people only understand the language of violence and that society must protect those who are most vulnerable. Those against its restoration argued that too many people are found "guilty" of murder when they are innocent – and it does not stop murder. The death penalty remains in over 100 countries, and Amnesty International believes that some 50,000 executions have been carried out in the world since 1980. Christians are permanently reminded that Jesus was unjustly put to death on a Roman cross.

Discussion Questions

1 Weigh up the arguments for and against capital punishment. Which do you think are the most convincing? Would you support the restoration of the death penalty? If so, why? If not, why not?

2 Some 60 per cent of all murders are carried out by people known to the murdered person, usually from their own family. What does that tell you about murder – and the suitability of the death penalty?

Divorce

In the New Testament
Matthew 19.3–12
Mark 10.2–12
Luke 16.18
Romans 7.2–3
1 Corinthians
7.10–11,27

Out of the 450,000 marriages each year in Great Britain, about 180,000 will end in divorce. This number has risen dramatically since the Divorce Reform Act was passed in 1969, allowing people to divorce if they could show that their marriage "had irretrievably broken down". Adultery, cruelty or desertion could be counted as evidence that this had happened. Seventy-five per cent of all couples divorcing have one or more children under sixteen. At the moment, 1,500,000 children are affected by the divorce of their parents. In the time of Jesus, only a man could obtain a divorce, which he did by issuing a certificate of divorce to his wife and sending her away from the family home.

The attitude of Jesus towards divorce is far from clear. He taught that nothing can break the vows of marriage, but, on occasions, suggested that a person can divorce if adultery had taken place.

Discussion Questions

1 The Roman Catholic Church does not allow divorce in any circumstances. Do you think that this is a reasonable attitude to adopt today?

2 Three out of every four divorces involve children. What is the impact on children if their parents divorce? Are there occasions when a divorce might be preferable to two unhappy people staying together?

Euthanasia

In the New Testament
Luke 12.4–7
1 Corinthians 15.55–57

Euthanasia – the right to seek "a good, easy death" – is a very controversial subject. Those in favour argue that everyone should have the right to choose when to end their own life, since a speedy death saves many people – patient and relatives – unnecessary suffering. Both the Roman Catholic Church and the Church of England oppose euthanasia, which is illegal in Great Britain, on the grounds that it treats human beings like animals and robs God of the right to decide when a person should die. In recent years the Hospice Movement has provided many beds for terminally ill patients to die with dignity. Euthanasia is not, as such, mentioned in the New Testament, although some principles can be found there to help in the debate.

Discussion Questions

1 Do you think that each person has the right to decide when their life will end – or does that decision rest with God alone?

2 What dangers might arise if euthanasia were legalized?

3 Hospices control pain and help people to die with dignity. Do you think that this is the way forward?

Homosexuality

In the New Testament
Romans 1.21–31
1 Corinthians 6.9–10

Homosexuality (from the Greek word *homo* meaning "same") refers to sexual relationships between people of the same sex – male or female. World-wide, millions of people have adopted a homosexual – or gay – lifestyle. It was in 1967 that sexual relationships between men became legal in Great Britain for consenting adults aged 21 and over. In 1994, the age limit was reduced to 18. (British law had not recognized the possibility of female homosexual behaviour and thus had never actually prohibited it.) Figures suggest that there are about 2,000,000 practising male homosexuals in Great Britain and 750,000 lesbians (female homosexuals).

Most of the Christian Churches draw a distinction between homosexual feelings and homosexual acts. Taking their lead from the New Testament they condemn homosexual acts as being against the will of God. Roman Catholic teaching calls such acts "unnatural" whilst the Church of England finds them unacceptable, especially for the clergy. Not all Christians agree, however, and growing numbers are

306

pressing for the Churches to take a more positive view of homosexual relationships.

> ### Discussion Questions
> **1** Why do you think that almost all Christian Churches draw a distinction between homosexual feelings and homosexual acts?
> **2** The law in Great Britain allows heterosexual sex at 16 but outlaws homosexual relationships until 18. Do you think that this is right – or fair?

Marriage

In the New Testament
Matthew 19.4–6
Mark 10.6–8
John 8.3–11
1 Corinthians 7.3–4
Ephesians 5.28–33

Each year about 300,000 couples marry in Great Britain. Almost 50 per cent of these weddings take place in a religious place of worship – church, synagogue, mosque, temple, etc. The remainder are performed in a Register Office. Ninety-eight per cent of people in Great Britain marry, with over 90 per cent of women and 80 per cent of men marrying before their 30th birthday.

Only couples marrying in a church go through a Christian ceremony. This ceremony emphasizes that God has given us marriage so that two people can live together and support each other, can enjoy a sexual relationship and can bring up children in a secure environment. The ring that is placed on the woman's finger – and often the man's as well – is a symbol of the couple's eternal love for each other. The ceremony assumes that the couple will be together "until death us do part".

> ### Discussion Questions
> **1** Why do you think that people marry?
> **2** What are the essential differences between marrying in a church and marrying in a Register Office? Which of the two locations would you feel happier marrying in? Can you explain why?

Money

In the New Testament
Matthew 6.24;
18.23–25
Mark 10.17–21
Luke 12.15; 18.25
2 Corinthians 9.7–8
1 Timothy 6.9–10

In the ancient world, people bartered their goods for those of someone else before learning to exchange goods for small pieces of metal. Money soon came to have a symbolic rather than actual value – as today when money changes hands in the forms of banknotes, cheques, debit or credit cards, etc.

The lack of money leads to poverty, yet possessing money does not guarantee happiness. According to the Citizen's Advice Bureau, the average British family now owes money to four different companies and carries three credit cards. The Bureau goes on to report that debt is a major cause of unhappiness – it now advises more people about debt than any other problem.

Discussion Questions

1 Is the love of money the root of all evil? Find out what Paul said in 1 Timothy 6.10. Do you agree with him? Why can the love of money be so dangerous and what can it lead to?

2 In Matthew 6.24 Jesus said that a person cannot serve God and mammon (money). What do you think it means to talk about people "serving" money? Do you think that many people today "serve" money?

Pollution

In the New Testament
Romans 8.18–25

Pollution of the global environment is taking place on a massive scale. This is particularly alarming for Christians, since one of their fundamental beliefs is that God made the world and was very pleased with his handiwork. The story of creation in the Old Testament book of Genesis (chapters 1 and 2) underlines the fact that the human race has been entrusted with looking after creation as its "stewards" (custodians). The last few centuries, however, have been ones in which the human race has gone a long way towards destroying the planet – with global warming, the destruction of the ozone layer, the burning of large tracts of rainforests and the pollution of the earth, the air and the water supplies amongst the many problems.

All of these problems were, of course, unknown in the time of the New Testament. The early Christians inherited the Jewish awareness that the world of creation was a gift from God – and should be looked after accordingly. Whilst Jesus used the natural world as the background to many of his parables, he himself had little to say about caring for it – perhaps he did not think it was necessary.

Discussion Questions

1 Much of the pollution and destruction of the natural world is due to the way we live. Which aspects of modern life do you think are particularly destructive?

2 What needs to be done if the human race is to have any kind of long-term future in the world?

Poverty

In the New Testament
Matthew 6.19–34;
25.31–46
Luke 6.20; 16.19–31
James 2.1–19
1 John 3.17–18

As far as world poverty is concerned the world can be divided into two parts – the North or Developed World, and the South or Developing World. In the poor, Developing World, there is a very high level of malnutrition; a largely uneducated population; a high level of disease and illness; a high rate of infant mortality with many babies dying, and a low life expectancy. In many countries few adults can expect to pass their 45th birthday. The poor countries have 75 per cent of the world's population but only 25 per cent of its resources. As a result, the rich are getting much richer and the poor much poorer.

The poor were given a very special place in the teaching of Jesus. At a time when many people believed that wealth was a sign of God's blessing, Jesus spoke of a Kingdom of God in which the first will be last and the last first (Matthew 19.30).

Discussion Questions

1 How did the teaching of Jesus on the poor and Kingdom of God differ from the attitude of the people of his time?
2 "If you are going to be serious about Christianity then you must do something about poverty." Do you think this is true?

Punishment

In the New Testament
Matthew 5.38–39; 7.1;
18.22–35
Luke 23.34
1 Peter 2.13–14

Anyone found guilty of committing a crime in the United Kingdom will be punished by a court of law. The punishment, which must fit the crime, can range from probation, community service or a fine to imprisonment. What, though, is punishment all about? What is society trying to accomplish when it sentences a criminal? There are four reasons why a person is punished. First, there is retribution. This is simply making a person pay for what they have done. Then there is the need to protect other people in society. Removing a person from circulation, for instance, makes it impossible for them to commit another crime – at least, until they are released. Thirdly, punishment is intended to act as a deterrent – to persuade the person, or others, not to commit a similar crime. Lastly, punishment is intended to reform the criminal by providing an opportunity for him or her to reflect on what they have done.

The New Testament attitude towards punishment is to steer a path between punishment and forgiveness. Whilst a person should be punished for their wrong-doing, the way of forgiveness should always be open.

Discussion Questions

1 What are the four aims of punishment? Do you agree that all of them are important?
2 What are some of the problems that might arise if one accepts the Christian approach of combining punishment and forgiveness?

Racism

In the New Testament
Luke 7.1–10; 10.25–36
Acts 11.1–18
Galatians 3.26–29
Colossians 3.11

"Racism" is the belief that one race is superior to another and acting on that belief. "Prejudice" is an attitude of mind which allows a person to "prejudge" others from a different racial group. "Discrimination" takes place when the prejudice, an attitude of mind, is applied in the real world – when a person is unfairly treated because of his or her racial origins. Many countries, including Britain, have passed laws to ensure that all their citizens are treated fairly in such areas as employment, housing and education. However, such laws are notoriously difficult to apply. How do you prove, for example, that someone has been passed over for a job simply because of the colour of their skin?

Christians are committed to the belief that all people are equal in God's sight – black and white. No race is, in any way, superior to another. Everyone has been created by God and so must be equal. Any distinctions between human beings on the basis of colour, class or gender are ruled out.

Discussion Questions

1 Why do you think that racial discrimination and prejudice are almost always directed towards people who are not white? Why are they rarely directed towards white people as well?
2 By common consent, laws against racial discrimination fail to change the attitudes of people who are prejudiced. Do you think that it is possible to change such attitudes? If so, how would you set about it?

Sex

In the New Testament
Matthew 5.27–30
1 Corinthians 6.18–20;
7.8–9
Galatians 3.26—4.7

Human beings, unlike the remainder of the animal creation, find that sex involves far more than simple reproduction. They alone find that sexual activity is a pleasurable and meaningful activity in its own right. Contraception (birth-control) allows human beings now to separate making love from the simple need to create new life. Sexual activity can be seen as a God-given activity which demands total commitment and trust if it is to be really meaningful. This means that it should never be used by one person simply to satisfy their own lust (sexual desire). That is a denial of everything that is beautiful and pure about sex when it is the expression of a growing and life-long relationship between two people. Sexual intercourse is so special that, in the New Testament, it is likened to the relationship which exists between Christ and his Church.

Discussion Questions

1 Paul had some controversial things to say about sex and marriage. You can read one of his comments in 1 Corinthians 7.8–9. What exactly do you think he was saying? Do you agree with him?
2 Why do many people think that sex outside marriage is perfectly acceptable? What arguments might a Christian put forward to support the belief that marriage is the best place for sex?

Suffering

In the New Testament
Matthew 10.28
Luke 4.38–39
John 9.2–3
Romans 5.12
1 Corinthians 11.29–30

Christians believe in a good and loving God who made and sustains all forms of life. Why, then, is there so much suffering in the world? Natural disasters kill thousands of people every year. Babies and adults die in large numbers from malnutrition. Children are born with incurable diseases or severe disabilities. Parents are snatched away

prematurely from their families through illness and accident. Christ
anguish about suffering is made even more acute by the unfairness of
all. Some people suffer much more than others. Many pass from birth
to death barely knowing what it is to suffer, whilst others have hardly
known a moment free from pain.

In the New Testament, a few answers are suggested to the problem of
suffering – that it is the direct result of sin, that suffering comes from
the activity of Satan, or from human free-will. Christians would also
point out that God himself suffered when Jesus, God's Son, was
crucified.

Discussion Questions

1 What do you think it is about suffering that most troubles the man or woman
   who believes in a loving God?
2 Look at the answers suggested in the text to the problem of suffering and add
   any of your own. Do they begin to provide an answer? Some religious people
   fall back on faith in God who knows and loves his creation. Do you think this
   is a suitable answer?
3 Do you think that suffering can usually be traced back to a human source? In
   your experience, can good often come out of suffering?

War and Peace

In the New Testament
Matthew 5.9,39;
22.6–7; 26.47–52
Luke 19.41–44
1 Corinthians 3.3
James 4.1–2

During the 20th century, over 100 million people have been killed in
war and armed conflict. During the Second World War, 90 per cent of
those killed were civilians. Since 1945 there have been more than 250
wars throughout the world and many of these have been "civil wars".
In one recent civil war, alone, more than 500,000 civilians were killed.
Such wars have not only brought widespread death and destruction but
have also created over 15,000,000 refugees – people without a home. In
addition, war destroys homes, crops, water and power supplies,
hospitals and schools as well as using up vast amounts of money.
Developed Western countries spend 20 times more on developing their
war machine than they do on helping the poorer parts of the world.

Although most people feel that war should be avoided if at all possible,
few are "pacifists" – turning their backs on all forms of war and
violence. Jesus, though, did teach his followers that they should not use
violence in any circumstances – Matthew 5.39.

Discussion Questions

1 Read Matthew 5.38–39 and 26.52. Do these verses suggest that Christians
   should adopt a pacifist approach to war and violence? Do you think that such
   an approach is realistic or are there exceptions to every rule?
2 Find out all that you can about "Just wars" and "Holy Wars". What is the
   difference between them?

Women and Men

.....y 2.8–15
Titus 2.3–5
1 Peter 3.1–7

There is an enormous difference between the ways that men and
women are treated world-wide. Women, although they do 65 per cent
of the world's work and produce 50 per cent of its food, only receive 10
per cent of its income and own 1 per cent of its property. Men make up
over 90 per cent of the world's leaders and earn 25 per cent more for
doing the same work as women. In the developing world, women are
still expected to combine domestic work, child-rearing and physical
work. In the Developed World, they are often expected to combine
raising a family and holding down a full-time occupation. In Great
Britain, the Sex Discrimination Act (1975) has not prevented over 90
per cent of the top jobs in industry being held by men.

There are strong indications of sexual inequality in the New Testament.
Although Jesus treated women as equal to men (women play a
particularly prominent role in Luke), Paul insisted that women should
keep quiet in the Christian community. They should also accept the
domination of men in the marriage relationship – 1 Timothy 2.8–15.

Discussion Questions

1 Many people believe that a woman should be a mother first and a worker
second. Do you agree with this? Do you think that there will always be a
conflict if a woman tries to fulfil both roles at the same time?

2 Do you think that society could, and should, do more to help women who
want to have a family and yet want to continue with their career? If so, how
do you think this might be done?

Glossary of Terms, People and Places

A

Abraham Also known as Abram, the first Patriarch of Israel who lived about 1800 BCE. He travelled with his family from Ur in the Chaldees to the Promised Land of Canaan. According to God's promise, he had a son, Isaac, when he and his wife, Sarah, were old. In the New Testament, Abraham is held up as a person of great faith and as second only to Moses among the great figures in Jewish history.

Adultery Sexual relations with a person who is married to someone else – forbidden by the seventh of the Ten Commandments. Adultery carried a penalty of death in the Jewish community in the first century, and is condemned by Jesus (Matthew 5.28).

Agrippa, Herod Grandson of Herod the Great. In 37 CE he was given the former tetrarchies of Philip and Antipas, made King of Judea and Samaria in 41 CE, and reigned until 44 CE. Herod Agrippa ordered the death of James who was a disciple of Jesus.

Andrew Disciple of Jesus, brother of Simon Peter, Andrew was fishing with his brother when Jesus called them to follow him (Mark 1.16–18). He may have been martyred by being crucified on an X-shaped cross.

Angel Greek word meaning a "messenger". In the Gospels, angels from God helped Jesus when he was tempted (Mark 1.13).

Annas The Jewish High Priest between 6 and 15 CE, who was later replaced by his son-in-law, Caiaphas, but continued to hold power. He presided over the hearing of the case against Jesus before it was passed to Caiaphas (John 18.12–14).

Antioch A prosperous town north of Syria visited by both Peter and Paul.

Apostle A person who is sent to carry a message. The eleven disciples (following the death of Judas) became apostles after the ascension. The number of disciples was made up to twelve by the addition of Matthias. This group was sent by Jesus after his resurrection to preach the Good News of the Gospel to all the world.

Aramaic Language closely related to Hebrew, spoken in Palestine at the time of Jesus amongst the general population. It is likely that Jesus spoke in this language.

Ascension When Jesus went up (ascended) into heaven, 40 days after rising from the dead (Acts 1.6–11).

Augustus Title given to Octavian when he became Roman emperor in 27 BCE. Augustus was emperor at time of the birth of Jesus, and looked upon himself as God on earth and demanded worship as such.

B

Baptism From a Greek word meaning "to dip in" or "wash". Gentiles who wanted to become Jews were baptized in water. The practice was used by John the Baptist who baptized many, including Jesus (Matthew 3.13–17), as a mark of repentance, and then by early Christians as an initiation ceremony for those joining the Church.

Barabbas Name of the nationalist leader held in prison at time of arrest of Jesus, released by Pontius Pilate instead of Jesus when people demanded the death of Jesus (Mark 15.6–15).

Barnabas A Cypriot and Levite who played an important role in the early Church, Barnabas travelled with Paul on missionary journeys, although he later fell out with him.

Bartholomew One of the twelve disciples, called Nathanael in John.

Beatitudes Word applied to part of the Sermon on the Mount (Matthew 5—7) which opens with a series of blessings (beatitudes) related to the arrival of the Kingdom of God.

Bethlehem Small town about 8 km south of Jerusalem, mentioned frequently in the Old Testament. Bethlehem was the birthplace of Jesus in the Gospels, although his home town was Nazareth.

C

Caesarea Philippi An inland city on the River Jordan at the foot of Mount Hermon. Herod the Great built a temple there to Caesar Augustus who had given him the city, which was the scene of Peter's important declaration that Jesus was God's Messiah (Matthew 16.13–20).

Caiaphas   Son-in-law and successor of Annas as Jewish High Priest, in office between 18 and 37 CE. Caiaphas held the first trial of Jesus after his arrest before delivering him over to Pontius Pilate (Mark 14.53–65).

Calvary   "Golgotha" in Aramaic, described in the Gospels as "the place of the skull" (Mark 15.22), situated outside the city of Jerusalem and close to an important road. It was here that Jesus was crucified.

Cana   A village in Galilee, scene of the first miracle of Jesus according to John's Gospel (John 2.1–11), and also where Jesus healed a government official's son (John 4.46–54).

Capernaum   Village on the north-western shore of Lake Galilee. Jesus made his early home in the village and healed the slave of a centurion there (Luke 7.1–10).

Centurion   There were sixty centurions (officers) in a Roman legion. They held officer rank and were men of status in the community.

Christian   Name first applied to followers of Jesus (the Christ, or Messiah) by their enemies. First heard in Antioch of Syria (Acts 11.26), it was soon accepted by Christians themselves.

Church   A word rarely used in the Gospels, in the letters it always means a community of Christians and is never used to refer to a building as it is today.

Circumcision   The removal or the cutting off of the foreskin of the male penis, a Jewish practice to initiate male children into the covenant of Abraham. This practice was rejected as an important part of the faith by the early Christian Church when large numbers of Gentiles (non-Jews) came to believe in Jesus.

Corinth   Important Greek city, with a reputation for encouraging sexual orgies and a temple dedicated to Aphrodite (the goddess of love). Paul founded a church there and sent two letters to the Christian community in Corinth which are found in the New Testament.

Cross   Instrument of torture and execution used by the Romans. An upright stake was placed in the ground to which a convict was either nailed or tied, having carried the cross-beam to the place of execution.

D

Damascus   An ancient city in Syria. Paul was travelling towards the city in search of

Christians to persecute when he heard Jesus speaking to him from heaven (Acts 9.1–19).

David   Presented in the Old Testament as Israel's ideal king of whom a descendant was to be the Messiah.

Day of Judgement   A popular Jewish belief that the day would come when God intervened to save Jews from their enemies. From early days, Christians looked forward to the day (the "Second Coming") when Jesus would return to the earth in power, and all people would appear before God to be judged.

Devil   The Devil or Satan tempted Jesus in the wilderness (Matthew 4.1–11).

Disciple   Word only used in Gospels and Acts to refer to the original twelve followers of Jesus and many later followers. Disciples are those learning under the "discipline" of Jesus.

Divorce   The legal ending of a marriage, a matter debated fiercely by the Jewish rabbis. Jesus appears to reject divorce with the single exception of unfaithfulness (Matthew 19.9). Paul allowed divorce if the person seeking one was a pagan (non-believer) married to a Christian (1 Corinthians 7.12).

E

Elijah   An Old Testament prophet whom many Jews believed would return as herald to the Messiah. John the Baptist and Jesus himself were both thought by some to be Elijah. Elijah (representing the prophets) appeared with Moses (the giver of the Law) alongside Jesus at his transfiguration (Mark 9.2–13).

Elizabeth   Wife of the priest Zechariah, Elizabeth gave birth to John the Baptist after years of infertility (Luke 1.5–80). Mary, the mother of Jesus, visited Elizabeth, her cousin, when both women were pregnant (Luke 1.39–45).

Ephesus   A prosperous port on the west coast of Asia Minor, with a temple dedicated to Artemis (Diana) which was one of seven wonders of the ancient world. Paul left the city in a hurry after he had criticized the worship of Diana.

F

Fasting   Going without food for religious reasons – a common activity in biblical times. Linked with prayer as a sign of human humility, fasting precedes many important events in New Testament such as the temptations of Jesus (Matthew 4.2).

G

Gabriel   The most prominent angel mentioned in the New Testament. He delivered special revelations to Zechariah and Mary about the births of John the Baptist and Jesus (Luke 1.8–20 and 1.26–38).

Galilee   Galilee was the northern part of Palestine. Lake Galilee (sometimes called Lake Gennesaret or Like Tiberias) was a fresh-water lake which separated the two parts of the River Jordan. Subject to sudden squalls and storms (Mark 4.35–41), fishing remains an important industry on its shores today.

Gentiles   Name used by Jews to describe the rest of humankind who were not Jewish.

Gethsemane   Name of the garden on the Mount of Olives where Jesus prayed in agony before his arrest (Mark 14.32).

Golgotha   Aramaic word translated as "place of the skull" (Mark 15.22), presumably to describe shape of hill on which Jesus was crucified. The Latin word for the place is Calvary.

Gospel   The English word means "Good News", a term used by Jesus as he proclaimed the coming of God's Kingdom (Mark 1.15). In the second century, the word was used as a title for certain Christian books – the Gospels.

H

Heaven   The place where God and Jesus reside, a place of joy (Luke 15.7) and peace (Luke 19.38), the home of all those who have died believing in God.

Hell   A place of eternal torment for those who are too wicked to go to heaven.

Herod Antipas   Ruler of Galilee from 4 CE to 36 CE, who imprisoned and executed John the Baptist (Mark 6.14–29).

Herod the Great   King who governed Palestine under the Romans from 40–4 BCE, the king who tried to kill Jesus by killing all boys in Bethlehem under the age of two (Matthew 2.16–17).

Herodians   Described in Mark 12.13 and Matthew 22.16 as joining with Pharisees in putting difficult question to Jesus, they were followers of Herod Antipas who had John the Baptist put to death.

High Priest   Appointed by the Romans, spokesman for the people to God and for God to the people. Annas and his son-in-law Caiaphas are two High Priests mentioned in Gospels.

Holy Spirit   Third person of the Christian Trinity with the Father and the Son, given by God to the early Christians on the Day of Pentecost (Acts 2.1–13). An unseen, life-giving force, the Spirit is given to each person who believes in Jesus.

J

James   Disciple of Jesus who was the brother of John, he became leader of the church in Jerusalem after the Day of Pentecost and was later beheaded by King Agrippa (Acts 12.2).

Jerusalem   The key city in the New Testament, the capital city in which the Temple was situated and also the place in which Jesus was executed. Destroyed by the Romans in 70 CE, Jerusalem is highly venerated today by Jews, Christians and Muslims.

Jew   Member of the people descended from Abraham and Isaac who share a common religion and culture and who regard Jerusalem and the area around it as their homeland.

John   John, the son of Zebedee (Mark 10.35) became with his brother James and Peter the closest friends of Jesus. John was traditionally thought to be the "beloved disciple" of John 13.23 and author of John's Gospel, three letters and Revelation.

John the Baptist   Cousin of Jesus, he was called a "forerunner" because his preaching prepared the people for Jesus, whom he later baptized (Mark 1.9–11). Imprisoned by Herod for describing his marriage to Herodias as illegal under Jewish Law and later executed (Mark 6.18).

Jordan   The river which runs from the north of the Sea of Galilee to the Dead Sea, about 320 km long and ends some 365 m below sea level. Jesus, along with many others, was baptized by John the Baptist in the Jordan.

Joseph   The husband of Mary, the mother of Jesus, and a descendant of King David. Unlike Mary, he disappears from the Gospel story after the childhood of Jesus.

Judaism   The religion of the Jewish people down to the present day.

Judas Iscariot   One of the twelve disciples, he betrayed Jesus to the religious authorities. Judas later suffered remorse and took his own life (Matthew 27.5).

K

Kingdom of God/Kingdom of heaven   The central theme of the teaching of Jesus according to the Gospels, the rule of God on earth which Jesus came to set up, the subject of many parables told by Jesus.

L

Law   In the New Testament, the word largely refers, as it did for the Jews, to the Torah, the first five books of the Old Testament (Genesis, Exodus, Leviticus, Deuteronomy and Numbers). Jesus insisted that he did not come to destroy the Law but to show its real meaning.

Last Supper   The last meal that Jesus ate with his disciples before his arrest, trial and death, the name is taken from Paul's reference to it (1 Corinthians 11.20). Most people think that Jesus was celebrating a Passover meal with his disciples.

Lazarus   A friend of Jesus who lived in Bethany with his sisters Martha and Mary. John's Gospel records that Jesus raised Lazarus from the dead (John 11.1–44). A character named Lazarus also appears in one of Jesus' parables (Luke 16.19–21).

Leprosy   The leprosy of biblical times was a skin complaint causing greenish or reddish spots on the body. This disease was believed to be contagious and so sufferers were banished outside cities and towns. Jesus healed several lepers (e.g. Luke 17.11–19).

Levi   Also called Matthew, one of the twelve disciples of Jesus, a tax collector (Matthew 9.9) and traditionally the author of Matthew's Gospel.

Lord's Prayer   Known as the "Our Father" among Roman Catholics, the prayer taught by Jesus to his disciples at their request (Matthew 6.9–13).

Luke   A doctor and companion of Paul, Luke was the author of Gospel that bears his name and also the Acts of the Apostles.

M

Mark   A Jew who set out with Barnabas and Paul on their first missionary journey, but turned back and upset Paul. Mark wrote the shortest and first Gospel in which he set down the recollections of Peter.

Martha   The sister of Mary and a friend of Jesus in Bethany. Martha resented her sister talking with Jesus while she (Martha) performed household chores. Martha and Mary were sisters of Lazarus who was brought back to life by Jesus (John 11.17–44).

Mary   Sister of Martha and Lazarus.

Matthew   Also called Levi, one of the twelve disciples of Jesus, a tax-collector (Matthew 9.9) and traditionally author of Matthew's Gospel.

Messiah   Meaning "the anointed one", this title was given to the Saviour of the Jewish people whose coming was foretold by the Old Testament prophets. Jesus is proclaimed by Peter at first and then by others as the Messiah or Christ (the Greek word for "anointed one").

Miracle   The writers of the Bible believed that God could intervene in the lives of the people in the world. The Gospels record many occasions when Jesus changed events, such as healing people and altering the course of nature.

Moses   The leader of the Israelites in the Old Testament who led them out of slavery in Egypt and passed on God's Law (the Torah) to them on Mount Sinai. Moses appeared with Elijah when Jesus was transfigured (Mark 9.2–13).

Mount of Olives   A hill to the east of Jerusalem on which the Garden of Gethsemane was situated. Jesus prayed there, and Luke says that Jesus went into heaven from there (Luke 24.50).

N

Nathanael   Disciple (also called Bartholomew) mentioned in John's Gospel, he was greeted by Jesus as an Israelite with "nothing false in him" (John 1.47).

P

Parable   A story told by Jesus which carried a moral or religious message. The Gospels are full of such stories told by Jesus to the crowd and also to his disciples. Important sayings were often attached to the end of the parables.

Paradise   The word used to describe the bliss of life in the Garden of Eden, the destination of the virtuous in the age to come, promised by Jesus to one of the two thieves executed with him (Luke 23.43).

Passover   The annual Jewish festival which commemorated the delivery of the Israelites from slavery in Egypt, a family meal still celebrated each year by Jews today.